"THE LORD IS MY STRENGTH AND MY PRAISE: AND HE IS BECOME
MY SALVATION. YOU SHALL DRAW WATERS WITH JOY OUT OF
THE SAVIOUR'S FOUNTAINS." Isai. 12, 2, 3.

THE RACCOLTA

A MANUAL OF INDULGENCES
PRAYERS AND DEVOTIONS
ENRICHED WITH INDULGENCES

Authorized by the Holy See

ENCHIRIDION
INDULGENTIARUM

PRECES ET PIA OPERA

IN FAVOREM OMNIUM CHRISTIFIDELIUM VEL QUORUM-
DAM COETUUM PERSONARUM INDULGENTIIS DITATA ET
OPPORTUNE RECOGNITA

TYPIS POLYGLOTTIS VATICANIS MCML

VERSIO ANGLICA

cura et studio

R. D. Josephi P. Christopher
Illmi. et Rmi. D. Caroli E. Spence

Antistitis Urbani S.S. Pii PP. XII

atque

Illmi et Rmi. D. Joannis F. Rowan

Antistitis Urbani S.S. Pii P.P. XII

**cum permissu Sanctae Sedis
concinnata**

Omnes preces, quæ in Editione Typica latine conscriptæ sunt, in hoc
libro et anglice et latine eduntur, reliquæ vero nonnisi anglice

Apud BENZIGER FRATRES
SUMMI PONTIFICIS ET SACRÆ
RITUUM CONGREGATIONIS TYPOGRAPHOS

NEO EBORACI

BOSTONIÆ, CINCINNATI, CHICAGIÆ, SANCTI FRANCISCI

1957

THE RACCOLTA

or

A MANUAL OF INDULGENCES

PRAYERS AND DEVOTIONS
ENRICHED WITH INDULGENCES

IN FAVOR OF ALL THE FAITHFUL IN CHRIST
OR OF CERTAIN GROUPS OF PERSONS AND
NOW OPPORTUNELY REVISED

Edited and in part newly translated into English from the 1950
official edition "Enchiridion Indulgentiarum—Preces et Pia
Opera" issued by the Sacred Penitentiary Apostolic.

by

The Rev. Joseph P. Christopher, Ph.D.

The Catholic University of America, Washington, D.C.

The Rt. Rev. Charles E. Spence, M.A. (Oxon.)

St. Gregory's Seminary, Cincinnati, Ohio

and

The Rt. Rev. John F. Rowan, D.D.,

St. Charles Seminary, Philadelphia, Pa.

By authorization of the Holy See

All prayers originally in Latin in the Typical Edition are given in
English and Latin. Other prayers in English only

MARTINO FINE BOOKS
Eastford, CT
2017

Martino Fine Books
P.O. Box 913,
Eastford, CT 06242 USA

ISBN 978-1-68422-125-7

Copyright 2017
Martino Fine Books

Cover Design Tiziana Matarazzo

Printed in the United States of America On 100% Acid-Free Paper

THE RACCOLTA

or

A MANUAL OF INDULGENCES

PRAYERS AND DEVOTIONS
ENRICHED WITH INDULGENCES

IN FAVOR OF ALL THE FAITHFUL IN CHRIST
OR OF CERTAIN GROUPS OF PERSONS AND
NOW OPPORTUNELY REVISED

Edited and in part newly translated into English from the 1950
official edition "Enchiridion Indulgentiarum—Preces et Pia
Opera" issued by the Sacred Penitentiary Apostolic.

by

The Rev. Joseph P. Christopher, Ph.D.

The Catholic University of America, Washington, D. C.

The Rt. Rev. Charles E. Spence, M. A. (Oxon.)

St. Gregory's Seminary, Cincinnati, Ohio

and

The Rt. Rev. John F. Rowan, D.D.,

St. Charles Seminary, Philadelphia, Pa.

By authorization of the Holy See

All prayers originally in Latin in the Typical Edition are given in
English and Latin. Other prayers in English only

BENZIGER BROTHERS, Inc.

PRINTERS TO THE HOLY SEE AND
THE SACRED CONGREGATION OF RITES

NEW YORK

BOSTON, CINCINNATI, CHICAGO, SAN FRANCISCO

1957

MADE IN U. S. A.

SACRA PAENITENTIARIA APOSTOLICA

OFFICIUM DE INDULGENTIIS
BEATISSIME PATER

FRANCISCUS CARDINALIS SPELLMAN, Archiepiscopus Neo-Eboracensis, ad Solium Sanctitatis Tuæ inclinatus, humiliter petit licentiam ut typis edi liceat, idiomate anglico, in sua archidiœcesi, Collectio authentica, anno 1950 edita, cui titulus: "Enchiridion Indulgentiarum— Preces et pia Opera in favorem omnium christifidelium vel quorumdam cœtuum personarum Indulgentiis ditata et opportune recognita." Et Deus, etc. . . .

DIE 30 MAJI 1951

SACRA PÆNITENTIARIA APOSTOLICA, vi facultatum a Ssmo D. N. Pio Pp. XII sibi tributarum, benigne annuit pro gratia iuxta preces, dummodo Em̃o Oratori de fidelitate versionis constet. Contrariis quibuslibet minime obstantibus.

N. card. Canali   *S. Luzio Regens*

Pænitentiarius Major

English Translation of Above

MOST HOLY FATHER: Francis Cardinal Spellman, Archbishop of New York, in obeisance before the throne of Your Holiness, humbly requests permission for the printing, in his Archdiocese, of an English translation of the authentic Collection of prayers published in 1950 under the title: "Enchiridion Indulgentiarum"—*Preces et pia Opera in favorem omnium christifidelium vel quorumdam cœtuum personarum Indulgentiis ditata et opportune recognita.*

May 30, 1951: The Sacred Penitentiary Apostolic, by virtue of the faculties given it by His Holiness, Pope Pius XII, hereby graciously grants the petition as set forth, provided that His Eminence, the petitioner, is sure of the fidelity of the translation. All to the contrary notwithstanding: By order of his Eminence.

N. Card. Canali, Major Penitentiary, S. Luzio, Regent.

IMPRIMATUR

Franciscus Card. Spellman

Archiepiscopus Neo-Eboracensis

NEO EBORACI

IN FESTO SANCTAE FRANCISCAE XAVERII CABRINI, 1951

In response to a petition of His Eminence, Francis Cardinal Spellman, Archbishop of New York, the Holy See, by a Rescript of the Sacred Penitentiary dated May 30, 1951, has authorized Benziger Brothers, Inc., to publish an English version of the work known as "Enchiridion Indulgentiarum—Preces et pia Opera," issued by the Vatican Press in the year 1950.

SACRED APOSTOLIC PENITENTIARY

OFFICE OF INDULGENCES

DECREE

Since the volume entitled "Prayers and Devotions" (*Preces et Pia Opera*) , published in 1937, is no longer in print, this Sacred Apostolic Penitentiary has decided to reprint the book, especially in view of the fact that not a few of the faithful, as well as priests and bishops, in many places have requested it. However, before carrying their decision into effect, this Office deemed it advisable to review the entire work carefully, to delete certain portions which appeared to be somewhat unsatisfactory, and to add some material which has been indulgenced since the appearance of the first edition.

Now the rules according to which this Manual has been compiled and arranged in its present form are the same as before; and its purpose is identical: namely, that there should be an authentic collection in one volume of all the Papal grants of indulgences to serve as a safe guide to general devotion.

Accordingly, this volume contains the prayers and devotions which have been indulgenced by the Sovereign Pontiffs up to the present time, and which are still valid; including those indulgences granted in favor of all the faithful as well as those given to certain groups of persons. All other general grants of indulgences that are not contained in this Manual are hereby abrogated.

It is, therefore, to be hoped that this work will yield a rich harvest of spiritual benefits, and that it will go far towards fostering a sincere and solid piety.

As was altogether necessary, the entire matter was submitted to the judgment of the august Pontiff Pius XII; in an audience granted to the undersigned Major Cardinal Penitentiary on the 29th of December 1949, His Holiness approved this collection of prayers and devotions as published by the Vatican Press; he further abrogated all general grants of indulgences not herein contained and ordered that this should be considered the only authentic collection.

Nothing to the contrary, though deserving of special mention, is to nullify the force of this decree.

Dated at Rome, from the Sacred Apostolic Penitentiary, the 30th day of January 1950.

NICHOLAS CARDINAL CANALI
Major Penitentiary

S. Luzio, *Regent.*

PREFACE

1. This Collection includes general indulgences that have been granted by the Supreme Pontiffs for the whole world down to the end of the year 1949, either in favor of all the faithful or of certain groups of the faithful, for the gaining of which there is not required a blessing imparted by a priest, religious or secular (having the proper faculties), to religious articles, or a visit to some definite pious place, or enrollment in some pious sodality.

However, an appendix has been added containing indulgences granted for visiting certain pious places in Rome.

2. The prayers and pious practices with indulgences granted by the Supreme Pontiffs at the time and in the manner above mentioned, and which are now published with certain alterations, possess their indulgences, not in the old form, but in the new one; moreover, those which are not found in this Collection lose their indulgences.

3. The prayers have been published in the same language in which they were indulgenced; as to translations, canon 934, § 2 of the Code of Canon Law is to be observed.

4. The conditions ordinarily prescribed for gaining the plenary indulgences contained in this Collection and designated by the familiar phrase "on the usual conditions" are the following: confession, Communion, a visit to a church or public oratory, or even a semi-public oratory (in the case of those who may lawfully use the latter according to canon 929), and prayer for the intentions of the Supreme Pontiff. In cases, however, where all the aforesaid conditions are not required, those which are necessary are separately mentioned in the proper places.

5. As to the manner of observing the conditions required for gaining plenary indulgences, and as to the rules for gaining indulgences in general, canons 925-936 of the Code of Canon Law should be carefully studied.

6. The indulgences attached to religious exercises which consist of several acts to be performed on the same day, or on successive days, or at different times, such as triduums, novenas, etc., are gained only when all the acts have been performed, and all the conditions fulfilled, unless otherwise stated, e. g., when it is stated that "on any one of the nine days, etc.", this or a similar expression is to be understood in the sense that the indulgences can be obtained on one or several of those days independently of the others.

7. Religious exercises are said to be performed publicly, only when they are held in common in churches or in public or semi-public oratories (in the case of those who may lawfully use the latter). In other cases they are understood to be performed privately.

8. Whenever it is considered advisable to conclude devotions that are being carried on publicly in churches, in public or (in the case of those who may lawfully use them) semi-public oratories for an entire month, on a feast-day which is not the last day of the same month, either in order that the faithful who are participating may more easily receive the sacraments of penance and the Holy Eucharist towards the end of the devotions or for any other just cause, it is permitted to begin the exercise on any day of that month which is customary for those devotions, or on any day of the preceding month, provided that the devotions be continued for the space of thirty days (**S. P. Ap., March 10, 1941**).

9. This Collection contains only those grants of indulgences, of which authentic documents are preserved in the archives of the Sacred Penitentiary.

10. If any doubt arises, especially concerning the meaning of the grants or the conditions for gaining the indulgences, it is to be settled from this Collection, in addition to the general rules that govern this subject.

THE CANONS ON INDULGENCES*

TAKEN FROM THE CODE OF CANON LAW

Art. I.   Of the Granting of Indulgences

Can. 911.   All men are to value indulgences highly: that is to say, the remission before God of the temporal punishment due to sin even after its guilt has been forgiven, which ecclesiastical authority grants from the treasury of the Church in behalf of the living after the manner of an absolution, and in behalf of the dead after the manner of an intercession.

Can. 917.   § 1. On the day of the Commemoration of all the Faithful Departed, all Masses enjoy the same privilege as if they were celebrated at a privileged altar.[1]

§ 2. All the altars of a church are privileged during the Forty Hours' devotion.

Can. 919.   § 1. . . . .

§ 2. In publishing books, pamphlets, etc., in which grants of indulgences for various prayers or pious practices are set forth, the prescription of canon 1388 is to be observed.[2]

Can. 920.   Those who have obtained from the Supreme Pontiff grants of indulgences for all the faithful are obliged, under pain of nullity of the favor obtained, to present authentic copies of these same grants to the Sacred Penitentiary.

Can. 921.   § 1. A plenary indulgence granted for feasts of Our Lord Jesus Christ or for feasts of the Blessed Virgin Mary, is understood to be granted only for feasts which are found in the universal calendar.

§ 2. A plenary or partial indulgence granted for feasts of the Apostles, is understood to be granted only for the feasts of their nativity.

§ 3. A plenary indulgence granted as daily, either perpetually or for a certain period of time, to those who

---

* The footnotes for these Canons will be found on pp. xv and xvi.

visit a certain church or public oratory, is to be understood in the sense that it can be gained on any day, but only once a year, by any one of the faithful, unless it is expressly stated otherwise in the decree.

Can. 922. Indulgences attached to feasts or solemn prayers, or the prayers of a novena, a seven days' devotion or a triduum, which are performed before or after a Feast or even during its Octave, are understood to be transferred to the day to which these feasts are lawfully transferred, if the transferred feast has an Office and a Mass without solemnity or external celebration and if the transference is made perpetually, or if the solemnity and external celebration of the feast are transferred either for a time or perpetually.

Can. 923. To gain an indulgence appointed for a particular day, if a visit to a church or oratory is required,[3] this can be done from noon of the previous day up to midnight of the appointed day.

Can. 924. § 1. . . .

§ 2. Indulgences attached to rosaries or other sacred objects cease only when the rosaries or other objects completely cease to exist or are sold.

Art. II. Of Acquiring Indulgences

Can. 925. § 1. In order that a person may be capable of gaining indulgences for himself, he must be baptized, not excommunicated, in the state of grace at least at the end of the prescribed works, and the subject of the grantor.

§ 2. Moreover, in order that one who is capable may actually gain the indulgences, he must have at least a general intention of acquiring them and must fulfil the prescribed works at the appointed time and in an appropriate manner according to the general sense of the grant.

Can. 926. A plenary indulgence is understood to be so granted that if one should be unable to gain it fully, he will nevertheless gain it partially, in keeping with the disposition that he has.

Can. 928. § 1. A plenary indulgence, unless it be otherwise expressly stated, can be gained only once a day, even though the prescribed work be performed several times.

§ 2. A partial indulgence, unless the contrary be expressly stated, can be gained frequently throughout the day, whenever the prescribed work is repeated.

Can. 929. The faithful of either sex who, in the pursuit of perfection, or for the purpose of training or education, or even for the sake of health, lead a community life in houses lacking a church or public chapel but established with the consent of the Ordinary, and likewise all persons who live there to wait upon them, whenever to gain an indulgence a visit is prescribed to some unspecified church or public oratory, can visit the chapel of their own house in which they lawfully fulfil their obligation of hearing Mass, provided that they duly perform the other works enjoined.

Can. 930. No one gaining an indulgence can apply it to others who are still living; but all indulgences granted by the Roman Pontiff, unless the contrary is evident, are applicable to the souls in purgatory.

Can. 931. § 1. The confession which may be required for gaining any particular indulgences can be made within the eight days which immediately precede the day to which the indulgences are appointed; and the Communion may take place on the previous day; or again both conditions may be satisfied within the following eight days.

§ 2. Likewise, to gain indulgences for pious exercises conducted for three days or for a week, etc., the confession and Communion may be made within the eight days immediately following the close of the exercises.

§ 3. The faithful who are accustomed, unless lawfully hindered, to approach the sacrament of penance at least twice a month, or to receive Holy Communion in the state of grace and with a right and devout intention daily, although they may abstain from it once or twice during the week, can gain all indulgences, even without the actual confession which would otherwise be necessary for gaining them, except the indulgences of an ordinary or extraordinary jubilee, or those granted in the form of a jubilee.

Can. 932. An indulgence cannot be gained by a work to which one is already bound by law or precept, unless it is expressly stated otherwise in the grant of the same; one, however, who performs a work imposed upon him as a sacramental penance and enriched with indulgences, may at one and the same time fulfil his penance and gain the indulgences.

Can. 933. To one and the same thing or place several indulgences can be attached for various reasons; but by one and the same work, to which by different titles various indulgences are attached, one cannot gain these several indulgences, unless the required work be confession or Communion, or unless the contrary be explicitly stated.

Can. 934. § 1. If, in order to gain certain indulgences, prayer in general according to the intentions of the Supreme Pontiff[4] be prescribed, merely mental prayer does not suffice; the vocal prayer, however, may be selected at the choice of the faithful, unless a particular prayer is assigned.

§ 2. If a particular prayer should be assigned, the indulgences can be gained in whatever language it may be recited, provided that the translation be officially correct, either by virtue of a declaration of the Sacred Penitentiary, or of one of the local Ordinaries of the place where the language into which the prayer has been translated is commonly used; but the indulgences cease entirely if there has been any addition, omission or interpolation.[5]

§ 3. To gain the indulgences it is sufficient to recite the prayer alternately with a companion, or to follow it in one's mind while it is being recited by another.[6]

Can. 935. The pious exercises enjoined for gaining indulgences can be commuted into others by any confessor, in behalf of those who are prevented from performing them by some lawful impediment.

Can. 936. Deaf-mutes can gain indulgences attached to public prayers, if, in company with others of the faithful who are praying in the same place, they raise their hearts and minds to God; and, if there is question of private prayers, it is enough for them to repeat them in their minds, or to express them by signs, or even merely to run over them with their eyes.

FOOTNOTES

[1] All Masses celebrated during the Octave of the Commemoration of all the Faithful Departed enjoy the same privilege, but only in behalf of the soul for whom they are applied (S. P. Ap., Oct. 31, 1934: Acta Apost. Sedis, vol. xxvi, p. 606).

[2] Can. 1388. 1. No books of indulgences, summaries, pamphlets, leaflets, etc., in which grants of indulgences are contained, are to be published without the leave of the local Ordinary.

2. Moreover, the express permission of the Apostolic See is required to make it lawful to publish in any language, not only the authentic Collection of prayers and devotions to which the Apostolic See has attached indulgences, but even a list of the apostolic indulgences, or a summary of indulgences, either previously made but never approved, or now for the first time assembled from various grants.

[3] The condition of "visiting a church, or public or semi-public oratory (in the case of those who may lawfully use the latter)" is fulfilled by entering the church or oratory with at least a general or implicit intention of honoring God Himself or His Saints, and making use of some form of prayer, or indeed the prescribed form, if any has been imposed by the grantor of the indulgence, or any other form, vocal or even mental, in accordance with the piety and devotion of the individual (S. P. Ap., Sept. 20, 1933; Acta Ap. Sedis, vol. xxv, p. 446).

The requisites for a visit to a church or oratory are to be observed likewise in visiting a sacred image or an altar.

[4] a) The phrase "praying according to the intentions of the Sovereign Pontiff" is readily fulfilled by adding to the other prescribed works the recitation of one *Our Father, Hail Mary* and *Glory be to the Father,* the faithful being left entirely free, according to the rule of can. 934, § 1, to recite any other prayer in keeping with each one's

affection and devotion towards the Roman Pontiff (S. P. Ap., Sept. 20, 1933; Acta Ap. Sed., vol. xxv, p. 446) .

b) In order to gain plenary indulgences which are to be obtained as often as the prescribed work is performed, and for which a visit to some church is enjoined, it is necessary and sufficient to say at least six times at each visit *Our Father, Hail Mary,* and *Glory be to the Father* (S. P. Ap., July 5, 1930; Acta Ap. Sed., vol. xxii, p. 363) .

[5] Indulgences wholly cease because of any addition, omission or interpolation which alter the prayers substantially (S. P. Ap., Nov. 26, 1934; Acta Ap. Sed., vol. xxvi, p. 643) .

[6] a) Indulgences attached to invocations and so-called ejaculations, can be gained even by reciting them merely mentally (S. P. Ap., Dec. 7, 1933; Acta Ap. Sed., vol. xxvi, p. 35) .

b) Whenever, either on account of manual labor or some other reasonable cause, there arises an impediment to holding in one's hand a rosary or crucifix, which has been blessed to enable the faithful thereby to gain the indulgences either of the Holy Rosary or of the Way of the Cross, these same indulgences may be gained, provided that, during the aforesaid recitation, the faithful have upon their person, in some manner or other, a blessed rosary or crucifix (S. P. Ap., Nov. 9, 1933; Acta Ap. Sed., vol. xxv, p. 502) .

ABBREVIATIONS USED IN THIS BOOK

S. P. Ap., the Sacred Penitentiary Apostolic.

S. C. Ind., the Sacred Congregation of Indulgences.

S. C. de Prop. Fide, the Sacred Congregation for the Propagation of the Faith.

exhib., exhibited; said of documents being presented to the respective Congregations.

PART I

IN FAVOR OF
ALL THE FAITHFUL

THE MOST HOLY TRINITY
THE BLESSED VIRGIN MARY
THE ANGELS AND SAINTS
FOR THE FAITHFUL DEPARTED
FOR SPECIAL OCCASIONS

GLORIA PATRIET FILIO+++ +++ ET PIRITUI ANCTO+

CHAPTER I
THE TRIUNE GOD

I

EJACULATIONS AND INVOCATIONS

1

To the King of ages, immortal and invisible, the only God, be honor and glory for ever and ever. Amen (Roman Breviary) ·

An indulgence of 500 days.
A plenary indulgence on the usual conditions, if this ejaculation is recited devoutly every day for a month(S. P. Ap., June 7, 1921 and Dec. 9, 1932) ·

Regi sæculórum immortáli et invisíbili, soli Deo honor et glória in sǽcula sæculórum. Amen (ex *Breviario Romano*) ·

2

Holy, Holy, Holy Lord God of Hosts: the heavens and the earth are full of Thy glory (Roman Missal) ·

An indulgence of 500 days.
A plenary indulgence on the usual conditions, if this ejaculation is devoutly recited every day for a month(S. C. Ind., June 6, 1769 and June 26, 1770; S. P. Ap., March 23, 1936 and May 25, 1949)

Sanctus, Sanctus, Sanctus Dóminus Deus Sábaoth: pleni sunt cæli et terra glória tua (ex *Missali Romano*)·

3

With all our heart and voice, we acknowledge, we praise and we bless Thee, God the Father unbegotten, Thee, the only-begotten Son, Thee, the Holy Ghost the Paraclete, O holy and undivided Trinity (Roman Missal)·

An indulgence of 500 days.
A plenary indulgence on the usual conditions, when this prayer is devoutly repeated every day for a month (S. C. Ind., July 2, 1816; S. P. Ap., Sept. 28, 1936)·

Te Deum Patrem ingénitum, te Fílium unigénitum, te Spíritum Sanctum Paráclitum, sanctam et indivíduam Trinitátem, toto corde et ore confitémur, laudámus atque benedícimus (ex *Missali Romano*)·

4

May the most just, the most high and the most lovable will of God be in all things done, praised and evermore exalted.

An indulgence of 500 days.
A plenary indulgence on the usual conditions, if the daily devout recitation of this ejaculation is continued for a month.
A plenary indulgence at the hour of death, to be gained by those who have often recited it during life and who, after confession and Communion or at least an act of contrition, shall invoke the Name of Jesus, orally if possible, or at least in their heart, and accept death from the hand of the Lord with resignation as being the wages of sin (S. C. Ind., May 19, 1818; S. P. Ap., Dec. 9, 1932)·

Fiat, laudétur atque in ætérnum superexaltétur iustíssima, altíssima et amabilíssima volúntas Dei in ómnibus.

5

My God and my all.

An indulgence of 300 days (S. C. Ind., May 4, 1888; S. P. Ap., June 15, 1935).

Deus meus et ómnia.

6

My God, grant that I may love Thee, and let the only reward of my love be to love Thee more and more.

An indulgence of 300 days (S. C. Ind., March 15, 1890; S. P. Ap., March 23, 1936).

7

My God, my only Good, Thou art all mine; may I be always Thine.

An indulgence of 300 days.

A plenary indulgence on the usual conditions, if this invocation is said daily for a month with pious dispositions (Apostolic Brief, March 13, 1902, exhib. March 17, 1902)

8

Blessed be the Name of the Lord!

An indulgence of 500 days, as often as this ejaculation is devoutly recited upon hearing blasphemies against God (S. C. Ind., Nov. 28, 1903; S. P. Ap., Dec. 9, 1932).

Sit Nomen Dómini benedíctum!

9

My God, I give Thee thanks for what Thou givest, and for what Thou takest away; Thy will be done.

An indulgence of 300 days (Pius X, Rescript in his own hand, May 29, 1906, exhib. June 28, 1922; S. P. Ap., May 22, 1934).

Deus meus, grátias tibi ago pro eo quod das, pro eo quod súbtrahis. Fiat volúntas tua.

10

My God, make us to be of one mind in the truth and of one heart in charity.

An indulgence of 300 days (Pius X, Rescript in his own hand, May 16, 1908, exhib. May 30, 1908).

11

T each me, O Lord, to do Thy will, for Thou art my God (Psalm 142, 10) .

An indulgence of 500 days.

A plenary indulgence on the usual conditions, when the daily recitation of this invocation is continued for a month (S. P. Ap., Jan. 20, 1921 and Oct. 4, 1933) .

D oce me, Dómine, fácere voluntátem tuam, quia Deus meus es Tu (Ps. CXLII, 10) .

12

a) O Most Holy Trinity, I adore Thee who art dwelling by Thy grace within my soul.

b) O Most Holy Trinity, who art dwelling by Thy grace within my soul, make me love Thee more and more.

c) O Most Holy Trinity, who art dwelling by Thy grace within my soul, sanctify me more and more.

d) Abide with me, O Lord, be Thou my true joy.

An indulgence of 300 days for each of the above prayers even when recited separately(S. P. Ap., April 26, 1921 and Oct. 23, 1928) .

a) O sanctíssima Trínitas, adóro te habitántem per grátiam tuam in ánima mea.

b) O sanctíssima Trínitas, hábitans per grátiam tuam in ánima mea, fac ut magis ac magis amem te.

c) O sanctíssima Trínitas, hábitans per grátiam tuam in ánima mea, magis magísque sanctífica me.

d) Mane mecum, Dómine, sis verum meum gáudium.

13

M y God, pour forth Thy blessings and Thy mercies upon all persons andupon all souls in purgatory for whom, by reason of

charity, gratitude and friendship, I am bound
or desire to pray.   Amen.

An indulgence of 300 days (Apostolic Brief, Dec. 13, 1922)

14

O God, be merciful to me, the sinner (Luke
18, 13)

An indulgence of 500 days (S. P. Ap., Jan. 25, 1923 and March
23, 1936)

Deus, propítius esto mihi peccatóri (Luc. XVIII,
13)

15

O God, Thou art all-powerful, make me a
saint (St. Alphonsus M. de' Liguori)

An indulgence of 500 days (Apostolic Brief, Jan. 26, 1924; S. P.
Ap., Feb. 12, 1934)

16

a) Holy God, Holy Strong One, Holy
Immortal One, have mercy on us.
b) To Thee be praise, to Thee be glory, to
Thee be thanksgiving through endless ages,
O Blessed Trinity (Roman Missal)

An indulgence of 500 days for each invocation even when recited
separately.

A plenary indulgence on the usual conditions, if either ejaculation is recited daily with devotion for an entire month (Apostolic
Brief, Feb. 13, 1924; S. P. Ap., Dec. 9, 1932)

a) Sanctus Deus, Sanctus fortis, Sanctus immortális, miserére nobis.
b) Tibi laus, tibi glória, tibi gratiárum áctio in
sǽcula sempitérna, o beáta Trínitas (ex *Missali
Romano*)

17

Blessing and glory and wisdom and thanksgiving, honor, might and power be unto
our God for ever and ever.   Amen (Apocalypse 7, 12).

An indulgence of 500 days.

A plenary indulgence on the usual conditions, for the devout repetition of this ejaculation daily for a month (S. P. Ap., March 20, 1931).

B enedíctio, et cláritas, et sapiéntia et gratiárum áctio, honor, virtus et fortitúdo Deo nostro in sǽcula sæculórum. Amen (Apoc., VII, 12).

18

K eep me, O Lord, as the apple of Thine eye; beneath the shadow of Thy wings protect me (Psalm 16, 8).

An indulgence of 500 days.

A plenary indulgence on the usual conditions, when this invocation is repeated with devotion every day for a month (S. P. Ap., Nov. 22, 1931).

C ustódi me, Dómine, ut pupíllam óculi; sub umbra alárum tuárum prótege me (Ps. XVI, 8).

19

I nto Thy hands, O Lord, I commend my spirit (Psalm 30, 6).

An indulgence of 500 days.

A plenary indulgence on the usual conditions, when the invocation has been devoutly recited every day for a month (S. P. Ap., Jan. 20, 1932).

I n manus tuas, Dómine, comméndo spíritum meum (Ps. XXX, 6).

20

O God, come unto my assistance: O Lord, make haste to help me (Psalm 69, 2).

An indulgence of 500 days.

A plenary indulgence on the usual conditions, provided that this devout invocation is recited daily for a month (S. P. Ap., April 28, 1933).

D eus, in adiutórium meum inténde: Dómine, ad adiuvándum me festína (Ps. LXIX, 2).

21

Vouchsafe, O Lord, this day (*or* this night) to keep us without sin (Ambrosian Hymn).

The faithful, who devoutly recite the above invocation morning or evening, are granted:

An indulgence of 500 days.

A plenary indulgence on the usual conditions, if they devoutly repeat this invocation every day for a month (S. P. Ap., June 15, 1934).

Dignáre, Dómine, die isto (*vel* nocte ista) sine peccáto nos custodíre (ex *Hymno Ambrosiano*).

22

Deliver me, O Lord, from mine enemies (Psalm 58, 2).

An indulgence of 500 days (S. P. Ap., Nov. 22, 1934).

Eripe me, Dómine, de inimícis meis (Ps. LVIII, 2).

23

O Lord, reward us not according to our sins which we have done, neither according to our iniquities (Psalm 102, 10).

An indulgence of 500 days.

A plenary indulgence on the usual conditions, if this invocation is said devoutly every day for an entire month (S. P. Ap., Feb. 10, 1935).

Dómine, non secúndum peccáta nostra quæ fécimus nos, neque secúndum iniquitátes nostras retríbuas nobis (Ps. CII, 10).

24

O Lord, remember not our former iniquities, and be merciful to our sins for Thy Name's sake (Psalm 78, 8-9).

An indulgence of 500 days.

A plenary indulgence on the usual conditions, if this invocation is said daily for a month with devotion (S. P. Ap., Oct. 4, 1936).

Dómine, ne memíneris iniquitátum nostrárum antiquárum et propítius esto peccátis nostris propter nomen tuum (Ps. LXXVIII, 8-9).

25

O praise the Lord, all ye nations: praise Him, all ye peoples.

For His mercy is confirmed upon us: and the truth of the Lord remaineth for ever (Psalm 116).

An indulgence of 500 days.

An indulgence of three years, if this prayer is said publicly.

A plenary indulgence on the usual conditions, when it has been repeated with devotion daily for the entire month (S. P. Ap., Dec. 22, 1936).

Laudáte Dóminum, omnes gentes; laudáte eum, omnes pópuli: quóniam confirmáta est super nos misericórdia eius et véritas Dómini manet in ætérnum (Ps. CXVI).

26

Holy Trinity, one God, have mercy on us.

An indulgence of 500 days.

A plenary indulgence on the usual conditions, provided that the devout recitation of this invocation shall be continued daily for an entire month (S. P. Ap., Jan. 16, 1939).

Sancta Trínitas, unus Deus, miserére nobis.

27

From all sin deliver me, O Lord.

An indulgence of 500 days.

A plenary indulgence on the usual conditions, if this invocation is devoutly recited every day for a month (S. P. Ap., June 11, 1939).

Ab omni peccáto líbera me, Dómine.

28

Lord, I fear Thy justice, I implore Thy mercy; deliver me not to everlasting pains, grant that I may possess Thee in the midst of everlasting joys.

An indulgence of 300 days (S. P. Ap., Dec. 18, 1940).

Dómine, iustítiam tuam tímeo, misericórdiam tuam implóro; ne ætérnis pœnis tradas me, ut in ætérnis gáudiis fruar te.

29

All through Thee, with Thee, and in Thee, O my God!

An indulgence of 300 days (S. P. Ap., March 26, 1941).

30

Most Holy Trinity, we adore Thee and through Mary we implore Thee. Give unto all mankind unity in the faith and courage faithfully to confess it.

An indulgence of 300 days.

A plenary indulgence on the usual conditions, if this invocation is recited daily for an entire month (S. P. Ap., Feb. 9, 1943).

Sanctíssima Trínitas, adorámus te et per Maríam rogámus te. Da ómnibus unitátem in fide eámque fidéliter confiténdi ánimum.

31

Lord, save us, we perish!

An indulgence of 500 days.

A plenary indulgence on the usual conditions, if this invocation is devoutly repeated every day for a month (S. P. Ap., Aug. 18, 1943).

Dómine, salva nos, perímus!

32

Thy will be done!

The faithful, who in the midst of the adversities of this life raise their minds in confidence to God and recite this ejaculation in a spirit of devotion, are granted:

An indulgence of 500 days.

A plenary indulgence on the usual conditions, if they continue its devout recitation daily for a month (S. P. Ap., July 10, 1944).

Fiat volúntas tua!

33

O merciful Lord, Thou art never weary of speaking to my poor heart; grant me grace that, if today I hear Thy voice, my heart may not be hardened (R. Cardinal Merry del Val) .

An indulgence of 300 days (S. P. Ap., June 8, 1949).

34

L ord, I am nothing, but, although nothing, I adore Thee (R. Cardinal Merry del Val).

An indulgence of 300 days (S. P. Ap., June 8, 1949).

35

L ord, I am my own enemy, when I seek my peace apart from Thee (R. Cardinal Merry del Val).

An indulgence of 300 days (S. P. Ap., June 8, 1949).

II
ACTS OF THE THEOLOGICAL VIRTUES AND OF CONTRITION
36

The faithful who make acts of the theological virtues as well as the act of contrition, using any formula set forth in catechisms approved by lawful ecclesiastical authority, may obtain:

An indulgence of three years for each of the aforesaid acts;

A plenary indulgence on the usual conditions, if they recite any of the aforesaid acts daily for an entire month;

A plenary indulgence at the hour of death, if they have been accustomed to make these acts frequently during life and moreover, after confession and Communion or at least being contrite, they shall pronounce the Name of Jesus with their lips if possible, or at least in their heart, and accept death patiently from the hand of God as the wages of sin (S. C. Ind., Jan. 28, 1756; S. P. Ap., Feb. 17, 1932).

37

My God, I believe in Thee, I hope in Thee, I love Thee above all things with all my soul, with all my heart and with all my strength; I love Thee because Thou art infinitely good and worthy of being loved; and because I love Thee, I repent with all my heart of having offended Thee; have mercy on me, a sinner. Amen.

An indulgence of 300 days (S. C. Ind., Nov. 21, 1885; S. P. Ap., March 23, 1936) ·

Deus meus, credo in te, spero in te, amo te super ómnia ex tota ánima mea, ex toto corde meo, ex totis víribus meis: amo te quia es infiníte bonus et dignus qui améris; et quia amo te, me pǽnitet ex toto corde te offendísse: miserére mihi peccatóri. Amen.

38

Lord, increase our faith (Luke 17, 5) ·

An indulgence of 500 days.

A plenary indulgence on the usual conditions, if the invocation is devoutly recited every day for a month (S. C. Ind., March 20, 1908; S. P. Ap., April 15, 1935) ·

Dómine, adáuge nobis fidem (Luc. XVII, 5) ·

39

My God, I love Thee.

An indulgence of 300 days (Apostolic Brief, Dec. 30, 1919) ·

40

I believe in Thee, I hope in Thee, I love Thee, I adore Thee, O Blessed Trinity, one God; have mercy on me now and at the hour of my death and save me.

An indulgence of 300 days (S. P. Ap., June 2, 1921) ·

In te credo, in te spero, te amo, te adóro, beáta Trínitas unus Deus, miserére mei nunc et in hora mortis meæ et salva me.

41

O my soul, love the Love that loves thee from eternity (R. Cardinal Merry del Val).

An indulgence of 300 days (S. P. Ap., June 8, 1949).

O ánima mea, ama Amórem ab ætérno te amántem. (R. Cardinal Merry del Val.)

42

A lmighty and everlasting God, give unto us an increase of faith, hope and charity; and, that we may deserve to obtain that which Thou dost promise, make us to love that which Thou dost command. Through Christ our Lord. Amen (Roman Missal).

An indulgence of five years.

A plenary indulgence on the usual conditions, when the daily recitation of this prayer is continued for a month (S. P. Ap., Nov. 22, 1934).

O mnípotens sempitérne Deus, da nobis fídei, spei et caritátis augméntum; et, ut mereámur ássequi quod promíttis, fac nos amáre quod præcipis. Per Christum Dóminum nostrum. Amen (ex *Missali Romano*).

43

I believe in God the Father Almighty, Creator of heaven and earth. And in Jesus Christ, His only Son, Our Lord: Who was conceived by the Holy Ghost, born of the Virgin Mary, suffered under Pontius Pilate, was crucified, died, and was buried; He descended into hell; the third day He rose again from the dead; He ascended into heaven; sitteth at the right hand of God the Father Almighty; from thence He shall come to judge the living and the dead. I believe in the Holy Ghost, the Holy Catholic Church, the communion of Saints, the forgiveness of sins, the resurrection of the body, and life everlasting. Amen.

An indulgence of 5 years.

A plenary indulgence, on the usual conditions, provided that the Apostles' Creed, as given above, be recited daily for a month in a spirit of devotion (S. P. Ap., April 12, 1940).

Credo in Deum, Patrem omnipoténtem, Creatórem cæli et terræ. Et in Jesum Christum, Fílium ejus únicum, Dóminum nostrum: qui concéptus est de Spíritu Sancto, natus ex María Vírgine, passus sub Póntio Piláto, crucifíxus, mórtuus, et sepúltus; descéndit ad ínferos; tértia die resurréxit a mórtuis; ascéndit ad cælos; sedet ad déxteram Dei Patris omnipoténtis; inde ventúrus est judicáre vivos et mórtuos. Credo in Spíritum Sanctum, sanctam Ecclésiam cathólicam, Sanctórum communiónem, remissiónem peccatórum, carnis resurrectiónem, vitam ætérnam. Amen.

44

I believe in one God, the Father Almighty, maker of heaven and earth, and of all things visible and invisible. And in one Lord Jesus Christ, the only-begotten Son of God, and born of the Father before all ages; God of God, light of light, true God of true God; begotten, not made, being of one substance with the Father; by Whom all things were made; Who for us men and for our salvation came down from heaven; and was incarnate by the Holy Ghost of the Virgin Mary and was made man; He was crucified also for us; suffered under Pontius Pilate and was buried; and the third day He rose again according to the Scriptures; and ascended into heaven;

He sitteth at the right hand of the Father; and He shall come again with glory to judge both the living and the dead; and of His kingdom there shall be no end. And in the Holy Ghost, the Lord and Giver of life; Who proceedeth from the Father and the Son; Who with the Father and the Son together is adored and glorified; Who spoke by the Prophets. And one, holy, catholic and apostolic Church. I confess one baptism for the remission of sins. And I look for the resurrection of the dead and the life of the world to come. Amen.

The faithful, who during the sacrifice of the Mass devoutly recite the foregoing Creed in union with the celebrant, are granted:

An indulgence of 7 years (S. P. Ap., May 4, 1940)

Credo in unum Deum, Patrem omnipoténtem, factórem cæli et terræ, visibílium ómnium et invisibílium. Et in unum Dóminum Jesum Christum, Fílium Dei unigénitum, et ex Patre natum ante ómnia sǽcula; Deum de Deo, lumen de lúmine, Deum verum de Deo vero; génitum, non factum, consubstantiálem Patri; per quem ómnia facta sunt; qui propter nos hómines, et propter nostram salútem descéndit de cælis; et incarnátus est de Spíritu Sancto ex María Vírgine et homo factus est; crucifíxus étiam pro nobis; sub Póntio Piláto passus, et sepúltus est; et resurréxit tértia die secúndum Scriptúras; et ascéndit in cælum; sedet ad déxteram Patris; et íterum ventúrus est cum glória judicáre vivos et mórtuos; cujus regni non erit finis. Et in Spíritum Sanctum, Dóminum et vivificántem; qui ex Patre Filíoque procédit; qui cum Patre et Fílio simul adorátur et conglorificátur; qui locútus est per Prophétas. Et unam, sanctam, cathólicam et apostólicam Ecclésiam. Confíteor unum baptísma in remissiónem peccatórum. Et exspécto resurrectiónem mortuórum et vitam ventúri sǽculi. Amen.

III

ACTS OF ADORATION AND THANKSGIVING FOR THE
BENEFITS WHICH ACCRUE TO MANKIND FROM THE
INCARNATION OF THE SON OF GOD

45

Most Holy Trinity, Father, Son and Holy Spirit, behold us prostrate in Thy divine presence. We humble ourselves profoundly and beg of Thee the forgiveness of our sins.

I. We adore Thee, Almighty Father, and with hearts overflowing we thank Thee that Thou hast given us Thy divine Son Jesus to be our Redeemer, and that He hath bequeathed Himself to us in the most august Eucharist even to the end of the world, revealing unto us the wondrous love of His Heart in this mystery of faith and love.

Glory be to the Father, *etc.*

II. O Word of God, dear Jesus our Redeemer, we adore Thee and with hearts overflowing we thank Thee for having taken human flesh upon Thee and become for our redemption both Priest and Victim in the sacrifice of the Cross, a sacrifice which, through the exceeding love of Thy Sacred Heart, Thou dost renew upon our altars at every moment. O High Priest, O divine Victim, give us the grace to honor Thy holy sacrifice in the most adorable Eucharist with the homage of Mary most holy and of all Thy holy Church, triumphant, suffering and mili-

tant. We offer ourselves wholly to Thee; of
Thine infinite goodness and mercy do Thou
accept our offering, unite it to Thine own and
grant us Thy blessing.

Glory be to the Father, *etc.*

III. O Divine Spirit the Paraclete, we
adore Thee and with hearts overflowing we
give Thee thanks that Thou hast, with such
great love for us, wrought the ineffable blessing of the Incarnation of the Word of God, a
blessing which is being continually extended
and enlarged in the most august Sacrament
of the Eucharist. Ah, by this adorable mystery of the love of the Sacred Heart of Jesus,
do Thou grant unto us and all poor sinners
Thy holy grace. Pour forth Thy holy gifts
upon us and upon all redeemed souls, and in
an especial manner upon the visible Head of
the Church, the supreme Roman Pontiff, upon all Cardinals, Bishops and Pastors of
souls, upon priests and all other ministers of
Thy sanctuary. Amen.

Glory be to the Father, *etc.*

An indulgence of 3 years (S. C. Ind., Mar. 22, 1905; S. P. Ap.,
Dec. 9, 1932).

46

I adore Thee O God, I count myself as
nothing before Thy divine Majesty. Thou
alone art Being, Life, Truth, Beauty and
Goodness. I glorify Thee, I praise Thee, I
give Thee thanks and I love Thee, all helpless
and unworthy as I am, in union with Thy dear
Son, Jesus Christ, our Saviour and our
Brother, in the merciful kindness of His Heart

and through His infinite merits. I desire to serve Thee, to please Thee, to obey Thee and to love Thee always, in union with Mary Immaculate, Mother of God and our Mother, loving also and serving my neighbor for the love of Thee.

Wherefore give me Thy Holy Spirit, to enlighten me, to correct me and to guide me in the way of Thy commandments and in all perfection, the while I look for the happiness of heaven, where we shall glorify Thee for ever and ever. Amen.

An indulgence of 500 days once a day (Pius X, Rescript in his own hand, Feb. 28, 1906, exhib. April 18, 1906; S. P. Ap., April 18, 1933).

IV

PIOUS PRACTICES

47

The faithful who recite devoutly three times the doxology "Glory be to the Father" etc., early in the morning, and at noon and in the evening, with the intention of giving thanks to the Most Holy Trinity for the excellent gifts and privileges granted to the B. V. Mary, may gain:

An indulgence of 500 days for each recitation corresponding to each of the aforesaid parts of the day.

A plenary indulgence on the usual conditions, if they perform the threefold recitation daily for a month with a devout heart (S. C. Ind., July 11, 1815; S. P. Ap., March 23, 1936).

48

The faithful who devoutly offer any prayers in honor of the Most Holy Trinity with the intention of continuing them for nine successive days, may gain:

An indulgence of 7 years once each day;

A plenary indulgence on the usual conditions at the end of the novena (S. C. Ind., Aug. 8, 1847; S. P. Ap., Mar. 18, 1932).

V

PRAYERS

49

Almighty and everlasting God, who hast given unto us Thy servants grace by the profession of the true faith, to acknowledge the glory of the eternal Trinity, and, in the power of Thy divine Majesty, to worship the Unity; we beseech Thee, that by our steadfastness in this same faith, we may evermore be defended from all adversities. Through Christ our Lord. Amen (Roman Missal).

An indulgence of 5 years.

A plenary indulgence on the usual conditions, if this prayer is said devoutly every day for a month (S. C. Ind., July 2, 1816; S. P. Ap., March 23, 1936).

Omnípotens sempitérne Deus, qui dedísti fámulis tuis in confessióne veræ fídei, ætérnæ Trinitátis glóriam agnóscere, et in poténtia maiestátis adoráre Unitátem: quæsumus, ut eiúsdem fídei firmitáte ab ómnibus semper muniámur advérsis. Per Christum Dóminum nostrum. Amen (*ex Missali Romano*).

50

Of Thy tender mercy, we beseech Thee, O Lord, loose the bonds of our sins, and through the intercession of Mary, the blessed and ever-Virgin Mother of God, together with that of Saint Joseph and Thy blessed Apostles Peter and Paul, and of all Thy Saints, keep us Thy servants and our dwelling places in all holiness; cleanse from sin and endue with virtue all those who are joined to us by kindred, affinity and friendship; grant unto us peace and safety; remove far from us our enemies, both visible and invisible; repress all our carnal desires: grant us wholesome air; bestow Thy charity upon our friends and enemies; guard Thy city; preserve our Pontiff N.; defend all prelates and princes and Thine entire Christian people from every adversity. Let Thy blessing be evermore upon us, and do Thou grant unto all the faithful departed rest everlasting. Amen.

An indulgence of 3 years.

A plenary indulgence on the usual conditions, provided that the devout recitation of this prayer be continued daily for a month (Leo XII, Rescript in his own hand, July 9, 1828; S. P. Ap., Dec. 9, 1932).

Pietáte tua, quæsumus Dómine, nostrórum solve víncula peccatórum, et intercedénte beáta sempérque Vírgine Dei Genitríce María cum beáto Ioseph ac beátis Apóstolis tuis Petro et Paulo et ómnibus Sanctis, nos fámulos tuos et loca nostra in omni sanctitáte custódi; omnes consanguinitáte, affinitáte ac familiaritáte nobis coniúnctos a vítiis purga, virtútibus illústra; pacem et salútem nobis tríbue; hostes visíbiles et invisíbiles rémove; carnália desidéria repélle: áërem salúbrem indúlge; amícis et inimícis nostris caritátem largíre; Urbem tuam custódi; Pontíficem nostrum N. consérva; omnes Prælátos, Príncipes cunctúmque pópulum christiánum ab omni adversitáte defénde. Benedíctio tua sit super nos semper, et ómnibus fidélibus defúnctis réquiem ætérnam concéde. Amen.

51

O Lord Omnipotent, who permittest evil that Thou mayest draw good therefrom, give ear to our humble petitions, whereby we beg of Thee the grace of being faithful unto death, evermore conforming ourselves to Thy most holy will.

An indulgence of 500 days (S. C. Ind., July 19, 1879; S. P. Ap., March 29, 1936).

52

R eceive, O Lord, all my liberty. Take my memory, my understanding, and my entire will. Whatsoever I have or hold, Thou hast given me; I give it all back to Thee and commit it wholly to be governed by Thy will. Thy love and Thy grace give unto me, and I am rich enough and ask for nothing more (St. Ignatius Loyola).

An indulgence of 3 years.

A plenary indulgence on the usual conditions, if this act of oblation is made daily with a devout spirit for an entire month (S. C. Ind., May 26, 1883; S. P. Ap., Dec. 4, 1932).

S úscipe, Dómine, univérsam meam libertátem. Accipe memóriam, intelléctum atque voluntátem omnem. Quidquid hábeo vel possídeo mihi largítus es: id tibi totum restítuo ac tuæ prorsus voluntáti trado gubernándum. Amórem tui solum cum grátia tua mihi dones, et dives sum satis, nec áliud quidquam ultra posco (S. Ignatius de Loyola).

53

O mnipotence of the Father, help my frailty and save me from the depths of misery.

Wisdom of the Son, direct all my thoughts, words and deeds.

Love of the Holy Ghost, be Thou the source of all the operations of my mind, that they may ever be conformed to God's good pleasure.

An indulgence of 500 days (S. C. Ind., March 15, 1890; S. P. Ap., Sept. 12, 1936).

O mnipoténtia Patris, ádiuva fragilitátem meam et e profúndo misériæ éripe me.

Sapiéntia Fílii, dírige cogitatiónes, verba et actiónes meas omnes.

Amor Spíritus Sancti, esto cunctárum ánimæ meæ

operatiónum princípium, quo iúgiter sint divíno bene-
plácito confórmes.

54

O Lord our God, we offer Thee our hearts united in the strongest and most sincere love of brotherhood; we pray that Jesus in the Blessed Sacrament may be the daily food of our souls and bodies; that Jesus may be established as the center of our affections, even as He was for Mary and Joseph. Finally, O Lord, may sin never disturb our union on earth; and may we be eternally united in heaven with Thee and Mary and Joseph and with all Thy Saints. Amen.

An indulgence of 500 days (S. P. Ap., Dec. 23, 1919 and March 23, 1935).

55

Into Thy hands, O Lord, and into the hands of Thy holy Angels, I commit and entrust this day my soul, my relations, my benefactors, my friends and enemies, and all Thy Catholic people. Keep us, O Lord, through the day, by the merits and intercession of the Blessed Virgin Mary and of all Thy Saints, from all vicious and unruly desires, from all sins and temptations of the devil, and from sudden and unprovided death and the pains of hell. Illuminate my heart with the grace of Thy Holy Spirit; grant that I may ever be obedient to Thy commandments; suffer me not to be separated from Thee, O God, who livest and reignest with God the Father and the same Holy Spirit for ever and ever. Amen (St. Edmund).

An indulgence of 3 years.

A plenary indulgence on the usual conditions, for the daily devout repetition of this prayer for a month (S. P. Ap., May 27, 1921 and Mar. 28, 1934).

56

I vow and consecrate to God all that is in me: my memory and my actions to God the Father; my understanding and my words to God the Son; my will and my thoughts to God the Holy Ghost; my heart, my body, my tongue, my senses and all my sorrows to the sacred Humanity of Jesus Christ, "who was contented to be betrayed into the hands of wicked men and to suffer the torment of the Cross" (St. Francis de Sales).

An indulgence of 3 years.

A plenary indulgence on the usual conditions, if this act of oblation is devoutly repeated every day for a month (S. P. Ap., Sept. 22, 1922 and May 12, 1934).

57

In order that I may be a living act of perfect love, I offer myself as a whole burnt offering to Thy tender love, beseeching Thee to consume me continually, letting my soul overflow with the floods of infinite tenderness that are found in Thee, that so I may become a martyr of Thy love, O my God! Let this martyrdom make me ready to appear before Thee and at last cause me to expire; let my soul cast itself without delay into the everlasting arms of Thy merciful love. With every beat of my heart I desire, O my dearly Beloved, to renew this offering an infinite number of times, until that day when the shadows shall vanish and I shall be able to retell my love in an eternal face-to-face with Thee! (St. Theresa of the Child Jesus).

An indulgence of 3 years.
A plenary indulgence on the usual conditions, if this act of oblation is repeated devoutly every day for a month (S. P. Ap., July 31, 1923 and Dec. 23, 1935).

58

M ost Holy Trinity, Godhead indivisible, Father, Son and Holy Spirit, our first beginning and our last end, since Thou hast made us after Thine own image and likeness, grant that all the thoughts of our minds, all the words of our tongues, all the affections of our hearts and all our actions may be always conformed to Thy most holy will, to the end that after having seen Thee here below in appearances and in a dark manner by the means of faith, we may come at last to contemplate Thee face-to-face in the perfect possession of Thee for ever in paradise. Amen.

An indulgence of 3 years (S. P. Ap., June 8, 1934 and June 1, 1936).

59

G rant, we beseech Thee, Almighty God, that we may so please Thy Holy Spirit by our earnest entreaties, that we may by His grace both be freed from all temptations and merit to receive the forgiveness of our sins. Through Christ our Lord. Amen (Roman Missal).

An indulgence of 5 years.
A plenary indulgence on the usual conditions, for the daily recitation of this prayer throughout a month (S. P. Ap., Nov. 22, 1934).

Concéde, quæsumus, omnípotens Deus, sanctum nos Spíritum votis promeréri sédulis, quátenus eius grátia et ab ómnibus liberémur tentatiónibus, et peccatórum nostrórum indulgéntiam percípere mereámur. Per Christum Dóminum nostrum. Amen (ex *Missali Romano*).

60

Lord God Almighty, who hast safely brought us to the beginning of this day, defend us in the same by Thy mighty power, that this day we may fall into no sin, but that all our words may so proceed, and all our thoughts and actions may be so directed as as to do always that which is just in Thy sight. Through Christ our Lord. Amen (Roman Breviary).

The faithful who recite this prayer devoutly in the morning may gain:

An indulgence of 5 years;

A plenary indulgence on the usual conditions, if they persevere in its devout recitation for a month (S. P. Ap., Oct. 15, 1935).

Dómine Deus omnípotens, qui ad princípium huius diéi nos perveníre fecísti: tua nos hódie salva virtúte; ut in hac die ad nullum declinémus peccátum, sed semper ad tuam iustítiam faciéndam nostra procédant elóquia, dirigántur cogitatiónes et ópera. Per Christum Dóminum nostrum. Amen (ex *Breviario Romano*).

61

I adore Thee, O my God, and I love Thee with all my heart. I give Thee thanks that Thou hast created me, made me a Christian, and preserved me this night. I offer Thee the actions of this day, grant that all of them may be according to Thy holy Will, and for Thy greater glory. Save me from sin and from all evil. Let Thy grace be always with me. Amen.

To the faithful, who recite this prayer with a devout heart, there is granted:

An indulgence of 500 days (S. P. Ap., October 10, 1940).

62

V isit, we beseech Thee, O Lord, this dwelling, and drive far from it all snares of the enemy; let Thy holy Angels dwell herein, to preserve us in peace; and let Thy blessing be always upon us. Through Christ our Lord. Amen (Roman Breviary).

The faithful who recite this prayer in the evening with a spirit of devotion may gain:

An indulgence of 5 years;

A plenary indulgence on the usual conditions, if they continue to recite the same for a month (S. P. Ap., July 16, 1936).

V ísita, quæsumus Dómine, habitatiónem istam, et omnes insídias inimíci ab ea longe repélle: Angeli tui sancti hábitent in ea, qui nos in pace custódiant; et benedíctio tua sit super nos semper. Per Christum Dóminum nostrum. Amen (ex *Breviario Romano*).

63

I adore Thee, my God, and I love Thee with all my heart. I give Thee thanks for having created me, for having made me a Christian, and for having preserved me this day. Pardon me for the evil I have done today; if I have done anything good, do Thou accept it. Keep me while I take my rest and deliver me from all dangers. May Thy grace be always with me. Amen.

The faithful, who recite the foregoing prayer with devotion in the evening, are granted:

An indulgence of 500 days (S. P. Ap., Oct. 10, 1940).

64

O God, Thou who art one in nature and three in persons, Father, Son, and Holy Spirit, first cause and last end of all creatures, the infinite Good, incomprehensible and ineffable, my Creator, my Redeemer, and my Sanctifier, I believe in Thee, I hope in Thee, and I love Thee with all my heart.

In the midst of Thine infinite happiness, Thou didst choose me, through no merits of mine, in preference to countless other creatures, who would doubtless have corresponded with Thy blessings better than I have done; Thou didst love me from eternity; and when my hour in time had come, Thou didst draw me from nothingness into earthly existence and didst bestow upon me Thy grace, as a pledge of everlasting life.

From the depths of my misery, I adore Thee and I give Thee thanks. Thy holy Name was invoked over my cradle to be my profession of faith, my plan of action, and the only goal of my earthly pilgrimage; grant, O most Holy Trinity, that I may ever be inspired by this faith, and may carry out this plan with perseverance, so that, when I have reached the end of my journey upon earth, I may be able to fix my gaze upon the blessed splendors of Thy glory.

The faithful, who recite this prayer devoutly on the feast of the Most Holy Trinity, are granted:

An indulgence of 3 years.

A plenary indulgence on the usual conditions (S. P. Ap., May 10, 1941).

O Ω N
QUI ES N___COELIS +

CHAPTER II
GOD THE FATHER
PRAYERS

65

O Father of mercies, from whom cometh all that is good, I offer my humble petitions unto Thee through the Most Sacred Heart of Jesus, Thy dearly beloved Son, our Lord and Redeemer, in whom Thou art always well pleased and who loves Thee so much; vouchsafe to grant me the grace of a lively faith, a firm hope and an ardent charity toward Thee and toward my neighbor. Grant me also the grace to be truly penitent for all my sins together with a firm purpose of never offending Thee again; that so I may be enabled to live always according to Thy divine good-pleasure, to do Thy most holy will in all things with a generous and willing heart, and to persevere in Thy love even to the end of my life. Amen.

An indulgence of 3 years (S. C. Ind., April 21, 1818; S. P. Ap., March 23, 1936).

O Pater misericordiárum, fons omnis boni, te supplex exóro per sacratíssimum tuíque amantíssimum Cor Iesu dilectíssimi Fílii tui, Dómini et Re-

29

demptóris nostri, in quo tibi semper bene compláces, dignáre concédere mihi grátiam vivæ fídei, firmæ spei et ardéntis caritátis erga te et próximum meum: ínsuper grátiam vere doléndi de ómnibus peccátis meis una cum firmíssimo propósito te in pósterum numquam offendéndi; ut secúndum divínum beneplácitum tuum semper vívere, voluntátem tuam sanctíssimam corde magno et ánimo volénti in ómnibus adimplére, et in amóre tuo usque ad finem vitæ meæ perseveráre váleam. Amen.

66

O holy Lord, Father almighty, everlasting God, for the sake of Thy bounty and that of Thy Son, who for me endured suffering and death; for the sake of the most excellent holiness of His Mother and the merits of all the Saints, grant unto me a sinner, unworthy of all Thy blessings, that I may love Thee only, may ever thirst for Thy love, may have continually in my heart the benefits of Thy passion, may acknowledge my own wretchedness and may desire to be trampled upon and be despised by all men; let nothing grieve me save guilt. Amen (St. Bonaventure).

An indulgence of 3 years.

A plenary indulgence on the usual conditions, when this prayer is said devoutly every day for a month (Pius IX, Rescript in his own hand, April 11, 1874; S. P. Ap., Dec. 13, 1932).

Dómine sancte, Pater omnípotens, ætérne Deus, propter tuam largitátem et Fílii tui, qui pro me sustínuit passiónem et mortem, et Matris eius excellentíssimam sanctitátem, atque ómnium Sanctórum mérita, concéde mihi peccatóri, et omni tuo benefício indígno, ut te solum díligam, tuum amórem semper sítiam, benefícium passiónis contínuo in corde hábeam, meam misériam recognóscam, et ab ómnibus conculcári et contémni cúpiam; nihil me contrístet nisi culpa. Amen (S. Bonaventura).

67

O God, who in the glorious Transfiguration of Thine only-begotten Son didst
confirm the mysteries of faith by the witness
of the Fathers, and in wondrous wise didst
foretoken the perfect adoption of sons by the
voice descending from the shining cloud : mercifully grant unto us to be made co-heirs with
the very King of glory and bestow upon us a
partaking of His glory. Through the same
Christ our Lord. Amen (Roman Missal).

An indulgence of 5 years.
A plenary indulgence on the usual conditions, when this prayer
has been devoutly repeated every day for a month (S. C. Ind.,
Dec. 14, 1889; S. P. Ap., March 26, 1936).

D eus, qui fídei sacraménta, in Unigéniti tui gloriósa
Transfiguratióne, patrum testimónio roborásti,
et adoptiónem filiórum perféctam, voce delápsa in
nube lúcida, mirabíliter præsignásti; concéde propítius, ut ipsíus Regis glóriæ nos coherédes effícias
et eiúsdem glóriæ tríbuas esse consórtes. Per
eúmdem Christum Dóminum nostrum. Amen (ex
Missali Romano)

68

E ternal Father, I offer Thee the sacrifice
wherein Thy dear Son Jesus offered
Himself upon the Cross and which He now
renews upon this altar, to adore Thee and to
render to Thee that honor which is Thy due,
acknowledging Thy supreme dominion over
all things and their absolute dependence on
Thee, for Thou art our first beginning and
our last end ; to give Thee thanks for countless
benefits received ; to appease Thy justice provoked to anger by so many sins, and to offer
Thee worthy satisfaction for the same; and
finally to implore Thy grace and mercy for

myself, for all those who are in tribulation and distress, for all poor sinners, for the whole world and for the blessed souls in purgatory.

An indulgence of 3 years for devoutly making this act of oblation at the beginning of Mass.

A plenary indulgence, if this act of devotion is performed on every holy day of obligation for one month, even if it is said at a Mass of obligation, provided one has gone to confession, received Holy Communion, and prayed according to the intention of the Sovereign Pontiff (Pius X, Audience July 5, 1904, exhib. July 8, 1904; S. P. Ap., Nov. 24, 1936).

69

Eternal Father, I offer unto Thee the infinite satisfaction which Jesus rendered to Thy justice in behalf of sinners upon the tree of the Cross; and I pray that Thou wouldst make the merits of His Precious Blood available to all guilty souls to whom sin has brought death; may they rise again to the life of grace and glorify Thee for ever.

Eternal Father, I offer Thee the fervent devotion of the Sacred Heart of Jesus in satisfaction for the lukewarmness and cowardice of Thy chosen people, imploring Thee by the burning love which made Him suffer death, that it may please Thee to rekindle their hearts now so lukewarm in Thy service, and to set them on fire with Thy love, that they may love Thee for ever.

Eternal Father, I offer Thee the submission of Jesus to Thy will, and I ask of Thee, through His merits, the fulness of all grace and the accomplishment of all Thy holy will. Blessed be God! (St. Margaret M. Alacoque).

An indulgence of 3 years.

A plenary indulgence on the usual conditions, if this act of oblation has been made daily with devotion throughout an entire month (S. P. Ap., April 8, 1920 and Dec. 13, 1932).

JESU++ CHRISTE ++FILI EI VIVI

CHAPTER III
GOD THE SON

ART. I
THE LORD JESUS CHRIST

I
EJACULATIONS AND INVOCATIONS

70

M y Jesus, mercy (St. Leonard of Port Maurice).

An indulgence of 300 days.

A plenary indulgence on the usual conditions, when this invocation is devoutly recited every day for a month (S. C. Ind., Sept. 24, 1846; Apostolic Brief, May 20, 1911; S. P. Ap., Dec. 17, 1932).

71

S weetest Jesus, be not my Judge, but my Saviour (St. Jerome Emilian).

An indulgence of 300 days.

A plenary indulgence on the usual conditions, if this invocation is devoutly said every day for a month (S. C. Ind., Aug. 11, 1851 and Nov. 29, 1853; S. P. Ap., Oct. 22, 1935).

D ulcíssime Iesu, non sis mihi Iudex, sed Salvátor (S. Hieronymus Aemilianus).

72

J esus, my God, I love Thee above all things.

An indulgence of 300 days (Pius IX, Rescript in his own hand, May 7, 1854; S. P. Ap., July 28, 1932).

I esu, Deus meus, super ómnia amo te.

73
Jesus, Son of David, have mercy on me
(Luke 18, 38).

An indulgence of 500 days.

A plenary indulgence on the usual conditions, if the daily recitation of this invocation is continued for a month (S. C. Ind., Feb. 27, 1886; S. P. Ap., March 15, 1934).

I esu, fili David, miserére mei (Luc. XVIII, 38).

74
O my Jesus, Thou who art very Love, enkindle in my heart that divine fire which consumes the Saints and transforms them into Thee.

An indulgence of 300 days (S. C. Ind., Feb. 6, 1893; S. P. Ap., May 8, 1935).

75
J esus Christ, Son of the living God, light of the world, I adore Thee; for Thee I live, for Thee I die. Amen.

An indulgence of 300 days (Pius X, Rescript in his own hand, June 19, 1909; S. C. of the Holy Office, July 1, 1909; S. P. Ap., Sept. 20, 1933).

I esu Christe, Fili Dei vivi, lux mundi, te adóro, tibi vivo, tibi mórior. Amen.

76
J esus, I live for Thee; Jesus, I die for Thee; Jesus, I am Thine in life and in death. Amen.

An indulgence of 300 days.

A plenary indulgence on the usual conditions, when this invocation has been devoutly repeated every day for a month (S. C. of the Holy Office, Dec. 3, 1914; S. P. Ap., Dec. 15, 1949).

I esu, tibi vivo - Iesu, tibi mórior - Iesu, tuus sum ego in vita et in morte. Amen.

77

O Jesus, life eternal in the bosom of the Father, life of souls made in Thine own likeness, in the name of Thy love reveal Thy Heart and make It known!

An indulgence of 300 days (Pius X, Rescript in his own hand, March 11, 1907; S. C. of the Holy Office, July 8, 1915).

78

O Jesus, the friend of little children, bless the little children of the whole world.

An indulgence of 300 days (Benedict XV, Rescript in his own hand, Jan. 9, 1920, exhib. Jan. 12, 1920; S. P. Ap., June 27, 1932).

79

Thou art the Christ, the Son of the living God (Matt. 16, 16).

An indulgence of 500 days when said before the Blessed Sacrament, even when It is reserved in the tabernacle.

A plenary indulgence once a month when this devout homage is offered daily, on condition of confession, Communion and prayer for the intention of the Sovereign Pontiff (Apostolic Brief, June 9, 1920; S. P. Ap., Jan. 12, 1934).

Tu es Christus, Fílius Dei vivi (Matt. XVI, 16).

80

Blessed be Jesus Christ and His most pure Mother!

An indulgence of 300 days (S. P. Ap., Nov. 8, 1921).

81

Jesus, for love of Thee, with Thee and for Thee.

An indulgence of 300 days (S. P. Ap., Feb. 9, 1922 and July 3, 1936)

I esu, amóre tui, tecum et pro te.

82

O Jesus, Son of the living God, have mercy on us!

O Jesus, Son of the Virgin Mary, have mercy on us!

O Jesus, King and center of all hearts, grant that peace may be in Thy kingdom.

An indulgence of 300 days when said conjointly (S. P. Ap., March 14, 1923).

O Iesu, Fili Dei vivi, miserére nobis!

O Iesu, Fili Maríæ Vírginis, miserére nobis!

O Iesu, rex et centrum ómnium córdium, fac ut fiat pax in regno tuo.

83

O Jesus, with all my heart I cling to Thee.

An indulgence of 300 days (Apostolic Brief, June 10, 1923).

O Iesu, toto corde tibi adhǽreo.

84

O Jesus, be to me Jesus, and save me.

An indulgence of 300 days.

A plenary indulgence on the usual conditions, for the daily and devout recitation of this invocation through one month (S. P. Ap., Nov. 22, 1934).

O Iesu, esto mihi Iesus et salva me.

85

Christ Jesus, my helper and my Redeemer (St. Augustine).

An indulgence of 300 days.

A plenary indulgence on the usual conditions, when this invocation is said with devotion daily for a month (S. P. Ap., Feb. 9, 1935).

Christe Iesu, adiútor meus et redémptor meus (S. Augustinus).

86

L ord Jesus Christ, Thou only art holy, Thou only art the Lord, Thou only art the Most High.

An indulgence of 500 days.

A plenary indulgence on the usual conditions, provided that the daily recitation of this ejaculation be continued for a month (S. P. Ap., Oct. 19, 1936).

D ómine Iesu Christe, Tu solus Sanctus, Tu solus Dóminus, Tu solus Altíssimus.

87

O Jesus, grant that I may be Thine, wholly Thine, forever Thine.

An indulgence of 300 days (S. P. Ap., Dec. 9, 1936).

88

L ord Jesus, let me know myself and know Thee,
And desire nothing save only Thee.
Let me hate myself and love Thee.
Let me do everything for the sake of Thee.
Let me humble myself and exalt Thee.
Let me think nothing except Thee.
Let me die to myself and live in Thee.
Let me accept whatever happens as from Thee.
Let me banish self and follow Thee,
And ever desire to follow Thee.
Let me fly from myself and take refuge in Thee,
That I may deserve to be defended by Thee.
Let me fear for myself, let me fear Thee,
And let me be among those who are chosen by Thee.

Let me distrust myself and put my trust in Thee.

Let me be willing to obey for the sake of Thee.

Let me cling to nothing save only to Thee, And let me be poor because of Thee.

Look upon me, that I may love Thee.

Call me that I may see Thee,

And for ever enjoy Thee.   Amen.

(St. Augustine).

An indulgence of 500 days.

A plenary indulgence on the usual conditions, if these invocations are devoutly repeated daily for a month (Apostolic Brief, Sept. 25, 1883; S. P. Ap., Dec. 17, 1932).

Dómine Iesu, nóverim me, nóverim te,
Nec áliquid cúpiam nisi te.

Oderim me et amem te.

Omnia agam propter te.

Humíliem me, exáltem te.

Nihil cógitem nisi te.

Mortíficem me et vivam in te.

Quæcúmque evéniant accípiam a te.

Pérsequar me, sequar te,

Sempérque optem sequi te.

Fúgiam me, confúgiam ad te,

Ut mérear deféndi a te.

Tímeam mihi, tímeam te,

Et sim inter eléctos a te.

Diffídam mihi, fidam in te.

Obedíre velim propter te.

Ad nihil affíciar nisi ad te,

Et pauper sim propter te.

Aspice me, ut díligam te.

Voca me, ut vídeam te,

Et in ætérnum fruar te.   Amen.

(S. Augustinus).

89

Lamb of God, who takest away the sins of the world, grant us Thy peace.

An indulgence of 30 days.

A plenary indulgence on the usual conditions, if this prayer is said devoutly every day for a month (S. P. Ap., Apr. 22, 1939).

Agnus Dei, qui tollis peccáta mundi, dona nobis pacem.

90

All honor, laud and glory be,
O Jesu, Virgin-born to Thee:
All glory, as is ever meet,
To Father and to Paraclete.

An indulgence of 500 days.

A plenary indulgence on the usual conditions, provided that the daily, devout recitation of this prayer be continued for a month (S. P. Ap., Mar. 20, 1940).

Iesu, tibi sit glória,
Qui natus es de Vírgine,
Cum Patre et almo Spíritu
In sempitérna sǽcula.

91

Grant unto us, Thy servants, O Lord Jesus Christ, to be protected at all times and in all places by the patronage of Blessed Mary, Thy Virgin Mother.

An indulgence of 300 days (S. P. Ap., Oct. 7, 1940).

Da nobis fámulis tuis, Dómine Iesu Christe, beátæ Maríæ Vírginis Matris tuæ semper et ubíque patrocínio prótegi.

92

O sweetest Jesus, hide me in Thy Sacred Heart, permit me not to be separated from Thee, defend me from the evil foe.

An indulgence of 300 days (S. P. Ap., Jan. 12, 1941).

Iesu dulcíssime, in tuo sacratíssimo Corde abscónde me, ne permíttas me separári a te, ab hoste malígno defénde me.

93

L ord, Jesus,
    Through Thine infant cries when Thou
wast born for me in the manger,
    Through Thy tears when Thou didst die
for me on the Cross,
    Through Thy love as Thou livest for me in
the tabernacle,
    Have mercy on me and save me.

An indulgence of 300 days.

A plenary indulgence on the usual conditions, for the daily, devout recitation of this invocation for an entire month (S. P. Ap., Jan. 20, 1941).

D ómine Iesu,
    per vagítus Tui in præsépio pro me nascéntis,
    per lácrimas Tui in cruce pro me moriéntis,
    per amórem Tui in tabernáculo pro me vivéntis,
    miserére mei et salva me.

94

M y dearest Jesus, teach me to be patient,
    when all the day long my heart is
troubled by little, but vexatious crosses (R. Card. Merry del Val).

An indulgence of 300 days (S.P.Ap., June 8, 1949).

NOTE.— Another invocation to be said when making or mending liturgical vestments is found under n. 710.

II

AN ACT OF ADORATION AND THANKSGIVING

95

W e adore Thee, most holy Lord Jesus
    Christ, here and in all Thy churches
that are in the whole world, and we bless
Thee; because by Thy holy Cross Thou hast
redeemed the world (Testament of St. Francis of Assisi, Conf.).

An indulgence of 7 years, if the aforesaid act of adoration is recited on bended knees, when entering or leaving a church, a public oratory or semipublic oratory (in the case of those who may lawfully use the latter).

A plenary indulgence once a month, if the aforesaid act is recited at least once a day, on condition of confession, Communion and prayer for the intention of the Sovereign Pontiff (S. P. Ap., Aug. 3, 1917 and March 18, 1932).

Adorámus te, sanctíssime Dómine Iesu Christe, hic et ad omnes Ecclésias tuas, quæ sunt in toto mundo, et benedícimus tibi; quia per sanctam Crucem tuam redemísti mundum (ex testamento S. Francisci Assisii Conf.)

III

AN ACT OF CONSECRATION

96

The Consecration of oneself to Jesus Christ, Incarnate Wisdom, by the hands of Mary

O Eternal and Incarnate Wisdom, most sweet and adorable Jesus, true God and true Man, only Son of the Eternal Father and of Mary ever Virgin, I adore Thee profoundly in the bosom and the splendor of Thy Father through eternity, and in the virginal womb of Mary, Thy most worthy Mother, at the time of Thine Incarnation.

I return Thee thanks for that Thou didst empty Thyself, taking upon Thee the form of a slave, to deliver me from the cruel slavery of the devil. I praise Thee and glorify Thee for that Thou didst willingly become subject in all things to Mary, Thy holy Mother, in order to make me through her Thy faithful slave. But alas, ungrateful and faithless that I am, I have not kept the promises I made Thee so solemnly in my baptism. Nay, I have utterly failed to do my bounden duty; I am no more worthy to be called Thy son nor Thy slave, and since there is nothing in me that does not provoke Thy rebukes and Thine indignation, I dare no longer approach alone unto Thy sacred and august Majesty. Wherefore I have recourse to the intercession of Thy most holy Mother, whom Thou hast given me to be my intercessor with Thee; and it is by this means that I hope to obtain from Thee the grace of contrition, the pardon of my sins, and the gift of abiding wisdom.

For which reason I salute thee, O Mary Immaculate, living tabernacle of the Divinity, wherein the eternal Wisdom lies hidden to be adored by Angels and men. I salute thee, O Queen of heaven and earth, to whose dominion is subject all that is less than God. I salute thee, O sure refuge of sinners, whose mercy faileth none; graciously hear my prayers for divine wisdom, and to this end receive the vows and oblations which my lowliness offers unto thee.

I. N . . . , a faithless sinner, renew and ratify this day at thy hands my baptismal vows. I renounce Satan for ever and all his works and pomps, and I give myself wholly to Jesus Christ, the Incarnate Wisdom, to bear my cross after Him all the days of my life. And in order that I may be more faithful to Him than I have hitherto been, I choose thee this day, O Mary, in the presence of the whole court of heaven for my Mother and my Mistress.

I deliver and consecrate to thee, after the manner of a bond-slave, my body and my soul, my interior and exterior goods, and even the value of my good works, past, present and future, leaving thee the full and entire right to dispose of me and of all that belongs to me, without exception, according to thy good pleasure and the greater glory of God both in time and in eternity.

Accept, O gracious Virgin, this little offering of my bondage, in honor of and in union with that submission which the Eternal Wisdom willed to show toward thy Motherhood; as a mark of homage to that dominion which thou and thy divine Son have over me, a wretched worm and a miserable sinner; in thanksgiving for the privileges with which the Most Holy Trinity has favored thee. I protest that henceforth I wish, as thy true slave, to seek thine honor and to obey thee in all things.

O Mother most admirable, present me to thy Son, as His slave for ever, in order that, having purchased me through thee, He may receive me through thee. O Mother of mercy, procure for me the grace of obtaining true wisdom from God and of being set thereby in the number of those whom thou lovest, whom thou teachest, whom thou guidest, whom thou dost sustain and protect as thy children and thy slaves.

O faithful Virgin, render me in all things so perfect a disciple, imitator and slave of the Incarnate Wisdom, Jesus Christ thy Son, that through thine intercession and example I may come to the fulness of His stature on earth and the plenitude of His glory in heaven. Amen (S. L. M. Grignion de Montfort).

A plenary indulgence on the usual conditions on the Feast of the Immaculate Conception and on the 28th day of April (Pius X, Rescript in his own hand, Dec. 24, 1907, exhib. Jan. 22, 1908; S. C. of the Holy Office, Dec. 7, 1927).

IV

PRAYERS

97

L ord Jesus Christ, in union with that divine intention wherewith on earth Thou didst offer to God Thy praises through Thy Most Sacred Heart, and dost now offer them in the Sacrament of the Eucharist everywhere on earth even to the end of time, I most gladly offer Thee throughout this entire day, all my thoughts and intentions, all my affections and desires, all my words and deeds, in imitation of the most sacred Heart of the blessed and ever Virgin Mary Immaculate.

An indulgence of 3 years once a day.

A plenary indulgence on the usual conditions, when this act of offering has been devoutly recited each day for a month (S. C. Ind., Dec. 19, 1885; S. P. Ap., March 10, 1933).

D ómine Iesu Christe, in unióne illíus divínæ intentiónis, qua in terris per sanctíssimum Cor tuum laudes Deo persolvísti et nunc in Eucharístiæ Sacraménto ubíque terrárum persólvis usque ad consummatiónem sǽculi, ego per hanc diem íntegram, ad imitatiónem sacratíssimi Cordis beátæ Maríæ semper Vírginis immaculátæ, tibi libentíssime óffero omnes meas intentiónes et cogitatiónes, omnes meos afféctus et desidéria, ómnia mea ópera et verba.

98

G rant me Thy grace, most merciful Jesus,
that it may be with me and work with
me and persevere with me even to the end.

Grant that I may always desire and will
that which is to Thee most acceptable and
most dear.

Let Thy will be mine, and let my will ever
follow Thine and agree perfectly with it.

Let my willing and not-willing be all one
with Thine, and let me not be able to will or
not will anything else but what Thou willest
or willest not (Imitation of Christ, bk. 3, ch. 15, v. 3).

An indulgence of 3 years.
A plenary indulgence on the usual conditions, once a month,
for the daily and devout recitation of this prayer (S. C. Ind., Feb.
27, 1886; S. P. Ap., Dec. 17, 1932).

C oncéde mihi, benigníssime Iesu, grátiam tuam,
ut mecum sit et mecum labóret mecúmque in
finem usque persevéret.

Da mihi hoc semper desideráre et velle, quod tibi
magis accéptum est et cárius placet.

Tua volúntas mea sit, et mea volúntas tuam semper
sequátur, et óptime ei concórdet.

Sit mihi unum velle et nolle tecum, nec áliud posse
velle aut nolle, nisi quod Tu vis et nolis. Amen
(De Imit. Chr. lib. III, c. XV, v. 3).

99

J esus Christ my God, I adore Thee and
thank Thee for all the graces Thou hast
given me this day. I offer Thee my sleep and
all the moments of this night, and I beseech
Thee to keep me without sin. Wherefore I
put myself within Thy sacred Side and under
the mantle of our Lady, my Mother. Let
Thy holy Angels stand about me and keep me

in peace; and let Thy blessing be upon me
(St. Alphonsus M. de' Liguori).

The faithful who recite this prayer in the evening before falling asleep may gain:

An indulgence of 3 years once a day;

A plenary indulgence once a month on the usual conditions for the daily devout repetition of the same (S. C. Ind., June 30, 1893; S. P. Ap., Dec. 18, 1935).

100

O Jesus, my Saviour and Redeemer, Son of the living God, behold we kneel before Thee and offer Thee our reparation; we would make amends for all the blasphemies uttered against Thy holy Name, for all the injuries done to Thee in the Blessed Sacrament, for all the irreverence shown toward Thine immaculate Virgin Mother, for all the calumnies and slanders spoken against Thy spouse, the holy Catholic and Roman Church. O Jesus, who hast said: "If you ask the Father anything in My name, He will give it you", we pray and beseech Thee for all our brethren who are in danger of sin; shield them from every temptation to fall away from the true faith; save those who are even now standing on the brink of the abyss; to all of them give light and knowledge of the truth, courage and strength for the conflict with evil, perseverance in faith and active charity! For this do we pray, most merciful Jesus, in Thy Name, unto God the Father, with whom Thou livest and reignest in the unity of the Holy Ghost world without end. Amen.

An indulgence of 500 days once a day.

A plenary indulgence once a month, on the usual conditions, when this prayer has been said devoutly every day (S. C. Ind., May 13, 1903; S. P. Ap., March 5, 1936).

101

Our sins, O Lord, darken our understanding and hide from us the blessing of loving Thee as Thou dost merit. Enlighten our minds with a ray of Thy divine light. Thou art the Friend, the Redeemer and the Father of him who turns penitent to Thy Sacred Heart; we, too, turn penitent to Thee, Jesus, we hope in Thee, for we know that our salvation cost Thee Thy death upon the Cross and moved Thee to remain continually in the Blessed Sacrament, in order to unite Thyself with us as often as we desire. We, O Lord, to give Thee thanks for the great love Thou bearest toward us, promise Thee, by the help of Thy grace, to receive Thee in Thy Sacrament as often as we can, and to sing Thy praises in church and in every place, without human respect. Lord, we beseech Thee, trusting in Thy Most Sacred Heart, that Thou wouldst call all men to receive Thee daily at the altar, according to Thy burning desire.

An indulgence of 500 days (Pius X, Audience June 26, 1906; exhib. July 6, 1906; S. P. Ap., Nov. 25, 1934).

102

O Jesus, Son of the glorious Virgin Mary, and only Son of the living God, I adore Thee and acknowledge Thee as my God, the only true God, unique and infinitely perfect, who hast made out of nothing all things that are outside of Thee, and who dost preserve and govern them with infinite wisdom, sovereign goodness and supreme power; I beg of Thee, by the mysteries that were fulfilled in Thy sacred Humanity, to cleanse me in Thy Blood from all my past sins; pour forth abundantly upon me Thy Holy Spirit, together with His grace, His virtues and His gifts; make me believe in Thee, hope in Thee, love Thee and labor to merit Thee in each of my actions; give Thyself to me one day, in the brightness of Thy glory, in the midst of the assembly of all Thy Saints.   Amen.

An indulgence of 500 days once a day (S. C. of the Holy Office, Jan. 22, 1914; S. P. Ap., Sept. 8, 1933).

103

Our Lord Jesus Christ, we have recourse to Thee, Holy God, Mighty God, Immortal God, have mercy on us and on all mankind.   Cleanse us in Thy Precious Blood from all our sins and infirmities.   My Jesus, I believe in Thee, I hope in Thee, I love Thee, I give myself to Thee.

An indulgence of 300 days (Benedict XV, Rescript in his own hand, Dec. 21, 1916, exhib. Apr. 20, 1917; S. P. Ap., Oct. 20, 1935).

104

Lord Jesus, I unite myself to Thy perpetual, unceasing, universal sacrifice.   I offer myself to Thee every day of my life and every moment of every day, according to Thy most holy and adorable will.   Thou hast been the victim of my salvation, I wish to be the victim of Thy love.   Accept my desire, take my offering, graciously hear my prayer.   Let me live

for love of Thee, let me die for love of Thee;
let my last heartbeat be an act of perfect love!

An indulgence of 500 days once a day (S. P. Ap., June 5, 1919
and Dec. 17, 1932).

105

O Jesus! I come to Thee! Thou art the
Way that I would follow in obedience
to Thy commandments, Thy counsels and
Thine example; let me walk after Thee in the
way of obedience, of self-denial and of sacrifice, which leads to heaven and Thee! O
Jesus, Thou art the Truth; Thou art "the
true Light which enlighteneth every man
coming into this world". I believe in Thee!
I believe in Thy Gospel; I would know Thee
in order to love Thee; I would make Thee
known in order to make Thee loved. O Jesus!
Thou art the Life, through Thy sanctifying
grace which is the life of our souls; through
Thy words which are "the words of everlasting life"; through Thy Eucharist which is
"the living bread come down from heaven";
through Thy Heart which is the fountain of
life for individual souls and for society. I
cling to Thy Word with all my heart; I hunger for the living Bread of Thy Eucharist; I
open my heart without reserve to the life-
giving streams from Thy Sacred Heart; I
unite myself inwardly to all Its intentions.
Ah, may this divine Heart reign universally
over the children of the Church and over all
humanity. Amen.

An indulgence of 500 days.
A plenary indulgence once a month on the usual conditions,

for the daily devout recitation of this prayer (S. P. Ap., Dec. 1, 1920 and Dec. 28, 1932).

106

My Lord Jesus Christ, Son of the living God, I humbly beseech Thee to scatter the darkness of my mind, and to give me lively faith, firm hope and burning love. Grant, O my God, that I may know Thee well and may do all things in Thy light and in conformity to Thy holy will. Amen.

An indulgence of 500 days.
A plenary indulgence once a month on the usual conditions, for the daily recitation of this prayer in a spirit of devotion (S. P. Ap., May 30, 1921 and July 23, 1936).

107

O Jesus our Saviour, give us Thy blessing, deliver us from everlasting death, assist Thy holy Church, give peace to all nations, deliver the holy souls suffering in purgatory.

An indulgence of 500 days S. P. Ap., Nov. 29, 1923 and Feb. 15, 1933).

108

O Lord God, King of heaven and earth, may it please Thee this day to order and to hallow, to rule and to govern our hearts and our bodies, our thoughts, our words and our works, according to Thy law and in the doing of Thy commandments, that we, being helped by Thee, may here and hereafter worthily be saved and delivered by Thee, O Saviour of the world, who livest and reignest for ever and ever. Amen (Roman Breviary).

The faithful who devoutly recite this prayer in the morning may gain:
An indulgence of 5 years;
A plenary indulgence once a month on the usual conditions for the daily devout recitation thereof (S. P. Ap., Apr. 8, 1934).

Dirígere et sanctificáre, régere et gubernáre dignáre, Dómine Deus, Rex cæli et terræ, hódie
corda et córpora nostra, sensus, sermónes et actus
nostros in lege tua et in opéribus mandatórum tuórum; ut hic et in ætérnum, te auxiliánte, salvi et
líberi esse mereámur, Salvátor mundi: Qui vivis et
regnas in sǽcula sæculórum.   Amen (ex *Breviario
Romano*).

109

Deliver me, Lord Jesus Christ, from all
my iniquities and from every evil, make
me ever hold fast to Thy commandments
and never allow me to be separated from
Thee (Roman Missal).

An indulgence of 5 years.

A plenary indulgence on the usual conditions, provided that the
devout recitation of this prayer be continued daily for an entire
month (S. P. Ap., Nov. 12, 1938).

Líbera me, Dómine Iesu Christe, ab ómnibus iniquitátibus meis et univérsis malis, fac me tuis
semper inhærére mandátis et a te numquam separári
permíttas (ex *Missali Romano*).

110

We offer Thee, Lord Jesus Christ, the
merits of Mary, Thy mother and ours,
as she stood beneath the Cross, in order that,
by her tender intercession, we may obtain
the happy fruits of Thy Passion and Death.

An indulgence of 300 days.

A plenary indulgence on the usual conditions, if this act of
oblation is made daily throughout an entire month (S. P. Ap.,
Mar. 20, 1939).

Tibi offérimus, Dómine Iesu Christe, mérita Maríæ,
Matris tuæ et nostræ, stantis juxta Crucem, ut, suo
piíssimo intervéntu, Passiónis ac Mortis tuæ efféctum
felícem consequámur

111

O dearly beloved Word of God, teach me to be generous, to serve Thee as Thou dost deserve, to give without counting the cost, to fight without fretting at my wounds, to labor without seeking repose, to be prodigal of myself without looking for any other reward save that of knowing that I do Thy holy will (R. Card. Merry del Val).

An indulgence of 500 days.

A plenary indulgence on the usual conditions, if this prayer is said devoutly every day for a month (S. P. Ap., June 8, 1949).

112

Change my heart, O Jesus, Thou who didst empty Thyself for love of me! Make known to my spirit how excellent were Thy sacred humiliations. Let me begin this day, illumined by Thy divine light, to do away with that portion of the natural man, that still lives undiminished in me. This is the chief source of my misery, this the barrier that I constantly oppose to Thy love (R. Card. Merry del Val).

An indulgence of 500 days.

A plenary indulgence on the usual conditions, for the devout repetition of this prayer every day for a month (S. P. Ap., June 8, 1949).

Art. II

IN HONOR OF
THE MOST HOLY NAME OF JESUS

I

AN INVOCATION

113

The faithful who devoutly invoke the holy Name of Jesus may gain:

An indulgence of 300 days;

A plenary indulgence on the usual conditions, when they repeat this invocation daily for a month;

A plenary indulgence at the hour of death, if they have been accustomed to invoke the holy Name frequently during life, provided that, after confession and Communion, or at least an act of contrition, they devoutly invoke the holy Name of Jesus with their lips if possible, otherwise in their hearts, and accept death with resignation from the hand of God as the wages of sin (S. C. Ind., Sept. 5, 1759 and Oct. 10, 1904; S. P. Ap., Dec. 9, 1933).

II

THE LITANY OF THE MOST HOLY NAME OF JESUS

114

Lord, have mercy on us.
Christ, have mercy on us.
Lord, have mercy on us.
Jesus, hear us.
Jesus, graciously hear us.
God the Father of Heaven, have mercy on us
God the Son, Redeemer of the world,
have mercy on us
God the Holy Ghost, have mercy on us
Holy Trinity, one God have mercy on us
Jesus, Son of the living God, have mercy on us
Jesus, splendor of the Father,
have mercy on us
Jesus, brightness of eternal light,
have mercy on us
Jesus, King of glory, have mercy on us
Jesus, sun of justice, have mercy on us
Jesus, Son of the Virgin Mary,
have mercy on us
Jesus, most amiable, have mercy on us
Jesus, most admirable, have mercy on us
Jesus, the mighty God, have mercy on us

Jesus, father of the world to come,
>have mercy on us

Jesus, Angel of great counsel,
>have mercy on us

Jesus, most powerful,   have mercy on us
Jesus, most patient,   have mercy on us
Jesus, most obedient,   have mercy on us
Jesus, meek and humble of heart,
>have mercy on us

Jesus, lover of chastity,   have mercy on us
Jesus, lover of us,   have mercy on us
Jesus, God of peace,   have mercy on us
Jesus, author of life,   have mercy on us
Jesus, example of virtues, have mercy on us
Jesus, zealous lover of souls,
>have mercy on us

Jesus, our God,   have mercy on us
Jesus, our refuge,   have mercy on us
Jesus, father of the poor, have mercy on us
Jesus, treasure of the faithful,
>have mercy on us

Jesus, good Shepherd,   have mercy on us
Jesus, true light,   have mercy on us
Jesus, eternal wisdom,   have mercy on us
Jesus, infinite goodness,   have mercy on us
Jesus, our way and our life, have mercy on us
Jesus, joy of Angels,   have mercy on us
Jesus, King of Patriarchs, have mercy on us
Jesus, Master of the Apostles,
>have mercy on us

Jesus, Teacher of the Evangelists,
>have mercy on us

Jesus, strength of Martyrs, have mercy on us
Jesus, light of Confessors, have mercy on us

Jesus, purity of Virgins,   have mercy on us
Jesus, crown of all Saints, have mercy on us
Be merciful,   spare us, O Jesus
Be merciful,   graciously hear us, O Jesus
From all evil,   deliver us, O Jesus
From all sin,   deliver us, O Jesus
From Thy wrath,   deliver us, O Jesus
From the snares of the devil,
                  deliver us, O Jesus
From the spirit of fornication,
                  deliver us, O Jesus
From everlasting death, deliver us, O Jesus
From the neglect of Thine inspirations,
                  deliver us, O Jesus
By the mystery of Thy holy Incarnation,
                  deliver us, O Jesus
By Thy Nativity,   deliver us, O Jesus
By Thine Infancy,   deliver us, O Jesus
By Thy most divine life, deliver us, O Jesus
By Thy labors,   deliver us, O Jesus
By Thine agony and Passion,
                  deliver us, O Jesus
By Thy Cross and dereliction,
                  deliver us, O Jesus
By Thy sufferings,   deliver us, O Jesus
By Thy death and burial, deliver us, O Jesus
By Thy Resurrection,   deliver us, O Jesus
By Thine Ascension,   deliver us, O Jesus
By Thine institution of the most Holy
  Eucharist,   deliver us, O Jesus
By Thy joys,   deliver us, O Jesus
By Thy glory,   deliver us, O Jesus
Lamb of God, Who takest away the sins of
  the world, spare us, O Jesus.

Lamb of God, Who takest away the sins of the world, hear us, O Jesus.

Lamb of God, Who takest away the sins of the world, have mercy on us, O Jesus.

Jesus, hear us.

Jesus, graciously hear us.

Let us pray.

O Lord Jesus Christ, who hast said: Ask and ye shall receive, seek and ye shall find, knock and it shall be opened unto you; mercifully attend to our supplications, and grant us the gift of Thy divine charity, that we may ever love Thee with our whole heart and with all our words and deeds, and may never cease from praising Thee.

Make us, O Lord, to have a perpetual fear and love of Thy holy Name, for Thou never failest to help and govern those whom Thou dost bring up in Thy steadfast love: who livest and reignest for ever and ever. Amen.

An indulgence of 7 years.

A plenary indulgence once a month on the usual conditions, for the daily and devout recitation of this litany (S. C. Ind., Jan. 16, 1886; S. P. Ap., Jan. 2, 1933).

K ýrie, eléison.
     Christe, eléison.
Kyrie, eléison.
Iesu, audi nos.
Iesu, exáudi nos.

Pater de cælis, Deus,	miserére nobis
Fili, Redémptor mundi, Deus,	miserére
Spíritus Sancte, Deus,	miserére
Sancta Trínitas, unus Deus,	miserére
Iesu, Fili Dei vivi,	miserére

Iesu, splendor Patris,	miserére
Iesu, candor lucis ætérnæ,	miserére
Iesu, rex glóriæ,	miserére
Iesu, sol iustítiæ,	miserére
Iesu, Fili Maríæ Vírginis,	miserére
Iesu amábilis,	miserére
Iesu admirábilis,	miserére
Iesu, Deus fortis,	miserére
Iesu, pater futúri sǽculi,	miserére
Iesu, magni consílii ángele,	miserére
Iesu potentíssime,	miserére
Iesu patientíssime,	miserére
Iesu obedientíssime,	miserére
Iesu, mitis et húmilis corde,	miserére
Iesu, amátor castitátis,	miserére
Iesu, amátor noster,	miserére
Iesu, Deus pacis,	miserére
Iesu, auctor vitæ,	miserére
Iesu, exémplar virtútum,	miserére
Iesu, zelátor animárum,	miserére
Iesu, Deus noster,	miserére
Iesu, refúgium nostrum,	miserére
Iesu, pater páuperum,	miserére
Iesu, thesáure fidélium,	miserére
Iesu, bone pastor,	miserére
Iesu, lux vera,	miserére
Iesu, sapiéntia ætérna,	miserére
Iesu, bónitas infiníta,	miserére
Iesu, via et vita nostra,	miserére
Iesu, gáudium Angelórum,	miserére
Iesu, rex Patriarchárum,	miserére
Iesu, magíster Apostolórum,	miserére
Iesu, doctor Evangelistárum,	miserére
Iesu, fortitúdo Mártyrum,	miserére
Iesu, lumen Confessórum,	miserére
Iesu, púritas Vírginum,	miserére
Iesu, coróna Sanctórum ómnium,	miserére
Propítius esto,	parce, nobis, Iesu
Propítius esto,	exáudi nos, Iesu
Ab omni malo,	líbera nos, Iesu
Ab omni peccáto,	líbera

Ab ira tua,	líbera
Ab insídiis diáboli,	líbera
A spíritu fornicatiónis,	líbera
A morte perpétua,	líbera
A negléctu inspiratiónum tuárum,	líbera
Per mystérium sanctæ Incarnatiónis tuæ,	líbera
Per nativitátem tuam,	líbera
Per infántiam tuam,	líbera
Per diviníssimam vitam tuam,	líbera
Per labóres tuos,	líbera
Per agoníam et passiónem tuam,	líbera
Per crucem et derelictiónem tuam,	líbera
Per languóres tuos,	líbera
Per mortem et sepultúram tuam,	líbera
Per resurrectiónem tuam,	líbera
Per ascensiónem tuam,	líbera
Per sanctíssimæ Eucharístiæ institutiónem tuam,	líbera
Per gáudia tua,	líbera
Per glóriam tuam,	líbera

Agnus Dei, qui tollis peccáta mundi, parce nobis, Iesu.

Agnus Dei, qui tollis peccáta mundi, exáudi nos, Iesu.

Agnus Dei, qui tollis peccáta mundi, miserére nobis, Iesu.

Iesu, audi nos.

Iesu, exáudi nos.

Oremus.

Dómine Iesu Christe, qui dixísti: Pétite et accipiétis; quǽrite et inveniétis; pulsáte et aperiétur vobis; quǽsumus, da nobis peténtibus diviníssimi tui amóris afféctum, ut te toto corde, ore et ópere diligámus et a tua nunquam laude cessémus.

Sancti Nóminis tui, Dómine, timórem páriter et amórem fac nos habére perpétuum, quia numquam tua gubernatióne destítuis, quos in soliditáte tuæ dilectiónis instítuis: Qui vivis et regnas in sǽcula sæculórum. Amen.

III

HYMNS

115

Iesu, dulcis memoria

J esus, the very thought of Thee
  With sweetness fills the breast!
Yet sweeter far Thy face to see
  And in Thy presence rest.

No voice can sing, no heart can frame,
  Nor can the memory find,
A sweeter sound than Jesus' name,
  The Saviour of mankind.

O hope of every contrite heart!
  O joy of all the meek!
To those who fall, how kind Thou art!
  How good to those who seek!

But what to those who find? Ah! this
  Nor tongue nor pen can show—
The love of Jesus, what it is,
  None but His loved ones know.

Jesus! our only hope be Thou,
  As Thou our prize shalt be;
In Thee be all our glory now,
  And through eternity. Amen.

(Roman Breviary, tr. E. Caswall).

An indulgence of 5 years.

A plenary indulgence once a month on the usual conditions, for the daily and devout recitation of this hymn(S. C. Ind., June 13, 1815; S. P. Ap., May 21, 1935).

I esu, dulcis memória,
  Dans vera cordis gáudia;
Sed super mel et ómnia
Eius dulcis præséntia.

Nil canítur suávius,
Nil audítur iucúndius,
Nil cogitátur dúlcius,
Quam Iesus Dei Fílius.

Iesu, spes pæniténtibus,
Quam pius es peténtibus,
Quam bonus te quæréntibus,
Sed quid inveniéntibus?

Nec lingua valet dícere,
Nec líttera exprímere,
Expértus potest crédere
Quid sit Iesum dilígere.

Sis, Iesu, nostrum gáudium,
Qui es futúrum præmium:
Sit nostra in te glória
Per cuncta semper sæcula.   Amen.

(ex *Breviario Romano*).

116
Iesu decus angelicum

O Jesus, Thou the beauty art
Of Angel worlds above!
Thy name is music to the heart,
Enchanting it with love!
Celestial sweetness unalloyed!
Who eat Thee hunger still,
Who drink of Thee still feel a void
Which naught but Thou can fill!

O my sweet Jesus! hear the sighs
Which unto Thee I send!
To Thee my inmost spirit cries,
My being's hope and end!
Stay with us, Lord, and with Thy light
Illume the soul's abyss;
Scatter the darkness of our night
And fill the world with bliss.

O Jesu! spotless Virgin flower!
Our life and joy! to Thee
Be praise, beatitude and power,
Through all eternity! Amen.

(Roman Breviary, tr. E. Caswall).

An indulgence of 5 years.

A plenary indulgence once a month on the usual conditions, when this hymn is said daily (S. P. Ap., Nov. 22, 1934).

I esu, decus angélicum,
In aure dulce cánticum,
In ore mel miríficum,
In corde nectar cǽlicum.

Qui te gustant, esúriunt,
Qui bibunt, adhuc sítiunt;
Desideráre nésciunt,
Nisi Iesum, quem díligunt.

O Iesu mi dulcíssime,
Spes suspirántis ánimæ!
Te quærunt piæ lácrimæ,
Te clamor mentis íntimæ,

Mane nobíscum, Dómine,
Et nos illústra lúmine;
Pulsa mentis calígine,
Mundum reple dulcédine.

Ieus, flos Matris Vírginis,
Amor nostræ dulcédinis,
Tibi laus, honor nóminis,
Regnum beatitúdinis. Amen.

(ex *Breviario Romano*).

117

Iesu Rex admirabilis

O Jesus, King most wonderful!
Thou Conqueror renowned!
Thou Sweetness most ineffable!
In whom all joys are found!

When once Thou visitest the heart,
    Then truth begins to shine;
Then earthly vanities depart;
    Then kindles love divine.

O Jesu! Light of all below!
    Thou Fount of life and fire!
Surpassing all the joys we know,
    And all we can desire.

May every heart confess Thy name,
    And ever Thee adore;
And seeking Thee, itself inflame
    To seek Thee more and more.

Thee may our tongues for ever bless;
    Thee may we love alone;
And ever in our lives express
    The image of Thine own.   Amen.

(Roman Breviary, tr. E. Caswall).

An indulgence of 5 years.

A plenary indulgence once a month on the usual conditions,
when this hymn has been said daily (S. C. Ind., June 13, 1815;
S. P. Ap., July 16, 1936).

I esu, Rex admirábilis
    Et triumphátor nóbilis,
Dulcédo ineffábilis,
Totus desiderábilis.

    Quando cor nostrum vísitas,
Tunc lucet ei véritas,
Mundi viléscit vánitas,
Et intus fervet cáritas.

    Iesu, dulcédo córdium,
Fons vivus, lumen méntium,
Excédens omne gáudium
Et omne desidérium.

    Iesum omnes agnóscite,
Amórem eius póscite;

Iesum ardénter quǽrite,
Quæréndo inardéscite.
  Te nostra, Iesu, vox sonet,
Nostri te mores éxprimant;
Te corda nostra díligant
Et nunc, et in perpétuum.   Amen.

(ex *Breviario Romano*).

IV

DEVOUT PRACTICES

118

The faithful who, during the month of January, perform some special act of devotion in honor of the holy Name of Jesus are granted:

An indulgence of 7 years once on any day of the month;

A plenary indulgence on the usual conditions, if this act of devotion is repeated daily for the entire month (**Apostolic Brief, Dec. 21, 1901; S. P. Ap., Jan. 2, 1933**).

119

The faithful who recite five times the doxology *Glory be to the Father* together with the ejaculation:

Blessed be the most holy Name of Jesus without end!

may gain:

An indulgence of 300 days (**Pius X, Audience Nov. 19, 1906, exhib. Nov. 26, 1906**).

120

The faithful who, after confession and Communion, visit some church or oratory, public or even semi-public (in the case of those who may lawfully use the latter), on the Feast of the most holy Name of Jesus and pray for the intentions of the Sovereign Pontiff may gain:

A plenary indulgence (**Pius X, Audience Nov. 19, 1906, exhib. Nov. 26, 1906; S. P. Ap., May 17, 1927**).

V

PRAYERS

121

O good Jesu, according to Thy great mercy, have mercy on me. O most merciful Jesu, by that Precious Blood which Thou didst will to shed for sinners, I beseech Thee to wash away all mine iniquities and to look graciously upon me, a poor and unworthy sinner, as I call upon Thy holy Name. Therefore, O Jesus, do Thou save me for Thy holy Name's sake.

An indulgence of 500 days (S. C. Ind., Nov. 26, 1876; S. P. Ap., Dec. 17, 1932).

O bone Iesu, secúndum magnam misericórdiam tuam miserére mei. O clementíssime Iesu, te déprecor per illum Sánguinem pretiósum, quem pro peccatóribus effúndere voluísti, ut ábluas omnes iniquitátes meas et in me respícias míserum et indígnum invocántem tuum sanctum Nomen. Ergo, Iesu, propter Nomen sanctum tuum salva me.

122

O God, who didst appoint Thine only-begotten Son to be the Saviour of mankind and didst command His name to be called Jesus; mercifully grant that we may enjoy the vision of Him in heaven, whose holy Name we venerate on earth. Through the same Christ our Lord. Amen (Roman Missal).

An indulgence of 5 years.

A plenary indulgence once a month on the usual conditions, if this prayer is said devoutly every day (S. P. Ap., Nov. 22, 1934).

Deus, qui unigénitum Fílium tuum constituísti humáni géneris Salvatórem et Iesum vocári iussísti: concéde propítius, ut, cuius sanctum Nomen

venerámur in terris, eius quoque adspéctu perfruá-
mur in cælis. Per eúmdem Christum Dóminum
nostrum. Amen (ex *Missali Romano*).

Art. III
THE INFANT JESUS
I
PIOUS EXERCISES
123

a) **T**he faithful who, in order to return thanks to
God the Father for the benefits conferred
upon mankind by the Incarnation of the Word, devoutly assist at midnight Mass on the Feast of the
Nativity of our Lord, may gain:

An indulgence of 10 years;
A plenary indulgence, if they have gone to confession and Communion and prayed for the intentions of the Holy Father.

b) Those who assist at Matins or Lauds and follow
the singing of the psalms and lessons, either by devoutly reading them or with pious meditations on
the Incarnation of the Word of God, or prayers,
may gain:

An indulgence of 10 years (**Apostolic Brief, Oct. 22, 1586; S. P.
Ap., Apr. 2, 1936**).

124
A NOVENA BEFORE THE FEAST OF THE
NATIVITY OF OUR LORD

The faithful who devoutly take part in a public
novena before the Feast of the Nativity of our
Lord in honor of the divine Infant Jesus, may gain:

An indulgence of 10 years on any day;
A plenary indulgence on condition of confession, communion
and prayer for the intention of the Sovereign Pontiff, if they assist
at five, at least, of the exercises.

To those who, at the aforesaid season, offer their
prayers or other acts of devotion to the divine
Infant privately, with the intention of continuing them
for nine successive days, is granted:

An indulgence of 7 years once on any day;

A plenary indulgence on the usual conditions, at the end of the novena; but where a public novena is held, this indulgence can be gained only by those who are legitimately hindered from attending the public exercises (Secr. Mem., Aug. 12, 1815; S. C. Ind., July 9, 1830; S. P. Ap., Feb. 21, 1933).

125

PRAYERS FOR A NOVENA FROM THE 16TH TO THE
24TH DAY OF ANY MONTH

I. Eternal Father, I offer to Thine honor and glory, for my eternal salvation and for the salvation of the whole world, the mystery of the birth of our divine Redeemer.
Glory be to the Father, *etc.*

II. Eternal Father, I offer to Thine honor and glory, for my eternal salvation and for the salvation of the whole world, the sufferings of the most holy Virgin and Saint Joseph on that long and weary journey from Nazareth to Bethlehem, and the anguish of their hearts at not finding a place of shelter when the Saviour of the world was about to be born.
Glory be to the Father, *etc.*

III. Eternal Father, I offer to Thine honor and glory, for my eternal salvation and for the salvation of the whole world, the sufferings of Jesus in the manger where He was born, the cold He suffered, the tears He shed and His tender infant cries.
Glory be to the Father, *etc.*

IV. Eternal Father, I offer to Thine honor and glory, for my eternal salvation and for the salvation of the whole world, the pain which the divine Child Jesus felt in His tender Body, when He submitted to the rite of circumcision: I offer Thee that Precious Blood which He then first shed for the salvation of all mankind.

Glory be to the Father, *etc.*

V. Eternal Father, I offer to Thine honor and glory, for my eternal salvation and for the salvation of the whole world, the humility, mortification, patience, charity and all the virtues of the Child Jesus; I thank Thee, I love Thee, and I bless Thee infinitely for this ineffable mystery of the Incarnation of the Word of God.

Glory be to the Father, *etc.*

℣. The Word was made flesh;
℞. And dwelt amongst us.

Let us pray.

O God, whose only-begotten Son hath appeared in the substance of our flesh; grant, we beseech Thee, that through Him, whom we acknowledge to have been outwardly like unto us, we may deserve to be renewed in our inward selves. Who liveth and reigneth with Thee for ever and ever. Amen.

An indulgence of 7 years once on any day.

A plenary indulgence on the usual conditions at the close of the novena (S. C. Ind., Sept. 23, 1846; S. P. Ap., Oct. 14, 1934).

II
PRAYERS
126

℣. O God, come unto my assistance!
℞. O Lord, make haste to help me!

℣. Glory be to the Father, and to the Son, and to the Holy Ghost;

℞. As it was in the beginning, is now, and ever shall be, world without end.   Amen.

Our Father.

I. Jesu, sweetest Child, who didst come down from the bosom of the Father for our salvation, who wast conceived by the Holy Ghost, who didst not abhor the Virgin's womb, and who, being the Word made flesh, didst take upon Thee the form of a servant, have mercy on us.

℞. Have mercy on us, Child Jesus, have mercy on us.

Hail Mary.

II. Jesu, sweetest Child, who by means of Thy Virgin Mother didst visit Saint Elisabeth, who didst fill Thy forerunner, John the Baptist, with Thy Holy Spirit and didst sanctify him in his mother's womb, have mercy on us.

℞. Have mercy on us, Child Jesus, have mercy on us.

Hail Mary.

III. Jesu, sweetest Child, who, enclosed for nine months in Thy Mother's womb, wast looked for with eager expectation by the Virgin Mary and Saint Joseph, and wast offered by God the Father for the salvation of the world, have mercy on us.

℞. Have mercy on us, Child Jesus, have mercy on us.

Hail Mary.

IV. Jesu, sweetest Child, born in Bethlehem of the Virgin Mary, wrapped in swaddling clothes and laid in a manger, announced by Angels and visited by shepherds, have mercy on us.

℟. Have mercy on us, Child Jesus, have mercy on us.

Hail Mary.

> All honor, laud, and glory be,
> O Jesu, Virgin-born, to Thee;
> All glory, as is ever meet,
> To Father and to Paraclete.   Amen.

℣. Christ is near to us;

℟. Come, let us adore Him.

Our Father.

V. Jesu, sweetest Child, wounded after eight days in Thy circumcision, called by the glorious Name of Jesus, and at once by Thy Name and by Thy Blood foreshown as the Saviour of the world, have mercy on us.

℟. Have mercy on us, Child Jesus, have mercy on us.

Hail Mary.

VI. Jesu, sweetest Child, manifested by the leading of a star to the three Wise Men, worshiped in the arms of Thy Mother, presented with the mystic gifts of gold, frankincense and myrrh, have mercy on us.

℟. Have mercy on us, Child Jesus, have mercy on us.

Hail Mary.

VII. Jesu, sweetest Child, presented in the temple by Thy Virgin Mother, taken up in

Simeon's arms, and revealed to Israel by Anna, a prophetess, have mercy on us.

℟. Have mercy on us, Child Jesus, have mercy on us.

Hail Mary.

VIII. Jesu, sweetest Child, sought by wicked Herod to be slain, carried with Thy Mother into Egypt by Saint Joseph, rescued from the cruel slaughter, and glorified by the praises of the martyred Innocents, have mercy on us.

℟. Have mercy on us, Child Jesus, have mercy on us.

Hail Mary.

> All honor, laud and glory be,
> O Jesu, Virgin-born, to Thee;
> All glory, as is ever meet,
> To Father and to Paraclete. Amen.

℣. Christ is near to us.
℟. O come and let us worship.
Our Father.

IX. Jesu, sweetest Child, who didst dwell in Egypt with most holy Mary and the Patriarch, Saint Joseph until the death of Herod, have mercy on us.

℟. Have mercy on us, Child Jesus, have mercy on us.

Hail Mary.

X. Jesu, sweetest Child, who didst return from Egypt to the land of Israel with Thy parents, suffering many hardships in the way, and didst enter into the city of Nazareth, have mercy on us.

℟. Have mercy on us, Child Jesus, have mercy on us.

Hail Mary.

XI. Jesu, sweetest Child, who didst dwell most holily in the holy house at Nazareth, in subjection to Thy parents, wearied by poverty and toil, and didst increase in wisdom, age and grace, have mercy on us.

℟. Have mercy on us, Child Jesus, have mercy on us.

Hail Mary.

XII. Jesu, sweetest Child, brought to Jerusalem at twelve years of age, sought by Thy parents sorrowing and found with joy after three days in the midst of the Doctors, have mercy on us.

℟. Have mercy on us, Child Jesus, have mercy on us.

Hail Mary.

All honor, laud, and glory be,
O Jesu, Virgin-born to Thee;
All Glory, as is ever meet,
To Father and to Paraclete. Amen.

(For Christmas Day and its Octave):

℣. The Word was made flesh, alleluia.

℟. And dwelt amongst us, alleluia.

(For the Epiphany and its Octave):

℣. Christ hath manifested Himself to us, alleluia.

℟ O come and let us worship, alleluia.

(Throughout the year):

℣. The Word was made flesh,

℟. And dwelt amongst us.

Let us pray.

Almighty and everlasting God, Lord of heaven and earth, who dost reveal Thyself to little ones; grant, we beseech Thee, that we, venerating with due honor the sacred mysteries of Thy Son, the Child Jesus, and copying them with due imitation, may be enabled to enter the kingdom of heaven which Thou hast promised to little children. Through the same Christ our Lord. Amen.

An indulgence of 5 years once a day.

A plenary indulgence on the usual conditions when these prayers are said devoutly on the 25th day of any month (S. C. Ind., Nov. 23, 1819; S. P. Ap., June 8, 1935).

℣. Deus, in adiutórium meum inténde:
℟. Dómine, ad adiuvándum me festína.
℣. Glória Patri et Fílio et Spirítui Sancto,
℟. Sicut erat in princípio et nunc et semper, et in sǽcula sæculórum. Amen.
Pater noster.

I. Iesu Infans dulcíssime, e sinu Patris propter nostram salútem descéndens, de Spíritu Sancto concéptus, Vírginis úterum non horrens, et Verbum caro factum, formam servi accípiens, miserére nostri.
℟. Miserére nostri, Iesu Infans, miserére nostri. Ave María.

II. Iesu Infans dulcíssime, per Vírginem Matrem tuam vísitans Elísabeth, Ioánnem Baptístam Præcursórem tuum Spíritu Sancto replens, et adhuc in útero matris suæ sanctíficans, miserére nostri.
℟. Miserére, *etc.* Ave María.

III. Iesu Infans dulcíssime, novem ménsibus in útero clausus, summis votis a María Vírgine et a sancto Ioseph expectátus, et a Deo Patri pro salúte mundi oblátus, miserére nostri.
℟. Miserére, *etc.* Ave María.

IV. Iesu Infans dulcíssime, in Béthlehem ex Vírgine María natus, pannis involútus, in præsépio reclinátus, ab Angelis annuntiátus et a pastóribus visitátus, miserére nostri.

℟. Miserére, *etc.* Ave María.
> Iesu, tibi sit glória,
> Qui natus es de Vírgine,
> Cum Patre et almo Spíritu,
> In sempitérna sæcula. Amen.

℣. Christus prope est nobis.
℟. Veníte, adorémus.
Pater noster.

V. Iesu Infans dulcíssime, in Circumcisióne post dies octo vulnerátus, glorióso Iesu nómine vocátus, et in nómine simul et sánguine Salvatóris offício præsignátus, miserére nostri.

℟. Miserére, *etc.* Ave María.

VI. Iesu Infans dulcíssime, stella duce tribus Magis demonstrátus, in sinu Matris adorátus, et mysticis munéribus, auro, thure et myrrha donátus, miserére nostri.

℟. Miserére, *etc.* Ave María.

VII. Iesu Infans dulcíssime, in templo a Matre Vírgine præsentátus, inter bráchia a Simeóne amplexátus, et ab Anna prophetíssa Isräel revelátus, miserére nostri.

℟. Miserére, *etc.* Ave María.

VIII. Iesu Infans dulcíssime, ab iníquo Heróde ad mortem quæsítus, a sancto Ioseph in Aegyptum cum Matre deportátus, a crudéli cæde sublátus, et præcóniis Mártyrum Innocéntium glorificátus, miserére nostri.

℟. Miserére, *etc.* Ave María.

> Iesu, tibi sit glória,
> Qui natus es de Vírgine
> Cum Patre et almo Spíritu
> In sempitérna sæcula. Amen.

℣ Christus prope est nobis.

℟. Veníte, adorémus.
Pater noster.

IX. Iesu Infans dulcíssime, in Aegyptum cum María sanctíssima et Patriárcha sancto Ioseph usque ad óbitum Heródis commorátus, miserére nostri.
℟. Miserére, *etc.* Ave María.

X. Iesu Infans dulcíssime, ex Aegypto cum Paréntibus in terram Isräel revérsus, multos labóres in itínere perpéssus, et in civitáte Názareth ingréssus, miserére nostri.
℟. Miserére, *etc.* Ave María.

XI. Iesu Infans dulcíssime, in sancta Nazaréna domo, súbditus Paréntibus, sanctíssime commorátus, paupertáte et labóribus faticátus, in sapiéntiæ, ætátis et grátiæ proféctu confortátus, miserére nostri.
℟. Miserére, *etc.* Ave María.

XII. Iesu Infans dulcíssime, in Ierúsalem duodénnis ductus, a Paréntibus cum dolóre quæsítus, et post tríduum cum gáudio inter Doctóres invéntus, miserére nostri.
℟. Miserére, *etc.* Ave María.

Iesu, tibi sit glória,
Qui natus es de Vírgine
Cum Patre et almo Spíritu
In sempitérna sǽcula. Amen.

Die Nativitatis Domini et per Octavam:
℣. Verbum caro factum est, allelúia.
℟. Et habitávit in nobis, allelúia.

In Epiphania Domini et per Octavam:
℣. Christus manifestávit se nobis, allelúia.
℟. Veníte, adorémus, allelúia.

Per annum:
℣. Verbum caro factum est,
℟. Et habitávit in nobis.

Orémus.

Omnípotens sempitérne Deus, Dómine cæli et terræ, qui te revélas párvulis; concéde, quǽsumus, ut nos sacrosáncta Fílii tui Infántis Iesu

mystéria digno honóre recoléntes, dignáque imitatióne sectántes, ad regnum cælórum promíssum
párvulis perveníre valeámus. Per eúmdem Christum Dóminum nostrum. Amen.

III
PRAYERS
127

Most dear Lord Jesus Christ, who, being
made a Child for us, didst will to be
born in a cave to free us from the darkness of
sin, to draw us unto Thee, and to set us on
fire with Thy holy love; we adore Thee as our
Creator and Redeemer, we acknowledge
Thee and choose Thee for our King and Lord,
and for tribute we offer Thee all the affection
of our poor hearts. Dear Jesus, our Lord and
God, graciously accept this offering, and that
it may be worthy of Thine acceptance, forgive
us our sins, enlighten us, and inflame us
with that sacred fire which Thou camest to
bring upon the earth and to enkindle in our
hearts. May our souls thus become an altar,
on which we may offer Thee the sacrifice of
our mortifications; grant that we may ever
seek Thy greater glory here on earth, so that
one day we may come to enjoy Thine infinite
loveliness in heaven. Amen.

An indulgence of 3 years.

A plenary indulgence once a month on the usual conditions for
the daily recitation of this prayer(S. C. Ind., Jan. 18, 1894; S. P.
Ap., Feb. 21, 1933).

128

O divine Infant, who, after the wonders
of Thy birth in Bethlehem, wishing to
extend to the whole world Thine infinite

mercy, didst call the Wise Men by heavenly inspiration to Thy crib, which was thus converted into a throne of royal grandeur, and didst graciously receive those holy men, who were obedient to the divine call and hastened to Thy feet, acknowledging Thee and worshiping Thee as the Prince of Peace, the Redeemer of mankind, and the very Son of God; ah, renew in us the proofs of Thy goodness and almighty power; enlighten our minds, strengthen our wills, and inflame our hearts to know Thee, to serve Thee, and to love Thee in this life, meriting thus to enjoy Thee eternally in the life to come.

An indulgence of 500 days (S. P. Ap., July 14, 1924 and Jan. 15, 1935).

129

Eight days being passed, the Child was circumcised and His name was called Jesus."

In order to melt the hard and frozen heart of sinful man, O divine Infant, the cold, the poverty, and the tears of Thy manger were not to be enough. Behold, even while the heavenly light and the echo of the angelic harmonies were not yet spent above Thy head, a knife of stone passed over Thy sacred flesh, work of the Holy Spirit, and drew from thence some drops of blood. Now, in the morning of life, those drops are few; but at eventide Thou wilt shed it all even to its last drop. Ah, make us also understand that we cannot escape the necessity of expiating our guilt and of recovering our freedom of spirit through mortification of the base instincts of our flesh.

The grandeur of Thy name, O Jesus, went before, accompanied, and followed Thy coming upon earth. From eternity the Father carried that name written in golden letters in His mind, and at the dawn of creation angelic harps intoned a hymn of praise to it, and the holy men of old greeted it from afar with a joyous heart-beat of hope. At its first echoes in the universe, the heavens opened, earth breathed again, and hell trembled. Its history records nothing but triumphs. For twenty centuries it has been the watch-word of true believers, who have always found in it, and will continue to find therein, the inspiration and the impelling power to reach the most exalted heights of virtue. It will ever be the sweetest name of all; it was spoken over Thy manger and inscribed upon the Cross; and through all the years it will bring to man's remembrance Him who loved us even unto death.

O Jesus, take full possession of our hearts, and make them live by Thy love only, until they consecrate their final beating to Thee.

The faithful, who on the feast of the Circumcision of Our Lord recite this prayer with devotion, are granted:

An indulgence of 3 years;

A plenary indulgence on the usual conditions (S. P. Ap., May 4. 1941).

130

At Thy birth, O Jesus, a star of wondrous splendor shone forth in the Eastern skies, and led to Bethlehem the Magi, those

envoys of far-distant, pagan peoples, even
as the Angel, bathed in heavenly light, was
summoning to Thy manger the shepherds,
as representatives of the chosen people. For
the Gentiles as well as the Jews, must needs
recognize in Thee, a poor and helpless Infant,
the almighty King of Ages, the Saviour of
mankind. Neither sceptre nor diadem dis-
closed Thy kingly state; no sweet harmonies,
no hosts of Angels mustering round Thy crib
revealed Thy divine nature; but the star,
shining above Thy wretched stable, pointed
to the heavens, the earth, and the entire
universe as Thine absolute possessions; even
as the Magi, who at the inspiration of Thy
grace, coming promptly from afar, caring
naught for dangers, overcoming every difficulty, and embracing every sacrifice, reached
Thy feet and kneeling down in reverence
offered Thee their gifts of gold, frankincense
and myrrh. Thirsting for God, they had
gone eagerly in search of Thee, and Thou
didst reveal Thyself to them in a wonderful
manner, while still in Thy crib, filling them
with ineffable joys and transforming them
into the first messengers of Thy glories to
the peoples of the Orient.

After the appearance of the star, which
sufficed to render the Magi Thy ardent followers, with what marvels, O Jesus, didst
Thou demonstrate Thy divinity! Yet what
darkness still overshadows our poor minds!
How reluctantly our wills give way to the
loving impulses of Thy grace, even when they

do not openly resist Thee! Give us, therefore, O Jesus, the strength to reply ever
promptly and generously to Thy call, and
grant that the divine light of faith, which
was enkindled by Thee within us while still
in our cradles, may ever accompany us on
the road of life, until, blessed at last in
Heaven, we shall be able to fix our eyes upon
Thee in the light of glory.

The faithful, who devoutly recite this prayer on the
solemn feast of the Epiphany of Our Lord, are granted:

An indulgence of 3 years;

A plenary indulgence on the usual conditions (S. P. Ap., May 4,
1941).

Art. IV
JESUS IN THE BLESSED SACRAMENT

I
EJACULATORY PRAYERS AND INVOCATIONS

131

Soul of Christ, be my sanctification.
Body of Christ, be my salvation.
Blood of Christ, fill all my veins.
Water from Christ's side, wash out my stains.
Passion of Christ, my comfort be.
O good Jesu, listen to me.
In Thy wounds I fain would hide,
Ne'er to be parted from Thy side.
Guard me should the foe assail me.
Call me when my life shall fail me.
Bid me come to Thee above,
With all Thy Saints to sing Thy love,
World without end.   Amen.

An indulgence of 300 days.

An indulgence of 7 years, if recited after Holy Communion.

A plenary indulgence once a month on the usual conditions, when this prayer has been said devoutly every day. (S. C. Ind., Jan. 9, 1854).

Anima Christi, sanctífica me. — Corpus Christi, salva me. — Sanguis Christi, inébria me. —Aqua láteris Christi, lava me. — Pássio Christi, confórta me. — O bone Iesu, exáudi me. — Intra tua vúlnera abscónde me. — Ne permíttas me separári a te. — Ab hoste malígno defénde me. — In hora mortis meæ voca me: — Et iube me veníre ad te, — Ut cum Sanctis tuis laudem te. — In sǽcula sæculórum. Amen.

132

a) **Hail, saving Victim, offered for me and for all mankind upon the gibbet of the Cross.**

b) **Hail, Precious Blood, flowing from the wounds of our crucified Lord Jesus Christ, and washing away the sins of the whole world.**

c) **Be mindful, O Lord, of Thy creature, whom Thou hast redeemed by Thy Precious Blood.**

An indulgence of 500 days for each of these ejaculations, even when separately recited, if said during the elevation in the Mass (S. C. Ind., June 30, 1893; S. P. Ap., Feb. 25, 1933).

a) Salve, salutáris Víctima, pro me et omni humáno génere in patíbulo Crucis obláta.

b) Salve, pretióse Sanguis, de vulnéribus Crucifíxi Dómini nostri Iesu Christi prófluens, et peccáta totíus mundi ábluens.

c) Recordáre, Dómine, creatúræ tuæ, quam tuo pretióso Sánguine redemísti.

133

My Lord and my God!

The faithful who, at the elevation of the Sacred Host during Mass or when It is solemnly exposed, recite this ejaculation with faith, piety and love, are granted:

An indulgence of 7 years;

A plenary indulgence once a week, if this pious practice is followed daily, on conditions of confession, Communion and prayer for the intentions of the Sovereign Pontiff (Pius X, Rescript in his own hand, May 18, 1907, exhib. June 12, 1907; S. P. Ap., June 21, 1927 and Jan. 26, 1937).

Dóminus meus et Deus meus!

134

O Jesus in the Blessed Sacrament, have mercy on us!

An indulgence of 300 days (Apostolic Brief, May 20, 1911).

O Iesu in sanctíssimo Sacraménto, miserére nobis!

135

Praise and adoration ever more be given to the most holy Sacrament.

An indulgence of 300 days.

A plenary indulgence on the usual conditions once a month for its daily and devout repetition (S. C. of the Holy Off., Apr. 10, 1913).

Laudétur et adorétur in ætérnum sanctíssimum Sacraméntum.

136

O Sacrament most holy, O Sacrament divine!
All praise and all thanksgiving be every moment Thine!

An indulgence of 300 days.

An indulgence of 3 years, when this ejaculation is recited in the presence of the Blessed Sacrament.

A plenary indulgence on the usual conditions, if the daily recitation of this ejaculation is continued for a whole month (Pius VI, Secr. a suppl. libell., May 24, 1776; Holy Office, Apr. 10, 1913 and Apr. 15, 1915; S. P. Ap., July 12, 1941).

137

I adore Thee every moment,
   O living Bread from heaven,
Great Sacrament!

An indulgence of 300 days.
An indulgence of 3 years, when recited before the Blessed Sacrament.
A plenary indulgence on the usual conditions, if this ejaculation
is repeated daily for an entire month (S. P. Ap., June 4, 1934 and
July 12, 1941).

138

O saving Victim! opening wide
   The gate of heaven to man below!
Our foes press on from every side:
   Thine aid supply, Thy strength bestow.
To Thy great Name be endless praise,
   Immortal Godhead, One in Three!
Oh, grant us endless length of days,
   In our true native land with Thee.   Amen.

(Roman Breviary, tr. E. Caswall).

An indulgence of 5 years.
An indulgence of 7 years, when this invocation is recited before
the Blessed Sacrament.
A plenary indulgence on the usual conditions, if this invocation
is devoutly repeated every day for a month (S. P. Ap., June 4, 1934
and July 12, 1941).

O salutáris Hóstia,
   Quæ cæli pandis óstium,
Bella premunt hostília;
Da robur, fer auxílium.
   Uni trinóque Dómino
Sit sempitérna glória,
Qui vitam sine término
Nobis donet in pátria.   Amen.

(ex *Breviario Romano*).

139

Blessed is He that cometh in the name of
   the Lord; Hosanna in the highest (Roman
Missal).

The faithful, who devoutly recite this prayer after the consecration in the Mass, are granted:

An indulgence of 500 days;
A plenary indulgence once a month on the usual conditions, if they recite it daily (S. P. Ap., Nov. 22, 1934).

B enedíctus qui venit in nómine Dómini: Hosánna in excélsis (ex *Missali Romano*).

140

V ery Bread, good Shepherd, tend us,
    Jesu, of Thy love befriend us,
Thou refresh us, Thou defend us,
Thine eternal goodness send us
In the land of life to see.
Thou Who all things canst and knowest,
Who on earth such food bestowest,
Grant us with Thy Saints, though lowest,
Where the heavenly feast Thou shewest,
Fellow-heirs and guests to be.   Amen.

(Roman Missal).

An indulgence of 5 years.
An indulgence of 7 years, if this invocation is recited in the presence of the Blessed Sacrament.
A plenary indulgence on the usual conditions, when this invocation has been devoutly repeated every day for a month (S. P. Ap., June 15, 1935 and July 12, 1941).

B one pastor, panis vere,
    Iesu, nostri miserére:
Tu nos pasce, nos tuére:
Tu nos bona fac vidére
In terra vivéntium.
    Tu, qui cuncta scis et vales;
Qui nos pascis hic mortáles;
Tuos ibi commensáles,
Coherédes et sodáles
Fac sanctórum cívium.   Amen.

(ex *Missali Romano*).

141
Hail true Body born of Mary the Virgin.

An indulgence of 500 days;

A plenary indulgence on the usual conditions, if this ejaculation has been recited devoutly every day for a month (S. P. Ap., June 23, 1939).

Ave verum Corpus natum ex María Vírgine.

II
ACTS OF ADORATION

142

The faithful who recite some prayer at the sound of the bell for the elevation at Mass, wherever they may be, are granted:

An indulgence of 300 days (Gregory XIII, Constitution *"Ad excitandum,"* Apr. 10, 1580; S. P. Ap., Feb. 25, 1933).

143

The faithful who devoutly accompany the Blessed Sacrament when It is carried to the sick as Viaticum are granted:

An indulgence of 7 years, if they accompany It with lights;

An indulgence of 5 years, if without lights;

An indulgence of 3 years, if, being lawfully hindered, they send another to carry a light for them;

An indulgence of 100 days, if they recite at least one Our Father and one Hail Mary while the Blessed Sacrament is being carried although they are unable to accompany   (Paul V, Nov. 3, 1606; Innocent XI, Oct. 1, 1678; Innocent XII, Constit. *"Debitum Pastoralis Officii,"* Jan. 5, 1695; S. P. Ap., Mar. 18, 1932).

144

The faithful who accompany the Blessed Sacrament, with or without lights, when It is being carried solemnly to the sick, are granted:

A plenary indulgence upon the addition of confession, Communion, and prayer for the intentions of the Sovereign Pontiff (S. P. Ap., Sept. 25, 1933).

145

The faithful who devoutly visit the Blessed Sacrament in the repository on Holy Thursday or Good Friday, and recite *Our Father, Hail Mary* and

Glory be, five times in order to return due thanks for the institution of the Holy Eucharist, and one *Our Father*, *Hail Mary* and *Glory be* for the intentions of the Sovereign Pontiff, are granted:

An indulgence of 15 years;

A plenary indulgence once each day, if in addition to confession they partake of the Eucharistic table (S. C. Ind., Mar. 7, 1815; S. P. Ap., May 20, 1935).

NOTE: The same indulgence may be gained in places where, with the approval of the Apostolic See, the custom obtains of exposing the Blessed Sacrament for the adoration of the faithful in Holy Week for a longer period than the two days above-mentioned (S. P. Ap., Mar. 20, 1936).

146

a) The faithful who pay the homage of a due genuflection before the Blessed Sacrament reserved in the tabernacle, at the same time reciting the following or similar ejaculation:

Jesus, My God, I adore Thee here present in the Sacrament of Thy love!

may gain:

An indulgence of 300 days;

b) If they duly genuflect on both knees before the Blessed Sacrament solemnly exposed to the adoration of the faithful, reciting the above-mentioned prayer, or one like it:

An indulgence of 500 days;

c) If they make some outward sign of reverence when passing a church or oratory where the Blessed Sacrament is reserved:

An indulgence of 300 days (Pius X, Rescript in his own hand, June 28, 1908, exhib., July 3, 1908; S. C. of the Holy Off., Mar. 22, 1917; S. P. Ap., Feb. 25, 1933).

147

The faithful who, upon entering a church, proceed at once to the Altar of the Blessed Sacrament and make even a brief adoration there, may gain:

An indulgence of 300 days (S. P. Ap., June 15, 1923).

148

The faithful who devoutly visit the Blessed Sacrament and recite five times *Our Father*, *Hail
Mary* and *Glory be*, and add one *Our Father*, *Hail
Mary* and *Glory be* for the intentions of the Sovereign Pontiff, are granted:

An indulgence of 10 years;

A plenary indulgence on condition of confession and Communion, if they devoutly perform this devotion for seven continuous days (Apostolic Brief, Sept. 15, 1876 and June 3, 1932).

149

The faithful who are hindered by sickness or some
other just cause from visiting the Blessed Sacrament in church, and who make such a visit in the
spirit of faith in the real Presence of Jesus in the
Blessed Sacrament at home or wherever they are detained, reciting five times *Our Father*, *Hail Mary*
and *Glory be*, with the addition of one *Our Father*,
Hail Mary and *Glory be* for the intentions of the
Sovereign Pontiff, are granted:

An indulgence of 5 years;

A plenary indulgence on the usual conditions, if they make such
a devout visit for seven continuous days provided that they are still
under the same lawful impediment (S. P. Ap., Apr. 12, 1935).

150

The faithful who take part in solemn Eucharistic
processions, whether held within a church or in
the public streets, are granted:

An indulgence of 5 years.

A plenary indulgence, on condition of sacramental confession,
Holy Communion, and prayers for the intention of the Sovereign
Pontiff (S. P. Ap., Sept. 25, 1933 and July 10, 1936).

III

FIRST COMMUNION

151

The faithful who receive Holy Communion for the
first time or who are present at the first Communion of others, are granted:

A plenary indulgence on the usual conditions (S. C. Ind., July 12, 1905; S. P. Ap., May 17, 1927).

152

a) The faithful who instruct children for their first Holy Communion for at least half an hour, are granted:

An indulgence of 500 days.

b) Those, moreover, who recite the following prayer:

O Jesus, who hast loved us with such exceeding great love as to give us the ineffable gift of the Holy Eucharist, inflame us with a burning zeal to promote Thy glory by preparing worthily the little children who are to approach Thy holy table for the first time. Protect, O Sacred Heart of Jesus, these young souls from the assaults of evil, strengthen their faith, increase their love and endow them with all the virtues that will make them worthy to receive Thee. Amen.

Saint John the Baptist, forerunner of the Messias, prepare the way for Jesus in the hearts of these children.

Saint Tarcisius, keep safe the children who are making their first Communion;

may gain:

An indulgence of 500 days (Pius X, Rescript in his own hand, Oct. 21, 1908, exhib., Nov. 14, 1908; S. P. Ap., Apr. 16, 1936).

IV

PRAYERS BEFORE COMMUNION

153

As the hart panteth after the water-springs, so panteth my soul after Thee, O God (Psalm 41, 2).

An indulgence of 500 days.

A plenary indulgence once a month for the daily recitation of this invocation, on condition of confession, a visit to some church or public oratory and prayer for the intentions of the Sovereign Pontiff (S. P. Ap., Apr. 23, 1932).

Quemádmodum desíderat cervus ad fontes aquárum, ita desíderat ánima mea ad te, Deus (Ps. XLI, 2).

154

Come, O Lord, and tarry not (Roman Breviary).

An indulgence of 500 days.

A plenary indulgence once a month for the daily recitation of this act of desire on condition of sacramental confession, a visit to a church or public oratory and prayer for the intentions of the Sovereign Pontiff (S. P. Ap., May 12, 1934).

Veni, Dómine, et noli tardáre (ex *Breviario Romano*).

155

Let the receiving of Thy Body, O Lord Jesus Christ, which I, though unworthy, do presume to receive, turn not to me for judgment and condemnation, but, according to Thy mercy, let it be profitable to me for the receiving of protection and healing, both of soul and body: Who livest and reignest for ever and ever. Amen (Roman Missal).

An indulgence of 5 years.

A plenary indulgence, upon the addition of sacramental confession, a visit to a church or public oratory, and prayer for the intentions of the Sovereign Pontiff, if they have recited this prayer in a spirit of devotion every day for an entire month (S. P. Ap., Mar. 15, 1935).

Percéptio Córporis tui, Dómine Iesu Christe, quod ego indígnus súmere præsúmo, non mihi provéniat in iudícium et condemnatiónem; sed pro tua pietáte prosit mihi ad tutaméntum mentis et córporis et ad medélam percipiéndam: Qui vivis et regnas in sæcula sæculórum. Amen. (ex *Missali Romano*).

156

L ord, I am not worthy that Thou shouldst enter under my roof; but only say the word and my soul shall be healed (Roman Missal).

An indulgence of 500 days, if thrice repeated.

A plenary indulgence, if this prayer is recited three times daily for an entire month, upon the addition of sacramental confession, a visit to a church or public oratory, and prayer for the intentions of the Sovereign Pontiff (S. P. Ap., Nov. 22, 1936).

D ómine, non sum dignus ut intres sub tectum meum, sed tantum dic verbo et sanábitur ánima mea (ex *Missali Romano*).

157

T he Body of Our Lord Jesus Christ preserve my soul unto everlasting life. Amen. (Roman Missal).

An indulgence of 500 days.

A plenary indulgence, if the daily recitation of this invocation shall be continued for an entire month, upon the addition of sacramental confession, a visit to a church or public oratory, and prayer for the intentions of the Sovereign Pontiff (S. P. Ap., June 10, 1940).

C orpus Dómini nostri Iesu Christi custódiat ánimam meam in vitam ætérnam. Amen (ex *Missali Rom.*)

158

A lmighty and everlasting God, behold I come to the Sacrament of Thine onlybegotten Son, our Lord Jesus Christ: I come as one infirm to the physician of life, as one unclean to the fountain of mercy, as one blind to the light of everlasting brightness, as one poor and needy to the Lord of heaven and earth. Therefore I implore the abundance of Thy measureless bounty that Thou wouldst vouchsafe to heal my infirmity, wash my uncleanness, enlighten my blindness, enrich my poverty and clothe my nakedness, that I may receive the Bread of Angels, the King of kings, the Lord of lords, with such reverence and humility, with such sorrow and devotion, with such purity and faith, with such purpose and intention as may be profitable to my soul's salvation. Grant unto me, I pray, the grace of receiving not only the Sacrament of our Lord's Body and Blood, but also the grace and power of the Sacrament. O most gracious God, grant me so to receive the Body of Thine only-begotten Son, our Lord Jesus Christ, which He took from the Virgin Mary, as to merit to be incorporated into His mystical Body, and to be numbered amongst His members. O most loving Father, give me grace to behold forever Thy beloved Son with His face at last unveiled, whom I now purpose to receive under the sacramental veil here below. Amen (St. Thomas Aquinas).

An indulgence of 3 years.

A plenary indulgence once a month for the daily recitation of this prayer on condition of confession, a visit to some church or public oratory and prayers for the intentions of the Sovereign Pontiff (S. P. Ap., Dec. 10, 1936).

Omnípotens sempitérne Deus, ecce accédo ad Sacraméntum unigéniti Fílii tui Dómini nostri Iesu Christi; accédo tamquam infírmus ad médicum vitæ, immúndus ad fontem misericórdiæ, cæcus ad lumen claritátis ætérnæ, pauper et egénus ad Dóminum cæli et terræ. Rogo ergo imménsæ largitátis tuæ abundántiam, quátenus meam curáre dignéris infirmitátem, laváre fœditátem, illumináre cæcitátem, ditáre paupertátem, vestíre nuditátem;

ut panem Angelórum, Regem regum et Dóminum dominántium tanta suscípiam reveréntia et humilitáte, tanta contritióne et devotióne, tanta puritáte et fide, tali propósito et intentióne, sicut éxpedit salúti ánimæ meæ. Da mihi, quæso, Domínici Córporis et Sánguinis non solum suscípere Sacraméntum, sed étiam rem et virtútem Sacraménti. O mitíssime Deus, da mihi Corpus unigéniti Fílii tui Dómini nostri Iesu Christi, quod traxit de Vírgine María, sic suscípere, ut córpori suo mýstico mérear incorporári, et inter eius membra connumerári. O amantíssime Pater, concéde mihi diléctum Fílium tuum, quem nunc velátum in via suscípere propóno, reveláta tandem fácie perpétuo contemplári. Amen (S. Thomas Aq.).

NOTE. A prayer to the Blessed Virgin Mary, to be recited before Communion, is found under n. 351.

V

THANKSGIVING AFTER COMMUNION

159

How delectable is the sweetness of Thy heavenly Bread! How admirable is the tranquillity and how perfect the peace of him who receives Thee, after the contrite and sincere confession of his sins! Be Thou blessed a thousand times, my Jesus! When I was in sin, I was unhappy; but now not only is my soul at peace, but I seem to have a foretaste of the peace of paradise! Ah, how true it is, that our hearts were made for Thee, my beloved Lord, and that they rest only when they rest in Thee! Therefore do I give Thee thanks and firmly purpose evermore to avoid sin and its occasions and to fix my abode in Thy divine Heart, whence I look for help to love Thee even unto death. Amen.

An indulgence of 500 days.

A plenary indulgence once a month for the daily repetition of this prayer on condition of sacramental confession, a visit to a church or public oratory and prayer for the intentions of the Sovereign Pontiff (S. C. Ind., June 3, 1896; S. P. Ap., Feb. 25, 1933).

160

I give Thee thanks, holy Lord, Father almighty, everlasting God, who hast vouchsafed to feed me, a sinner, Thine unworthy servant, for no merits of my own, but only out of the goodness of Thy great mercy, with the precious Body and Blood of Thy Son, our Lord Jesus Christ; and I pray Thee, that this holy Communion may be to me, not guilt for punishment, but a saving intercession for pardon.   Let it be to me an armor of faith and a shield of good-will.   Let it be to me a casting out of vices; a driving away of all evil desires and fleshly lusts; an increase of charity, patience, humility, obedience, and all virtues; a firm defense against the plots of all my enemies, both seen and unseen; a perfect quieting of all motions of sin, both in my flesh and in my spirit; a firm cleaving unto Thee, the only and true God, and a happy ending of my life.   And I pray Thee to deign to bring me, a sinner, to that ineffable Feast, where Thou with Thy Son and the Holy Ghost, art to Thy holy ones true light, full satisfaction, everlasting joy, consummate pleasure and perfect happiness.   Amen (St. Thomas Aquinas).

An indulgence of 3 years.

A plenary indulgence once a month for the daily recitation of this prayer on condition of sacramental confession, a visit to some church or public oratory and prayers for the intentions of the Sovereign Pontiff (S. P. Ap., Nov. 22, 1934).

Grátias tibi ago, Dómine sancte, Pater omnípotens, ætérne Deus, qui me peccatórem indígnum fámulum tuum, nullis meis méritis, sed sola dignatióne misericórdiæ tuæ satiáre dignátus es pretióso Córpore et Sánguine Fílii tui Dómini nostri Iesu Christi. Et precor, ut hæc sancta commúnio non sit mihi reátus ad pœnam, sed intercéssio salutáris ad véniam. Sit mihi armatúra fídei et scutum bonæ voluntátis. Sit vitiórum meórum evacuátio, concupiscéntiæ et libídinis exterminátio, caritátis et patiéntiæ humilitátis et obediéntiæ, omniúmque virtútum augmentátio; contra insídias inimicórum ómnium tam visibílium quam invisibílium firma defénsio; mótuum meórum tam carnálium quam spirituálium perfécta quietátio, in te uno ac vero Deo firma adhǽsio, atque finis mei felix consummátio. Et precor te, ut ad illud ineffábile convívium me peccatórem perdúcere dignéris, ubi tu cum Fílio tuo et Spíritu Sancto Sanctis tuis es lux vera, satíetas plena, gáudium sempitérnum, iucúnditas consummáta et felícitas perfécta. Amen (S. Thomas Aquin.).

161

My Lord Jesus Christ, most sweet and most kind, who even now, of Thy great goodness, hast entered into this poor and humble abode, adorn it and enrich it with Thy treasures, that it may be made worthy of Thine indwelling. Take up Thy rest therein, that my heart may find its rest in Thee alone. Let it not suffice Thee, O Lord, to have given me Thy sacred Body; give me also the treasures of grace which Thou bringest with Thee; for it will profit me little to eat the Bread of life, if I remain unfed by Thy grace. Give me, O Lord, a heart completely transformed into Thee by love; give me a life that shall be all Thine, a quiet death that

shall be the beginning of eternal life. That
is what I look for, pray and hope for from
Thee, my eternal God, by virtue of this
Blessed Sacrament. Amen.

An indulgence of 500 days(S. P. Ap., July 8, 1935).

162

O Lord Jesus Christ, Son of the living
God, who according to the will of the
Father, with the cooperation of the Holy
Spirit, hast by Thy death given life unto the
world, deliver me by Thy most sacred Body,
which I, unworthy, have presumed to receive, from all my iniquities and from every
evil, and make me ever to hold fast to Thy
commandments and suffer me never to be
separated from Thee.

An indulgence of 500 days.

A plenary indulgence, if this prayer is devoutly recited every day
for a month and moreover, sacramental confession, a visit to a
church or public oratory, and prayers for the intention of the
Sovereign Pontiff are added thereto(S. P. Ap., May 14, 1940).

D omine Iesu Christe, Fili Dei vivi, qui ex voluntáte
Patris, cooperánte Spíritu Sancto, per mortem
tuam mundum vivificásti, líbera me per sacrosánctum
Corpus tuum, quod ego indígnus súmere præsúmpsi,
ab ómnibus iniquitátibus meis et univérsis malis, et
fac me tuis semper inhærére mandátis et a te numquam
separári permíttas.

NOTE.— Invocations to be said after Communion are found under
n. 131.

VI

A PRAYER TO FOSTER THE PRACTICE OF
DAILY COMMUNION

163

O sweetest Jesu, Thou who camest into
the world to give all souls the life of Thy
grace, and who, to preserve and nourish it in

them, hast willed to be at once the daily cure
of their daily infirmities and their daily sus-
tenance; we humbly beseech Thee, by Thy
Heart all on fire with love for us, to pour forth
upon them all Thy divine Spirit, so that those
who are unhappily in mortal sin, may turn
to Thee and regain the life of grace which
they have lost, and those who, through Thy
gift, are already living this divine life, may
draw near daily, when they can, to Thy sacred
table, whence, by means of daily Communion, they may receive daily the antidote of
their daily venial sins, and may every day
foster within themselves the life of grace; and
being thus ever more and more purified, may
come at last to the possession of that eternal
life which is happiness with Thee.   Amen.

An indulgence of 500 days once a day.

A plenary indulgence once a month on the usual conditions,
when this prayer is said every day (Pius X, Audience of May 30,
1905, exhibited June 3, 1905; S. P. Ap., May 17, 1935).

NOTE.—Another prayer addressed to our Lady of the Blessed
Sacrament is found under n. 418.

VII

AN ACT OF SPIRITUAL COMMUNION

164

To the faithful who make an act of spiritual Communion, using any formula they may choose,
there is granted:

An indulgence of 3 years;

A plenary indulgence once a month on the usual conditions
when the act is performed every day of the month (S. P. Ap., Mar.
7, 1927 and Feb. 25, 1933).

The following forms of prayer are given as examples
of spiritual Communion:

a) **M**y Jesus, I believe that Thou art present in the Blessed Sacrament. I love Thee above all things and I desire Thee in my soul. Since I cannot now receive Thee sacramentally, come at least spiritually into my heart. As though thou wert already there, I embrace Thee and unite myself wholly to Thee; permit not that I should ever be separated from Thee (St. Alphonsus Maria de' Liguori).

b) **A**t Thy feet, O my Jesus, I prostrate myself and I offer Thee the repentance of my contrite heart, which is humbled in its nothingness and in Thy holy presence. I adore Thee in the Sacrament of Thy love, the ineffable Eucharist. I desire to receive Thee into the poor dwelling that my heart offers Thee. While waiting for the happiness of sacramental Communion, I wish to possess Thee in spirit. Come to me, O my Jesus, since I, for my part, am coming to Thee! May Thy love embrace my whole being in life and in death. I believe in Thee, I hope in Thee, I love Thee. Amen (Raphael Cardinal Merry del Val).

VIII
HYMN, RHYTHM AND SEQUENCE
165
Hymn
Pange, lingua, gloriosi

Sing, my tongue, the Saviour's glory,
  Of His Flesh the mystery sing;
Of the Blood, all price exceeding,
  Shed by our immortal King,

Destined, for the world's redemption,
  From a noble womb to spring.
Of a pure and spotless Virgin
  Born for us on earth below,
He, as Man with man conversing,
  Stay'd, the seeds of truth to sow;
Then He closed in solemn order
  Wondrously His life of woe.

On the night of that Last Supper,
  Seated with His chosen band,
He the Paschal victim eating,
  First fulfils the Law's command;
Then, as Food to His Apostles
  Gives Himself with His own hand.

Word made Flesh, the bread of nature
  By His word to Flesh He turns;
Wine into His Blood He changes:—
  What though sense no change discerns?
Only be the heart in earnest,
  Faith her lesson quickly learns.

Therefore, we, before It bending,
  This great Sacrament adore;
Types and shadows have their ending
  In the new rite evermore:
Faith, our outward sense amending,
  Maketh good defects before.

Honor, laud, and praise addressing
  To the Father and the Son,
Might ascribe we, virtue, blessing,
  And eternal benison:
Holy Ghost, from both progressing,
  Equal laud to Thee be done.   Amen.

(tr. E. Caswall)

℣. Thou didst send them bread from heaven,

℟. Having in itself every delight.

Let us pray.

O God, who under this wonderful Sacrament hast left us a memorial of Thy Passion: grant us, we beseech Thee, so to reverence the sacred mysteries of Thy Body and Thy Blood, that we may ever feel within ourselves the fruit of Thy redemption: Who livest and reignest for ever and ever. Amen (Roman Breviary).

An indulgence of 7 years.

An indulgence of 5 years, when only the last two stanzas are said with the versicles and prayer.

An indulgence of 10 years, if this hymn or its last two stanzas together with the versicle and prayer are recited before the Blessed Sacrament.

A plenary indulgence on the usual conditions, if the entire hymn, or at least, the last two stanzas with the versicle and prayer, are said every day for a month (S. C. Ind., Aug. 24, 1818; S. P. Ap., Sept. 15, 1935 and July 12, 1941).

Hymnus

Pange, língua, gloriósi
Córporis mystérium,
Sanguinísque pretiósi,
Quem in mundi prétium,
Fructus ventris generósi,
Rex effúdit géntium.

Nobis datus, nobis natus
Ex intácta Vírgine,
Et in mundo conversátus
Sparso verbi sémine,
Sui moras incolátus
Miro clausit órdine.

In suprémæ nocte cœnæ
Récumbens cum frátribus,

Observáta lege plene
Cibis in legálibus,
Cibum turbæ duodénæ
Se dat suis mánibus.

Verbum caro, panem verum
Verbo carnem éfficit,
Fitque sanguis Christi merum;
Et si sensus déficit,
Ad firmándum cor sincérum
Sola fides súfficit.

Tantum ergo Sacraméntum
Venerémur cérnui:
Et antíquum documéntum
Novo cedat rítui:
Præstet fides suppleméntum
Sénsuum deféctui.

Genitóri Genitóque
Laus et iubilátio,
Salus, honor, virtus quoque
Sit et benedíctio:
Procedénti ab utróque
Compar sit laudátio. Amen.

℣ Panem de cælo præstitísti eis,
℟. Omne delectaméntum in se habéntem.

Orémus.

Deus, qui nobis sub Sacraménto mirábili Passiónis tuæ memóriam reliquísti: tríbue, quæsumus, ita nos Córporis et Sánguinis tui sacra mystéria venerári, ut redemptiónis tuæ fructum in nobis iúgiter sentiámus: Qui vivis et regnas in sǽcula sæculórum. Amen (**ex** *Breviario Romano*).

166

Rhythm

Adoro te devote

O Godhead hid, devoutly I adore Thee,
Who truly art within the forms before
me;

To Thee my heart I bow with bended knee,
As failing quite in contemplating Thee.

Sight, touch, and taste in Thee are each
deceived;
The ear alone most safely is believed:
I believe all the Son of God has spoken,
Than Truth's own word there is no truer
token.

God only on the Cross lay hid from view;
But here lies hid at once the Manhood too:
And I, in both professing my belief,
Make the same prayer as the repentant thief.

Thy wounds, as Thomas saw, I do not see;
Yet Thee confess my Lord and God to be:
Make me believe Thee ever more and more;
In Thee my hope, in Thee my love to store.

O thou Memorial of our Lord's own dying!
O Bread that living art and vivifying!
Make ever Thou my soul on Thee to live;
Ever a taste of Heavenly sweetness give.

O loving Pelican! O Jesu, Lord!
Unclean I am, but cleanse me in Thy Blood;
Of which a single drop, for sinners spilt,
Is ransom for a world's entire guilt.

Jesu! Whom for the present veil'd I see,
What I so thirst for, O vouchsafe to me:
That I may see Thy countenance unfolding,
And may be blest Thy glory in beholding.
Amen.

(St. Thomas Aquinas, tr. E. Caswall.)

An indulgence of 5 years.

An indulgence of 7 years, if this hymn (rhythm), or only its last stanza, is recited before the Blessed Sacrament.

A plenary indulgence on the usual conditions, when this hymn is said daily for a month (S. C. Ind., June 15, 1895; S. P. Ap., March 12, 1936 and July 12, 1941).

Rhythmus

Adóro te devóte, latens Déitas,
Quæ sub his figúris vere látitas;
Tibi se cor meum totum súbiicit,
Quia te contémplans, totum déficit.

Visus, tactus, gustus in te fállitur,
Sed audítu solo tuto créditur;
Credo quidquid dixit Dei Fílius,
Nil hoc verbo veritátis vérius.

In Cruce latébat sola Déitas.
At hic latet simul et humánitas:
Ambo tamen credens, atque cónfitens,
Peto quod petívit latro pǽnitens.

Plagas, sicut Thomas, non intúeor,
Deum tamen meum te confíteor:
Fac me tibi semper magis crédere,
In te spem habére, te dilígere.

O memoriále mortis Dómini,
Panis vivus vitam præstans hómini:
Præsta meæ menti de te vívere,
Et te illi semper dulce sápere.

Pie pellicáne Iesu Dómine,
Me immúndum munda tuo Sánguine:
Cuius una stilla salvum fácere
Totum mundum quit ab omni scélere.

Iesu, quem velátum nunc aspício,
Oro, fiat illud, quod tam sítio,
Ut te reveláta cernens fácie,
Visu sim beátus tuæ glóriæ. Amen.

(S. Thomas Aquin.).

167

Sequence

Lauda Sion Salvatorem

Laud, O Sion, thy salvation,
Laud with hymns of exultation
   Christ, thy King and Shepherd true.

Spend thyself, His honor raising,
Who surpasseth all thy praising;
   Never canst thou reach His due.

Sing today, the mystery showing
Of the living, life-bestowing
   Bread before thee set.

E'en the same of old provided,
Where the twelve, divinely guided,
   At the holy Table met.

Full and clear ring out thy chanting,
Joy nor sweetest grace be wanting
   To thy heart and soul today;

When we gather up the measure
Of that Supper and its treasure,
   Keeping feast in glad array.

Lo, the new King's Table gracing,
This new Passover of blessing
   Hath fulfilled the elder rite:

Now the new the old effaceth,
Truth revealed the shadow chaseth,
   Day is breaking on the night.

His own act, at supper seated,
Christ ordained to be repeated,
   In His memory divine.

Wherefore, now, with adoration,
We the Host of our salvation
　Consecrate from bread and wine.

This the truth to Christians given—
Bread becomes His Flesh from heaven,
　Wine becomes His holy Blood.

Doth it pass thy comprehending?
Faith, the law of sight transcending,
　Leaps to things not understood.

Yea, beneath these signs are hidden
Glorious things to sight forbidden:
　Look not on the outward sign.

Wine is poured and Bread is broken,
But in either sacred token
　Christ is here by power divine.

Whoso of this Food partaketh,
Rendeth not the Lord nor breaketh:
　Christ is whole to all that taste.

Thousands are, as one, receivers,
One, as thousands of believers,
　Takes the food that cannot waste.

Good and evil men are sharing
One repast, a doom preparing
　Varied as the heart of man.

Doom of life or death awarded,
As their days shall be recorded
　Which from one beginning ran.

When the Sacrament is broken,
Doubt not in each severed token,
Hallowed by the word once spoken,
　Resteth all the true content:

Naught the precious Gift divideth,
Breaking but the sign betideth,
He Himself the same abideth,
    Nothing of His fulness spent.

Lo! the Angels' Food is given
To the pilgrim who hath striven;
See the children's Bread from heaven,
    Which on dogs may not be spent.

Truth, the ancient types fulfilling,
Isaac bound, a victim willing,
Paschal lamb, its life-blood spilling,
    Manna to the fathers sent.

Very Bread, good Shepherd, tend us,
Jesu, of Thy love befriend us,
Thou refresh us, Thou defend us,
Thine eternal goodness send us
    In the land of life to see:

Thou Who all things canst and knowest,
Who on earth such Food bestowest,
Grant us with Thy Saints, though lowest,
Where the heavenly Feast Thou showest,
    Fellow-heirs and guests to be.   Amen.

(Roman Missal; tr. cento).

An indulgence of 7 years, on the Feast of Corpus Christi and
during its Octave.

A plenary indulgence on the usual conditions, if the sequence
is duly recited on the aforesaid Feast and on each day of the
Octave (S. P. Ap., Nov. 28, 1936).

Sequentia

Lauda, Sion, Salvatórem,
    Lauda ducem et pastórem
In hymnis et cánticis.

Quantum potes, tantum aude:
Quia maior omni laude,
Nec laudáre súfficis.

Laudis thema speciális
Panis vivus et vitális
Hódie propónitur.

Quem in sacræ mensa cœnæ
Turbæ fratrum duodénæ
Datum non ambígitur.

Sit laus plena, sit sonóra,
Sit iucúnda, sit decóra
Mentis iubilátio.

Dies enim solémnis ágitur,
In qua mensæ prima recólitur
Huius institútio.

In hac mensa novi regis,
Novum Pascha novæ legis,
Phase vetus términat.

Vetustátem nóvitas,
Umbram fugat véritas,
Noctem lux elíminat.

Quod in cœna Christus gessit,
Faciéndum hoc expréssit
In sui memóriam.

Docti sacris institútis,
Panem, vinum, in salútis
Consecrámus hóstiam.

Dogma datur christiánis,
Quod in carnem transit panis,
Et vinum in sánguinem.

Quod non capis, quod non vides,
Animósa firmat fides,
Præter rerum órdinem.

Sub divérsis speciébus,
Signis tantum, et non rebus,
Latent res exímiæ.

Caro cibus, sanguis potus:
Manet tamen Christus totus,
Sub utráque spécie.

A suménte non concísus,
Non confráctus, non divísus:
Integer accípitur.

Sumit unus, sumunt mille:
Quantum isti, tantum ille:
Nec sumptus consúmitur.

Sumunt boni, sumunt mali:
Sorte tamen inæquáli,
Vitæ vel intéritus.

Mors est malis, vita bonis:
Vide paris sumptiónis
Quam sit dispar éxitus.

Fracto demum Sacraménto,
Ne vacílles, sed meménto,
Tantum esse sub fragménto,
Quantum toto tégitur.

Nulla rei fit scissúra:
Signi tantum fit fractúra:
Qua nec status, nec statúra
Signáti minúitur.

Ecce panis angelórum,
Factus cibus viatórum:
Vere panis filiórum,
Non mitténdus cánibus.

In figúris præsignátur,
Cum Isaac immolátur:
Agnus paschæ deputátur:
Datur manna pátribus.

Bone pastor, panis vere,
Iesu, nostri miserére:
Tu nos pasce, nos tuére:
Tu nos bona fac vidére
In terra vivéntium.

Tu, qui cuncta scis et vales:
Qui nos pascis hic mortáles:
Tuos ibi commensáles,
Coherédes et sodáles
Fac sanctórum cívium. Amen.

(ex *Missali Romano*).

IX

PIOUS PRACTICES

168
The Holy Hour

The faithful, who take part for an entire hour in the public exercise known as the "Holy Hour," in any church, public or semi-public oratory (if they may lawfully make use of the latter), in order to venerate the Passion and Death of Jesus Christ, and to worship and meditate upon the burning love whereby He was led to institute the Holy Eucharist, may gain:

A plenary indulgence, provided that they atone for their sins in sacramental confession, receive Holy Communion and pray for the intentions of the Sovereign Pontiff.

Those, who being at least contrite, perform this pious exercise, whether publicly or privately, may gain:

An indulgence of 10 years (Secr. Mem., Feb. 14, 1815 and Apr. 6, 1816; S. C. Ind., June 18, 1876; S. P. Ap., Mar. 21, 1933).

169
Solemn Exposition of the Blessed Sacrament

a) The solemn exposition of the Blessed Sacrament in the form which is known as the "Forty Hours' Prayer" is, properly speaking, that which is carried out according to the "Instruction" of Pope Clement VIII, "*Graves et diuturnœ*," which is therefore called the Clementine Instruction; this form of exposition was first introduced in Rome on the 25th day of November in the year 1592, and afterwards came into use in many other places as well.
In keeping with the rules laid down in this Instruc-

tion, which is still strictly observed in Rome, the Blessed Sacrament is exposed to the public adoration of the faithful in the ostensorium about noon on one day, which is counted as the first, and remains so exposed, without any interruption even at night, until noon of the third day following.

During the course of this exposition, if a visit is made to the Blessed Sacrament, as is prescribed in n. 148 above, there is granted:

An indulgence of 15 years;

A plenary indulgence on each of the days of the exposition, provided that the faithful make their confession and receive Holy Communion;

The altars of the church are "privileged" during the exposition.

b) Where, however, the solemn exposition according to the Clementine Instruction cannot, in the judgment of the local Ordinary, be carried out, it is held in a manner which may be called "ad instar," as follows: The Blessed Sacrament is exposed in the ostensorium to the adoration of the faithful during the course of the morning or about midday and remains so exposed until midday or evening on the third day, except that the exposition is interrupted each evening.

The same indulgences, including the privileged altars, are granted for this form of the Forty Hours' Prayer as for the strict Clementine form.

c) Where the Blessed Sacrament is exposed continuously in the ostensorium, for at least a month, even though the exposition be interrupted at night, the following indulgences are granted for visits to the Blessed Sacrament, according to the prescriptions of n. 148 above:

An indulgence of 15 years;

A plenary indulgence once each week, on condition of confession and Communion.

The altars are "privileged" each day of the exposition.

d) Whenever no other provision is made for gaining some indulgence, a visit to the Blessed Sacrament publicly exposed will suffice to gain:

An indulgence of 10 years (S. C. Ind., Dec. 8, 1897; S. C. of the Holy Office, Jan. 22, 1914; canon 917, No. 2 of the Code of Canon Law; S. P. Ap., July 24, 1933).

170
A Novena before the Feast of Corpus Christi

The faithful, who devoutly take part in a public novena before the Feast of Corpus Christi, may gain:

An indulgence of 10 years each day of the novena;

A plenary indulgence, if they assist at five of the novena exercises, make their confession, receive Holy Communion and pray for the intentions of the Sovereign Pontiff.

Those who, at the aforesaid season, privately offer their prayers and devout homage in honor of the most holy Body of Christ with the intention of so continuing for nine successive days, may obtain:

An indulgence of 7 years once each day;

A plenary indulgence on the usual conditions at the end of the novena; however, where a public novena is held, these indulgences are available only to those who are legitimately hindered from assisting at the public exercises (S. C. Ind., May 8, 1907; S. P. Ap., Feb. 25, 1933).

171
The Feast and the Octave of Corpus Christi

The faithful, who visit the Blessed Sacrament, as explained above (n. 148), on the Feast of Corpus Christi and during the Octave, may obtain:

A plenary indulgence on each day, on condition of confession and Communion (S. P. Ap., June 16, 1933 and Sept. 15, 1949).

NOTE.—With respect to the solemn Eucharistic procession which is usually held on the Feast of Corpus Christi, or during the Octave, consult n. 150.

172
A Triduum during the Octave of Corpus Christi

The faithful who assist at the solemn services which are to be held in all Cathedrals and parish churches, according to the Letter of the Sacred Congregation of Indulgences (**Apr. 10, 1907**), on the Friday, Saturday and Sunday within the Octave of Corpus Christi, or at some other season of the year, even with a change of the days of the week (S. C. Ind., **Apr. 8, 1908**) to be chosen at the discretion of the Ordinary, may obtain:

An indulgence of 10 years on any day of the triduum;

A plenary indulgence on the third day, if they have been present every day and have gone to confession and Communion.

Furthermore, those who take part in a corporate Communion in some church on any one of the three days, may gain:

A plenary indulgence, if they have confessed their sins and prayed for the intentions of the Sovereign Pontiff (S. C. Ind., Apr. 10, 1907; S. P. Ap., Mar. 18, 1932).

173
The Offering of Holy Mass in Reparation

The faithful, who make an offering and have the sacrifice of the Mass said in reparation for the insults offered by mankind to the most holy Sacrament of the Eucharist, may gain:

A plenary indulgence on the usual conditions (Pius X, Rescript in his own hand, Nov. 15, 1907, exhib., Nov. 19, 1907).

174
A Pious Exercise of Reparation

The faithful who spend some time in meditation or devout prayers on any one of the nine days that they have chosen, to make reparation for the injuries offered by men to the Blessed Sacrament, may gain:

An indulgence of 7 years.

Moreover, those who assist at Mass during this devout exercise may, on each occasion, obtain:

An indulgence of 10 years.

At the end of the novena they may gain:

A plenary indulgence on the usual conditions (Pius X, Rescript in his own hand, Nov. 15, 1907, exhib., Nov. 19, 1907; Bene-

dict XV, Rescript in his own hand, Nov. 25, 1916, exhib., Dec. 30,
1916; S. P. Ap., May 21, 1933).

175
The Eucharistic Month

The faithful who, during one month of the year, devoutly offer their prayers and homage in honor
of the Blessed Sacrament may obtain:

An indulgence of 7 years once on each day of the month;

A plenary indulgence on the usual conditions, if they perform
this devout exercise every day of the month (S. P. Ap., July 3,
1928 and Mar. 18, 1932).

176
The Eucharistic Day

The faithful who, on the so-called "Eucharistic
Day," during which the Blessed Sacrament is exposed for public adoration, make a visit according to
the prescriptions of n. 148 above, may obtain:

An indulgence of 15 years;

A plenary indulgence once on condition of sacramental confession
and Holy Communion (S. P. Ap., April 10, 1934).

X
ACTS OF ADORATION, REPARATION AND THANKSGIVING

177
An Act of Adoration and Thanksgiving

I adore Thee, Eternal Father, and I give
Thee thanks for the infinite love, with
which for my redemption Thou didst deign
to send Thine only-begotten Son to be the
food of my soul. I offer Thee all the acts of
adoration and thanksgiving that are offered
to Thee by the Angels and Saints in heaven
and by the just on earth. I praise Thee, I
love Thee, and I thank Thee, with all the
praises, love and thanksgiving wherewith

Thine own Son praises Thee, loves Thee and thanks Thee. And I pray Thee to grant that He may be known, loved, honored, thanked and worthily received by all men in this Most Blessed Sacrament.

Our Father, Hail Mary, Glory be.

I adore Thee, Eternal Son, and I thank Thee for the infinite love which caused Thee to become incarnate for me, to be born in a stable, to be brought up in the carpenter's shop, and to be willing to endure hunger, thirst, cold, fatigue, hardships, contempt, persecution, scourges, thorns, nails and death on the hard wood of the Cross. I thank Thee, in company with Thy whole Church, militant and triumphant, for the infinite love with which Thou didst institute the Blessed Sacrament to be the food of my soul. I adore Thee in all the consecrated Hosts throughout the whole world. I give Thee thanks also on behalf of those who know Thee not and who fail to thank Thee. Would that I could lay down my life to cause Thee to be known, loved and honored by all men in this Sacrament of love, and to put an end to all the irreverences and sacrileges that are committed against Thee! I love Thee, my Jesus, and I desire to love Thee and receive Thee with all the love, purity and affection of Thy most holy Mother, and with the perfect love of Thine own Sacred Heart. Ah, most loving Spouse of my soul, come to me in Thy Sacrament and bring forth in me all those fruits for the sake of which Thou comest to us, and grant that I may die rather than ever receive Thee unworthily.

Our Father, Hail Mary, Glory be.

I adore Thee, Eternal Spirit, and I give Thee thanks for the infinite love with which Thou hast wrought the ineffable mystery of the Incarnation, and for the infinite charity wherewith Thou didst form out of the most pure blood of the Blessed Virgin Mary the sacred Body of Jesus, which in this Sacrament is the food of my soul. I pray Thee to enlighten my mind and purify my heart and the hearts of all men, that they may come to know this great gift of Thy love, and may receive this Blessed Sacrament in all worthiness.

Our Father, Hail Mary, Glory be.

The faithful who recite these prayers devoutly before the Blessed Sacrament, may obtain:

An indulgence of 3 years;

A plenary indulgence on the first Thursday of each month on condition of confession, Holy Communion and prayers for the intentions of the Sovereign Pontiff (Secret. Mem., Oct. 17, 1796: S. P. Ap., March 31, 1931).

178

An Act of Adoration and Reparation

I adore Thee profoundly, O my Jesus, in Thy sacramental form; I acknowledge Thee to be true God and true Man, and by this act of adoration I intend to atone for the coldness of so many Christians who pass before Thy churches and sometimes before the very Tabernacle in which Thou art pleased to remain at all hours with loving impatience to give Thyself to Thy faithful people, and do not so much as bend the knee before Thee, and who, by their indifference proclaim that they grow weary of this heavenly manna, like the people of Israel in the wilderness. I offer Thee in reparation for this grievous negligence, the Most Precious Blood which Thou didst shed from Thy five wounds, and especially from Thy sacred Side, and entering therein, I repeat a thousand times with true recollection of spirit:

O Sacrament most holy! O Sacrament divine!

All praise and all thanksgiving be every moment Thine.

Our Father, Hail Mary, Glory be.

II. Profoundly I adore Thee, my Jesus; I acknowledge Thy presence in the Blessed Sacrament, and by this act of adoration I intend to atone for the carelessness of so many Christians who see Thee carried to poor sick people to strengthen them for the great journey to eternity, and leave Thee unescorted, nay, who scarcely give Thee any outward marks of reverence. I offer Thee in reparation for such coldness, the Most Precious Blood which Thou didst shed from Thy five wounds and especially from Thy sacred Side, and entering therein I say again and again with my heart full of devotion:

O Sacrament most holy, *etc.*
Our Father, Hail Mary, Glory be.

III. Profoundly I adore Thee, my Jesus, true Bread of life eternal, and by my adoration I intend to compensate Thee for the many wounds which Thy Heart suffers daily in the profaning of churches where Thou art pleased to dwell beneath the sacramental veils to be adored and loved by all Thy faithful people; and in reparation for so many acts of irreverence, I offer Thee the Most Precious Blood which Thou didst shed from Thy five wounds and especially from Thy sacred Side, and entering therein with recollected spirit I repeat every instant:

O Sacrament most holy, *etc.*
Our Father, Hail Mary, Glory be.

IV. Profoundly I adore Thee, my Jesus, the living Bread which cometh down from heaven, and by this act of adoration, I intend to atone for all the many acts of irreverence which are committed all the day long by Thy faithful when they assist at Holy Mass, wherein through Thine exceeding love Thou dost renew in an unbloody manner the self-same sacrifice which Thou didst once offer on Calvary for our salvation. I offer Thee in atonement for such base ingratitude the Most Precious Blood which Thou didst shed from Thy five wounds and especially from Thy sacred Side, and entering therein with sincere devotion, I unite my voice to that of the Angels who stand around Thee in adoration, saying with them:

O Sacrament most holy, *etc.*

Our Father, Hail Mary, Glory be.

V. Profoundly I adore Thee, my Jesus, true Victim of expiation for our sins, and I offer Thee this act of adoration to atone for the sacrilegious outrages Thou dost suffer from so many ungrateful Christians who dare to draw near to receive Thee with mortal sin upon their souls. In reparation for such hateful sacrileges I offer Thee the last drops of Thy Most Precious Blood, which Thou didst shed from Thy sacred wounds and especially from the wound in Thy sacred Side, and entering therein with a devout heart, I adore Thee, I bless and I love Thee, and I repeat with all the hearts who are devoted to the Blessed Sacrament:

O Sacrament most holy, *etc.*

Our Father, Hail Mary, Glory be.

An indulgence of 7 years.

A plenary indulgence once a month on the usual conditions for its daily recitation (S. C. of Rites, Aug. 26, 1814; S. P. Ap., Feb. 25, 1933).

179
An Act of Reparation

With that profound humility which the Faith itself inspires in me, O my God and Saviour Jesus Christ, true God and true man, I love Thee with all my heart, and I adore Thee who art hidden here, in reparation for all the irreverences, profanations and sacrileges which Thou receivest in the most adorable Sacrament of the Altar.

I adore Thee, O my God, if not so much as Thou art worthy to be adored nor so much as I am bound to do, yet as much as I am able; would that I could adore Thee with that perfect worship which the Angels in heaven are enabled to offer Thee. Mayest Thou, O my Jesus, be known, adored, loved and thanked by all men at every moment in this most holy and divine Sacrament. Amen.

An indulgence of 500 days.

A plenary indulgence once a month on the usual conditions for the daily repetition of this prayer (S. C. Ind., Jan. 21, 1815; S. P. Ap., Oct. 4, 1935).

XI

PRAYERS

180

O sacred banquet, in which Christ is received, the memory of His Passion is renewed, the mind is filled with grace, and a pledge of future glory is given to us.

℣. Thou didst give them bread from heaven:

℟. Containing in itself all sweetness.

Let us pray.

O God, who under a wonderful Sacrament hast left us a memorial of Thy Passion; grant us, we beseech Thee, so to reverence the sacred mysteries of Thy Body and Blood, that we may ever feel within ourselves the fruit of Thy Redemption: Who livest and reignest for ever and ever. Amen.

In Paschaltide the following prayer is said:

Let us pray.

Pour upon us, O Lord, the Spirit of Thy love, to make us of one heart, whom, by Thy tender mercy, Thou hast filled with the paschal sacrament. Through Our Lord Jesus Christ, Thy Son, Who with Thee liveth and reigneth in the unity of the same Holy Spirit, God, for ever and ever. Amen.

An indulgence of 7 years.

An indulgence of 10 years, if these prayers are recited before the Blessed Sacrament.

A plenary indulgence once a month on the usual conditions for the daily recitation of the above antiphon together with the versicle and prayer (S. P. Ap., June 4, 1934, July 12, 1941 and Sept. 29, 1949).

O sacrum convívium, in quo Christus súmitur: recólitur memória passiónis eius; mens implétur grátia et futúræ glóriæ nobis pignus datur.

℣. Panem de cælo præstitísti eis;

℟. Omnem delectaméntum in se habéntem.

Orémus.

Deus, qui nobis sub Sacraménto mirábili Passiónis tuæ memóriam reliquísti; tríbue, quæsumus, ita nos Córporis et Sánguinis tui sacra mystéria venerári, ut redemptiónis tuæ fructum in nobis iúgiter sentiámus: Qui vivis et regnas in sæcula sæculórum. Amen.

Tempore paschali sequens dicitur oratio:

Orémus.

Spíritum nobis, Dómine, tuæ caritátis infúnde, ut, quos Sacraméntis paschálibus satiásti, tua fácias pietáte concórdes. Per Dóminum nostrum Iesum Christum Fílium tuum, qui tecum vivit et regnat in unitáte eiúsdem Spíritus Sancti Deus per ómnia sæcula sæculórum. Amen.

XII

PRAYERS

181

Behold, O my most loving Jesus, how far Thine exceeding love hath reached! Of Thine own Flesh and Most Precious Blood Thou hast prepared for me a divine table in order to give Thyself wholly to me. What hath impelled Thee to such transports of love? Nothing else surely save Thy most loving Heart. O adorable Heart of my Jesus, burning furnace of divine charity, receive my heart within Thy most sacred wound; to the end that in this school of love, I may learn to make a return of love to the God who hath given me such wondrous proofs of His love. Amen.

An indulgence of 500 days.

A plenary indulgence once a month on the usual conditions for the daily recitation of this prayer (**Secr. Mem.,** Feb. 9, 1818; S. P. Ap., July 15, 1932).

182

O my Lord Jesus Christ, who for the love Thou bearest mankind, dost remain night and day in this Sacrament, all full of tenderness and love, expecting, inviting and receiving all those who come to visit Thee; I believe that Thou art present in the Sacrament of the altar; I adore Thee from the depths of my own nothingness and thank Thee for all the favors Thou hast bestowed upon me; and especially for having given me Thyself in this Sacrament, and Thy most holy

Mother Mary as my advocate; and for having called me to visit Thee in this church. I pay my homage this day to Thy most loving Heart and this I intend to do for three intentions: first, in thanksgiving for this great gift; secondly, in reparation for all the insults Thou hast received from Thine enemies in this Sacrament; thirdly, by this visit I intend to adore Thee in all places upon the earth, where Thou art least adored and most neglected in Thy Sacrament. My Jesus, I love Thee with my whole heart. I repent of having in the past so many times displeased Thine infinite goodness. I purpose with the help of Thy grace never more to offend Thee in the future; and at this moment, wretched as I am, I consecrate myself wholly to Thee. I give to Thee and utterly renounce my entire will, all my affections, all my desires, and all that I possess. From this day forth do with me and with all that is mine whatever is pleasing in Thy sight. I ask and desire only Thy holy love, final perseverance and the perfect fulfilment of Thy will. I commend to Thee the souls in purgatory, especially those who were most devoted to this Blessed Sacrament and to Blessed Mary; I commend to Thee in like manner all poor sinners. Finally, my dear Saviour, I unite all my affections with those of Thy most loving Heart, and thus united I offer them to Thine eternal Father, and I pray Him in Thy name graciously to accept and answer them for love of Thee (St. Alphonsus M. de' Liguori).

The faithful who devoutly recite this prayer in the presence of the Blessed Sacrament, are granted:

An indulgence of 5 years.

A plenary indulgence once a month if its daily recitation is persevered in for the entire month and, in addition, make their confession, receive Holy Communion and pray for the intentions of the Sovereign Pontiff (Pius IX, Rescript in his own hand, Sept. 7, 1854; S. P. Ap., Feb. 25, 1933).

183

I adore Thee, O Jesus, true God and true Man, here present in the Holy Eucharist, humbly kneeling before Thee and united in spirit with all the faithful on earth and all the blessed in heaven. In deepest gratitude for so great a blessing, I love Thee, my Jesus, with my whole heart, for Thou art all perfect and all worthy of love.

Give me grace nevermore in any way to offend Thee, and grant that I, being refreshed by Thy Eucharistic presence here on earth, may be found worthy to come to the enjoyment with Mary of Thine eternal and ever-blessed presence in heaven. Amen.

An indulgence of 3 years once a day (S. C. of the Holy Off., March 18, 1909; S. P. Ap., Oct. 30, 1934).

Te, Iesu, verum Deum et Hóminem hic in sancta Eucharístia præséntem, in génua humíllime provolútus, cum fidélibus terræ et Sanctis cæli mente coniúnctus, adóro; ac pro tanto benefício íntime gratus, te, Iesu, infiníte perféctum atque infiníte amábilem ex toto corde díligo.

Da mihi grátiam ne ullo modo te unquam offéndam, atque ut, tua hac in terra eucharística præséntia recreátus, ad tua ætérna ac beáta in cælis præséntia una cum María perfruéndum mérear veníre. Amen.

184

O my God, I firmly believe that Thou art really and corporally present in the Blessed Sacrament of the altar. I adore Thee here present from the very depths of my heart, and I worship Thy sacred presence with all possible humility. O my soul, what joy to have Jesus Christ always with us, and to be able to speak to Him, heart to heart, with all confidence. Grant, O Lord, that I, having adored Thy divine Majesty here on earth in this wonderful Sacrament, may be able to adore It eternally in heaven. Amen.

An indulgence of 500 days (Apostolic Brief, May 7, 1921; S. P. Ap., Jan. 22, 1935).

185

Throughout the year, O Jesus, thou dost remain humbly hidden within the tabernacle, awaiting, receiving, and hearing the souls who come to Thy feet in search of sympathy and consolation in their sorrows, light and support in the trials of life. Only on this day, leaving Thy silent loneliness, Thou goest forth, passing in triumph and benediction through the streets and squares of the cities in a maze of lights and music, incense and flowers, in the midst of joyous multitudes, who fall down in adoration before Thee.

In the synagogue of Capharnaum, the unbelieving throng, rebelling against Thy words of faith and love, deserted Thee; but in the Upper Room that last evening of Thine earthly life, when the dark clouds of betrayal were already settling upon Thy sorrowful soul, Thou didst make Thy divine promise a reality, perpetuating in the institution of the Holy Eucharist, as in a living memorial, the infinite love with which Thy Heart was over-flowing towards mankind. By means of this august Sacrament, Thou wouldst prolong Thy presence in the world even to the end of time; and the souls of men, seated at Thy heavenly banquet, were to taste inwardly the sweet irradiations of Thy grace and the ineffable delights of Thy love.

O Jesus, make me feel the overwhelming attraction of Thy silent tabernacle, which has ever drawn not only the little ones, but has always been and will continue to be the joy of pure and great souls. Grant me a living faith and an ardent love for Thee hidden under the sacramental species, so that, frequently drawing near to Thy table where the "Bread of Life" is set out, I may receive the germ of a life that will not die.

The faithful, who recite this prayer with devotion on the Feast of Corpus Christi, are granted:

An indulgence of 3 years.
A plenary indulgence on the usual conditions (S. P. Ap., May 10, 1941).

Art. V
JESUS CRUCIFIED
I
EJACULATIONS AND INVOCATIONS
186

The Cross is my sure salvation.
The Cross it is that I worship evermore.
The Cross of our Lord is with me.
The Cross is my refuge. (St. Thomas Aquinas).

An indulgence of 300 days.

A plenary indulgence once a month on the usual conditions for the daily recitation of these invocations (Pius IX, Rescript in his own hand, Jan. 21, 1874; S. P. Ap., March 10, 1933).

Crux mihi certa salus.
Crux est quam semper adóro.
Crux Dómini mecum.
Crux mihi refúgium.
(S. Thomas Aq.)

187

Hail, O Cross, our only hope.

An indulgence of 500 days.

A plenary indulgence once a month on the usual conditions for the daily repetition of this ejaculation (S. P. Ap., March 20, 1934).

O Crux, ave, spes única.

188

By the sign of the holy Cross, deliver us from our enemies, O our God (Roman Breviary).

An indulgence of 3 years.

A plenary indulgence on the usual conditions, if the daily recitation of this invocation is prolonged for an entire month (S. P. Ap., Aug. 1, 1934).

NOTE:— Another invocation is found under n. 132, a.

Per signum Crucis de inimícis nostris líbera nos, Deus noster (ex *Breviario Romano*).

II
OFFICES OF THE PASSION OF OUR LORD JESUS CHRIST
189
The Office of Tenebræ

The faithful who are present at the Office of Tenebræ on Wednesday, Thursday and Friday of Holy Week, and follow the singing of the Psalms and Lessons, either by reading them devoutly or with pious meditations on the Passion of our Lord, or other prayers according to each one's capacity, may gain:

An indulgence of 10 years on each of these days;

A plenary indulgence if they are present at this devout exercise on all three days and, in addition, make their confession, receive Holy Communion and pray for the intentions of the Sovereign Pontiff (S. P. Ap., March 16, 1935).

190
The Little Office of the Passion of our Lord Jesus Christ

The faithful who recite the little Office of the Passion of our Lord Jesus Christ, in keeping with the prescriptions of canon 932 of the Code of Canon Law, may gain:

An indulgence of 300 days for each hour of this Office;

An indulgence of 7 years for the entire Office;

A plenary indulgence once a month on the usual conditions for the daily recitation of the same (S. P. Ap., April 6, 1934).

III
ACTS OF ADORATION AND THANKSGIVING
191

We adore Thee, O Christ, and we bless Thee; because by Thy holy Cross Thou hast redeemed the world.

An indulgence of 3 years (S. P. Ap., Feb. 2, 1934).

The faithful who recite the Apostles' Creed in conjunction with the above short prayer in a spirit of devotion to the Passion and Death of our Lord Jesus Christ, are granted:

An indulgence of 10 years;

A plenary indulgence once a month on the usual conditions for the daily recitation of the same (S. P. Ap., Feb. 20, 1934).

Adorámus te, Christe, et benedícimus tibi; quia per sanctam Crucem tuam redemísti mundum.

192

Lord, I give Thee thanks for that Thou didst die upon the Cross for my sins (St. Paul of the Cross).

An indulgence of 300 days.

A plenary indulgence on the usual conditions, if this invocation is repeated daily for a month (S. P. Ap., Jan. 18, 1918 and March 10, 1933)

IV

HYMN

193

Vexilla Regis prodeunt

The royal banners forward go;
The Cross shines forth in mystic glow,
Where Life for sinners death endured,
And life by death for man procured.

Where deep for us the spear was dyed,
Life's torrent rushing from His side,
To wash us in that precious flood
Where mingled, Water flowed, and Blood.

Fulfilled is all that David told
In true prophetic song of old;
"Amidst the nations, God," saith he,
"Hath reigned and triumphed from the Tree."

O Tree of beauty! Tree of light!
O Tree with royal purple dight!
Elect on whose triumphal breast
Those holy Limbs should find their rest.

On whose dear arms, so widely flung,
The weight of this world's ransom hung:
The price of human kind to pay
And spoil the spoiler of his prey.

O Cross, our one reliance, hail,
Thou glory of the saved, avail*
To give fresh merit to the Saint,
And pardon to the penitent.

---

* Instead of: *"Thou glory of the saved,"* during Passiontide, say: *"This holy Passiontide"*; during the Paschal Season: *"Thou joy of Eastertide"*; on the Feast of the Exaltation of the Holy Cross: *"On this triumphant day."*

To Thee, Eternal Three in One,
Let homage meet by all be done;
Whom by the Cross Thou dost restore,
Preserve and govern evermore.   Amen.

(Roman Breviary, tr. J. M. Neale).

An indulgence of 5 years.
A plenary indulgence on the usual conditions for the daily reci-
tation of this hymn throughout an entire month (S. C. Ind.,
Jan. 16, 1886; S. P. Ap., April 29, 1934).

Hymnus

Vexílla Regis pródeunt,
   Fulget Crucis mystérium,
Qua vita mortem pértulit,
Et morte vitam prótulit.

Quæ vulneráta lánceæ
Mucróne diro, críminum
Ut nos laváret sórdibus,
Manávit unda et sánguine.

Impléta sunt quæ cóncinit
David fidéli cármine,
Dicéndo natiónibus:
Regnávit a ligno Deus.

Arbor decóra et fúlgida,
Ornáta regis púrpura,
Elécta digno stípite
Tam sancta membra tángere.

Beáta, cuius bráchiis
Prétium pepéndit sǽculi,
Statéra facta córporis,
Tulítque prædam tártari.

O Crux, ave, spes única,
Gentis redémptæ glória![1]
Piis adáuge grátiam,
Reísque dele crímina.

---

[1] Loco: *Gentis redémptæ glória, dictur:* Tempore Passionis: *Hoc Passiónis témpore!*—Tempore Paschali: *Paschále quæ fers gáudium!*—In festo Exaltationis S.
Crucis: *In hac triúmphi glória.*

Te, fons salútis, Trínitas,
Colláudet omnis spíritus:
Quibus Crucis victóriam
Largíris, adde præmium. Amen.

(ex *Breviario Romano*).

V

THE WAY OF THE CROSS

194

The faithful who with at least a contrite heart, whether singly or in company, perform the pious exercise of the Way of the Cross, when the latter has been legitimately erected according to the prescriptions of the Holy See, may gain:

A plenary indulgence as often as they perform the same;

Another plenary indulgence, if they receive Holy Communion on the same day, or even within a month after having made the Stations ten times;

An indulgence of 10 years for each station, if for some reasonable cause they are unable to complete the entire Way of the Cross.

The same indulgences are valid for the following:

a)   Those at sea, prisoners, sick persons and those who live in pagan countries, as well as those who are lawfully hindered from making the Stations in their ordinary form, provided that they hold in their hand a Crucifix, blessed for this purpose by a Priest with the proper faculties, and recite devoutly with a contrite heart and with a pious reflection on the Passion of our Lord, the *Our Father*, *Hail Mary* and *Glory be*, twenty times, namely, one for each Station, five in honor of the five sacred Wounds of our Lord, and one for the intentions of the Sovereign Pontiff. If reasonably prevented from saying all, they are entitled to a partial indulgence of 10 years for each recitation of *Our Father*, *Hail Mary* and *Glory be*.

b)   The sick who on account of their condition cannot without serious inconvenience or difficulty perform the Way of the Cross in its ordinary form or in the shorter form described in paragraph a), may gain all the indulgences, provided that they devoutly and contritely kiss, or at least fix their eyes upon a Crucifix, duly blessed for this purpose, which is held before them by a priest or some other person, and recite, if possible, some short prayer or ejaculation in memory of the Passion and Death of our Lord Jesus Christ (Clement XIV, Audience, Jan. 26, 1773; S. C. Ind., Sept. 16, 1859; S. P. Ap., March 25, 1931, Oct. 20, 1931, March 18, 1932 and March 20, 1946).

VI
PIOUS EXERCISES

195

The faithful, who on Good Friday strive to meditate for three continuous hours, publicly or privately, on the sufferings of the dying Saviour and the sacred Words which He said on the Cross, or who recite Psalms, hymns and other vocal prayers, may gain:

A plenary indulgence, on condition of confession, Communion on Holy Thursday or during Easter Week, and prayer for the intentions of the Holy Father.

Those who pray in like manner, as described above, on other Fridays of the year for at least a quarter of an hour, in memory of the divine Agony, may gain:

An indulgence of 7 years on each and every Friday;

A plenary indulgence on the usual conditions on the last Friday of any month, provided that they have performed this devout exercise on the preceding Fridays (S. C. Ind., Feb. 14, 1815; S. P., Ap., Sept. 8, 1932).

196

On any Friday of any week, if the *Our Father, Hail Mary* and *Glory be* are devoutly recited seven times before an image of our Lord Jesus Christ Crucified, the faithful may gain:

An indulgence of 7 years;

A plenary indulgence on the usual conditions, provided that these devout prayers have been recited on all the Fridays of the month (S. C. Ind., Aug. 4, 1837; S. P. Ap., Mar. 10, 1933).

197

The faithful who on Friday at any hour according to the local custom, at the sound of the bell in memory of the Passing of our Lord Jesus Christ, recite five times *Our Father, Hail Mary* and *Glory be*, on bended knees, if this can be conveniently done, and add moreover for the intention of the Holy Father, this prayer:

We adore Thee, O Christ, and we bless Thee;

Because by Thy holy Cross Thou hast redeemed the world,

or some similar prayer, may gain:

An indulgence of 10 years;

A plenary indulgence on the usual conditions, if they devoutly perform this devotion on each Friday for a month (S. P. Ap., Jan. 30, 1933).

The same indulgences can be gained in places where it is not the custom to sound a bell, if the prayers are said, either in the first hours after midday in which, according to the ancient reckoning, the ninth hour fell, at which time, as the holy Evangelists testify, Jesus Christ breathed forth His spirit on the Cross, or at another hour at which the aforesaid commemoration is wont to be made according to the custom of divers places. (S. P. Ap., Dec. 28, 1935).

198

The faithful, who in memory of the five Wounds of our Lord Jesus Christ say five times *Our Father*, *Hail Mary* and *Glory be*, together with the following verse:

Holy Mother, pierce me through;
In my heart each wound renew
Of my Saviour crucified.

may obtain:

An indulgence of 3 years;

A plenary indulgence once a month on the usual conditions for the daily recitation of the same (S. P. Ap., July 9, 1934).

VII

PRAYERS IN HONOR OF THE FIVE WOUNDS OF
OUR LORD JESUS CHRIST

199

O good Jesus, within Thy wounds hide me.

An indulgence of 300 days (S. P. Ap., Dec. 21, 1936).

O bone Iesu, intra tua vúlnera abscónde me.

200

℣. O God, come unto my assistance.

℟. O Lord, make haste to help me.

℣. Glory be to the Father, and to the Son, and to the Holy Ghost;

℟. As it was in the beginning, is now, and ever shall be, world without end. Amen.

My dearest Lord Jesus Crucified, bending low before Thee, with Mary most holy and with all the Angels and Saints in paradise, I adore the most holy Wound in Thy right Hand. I give Thee thanks for the infinite love, wherewith Thou didst will to suffer so many bitter pains because of my sins which I detest with all my heart; I implore Thee to grant graciously to Thy holy Church victory over all her enemies, and to all her children grace to walk in holiness in the way of Thy commandments.

Our Father, Hail Mary, Glory be.

My dearest Lord Jesus Crucified, bending low before Thee, together with Mary most holy and with all the Angels and Saints in paradise, I adore the sacred Wound in Thy left Hand, and I beseech Thee for grace for all poor sinners, for the dying, and especially for those who will not be reconciled to Thee.

Our Father, Hail Mary, Glory be.

My dearest Lord Jesus Crucified, bending low before Thee, with Mary most holy, and with all the Angels and Saints in paradise, I adore the sacred Wound in Thy right Foot, and I beg of Thee this grace, that countless flowers of holiness may blossom among the clergy and all those who are consecrated to Thee.

Our Father, Hail Mary, Glory be.

My dearest Lord Jesus Crucified, bending low before Thee, with Mary most holy and with all the Angels and Saints in paradise, I adore the sacred Wound in Thy left Foot, and implore Thee to deliver the holy souls in purgatory, and especially those who in life were most devout toward Thy sacred Wounds.

Our Father, Hail Mary, Glory be.

My dearest Lord Jesus Crucified, bending low before Thee, with Mary most holy and with all the Angels and Saints in paradise, I adore the sacred Wound in Thy most holy Side, and I pray Thee to bless and graciously hear all those who have recommended themselves to my prayers.

Our Father, Hail Mary, Glory be.

℣. O Virgin most sorrowful,

℟. Pray for us (*to be said thrice*).

My Crucified Jesus, confirm these prayers by the merits of Thy Passion; give me holiness of life, the grace to receive Thy holy Sacraments at the hour of my death, and glory everlasting.   Amen.

An indulgence of 3 years (S. C. of the Holy Off., May 6, 19'5; S. P. Ap., Jan. 15, 1935).

201

Behold, O good and sweetest Jesu, I cast myself upon my knees in Thy sight, and with the most fervent desire of my soul I pray and beseech Thee to impress upon my heart lively sentiments of faith, hope and charity, true repentance for my sins and a most firm purpose of amendment: whilst with deep affection and grief of soul I consider within myself and mentally contemplate Thy five most precious Wounds, having before mine eyes that which David, the prophet, long ago spoke in Thine own person concerning Thee, my Jesus: *They have pierced my hands and my feet; they have numbered all my bones* (Psalm 21, 17 and 18).

The faithful, who recite this prayer devoutly before an image of Jesus Christ Crucified, may gain:

An indulgence of 10 years; a plenary indulgence if, moreover, they go to confession, receive Holy Communion and pray for the intentions of the Sovereign Pontiff (S. C. Ind., July 31, 1858; S. P. Ap., Feb. 2, 1934).

E n ego, o bone et dulcíssime Iesu, ante conspéctum tuum génibus me provólvo ac máximo ánimi ardóre te oro atque obtéstor, ut meum in cor vívidos fídei, spei et caritátis sensus, atque veram peccatórum meórum pæniténtiam, éaque emendándi firmíssimam voluntátem velis imprímere: dum magno ánimi afféctu et dolóre tua quinque Vúlnera mecum ipse consídero, ac mente contémplor, illud præ óculis habens, quod iam in ore ponébat tuo David Prophéta de te, o bone Iesu: *Fodérunt manus meas et pedes meos; dinumeravérunt ómnia ossa mea* (Ps. xxi v. 17 et 18).

202

O God, who by the Passion of Thine only-begotten Son, and by the shedding of His Precious Blood through His five Wounds, didst restore human nature when it was lost by sin; grant us, we beseech Thee, that we who venerate on earth the Wounds suffered by Him, may be found worthy to obtain in heaven the fruits of that same Most Precious Blood. Through the same Christ our Lord. Amen (Roman Missal).

An indulgence of 5 years.
A plenary indulgence once a month on the usual conditions for the daily recitation of this prayer(S. P. Ap., Dec. 12, 1936).

Deus, qui Unigéniti Fílii tui passióne, et per quinque Vúlnera eius Sánguinis effusióne humánam natúram peccáto pérditam reparásti; tríbue nobis, quæsumus, ut qui ab eo suscépta Vúlnera venerámur in terris, eiúsdem pretiosíssimi Sánguinis fructum cónsequi mereámur in cælis. Per eúmdem Christum Dóminum nostrum. Amen (ex *Missali Romano*).

203

Grant, Lord Jesus Christ, that we who devoutly worship Thy five most precious Wounds, may keep them deeply impressed upon our hearts both in our life and in our deeds.

Glory be (*five times*).

An indulgence of 3 years(S. P. Ap., Dec. 12, 1936).

Fac, Dómine, Iesu Christe, ut qui Vúlnera tua devóte cólimus, hæc in nostris córdibus impréssa, móribus et vita teneámus.
Quinquies Glória Patri.

VIII

PRAYERS IN COMMEMORATION OF THE SEVEN WORDS SPOKEN BY JESUS ON THE CROSS

204

℣. O God, come unto my assistance.
℟. O Lord, make haste to help me.
℣. Glory be, *etc.*
℟. As it was, *etc.*

FIRST WORD

Father, forgive them, for they know not what they do.

Dear Jesu, who for love of me dost suffer upon the Cross in order to pay with Thy sufferings the debt of my sins and dost open Thy divine lips to obtain for me their remission from the eternal justice of God, have pity on all the faithful who are in their last agony and upon me; and when I shall come to that final hour, by the merits of Thy Most Precious Blood which was shed for our salvation, give me such a lively sorrow for my sins as shall cause my soul to expire in the bosom of Thine infinite mercy.

Glory be to the Father, *etc.* (*three times*).

Have mercy on us, O Lord, have mercy on us.

My God, I believe in Thee, I hope in Thee, I love Thee and I repent of having offended Thee by my sins.

SECOND WORD

This day shalt thou be with Me in paradise

Dear Jesu, who for love of me dost hang in agony upon the Cross, and with such readiness and bounty dost respond to the faith of the good thief who in the midst of Thy humiliation acknowledges Thee to be the Son of God, and dost assure him of paradise, have pity on all the faithful who are in their agony and upon me; and when I shall come to my latter end, by the merits of Thy Most Precious

Blood, inspire in my soul a faith so firm and constant that it shall not waver at any suggestions of the evil spirit; so may I obtain the reward of Thy holy paradise.

Glory be to the Father, *etc.* (*three times*).

Have mercy, *etc.* (*as above*).

My God, *etc.* (*as above*).

THIRD WORD

Behold thy mother; behold thy son.

Dear Jesu, who for love of me dost hang in agony upon the Cross, and who, forgetting Thine own sufferings, dost bequeath to me Thy most holy Mother as a pledge of Thy love, in order that, through her, I may be enabled to have recourse to Thee with all confidence in my greatest necessities, have pity on all the faithful who are in their agony and upon me; and when I shall come to my latter end, by the interior martyrdom of Thy dear Mother, inspire in my heart a firm trust in the infinite merits of Thy Most Precious Blood, whereby I may be able to escape the eternal damnation which I have merited by my sins.

Glory be to the Father, *etc.* (*three times*).

Have mercy, *etc.*

My God, *etc.* (*as above*).

FOURTH WORD

My God, my God, why hast Thou forsaken Me?

Dear Jesu, who for love of me dost hang in agony upon the Cross, and who, adding suffering to suffering, besides Thy bodily pains, dost endure with infinite patience the most painful affliction of spirit at being abandoned by Thine eternal Father, have pity on all the faithful who are in their agony and upon me; and when I shall come to the hour of death, by the merits of Thy Most Precious Blood, give me the grace of suffering with true patience all the pains and agony of my death-struggle, so that by uniting my sufferings to Thine, I may be able at the last to share Thy glory in paradise.

Glory be to the Father, *etc.* (*three times*).
Have mercy, *etc.*
My God, *etc.*

FIFTH WORD

I thirst.

Dear Jesu, who for love of me dost hang in agony upon the Cross, and who, not yet satisfied with so many reproaches and sufferings, wouldst suffer even more, if thereby all men might be saved, showing thus that the whole torrent of Thy Passion is not enough to slake the thirst of Thy loving Heart, have pity on all the faithful who are in their agony and upon me; and when I shall come to my final hour, by the merits of Thy Most Precious Blood, enkindle so great a fire of love within my heart as shall cause it to die for very desire of being united to Thee through all eternity.

Glory be to the Father, *etc.* (*three times*).
Have mercy, *etc.*
My God, *etc.*

SIXTH WORD

All is finished.

Dear Jesu, who for love of me dost hang in agony upon the Cross, and from that pulpit of truth dost proclaim that Thou hast finished the work of our redemption, whereby man, from being a child of wrath and perdition, has been made a son of God and an heir of heaven, have pity on all the faithful who are in their agony and upon me; and when I shall come to my last hour, by the merits of Thy Most Precious Blood, detach me wholly from the world and from myself, giving me the grace to offer Thee from my heart the sacrifice of my life in expiation of my sins.

Glory be to the Father, *etc.* (*three times*). Have mercy, *etc.* My God, *etc.*

SEVENTH WORD

Father, into Thy hands I commend my spirit.

Dear Jesu, who for the love of me dost hang in agony upon the Cross, and who to complete this great sacrifice dost embrace the will of Thine eternal Father, resigning Thy spirit into His hands, and then dost bow Thy head and die, have pity on all the faithful who are in their agony and upon me; and when I shall come to my latter end, by the merits of Thy Most Precious Blood give me a perfect conformity to Thy divine will, so that I may be ready to live or die, as it shall

please Thee; nor do I desire anything else
except the perfect fulfilment in me of Thine
adorable will.

Glory be to the Father, *etc.* (*three times*).
Have mercy, *etc.*   My God, *etc.*

Prayer to the Sorrowful Mother

Most holy Mother of sorrows, by that soul-
piercing martyrdom thou didst undergo at
the foot of the Cross during the three hours'
agony of Jesus, deign to assist me also, who
am the child of thy sorrows, in my agony, so
that by thine intercession I may be found
worthy to pass from my deathbed to thy
blessed society in paradise.

℣. From a sudden and unprovided death,
℟. Deliver me, O Lord.
℣. From the snares of the devil,
℟. Deliver me, O Lord.
℣. From everlasting death,
℟. Deliver me, O Lord.

Let us pray.

O God, who for the salvation of mankind
hast made for us in the most bitter death of
Thy Son both an example and a refuge; grant,
we beseech Thee, that we may be found
worthy to obtain the fruit of His great love in
our final peril at the hour of death, and to be
made partakers of our Redeemer's glory.
Through the same Christ our Lord.   Amen.

An indulgence of 7 years.

A plenary indulgence on the usual conditions, if this prayer is
recited daily for a month (S. C. Rit., Aug. 26, 1814; S. C. Ind., Dec.
8, 1897; S. P. Ap., May 27, 1935)

IX
PRAYERS

205

O God, who for the redemption of the world didst will to be born amongst men, to be circumcised, to be rejected by the Jews, to be betrayed by the traitor Judas with a kiss, to be bound with cords, to be led to slaughter as an innocent lamb, to be shamelessly exposed to the gaze of Annas, Caiphas, Pilate and Herod, to be accused by false witnesses, to be tormented by scourges and insults, defiled with spitting, crowned with thorns, smitten with blows, struck with a reed, blindfolded, stripped of Thy garments, fastened to the Cross with nails, lifted on the Cross, reckoned among thieves, given gall and vinegar to drink and wounded with a spear; do Thou, O Lord, by these Thy most holy sufferings, upon which I unworthily meditate, and by Thy holy Cross and death, deliver me from the pains of hell, and vouchsafe to bring me where Thou didst bring the penitent thief who was crucified with Thee, Who with the Father and the Holy Ghost livest and reignest, one God, world without end. Amen.

Our Father, Hail Mary, Glory be (*five times*).

An indulgence of 3 years.

An indulgence of 5 years, if this prayer is recited on Fridays in Lent.

A plenary indulgence on the usual conditions, if this prayer is said with devotion daily for an entire month (S. C. Ind., Aug. 25, 1820; S. P. Ap., Oct. 6, 1933; March 7, 1941).

Deus, qui pro redemptióne mundi voluísti nasci, circumcídi, a Iudæis reprobári, a Iuda traditóre ósculo tradi, vínculis alligári, sicut agnus ínnocens ad víctimam duci atque conspéctibus Annæ, Cáiphæ, Piláti et Heródis indecénter offérri, a falsis téstibus accusári, flagéllis et oppróbriis vexári, sputis cónspui, spinis coronári, cólaphis cædi, arúndine pércuti, fácie velári, véstibus éxui, cruci clavis affígi, in cruce levári, inter latrónes deputári, felle et acéto potári et láncea vulnerári, Tu, Dómine, per has sanctíssimas pœnas tuas, quas ego indígnus récolo, et per sanctam Crucem et Mortem tuam, líbera me a pœnis inférni et perdúcere dignéris, quo perduxísti latrónem tecum crucifíxum. Qui cum Patre et Spíritu Sancto vivis et regnas Deus per ómnia sǽcula sæculórum. Amen.

Quinquies Pater, Ave *et* Glória.

206

My divine Saviour, what didst Thou become, when for love of souls Thou didst suffer Thyself to be bound to the pillar? Ah! how truly then was fulfilled the word of the Prophet, saying of Thee that from head to foot Thou shouldst be all one wound, so as to be no longer recognizable! What shame Thou didst endure when they stripped Thee of Thy garments! What torments Thou didst undergo in that tempest of countless blows! In what torrents did Thy Most Precious Blood gush forth from Thy bursting veins!

I know well it was not so much the injustice of the Roman governor and the cruelty of the soldiers that scourged Thee as my sins. O accursed sins, that have cost Thee so many pains! Alas, what hardness of heart, when notwithstanding Thy manifold sufferings for me I have continued to offend Thee! But from this day forth it shall be so no longer. United to Thee by bonds of loyalty for ever, as long as I shall live, I shall seek to satisfy Thine offended justice. By the pains Thou didst suffer when bound to the pillar, by the scourges which tore Thine innocent Flesh, by the Blood which Thou didst shed in such abundance, have mercy on this unhappy soul of mine; deliver me today and always from the snares of the tempter; and when I have come to the end of my exile, bring me safely home to heaven with Thee.

An indulgence of 500 days (Leo XIII, Audience May 15, 1886; S. P. Ap., March 10, 1933).

207

Behold me at Thy feet, O Jesus of Nazareth, behold the most wretched of creatures, who comes into Thy presence humbled and penitent! Have mercy on me, O Lord, according to Thy great mercy! I have sinned and my sins are always before Thee. Yet my soul belongs to Thee, for Thou hast created it, and redeemed it with Thy Precious Blood. Ah, grant that Thy redeeming work be not in vain! Have pity on me; give me tears of true repentance; pardon me for I am Thy child; pardon me as Thou didst pardon the penitent thief; look upon me from Thy throne in heaven and give me Thy blessing.

I believe in God, etc.

An indulgence of 3 years (S. C. Ind., June 26, 1894; S. P. Ap., May 12, 1931).

208

O Jesus, who in Thy bitter Passion didst become "the most abject of men, a man of sorrows," I venerate Thy sacred Face whereon there once did shine the beauty and sweetness of the Godhead; but now It has become as it were the face of a leper! Nevertheless under those disfigured features, I recognize Thine infinite Love, and I am consumed with desire to love Thee and make Thee loved by all men. The tears which well up so abundantly in Thy sacred eyes appear to me as so many precious pearls that I love to gather up, in order to purchase the souls of poor sinners by means of their infinite value. O Jesus, whose adorable Face ravishes my heart, I implore Thee to fix deep within me Thy divine image and to set me on fire with Thy love, that so I may be found worthy to come to the contemplation of Thy glorious Face in heaven. Amen.

An indulgence of 500 days (S. C. of the Holy Office, June 10, 1915; S. P. Ap., April 5, 1931).

209

O my crucified God, behold me at Thy feet; deign to cast me not out, now that I appear before Thee as a sinner. I have offended Thee exceedingly in the past, my Jesus, but it shall be so no longer. Before Thee, my God, I put all my sins . . . ; I have now considered them and behold, they do not deserve Thy pardon; but do Thou cast one glance upon Thy sufferings and see how great is the worth of that Precious Blood that flows from Thy veins. O my God, at this hour close Thine eyes to my want of merit and open them to Thine infinite merit, and since Thou hast been pleased to die for my sins, grant me forgiveness for them all, that I may no longer feel the burden of my sins, for this burden, dear Jesus, oppresses me beyond measure. Assist me, my Jesus, for I desire to become good whatsoever it may cost; take away, destroy, utterly root out all that Thou findest in me contrary to Thy holy will. At the same time I pray Thee, O Jesus, to enlighten me, that I may be able to walk in Thy holy light (Blessed Gemma Galgani).

An indulgence of 500 days.

A plenary indulgence on the usual conditions, if this prayer is recited with devotion every day for a month (S. P. Ap., Feb. 16, 1934 and Nov. 26, 1934).

210

Assist us, O Lord our God; and defend us evermore by the might of Thy holy Cross, in whose honor Thou makest us to rejoice. Through Christ our Lord. Amen (Roman Missal).

An indulgence of 5 years.

A plenary indulgence once a month on the usual conditions, when it has been recited daily with devout dispositions (S. P. Ap., Sept. 14, 1934).

Adésto nobis, Dómine Deus noster; et quos sanctæ Crucis lætári facis honóre, eius quoque perpétuis defénde subsídiis. Per Christum Dóminum nostrum. Amen (ex *Missali Romano*).

211

O God, who for our sake didst will Thy Son to undergo the torments of the Cross, that Thou mightest drive far from us the power of the enemy; grant unto us Thy servants that we may attain to the grace of His Resurrection. Through the same Christ our Lord. Amen (Roman Missal)·

An indulgence of 5 years.

A plenary indulgence once a month on the usual conditions for the daily recitation of this prayer (S. P. Ap., Nov. 22, 1934)·

Deus, qui pro nobis Fílium tuum Crucis patíbulum subíre voluísti, ut inimíci a nobis expélleres potestátem: concéde nobis fámulis tuis; ut resurrectiónis grátiam consequámur. Per eúmdem Christum Dóminum nostrum. Amen (ex Missali Romano)·

212

O God, Who didst will to hallow the standard of the life-giving Cross by the Precious Blood of Thine only-begotten Son; grant, we beseech Thee, that they who rejoice in honoring the same holy Cross, may rejoice also in Thine ever-present protection. Through the same Christ our Lord. Amen (Roman Missal)·

An indulgence of 5 years.

A plenary indulgence on the usual conditions when this prayer has been devoutly said every day for a month (S. P. Ap., Feb. 7, 1935)·

Deus, qui unigéniti Fílii tui pretióso Sánguine, vivíficæ Crucis vexíllum sanctificáre voluísti: concéde, quæsumus, eos qui eiúsdem sanctæ Crucis gaudent honóre, tua quoque ubíque protectióne gaudére. Per eúmdem Christum Dóminum nostrum. Amen (ex Missali Romano)·

213

Lord Jesus Christ, Son of the living God, who at the sixth hour didst mount the gibbet of the Cross for the redemption of the world and didst shed Thy Precious Blood for the remission of our sins, we humbly beseech Thee, that Thou wouldst grant us the grace after death to enter with joy the gates of paradise. Who livest and reignest for ever and ever. Amen (Roman Missal).

An indulgence of 5 years.
A plenary indulgence on the usual conditions, if this prayer is devoutly said every day for a month (S. P. Ap., July 18, 1936).

Dómine Iesu Christe, Fili Dei vivi, qui hora sexta pro redemptióne mundi Crucis patíbulum ascendísti et Sánguinem tuum pretiósum in remissiónem peccatórum nostrórum fudísti; te humíliter deprecámur, ut post óbitum nostrum paradísi iánuas nos gaudénter introíre concédas: Qui vivis et regnas in sǽcula sæculórum. Amen (ex *Missali Romano*).

214

O Jesus, Who by reason of Thy burning love for us hast willed to be crucified and to shed Thy Most Precious Blood for the redemption and salvation of our souls, look down upon us here gathered together in remembrance of Thy most sorrowful Passion and Death, fully trusting in Thy mercy; cleanse us from sin by Thy grace, sanctify our toil, give unto us and unto all those who are dear to us our daily bread, sweeten our sufferings, bless our families, and to the nations so sorely afflicted, grant Thy peace, which is the only true peace, so that by obeying Thy commandments we may come at last to the glory of heaven. Amen.

The faithful, who recite this prayer with devotion at three o'clock on Good Friday, the hour when Our Lord Jesus Christ expired on the Cross, are granted:

An indulgence of 500 days (S. P. Ap., Jan. 15, 1940).

Art. VI
IN HONOR OF THE
MOST PRECIOUS BLOOD OF JESUS

I
INVOCATION

215

W e therefore pray Thee, help Thy serv-ants: whom Thou hast redeemed with Thy Precious Blood (Ambrosian Hymn).

An indulgence of 300 days (S. P. Ap., March 23, 1933).

T e ergo quæsumus, tuis fámulis súbveni, quos pre-tióso Sánguine redemísti (ex *Hymno Ambro-siano*).

NOTE:— Another invocation is found under n. 132-b.

II
HYMN
Salvete, Christi vulnera

216

H ail, Holy Wounds of Jesus, hail!
Sweet pledges of the saving Rood!
Whence flow the streams that never fail—
The purple streams of His dear Blood.

Brighter than brightest stars ye show,
Than sweetest rose your scent more rare,
No Indian gem may match your glow,
No honey's taste with yours compare.

Portals are ye to that dear Home,
Wherein our wearied souls may hide,
Whereto no angry foe can come,
The heart of Jesus Crucified.

What countless stripes our Jesus bore,
All naked left in Pilate's hall,
What copious floods of purple gore
Through rents in His torn garments fall.

His comely brow, O shame and grief,
By the sharp, thorny crown is riven,
Through hands and feet, without relief
The cruel nails are deeply driven.

But when for our poor sakes He died,
A willing Priest, by love subdued,
The soldier's spear transfixed His side—
Forth flowed the water and the blood.

Beneath the winepress of God's wrath,
To save our souls from endless pains,
Still hour by hour His Blood pours forth
Till not a single drop remains.

Come, bathe you in that healing flood,
All ye who mourn with sin opprest,
Your only hope in Jesus' Blood,
His Sacred Heart your only rest.

All praise to Him, the eternal Son,
At God's right hand enthroned above,
Whose Blood the world's redemption won,
Whose Spirit seals the gifts of love. Amen.

(Roman Breviary, tr. by H. N. Oxenham).

An indulgence of 5 years.

A plenary indulgence once a month on the usual conditions for
its daily devout recitation (S. P. Ap., Nov. 22, 1934).

Hymnus

Salvéte, Christi vúlnera,
  Imménsi amóris pígnora,
Quibus perénnes rívuli
Manant rubéntis sánguinis.

Nitóre stellas víncitis,
Rosas odóre et bálsama,
Prétio lapíllos Indicos,
Mellis favos dulcédine.

Per vos patet gratíssimum
Nostris asylum méntibus;
Non huc furor minántium
Unquam pénetrat hóstium.

Quot Iesus in prætório
Flagélla nudus éxcipit!
Quot scissa pellis úndique
Stillat cruóris gúttulas!

Frontem venústam, proh dolor!
Coróna pungit spínea,
Clavi retúsa cúspide
Pedes manúsque pérforant.

Postquam sed ille trádidit
Amans volénsque spíritum,
Pectus ferítur láncea,
Geminúsque liquor éxsilit.

Ut plena sit redémptio,
Sub torculári stríngitur,
Suíque Iesus ímmemor,
Sibi nil resérvat sánguinis.

Veníte, quotquot críminum
Funésta labes ínficit:
In hoc salútis bálneo
Qui se lavat, mundábitur.

Summi ad Paréntis déxteram
Sedénti habénda est grátia,
Qui nos redémit sánguine,
Sanctóque firmat Spíritu.   Amen.

(ex *Breviario Romano*)

III

A DEVOUT EXERCISE FOR THE MONTH OF JULY

217

The faithful, who during the month of July devoutly take part in the public exercise which is held in honor of the Most Precious Blood of our Lord Jesus Christ, may gain:

An indulgence of 10 years on any day of the month;

A plenary indulgence upon the addition of sacramental confession, Holy Communion, and prayer for the intentions of the Sovereign Pontiff, if they are present at ten of the exercises at least.

Those who during this month perform privately certain pious practices in honor of the same Precious Blood, may gain:

An indulgence of 7 years once on each day;

A plenary indulgence on the usual conditions, if they persevere in their prayers throughout the month; where, however, a public exercise is held, this indulgence is available only to those who are legitimately hindered from taking part in it (S. C. Ind., June 4, 1850; S. P. Ap., May 12, 1931).

IV

PRAYERS

218

O Precious Blood of Jesus, infinite price of sinful man's redemption, both drink and laver of our souls, Thou who dost plead continually the cause of man before the throne of infinite mercy; from the depths of my heart, I adore Thee, and so far as I am able, I would requite Thee for the insults and outrages which Thou dost continually receive from human beings, and especially from those who rashly dare to blaspheme Thee. Who would not bless this Blood of infinite value? Who doth not feel within himself the fire of the love of Jesus who shed it all for us? What would be my fate, had I not been redeemed by this divine Blood? Who hath drawn it from the veins of my Saviour, even to the last drop? Ah, this surely was the work of love. O infinite love, which has given us this saving balm! O balm beyond all price, welling up from the fountain of infinite love, grant that every heart and every tongue may be enabled to praise Thee, magnify Thee and give Thee thanks both now and for evermore. Amen.

An indulgence of 500 days (Pius VII, Oct. 18, 1815; S. P. Ap., June 25, 1932).

219

Eternal Father, I offer Thee the Most Precious Blood of Jesus Christ in atonement for my sins, and in supplication for the holy souls in purgatory and for the needs of holy Church.

An indulgence of 500 days.

An indulgence of 3 years, if this prayer is recited during the month of July.

A plenary indulgence on the usual conditions for the daily recitation of this act of oblation for an entire month (Pius VII, Sept. 22, 1817; S. P. Ap., March 10, 1933 and April 3, 1941).

220

Eternal Father, I offer Thee the merits of the Precious Blood of Jesus, Thy beloved Son, my Saviour and my God, for the spread and exaltation of my dear Mother, Thy holy Church, for the preservation and welfare of her visible Head, the sovereign Roman Pontiff, for the Cardinals, Bishops and Pastors of souls, and for all the ministers of the sanctuary.

Glory be to the Father, etc.
Blessed and praised for evermore be Jesus,
Who hath saved us with His Blood!

II. Eternal Father, I offer Thee the merits
of the Precious Blood of Jesus, Thy beloved
Son, my Saviour and my God, for peace and
concord among Catholic kings and princes,
for the humbling of the enemies of our holy
faith and for the welfare of all Thy Christian
people.

Glory be to the Father, etc.
Blessed and praised, etc.

III. Eternal Father, I offer Thee the merits
of the Precious Blood of Jesus, Thy beloved
Son, my Saviour and my God, for the conversion of unbelievers, the rooting-up of all
heresies and the conversion of sinners.

Glory be to the Father, etc.
Blessed and praised, etc.

IV. Eternal Father, I offer Thee the merits
of the Precious Blood of Jesus, Thy beloved
Son, my Saviour and my God, for all my
relations, friends and enemies, for those in
need, in sickness and in tribulation, and for
all those for whom Thou knowest that I am
bound to pray, and willest that I should pray.

Glory be to the Father, etc.
Blessed and praised, etc.

V. Eternal Father, I offer Thee the merits
of the Precious Blood of Jesus, Thy beloved
Son, my Saviour and my God, for all those
who are to pass this day to the other life,
that Thou wouldst deliver them from the

pains of hell, and admit them with all speed
to the possession of Thy glory.
  Glory be to the Father, etc.
  Blessed and praised, etc.

  VI. Eternal Father, I offer Thee the merits
of the Precious Blood of Jesus, Thy beloved
Son, my Saviour and my God, for all men
who are lovers of this great treasure and who
are united with me in adoring and glorifying
It and who labor to spread this devotion.
  Glory be to the Father, etc.
  Blessed and praised, etc.

  VII. Eternal Father, I offer Thee the
merits of the Precious Blood of Jesus, Thy
beloved Son, my Saviour and my God, for all
my needs, both temporal and spiritual, as
an intercession for the holy souls in purgatory, and in an especial manner for those
who were most devoted to this price of our
redemption, and to the sorrows and sufferings of our dear Mother, Mary most holy.
  Glory be to the Father, etc.
  Blessed and praised, etc.

  Glory to the Blood of Jesus both now and
for evermore and through the everlasting
ages.   Amen.
  An indulgence of 3 years.
  A plenary indulgence on the usual conditions for the daily recitation of this act of oblation for a month (Pius VII, Sept. 22, 1817;
S. P. Ap., May 12, 1931).

221

L ord Jesus Christ, who camest down from
  heaven to earth from the bosom of the
Father, and didst shed Thy Precious Blood

for the remission of our sins: we humbly
beseech Thee, that in the day of judgment
we may deserve to hear, standing at Thy
right hand: "Come, ye blessed." Who livest
and reignest for ever and ever. Amen
(Roman Missal).

An indulgence of 5 years.
A plenary indulgence once a month on the usual conditions for
the daily repetition of this prayer (S. P. Ap., Nov. 22, 1934).

D ómine Iesu Christe, qui de cælis ad terram de
sinu Patris descendísti et Sánguinem tuum
pretiósum in remissiónem peccatórum nostrórum
fudísti: te humíliter deprecámur, ut in die iudícii ad
déxteram tuam audíre mereámur: Veníte benedícti.
Qui vivis et regnas in sǽcula sæculórum. Amen
(ex *Missali Romano*).

222

A lmighty, and everlasting God, who hast
appointed Thine only-begotten Son to
be the Redeemer of the world, and hast been
pleased to be reconciled unto us by His Blood,
grant us, we beseech Thee, so to venerate
with solemn worship the price of our salvation, that the power thereof may here on
earth keep us from all things hurtful, and
the fruit of the same may gladden us for ever
hereafter in heaven. Through the same
Christ our Lord. Amen (Roman Missal).

An indulgence of 5 years.
A plenary indulgence on the usual conditions once a month for
the daily devout recitation of this prayer (S. P. Ap., July 15, 1035).

O mnípotens sempitérne Deus, qui unigénitum
Fílium tuum mundi Redemptórem constituísti,
ac eius Sánguine placári voluísti: concéde quǽsumus,
salútis nostræ prétium solémni cultu ita venerári,
atque a præséntis vitæ malis eius virtúte deféndi in

terris, ut fructu perpétuo lætémur in cælis. Per eúmdem Christum Dóminum nostrum. Amen (ex *Missali Romano*).

Art. VII

THE MOST SACRED HEART OF JESUS

I

EJACULATIONS AND INVOCATIONS

223

May the Sacred Heart of Jesus be loved in every place.

An indulgence of 300 days (Pius IX, Rescript in his own hand, Sept. 20, 1860; S. P. Ap., March 10, 1933).

224

Sweet Heart of my Jesus, grant that I may ever love Thee more.

An indulgence of 300 days.

A plenary indulgence once a month on the usual conditions, for the daily and devout repetition of this ejaculation (S. C. Ind., Nov. 26, 1876).

225

Heart of Jesus, burning with love for us, set our hearts on fire with love of Thee

(Roman Breviary).

An indulgence of 500 days.

A plenary indulgence on the usual conditions, when this invocation is said with devotion every day for a month (S. C. Ind., July 16, 1893; S. P. Ap., March 10, 1933).

Cor Iesu, flagrans amóre nostri, inflámma cor nostrum amóre tui (ex *Breviario Romano*).

226

Heart of Jesus, I put my trust in Thee!

An indulgence of 300 days.

A plenary indulgence once a month on the usual conditions, when its daily recitation is continued for a month (Pius X, Rescript in his own hand, May 27, 1905, exhib. Aug. 19, 1905; Audience, June 5, 1906; S. C. Ind., June 27, 1906).

227

J esus, meek and humble of heart, make our heart like unto Thy Heart (Roman Breviary).

An indulgence of 500 days.

A plenary indulgence once a month on the usual conditions for the devout recitation of this invocation every day (Pius X, Rescript in his own hand, Sept. 13, 1905, exhib. Sept. 15, 1905; S. P. Ap., March 10, 1933).

I esu, mitis et húmilis corde, fac cor nostrum secúndum Cor tuum (ex *Breviario Romano*).

228

Sacred Heart of Jesus, Thy kingdom come!

An indulgence of 300 days (Pius X, Audience, June 29, 1906, exhib. July 6, 1906).

229

D ivine Heart of Jesus, convert sinners, save the dying, deliver the holy souls in purgatory.

An indulgence of 300 days (Pius X, Rescript in his own hand, July 13, 1906, exhib. Nov. 5, 1906).

230

S acred Heart of Jesus, I believe in Thy love for me.

An indulgence of 300 days (Pius X, Rescript in his own hand, July 29, 1907, exhib. July 18, 1908).

231

G lory, love and thanksgiving be to the Sacred Heart of Jesus!

An indulgence of 300 days (S. C. Ind., Jan. 8, 1908; S. P Ap., Nov. 15. 1927).

232

O Heart of love, I put all my trust in Thee; for I fear all things from my own weakness, but I hope for all things from Thy goodness (St. Margaret Mary Alacoque).

An indulgence of 300 days.

A plenary indulgence once a month on the usual conditions, if this invocation is repeated daily with devotion (Pius X, Rescript in his own hand, May 30, 1908; exhib. June 3, 1908; S. P. Ap., March 10, 1935).

233

S weet Heart of Jesus, have mercy on us and on our erring brethren.

An indulgence of 300 days (Pius X, Rescript in his own hand, Aug. 13, 1908, exhib. Oct. 13, 1908; S. P. Ap., May 7, 1934).

234

A ll for Thee, Most Sacred Heart of Jesus.

An indulgence of 300 days (S. C. of the Holy Office, Nov. 26, 1908).

235

S acred Heart of Jesus, mayest Thou be known, loved and imitated!

An indulgence of 300 days once a day (S. P. Ap., March 15, 1918).

236

S acred Heart of Jesus, protect our families.

An indulgence of 300 days.

A plenary indulgence once a month on the usual conditions, if this devout invocation is repeated daily (S. P. Ap., June 7, 1918 and March 2, 1932).

237

S weet Heart of Jesus, be my love.

An indulgence of 300 days (S. P. Ap., Jan. 13, 1920).

D ulce Cor Iesu, sis amor meus.

238

S acred Heart of Jesus, I give myself to Thee through Mary.

An indulgence of 300 days.

A plenary indulgence on the usual conditions, for the daily repetition of this invocation for a month (S. P. Ap., June 19, 1920; March 1, 1923 and April 23, 1936).

239

S acred Heart of Jesus, strengthened in Thine agony by an Angel, strengthen us in our agony.

An indulgence of 300 days (S. P. Ap., June 26, 1920 and Sept. 9, 1936).

240

S acred Heart of Jesus, let me love Thee and make Thee loved.

An indulgence of 300 days (Benedict XV, Rescript in his own hand, July 29, 1920, exhib. Jan. 18, 1927; S. P. Ap., March 12, 1949).

241

S acred Heart of Jesus, convert all poor blasphemers!

An indulgence of 300 days.

A plenary indulgence once a month on the usual conditions, if this invocation is repeated daily (S. P. Ap., Nov. 20, 1925 and April 22, 1949).

242

M ost Sacred Heart of Jesus, have mercy on us.

An indulgence of 500 days.

A plenary indulgence on the usual conditions, if this invocation is devoutly repeated every day for a month (S. P. Ap., Nov. 22, 1934).

C or Iesu sacratíssimum, miserére nobis.

NOTE:—With regard to the saying of this invocation after the celebration of Low Mass, see n. 675.

243

M ost sweet Heart of Jesus, grant that peace, the fruit of justice and charity, may reign throughout the world.

An indulgence of 300 days (Pius XII, Rescript in his own hand, Dec. 21, 1939, exhibited Jan. 15, 1940; S. P. Ap., July 16, 1949).

II

THE LITTLE OFFICE

244

The faithful who recite devoutly the little Office of the Sacred Heart of Jesus may gain:

An indulgence of 7 years;

A plenary indulgence on the usual conditions, provided that they recite it daily for a month (Apostolic Brief, Dec. 12, 1901 and March 1, 1904; S. P. Ap., March 18, 1932).

III

THE LITANY

245

Lord, have mercy on us.
Christ, have mercy on us.
Lord, have mercy on us.
Christ, hear us.
Christ, graciously hear us.
God, the Father of Heaven, have mercy on us
God the Son, Redeemer of the world,
have mercy on us
God the Holy Ghost, have mercy on us
Holy Trinity, one God, have mercy on us
Heart of Jesus, Son of the Eternal Father,
have mercy on us
Heart of Jesus, formed by the Holy Ghost in the Virgin Mother's womb,
have mercy on us
Heart of Jesus, substantially united to the Word of God, have mercy on us
Heart of Jesus, of infinite majesty,
have mercy on us
Heart of Jesus, holy temple of God,
have mercy on us

Heart of Jesus, tabernacle of the Most
  High,   have mercy on us
Heart of Jesus, house of God and gate
  of Heaven,   have mercy on us
Heart of Jesus, glowing furnace of charity,
                                     have mercy on us
Heart of Jesus, vessel of justice and love,
                                     have mercy on us
Heart of Jesus, full of goodness and love,
                                     have mercy on us
Heart of Jesus, abyss of all virtues,
                                     have mercy on us
Heart of Jesus, most worthy of all praise,
                                     have mercy on us
Heart of Jesus, King and center of all
  hearts,   have mercy on us
Heart of Jesus, wherein are all the treasures
  of wisdom and knowledge,
                                     have mercy on us
Heart of Jesus, wherein dwelleth all the
  fulness of the Godhead, have mercy on us
Heart of Jesus, in Whom the Father is
  well pleased,   have mercy on us
Heart of Jesus, of Whose fulness we have
  all received,   have mercy on us
Heart of Jesus, desire of the everlasting
  hills,   have mercy on us
Heart of Jesus, patient and rich in mercy,
                                     have mercy on us
Heart of Jesus, rich unto all who call
  upon Thee,   have mercy on us
Heart of Jesus, fount of life and holiness,
                                     have mercy on us

Heart of Jesus, propitiation for our offenses,
                    have mercy on us
Heart of Jesus, overwhelmed with
    reproaches,   have mercy on us
Heart of Jesus, bruised for our iniquities,
                    have mercy on us
Heart of Jesus, obedient even unto death,
                    have mercy on us
Heart of Jesus, pierced with a lance,
                    have mercy on us
Heart of Jesus, source of all consolation,
                    have mercy on us
Heart of Jesus, our life and resurrection,
                    have mercy on us
Heart of Jesus, our peace and reconciliation,
                    have mercy on us
Heart of Jesus, victim for our sins,
                    have mercy on us
Heart of Jesus, salvation of those who
    hope in Thee,   have mercy on us
Heart of Jesus, hope of those who die in
    Thee,   have mercy on us
Heart of Jesus, delight of all Saints,
                    have mercy on us

Lamb of God, Who takest away the sins of
    the world, spare us, O Lord.
Lamb of God, who takest away the sins of
    the world, graciously hear us, O Lord.
Lamb of God, Who takest away the sins of
    the world, have mercy on us.

℣. Jesus, meek and humble of Heart,
℟. Make our hearts like unto Thine.

Let us pray.

Almighty and everlasting God, look upon the Heart of Thy well-beloved Son and upon the praise and satisfaction which He offers unto Thee in the name of sinners; and do Thou of Thy great goodness grant them pardon when they seek Thy mercy, in the name of the same Thy Son, Jesus Christ, who liveth and reigneth with Thee for ever and ever. Amen.

An indulgence of 7 years.

A plenary indulgence on the usual conditions, when this Litany together with its versicle and prayer are devoutly said every day for a month (S. C. of Rites, the document being exhibited April 2, 1899; S. P. Ap., March 10, 1933).

Kýrie, eléison.
Christe, eléison.
Kýrie, eléison.
Christe, audi nos.
Christe, exáudi nos.

Pater de cælis, Deus,	miserére nobis
Fili, Redémptor mundi, Deus,	miserére
Spíritus Sancte, Deus,	miserére
Sancta Trínitas, unus Deus,	miserére
Cor Iesu, Fílii Patris ætérni,	miserére
Cor Iesu, in sinu Vírginis Matris a Spíritu Sancto formátum,	miserére
Cor Iesu, Verbo Dei substantiáliter unítum,	miserére
Cor Iesu, maiestátis infinítæ,	miserére
Cor Iesu, templum Dei sanctum,	miserére
Cor Iesu, tabernáculum Altíssimi,	miserére
Cor Iesu, domus Dei et porta cæli,	miserére
Cor Iesu, fornax ardens caritátis,	miserére
Cor Iesu, iustítiæ et amóris receptáculum,	miserére
Cor Iesu, bonitáte et amóre plenum,	miserére
Cor Iesu, virtútum ómnium abýssus,	miserére

Cor Iesu, omni laude digníssimum, miserére
Cor Iesu, rex et centrum ómnium córdium, miserére
Cor Iesu, in quo sunt omnes thesáuri sapiéntiæ et sciéntiæ, miserére
Cor Iesu, in quo hábitat omnis plenitúdo divinitátis, miserére
Cor Jesu, in quo Pater sibi bene complácuit, miserére
Cor Iesu, de cuius plenitúdine omnes nos accépimus, miserére
Cor Iesu, desidérium cóllium æternórum, miserére
Cor Iesu, pátiens et multæ misericórdiæ, miserére
Cor Iesu, dives in omnes qui ínvocant te, miserére
Cor Iesu, fons vitæ et sanctitátis, miserére
Cor Iesu, propitiátio pro peccátis nostris, miserére
Cor Iesu, saturátum oppróbriis, miserére
Cor Iesu, attrítum propter scélera nostra, miserére
Cor Iesu, usque ad mortem obédiens factum, miserére
Cor Iesu, láncea perforátum, miserére
Cor Iesu, fons totíus consolatiónis, miserére
Cor Iesu, vita et resurréctio nostra, miserére
Cor Iesu, pax et reconciliátio nostra, miserére
Cor Iesu, víctima peccatórum, miserére
Cor Iesu, salus in te sperántium, miserére
Cor Iesu, spes in te moriéntium, miserére
Cor Iesu, delíciæ Sanctórum ómnium, miserére

Agnus Dei, qui tollis peccáta mundi, parce nobis, Dómine.
Agnus Dei, qui tollis peccáta mundi, exáudi nos, Dómine.
Agnus Dei, qui tollis peccáta mundi, miserére nobis.

℣. Iesu, mitis et húmilis Corde,
℞. Fac cor nostrum secúndum Cor tuum.

Orémus.

O mnípotens sempitérne Deus, réspice in Cor dilectíssimi Fílii tui et in laudes et satisfactiónes,
quas in nómine peccatórum tibi persólvit, iísque
misericórdiam tuam peténtibus, tu véniam concéde
placátus in nómine eiúsdem Fílii tui Iesu Christi: Qui
tecum vivit et regnat in sǽcula sæculórum. Amen.

IV

HYMNS

246

Cor, arca legem continens

O Heart! thou ark where lies the law,
   Not of the servitude of old,
But that from which we pardon draw,
   And grace and mercies manifold.

Heart, the pure and stainless shrine
   Where that new covenant has lain:
Temple than Salem's more divine;
   Veil, better than its veil in twain.

With such a wound as must appear
   Love willed that Thou shouldst wounded be,
That we might all the wounds revere,
   Which love doth bear invisibly.

'Neath this, love's symbol, suffering twice,
   Things mystical and bloody both
Christ, as a priest, in sacrifice
   To Heaven uplifted, nothing loth.

Who would not love for love repay?
   What man, redeemed, could love refuse
To this Heart, or herein, for aye,
   His tabernacle fail to choose?

Jesu, to Thee be glory given,
  Who from Thy Heart dost grace outpour;
To Father and to Paraclete
  Be endless praise for evermore.   Amen.

(Roman Breviary; tr. J. Fitzpatrick).

An indulgence of 5 years.

A plenary indulgence on the usual conditions, for the daily recitation of this hymn throughout a month (S. P. Ap., June 23, 1935).

COR, arca legem cóntinens
  Non servitútis véteris,
Sed grátiæ, sed véniæ,
  Sed et misericórdiæ.

  Cor, sanctuárium novi
Intemerátum fœderis,
  Templum vetústo sánctius,
Velúmque scisso utílius.

  Te vulnerátum cáritas
Ictu paténti vóluit,
  Amóris invisíbilis
Ut venerémur vúlnera.

  Hoc sub amóris sýmbolo
Passus cruénta et mýstica,
  Utrúmque sacrifícium
Christus sacérdos óbtulit.

  Quis non amántem rédamet?
Quis non redémptus díligat,
  Et Corde in isto séligat
Aetérna tabernácula?

  Iesu, tibi sit glória,
Qui Corde fundis grátiam
  Cum Patre et almo Spíritu
In sempitérna sǽcula.   Amen.

(ex *Breviario Romano*).

247

Auctor beate sæculi

J esu! Creator of the world,
  Of all mankind Redeemer blest,
True God of God, in Whom we see
  Thy Father's image clear expressed!

Thee, Saviour, love alone constrained
  To make our mortal flesh Thine own,
And, as a second Adam, come
  For the first Adam to atone.

That selfsame love which made the sky,
  Which made the sea and stars, and earth,
Took pity on our misery,
  And broke the bondage of our birth.

O Jesus! in Thy Heart divine
  May that same love for ever glow!
Forever mercy to mankind
  From that exhaustless fountain flow!

For this the Sacred Heart was pierced,
  And both with blood and water ran—
To cleanse us from the stains of guilt,
  And be the hope and strength of man.

Jesu, to Thee be glory given,
  Who from Thy Heart dost grace outpour,
To Father and to Paraclete
  Be endless praise for evermore.   Amen.

(Roman Breviary, tr. E. Caswall).

An indulgence of 5 years.
A plenary indulgence on the usual conditions, if this hymn is
devoutly recited every day for a month (S. P. Ap., March 12, 1936).

Auctor beáte sæculi,
Christe, Redémptor ómnium,
Lumen Patris de lúmine,
Deúsque verus de Deo.

Amor coëgit te tuus
Mortále corpus súmere,
Ut, novus Adam, rédderes,
Quod vetus ille abstúlerat.

Ille amor almus ártifex
Terræ marísque et síderum,
Erráta patrum míserans
Et nostra rumpens víncula.

Non Corde discédat tuo
Vis illa amóris ínclyti:
Hoc fonte gentes háuriant
Remissiónis grátiam.

Percússum ad hoc est láncea,
Passúmque ad hoc est vúlnera,
Ut nos laváret sórdibus,
Unda fluénte et sánguine.

Iesu, tibi sit gloria,
Qui Corde fundis grátiam
Cum Patre et almo Spíritu
In sempitérna sǽcula. Amen.

(ex *Breviario Romano*).

V

PIOUS PRACTICES

248

The faithful who recite the *Our Father*, *Hail Mary*,
and *Glory be* together with the invocation

*Sweet Heart of my Jesus, grant that I may
love Thee more and more:*

before an image of the Sacred Heart of Jesus may
gain:

An indulgence of 500 days;

A plenary indulgence once a month on the usual conditions, if
they perform this act of devotion daily (**Pius VI, Audience, Jan.
2, 1799; S. P. Ap., March 10, 1933**).

249

The faithful who devoutly visit a church or public oratory where the Feast of the Sacred Heart
of Jesus is being celebrated (even though it has been

transferred with the consent of the Ordinary) may gain:

A plenary indulgence on condition of confession, Holy Communion and prayer for the intentions of the Sovereign Pontiff (Secret Mem., July 7, 1815; S. P. Ap., Nov. 4, 1934).

250

The faithful who devoutly assist at a public novena in honor of the Sacred Heart of Jesus, immediately before the Feast or at some other time during the year, may gain:

An indulgence of 10 years on any day;

A plenary indulgence on condition of confession, Holy Communion and prayer for the intentions of the Sovereign Pontiff, provided that they assist at this devout exercise on at least five days.

Those who at the aforesaid times perform their devotions privately in honor of the Sacred Heart of Jesus, with the intention of so continuing for nine successive days, may gain:

An indulgence of 7 years once each day;

A plenary indulgence on the usual conditions at the end of the novena; but where this is performed publicly, this indulgence can be gained only by those who are lawfully prevented from taking part in the public exercises (S. C. Ind., Jan. 13, 1818; Pius IX, Audience, Jan. 3, 1849; S. C. of Bishops and Religious, Jan. 28, 1850; S. C. Ind., Nov. 26, 1876; S. P. Ap., Feb. 22, 1935).

251
THE BADGE OF THE SACRED HEART

The faithful who devoutly wear a badge of white wool, suspended from the neck after the manner of a small scapular, with a likeness of the Sacred Heart of Jesus embroidered thereon or otherwise attached, and with the following, or similar words, printed upon it: *Cease, the Heart of Jesus is with us*, or even without any inscription at all, if they say *Our Father*, *Hail Mary* and *Glory be*, may gain:

An indulgence of 500 days, once a day (Pius IX, Rescript in his own hand, Oct. 28, 1872, exhib. Dec. 18, 1872; Apostolic Brief, March 28 and June 20, 1873; S. P. Ap., April 8, 1936).

252

a) The faithful who devoutly assist at the public exercises in honor of the Sacred Heart of Jesus on the First Friday of the month may gain:

A plenary indulgence, provided that they make their confession, receive Holy Communion and pray for the intentions of the Sovereign Pontiff.

If however on the First Friday they recite privately some prayers in reparation for the injuries offered to the Sacred Heart of Jesus they may gain:

A plenary indulgence on the usual conditions; if however, a public service is held, this latter indulgence can be gained only by those who are lawfully prevented from assisting at such service.

b) The faithful who recite devout prayers of reparation on other Fridays of the year may gain:

An indulgence of 7 years once on each Friday (S. C. Ind., Sept. 7, 1897; S. P. Ap., June 1, 1934 and May 15, 1949).

253
A MONTH DEDICATED TO THE
MOST SACRED HEART OF JESUS

The faithful who devoutly take part in public services in honor of the Sacred Heart of Jesus during the month of June, or some other, according to the prudent judgment of the most Reverend Ordinary, may gain:

An indulgence of 10 years on any day of the month;

A plenary indulgence, if they are present at these services on at least ten days of the month and, in addition, make their confession, receive Holy Communion and pray for the intentions of the Sovereign Pontiff.

Those who perform their devotions privately during such a month may gain:

An indulgence of 7 years once on any day of the month;

A plenary indulgence on the usual conditions, provided that they perform these devotions daily throughout the month and are lawfully excused from taking part in public exercises where the latter are held (S. C. Ind., May 8, 1873 and May 30, 1902; S. P. Ap., March 1, 1933).

Moreover, if the month dedicated to the Sacred Heart is solemnly celebrated, namely, with a sermon either daily or in the form of a retreat (with at least two discourses each day) for a period of eight days, whether in a church, public oratory or semi-public oratory (for those who may lawfully make use of the latter), there is granted:

1° A plenary indulgence for each visit made on the day on which the month is closed, to be gained by those who have been present at ten at least of the sermons and prayers, or have assisted at all the exercises of the retreat (performing their devotions from time to time), if they make their confession, receive Holy Communion and say the *Our Father, Hail Mary* and *Glory be* six times at each visit for the intentions of the Sovereign Pontiff;

2° a) An indulgence of 500 days, for those who perform some work of piety that this devout practice may be more widely spread or receive an increase;

b) A plenary indulgence as often as they receive Holy Communion during the aforesaid month, on condition of confession, a visit to a church or public oratory and prayer for the intentions of the Sovereign Pontiff;

3° The indult of a personal "privileged" altar on the final day of the month, to the preachers and rectors of churches or oratories where the aforesaid service is solemnly held (S. C. Ind., Aug. 8, 1906; Pius X in a private audience, the document having been exhibited on Jan. 26, 1908; S. P. Ap., Nov. 15, 1927 and July 5, 1930).

254

The faithful, on any of the five Fridays immediately preceding the Feast of the Sacred Heart of Jesus, if they receive Holy Communion, may gain:

A plenary indulgence, if they make their confession, visit some church or public oratory and pray for the intentions of the Sovereign Pontiff (Apostolic Brief, June 3, 1924; S. P. Ap., April 26, 1930).

VI
CHAPLET
255

℣. O God, come unto my assistance;
℟. O Lord, make haste to help me.
℣. Glory be to the Father, *etc.*
℟. As it was in the beginning, *etc.*

I. My most loving Jesus, when I consider Thy tender Heart and behold It full of mercy and tenderness toward sinners, my own heart is filled with joy and confidence that I shall be kindly welcomed by Thee. Alas, how many times have I sinned! But now, with Peter and with Magdalen, I weep for my sins and detest them because they offend Thee, who art infinite Goodness. Ah, mercifully grant me pardon for them all; and let me die, I ask it through Thy Sacred Heart, let me die rather than offend Thee again; at least let me live only to love Thee in return.

Our Father once and *Glory be* five times.
Sweet Heart of my Jesus,
Make me love Thee ever more and more.

II. My Jesus, I bless Thy most humble Heart, and I give Thee thanks that, in giving It to me to be my example, not only dost Thou urge me with strong pleadings to imitate It, but even at the cost of Thine own great humiliations, Thou dost point out and make plain to me the way of salvation. Fool and ingrate that I am, how far have I gone astray! Pardon me; no longer shall pride rule in me, but with a humble heart will I follow Thee through the midst of tribulations and thus obtain my peace and salvation. Do Thou give me strength and I will bless Thy Sacred Heart for ever.

Our Father once and *Glory be* five times.
Sweet Heart, *etc.*

III. My Jesus, I am filled with admiration at the exceeding patience of Thy Sacred Heart, and I thank Thee for having given us so many wondrous examples of unwearied patience. It grieves me that these Thine examples vainly reproach me for my excessive delicacy, shrinking as I do from the slightest pain. O my dear Jesus, pour into my heart a fervent and abiding love of tribulations, of crosses, of mortification and penance, so that, by following Thy footsteps to Calvary, I may likewise come with Thee to the joys of paradise.

Our Father once and *Glory be* five times. Sweet Heart, *etc.*

IV. At the sight of the great meekness of Thy Heart, dear Jesus, I shudder at my own, so unlike to Thine. Unhappily I am disquieted and complain even at a hint, a gesture, a word that thwarts me! Ah, pardon all my violence, and give me the grace henceforward to imitate in every contradiction Thine own unchanging meekness, thus to enjoy a perpetual and holy peace.

Our Father once and *Glory be* five times. Sweet Heart, *etc.*

V. Let all men sing the praises, O Jesus, of Thy most generous Heart, the Conqueror of death and hell, for well It merits every praise. I am more than ever ashamed when I behold my own heart so cowardly that it trembles at every idle word out of human respect; but it shall be so no longer; from Thee I implore strength so courageous, that after fighting and conquering on earth, I may hereafter triumph joyfully with Thee in heaven.

Our Father once and *Glory be* five times. Sweet Heart, *etc.*

Let us turn to Mary, dedicating ourselves yet more and more to her, and filled with confidence in her maternal heart let us say to her:

Through the high worth of thy most sweet Heart, obtain for me, O mighty Mother of God and my Mother, a true and lasting devotion to the Sacred Heart of Jesus thy Son; to the end that I may take up my abode, with all my thoughts and affections, in that Sacred Heart, and may faithfully fulfil my every duty, and serve Jesus with a ready heart every day of my life, and especially this present day.

℣. Heart of Jesus, burning with love of us,
℟. Make our hearts to burn with love of Thee.

Let us pray.

May Thy Holy Spirit, we beseech Thee, O Lord, enkindle in us that fire which our Lord Jesus Christ sent upon the earth from the innermost recesses of His Sacred Heart, and which He willed should burn with exceeding warmth: Who liveth and reigneth with Thee in the unity of the same Holy Spirit for ever and ever. Amen.

An indulgence of 7 years.

A plenary indulgence on the usual conditions for the daily recitation of this chaplet throughout one month (S. C. Ind., March 20, 1815; S. P. Ap., March 10, 1933).

VII

ACTS OF REPARATION AND CONSECRATION

256

ACT OF REPARATION

O sweetest Jesus, Thou dost pour forth Thy love abundantly on men, while they repay Thee most ungratefully with neglect, indifference and contempt. Behold us humbly kneeling before Thine altar (*outside a church or oratory say:*in Thy presence); we would fain repair this heartless ingratitude on the part of men, and the manifold injuries that are everywhere done to Thy most loving Heart, by a special act of homage.

Yet we are not unmindful that we, too, have had our part in this unworthy behavior; therefore are we moved to deep contrition, and, above all, we beg Thy mercy for ourselves; we are ready to atone, by this voluntary act of expiation, for the crimes which we ourselves have committed, as also for the sins of those who, straying far from the way of salvation, either refuse, in the blindness of their unbelief, to follow Thee, the Shepherd and Guide of their souls, or who trample upon the vows of their Baptism and shake off the sweet yoke of Thy law.

Not only are we anxious to expiate all these deplorable crimes, but in an especial manner do we purpose to make reparation for these following: immodesty and shameful excesses in life and dress; the many snares of corruption laid for the souls of the innocent; the neglect of holydays; the hateful blasphemies that are hurled against Thee and Thy Saints; the reproaches uttered against Thy Vicar on earth and all the priestly order; the neglect, also, of the very Sacrament of Thy love, as well as its profanation by horrifying sacrilege; and finally the public sins of the nations in rebellion against the just rights and the teaching authority of the Church established by Thee.

Would that we were able to atone for all these outrages even to the shedding of our blood! Meanwhile, in order to atone for the violations of the honor due to Thee, we offer unto Thee that selfsame satisfaction which of old Thou didst offer to the Father upon the holy Cross and which from day to day Thou dost continually renew upon the altars of Thy Church. To this we add the expiatory merits of Thy Virgin Mother, of all Thy Saints and of the devout faithful upon earth. With all our hearts we promise to atone, Thy grace assisting us, for our own past sins and those of all other men, as also for our coldness towards Thine exceeding great love, by a firm faith, spotless purity of life and the perfect fulfilment, so far as in us lies, of the law of the Gospel, and in particular of the precept of charity.

We likewise pledge ourselves in accordance with our strength to prevent such injuries from being done to Thee, and to invite as many as we can to follow Thee. Accept, we pray Thee, most gracious Jesus, through the intercession of Our Lady of Reparation, this our free-will offering of reparation, and be Thou pleased to keep us, by the great gift of final perseverance, faithful even unto death in our dutiful service of Thee, so that in the

end we may all come to that our true native
land, where Thou, with the Father and the
Holy Spirit, livest and reignest for ever and
ever. Amen.

An indulgence of 5 years.
A plenary indulgence once a month for the daily devout recitation of this prayer, on condition of confession, Communion and a
visit to some church or public oratory.

The faithful, moreover, who, on the Feast of the
Sacred Heart of Jesus, assist at this same act of reparation, adding thereto the Litany of the Sacred
Heart, in any church or oratory, even semi-public
(for those who lawfully frequent it), in the presence
of the Blessed Sacrament solemnly exposed, may
gain:

An indulgence of 7 years;
A plenary indulgence, provided that they atone for their sins in
sacramental confession and partake of the Eucharistic Table (S. P.
Ap., June 1, 1928 and March 18, 1932) ·
NOTE. As to certain versions cfr. Acta Ap. Sedis, 1928, p. 179
and following.

Actus reparationis

I esu dulcíssime, cuius effúsa in hómines cáritas,
tanta oblivióne, negligéntia, comtemptióne, in-
gratíssime repénditur, en nos, ante altária tua pro-
volúti, tam nefáriam hóminum socórdiam iniuriás-
que, quibus úndique amantíssimum Cor tuum affíci-
tur, peculiári honóre resarcíre conténdimus.

Attamen, mémores tantæ nos quoque indignitátis
non expértes aliquándo fuísse, índeque vehementís-
simo dolóre commóti, tuam in primis misericórdiam
nobis implorámus, parátis, voluntária expiatióne
compensáre flagítia non modo quæ ipsi patrávimus,
sed étiam illórum, qui, longe a salútis via aberrántes,
vel te pastórem ducémque sectári detréctant, in sua
infidelitáte obstináti, vel, baptísmatis promíssa con-
culcántes, suavíssimum tuæ legis iugum excussérunt.

Quæ deploránda crímina, cum univérsa expiáre
conténdimus, tum nobis síngula resarciénda propóni-

---

[1] Extra ecclesiam vel oratorium, loco: *altária tua*, dicatur: *conspéctum tuum*.

mus: vitæ cultúsque immodéstiam atque turpitú-
dines, tot corruptélæ pédicas innocéntium ánimis in-
strúctas, dies festos violátos, exsecránda in te tuósque
Sanctos iactáta maledícta atque in tuum Vicárium
ordinémque sacerdotálem convícia irrogáta, ipsum
dénique amóris divíni Sacraméntum vel negléctum
vel horréndis sacrilégiis profanátum, pública postré-
mo natiónum delícta, quæ Ecclésiæ a te institútæ
iúribus magisterióque reluctántur.

Quæ útinam crímina sánguine ipsi nostro elúere
possémus! Intérea ad violátum divínum honórem
resarciéndum, quam Tu olim Patri in Cruce satis-
factiónem obtulísti quamque quotídie in altáribus re-
nováre pergis, hanc eámdem nos tibi præstámus, cum
Vírginis Matris, ómnium Sanctórum, piórum quoque
fidélium expiatiónibus coniúnctam, ex ánimo spon-
déntes, cum prætérita nostra aliorúmque peccáta ac
tanti amóris incúriam firma fide, cándidis vitæ móribus, perfécta legis evangélicæ, caritátis potíssimum,
observántia, quantum in nobis erit, grátia tua favénte,
nos esse compensatúros, tum iniúrias tibi inferéndas
pro víribus prohibitúros, et quam plúrimos potuéri-
mus ad tui sequélam convocatúros. Excípias, quǽsumus, benigníssime Iesu, beáta Vírgine María Re-
paratríce intercedénte, voluntárium huius expiati-
ónis obséquium nosque in offício tuíque servítio
fidíssimos ad mortem usque velis, magno illo perse-
verántiæ múnere, continére, ut ad illam tandem
pátriam perveniámus omnes, ubi Tu cum Patre et
Spíritu Sancto vivis et regnas in sǽcula sæculórum.
Amen.

257

An Act of Reparation and Consecration

O most merciful Heart of Jesus, divine
mercy-seat, for whose sake the Eternal
Father has promised that He would always
hear our prayers!

I unite myself to Thee in offering to Thine
Eternal Father this poor and needy heart of

mine, contrite and humbled in His divine presence, and desirous of making complete reparation for the offenses that are committed against Him, especially those which Thou dost continually suffer in the Holy Eucharist, and more particularly those which I myself have unhappily so often committed. Would that I could wash them away with my tears, O Sacred Heart of Jesus, and blot out with my own heart's blood the ingratitude wherewith we have repaid Thy tender love. I unite my sorrow, slight as it is, with the mortal agony which caused Thy sweat to become as drops of blood in the Garden of Olives at the very thought of our sins. Do Thou offer it, dear Lord, to Thine Eternal Father in union with Thy Sacred Heart. Render Him infinite thanks for the manifold blessings which He constantly showers upon us, and let Thy love supply for our want of thankfulness and remembrance. Grant me grace always to present myself in a spirit of deepest reverence before the face of Thy divine Majesty, in order thus to repair in some measure the irreverences and outrages which I have dared to commit before Thee; grant also, that from this day forth, I may devote myself with all my might to drawing, both by word and example, many souls to know Thee and to experience the riches of Thy Heart. From this moment I offer and dedicate myself wholly to propagating the honor due to Thy most sweet Sacred Heart. I choose It as the object of all my affections

and desires, and from this hour forevermore
I set up in It my perpetual abode, thanking,
adoring and loving It with all my heart, inasmuch as It is the Heart of my Jesus, who is
worthy to be loved, the Heart of my King and
sovereign Lord, the Bridegroom of my soul,
my Shepherd and Master, my truest Friend,
my loving Father, my sure Guide, my unfailing protection and my everlasting blessedness. Amen.

An indulgence of 500 days.

A plenary indulgence once a month on the usual conditions for
the daily devout repetition of this prayer (S. P. Ap., April 19, 1923
and March 10, 1933).

258

An Act of Consecration

a) I,N . . . N . . . give myself and consecrate
to the Sacred Heart of our Lord Jesus
Christ, my person and my life, my actions,
pains and sufferings, so that I may be unwilling to make use of any part of my being save
to honor, love and glorify the Sacred Heart.

This is my unchanging purpose, namely,
to be all His, and to do all things for the love
of Him, at the same time renouncing with
all my heart whatever is displeasing to Him.

I therefore take Thee, O Sacred Heart, to
be the only object of my love, the guardian
of my life, my assurance of salvation, the
remedy of my weakness and inconstancy,
the atonement for all the faults of my life
and my sure refuge at the hour of death.

Be then, O Heart of goodness, my justifica-
tion before God Thy Father, and turn away

from me the strokes of His righteous anger.
O Heart of love, I put all my confidence in
Thee, for I fear everything from my own
wickedness and frailty, but I hope for all
things from Thy goodness and bounty.

Do Thou consume in me all that can displease Thee or resist Thy holy will; let Thy
pure love imprint Thee so deeply upon my
heart, that I shall nevermore be able to
forget Thee or to be separated from Thee;
may I obtain from all Thy loving kindness
the grace of having my name written in
Thee, for in Thee I desire to place all my
happiness and all my glory, living and dying
in very bondage to Thee. (St. Margaret Mary Alacoque).

An indulgence of 3 years.

A plenary indulgence once a month on the usual conditions for
the daily devout recitation of this prayer (S. C. Ind., June 1, 1897,
Jan. 13, 1898 and Apr. 21, 1908; S. P. Ap., Feb. 25, 1934).

259

b) **M**y most loving Jesus, I consecrate
myself to-day anew and without
reserve to Thy divine Heart. I consecrate to
Thee my body with all its senses, my soul with
all its faculties, and in short, my entire being. I consecrate to Thee all my thoughts,
words and deeds; all my sufferings and labors;
all my hopes, consolations and joys; and
chiefly do I consecrate to Thee this poor heart
of mine, to the end that it may love nothing
save only Thee, and may be consumed as a
victim in the fire of Thy love. Accept, O
Jesus, Thou dearest Spouse of my soul, the
desire which I have of consoling Thy divine

Heart, and of belonging to Thee for ever.
Take possession of me in such wise that from
this day forth I may have no other freedom,
save that of loving Thee, and no other life,
save that of suffering and dying for Thee: I
put my trust in Thee without reserve, and I
hope for the remission of my sins through
Thine infinite bounty. I place within Thy
hands all my cares and anxieties, especially
as touching my eternal salvation. I promise
to love Thee and honor Thee to the last
moment of my life, and to spread, as much
as I can, the worship of Thy most Sacred
Heart. Dispose of me, my Jesus, according
to Thy good pleasure; I would have no other
reward save Thy greater glory and Thy holy
love. Grant me grace to find my home in
Thy divine Heart; here would I pass every
day of my life; here would I breathe forth
my last breath; only do Thou establish in my
heart Thy dwelling place, the seat of Thy rest,
in order that we may thus remain inseparably united; and so may I one day be able to
praise Thee, love Thee and possess Thee for
ever in the kingdom of heaven, where I shall
sing without end the infinite mercies of Thy
Sacred Heart.

An indulgence of 500 days once a day (Leo XIII, Audience Dec.
11, 1902; S. C. Ind., Jan. 7, 1903; S. P. Ap., July 9, 1935).

260

c) **M**y loving Jesus, out of the grateful
love I bear Thee, and to make reparation for my unfaithfulness to grace, I give
Thee my heart, and I consecrate myself

wholly to Thee; and with Thy help I purpose
to sin no more.

The faithful who devoutly recite this act of consecration before an image of the Sacred Heart of
Jesus may obtain:

An indulgence of 300 days;

A plenary indulgence once a month on the usual conditions for
its daily devout recitation (Secret Mem., June 9, 1807; S. P. Ap.,
Mar. 15, 1936 and April 20, 1949).

NOTE: A formula for the consecration of the family to the Sacred
Heart of Jesus is found under n. 705.

VIII

PRAYERS

261

O divine Heart of Jesus, grant, I pray
Thee, eternal rest to the souls in purgatory, the final grace to those who are about
to die this day, true repentance to sinners,
the light of faith to pagans, and Thy blessing
to me and to all who are dear to me. To Thee,
therefore, O most merciful Heart of Jesus, I
commend all these souls, and in their behalf
I offer unto Thee all Thy merits in union
with the merits of Thy most blessed Mother
and of all the Angels and Saints, together
with all the Masses, Communions, prayers
and good works which are this day being
offered throughout Christendom.

An indulgence of 500 days (Apostolic Brief, Mar. 13, 1901; S. P.
Ap., Jan. 18, 1933 and Mar. 10, 1949).

O divínum Cor Iesu, præsta, quæso, animábus
purgántibus réquiem ætérnam, hódie moritúris
grátiam finálem, peccatóribus veram pæniténtiam, pa-
gánis fídei lucem mihi meísque ómnibus tuam benedictiónem. Tibi ergo, Cor Iesu piíssimum, omnes has
ánimas comméndo et pro ipsis tibi óffero ómnia tua
mérita una cum méritis beatíssimæ Matris tuæ om-

niúmque Sanctórum et Angelórum atque ómnibus Missárum sacrifíciis, sacris Communiónibus, oratiónibus et bonis opéribus, quæ hódie in toto christianórum orbe peragúntur.

262

O Most Holy Heart of Jesus, shower Thy blessings in abundant measure upon Thy holy Church, upon the Supreme Pontiff and upon all the clergy; to the just grant perseverance; convert sinners; enlighten unbelievers; bless our relations, friends and benefactors; assist the dying; deliver the holy souls in purgatory; and extend over all hearts the sweet empire of Thy love. Amen.

An indulgence of 500 days.

A plenary indulgence once a month on the usual conditions for the daily devout recitation of this prayer (S. C. Ind., June 16, 1906; S. P. Ap., June 23, 1934 and June 18, 1949).

263

O most holy Heart of Jesus, fountain of every blessing, I adore Thee, I love Thee, and with a lively sorrow for my sins, I offer Thee this poor heart of mine. Make me humble, patient, pure and wholly obedient to Thy will. Grant, good Jesu, that I may live in Thee and for Thee. Protect me in the midst of danger; comfort me in my afflictions; give me health of body, assistance in my temporal needs, Thy blessing on all that I do, and the grace of a holy death.

An indulgence of 500 days (Apostolic Brief, Dec. 4, 1915; S. P. Ap., Nov. 8, 1934).

264

I hail Thee, O Sacred Heart of Jesus, living and life-giving fountain of eternal life, infinite treasure of divinity, glowing furnace of divine love; Thou art my place of rest and my most sure refuge. My dear Saviour, enkindle my heart with that burning love wherewith Thine own is on fire; pour into my heart the manifold graces, of which Thy Heart is the source; let Thy will be mine, and let mine be for ever obedient to Thine. Amen.

An indulgence of 500 days (S. P. Ap., Feb. 5, 1935 and June 18, 1949).

265

O God, Who dost deign mercifully to bestow upon us infinite treasures of love in the Heart of Thy Son, which was wounded for our sins; grant, we beseech Thee, that we who pay Him the devout homage of our piety, may in like manner show unto Thee our due of worthy satisfaction. Through the same Christ our Lord. Amen (Roman Missal).

An indulgence of 5 years.

A plenary indulgence on the usual conditions for the daily recitation of this prayer through an entire month (S. P. Ap., Apr. 18, 1936).

Deus, qui nobis, in Corde Fílii tui, nostris vulneráto peccátis, infinítos dilectiónis thesáuros misericórditer largíri dignáris; concéde, quǽsumus, ut illi devótum pietátis nostræ præstántes obséquium, dignæ quoque satisfactiónis exhibeámus offícium. Per eumdem Christum Dóminum nostrum. Amen (ex *Missali Romano*).

266

Grant, we beseech Thee, Almighty God, that we who glory in the Most Sacred Heart of Thy dear Son and call to mind the chief benefits of His love toward us, may find equal joy in their achievement and in their saving effect. Through the same Christ our Lord. Amen.

An indulgence of 5 years.

A plenary indulgence on the usual conditions, for the devout repetition of this prayer daily for a month (S. P. Ap., Oct. 20, 1936).

Concéde, quǽsumus omnípotens Deus, ut qui in sanctíssimo dilécti Fílii tui Corde gloriántes, præcípua in nos caritátis eius benefícia recólimus, eórum páriter et actu delectémur et fructu. Per eúmdem Christum Dóminum nostrum. Amen.

267

Reveal Thy Sacred Heart to me, O Jesus, and show me Its attractions. Unite me to It for ever. Grant that all my aspirations and all the beats of my heart, which cease not even while I sleep, may be a testimonial to Thee of my love for Thee and may say to Thee: Yes, Lord, I am all Thine; the pledge of my allegiance to Thee rests ever in my heart and will never cease to be there. Do Thou accept the slight amount of good that I do and be graciously pleased to repair all my wrong-doing; so that I may be able to bless Thee in time and in eternity. Amen. (R. Card. Merry del Val).

An indulgence of 500 days.

A plenary indulgence, on the usual conditions, if this prayer is recited daily for a month (S. P. Ap., June 8, 1949).

Art. VIII

JESUS CHRIST THE KING

I

INVOCATIONS

268

Jesus, King and center of all hearts, by the coming of Thy kingdom, grant us peace.

An indulgence of 300 days (S. P. Ap., June 23, 1923).

I esu, rex et centrum ómnium córdium, per advén-
tum regni tui, dona nobis pacem.

269

Christ conquers! Christ reigns! Christ commands!

The faithful, who sing this praise of Jesus Christ, according to the modern custom, in their private or public
gatherings as well as in religious processions, with sentiments of devotion, as a testimonial of their faith in the
infinite royal dignity of Christ, are granted:

An indulgence of 500 days (S. P. Ap., April 26, 1941).

Christus vincit! Christus regnat! Christus ímperat!

II

A DEVOUT EXERCISE

270

T he faithful, who take part in a public novena or
triduum held immediately before the Feast of
Our Lord Jesus Christ the King in honor of the same
may gain:

An indulgence of 10 years each day;

A plenary indulgence, provided that they have been present at
five of the exercises of the novena or at the entire triduum, and
moreover go to confession, receive Holy Communion and pray for
the Holy Father's intention.

Those who make a private novena or triduum during the aforesaid time in honor of Jesus Christ the
King may gain:

An indulgence of 7 years once on any day of the exercises;

A plenary indulgence on the usual conditions at the close of the
novena or triduum; but where a public exercise is held, this indulgence is available only to those who are legitimately hindered from
assisting at the same (S. P. Ap., Nov. 21, 1936).

III

AN ACT OF DEDICATION OF THE HUMAN RACE

271

M ost sweet Jesus, Redeemer of the human
race, look down upon us humbly prostrate before Thine Altar (*outside a church or*

oratory say: in Thy presence). We are Thine, and Thine we wish to be; but to be more surely united with Thee, behold, each one of us freely consecrates himself today to Thy Most Sacred Heart.

Many, indeed, have never known Thee; many, too, despising Thy precepts have rejected Thee. Have mercy on them all, most merciful Jesus, and draw them to Thy Sacred Heart.

Be Thou King, O Lord, not only of the faithful who have never forsaken Thee, but also of the prodigal children who have abandoned Thee; grant that they may quickly return to their Father's house, lest they die of wretchedness and hunger.

Be Thou King of those who are deceived by erroneous opinions, or whom discord keeps aloof, and call them back to the harbor of truth and unity of faith, so that soon there may be but one flock and one Shepherd.

Grant, O Lord, to Thy Church assurance of freedom and immunity from harm; give peace and order to all nations, and make the earth resound from pole to pole with one cry: Praise to the divine Heart that wrought our salvation; to It be honor and glory for ever. Amen.

An indulgence of 5 years to the faithful who recite this prayer with contrite heart.

A plenary indulgence once a month on condition of confession, Communion and a visit to a church or public oratory for the daily pious recitation of this prayer.

The faithful who on the Feast of our Lord Jesus Christ the King take part in an act of dedication of the human race to the Most Sacred Heart of Jesus, according to the above formula, in any church, public or semi-public oratory (if they may lawfully use the latter), and in addition recite the Litany of the Sacred Heart in the presence of the Blessed Sacrament solemnly exposed, may gain:

An indulgence of 7 years;

A plenary indulgence on condition of confession and Holy Communion (S. P. Ap., July 18, 1959).

Iesu dulcíssime, Redémptor humáni géneris, réspice nos ad altáre[1] tuum humíllime provolútos. Tui sumus, tui esse vólumus; quo autem tibi coniúncti fírmius esse possímus, en hódie sacratíssimo Cordi tuo se quisque nostrum sponte dédicat.

Te quidem multi novére nunquam; te, spretis mandátis tuis, multi repudiárunt. Miserére utrorúmque, benigníssime Iesu, atque ad sanctum Cor tuum rape univérsos.

Rex esto, Dómine, nec fidélium tantum qui nullo témpore discessére a te, sed étiam prodigórum filiórum qui te reliquérunt: fac ut domum patérnam cito répetant, ne miséria et fame péreant.

Rex esto eórum, quos aut opiniónum error decéptos habet, aut discórdia separátos, eósque ad portum veritátis atque ad unitátem fídei révoca, ut brevi fiat unum ovíle et unus pastor.

Largíre, Dómine, Ecclésiæ tuæ secúram cum incolumitáte libertátem; largíre cunctis géntibus tranquillitátem órdinis; pérfice, ut ab utróque terræ vértice una résonet

---

[1] Extra ecclesiam vel oratorium, loco: *ad altáre*, dicatur: *ante conspéctum*.

vox: Sit laus divíno Cordi, per quod nobis parta salus: ipsi glória et honor in sæcula. Amen.

IV
PRAYER
272

O Christ Jesus, I acknowledge Thee to be the King of the universe; all that hath been made is created for Thee. Exercise over me all Thy sovereign rights. I hereby renew the promises of my Baptism, renouncing Satan and all his works and pomps, and I engage myself to lead henceforth a truly Christian life. And in an especial manner do I undertake to bring about the triumph of the rights of God and Thy Church, so far as in me lies. Divine Heart of Jesus, I offer Thee my poor actions to obtain the acknowledgment by every heart of Thy sacred kingly power. In such wise may the kingdom of Thy peace be firmly established throughout all the earth. Amen.

A plenary indulgence on the usual conditions once daily (S. P. Ap., Feb. 21, 1923).

Art. IX
THE HOLY FAMILY
JESUS, MARY AND JOSEPH
I
INVOCATIONS
273

Jesu, Mary and Joseph most kind,
Bless us now and in death's agony.

An indulgence of 300 days (S. C. Ind., June 9, 1906; S. P. Ap., March 25, 1933).

Nos, Iesu, María et Ioseph bone,
  Benedícite nunc et in mortis agóne.

274

The faithful who devoutly invoke the sacred names of Jesus, Mary and Joseph conjointly, may gain:

An indulgence of 7 years;

A plenary indulgence once a month on the usual conditions for the daily repetition of the invocation (Pius X, Rescript, in his own hand, June 8, 1906, exhibited June 16, 1906; S. P. Ap., March 18, 1932).

NOTE: For invocations for a happy death, see n. 636.

II
RESPONSORY PRAYERS
275

Jesus, Mary and Joseph, bless us and grant us the grace of loving Holy Church, as we are bound to do, above every earthly thing, and of ever showing forth our love by the witness of our deeds.

Our Father, Hail Mary, Glory be.

Jesus, Mary and Joseph, bless us and grant us the grace of openly professing, as we are bound to do, with courage and without human respect, the faith that we received of Thy gift in holy Baptism.

Our Father, Hail Mary, Glory be.

Jesus, Mary and Joseph, bless us and grant us the grace of sharing, as we are bound to do, in the defense and propagation of the Faith, when duty calls, whether by word or by the sacrifice of our fortunes and our lives.

Our Father, Hail Mary, Glory be.

Jesus, Mary and Joseph, bless us and grant us the grace of loving one another in mutual charity, as we are bound to do, and establish us in perfect harmony of thought, will and action, under the rule and guidance of our holy Pastors.

Our Father, Hail Mary, Glory be.

Jesus, Mary and Joseph, bless us and grant us the grace of conforming our lives fully, as we are bound to do, to the commandments of God's law and that of His holy Church, so as to live always in that charity which they set forth.

Our Father, Hail Mary, Glory be.

An indulgence of 3 years (S. C. Ind., May 17, 1890; S. P. Ap., July 27, 1935).

III

PRAYER

276

Lord Jesus Christ, who, being made subject to Mary and Joseph, didst consecrate domestic life by Thine ineffable virtues; grant that we, with the assistance of both, may be taught by the example of Thy holy Family and may attain to its everlasting fellowship. Who livest and reignest, world without end. Amen (Roman Missal).

An indulgence of 5 years.

A plenary indulgence on the usual conditions for the devout recitation of this prayer every day for a month (S. P. Ap., Sept. 3, 1936).

Dómine Iesu Christe, qui Maríæ, et Ioseph súbditus, domésticam vitam ineffabílibus virtútibus consecrásti: fac nos, utriúsque auxílio, Famíliæ sanctæ tuæ exémplis ínstrui et consórtium cónsequi sempitérnum: Qui vivis et regnas in sǽcula sæculórum. Amen (ex *Missali Romano*).

NOTE: A form for the dedication of the Christian family to the Holy Family of Jesus, Mary and Joseph is found under n. 706; a prayer for a happy death under n. 643.

VENI ++ SANCTE SPIRITUS EPLE TU- ORUM COR DA FIDELIUM

CHAPTER IV

GOD THE HOLY GHOST

I

INVOCATIONS

277

O Holy Spirit, Spirit of truth, come into our hearts; shed the brightness of Thy light upon the nations, that they may please Thee in unity of faith.

An indulgence of 300 days (S. C. Ind., July 31, 1897; S. P. Ap., Dec. 22, 1932).

Spíritus Sancte, Spíritus veritátis, veni in corda nostra; da pópulis claritátem lucis tuæ, ut in fídei unitáte tibi compláceant.

278

O Holy Spirit, sweet Guest of my soul, abide in me and grant that I may ever abide in Thee.

An indulgence of 300 days (S. P. Ap., April 26, 1921).

O Sancte Spíritus, dulcis hospes ánimæ meæ, mane mecum et fac ut ego máneam semper tecum.

279

God the Holy Ghost, have mercy on us.

An indulgence of 500 days.
A plenary indulgence, on the usual conditions, if the daily,

devout recitation of this invocation be continued for a month (S. P. Ap., Mar. 4, 1939) .

S píritus Sancte, Deus, miserére nobis.

280

May the grace of the Holy Spirit enlighten our senses and our hearts (Roman Breviary).

An indulgence of 500 days.

A plenary indulgence, on the usual conditions, provided that this invocation is recited daily with sentiments of devotion for a whole month (S. P. Ap., Feb. 24, 1940) .

S píritus Sancti grátia illúminet sensus et corda nostra (ex *Breviario Romano*) .

281

May our hearts be cleansed, O Lord, by the inpouring of the Holy Spirit, and may He render them fruitful by watering them with His heavenly dew (Roman Missal).

An indulgence of 500 days.

A plenary indulgence on the usual conditions for the daily recital of this invocation for a month (S. P. Ap., March 5, 1941) .

S ancti Spíritus, Dómine, corda nostra mundet infúsio, et sui roris íntima aspersióne fecúndet (ex *Missali Romano*) .

II

SEQUENCE FOR PENTECOST

282

C ome, Thou holy Paraclete,
And from Thy celestial seat
Send Thy light and brilliancy.

Father of the poor, draw near,
Giver of all gifts, be here,
Come, the soul's true radiancy.

Come, of comforters the best,
Of the soul the sweetest guest,
Come in toil refreshingly.

Thou in labor rest most sweet,
Thou art shadow from the heat,
Comfort in adversity.

O Thou light, most pure and blest,
Shine within the inmost breast
Of Thy faithful company.

Where Thou art not, man hath naught;
Ev'ry holy deed and thought
Comes from Thy divinity.

What is soiléd, make Thou pure;
What is woundéd, work its cure;
What is parched, fructify.

What is rigid, gently bend;
What is frozen, warmly tend;
Strengthen what goes erringly.

Fill Thy faithful, who confide
In Thy power to guard and guide,
With Thy sevenfold mystery.

Here Thy grace and mercy send;
Grant salvation in the end,
And in Heaven felicity. Amen.

(Roman Missal, tr. J. M. Neale).

An indulgence of 5 years.

A plenary indulgence once a month on the usual conditions for its daily devout recitation (Apostolic Brief, May 26, 1796; S. P. Ap., April 15, 1933).

Veni, Sancte Spíritus, et emítte cǽlitus lucis
tuæ rádium.
Veni, pater páuperum, veni, dator múnerum,
veni, lumen córdium.
Consolátor óptime, dulcis hospes ánimæ,
dulce refrigérium.
In labóre réquies, in æstu tempéries, in fletu
solátium.

O lux beatíssima, reple cordis íntima tuórum
fidélium.
Sine tuo númine nihil est in hómine, nihil est
innóxium.
Lava quod est sórdidum, riga quod est
áridum, sana quod est sáucium.
Flecte quod est rígidum, fove quod est
frígidum, rege quod est dévium.
Da tuis fidélibus in te confidéntibus sacrum
septenárium.
Da virtútis méritum, da salútis éxitum, da
perénne gáudium. Amen.

(ex *Missali Romano*)·

III

HYMN FOR PENTECOST

283

Come, Holy Ghost, Creator blest,
And in our souls take up Thy rest,
Come with Thy grace and heavenly aid,
And fill the hearts which Thou hast made.

To Thee, the Comforter, we cry,
To Thee, the gift of God most high,
The fount of life, the fire of love,
The soul's anointing from above.

The sevenfold gifts of grace are Thine,
O Finger of the hand Divine;
True promise of the Father Thou,
Who dost the tongue with speech endow.

Thy light to every thought impart,
And shed Thy love in every heart;
Our body's poor infirmity
With strength perpetual fortify.

Our mortal foe afar repel,
Grant us henceforth in peace to dwell;

If Thou be our preventing guide,
No evil can our steps betide.

Make Thou to us the Father known;
Teach us th' Eternal Son to own,
And Thee, Whose name we ever bless,
Of Both the Spirit to confess.

All glory while the ages run
Be to the Father and the Son,
Who rose from death; the same to Thee,
O Holy Ghost, eternally. Amen. (Roman Breviary,
tr. cento).

℣. Send forth Thy Spirit and they shall be created;
℟. And Thou shalt renew the face of the earth.

Let us pray.

O God, who didst teach the hearts of Thy faithful people by sending them the light of Thy Holy Spirit, grant us by the same Spirit to have a right judgment in all things, and evermore to rejoice in His holy comfort. Through Christ our Lord. Amen.

An indulgence of 5 years.

A plenary indulgence once a month on the usual conditions, for the daily recitation of this hymn with its versicle and prayer (Apostolic Brief, May 26, 1706; S. Cong. of Rites, June 20, 1889; S. P. Ap., Feb. 9, 1934).

Veni, Creátor Spíritus,
Mentes tuórum vísita,
Imple supérna grátia
Quæ Tu creásti péctora.

Qui díceris Paráclitus,
Altíssimi donum Dei,
Fons vivus, ignis cáritas
Et spiritális únctio.

Tu septifórmis múnere,
Dígitus patérnæ déxteræ,
Tu rite promíssum Patris
Sermóne ditans gúttura.

Accénde lumen sénsibus,
Infúnde amórem córdibus,
Infírma nostri córporis
Virtúte firmans pérpeti.

Hostem repéllas lóngius,
Pacémque dones prótinus;
Ductóre sic te prǽvio
Vitémus omne nóxium.

Per te sciámus da Patrem,
Noscámus atque Fílium,
Teque utriúsque Spíritum
Credámus omni témpore.

Deo Patri sit glória
Et Fílio qui a mórtuis
Surréxit, ac Paráclito
In sæculórum sǽcula. Amen.

(ex *Breviario Romano*) .

℣. Emítte Spíritum tuum et creabúntur;
℟. Et renovábis fáciem terræ.

Orémus.

Deus, qui corda fidélium Sancti Spíritus illustratióne docuísti: da nobis in eódem Spíritu recta sápere;
et de eius semper consolatióne gaudére. Per Christum Dóminum nostrum. Amen. (ex *Breviario Romano*) .

NOTE: For singing this hymn on the first day of the year, see
n. 681.

IV

DEVOUT EXERCISES

284

Prayers of the Novena before the Feast of Pentecost

The faithful who devoutly assist at the public novena in honor of the Holy Ghost immediately
preceding the Feast of Pentecost, may gain:

An indulgence of 10 years on any day of the novena;

A plenary indulgence, if they take part in at least five of the exercises, and moreover go to confession, receive Holy Communion and pray for the Holy Father's intention.

Those who make a private novena in honor of the Holy Ghost, either before Pentecost or at any other time in the year, may gain:

An indulgence of 7 years once on any day of their novena;

A plenary indulgence on the usual conditions at the close of the novena; but if a public novena is held, this indulgence is available only to those who are lawfully hindered from taking part in the same (Pius IX, Audience, Jan. 3, 1849; S. C. of Bishops and Regulars, Jan. 28, 1850; S. C. Ind., Nov. 26, 1876; Apostolic Brief, May 5, 1895; Encyclical Letter "Divinum illud munus," May 9, 1897; S. P. Ap., May 12, 1934).

285

The faithful, who recite seven times the doxology "Glory be to the Father, etc." with devotion in order to obtain the seven gifts of the Holy Ghost, are granted:

An indulgence of 3 years (Sacred Congregation for the Propagation of the Faith, Mar. 12, 1857; S. P. Ap., July 10, 1941).

V

A CHAPLET OF THE HOLY SPIRIT

286

I n the name of the Father, and of the Son, and of the Holy Ghost. Amen.

An Act of Contrition: O my God, I am sorry that I have sinned against Thee, because Thou art so good; with the help of Thy grace, I will sin no more.

The hymn, *"Come, Holy Ghost,"* etc., with the versicles and prayer as above, n. 283.

I— FIRST MYSTERY

Jesus is conceived by the Holy Ghost of the Virgin Mary

Meditation.—The Holy Ghost shall come upon thee, and the power of the Most High shall overshadow thee. Therefore also the Holy One which shall be born of thee shall be called the Son of God (Luke 1, 35).

Application.—Pray earnestly for the assistance of the Spirit of God and the intercession of Mary to imitate the virtues of Jesus Christ who is the pattern of every virtue, in order that you may be conformed to the image of the Son of God.

Our Father *and* Hail Mary *once;* Glory be *seven times.*

II—SECOND MYSTERY

The Spirit of the Lord rests upon Jesus

Meditation.—Now Jesus being baptized went up immediately from the water; and behold, the heavens were opened unto Him; and He saw the Spirit of God descending like a dove and coming upon Him (Matt. 3, 16).

Application.—Hold in highest esteem the precious gift of sanctifying grace which was infused into your heart in Baptism by the Holy Spirit. Keep the promises to whose observance you then bound yourself. By continual exercise increase your faith, your hope and your charity. Ever live as becomes a child of God and a member of the true Church of God, so that after this life you may receive heaven as your inheritance.

Our Father *and* Hail Mary *once*, Glory be *seven times.*

III— THIRD MYSTERY

Jesus is led by the Spirit into the desert

Meditation.—And Jesus being full of the Holy Ghost returned from the Jordan: and was led by the Spirit into the desert for the space of forty days, and was tempted by the devil (Luke 4: 1, 2).

Application.—Be ever thankful for the sevenfold gifts of the Holy Spirit given to you in Confirmation, for the Spirit of wisdom and understanding, of counsel and fortitude, of knowledge and piety, and of the fear of the Lord. Faithfully obey your divine Guide, so that you may act manfully in all the perils of this life and in all temptations, as becomes a perfect Christian and a strong athlete of Jesus Christ.

Our Father *and* Hail Mary *once*, Glory be *seven times*.

IV— FOURTH MYSTERY

The Holy Spirit in the Church

Meditation.—And suddenly there came from Heaven a sound as of a mighty wind coming, where they were sitting; and they were all filled with the Holy Ghost, speaking the wonderful works of God (Acts 2: 2, 4, 11).

Application.—Give thanks to God that He has made you a child of His Church which is always quickened and governed by His divine Spirit, who was sent into the world on the day of Pentecost. Hear and follow the sovereign Pontiff who teaches infallibly through the Holy Spirit, and the Church which is the pillar and ground of truth. Hold fast her doctrines, maintain her cause, defend her rights.

Our Father *and* **Hail Mary** *once*, **Glory be** *seven times*.

V—FIFTH MYSTERY

The Holy Spirit in the souls of the righteous

Meditation.—Know ye not that your members are the temple of the Holy Ghost who is in you? (1 Cor. 6, 19).

Extinguish not the Spirit (1 Thess. 5, 19).

And grieve not the Holy Spirit of God, in whom ye are sealed unto the day of redemption (Eph. 4, 30).

Application.—Be ever mindful of the Holy Spirit who is in you, and make every effort to be pure in mind and body. Faithfully obey His divine inspirations, that you may bring forth the fruits of the Spirit: which are charity, joy, peace, patience, kindness, goodness, long-suffering, meekness, faith, moderation, continence and chastity.

Our Father *and* **Hail Mary** *once*, **Glory be** *seven times*.

At the end say the Apostles' Creed: I belive in God, *etc.*, **as above under n. 43.**

An indulgence of 7 years.

A plenary indulgence once a month on the usual conditions for the daily devout repetition of this chaplet (Apostolic Brief, March 24, 1902; S. P. Ap., March 18, 1932).

VI

PRAYERS

287

Come, Holy Ghost, fill the hearts of Thy faithful and kindle in them the fire of Thy love.

℣. Send forth Thy Spirit, and they shall be created;

℟. And Thou shalt renew the face of the earth.

Let us pray.

O God, who didst teach the hearts of Thy faithful people by sending them the light of Thy Holy Spirit, grant us by the same Spirit to have a right judgment in all things, and evermore to rejoice in His holy comfort. Through Christ our Lord. Amen (Roman Missal).

An indulgence of 5 years.

A plenary indulgence on the usual conditions, when this prayer is recited daily for an entire month (S. C. Ind., May 8, 1907; S. P. Ap., Dec. 22, 1932).

Veni, Sancte Spíritus, reple tuórum corda fidélium et tui amóris in eis ignem accénde.

℣. Emítte Spíritum tuum et creabúntur;

℟. Et renovábis fáciem terræ.

Orémus.

Deus, qui corda fidélium Sancti Spíritus illustratióne docuísti: da nobis in eódem Spíritu recta sápere; et de eius semper consolatióne gaudére. Per Christum Dóminum nostrum. Amen.

(ex *Missali Romano*).

VII
PRAYERS

288

O Holy Spirit, Creator, mercifully assist Thy Catholic Church, and by Thy heavenly power strengthen and establish her against the assaults of all her enemies; and by Thy love and grace renew the spirit of Thy servants whom Thou hast anointed, that in Thee they may glorify the Father and His only-begotten Son, Jesus Christ our Lord. Amen.

An indulgence of 500 days (S. C. Ind., Aug. 26, 1889; S. P. Ap., Oct. 14, 1935).

O Creátor Sancte Spíritus, adésto propítius Ecclésiæ cathólicæ eámque contra inimicórum incúrsus tua supérna virtúte róbora et confírma, tua caritáte et grátia spíritum famulórum tuórum, quos unxísti, rénova, ut in te claríficent Patrem Filiúmque eius Unigénitum Iesum Christum Dóminum nostrum. Amen.

289

O Holy Spirit, divine Spirit of light and love, I consecrate to Thee my understanding, my heart and my will, my whole being for time and for eternity. May my understanding be always submissive to Thy heavenly inspirations and to the teachings of the holy Catholic Church, of which Thou art the infallible Guide; may my heart be ever inflamed with love of God and of my neighbor; may my will be ever conformed to the divine will, and may my whole life be a faithful imitation of the life and virtues of Our Lord and Saviour Jesus Christ, to whom

with the Father and Thee be honor and glory
for ever. Amen.

An indulgence of 500 days (Pius X, Rescript in his own hand,
June 1, 1908, exhib. June 5, 1908; S. P. Ap., May 25, 1936).

290

Come, Holy Ghost, Sanctifier all powerful,
God of love, Thou who didst fill the
Virgin Mary with grace, Thou who didst won-
derfully transform the hearts of the Apostles,
Thou who didst endow all Thy martyrs with
a miraculous heroism, come and sanctify us.
Illumine our minds, strengthen our wills,
purify our consciences, rectify our judgments, set our hearts on fire, and preserve us
from the misfortune of resisting Thine inspirations. Amen.

An indulgence of 500 days (S. P. Ap., Apr. 9, 1940 and Apr. 5,
1941).

291

O Holy Spirit, who on the solemn day of
Pentecost didst suddenly descend upon
the Apostles gathered in the Upper Room in
parted tongues as it were of fire and didst so
enlighten their minds, inflame their hearts,
and strengthen their wills, that thenceforth
they went through the entire world and
courageously and confidently proclaimed
everywhere the teaching of Christ and sealed
it with the shedding of their blood, renew,
we beseech Thee, the wondrous outpouring
of Thy grace in our hearts also.

How grievously our minds are afflicted
with ignorance concerning the nature and
dignity of those divine truths which form the

object of faith, without which no man may hope for salvation. How far men go astray from a just estimation of earthly goods, which too often are put before the soul itself. How often our hearts do not beat with love of the Creator as they ought, but rather with an ignoble lust for creatures. How often are we led by a false respect for human judgment, when we ought to profess openly the precepts of Jesus Christ and to reduce them to action with a sincere heart and with the loss, if need be, of our worldly substance. What weakness we manifest in embracing and carrying with a serene and willing heart the crosses of this life, which alone can make the Christian a worthy follower of his divine Master.

O Holy Spirit, enlighten our minds, cleanse our hearts, and give new strength to our wills; to such a degree, at least, that we may clearly recognize the value of our soul, and in like manner, despise the perishable goods of this world; that we may love God above all things, and, for the love of Him, our neighbor as ourselves; that we may not only be free from fear in professing our faith publicly, but rather may glory in it; finally, that we may accept not only prosperity but also adversity as from the hand of the Lord, with all confidence that He will turn all things into good for those who lovingly tend towards Him. Grant, we beseech Thee, that we, by constantly answering the sweet impulses of Thy grace and doing that which is good with a persevering heart, may deserve one day to receive the rich reward of glory everlasting. Amen.

The faithful, who recite this prayer devoutly on the solemn day of Pentecost, are granted:

An indulgence of 3 years;

A plenary indulgence on the usual conditions (S. P. Ap., May 31, 1941).

NOTE:—A prayer to the Holy Ghost to be said by those who are gathered together to transact any business in common is found under n. 682.

O Sancte Spíritus, qui sollémni Pentecóstes die repénte per dispertítas linguas tamquam ignis in Apóstolos descéndens, intra cænáculum congregátos, ita eórum mentes illuminásti, eórum ánimos incendísti, eorúmque voluntátes roborásti, ut inde per univérsum mundum proficisceréntur et ubicúmque animóse fidentérque Iesu Christi doctrínam annuntiárent, eámque suo profúso cruóre obsignárent, rénova, quǽsumus, in ánimas quoque nostras prodigiáles grátiæ tuæ effusiónes.

Quanta mentes nostræ ignorántia labórant circa natúram gravitatémque divinárum veritátum, quæ obiéctum fídei efficiunt, sine qua salútem némini speráre licet. Quot aberratiónes a iusta terrenórum bonórum æstimatióne, quæ sæpius ánimæ ípsimet anteponúntur. Quam sæpe corda nostra non—ut debent—Creatóris amóre pálpitant, sed ignobíliter creaturárum cupídine. Quam sæpe falso humáni iudícii respéctu impéllimur, cum debémus Iesu Christi præcépta palam profitéri, eáque sincére et cum rerum étiam iactúra in vitæ usum dedúcere. Quanta infírmitas in amplecténda ferendáque seréno libentíque ánimo huius vitæ cruce, quæ christiánum solúmmodo potest divíni Magístri sui discípulum dignum effícere.

O Sancte Spíritus, mentes nostras illúmina, corda nostra puríffica, voluntatésque nostras redíntegra; ita quidem ut infínitum ánimæ nostræ prétium plane cognoscámus, itémque peritúra huius mundi bona pro níhilo habeámus; ut Deum supra res omnes adamémus, eiúsque amóre próximos, quemádmodum nosmetípsos, diligámus; ut fidem nostram non modo palam demonstráre ne timeámus, sed de eádem pótius gloriémur; ut dénique non tantum res prósperas sed res etiam advérsas quasi de manu Domini accipiámus, confísi prorsus ómnia Eum in eórum bonum esse conversúrum, qui erga Eum amóre ferántur. Fac, quǽsumus, ut nos, suávibus grátiæ tuæ impulsiónibus constánter respondéntes ac perseveránti ánimo operántes bonum, amplíssimam sempitérnæ gloriæ messem aliquándo accípere mereámur. Amen.

CHAPTER V
THE MOST BLESSED VIRGIN MARY

Art. I
GENERAL DEVOTIONS TO THE BLESSED VIRGIN MARY

I
EJACULATIONS AND INVOCATIONS

292

The faithful who devoutly invoke the most holy name of Mary may gain:

An indulgence of 300 days;

A plenary indulgence once a month on the usual conditions for the daily devout repetition of the invocation;

A plenary indulgence at the hour of death if they have been wont to recite the aforesaid invocation frequently during life, and have gone to confession and received Holy Communion, or at least have made an act of contrition, invoking the holy Name of Jesus vocally if possible, otherwise in their hearts, and accepting death with resignation from God's hand, as the just punishment of their sins (S. C. Ind., Sept. 5, 1759; S. P. Ap., Nov. 12, 1932).

293

Vouchsafe that I may praise thee, O sacred Virgin;
Give me strength against thine enemies.

(Roman Breviary).

An indulgence of 300 days.

A plenary indulgence on the usual conditions, if this invocation is repeated daily for a month (S. C. Ind., Apr. 5, 1786; S. P. Ap., March 28, 1933).

209

Dignáre me laudáre te, Virgo sacráta;
Da mihi virtútem contra hostes tuos.

(ex *Breviario Romano*).

294

O Mary, Mother of God and Mother of mercy, pray for us and for all who have died in the embrace of the Lord.

An indulgence of 300 days (Leo XIII, Audience, Dec. 15, 1883; S. P. Ap., June 4, 1934).

295

Thou who wast a Virgin before thy delivery, pray for us.
Hail Mary, *etc.*
Thou who wast a Virgin in thy delivery, pray for us.
Hail Mary, *etc.*
Thou who wast a Virgin after thy delivery, pray for us.
Hail Mary, *etc.*

An indulgence of 300 days.
A plenary indulgence once a month on the usual conditions, if these invocations are repeated daily (S. C. Ind., May 20, 1893; S. P. Ap., Oct. 12, 1934).

Virgo ante partum, ora pro nobis.
Ave María.
Virgo in partu, ora pro nobis.
Ave María.
Virgo post partum, ora pro nobis.
Ave María.

296

Our Lady of Lourdes (of the Pillar, *or under another title approved by ecclesiastical authority*), pray for us.

An indulgence of 300 days (Apostolic Brief, June 25, 1902; S. C. Ind., Nov. 9, 1907 and Jan. 23, 1907; S. P. Ap., Nov. 15. 1927).

Dómina nostra de Lourdes (a Colúmna, *aut sub alio titulo ab Auctoritate ecclesiastica probato*), ora pro nobis.

297

My Mother, deliver me from mortal sin. Hail Mary *three times*.

An indulgence of 300 days (Apostolic Brief, Feb. 8, 1900; S. P. Ap., Jan. 7, 1935) ·

Mater mea, líbera me a peccáto mortáli.
Ter Ave María.

298

O Mary, bless this house where thy Name is always blessed.
Praise forever be to Mary Immaculate, the ever-Virgin Mother, blessed amongst women, the Mother of our Lord Jesus Christ, the Queen of Paradise.

An indulgence of 300 days (Pius X, Audience, Feb. 26, 1905, exhib. March 21, 1905) ·

299

O Mary, our hope, have pity on us.

An indulgence of 300 days (Pius X, Rescript in his own hand, Jan. 3, 1906, exhib. Jan. 8, 1906) ·

300

Mother of love, of sorrow and of mercy, pray for us.

An indulgence of 300 days (Pius X, Audience, May 14, 1908; S. C. Ind., May 30, 1908) ·

Mater amóris, dolóris et misericórdiæ, ora pro nobis.

301

Holy Mary, deliver us from the pains of hell.

An indulgence of 300 days (Holy Off., Jan. 22, 1914; S. P. Ap., March 28, 1933) ·

Sancta María, líbera nos a pœnis inférni.

302

My Mother, my hope.

An indulgence of 300 days (Benedict XV, Rescript in his own hand, Jan. 3, 1917, exhib. Jan. 27, 1917).

Mater mea, fidúcia mea.

303

O Virgin Mary , Mother of Jesus, make us saints (St. Joseph Benedict Cottolengo).

An indulgence of 300 days (S. P. Ap., June 21, 1918 and March 25, 1935).

304

Mother of mercy, pray for us.

An indulgence of 300 days (S. P. Ap., July 26, 1919 and May 31, 1927).

305

O Mary, Virgin Mother of God, pray to Jesus for me.

An indulgence of 300 days.

A plenary indulgence on the usual conditions, if this invocation is devoutly repeated every day for a month (S. P. Ap., April 7, 1921; March 28, 1933).

Virgo Dei Génitrix, María, deprecáre Iesum pro me.

306

O Mary, make me to live in God, with God, and for God.

An indulgence of 300 days (S. P. Ap., April 26, 1921).

O María, fac ut vivam in Deo, cum Deo et pro Deo.

307

O Mary, Mother of grace and Mother of mercy, do thou protect us from our enemy, and receive us at the hour of our death.

An indulgence of 300 days.

A plenary indulgence once a month on the usual conditions for the daily recitation of this invocation (S. P. Ap., Sept. 25, 1933).

María, Mater grátiæ, Mater misericórdiæ, Tu nos ab hoste prótege et mortis hora súscipe.

308

Remember, O Virgin Mother of God, when thou shalt stand before the face of the Lord, that thou speak favorable things in our behalf and that He may turn away His indignation from us (Roman Missal).

An indulgence of 300 days.

A plenary indulgence once a month on the usual conditions for the daily devout recitation of this invocation (S. P. Ap., Nov. 22, 1934).

Recordáre, Virgo Mater Dei, dum stéteris in conspéctu Dómini, ut loquáris pro nobis bona, et ut avértat indignatiónem suam a nobis (ex *Missali Romano*).

309

Bless us, Mary Maiden mild, bless us too, her tender Child.

An indulgence of 300 days (S. P. Ap., Feb. 4, 1935).

Nos cum prole pia benedícat Virgo María.

310

Thou art my Mother, O Virgin Mary: keep me safe lest I ever offend thy dear Son, and obtain for me the grace to please Him always and in all things.

An indulgence of 300 days (S. P. Ap., Oct. 26, 1935).

Tu es mea mater, Virgo María, defénde me ne in ætérnum lædam dilectíssimum Fílium tuum, et fac ut semper et per ómnia illi pláceam.

311

Blessed art thou, O Virgin Mary, by the Lord God most high, above all women upon the earth (Roman Missal).

An indulgence of 300 days.

A plenary indulgence once a month on the usual conditions for the daily devout repetition of this ejaculation (S. P. Ap., May 20, 1936) ·

Benedícta es Tu, Virgo María, a Dómino Deo excélso, præ ómnibus muliéribus super terram (ex *Missali Romano*) ·

312

Most high Queen of the universe, Mary ever Virgin, make intercession for our peace and salvation, thou who didst bear Christ the Lord, the Saviour of all mankind

(Roman Missal) ·

An indulgence of 300 days.
A plenary indulgence once a month on the usual conditions for the daily devout recitation of the invocation (S. P. Ap., Oct. 10, 1936) ·

Regína mundi digníssima, María perpétua, intercéde pro nostra pace et salúte, quæ genuísti Christum Dóminum Salvatórem ómnium (ex *Missali Romano*)

313

Draw us after thee, holy Mother.

An indulgence of 300 days (S. P. Ap., Oct. 10, 1938) ·

Trahe me post te, sancta Mater.

314

Pray for us, O holy Mother of God, that we may be made worthy of the promises of Christ (Roman Breviary) ·

An indulgence of 300 days.
A plenary indulgence on the usual conditions, when the daily recitation of this invocation has been continued for a month (S. P. Ap., Dec. 15, 1940) ·

Ora pro nobis, sancta Dei Génitrix, ut digni efficiámur promissiónibus Christi (ex *Breviario Romano*) ·

315

H oly Mary, Virgin Mother of God, intercede for me.

An indulgence of 300 days.
A plenary indulgence on the usual conditions, if this invocation is devoutly repeated every day for a month (S. P. Ap., Feb. 25, 1941).

Sancta María, Dei Génitrix Virgo, intercéde pro me.

316

R ejoice, O Virgin Mary, thou alone hast put down all heresies in the whole world.

An indulgence of 300 days (S. P. Ap., Mar. 30, 1941).

G aude, María Virgo, cunctas hǽreses sola interemísti in univérso mundo.

317

O Mary, may thy children persevere in loving thee!

An indulgence of 300 days (Pius XI, Rescr. in his own hand, May 9, 1922, exhib. Feb. 12, 1943).

O María, in amóre Tui persevérent fílii!

NOTE An invocation to the Blessed Virgin Mary for obtaining the grace of continence is found under n. 713.

II

THE LITTLE OFFICE

318

T he faithful who devoutly recite the little Office of the B. V. M. even though bound thereto, may gain:

An indulgence of 500 days for each hour of the same Office;
An indulgence of 10 years for the entire Office;
A plenary indulgence once a month for daily recitation of the entire Office, on the usual conditions (S. C. Ind., Nov. 17, 1887 and Dec. 8, 18'7, S. P. Ap., March 28, 1935).

III

THE LITANY OF LORETO

319

Lord, have mercy on us.
    Christ, have mercy on us.
Lord, have mercy on us.
Christ, hear us.
Christ, graciously hear us.
God the Father of heaven, have mercy on us
God the Son, Redeemer of the world,
                          have mercy on us
God the Holy Ghost,   have mercy on us
Holy Trinity, one God,   have mercy on us
Holy Mary,   pray for us
Holy Mother of God,   pray for us
Holy Virgin of virgins,   pray for us
Mother of Christ,   pray for us
Mother of divine grace,   pray for us
Mother most pure,   pray for us
Mother most chaste,   pray for us
Mother inviolate,   pray for us
Mother undefiled,   pray for us
Mother most amiable,   pray for us
Mother most admirable,   pray for us
Mother of good counsel,   pray for us
Mother of our Creator,   pray for us
Mother of our Saviour,   pray for us
Virgin most prudent,   pray for us
Virgin most venerable,   pray for us
Virgin most renowned,   pray for us
Virgin most powerful,   pray for us
Virgin most merciful,   pray for us
Virgin most faithful,   pray for us

Mirror of justice,	pray for us
Seat of wisdom,	pray for us
Cause of our joy,	pray for us
Spiritual vessel,	pray for us
Vessel of honor,	pray for us
Singular vessel of devotion,	pray for us
Mystical rose,	pray for us
Tower of David,	pray for us
Tower of ivory,	pray for us
House of gold,	pray for us
Ark of the covenant,	pray for us
Gate of Heaven,	pray for us
Morning star,	pray for us
Health of the sick,	pray for us
Refuge of sinners,	pray for us
Comforter of the afflicted,	pray for us
Help of Christians,	pray for us
Queen of Angels,	pray for us
Queen of Patriarchs,	pray for us
Queen of Prophets,	pray for us
Queen of Apostles,	pray for us
Queen of Martyrs,	pray for us
Queen of Confessors,	pray for us
Queen of Virgins,	pray for us
Queen of all Saints,	pray for us
Queen conceived without original sin,	pray for us
Queen assumed into heaven,	pray for us
Queen of the most holy Rosary,	pray for us
Queen of peace,	pray for us

Lamb of God, Who takest away the sins of the world, spare us, O Lord.

Lamb of God, Who takest away the sins of the world, graciously hear us, O Lord.

Lamb of God, Who takest away the sins of the world, have mercy on us.

℣. Pray for us, O holy Mother of God,
℟. That we may be made worthy of the promises of Christ.

Let us pray.

Grant, we beseech Thee, O Lord God, unto us Thy servants, that we may rejoice in continual health of mind and body; and, by the glorious intercession of blessed Mary ever Virgin, may be delivered from present sadness, and enter into the joy of Thine eternal gladness. Through Christ our Lord. Amen.

An indulgence of 7 years.

A plenary indulgence once a month on the usual conditions for the daily devout recitation of this Litany with its versicle and prayer (S. C. Ind., Sept. 30, 1817; S. P. Ap., March 28, 1933).

NOTE: The versicle and prayer can be changed for the various seasons without prejudice to the indulgences (S. P. Ap., Oct. 4, 1949).

Kýrie eléison.
Christe eléison.
Kýrie eléison.
Christe, audi nos.
Christe, exáudi nos.

Pater de cælis, Deus,	miserére nobis
Fili Redémptor mundi, Deus,	miserére
Spíritus Sancte, Deus,	miserére
Sancta Trínitas, unus Deus,	miserére
Sancta María,	ora
Sancta Dei Génitrix,	ora
Sancta Virgo Vírginum,	ora
Mater Christi,	ora
Mater divínæ grátiæ,	ora
Mater puríssima,	ora
Mater castíssima,	ora
Mater invioláta.	ora

Mater intemeráta,	ora
Mater amábilis,	ora
Mater admirábilis,	ora
Mater boni consílii,	ora
Mater Creatóris,	ora
Mater Salvatóris,	ora
Virgo prudentíssima,	ora
Virgo veneránda,	ora
Virgo prædicánda,	ora
Virgo potens,	ora
Virgo clemens,	ora
Virgo fidélis,	ora
Spéculum iustítiæ,	ora
Sedes sapiéntiæ,	ora
Causa nostræ lætítiæ,	ora
Vas spirituále,	ora
Vas honorábile,	ora
Vas insígne devotiónis,	ora
Rosa mýstica,	ora
Turris davídica,	ora
Turris ebúrnea,	ora
Domus áurea,	ora
Fœderis arca,	ora
Iánua cæli,	ora
Stella matutína,	ora
Salus infirmórum,	ora
Refúgium peccatórum,	ora
Consolátrix afflictórum,	ora
Auxílium Christianórum,	ora
Regína Angelórum,	ora
Regína Patriarchárum,	ora
Regína Prophetárum,	ora
Regína Apostolórum,	ora
Regína Mártyrum,	ora
Regína Confessórum,	ora
Regína Vírginum,	ora
Regína Sanctórum ómnium,	ora
Regína sine labe origináli concépta,	ora
Regína in cælum assúmpta,	ora
Regína sacratíssimi Rosárii,	ora
Regína pacis,	ora

Agnus Dei, qui tollis peccáta mundi, parce nobis, Dómine.

Agnus Dei, qui tollis peccáta mundi, exáudi nos, Dómine.

Agnus Dei, qui tollis peccáta mundi, miserére nobis.

℣. Ora pro nobis, sancta Dei Génitrix,

℞. Ut digni efficiámur promissiónibus Christi.

Orémus.

Concéde nos fámulos tuos, quǽsumus, Dómine Deus, perpétua mentis et córporis sanitáte gaudére: et gloriósa beátæ Maríæ semper Vírginis intercessióne, a præsénti liberári tristítia et ætérna pérfrui lætítia. Per Christum Dóminum nostrum. Amen.

IV
CANTICLE, HYMNS AND ANTIPHONS
320

My soul doth magnify the Lord: And my spirit hath rejoiced in God my Saviour.

Because He hath regarded the lowliness of His handmaid: for, behold, from henceforth all generations shall call me blessed.

For He that is mighty hath done great things to me: and holy is His Name.

And His mercy is from generation unto generations, to them that fear Him.

He hath showed might with His arm: He hath scattered the proud in the conceit of their heart.

He hath put down the mighty from their seat, and hath exalted the lowly.

He hath filled the hungry with good things: and the rich he hath sent empty away.

He hath received Israel His servant, being mindful of His mercy:

As He spoke to our fathers, to Abraham and to his seed for ever. (Luke 1, 46).

An indulgence of 3 years.

An indulgence of 5 years, if the canticle is recited on the feast of the Visitation of the Blessed Virgin Mary, or on any Saturday of the year.

A plenary indulgence once a month on the usual conditions for the daily recitation of this canticle (S. C. Ind., Sept. 20, 1879 and Feb. 22, 1888; S. P. Ap., Feb. 18, 1936 and April 12, 1940).

Magníficat ánima mea Dóminum:
Et exsultávit spíritus meus in Deo salutári meo.

Quia respéxit humilitátem ancíllæ suæ: ecce enim ex hoc beátam me dicent omnes generatiónes.

Quia fecit mihi magna qui potens est: et sanctum nomen eius.

Et misericórdia eius a progénie in progénies timéntibus eum.

Fecit poténtiam in bráchio suo: dispérsit supérbos mente cordis sui.

Depósuit poténtes de sede, et exaltávit húmiles.

Esuriéntes implévit bonis: et dívites dimísit inánes.

Suscépit Israël púerum suum, recordátus misericórdiæ suæ.

Sicut locútus est ad patres nostros, Abraham et sémini eius in sǽcula. (Luc. I, 46).

321
Ave maris stella

Hail thou star of ocean
God's own mother blest,
Ever sinless Virgin,
Gate of heavenly rest.

Oh! by Gabriel's Ave,
Uttered long ago,
Eva's name reversing
'Stablish peace below.

Break the captive's fetters,
Light on blindness pour;
All our ills expelling,
Every bliss implore.

Show thyself a Mother;
May the Word divine,
Born for us thine Infant,
Hear our prayers through thine.

Virgin all excelling,
Mildest of the mild;
Freed from guilt preserve us
Meek and undefiled.

Keep our life all spotless,
Make our way secure,
Till we find in Jesus,
Joy for evermore.

Through the highest Heaven
To the almighty Three,
Father, Son and Spirit
One same glory be.   Amen.

(Roman Breviary, tr. cento).

An indulgence of 3 years.

A plenary indulgence once a month on the usual conditions, for the devout daily recitation of this hymn throughout a month (S. C. Ind., Jan. 27, 1888; S. P. Ap., March 27, 1935).

Ave maris stella,
Dei Mater alma,
Atque semper Virgo,
Felix cæli porta.

Sumens illud Ave
Gabriélis ore,
Funda nos in pace
Mutans Hevæ nomen.

Solve vincla reis,
Profer lumen cæcis,
Mala nostra pelle,
Bona cuncta posce.

Monstra te esse matrem,
Sumat per te preces
Qui pro nobis natus
Tulit esse tuus.

Virgo singuláris,
Inter omnes mitis,
Nos culpis solútos,
Mites fac et castos.

Vitam præsta puram,
Iter para tutum,
Ut vidéntes Iesum
Semper collætémur.

Sit laus Deo Patri,
Summo Christo decus,
Spirítui Sancto,
Tribus honor unus. Amen.

(**ex** *Breviario Romano*).

322

O gloriosa virginum

O glorious Virgin, ever blest,
All daughters of mankind above,
Who gavest nurture from thy breast
To God, with pure maternal love.

What man hath lost in hapless Eve,
The Blossom sprung from thee restores;
Thou to the sorrowing here beneath
Hast opened heaven's eternal doors.

O gate, through which hath passed the King,
O hall, whence light shone through the gloom!
The ransomed nations praise and sing
The Offspring of thy Virgin womb.

All honor, laud and glory be,
O Jesu, Virgin-born, to Thee:
All glory, as is ever meet,
To Father and to Paraclete.
Amen (Roman Breviary, tr. cento).

An indulgence of 3 years.

A plenary indulgence once a month on the usual conditions if this hymn is devoutly recited every day (S. P. Ap., Nov. 22, 1934).

O gloriósa Vírginum
Sublímis inter sídera,
Qui te creávit, párvulum
Lacténte nutris úbere.

Quod Heva tristis ábstulit,
Tu reddis almo gérmine:
Intrent ut astra flébiles,
Cæli reclúdis cárdines.

Tu regis alti iánua,
Et aula lucis fúlgida:
Vitam datam per Vírginem
Gentes redémptæ pláudite.

Iesu, tibi sit glória,
Qui natus es de Vírgine,
Cum Patre et almo Spíritu,
In sempitérna sǽcula.   Amen.
(ex *Breviario Romano*).

323
Antiphon
Alma Redemptoris

Mother benign of our redeeming Lord,
  Star of the sea and portal of the skies,
Unto thy fallen people help afford—
Fallen, but striving still anew to rise.

Thou who didst once, while wondering worlds
    adored,
Bear thy Creator, Virgin then as now,

O by thy holy joy at Gabriel's word,
Pity the sinners who before thee bow (Roman
Breviary).
An indulgence of 5 years.

A plenary indulgence once a month on the usual conditions, if
the daily recitation of this antiphon is continued for a month
(S. P. Ap., Feb. 15, 1941).

Antiphona

Alma Redemptóris Mater, quæ pérvia cæli
Porta manes, et stella maris, succúrre cadénti,
Súrgere qui curat, pópulo: tu quæ genuísti,
Natúra miránte, tuum sanctum Genitórem,
Virgo prius ac postérius, Gabriélis ab ore
Sumens illud Ave, peccatórum miserére.
(ex *Breviario Romano*).

324

Antiphon
Ave, Regina cælorum

Hail, O Queen of heaven enthroned!
Hail, by Angels Mistress owned!
Root of Jesse, Gate of morn,
Whence the world's true Light was born:
Glorious Virgin, joy to thee,
Loveliest whom in heaven they see:
Fairest thou where all are fair,
Plead with Christ our sins to spare (Roman
Breviary).
An indulgence of 5 years.

A plenary indulgence on the usual conditions, when this antiphon has been repeated daily for a month (S. P. Ap., Feb. 15, 1941).

Antiphona

Ave, Regína cælórum,
Ave, Dómina Angelórum:
Salve, radix, salve, porta,
Ex qua mundo lux est orta:
Gaude, Virgo gloriósa,

Super omnes speciósa,
Vale, o valde decóra,
Et pro nobis Christum exóra.

(**ex** *Breviario Romano*) ·

V
DEVOUT EXERCISES

325

The faithful who during the month of May take part in *public* exercises in honor of the B. V. M. may gain:

An indulgence of 7 years on any day of the month;

A plenary indulgence if they assist at the exercises on at least ten days, and moreover go to confession, receive Holy Communion and pray for the Holy Father's intention.

Those who perform their devotions privately during the aforesaid month are granted:

An indulgence of 5 years once on any day of the month;

A plenary indulgence on the usual conditions, if they perform these devotions every day during the month; but where public exercises are held, this indulgence is granted only to those who are lawfully hindered from taking part in the same (Secret Mem. March 21, 1815; S. C. Ind., June 18, 1822; S. P. Ap., March 28, 1933) ·

326

The faithful who devoutly offer some prayers in honor of the Nativity, Presentation, Annunciation, Visitation, Expectation, Purification or Assumption of the B. V. M. at any season of the year, with the intention of continuing these prayers for nine days without interruption, are granted:

An indulgence of 5 years once on each day; a plenary indulgence on the usual conditions at the close of the novena (Pius IX, Audience, Jan. 3, 1849; S. C. of Bishops and Regulars, Jan. 28, 1850; S. C. Ind., Nov. 26, 1876; S. P. Ap., Dec. 16, 1935) ·

NOTE: For other novenas in honor of the B. V. M. under various titles, see nn. 361, 380, 388, 396.

A devout exercise of thanksgiving to the Most Holy Trinity for the gifts and privileges conferred on the B. V. M. is found under n. 47.

327

The faithful who devoutly recite the *Hail Mary* three times with the invocation "*Pray for me, O holy Mother of God,*" or another at their choice, before an image of our Lady, are granted:

An indulgence of 300 days;

A plenary indulgence on the usual conditions if this pious practice is performed daily for a month (S. P. Ap., May 24, 1936 and June 18, 1949).

VI

AN ACT OF REPARATION FOR BLASPHEMIES AGAINST THE B. V. M.

328

Most glorious Virgin Mary, Mother of God and our Mother, turn thine eyes in pity upon us, miserable sinners; we are sore afflicted by the many evils that surround us in this life, but especially do we feel our hearts break within us upon hearing the dreadful insults and blasphemies uttered against thee, O Virgin Immaculate. O how these impious sayings offend the infinite Majesty of God and of His only-begotten Son, Jesus Christ! How they provoke His indignation and give us cause to fear the terrible effects of His vengeance! Would that the sacrifice of our lives might avail to put an end to such outrages and blasphemies; were it so, how gladly we should make it, for we desire, O most holy Mother, to love thee and to honor thee with all our hearts, since this is the will of God. And just because we love thee, we will do all that is in our power to make thee honored and loved by all men. In the meantime do thou, our merciful

Mother, the supreme comforter of the afflicted, accept this our act of reparation which we offer thee for ourselves and for all our families, as well as for all who impiously blaspheme thee, not knowing what they say. Do thou obtain for them from Almighty God the grace of conversion, and thus render more manifest and more glorious thy kindness, thy power and thy great mercy. May they join with us in proclaiming thee blessed among women, the Immaculate Virgin and most compassionate Mother of God.

Hail Mary *three times*.

An indulgence of 5 years (S. C. Ind., March 21, 1885; S. P. Ap., April 6, 1935 and June 10, 1949).

IN REPARATION FOR INSULTS OFFERED TO THE B. V. M.

329

O blessed Virgin, Mother of God, look down in mercy from Heaven, where thou art enthroned as Queen, upon me, a miserable sinner, thine unworthy servant. Although I know full well my own unworthiness, yet in order to atone for the offenses that are done to thee by impious and blasphemous tongues, from the depths of my heart I praise and extol thee as the purest, the fairest, the holiest creature of all God's handiwork. I bless thy holy Name, I praise thine exalted privilege of being truly Mother of God, ever Virgin, conceived without stain of sin, Co-Redemptrix of the human race. I bless the Eternal Father who chose thee in an especial way for His daughter; I bless the

Word Incarnate who took upon Himself our nature in thy bosom and so made thee His Mother; I bless the Holy Spirit who took thee as His bride. All honor, praise and thanksgiving to the ever-blessed Trinity who predestined thee and loved thee so exceedingly from all eternity as to exalt thee above all creatures to the most sublime heights. O Virgin, holy and merciful, obtain for all who offend thee the grace of repentance, and graciously accept this poor act of homage from me thy servant, obtaining likewise for me from thy divine Son the pardon and remission of all my sins. Amen.

An indulgence of 500 days (Holy Office, Jan. 22, 1914; S. P. Ap., Dec. 4, 1934).

VII

THE CROWN OF TWELVE STARS

330

Let us offer praise and thanksgiving to the Most Holy Trinity, who hath shown us the Virgin Mary, clothed with the sun, the moon beneath her feet, and on her head a mystic crown of twelve stars.

℟. For ever and ever. Amen.

Let us praise and thank the divine Father, who elected her for His daughter.

℟. Amen. Our Father.

Praised be the divine Father, who predestined her to be the Mother of His divine Son.

℟. Amen. Hail Mary.

Praised be the divine Father, who preserved her from all stain in her conception.

℟ Amen. Hail Mary.

Praised be the divine Father, who adorned her at her birth with His most excellent gifts.

℞. Amen.   Hail Mary.

Praised be the divine Father, who gave her Saint Joseph to be her companion and most pure spouse.

℞. Amen.   Hail Mary.   Glory be to the Father.

Let us praise and thank the divine Son, who chose her for His Mother.

℞. Amen.   Our Father.

Praised be the divine Son, who became incarnate in her bosom and there abode for nine months.

℞. Amen.   Hail Mary.

Praised be the divine Son, who was born of her and was nourished at her breast.

℞. Amen.   Hail Mary.

Praised be the divine Son, who in His childhood willed to be taught by her.

℞. Amen.   Hail Mary.

Praised be the divine Son, who revealed to her the mystery of the redemption of the world.

℞. Amen.   Hail Mary.   Glory be to the Father.

Let us praise and thank the Holy Spirit, who took her for His spouse.

℞. Amen.   Our Father.

Praised be the Holy Spirit, who revealed first to her His Name of Holy Spirit.

℞. Amen.   Hail Mary.

Praised be the Holy Spirit, by whose operation she was at once Virgin and Mother.

℞. Amen. Hail Mary.

Praised be the Holy Spirit, by whose power she was the living temple of the ever-blessed Trinity.

℞. Amen. Hail Mary.

Praised be the Holy Spirit, by whom she was exalted in heaven above every living creature.

℞. Amen. Hail Mary. Glory be to the Father.

(St. Joseph Calasanctius).

An indulgence of 3 years.

A plenary indulgence on the usual conditions, if this devotion is repeated daily for a month (S. C. Ind., Jan. 8, 1838 and Aug. 17, 1898; Pius IX, Audience March 17, 1856; S. P. Ap., March 28, 1934 and June 12, 1949).

VIII

PRAYERS

331

a)

℣. The Angel of the Lord declared unto Mary.

℞. And she conceived of the Holy Ghost.

Hail Mary.

℣. Behold the handmaid of the Lord,

℞. Be it done unto me according to Thy word.

Hail Mary.

℣. And the Word was made flesh,

℞. And dwelt amongst us.

Hail Mary.

℣. Pray for us, O holy Mother of God,

℞. That we may be made worthy of the promises of Christ.

Let us pray.

Pour forth, we beseech Thee, O Lord, Thy
grace into our hearts; that, as we have known
the Incarnation of Christ Thy Son by the
message of an Angel, so by His Passion and
Cross we may be brought to the glory of the
Resurrection. Through the same Christ our
Lord. Amen.

b)

Queen of Heaven, rejoice, alleluia:
For He Whom thou didst merit to bear,
alleluia,
Hath risen, as He said, alleluia.
Pray for us to God, alleluia.
℣. Rejoice and be glad, O Virgin Mary,
alleluia,
℟. Because the Lord is truly risen, alleluia.

Let us pray.

O God, who by the Resurrection of Thy
Son, our Lord Jesus Christ, hast vouchsafed
to make glad the whole world: grant, we beseech Thee, that, through the intercession of
the Virgin Mary, His Mother, we may lay
hold of the joys of eternal life. Through the
same Christ our Lord. Amen (Roman Breviary).

The faithful who at dawn, at noon and at eventide,
or as soon thereafter as may be, devoutly recite the
Angelus, or at Eastertide the *Regina cæli*, with the
appropriate versicles and prayers, or who merely
say the *Hail Mary* five times, may gain:

An indulgence of 10 years each time;

A plenary indulgence on the usual conditions if they persevere
in this devout practice for a month (S. P. Ap., Feb. 20, 1933).

℣. Angelus Dómini nuntiávit Maríæ,
℞. Et concépit de Spíritu Sancto.
Ave María.
℣. Ecce ancílla Dómini,
℞. Fiat mihi secúndum verbum tuum.
Ave María.
℣. Et Verbum caro factum est,
℞. Et habitávit in nobis.
Ave María.
℣. Ora pro nobis, sancta Dei Génitrix.
℞. Ut digni efficiámur promissiónibus Christi.

Orémus.

Grátiam tuam, quǽsumus Dómine, méntibus nostris infúnde: ut qui, Angelo nuntiánte, Christi Fílii tui incarnatiónem cognóvimus, per passiónem eius et crucem ad resurrectiónis glóriam perducámur. Per eúmdem Christum Dóminum nostrum. Amen.

b)

Regína cæli lætáre, allelúia:
Quia quem meruísti portáre, allelúia,
Resurréxit, sicut dixit, allelúia.
Ora pro nobis Deum, allelúia.
℣. Gaude et lætáre, Virgo María, allelúia.
℞. Quia surréxit Dóminus vere, allelúia.

Orémus.

Deus, qui per resurrectiónem Fílii tui Dómini nostri Iesu Christi mundum lætificáre dignátus es: præsta quǽsumus, ut per eius Genitrícem Vírginem Maríam perpétuæ capiámus gáudia vitæ. Per eúmdem Christum Dóminum nostrum. Amen. (ex *Breviario Romano*).

IX

PRAYERS

332

Hail, holy Queen, Mother of mercy, hail, our life, our sweetness and our hope. To thee do we cry, poor banished children of

Eve: to thee do we sigh, mourning and weeping in this vale of tears. Ah then, our Advocate, turn thine eyes of mercy toward us, and after this our exile, show unto us the blessed fruit of thy womb, Jesus, O merciful, O loving, O sweet Virgin Mary!

(Roman Breviary).

An indulgence of 5 years.

An indulgence of 7 years, every day in May.

A plenary indulgence once a month on the usual conditions for the daily recitation of this prayer.

A plenary indulgence at the hour of death to be gained by those who have often recited this prayer during life, and who, after confession and Communion, or at least an act of contrition, shall invoke the holy Name of Jesus with their lips, if possible, or at least in their hearts, and accept death with resignation from the hand of God as the just punishment of sin (S. C. Ind., April 5, 1786; S. P. Ap., July 2, 1934 and Dec. 6, 1940).

Salve, Regína, mater misericórdiæ, vita, dulcédo et spes nostra, salve. Ad te clamámus éxsules fílii Hevæ; ad te suspirámus geméntes et flentes in hac lacrymárum valle. Eia ergo, advocáta nostra, illos tuos misericórdes óculos ad nos convérte. Et Iesum, benedíctum fructum ventris tui, nobis post hoc exsílium osténde, o clemens, o pia, o dulcis Virgo María (ex *Brevario Romano*).

333

We fly to thy patronage, O holy Mother of God; despise not thou our petitions in our necessities, but deliver us always from all dangers, O glorious and blessed Virgin (Roman Breviary).

An indulgence of 5 years.

A plenary indulgence on the usual conditions, if this prayer is said daily for a month.

A plenary indulgence to be gained at the hour of death by those who have been accustomed to recite this prayer frequently in life, provided that, having confessed their sins and received Holy Communion, or at least being duly contrite, they devoutly invoke the most holy Name of Jesus with their lips, if they can, but if not, in their heart and accept death at the hands of the Lord with resignation as the just punishment of their sins (S. C. Ind., April 5, 1786; S. P. Ap., Dec. 12, 1935)·

S ub tuum præsídium confúgimus, sancta Dei Génitrix; nostras deprecatiónes ne despícias in necessitátibus nostris, sed a perículis cunctis líbera nos semper, Virgo gloriósa et benedícta (ex *Breviario Romano*)·

334
PRAYERS FOR EVERY DAY OF THE WEEK

SUNDAY

B ehold, O Mother of God, at thy feet a wretched sinner who has recourse to thee and trusts in thee. I do not deserve that thou shouldst even look upon me; but I know that thou, seeing thy Son dead to save sinners, hast a great desire to assist them. O Mother of mercy, behold my miseries and have pity on me. I hear all men call thee the refuge of sinners, the hope of the hopeless, the help of that which is lost. Thou art, then, my refuge, my hope and my help. Thou must save me by thine intercession; aid me for the love of Jesus Christ; give thy hand to a fallen wretch who commends himself to thee. I know that thou art consoled in helping a sinner, when thou canst; wherefore help me now, for thou canst help me. By my sins I have lost the grace of God and my soul; but I put myself in thy hands; tell me what I must do to return to the grace of God, for I wish to do so at once. He sends me to thee, that thou mayest assist me; He wills that I should have recourse to thy mercy, in order that I may be helped to salvation not only by the merits of thy Son, but also by thy prayers. To thee, therefore, do I have recourse. Do thou pray to Jesus for me. Make known the good which thou canst do for him who puts his trust in thee. This is my firm hope. Amen.

Hail Mary *three times* in reparation for blasphemies against the B. V. M.

MONDAY

O Queen of Heaven, most holy Mary, once I was the slave of Satan, but now I dedicate myself to be thy servant for ever; I offer myself to thy perpetual honor and service. Accept me, then, as thy servant; ah, do not cast me out as I deserve. In thee, my Mother, have I set all my hope. I praise and thank almighty God, who in His mercy gives me this confidence in thee. True it is, in the past I have fallen miserably into sin; but I hope that I have already obtained pardon for them through the merits of Jesus Christ and through thine intercession. But this is not enough, dear Mother; one thought distresses me, and that is that I may turn back and lose the grace of God; the dangers are ever present, mine enemies sleep not, fresh temptations will assail me. Ah, protect me then, my Lady! Defend me against the assaults of hell and permit not that I should begin again to commit sin and offend Jesus, thy divine Son. No, may it never come to pass that I should begin again to suffer the loss of my soul, of paradise and of God. This is the grace that I ask of thee, O Mary, this is my one desire, this do thou obtain for me by thine intercession. This is my firm hope. Amen.

Hail Mary *three times, as above.*

TUESDAY

Most holy Mary, Mother of goodness and mercy, when I consider my sins and think of the moment of death, I am filled with trembling and confusion. O sweetest Mother, in the Blood of Jesus Christ and in thy intercession are all my hopes. O Comforter of the afflicted, do not abandon me at that hour; forget not to console me in that great affliction. If at present I am so tormented with remorse at the sight of my sins, the uncertainty of forgiveness, the danger of falling again and the rigor of God's justice, what will become of me at that dread hour? Ah, my Lady, before death shall come, do thou obtain for me true sorrow for my sins, sincere amendment and fidelity to God for the rest of my life. And when at length I come to the hour of death, O Mary, my only hope, do thou assist me in the dire torments in which I shall then find myself; strengthen me so that I may not despair at the sight of my sins, which the devil himself will set before me. Obtain for me the grace to call upon thee more frequently so that I may breathe forth my spirit with thy sweet name on my lips and the Name of thy dear Son. Thou hast imparted this grace to so many of thy devoted children; it is the grace that I desire and hope for myself. Amen.

Hail Mary *three times, as above.*

WEDNESDAY

O Mother of God, Mary most holy, how often have I merited hell by my sins! Even now the sentence might have been executed, perhaps on the occasion of my first sin, hadst thou not, in thy loving pity, restrained the hand of God's justice; and then, overcoming my hardness of heart, thou didst gently draw me to put my trust in thee. Alas, into how many more sins I might have fallen, by reason of the dangers which encompass me, hadst thou not, O dearest Mother, preserved me from them by the graces thou didst obtain for me. Ah, my Queen, what will thy mercy and the many favors thou hast done for me avail me, if I become the cause of my own condemnation? If once upon a time I did not love thee, now at any rate I do love thee, after God, above all things. Ah, permit not that I should turn my back upon thee and upon Almighty God who has granted me so many merciful favors through thy intercession. Wilt thou suffer one of thy servants, who loves thee, to be damned? O Mary, what sayest thou? Am I to bring about my own damnation? I shall do so, indeed, if I ever forsake thee. But who, henceforth, will have the heart to forsake thee? Who can forget the love which thou hast borne toward me? No, he is not lost who commends himself faithfully to thee and has recourse to thee. Ah, my dearest Mother, abandon me not to my own devices, for then I shall surely lose my soul; grant that I may always run to thy protection. Save me, for thou art my hope, save me from hell, but first from sin which alone can bring me down to the gates of hell.   Amen.

Hail Mary *three times, as above.*

THURSDAY

O Queen of Heaven, thou who sittest enthroned above all the choirs of Angels, nearest to God Himself, from this vale of tears I, a wretched sinner, salute thee and implore thee to turn thine eyes of mercy toward me. See, O Mary, the great dangers which encompass me now and in the future, so long as I shall live upon the earth, the danger of losing my soul, Heaven and God. In thee, dear Lady, do I put all my trust. I love thee and I would fain come quickly to see thee and praise thee in paradise. O Mary, when will that day come when I shall find myself in safety at thy feet? When shall I kiss that hand of thine, which has poured so many graces upon me? It is true, dearest Mother, that I have been many times ungrateful to thee during my life; but when I shall come safe home to heaven, there will I love thee every moment throughout eternity; and I will atone for my lack of gratitude by praising and thanking thee for ever. I give thanks to Almighty God who gives me such confidence in the Blood of Jesus Christ and in thy mighty intercession. Thy truly devoted servants have ever placed such confidence in thee and none has ever been confounded. Let me never be confounded, no, not even me. O Mary, pray to Jesus thy Son, even as I also am praying, to strengthen and evermore confirm these hopes of mine through the merits of His Passion. Amen.

Hail Mary *three times, as above.*

FRIDAY

O Mary, thou art the noblest, the most exalted, the purest, the fairest, the holiest of all things created! O that all men knew thee, dearest Lady, and loved thee as thou deservest! But I am consoled by the thought that so many holy souls in heaven and so many just men upon the earth live enthralled by thy goodness and beauty. Above all else I rejoice that God Himself loves thee alone more than all men and Angels. O my Queen, most worthy of love, I too love thee, miserable sinner that I am, but I love thee far too little; I desire a greater and more tender love of thee, and this thou must obtain for me; for love of thee is a great sign of predestination, and a grace granted by God to those who shall be saved. Therefore, dear Mother, I see that I am under exceeding obligation to thy divine Son; I see that He is deserving of infinite love. Thou hast no other desire but to see Him loved by men; do thou obtain for me the grace of an ardent love of Jesus Christ. Ah, obtain this grace for me, thou who dost obtain from God whatsoever thou desirest. I do not seek the things of earth, not honors, not riches; I seek only that which thy heart seeks most of all, to love God and Him alone. Can it be that thou art unwilling to assist me in this my desire which is so dear to Thee? Nay, thou art already giving me thy help; even now thou art praying for me. Pray, O Mary, pray and never cease to pray until thou shalt see me safe in paradise, where I shall be sure of possessing and loving my God together with thee, my dearest Mother, for ever and ever. Amen.

Hail Mary *three times, as above.*

SATURDAY

O my most holy Mother, I behold the graces which thou hast obtained for me, and the ingratitude which I have shown toward thee. The thankless soul is no longer worthy of blessings; but not even on this account will I lose confidence in thy mercy. O my mighty Advocate, have pity on me. Thou art the dispenser of all the graces that God grants to the miserable children of men, and to this end has He made thee so mighty, so rich and so kind, that thou mightest succor us in our need. I wish to be saved; in thy hands, therefore, I place my eternal salvation; to thee I commend my spirit. I wish to be inscribed among thy most special servants; drive me not away. Thou goest about seeking the wretched to comfort them: do not abandon a poor sinner who flies to thy protection. Speak thou for me; thy Son will do whatsoever thou shalt ask Him. Take me under thy protection, and this is enough for me; for if thou shield me, I shall fear nothing: not my sins, for I hope that thou wilt obtain their remission from Almighty God; not the evil spirits, for thou art mightier than the powers of hell; not even Jesus as my Judge, for one prayer of thine will turn away His anger. Do thou, therefore, protect me, dear Mother, and obtain for me the remission of all my sins, the love of Jesus, final perseverance, a happy death, and paradise at last. True it is, I do not deserve these graces, but if thou dost ask them for me from our Lord, I shall receive them. O Mary, my Queen, pray to Jesus for me; in thee do I put my trust; in this hope will I live and take my rest; and with this hope I wish to die. Amen (St. Alphonsus M. de' Liguori).

Hail Mary *three times, as above.*

An indulgence of 3 years, for each prayer.

A plenary indulgence on the usual conditions, if these prayers are devoutly recited throughout an entire month (S. C. Ind., June 21, 1808 and June 18, 1876; S. P. Ap., Nov. 24, 1935).

335

O Mother of God, Mary most holy, how many times by my sins have I merited the pains of hell! Even now the sentence might have been passed, perhaps on the occasion of my very first sin, hadst thou not in thy tender pity restrained the hand of divine Justice: and then overcoming my hardness of heart, thou drewest me gently to place my confidence in thee. And oh, how very often should I have fallen in the dangers which beset my steps hadst not thou, loving Mother that thou art, preserved me by the graces thou didst obtain for me. But oh, my Queen, what will thy pity and thy favors avail me, if after all, I became the cause of my own condemnation. If there was once a time when I loved thee not, yet now, next to God, I love thee above all things. Ah, permit not that I should turn my back on thee and on my God who, by means of thee, has granted me so many mercies. Wilt thou endure seeing one of thy servants who loves thee go down into hell? O Mary, what sayest thou? Shall I bring about my own condemnation? I shall most surely do so, if I forsake thee. But who would henceforth have the heart to forsake thee? Who could ever forget the love thou hast borne toward me? No, he assuredly is not lost who faithfully commends himself to thee and has recourse to thee. Ah, my dear Mother, leave me not to my own devices for then I shall surely die. Grant that I may always seek thy protection.

Save me, for thou art my hope, save me from the pains of hell, but especially from sin, which alone has power to condemn me to the flames of perdition (St. Alphonsus M. de' Liguori).

Hail Mary *three times.*

An indulgence of 3 years.

A plenary indulgence once a month on the usual conditions, if this prayer be recited daily (S. C. Ind., May 15, 1821; S. P. Ap., April 5, 1936) ·

336

I. I venerate thee with all my heart, O Virgin most holy, above all Angels and Saints in paradise, as the daughter of the Eternal Father, and to thee I consecrate my soul with all its powers.

Hail Mary.

II. I venerate thee with all my heart, O Virgin most holy, above all Angels and Saints in paradise, as the Mother of the only-begotten Son, and to thee I consecrate my body with all its senses.

Hail Mary.

III. I venerate thee with all my heart, O Virgin most holy, above all Angels and Saints in paradise, as the beloved Spouse of the Spirit of God, and to thee I consecrate my heart and all its affections, imploring thee to obtain for me from the Most Holy Trinity all the means of salvation.

Hail Mary.

An indulgence of 500 days.

A plenary indulgence once a month on the usual conditions, if this act of consecration is devoutly repeated every day (Leo XII, Rescript in his own hand, Oct. 21, 1823; S. C. Ind., June 18, 1876; S. P. Ap., Jan. 14, 1934) ·

337

Virgin most holy, Mother of the Word Incarnate, Treasurer of graces, and Refuge of us poor sinners; we fly to thy motherly affection with lively faith, and we beg of thee the grace ever to do the will of God.   Into thy most holy hands we commit the keeping of our hearts, asking thee for health of soul and body, in the certain hope that thou, our most loving Mother, wilt hear our prayer. Wherefore with lively faith we say:

Hail Mary *three times*.

An indulgence of 500 days. (S. C. Ind., Aug. 11, 1824; S. P. Ap., Sept. 21, 1935 and June 18, 1949)·

338

O most excellent, most glorious, most holy and ever inviolate Virgin Mary, Mother of our Lord Jesus Christ, Queen of the whole world and Mistress of every creature; thou forsakest no one, thou despisest no one, thou sendest away disconsolate no one who comes to thee with a pure and lowly heart; despise me not for my countless grievous sins, neither forsake me for my exceeding iniquities, nor for the hardness and uncleanness of my heart; cast me not away, who am thy servant, from thy grace and love. Graciously hear me, a miserable sinner, trusting in thy tender mercy; come to my assistance, O most loving Virgin Mary, in all my tribulations, trials and necessities; obtain for me of thy dear Son, Almighty God and our Lord Jesus Christ, the forgiveness and remission of all my sins, and the grace of fear and the love of thee; health likewise and chastity of body, and deliverance from all evils and dangers which beset both soul and body.

In my last moments do thou graciously assist me, and deliver my soul and the souls of my parents, brothers, sisters and friends, kinsmen and benefactors, and of all faithful Christians, both living and departed, from eternal darkness and from all evil, by the grace of Him whom thou didst bear in thy sacred womb for nine long months, and didst lay in the manger with thine own pure hands, even our Lord Jesus Christ thy Son who is blessed for ever.   Amen.

An indulgence of 500 days.

A plenary indulgence once a month on the usual conditions, if this prayer is devoutly recited every day (S. C. Ind., Jan. 30, 1828; S. P. Ap., March 10, 1936).

O excellentíssima, gloriosíssima atque sanctíssima semper intemeráta Virgo María, Mater Dómini nostri Iesu Christi, Regína mundi et totíus creatúræ Dómina, quæ nullum, qui ad te puro et húmili corde recúrrit, desolátum dimíttis, noli me despícere propter innumerabília et gravíssima peccáta mea, noli me derelínquere propter nímias iniquitátes meas, nec etiam propter durítiam et immundítiam cordis mei: ne abiícias me fámulum tuum a grátia tua et amóre tuo. Exáudi me míserum peccatórem in tua misericórdia et pietáte confidéntem; succúrre mihi, piíssima Virgo María, in ómnibus tribulatiónibus, angústiis et necessitátibus meis; et ímpetra mihi a dilécto Fílio tuo omnipoténte Deo et Dómino nostro Iesu Christo indulgéntiam et remissiónem ómnium peccatórum meórum et grátiam timóris et amóris tui, sanitátem quoque et castitátem córporis, et liberatiónem ab ómnibus malis et perículis ánimæ et córporis. In extrémis meis esto mihi pia auxiliátrix, et ánimam meam ac ánimas ómnium paréntum meórum, fratrum, sorórum et amicórum consanguineórum et benefactórum meórum omniúmque fidélium vivórum et defunctórum ab ætérna calígine et ab omni malo líbera, Illo auxiliánte, quem in tuo sacratíssimo útero novem ménsibus portásti et in præsépe tuis sanctis mánibus reclinásti, Dóminum nostrum

Iesum Christum Fílium tuum, qui est benedíctus in sæcula sæculórum. Amen.

339

Remember, O most gracious Virgin Mary, that never was it known that any one who fled to thy protection, implored thy help or sought thy intercession, was left unaided. Inspired with this confidence, I fly unto thee, O Virgin of virgins and Mother; to thee do I come, before thee I stand, sinful and sorrowful; O Mother of the Word Incarnate, despise not my petitions, but in thy mercy hear and answer me. Amen.

An indulgence of 3 years.

A plenary indulgence once a month on the usual conditions for the daily recitation of this prayer (S. C. Ind., Dec. 11, 1846; S. P. Ap., Sept. 8, 1935).

Memoráre, o piísima Virgo María, non esse audítum a sæculo, quemquam ad tua curréntem præsídia, tua implorántem auxília, tua peténtem suffrágia esse derelíctum. Ego tali animátus confidéntia ad te, Virgo Vírginum, Mater, curro; ad te vénio; coram te gemens peccátor assísto. Noli, Mater Verbi, verba mea despícere, sed audi propítia et exáudi. Amen.

340

Hail Mary, *etc.*

My Queen! my Mother! I give thee all myself, and, to show my devotion to thee, I consecrate to thee my eyes, my ears, my mouth, my heart, my entire self. Wherefore, O loving Mother, as I am thine own, keep me, defend me, as thy property and possession.

An indulgence of 500 days.

A plenary indulgence on the usual conditions, if this act of oblation is repeated every day for a month (S. C. Ind., Aug. 5, 1851; S. P. Ap., Nov. 21, 1936).

Ave María, *etc.*

O Dómina mea! O Mater mea! Tibi me totum óffero, atque, ut me tibi probem devótum, cónsecro tibi óculos meos, aures meas, os meum, cor meum, plane me totum. Quóniam ítaque tuus sum, o bona Mater, serva me, defénde me ut rem ac possessiónem tuam.

341

O blessed Virgin Mary, who can worthily repay thee thy just dues of praise and thanksgiving, thou who by the wondrous assent of thy will didst rescue a fallen world? What songs of praise can our weak human nature recite in thy honor, since it is by thy intervention alone that it has found the way to restoration? Accept, then, such poor thanks as we have here to offer, though they be unequal to thy merits; and, receiving our vows, obtain by thy prayers the remission of our offenses. Carry thou our prayers within the sanctuary of the heavenly audience, and bring forth from it the antidote of our reconciliation. May the sins we bring before Almighty God through thee, become pardonable through thee; may what we ask for with sure confidence, through thee be granted. Take our offering, grant us our requests, obtain pardon for what we fear, for thou art the sole hope of sinners. Through thee we hope for the remission of our sins, and in thee, O blessed Lady, is our hope of reward. Holy Mary, succour the miserable, help the faint-hearted, comfort the sorrowful, pray for thy people, plead for the clergy, intercede for all

women consecrated to God; may all who
keep thy holy commemoration feel now thy
help and protection. Be thou ever ready to
assist us when we pray, and bring back to us
the answers to our prayers. Make it thy
continual care to pray for the people of God,
thou who, blessed by God, didst merit to
bear the Redeemer of the world, who liveth
and reigneth, world without end. Amen
(St. Augustine) .

An indulgence of 3 years.

A plenary indulgence once a month on the usual conditions for
the daily recitation of this prayer (Secret Mem., May 19, 1854;
S. P. Ap., Feb. 5, 1932) .

O beáta Virgo María, quis tibi digne váleat iura
gratiárum ac laudum præcónia repéndere, quæ
singulári tuo assénsu, mundo succurrísti pérdito?
Quas tibi laudes fragílitas humáni géneris persólvat,
quæ solo tuo commércio recuperándi áditum invénit?
Accipe ítaque quascúmque éxiles, quascúmque méritis tuis ímpares gratiárum actiónes, et cum suscé-
peris vota, culpas nostras orándo excúsa. Admítte
nostras preces intra sacrárium exauditiónis et repórta nobis antídotum reconciliatiónis. Sit per te
excusábile quod per te ingérimus; fiat impetrábile
quod fida mente póscimus. Accipe quod offérimus,
redóna quod rogámus, excúsa quod timémus, quia
Tu es spes única peccatórum. Per te sperámus
véniam delictórum et in te, beatíssima, nostrórum est
expectátio præmiórum. Sancta María, succúrre
míseris; iuva pusillánimes; réfove flébiles; ora pro
pópulo; intérveni pro clero; intercéde pro devóto
femíneo sexu: séntiant omnes tuum iuvámen, quicúmque célebrant tuam sanctam commemoratiónem.
Assíste paráta votis poscéntium et repórta nobis
optátum efféctum. Sint tibi stúdia assídua oráre pro
pópulo Dei, quæ meruísti, benedícta, Redemptórem
ferre mundi, qui vivit et regnat in sæcuia sæculórum.
Amen (S. Augustinus) .

Most holy Virgin Immaculate, my Mother Mary, to thee who art the Mother of my Lord, the Queen of the universe, the advocate, the hope, the refuge of sinners, I who am the most miserable of all sinners, have recourse this day. I venerate thee, great Queen, and I thank thee for the many graces thou hast bestowed upon me even unto this day; in particular for having delivered me from the hell which I have so often deserved by my sins. I love thee, most dear Lady; and for the love I bear thee, I promise to serve thee willingly for ever and to do what I can to make thee loved by others also. I place in thee all my hopes for salvation; accept me as thy servant and shelter me under thy mantle, thou who art the Mother of mercy. And since thou art so powerful with God, deliver me from all temptations, or at least obtain for me the strength to overcome them until death. From thee I implore a true love for Jesus Christ. Through thee I hope to die a holy death. My dear Mother, by the love thou bearest to Almighty God, I pray thee to assist me always, but most of all at the last moment of my life. Forsake me not then, until thou shalt see me safe in heaven, there to bless thee and sing of thy mercies through all eternity. Such is my hope. Amen 'St Alphonsus M. de' Liguori).

The faithful who recite this prayer with devotion before an image of the B. V. Mary, may gain:

An indulgence of 3 years.

A plenary indulgence once a month on the usual conditions, if they recite it every day (Pius IX, Rescript in his own hand, Sept. 7, 1854; S. P. Ap., May 18, 1934).

343

O holy Mary, my Mistress, into thy blessed trust and special keeping, into the bosom of thy tender mercy, this day, every day of my life and at the hour of my death, I commend my soul and body; to thee I entrust all my hopes and consolations, all my trials and miseries, my life and the end of my life, that through thy most holy intercession and thy merits, all my actions may be ordered and disposed according to thy will and that of thy divine Son. Amen (St. Aloysius Gonzaga).

An indulgence of 3 years.

A plenary indulgence once a month on the usual conditions, if this prayer is recited daily (S. C. Ind., Mar. 15, 1890; S. P. Ap., Mar. 28, 1933).

O Dómina mea, sancta María, me in tuam benedíctam fidem ac singulárem custódiam et in sinum misericórdiæ tuæ, hódie et quotídie et in hora éxitus mei ánimam meam et corpus meum tibi comméndo: omnem spem et consolatiónem meam, omnes angústias et misérias meas, vitam et finem vitæ meæ tibi commítto, ut per tuam sanctíssimam intercessiónem et per tua mérita, ómnia mea dirigántur et disponántur ópera secúndum tuam tuíque Fílii voluntátem. Amen (S. Aloisius Gonzaga).

344

O Mary, crowned with stars, who hast the moon for thy footstool and who sittest enthroned above all the choirs of Angels, incline thine eyes toward this vale of tears, and hear the voice of one who puts all his hope and trust in thee.

Now thou dost rejoice in the endless bliss of paradise; but once thou didst endure the miseries of this our exile and thou knowest how bitter are the days of him who eats the bread of sorrow.

On Calvary thou didst hear a voice, well-known to thee, which said: "Woman, behold thy son"; that is to say, "a son in my stead". By these words thou wast appointed the Mother of all believers.

And without thee what life should we have, who are the unhappy children of Adam? Each of us has a sorrow that tries him, a grief that oppresses, a wound that rankles. All men run to thy protection, as to the haven of safety and the fountain of healing. When the waves rise high in the tempest, it is to thee the mariner turns and prays for calm. The orphan flies to thee, for he sees himself as a plant in a thirsty land, defenseless before all the whirlwinds of life. To thee the poor offer their supplications when they are in want of daily bread. And not even one is left without thy help and consolation.

O Mary, dear Mother, enlighten our minds, and warm our hearts; let that pure love which streams forth from thine eyes, spread itself abroad and bring forth those wondrous fruits which thy Son hath purchased for us by the shedding of His Blood, the while thou didst suffer most bitter torments at the foot of His Cross.

An indulgence of 500 days (Pius X, Rescript in his own hand, March 24, 1905, exhib. June 2, 1905; S. P. Ap., Sept. 23, 1936).

345

Majestic Queen of Heaven and Mistress of the Angels, thou didst receive from God the power and commission to crush the head of Satan; wherefore we humbly beseech thee, send forth the legions of heaven, that, under thy command, they may seek out all evil spirits, engage them everywhere in battle, curb their insolence, and hurl them back into the pit of hell. "Who is like unto God?"

O good and tender Mother, thou shalt ever be our hope and the object of our love.

O Mother of God, send forth the holy Angels to defend me and drive far from me the cruel foe.

Holy Angels and Archangels, defend us and keep us.

An indulgence of 500 days (S. C. Ind., July 8, 1908; S. P. Ap., March 28, 1935)-

346

O Mary, my dear Mother and mighty Queen, take and receive my poor heart with all its freedom and desires, all its love and affection, and all the virtues and graces with which it can be adorned. All that I am, all that I might be, my Lady and Queen, all that I have and hold in the order of nature as well as of grace, I have received from God through thy loving intercession; into thy sovereign hands I commit it all, that it may be returned to its noble original; wherefore we confess that thou art the channel whereby the graces of heaven descend upon us; thou art likewise the aqueduct which carries them back to their source; thou art, as it were, an electric wire, whereby we are put in direct communication with our heavenly Father; thou art the immaculate way which leads us safe to the Heart of God. Take,then, and accept all that I am, O Mary, Queen of every heart, and bind me to thee with the bonds of love, that I may be thine for ever, and may be able to say in truth: "I belong to Jesus through Mary." Thee only will I love, my Mother most pure; lend me thy heart; give me love for thee and for Jesus, and it is enough to make me happy and blessed in life, in death and in eternity. Amen.

An indulgence of 500 days.

A plenary indulgence once a month on the usual conditions for the daily recitation of this prayer(S. P. Ap., July 29, 1924 and July 12, 1933) ·

347

May we be assisted, we beseech Thee, O Lord, by the worshipful intercession of Thy glorious Mother, the ever-Virgin Mary; that we, who have been enriched by her perpetual blessings, may be delivered from all dangers, and through her loving kindness made to be of one heart and mind: Who livest and reignest world without end. Amen

(Roman Missal) ·

An indulgence of 3 years.

A plenary indulgence on the usual conditions if this prayer is recited every day for a month(S. P. Ap., Feb. 6, 1934) ·

Adiuvet nos, quǽsumus Dómine, gloriósæ tuæ Geni- trícis sempérque Vírginis Maríæ intercéssio veneránda: ut quos perpétuis cumulávit benefíciis, a cunctis perículis absolútos, sua fáciat pietáte concórdes: Qui vivis et regnas in sǽcula sæculórum. Amen (ex *Missali Romano*).

348

Grant, we beseech Thee, O Lord God, unto us Thy servants, that we may rejoice in continual health of mind and body; and, by the glorious intercession of blessed Mary ever Virgin, may be delivered from present sadness, and enter into the joy of Thine eternal gladness. Through Christ our Lord. Amen (Roman Missal).

An indulgence of 3 years.

A plenary indulgence once a month on the usual conditions for the daily repetition of this prayer (S. P. Ap., March 18, 1935).

Concéde nos fámulos tuos, quǽsumus, Dómine Deus, perpétua mentis et córporis sanitáte gaudére; et, gloriósæ beátæ Maríæ semper Vírginis intercessióne, a præsénti liberári tristítia et ætérna pérfrui lætítia. Per Christum Dóminum nostrum. Amen ex *Missali Romano*).

349

Holy Mary, be thou a help to the helpless, strength to the fearful, comfort to the sorrowful, pray for the people, plead for the clergy, intercede for all holy women consecrated to God; may all who keep thy sacred commemoration feel the might of thine assistance (Roman Breviary).

An indulgence of 3 years.

A plenary indulgence once a month on the usual conditions for the devout recitation of this prayer every day (S. P. Ap., May 29, 1936).

Sancta María, succúrre míseris, iuva pusillánimes, réfove flébiles, ora pro pópulo, intérveni pro clero, intercéde pro devóto femíneo sexu: séntiant omnes tuum iuvámen, quicúmque célebrant tuam sanctam commemoratiónem (ex *Breviario Romano*).

350

H ail, most gracious Mother of mercy, hail, Mary, for whom we fondly yearn, through whom we obtain forgiveness, who would not love thee? Thou art our light in uncertainty, our comfort in sorrow, our solace in the time of trial, our refuge from every peril and temptation. Thou art our sure hope of salvation, second only to thy only-begotten Son; blessed are they who love thee, Our Lady! Incline, I beseech thee, thy ears of pity to the entreaties of this thy servant, a miserable sinner; dissipate the darkness of my sins by the bright beams of thy holiness, in order that I may be acceptable in thy sight.

An indulgence of 500 days.

A plenary indulgence on the usual conditions, for the devout recitation of this prayer every day for a month (S. P. Ap., April 22, 1941) .

A ve, benigníssima misericórdiæ Mater, salve, véniæ conciliátrix optatíssima María, quis te non amet? Tu in rebus dúbiis lumen, et in mœróribus solátium, in angústiis levámen, in perículis et tentatiónibus refúgium. Tu post unigénitum tuum certa salus; beáti qui díligunt te, Dómina! Inclína, quæso, aures tuæ pietátis ad preces huius servi tui, huius míseri peccatóris; et calíginem vitiórum meórum rádiis tuæ sanctitátis díssipa, ut tibi pláceam.

351

O Mother of tender mercy, most Blessed Virgin Mary, I am a wretched and unworthy sinner, yet I fly to thee with all my heart and all my affection; I implore thy loving-kindness, that even as thou didst stand beside thy dear Son as He hung upon the Cross, so thou wilt mercifully deign to stand beside me, a miserable sinner, and beside all thy faithful people as we receive the most sacred Body of thy Son, to the end that we may be enabled to receive It worthily and fruitfully. Through the same Christ our Lord. Amen.

The faithful who recite this prayer before Holy Communion are granted:

An indulgence of 3 years;

A plenary indulgence, if they say it daily for a month, and in addition go to confession, visit some church or public oratory, and pray for the intentions of the Sovereign Pontiff (S. P. Ap., May 25, 1941).

O Mater pietátis et misericórdiæ, beatíssima Virgo María, ego miser et indígnus peccátor ad te confúgio toto corde et afféctu; et precor pietátem tuam ut, sicut dulcíssimo Fílio tuo in Cruce pendénti adstitísti, ita et mihi mísero peccatóri et fidélibus ómnibus sacrosánctum Fílii tui Corpus suméntibus cleménter adsístere dignéris, ut tua grátia adiúti, digne ac fructuóse illud súmere valeámus. Per eúmdem Christum Dóminum nostrum. Amen.

352

O Mary, my dear Mother, how much I love thee! And yet in reality how little! Thou dost teach me what I ought to know, for thou teachest me what Jesus is to me and what I ought to be for Jesus. Dearly beloved Mother, how close to God thou art, and how utterly filled with Him! In the measure that we know God, we remind ourselves of thee. Mother of God, obtain for me the grace of loving my Jesus; obtain for me the grace of loving thee! (R. Card. Merry del Val).

An indulgence of 500 days.

A plenary indulgence on the usual conditions, for the devout repetition of this prayer every day for a month (S. P. Ap., June 8, 1949).

Art. II
THE IMMACULATE CONCEPTION OF THE B. V. M.
I
EJACULATIONS AND INVOCATIONS
353

In thy Conception, O Virgin Mary, thou wast immaculate; pray for us to the Father whose Son Jesus, after He was conceived by the Holy Ghost, thou didst bring forth into the world.

An indulgence of 300 days (S. C. Ind., Nov. 21, 1793; S. P. Ap., April 24, 1933).

In Conceptióne tua, Virgo María, immaculáta fuísti; ora pro nobis Patrem, cuius Fílium Iesum de Spíritu Sancto concéptum peperísti.

354

To thee, O Virgin Mother, who wast never touched by any spot of original or actual sin, I commend and entrust the purity of my heart.

An indulgence of 300 days (S. C. of the Prop. of the Faith, Nov. 26, 1854; S. P. Ap., May 9, 1932).

355

O Mary, thou didst enter the world without stain; do thou obtain for me from God, that I may leave it without sin.

An indulgence of 300 days (Pius IX, Audience, March 27, 1863; S. P. Ap., Oct. 16, 1936).

356

Blessed be the holy and Immaculate Conception of the Blessed Virgin Mary, Mother of God.

An indulgence of 300 days.

A plenary indulgence once a month on the usual conditions, if this ejaculation be said devoutly every day (Apostolic Brief, Sept. 10, 1878; S. P. Ap., Nov. 8, 1934).

357

O Mary, conceived without sin, pray for us who have recourse to thee.

An indulgence of 300 days.

A plenary indulgence once a month on the usual conditions if this invocation be devoutly repeated daily (S. C. Ind., March 15, 1884; S. P. Ap., April 15, 1932) ·

358

Hail Mary, *etc.*

B y thine Immaculate Conception, O Mary, make my body pure and my spirit holy

(St. Alphonsus M. de' Liguori) ·

An indulgence of 300 days (Apostolic Brief, Dec. 5, 1904; S. P. Ap., March 27, 1935) ·

Ave, María, *etc.*

P er tuam immaculátam Conceptiónem, o María, redde purum corpus meum et sanctam ánimam meam (S. Alphonsus M. de Ligorio) ·

359

T hou art all fair, O Mary,
The original stain is not in thee.
Thou art the glory of Jerusalem,
Thou, the joy of Israël,
Thou, the great honor of our people
Thou, the advocate of sinners.
O Mary,
O Mary,
Virgin most prudent,
Mother most merciful,
Pray for us,
Intercede for us with our Lord Jesus Christ.

An indulgence of 500 days (S. C. Ind., Mar. 23, 1904; S. P. Ap., Dec. 19, 1936) ·

T ota pulchra es, María,
Et mácula originális non est in te.
Tu glória Ierúsalem,

Tu lætítia Israël,
Tu honorificéntia pópuli nostri,
Tu advocáta peccatórum.
O María,
O María,
Virgo prudentíssima,
Mater clementíssima,
Ora pro nobis,
Intercéde pro nobis ad Dóminum Iesum Christum.

II
THE LITTLE OFFICE

360

The faithful, who recite with devotion the little Office of the Immaculate Conception of the B. V. M., may obtain:

An indulgence of 7 years;

A plenary indulgence on the usual conditions if they recite the same daily for a month (Apostolic Brief, March 31, 1876; S. P. Ap., Oct. 23, 1928 and March 18, 1932)·

III
DEVOUT PRACTICES

361

The faithful who devoutly assist at a public novena in honor of the Immaculate Conception of the B. V. M., immediately preceding the 8th of December, may gain:

An indulgence of 7 years on each day;

A plenary indulgence, if they are present on at least five days and in addition go to confession, receive Holy Communion and pray for the intentions of the Holy Father.

Those who make a private novena at the aforesaid season may gain:

An indulgence of 5 years, once each day;

A plenary indulgence on the usual conditions at the close of the novena; but this indulgence is available only to those who are lawfully prevented from assisting at the public novena where one is held (Pius IX, Audience Jan. 3, 1849; S. C. of Bishops and Regulars, Jan. 28, 1850; S. C. Ind., Nov. 26, 1876; S. P. Ap., May 18, 1935)·

362

The faithful who recite with devotion the prayers entitled: "A devout seven days' supplication to the most holy Virgin Mother of God, immaculately conceived, for obtaining the grace of a godly life in Christ, and a happy death in the peace of the Lord, taken from the writings of the Seraphic Doctor, St. Bonaventure," may gain:

An indulgence of 7 years once a day.

A plenary indulgence on the usual conditions, on the Feast of the Immaculate Conception of the B. V. M. and on one day during the Octave, on the Feast of St. Joseph, Spouse of the Virgin Mother of God, on the Feast of St. Bonaventure, and once during the month of May, if this devout service is performed daily throughout an entire month immediately preceding the above-mentioned feasts and days (**Apostolic Brief, Dec. 9, 1856; S. P. Ap., March 18, 1932**).

363

The faithful on any one of seven successive Sundays that they choose, if they recite some devout prayers in honor of the Immaculate Conception of the B. V. M., may gain:

A plenary indulgence on the usual conditions (**S. C. of the Prop. of the Faith, Sept. 21, 1865; S. C. Ind., July 23, 1898; S. P. Ap., May 4, 1936**).

364

The faithful who perform some act of devotion in honor of the Immaculate Conception of the B. V. M. during the month of December may gain:

An indulgence of 5 years once, on any day;

A plenary indulgence, on the usual conditions, if they perform it daily throughout the month (**S. C. Ind., Nov. 13, 1907; S. P. Ap., April 24, 1933**).

365

The faithful who spend some time in devout prayers or meditations in honor of the B. V. M. Immaculate, on the first Saturday or Sunday of each month with the intention of persevering in the same practice for the space of twelve months, may gain:

A plenary indulgence, on the usual conditions, on each first Saturday or Sunday (**S. C. Ind., July 1, 1905; S. P. Ap., Nov. 15, 1927**).

366

The faithful may gain on each of the twelve Saturdays immediately preceding the feast of the Immaculate Conception of the B. V. M., if they devote some time to prayer or meditation in honor of that mystery:

A plenary indulgence on the usual conditions (Holy Office, Nov. 26, 1908).

367

a) The faithful who on the first Saturday of each month perform some special exercises of devotion in honor of the B. V. M. Immaculate, in order to make atonement for the blasphemies whereby the name and prerogatives of the same Blessed Virgin are reviled, may gain:

A plenary indulgence on the usual conditions (S. C. Holy Off., June 13, 1912).

b) Those who once in their lifetime perform such a devout exercise on the first Saturdays of eight successive months may gain, without prejudice to the above plenary indulgence:

A plenary indulgence at the hour of death, if, after confession and Communion, or at least being duly contrite, they invoke with their lips, if possible, otherwise in their hearts, the most holy Name of Jesus, and accept death with resignation from the Hand of God as the due punishment of their sins (Benedict XV, Rescript in his own hand, Nov. 9, 1920, exhib. Nov. 17, 1920).

IV
PRAYERS
368

O Virgin Immaculate, who wast pleasing in the Lord's sight and didst become His Mother, look graciously upon the wretched who implore thy mighty patronage. The wicked serpent, against whom the primal curse was hurled, continues none the less to wage war and to lay snares for the unhappy children of Eve. Ah, do thou, our blessed Mother, our Queen and Advocate, who from the first instant of thy conception didst crush the head of our enemy, receive the prayers that we unite single-heartedly to thine and conjure thee to offer at the throne of God, that we may never fall into the snares that are laid for us, in such wise that we may all come to the haven of salvation; and in the midst of so many dangers may holy Church and the fellowship of Christians everywhere sing once more the hymn of deliverance, victory and peace.   Amen.

An indulgence of 500 days (S. C. Ind., Jan. 11, 1905; S. P. Ap., Feb. 2, 1934).

369

O Virgin Immaculate, Mother of God and my Mother, from thy sublime height turn upon me thine eyes of pity.   Filled with confidence in thy goodness and knowing full well thy power, I beseech thee to extend to me thine assistance in the journey of life, which is so full of dangers for my soul.   And in order that I may never be the slave of the devil through sin, but may ever live with my heart humble and pure, I entrust myself wholly to thee.   I consecrate my heart to thee for ever, my only desire being to love thy divine Son Jesus.   Mary, none of thy devout servants has ever perished; may I too be saved.   Amen.

An indulgence of 500 days (S. P. Ap., May 17, 1919 and April 29, 1935).

370

Immaculate Mother of God, Queen of heaven, Mother of mercy, Advocate and Refuge of sinners, behold, I, enlightened and inspired by the graces obtained for me abundantly from the divine treasury through thy maternal affection, resolve this day and always to place my heart in thy hands to be consecrated to Jesus.

To thee, therefore, most Blessed Virgin, in the presence of the nine choirs of Angels and all the Saints, I now give it. Do thou, in my name, consecrate it to Jesus; and out of the filial confidence which I hereby make profession of, I am certain that now and always thou wilt do all thou canst to bring it to pass that my heart may ever wholly belong to Jesus, and may imitate perfectly the example of the Saints, and in particular that of Saint Joseph, thy most pure Spouse. Amen
(Bl. Vincent Pallotti) .

An indulgence of 3 years.

A plenary indulgence on the usual conditions, if this prayer is recited every day for a month (S. P. Ap., July 27, 1920 and Sept. 12, 1936) .

Immaculáta Mater Dei, Regína cælórum, Mater misericórdiæ, advocáta et refúgium peccatórum, ecce ego illuminátus et incitátus grátiis, a te matérna benevoléntia large mihi impetrátis ex thesáuro divíno, státuo nunc et semper dare in manus tuas cor meum Iesu consecrándum.

Tibi ígitur, beatíssima Virgo, coram novem choris Angelórum cunctísque Sanctis illud trado, Tu autem, meo nómine, Iesu id cónsecra; et ex fidúcia filiáli, quam profíteor, certum mihi est te nunc et semper quantum póteris esse factúram, ut cor meum iúgiter totum sit Iesu, ímitans perfectíssime Sanctos, præsértim sanctum Ioseph, Sponsum tuum puríssimum. Amen (Bl. Vincentius Pallotti) .

371

O pure and immaculate and likewise blessed Virgin, who art the sinless Mother of thy Son, the mighty Lord of the universe, thou who art inviolate and altogether holy, the hope of the hopeless and sinful, we sing thy praises. We bless thee, as full of every grace, thou who didst bear the God-Man: we all bow low before thee; we invoke thee and implore thine aid. Rescue us, O holy and inviolate Virgin, from every necessity that presses upon us and from all the temptations of the devil. Be our intercessor and advocate at the hour of death and judgment; deliver us from the fire that is not extinguished and from the outer darkness; make us worthy of the glory of thy Son, O dearest and most clement Virgin Mother. Thou indeed art our only hope most sure and sacred in God's sight, to whom be honor and glory, majesty and dominion for ever and ever world without end. Amen (St. Ephrem the Syrian).

An indulgence of 3 years.

A plenary indulgence on the usual conditions, if the daily recitation of this prayer be continued for a month (S. P. Ap., Dec. 21, 1920 and Jan. 9, 1933).

O pura et immaculáta, eadémque benedícta Virgo, magni Fílii tui universórum Dómini Mater inculpáta, íntegra et sacrosanctíssima, desperántium atque reórum spes, te collaudámus. Tibi ut grátia pleníssimæ benedícimus, quæ Christum genuísti Deum et Hóminem: omnes coram te prostérnimur: omnes te invocámus et auxílium tuum implorámus. Eripe nos, o Virgo sancta atque intemeráta, a quacúmque ingruénte necessitáte et a cunctis tentatiónibus diáboli. Nostra conciliátrix et advocáta in hora

mortis atque iudícii esto: nosque a futúro inexstin-
guíbili igne et a ténebris exterióribus líbera: et Fílii
tui nos glória dignáre, o Virgo et Mater dulcíssima
ac clementíssima. Tu síquidem única spes nostra es
securíssima et sanctíssima apud Deum, cui glória et
honor, decus atque impérium in sempitérna sæcula
sæculórum. Amen (S. Ephræm, C. D.).

372

O God, who by the Immaculate Conception of the Virgin didst make ready a
fitting habitation for Thy Son, we beseech
Thee that Thou who didst keep her clean
from all stain by the precious death of the
same Thy Son, foreseen by Thee, mayest
grant unto us in like manner to be made
clean through her intercession and so attain
unto Thee. Through the same Christ our
Lord. Amen (Roman Missal).

An indulgence of 3 years.

A plenary indulgence on the usual conditions, if this prayer is
recited daily for a month (S. C. Ind., March 23, 1904; S. P. Ap.,
May 4, 1936).

Deus, qui per immaculátam Vírginis Conceptiónem
dignum Fílio tuo habitáculum præparásti, quæsumus, ut qui ex morte eiúsdem Fílii tui prævísa eam
ab omni labe præservásti, nos quoque mundos, eius
intercessióne, ad te perveníre concédas. Per eúmdem Christum Dóminum nostrum. Amen (ex Missali Romano).

373

Most holy Virgin, who, being predestined
to become the Mother of God, wast
preserved by a singular privilege from original sin and filled with grace, confirmed in
grace and enriched with all the gifts of the
Holy Ghost, do thou accept, we pray, the

homage of our most lively admiration and of our most profound veneration, the expression of our intense and reverent affection.

Beholding in thee a relic of the earthly paradise that was lost to man, purer and more spotless than the snowy splendor of mountain tops bathed in light, in that magnificent act of treading upon the proud head of the infernal serpent, the heavens exulted, earth was filled with joy, and hell trembled with fear. With thee came the bright dawn of man's redemption from sin, and when the children of men, having for centuries anxiously scanned the horizon in expectation of a fairer day, raised their heads, they discovered thee on high like a radiant vision of paradise and saluted thee with a cry of holy enthusiasm: "Thou art all fair, O Mary, and in thee there is no original stain."

At our feet, O Mary, the muddy torrent of lust did not halt, as it did before thine, that torrent that still flows across the world and threatens continually to submerge our souls also. We bear about within us and perceive around us countless deadly incentives that cease not to urge us on to savor the foul pleasures of sensual passion. O good Mother, enfold us under thy mantle, protect us from the snares of the infernal enemy, renew in us our love of the angelic virtue, and grant that, by ever keeping vivid in our hearts the reflections of thy heavenly brightness, we may be able one day to sing to thee a hymn of love and glory in the world to come.

The faithful who devoutly recite this prayer on the feast of the Immaculate Conception of the B. V. M., are granted:

An indulgence of 3 years;

A plenary indulgence on the usual conditions (S. P. Ap., May 20, 1941) ·

374

O Mary, Mother of God and Mother of us, thou who by a singular privilege, in virtue of the foreseen death of our Redeemer, wast redeemed from the first moment of thy conception and preserved immune from every spot of original sin, we firmly believe in this thy privilege and we proclaim it aloud, saying: "Thou art all fair, O Mary, and in thee there is no stain"; thou art the Immaculate; thy raiment is white as snow; thy face shines like the sun; in thee we marvel at the brightness of eternal light and the spotless mirror of divine beauty. Like the divine Redeemer, thou art wholly and utterly fair, for in Him there can be no stain and thou art His most perfect reflection.

We all rejoice in the Lord, as we celebrate the feast that recalls this singular privilege of thine, O Mary, Mother of God and our Mother, and we unite ourselves to thee in magnifying and thanking Our Lord, who through thee hath done such wondrous deeds, and hath given us in thee good cause for rejoicing.

We would be ever worthy to love thee and to sing thy glories, O Mary, our Immaculate Mother, but we are by nature sons of wrath, and only by grace can we become thy children and acceptable unto thee. From thee we hope for assistance in obtaining the pardon of our sins, the strength to overcome our wicked passions, and to escape the snares laid for us by the world and the devil. Wherefore, O Immaculate Mother, Mary, inspire in us an intense hatred of sin, perfect contrition for the sins we have committed, and a lively fear of falling again into sin; make our hearts and our bodies immaculate, lest we be confounded forever; and so, being cleansed of sin, with our passions under control, and the enemies of our salvation overcome, with pure hearts burning with love of thee, may we be able to sing to thee with unfaltering voices: "Thou art all fair, O Mary, and in thee there is no original stain; thou art our glory, thou art our joy."

The faithful who on the feast of the Immaculate Conception of the B. V. M., devoutly recite this prayer are granted:

An indulgence of 3 years;

A plenary indulgence on the usual conditions (S. P. Ap., June 10, 1949).

Note: A prayer to the Blessed Virgin Mary, conceived without sin, for the conversion of non-Catholics is found under n. 627; one for a happy death under n. 642.

Art. III
THE BLESSED VIRGIN SORROWING

I
INVOCATIONS

375

Holy Mother, pierce me through,
In my heart each wound renew,
Of my Saviour crucified (Roman Missal).

An indulgence of 500 days.

A plenary indulgence on the usual conditions, if this invocation is devoutly repeated every day for a month (S. P. Ap , Aug. 1, 1934).

S ancta Mater, istud agas,
 Crucifíxi fige plagas
Cordi meo válide.

(**ex** *Missali Romano)*

NOTE: For the indulgences attached to the recitation five times of the *Our Father*, *Hail Mary*, and *Glory be* with the above stanza, see n. 198.

376

M ary most sorrowful, Mother of Christians, pray for us.

An indulgence of 300 days (Pius X, Audience June 4, 1906, exhib. June 27, 1906; S. P. Ap., Sept. 23, 1935).

377

Virgin most sorrowful, pray for us.

An indulgence of 300 days.

An indulgence of 5 years, if, in honor of the B. V. M. Sorrowing, the *Hail Mary* is devoutly recited 7 times followed by the above invocation once (S. P. Ap., Nov. 22, 1934).

Virgo dolorosíssima, ora pro nobis.

II

SEQUENCE

Stabat Mater

378

A t the Cross her station keeping,
 Stood the mournful Mother weeping,
Close to Jesus to the last.

Through her heart, His sorrow sharing,
All His bitter anguish bearing,
 Lo! the piercing sword had passed.

O how sad and sore distressed
Was that Mother, highly blessed,
 Of the sole-begotten One.

Woe-begone, with heart's prostration,
Mother meek, the bitter Passion
  Saw she of her glorious Son.

Who on Christ's dear Mother gazing,
In her trouble so amazing,
  Born of woman, would not weep?

Who on Christ's dear Mother thinking,
Such a cup of sorrow drinking,
  Would not share her sorrow deep?

For His people's sins rejected,
Saw her Jesus unprotected,
  Saw with thorns, with scourges rent:

Saw her Son from judgment taken,
Her Beloved in death forsaken,
  Till His spirit forth He sent.

Fount of love and holy sorrow,
Mother! may my spirit borrow
  Somewhat of thy woe profound;

Unto Christ, with pure emotion,
Raise my contrite heart's devotion,
  Love to read in every wound.

Those five wounds on Jesus smitten,
Mother! in my heart be written,
  Deep as in thine own they be;

Thou, thy Savior's Cross who bearest,
Thou, thy Son's rebuke who sharest.
  Let me share them both with thee.

In the Passion of my Maker,
Be my sinful soul partaker,
  Weep till death and weep with thee;

Mine with thee be that sad station,
There to watch the great salvation,
  Wrought upon the atoning tree.

Virgin, thou of virgins fairest,
May the bitter woe thou bearest,
  Make on me impression deep.

Thus Christ's dying may I carry,
With Him in His Passion tarry,
  And His wounds in memory keep.

May His wound both wound and heal me,
He enkindle, cleanse, anneal me,
  Be His Cross my hope and stay.

May He, when the mountains quiver,
From that flame which burns for ever,
  Shield me on the judgment day.

Jesus, may Thy Cross defend me,
And Thy Mother's prayer befriend me,
  Let me die in Thy embrace;

When to dust my dust returneth,
Grant a soul that to Thee yearneth,
  In Thy paradise a place.   Amen (tr. cento)

An indulgence of 7 years.

A plenary indulgence on the usual conditions, if this sequence is recited daily for a month (S. C. Ind., June 18, 1876; S. P. Ap., Aug. 1, 1934).

Stabat Mater dolorósa
  Iuxta Crucem lacrimósa,
  Dum pendébat Fílius.

Cuius ánimam geméntem,
  Contristátam et doléntem
  Pertransívit gládius.

O quam tristis et afflícta
Fuit illa benedícta
Mater Unigéniti!

Quæ mærébat et dolébat,
Pia Mater, dum vidébat
Nati pœnas ínclyti.

Quis est homo, qui non fleret
Matrem Christi si vidéret
In tanto supplício?

Quis non posset contristári
Christi Matrem contemplári
Doléntem cum Fílio?

Pro peccátis suæ gentis
Vidit Iesum in torméntis,
Et flagéllis súbditum.

Vidit suum dulcem Natum
Moriéndo desolátum,
Dum emísit spíritum.

Eja Mater, fons amóris,
Me sentíre vim dolóris
Fac, ut tecum lúgeam.

Fac, ut árdeat cor meum
In amándo Christum Deum,
Ut sibi compláceam.

Sancta Mater, istud agas,
Crucifíxi fige plagas
Cordi meo válide.

Tui Nati vulneráti,
Tam dignáti pro me pati,
Pœnas mecum dívide.

Fac me tecum pie flere,
Crucifíxo condoKLere,
Donec ego víxero.

Iuxta Crucem tecum stare,
Et me tibi sociáre
In planctu desídero.

Virgo vírginum præclára,
Mihi iam non sis amára,
Fac me tecum plángere.

Fac, ut portem Christi mortem,
Passiónis fac consórtem,
Et plagas recólere.

Fac me plagis vulnerári,
Fac me Cruce inebriári,
Et cruóre Fílii.

Flammis ne urar succénsus,
Per te, Virgo, sim defénsus
In die iudícii.

Christe, cum sit hinc exíre,
Da per Matrem me veníre
Ad palmam victóriæ.

Quando corpus moriétur,
Fac, ut ánimæ donétur
Paradísi glória.   Amen.

NOTE: The hymn entitled, "Ave Mater dolorosa", for a happy death is found under n. 640.

III

DEVOUT EXERCISES

379

The faithful who, between three o'clock on the afternoon of Good Friday and noon of the following day, spend some time in devout meditation or offer some prayers, either in public or in private, in honor of the B. V. M. Sorrowing, may gain:

A plenary indulgence on the usual conditions.

Those who at other seasons of the year perform the same devout exercises between three o'clock on Friday afternoon and noon of the following Sunday, may gain:

An indulgence of 5 years;

A plenary indulgence on the usual conditions, if they perform this devout exercise each week for a month (S. C. Ind., June 18, 1822; June 16, 1931).

380

The faithful who make a novena in honor of the B. V. M. Sorrowing, at any time during the year, may gain:

An indulgence of 5 years once, on any day;

A plenary indulgence on the usual conditions at the end of the novena(Pius IX, Audience Jan. 3, 1849; S. C. Bishops and Religious, Jan. 28, 1850; S. C. Ind., Nov. 26, 1876; S. P. Ap., July 31, 1935) .

381

The faithful who, during the month of September, perform their devotions in honor of the B. V. M. Sorrowing, may gain:

An indulgence of 5 years once, on any day of the month;

A plenary indulgence on the usual conditions, if they persevere daily in this devout practice throughout the entire month(Apostolic Brief, April 3, 1857; S. C. Ind., Nov. 26, 1876 and Jan. 27, 1888; S. P. Ap., Nov. 12, 1936) .

382

The faithful who, on any of the seven Fridays which immediately precede either Feast of the Sorrows of the B. V. M. recite seven times the *Our Father*, *Hail Mary* and *Glory be*, may gain:

An indulgence of 7 years;

A plenary indulgence on the usual conditions (Apostolic Brief, March 22, 1918; S. P. Ap., March 18, 1932) .

IV

PRAYERS

383

℣. O God, come unto my assistance;
℞. O Lord, make haste to help me.
℣. Glory be, *etc.*
℞. As it was, *etc.*

I. I grieve for thee, O Mary most sorrowful, in the affliction of thy tender heart at the prophecy of the holy and aged Simeon. Dear Mother, by thy heart so afflicted, obtain for me the virtue of humility and the gift of the holy fear of God.

Hail Mary.

II. I grieve for thee, O Mary most sorrowful, in the anguish of thy most affectionate heart during the flight into Egypt and thy sojourn there. Dear Mother, by thy heart so troubled, obtain for me the virtue of generosity, especially towards the poor, and the gift of piety.

Hail Mary.

III. I grieve for thee, O Mary most sorrowful, in those anxieties which tried thy troubled heart at the loss of thy dear Jesus. Dear Mother, by thy heart so full of anguish, obtain for me the virtue of chastity and the gift of knowledge.

Hail Mary.

IV. I grieve for thee, O Mary most sorrowful, in the consternation of thy heart at meeting Jesus as He carried His Cross. Dear Mother, by thy heart so troubled, obtain for me the virtue of patience and the gift of fortitude.

Hail Mary.

V. I grieve for thee, O Mary most sorrowful in the martyrdom which thy generous heart endured in standing near Jesus in His agony. Dear Mother, by thy heart afflicted in such wise, obtain for me the virtue of temperance and the gift of counsel.

Hail Mary.

VI. I grieve for thee, O Mary most sorrowful, in the wounding of thy compassionate heart, when the side of Jesus was struck by the lance and His Heart was pierced. Dear Mother, by thy heart thus transfixed, obtain for me the virtue of fraternal charity and the gift of understanding.

Hail Mary.

VII. I grieve for thee, O Mary most sorrowful, for the pangs that wrenched thy most loving heart at the burial of Jesus. Dear Mother, by thy heart sunk in the bitterness of desolation, obtain for me the virtue of diligence and the gift of wisdom.

Hail Mary.

℣. Pray for us, O Virgin most sorrowful,

℞. That we may be made worthy of the promises of Christ.

Let us pray.

Let intercession be made for us, we beseech Thee, O Lord Jesus Christ, now and at the hour of our death, before the throne of Thy mercy, by the blessed Virgin Mary, Thy Mother, whose most holy soul was pierced by a sword of sorrow in the hour of Thy bitter passion. Through Thee, Jesus Christ, Saviour of the world, who with the Father and the Holy Ghost livest and reignest world without end.   Amen.

An indulgence of 5 years.

An indulgence of 7 years each day in September.

A plenary indulgence once a month on the usual conditions, if these prayers are recited daily (Pius VII, Audience Jan. 14, 1815; S. P. Ap., Oct. 6, 1935 and April 3, 1941).

V

PRAYERS

384

Mary, most holy Virgin and Queen of Martyrs, accept the sincere homage of my filial affection. Into thy heart, pierced by so many swords, do thou welcome my poor soul. Receive it as the companion of thy sorrows at the foot of the Cross, on which Jesus died for the redemption of the world. With thee, O sorrowful Virgin, I will gladly suffer all the trials, contradictions, and infirmities which it shall please our Lord to send me. I offer them all to thee in memory of thy sorrows, so that every thought of my mind, and every beat of my heart may be an act of compassion and of love for thee. And do thou, sweet Mother, have pity on me, reconcile me to thy divine Son Jesus, keep me in His grace and assist me in my last agony, so that I may be able to meet thee in heaven and sing thy glories. Amen.

An indulgence of 500 days (S. C. Ind., Mar. 20, 1887; S. P. Ap., May 19, 1934 and June 18, 1949).

385

Most holy Virgin and Mother, whose soul was pierced by a sword of sorrow in the Passion of thy divine Son, and who in His glorious Resurrection wast filled with never-ending joy at His triumph; obtain for us who call upon thee, so to be partakers in the adversities of Holy Church and the sorrows of the Sovereign Pontiff, as to be found worthy to rejoice with them in the consolations for which we pray, in the charity and peace of the same Christ our Lord. Amen.

An indulgence of 500 days (Pius X, Rescript in his own hand, Jan. 25, 1906; exhib. Feb. 3, 1906; S. P. Ap., Feb. 27, 1936).

O Virgo et Mater sanctíssima, cuius ánimam in divíni Fílii tui passióne dolóris gládius pertransívit, et quæ in gloriósa eius resurrectióne perénnem triumphántis lætítiam percepísti; ímpetra nobis supplícibus tuis, ita sanctæ Ecclésiæ adversitátibus Summíque Pontíficis dolóribus consociári, ut optátis étiam consolatiónibus lætificári cum ipsis mereámur, in caritáte et pace eiúsdem Christi Dómini nostri. Amen.

Art. IV
THE MOST PURE HEART OF MARY
I
INVOCATIONS
386

Sweet Heart of Mary, be my salvation.

An indulgence of 300 days.

A plenary indulgence once a month on the usual conditions, if repeated daily (S. C. Ind., Sept. 30, 1852).

387

O Heart most pure of the Blessed Virgin Mary, obtain for me from Jesus a pure and humble heart.

An indulgence of 300 days.

A plenary indulgence once a month on the usual conditions for the daily devout repetition of this invocation (S. P. Ap., Jan. 13, 1922 and April 23, 1934).

II
DEVOUT EXERCISES
388

The faithful who devoutly recite prayers in honor of the most pure Heart of Mary, at any season of the year, with the intention of persevering in the same for nine consecutive days may gain:

An indulgence of 5 years, once on any day of the novena;

A plenary indulgence on the usual conditions at the end of the novena (Pius IX, Audience Jan. 3, 1849; S. C. of Bishops and Religious, Jan. 28, 1850; S. C. Ind., Nov. 26, 1876; S. P. Ap., April 29, 1933) .

389

The faithful who offer prayers or other acts of piety in honor of the immaculate Heart of Mary, on any day during the month of August, may gain:

An indulgence of 5 years, once.

Those who persevere in such a devout exercise daily throughout the month of August, may gain:

A plenary indulgence on the usual conditions (S. C. Holy Off., March 13, 1913; S. P. Ap., June 2, 1935) .

III
AN ACT OF CONSECRATION
390

O Mary, Virgin most powerful and Mother of mercy, Queen of Heaven and Refuge of sinners, we consecrate ourselves to thine immaculate heart.

We consecrate to thee our very being and our whole life; all that we have, all that we love, all that we are. To thee we give our bodies, our hearts and our souls; to thee we give our homes, our families, our country. We desire that all that is in us and around us may belong to thee, and may share in the benefits of thy motherly benediction. And that this act of consecration may be truly efficacious and lasting, we renew this day at thy feet the promises of our Baptism and our first Holy Communion. We pledge ourselves to profess courageously and at all times the truths of our holy Faith, and to live as befits Catholics who are duly submissive to all the directions of the Pope and the Bishops in communion with him. We pledge ourselves to keep the commandments of God and His Church, in particular to keep holy the Lord's Day. We likewise pledge ourselves to make the consoling practices of the Christian religion, and above all, Holy Communion, an integral part of our lives, in so far as we shall be able so to do. Finally, we promise thee, O glorious Mother of God and loving Mother of men, to devote ourselves whole-heartedly to the service of thy blessed cult, in order to hasten and assure, through the sovereignty of thine immaculate heart, the coming of the kingdom of the Sacred Heart of thine adorable Son, in our own hearts and in those of all men, in our country and in all the world, as in heaven, so on earth. Amen.

An indulgence of 3 years.

A plenary indulgence, on the usual conditions, if this act of consecration is repeated daily for a month (S. C. Ind., Feb. 21, 1907; S. P. Ap., April 29, 1933).

391

Queen of the most holy Rosary, help of Christians, refuge of the human race, victorious in all the battles of God, we prostrate ourselves in supplication before thy throne, in the sure hope of obtaining mercy and of receiving grace and timely aid in our present calamities, not through any merits of our own on which we do not rely, but only through the immense goodness of thy mother's Heart. In thee and in thy Immaculate Heart, at this grave hour of human history, do we put our trust; to thee we consecrate ourselves, not only with all of Holy Church, which is the mystical body of thy Son Jesus, and which is suffering in so many of her members, being subjected to manifold tribulations and persecutions, but also with the whole world, torn by discords, agitated with hatred, the victim of its own iniquities. Be thou moved by the sight of such material and moral degradation, such sorrows, such anguish, so many tormented souls in danger of eternal loss! Do thou, O Mother of mercy, obtain for us from God a Christ-like reconciliation of the nations, as well as those graces which can convert the souls of men in an instant, those graces which prepare the way and make certain the long desired coming of peace on earth. O Queen of peace, pray for us, and grant peace unto the world in the truth, the justice, and the charity of Christ. Above all, give us peace in our hearts, so that the kingdom of God may spread its borders in the tranquillity of order. Accord thy protection to unbelievers and to all those who lie within the shadow of death; cause the Sun of Truth to rise upon them; may they be enabled to join with us in repeating before the Saviour of the world: "Glory to God in the highest, and on earth peace to men of good will." Give peace to the nations that are separated from us by error or discord, and in a special manner to those peoples who profess a singular devotion toward thee; bring them back to Christ's one fold, under the one true Shepherd. Obtain full freedom for the holy Church of God; defend her from her enemies; check the ever-increasing torrent of immorality; arouse in the faithful a love of purity, a practical Christian life, and an apostolic zeal, so that the multitude of those who serve God may increase in merit and in number. Finally, even as the Church and all mankind were once consecrated to the Heart of thy Son Jesus, because He was for all those who put their hope in Him an inexhaustible source of victory and salvation, so in like manner do we consecrate ourselves forever to thee also and to thy Immaculate Heart, O Mother of us and Queen of the world; may thy love and patronage hasten the day when the kingdom of God shall be victorious and all the nations, at peace with God and with one another, shall call thee blessed and intone with thee, from the rising of the sun to its going down, the everlasting "Magnificat" of glory, of love, of gratitude to the Heart of Jesus, in which alone we can find truth, life, and peace (Pope Pius XII).

An indulgence of 3 years.

A plenary indulgence on the usual conditions, if this act of consecration is devoutly repeated every day for a month (Pius XII, Rescript from the Secretariate of State, Nov. 17, 1942, document exhibited, Nov. 19, 1942).

IV
PRAYERS

392

℣. O God, come unto my assistance;
℞. O Lord, make haste to help me.

℣. Glory be to the Father, *etc.*

℟. As it was, *etc.*

I. Immaculate Virgin, who being conceived without sin, didst direct every movement of thy most pure heart toward God, and wast always submissive to His divine will; obtain for me the grace to hate sin with all my heart and to learn from thee to live in perfect resignation to the will of God.

Our Father *once and* Hail Mary *seven times*.

II. O Mary, I wonder at that profound humility, which troubled thy blessed heart at the message of the Angel Gabriel, that thou hadst been chosen to be the Mother of the Son of the most high God, the while thou didst profess thyself His lowly handmaiden; ashamed at the sight of my own pride, I beg of thee the grace of a contrite and humble heart, so that, acknowledging my misery, I may come to attain the glory promised to those who are truly humble of heart.

Our Father *once and* Hail Mary *seven times*.

III. Blessed Virgin, who didst keep in thy heart the precious treasure of the words of Jesus thy Son and, pondering over the sublime mysteries therein contained, couldst live only for God, how am I confounded by the coldness of my heart! Ah, dear Mother, obtain for me the grace of meditating always on the holy law of God, and of seeking to follow thine example in the fervent practice of all the Christian virtues.

Our Father *once and* Hail Mary *seven times.*

IV. O glorious Queen of Martyrs, whose sacred heart, in the Passion of thy Son, was cruelly pierced by the sword foretold by the holy and aged Simeon; obtain for my heart true courage and holy patience to bear well the tribulations and trials of this wretched life; may I show myself to be thy true child by crucifying my flesh and all its desires in following the mortification of the Cross.

Our Father *once and* Hail Mary *seven times.*

V. O Mary, mystic rose, whose lovable heart, burning with the living fire of love, adopted us as thy children at the foot of the Cross, becoming thus our most tender Mother, make me experience the sweetness of thy motherly heart and the power of thine intercession with Jesus, in all the dangers that beset me during life, and especially at the dread hour of my death; in such wise may my heart be ever united to thine, and love Jesus both now and through endless ages. Amen.

Our Father *once and* Hail Mary *seven times.*

An indulgence of 3 years.

A plenary indulgence on the usual conditions, for the daily recitation of these prayers over the period of one month (S. C. Ind., Dec. 11, 1854; S. P. Ap., July 2, 1931).

V
A PRAYER
393

O Heart of Mary, Mother of God, and our Mother; Heart most worthy of love, in which the adorable Trinity is ever well-pleased, worthy of the veneration and love of all the Angels and of all men; Heart most like to the Heart of Jesus, of which thou art the perfect image; Heart, full of goodness, ever compassionate toward our miseries; deign to melt our icy hearts and grant that they may be wholly changed into the likeness of the Heart of Jesus, our divine Saviour. Pour into them the love of thy virtues, enkindle in them that divine fire with which thou thyself dost ever burn. In thee let Holy Church find a safe shelter; protect her and be her dearest refuge, her tower of strength, impregnable against every assault of her enemies. Be thou the way which leads to Jesus, and the channel, through which we receive all the graces needful for our salvation. Be our refuge in time of trouble, our solace in the midst of trial, our strength against temptation, our haven in persecution, our present help in every danger, and especially at the hour of death, when all hell shall let loose against us its legions to snatch away our souls, at that dread moment, that hour so full of fear, whereon our eternity depends. Ah, then most tender Virgin, make us to feel the sweetness of thy motherly heart, and the might of thine intercession with Jesus, and open to us a safe refuge in that very fountain of mercy, whence we may come to praise Him with thee in paradise, world without end. Amen.

An indulgence of 500 days.

A plenary indulgence on the usual conditions, provided that this prayer be devoutly recited every day for a month. (S. C. Ind., Aug. 18, 1807 and Feb. 1, 1816; S. P. Ap., Sept. 15, 1934) ·

Art. V
THE HOLY ROSARY OF THE BLESSED VIRGIN MARY
A) AS PRACTISED IN THE UNIVERSAL CHURCH

I. AN INVOCATION

394

Queen of the most holy Rosary, pray for us.

An indulgence of 300 days. (Holy Office, Oct. 1, 1915; S. P. Ap., Nov. 24, 1933).

Regina sacratíssimi Rosárii, ora pro nobis.

II. THE RECITATION OF THE ROSARY

395

a) The faithful, whenever they recite a third part of the Rosary with devotion, may gain:

An indulgence of 5 years. (Bull "Ea quæ ex fidelium", Sixtus IV, May 12, 1479; S. C. Ind., Aug. 29, 1899; S. P. Ap., March 18, 1932).

A plenary indulgence on the usual conditions, if they do this for an entire month. (Pius XII, Jan. 22, 1952).

b) If they recite a third part of the Rosary in company with others, whether in public or in private, they may gain:

An indulgence of 10 years, once a day;

A plenary indulgence on the last Sunday of each month, with the addition of confession, Communion and a visit to a church or public oratory, if they perform such a recitation at least three times in any of the preceding weeks.

If however they recite this together in a family group, besides the partial indulgence of 10 years, they are granted:

A plenary indulgence twice a month, if they perform this recitation daily for a month, go to confession, receive Holy Communion, and visit some church or public oratory. (S. C. Ind., May 12, 1851 and Aug. 29, 1899; S. P. Ap., Mar. 18, 1932 and July 26, 1946).

The faithful who daily recite a third part of the Rosary with devotion in a family group, besides the indulgences already granted under 395b), are also granted:

A plenary indulgence on condition of confession and Communion, on each Saturday, on two other days of the week, and on each of the Feasts of the Blessed Virgin Mary in the universal Calendar, namely, the Immaculate Conception, the Purification, the Apparition of Our Blessed Lady at Lourdes, the Annunciation, the Seven

Dolors (Friday in Passion Week), the Visitation, Our Lady of Mt. Carmel, Our Lady of the Snows, the Assumption, the Immaculate Heart of the Blessed Virgin Mary, the Nativity of the Blessed Virgin Mary, the Most Holy Name of Mary, the Seven Dolors (Sept. 15), Our Lady of Ransom, the Most Holy Rosary, the Maternity of the Blessed Virgin Mary, the Presentation of the Blessed Virgin Mary. (S. P. Ap., Oct. 11, 1954).

c) Those who piously recite a third part of the Rosary in the presence of the Blessed Sacrament publicly exposed or even reserved in the tabernacle, as often as they do this, may gain:

A plenary indulgence, on condition of confession and Communion. (Apostolic Brief, Sept. 4, 1927)

NOTE: 1. The decades may be separated, if the entire chaplet is completed on the same day. (S. C. Ind., July 8, 1908).

2. If, as is the custom during recitation of the Rosary, the faithful make use of a chaplet, they may gain other indulgences in addition to those enumerated above, if the chaplet is blessed by a religious of the Order of Preachers or another priest having special faculties. (S. C. Ind., April 13, 1726, Jan. 22, 1858 and Aug. 29, 1899).

III
DEVOUT EXERCISES
396

The faithful who at any time of the year devoutly offer their prayers in honor of our Lady of the Rosary, with the intention of continuing the same for nine consecutive days, may gain:

An indulgence of 5 years once on any day of the novena;

A plenary indulgence on the usual conditions at the close of the novena (Pius IX, Audience Jan. 3, 1849; S. C. Bishops and Religious, Jan. 28, 1850; S. C. Ind., Nov. 26, 1876; S. P. Ap., June 29, 1932).

397

The faithful who resolve to perform a devout exercise in honor of Our Lady of the Rosary for fifteen uninterrupted Saturdays (or these being impeded, for as many respective Sundays immediately following) if they devoutly recite at least a third part of the Rosary or meditate on its mysteries in some other manner may gain:

A plenary indulgence on the usual conditions, on any of these fifteen Saturdays, or corresponding Sundays (S. C. Ind., Sept. 21, 1889 and Sept. 17, 1892; S. P. Ap., Aug. 3, 1936).

398

The faithful who during the month of October recite at least a third part of the Rosary, either publicly or privately, may gain:

An indulgence of 7 years each day;

A plenary indulgence, if they perform this devout exercise on the Feast of the Rosary and throughout the Octave, and moreover, go to confession, receive Holy Communion and visit a church or public oratory;

A plenary indulgence, with the addition of confession, Communion and a visit to a church or public oratory, if they perform this same recitation of the holy Rosary for at least ten days after the Octave of the aforesaid Feast (S. C. Ind., July 23, 1898 and Aug. 29, 1899; S. P. Ap., March 18, 1932).

IV

A PRAYER

399

Queen of the most holy Rosary, in these times of such brazen impiety, manifest thy power with the signs of thine ancient victories, and from thy throne, whence thou dost dispense pardon and graces, mercifully regard the Church of thy Son, His Vicar on earth, and every order of clergy and laity, who are sore oppressed in the mighty conflict. Do thou, who art the powerful vanquisher of all heresies, hasten the hour of mercy, even though the hour of God's justice is every day provoked by the countless sins of men. For me who am the least of men, kneeling before thee in supplication, do thou obtain the grace I need to live righteously upon earth and to reign among the just in heaven, the while in company with all faithful Christians throughout the world, I salute thee and acclaim thee as Queen of the most holy Rosary:

Queen of the most holy Rosary, pray for us.

An indulgence of 500 days (Leo XIII, Audience July 3, 1886; S. P. Ap., April 29, 1933).

B) AS IT IS PRACTISED IN THE VALLEY OF POMPEII

I

A VISIT

400

The faithful who devoutly visit the Pompeian image of Our Lady of the holy Rosary, exposed for veneration in some church, public or semi-public oratory (this last for those who may lawfully use it), may gain:

An indulgence of 300 days;

A plenary indulgence on the 8th day of May and on the Feast of the holy Rosary, if, in addition, they make their confession, receive Holy Communion and pray for the intentions of His Holiness (Apostolic Brief, July 20, 1925).

II

A PRAYER TO BE SAID AT MIDDAY ON THE 8TH DAY OF MAY AND THE FIRST SUNDAY OF OCTOBER

401

I. O august Queen of victories, O Virgin-ruler of paradise, at whose powerful name the heavens rejoice and hell trembles for fear, O glorious Queen of the most holy Rosary, all of us, thy highly favored children whom thy goodness hath chosen to raise a temple to thee at Pompeii in this our day, here humbly kneeling at thy feet, on this most solemn day of the Feast of thy fresh triumphs on earth over false gods and devils, pour forth with tears the deepest affection of our hearts, and with the confidence of sons we show our miseries to thee.

Ah, from that throne of mercy where thou art seated in queenly state, turn thy pitying gaze upon us, O Mary, and upon our families, upon Italy, upon Europe and upon the universal Church; do thou have compassion upon us by reason of the miseries whereby we are encompassed, and the tribulations that make life bitter for us. See, dear Mother, how many perils to body and soul surround us, what calamities and afflictions oppress us! O Mother, stay the arm of thine unheeded Son's justice and win the hearts of sinners by thy mercy; for they are our brethren and thy children, for whom the Precious Blood of Jesus was shed and thine own most gentle heart was pierced by the sword of sorrow. Show unto all men this day that thou art indeed the Queen of peace and forgiveness.

Hail holy Queen, *etc.*

2. Too true it is, alas, that we, although we are thy children, have been among the first to begin to crucify Jesus afresh in our hearts by sin and to renew the piercing of thy tender heart. Yes, we confess it, we deserve the sharpest scourges of God's anger. None the less do thou remember how, on Calvary's heights, thou didst gather up the last drops of the Precious Blood and didst receive the final testament of the dying Sav-

iour. And that testament of a God, sealed by the Precious Blood of the God-Man, proclaimed thee our Mother, the Mother of sinners. Wherefore, just as thou art our Mother, so thou art likewise our advocate and our hope; to thee do we sigh, and stretch forth our hands in supplication, crying out for mercy.

Let compassion move thee, good Mother, compassion for us, for our souls, for our families, our relations and our friends, for our departed brethren, and above all, for our enemies and for the many souls who call themselves Christians and who, nevertheless, continue to wound the loving Heart of thy dear Son. We ask this day with tears for mercy, mercy upon the nations that have gone astray, upon the whole of Europe, upon the entire world, that all may return in penitence to thy heart. Have mercy upon them all, O Mother of mercy!

Hail holy Queen, *etc.*

3. What will it cost thee, O Mary, to hear our prayer? What will it cost thee to save us? Hath not Jesus placed in thy hands all the treasures of His grace and mercy? Thou sittest, crowned as a queen, at the right hand of thy Son, shining with undying glory, above all the choirs of Angels. Thy dominion reaches as far as the heavens, and to thee the earth and all creatures dwelling thereon are subject. Thy dominion reaches even down to the abyss of hell, and thou alone, O Mary,

dost save us from the hands of Satan. Thou art omnipotent through grace; thou, therefore, canst save us. But if thou sayest that thou art unwilling to help us because we are ungrateful children and undeserving of Thy protection, at least do tell us to whom we must go to be delivered from so many evils. Ah! no, thy motherly heart will not suffer thy children to be lost. The divine Child whom we see upon thy knees and the mystic chaplet in thy hand inspire us with confidence that we shall be heard. We put all our trust in thee; we cast ourselves at thy feet; we surrender ourselves, like helpless children, to the embrace of the tenderest of mothers. Today, yes, this very day, we look to receive from thee the graces for which we sigh.

Hail, holy Queen, *etc.*

Let us ask a blessing from Mary.

One last grace do we beg of thee, our Queen, and thou canst not deny it on this most solemn day. Grant unto all of us thy abiding love and, in a special manner, thy maternal blessing. No, we will not rise from before thy feet this day until thou bless us. At this very moment, O Mary, bless the Supreme Pontiff. To the former laurels of thy chaplet, to the ancient triumphs of thy Rosary, whence thou art called the Queen of Victories, add this favor also, O Mother: give victory to the cause of religion and peace to human society. Bless our Bishop and priests, especially those who are zealous for the honor of thy sanctuary. Finally bless all who are associated with thy new shrine at Pompeii, and all who cultivate and spread the devotion to thy most holy Rosary.

O blessed Rosary of Mary, sweet chain that binds us to God, bond of love that makes us one with the Angels, tower of salvation amid the attacks of hell, safe harbor in the universal shipwreck, we shall never forget thee. Thou shalt be our consolation in the hour of death's agony, thine shall be the last kiss of our ebbing life. The last whisper of our dying lips shall be thy sweet name, O Queen of the Rosary in the Vale of Pompeii, our dearest Mother, only refuge of sinners, sovereign comforter of the sorrowful. Be thou everywhere blessed, now and for ever, on earth and in heaven. Amen.

Hail, holy Queen, *etc.*

An indulgence of 7 years.

A plenary indulgence on the usual conditions (Apostolic Brief, July 20, 1925; S. P. Ap., March 18, 1932).

III

IMPETRATORY PRAYERS FOR A NOVENA OR A TRIDUUM

402

A Preparatory Prayer to St. Catherine

O Saint Catherine of Siena, my guardian and mistress, thou who from heaven dost assist thy clients when they recite Mary's Rosary, assist me at this hour and vouchsafe to join with me in this Novena to the Queen of the Rosary who hath set the throne of her graces in the Vale of Pompeii, so that through thine intercession, I may obtain the grace that I desire.   Amen.

℣. O God, come unto my assistance;
℟. O Lord, make haste to help me.
℣. Glory be, *etc.*
℟. As it was, *etc.*

1. O Virgin immaculate and Queen of the Rosary, in these days of dead faith and triumphant impiety, thou hast been pleased to set up thy throne as Queen and Mother, upon the ancient site of Pompeii, the dwelling place of pagans long since dead.   And from the place where once men worshiped false gods and demons, thou, as Mother of divine grace, dost in these our times scatter everywhere the treasures of heavenly mercies. Ah, from that throne where thou reignest as Queen of mercy, turn, dear Mother upon me also thine eyes of mercy, and have pity on me who have such great need of thy assistance.   Show thyself to me, as to so many others, a true Mother of mercy: "Show thyself a Mother"; while with all my heart I salute thee and call upon thee as my Sovereign and Queen of the most holy Rosary.

Hail, holy Queen, *etc.*

2. Humbly bending at the foot of thy throne, O great and glorious Lady, my soul venerates thee in the midst of the groans and anguish that oppress me beyond measure. In spite of the trials and tribulations wherewith I am encompassed, I raise my eyes with confidence to thee who hast deigned to choose

for thy earthly habitation the fields of poor and forsaken country folk. And there, facing the city and amphitheatre devoted to heathen pleasures, where now reign silence and ruin, thou, as the Queen of Victories, hast lifted up thy mighty voice to summon from Italy and from every quarter of the Catholic world, thy devoted children to build thee a shrine in thine honor. Ah, be thou moved to pity for this soul of mine which lies trampled in the mire. Have mercy on me, dear Lady, have mercy on me, for I am filled beyond measure with misery and humiliation. Thou who art the Help of Christians, draw me from the tribulations wherein I am miserably entangled. Thou who art our life, triumph over the death which threatens my soul in these dangers to which I find myself exposed; give me peace again, tranquillity, love and salvation.

Hail, holy Queen, *etc.*

3. Ah, the very thought that so many have been blessed only because they had recourse to thee with confidence, inspires me with fresh hope and courage to call upon thee to come to my assistance. Thou didst once promise Saint Dominic that whosoever desired the grace of God should obtain it by means of thy Rosary: now I, with rosary in hand, call upon thee, my Mother, to keep thy maternal promises. Nay, thou thyself in these our times dost work never-ceasing wonders to call thy children to honor thee in

thy shrine of Pompeii. Be thou pleased, therefore, to wipe away our tears and assuage our sorrows! With my heart upon my lips and with lively faith, I call upon thee and invoke thee: my Mother, dearest Mother, Mother fairest, Mother gentlest, help me! Mother and Queen of the holy Rosary of Pompeii, delay not to stretch forth thy mighty hand to save me, for delay, as thou seest, will bring me down to ruin.

Hail, holy Queen, *etc.*

4. To whom else can I have recourse, if not to thee, who art the solace of the wretched, the comfort of the desolate, the consolation of the afflicted? I confess it to thee, my soul is exceeding sorrowful, weighed down as it is by countless sins, it deserves the fire of hell, it is unworthy to receive thy favors. But art not thou the hope of the hopeless, the great mediatrix between man and God, our powerful advocate at the throne of the Most High, and the refuge of sinners? Ah, do thou only say the word in my behalf to thy divine Son, and He will hear and answer thee. Ask Him, then, O Mother, for this favor, of which I stand so much in need. · · · Thou alone canst obtain it for me; thou art my only hope, my consolation, my sweetness, my whole life. Such is my hope. Amen.

Hail, holy Queen, *etc.*

5. O Virgin and Queen of the Holy Rosary, thou art the Daughter of our heavenly Father, the Mother of God the Son, and the Bride of

the Spirit with His sevenfold gift. Thou canst obtain all things from the ever Blessed Trinity, thou must therefore obtain for me this favor which is so necessary for me, provided that it be no obstacle to my eternal salvation . . . ; I ask it of thee through thy Immaculate Conception, thy divine Motherhood, thy joys, thy sorrows and thy triumphs; I ask it of thee through the Heart of thy dear Jesus, and the nine months wherein thou didst carry Him in thy bosom, the hardships of His life, His bitter Passion, His death on the Cross, His most holy Name, the shedding of His Precious Blood; finally I ask it of thee through thine own most sweet heart and thy glorious name, O Mary, thou who art the star of the sea, our mighty mistress, the sea of sorrow, the gate of heaven, and the Mother of every grace. In thee I put my trust; from thee I hope for all things. It is thy task to save me. Amen.

Hail, holy Queen, *etc.*

℣. Make me worthy to praise thee, O sacred Virgin;

℟. Give me strength against thine enemies.

℣. Pray for us, O Queen of the most Holy Rosary,

℟. That we may be made worthy of the promises of Christ.

Let us pray.

O God, whose only begotten Son, by His life, death, and resurrection, hath purchased for us the rewards of everlasting life; grant, we beseech Thee, that we, who meditate upon these mysteries of the most holy Rosary of the Blessed Virgin Mary, may both imitate what they contain, and attain to what they promise. Through the same Christ our Lord. Amen.

Hail Mary, *etc.*

Prayer to St. Dominic and St. Catherine

O holy Priest of God and glorious Patriarch, Saint Dominic, thou who wast the friend, the well-beloved son and the confidant of the Queen of Heaven, and didst work so many miracles by the power of the holy Rosary; and thou, Saint Catherine of Siena, first daughter of this Order of the Rosary, and powerful mediator at Mary's throne with the Heart of Jesus, with whom thou didst exchange thy heart; do you, my beloved Saints, have regard to my necessities and pity the sad condition in which I now find myself. On earth you opened your hearts to the miseries of your fellow-men and your hands were strong to help them; now in heaven your charity hath not grown less nor hath your power waned. Pray, ah, pray for me to the Mother of the Rosary and to her divine Son, for I have great confidence that through your assistance I shall obtain the favor I so much desire. Amen.

Glory be, *etc., three times.*

In honor of St. Vincent Ferrer, Glory be, *etc.*

In honor of St. Thomas Aquinas, Glory be, *etc.*

An indulgence of 7 years on each of the days of the Novena or Triduum, if the devotions are held publicly in a church or public oratory.

An indulgence of 3 years on each day of the Novena or Triduum, if performed privately by the faithful.

A plenary indulgence, on the usual conditions, at the close of the exercise (Apostolic Brief, July 20, 1925; S. P. Ap., Nov. 15, 1927 and March 18, 1932).

IV

PRAYERS FOR A NOVENA OR TRIDUUM OF THANKSGIVING

403

℣. O God, come unto my assistance;
℞. O Lord, make haste to help me.
℣. Glory be to the Father, *etc.*
℞. As it was in the beginning, *etc.*

1. Behold me at thy knees, immaculate Mother of Jesus, who dost rejoice at being invoked as Queen of the Rosary in the Vale of Pompeii. With joy in my heart, and my mind filled with the most lively gratitude, I return to thee who art my most generous benefactor, my dearest Lady, the Queen of my heart, to thee who hast shown thyself my true Mother, the Mother who loves me exceedingly. I was filled with groanings and thou didst hear my cry; I was in affliction and thou didst comfort me; I was in the valley of the shadow of death and thou didst bring me peace. The sorrows and pains of death laid siege to my soul, and thou, dear Mother, from thy throne in Pompeii with one look of pity didst make me serene. Who hath ever turned to thee with confidence and

hath not been heard? If only the whole world knew thy great goodness, thy tender compassion for those who suffer, how all creation would have recourse to thee! Mayest thou be ever blessed, O Virgin and Queen of Pompeii, by me and by all others, both men and Angels, on earth and in heaven.

Glory be to the Father; Hail, holy Queen.

2. I return thanks to God and to thee, O Mother of God, for the fresh blessings that have been showered upon me through thy pity and loving-kindness. What a fate would mine have been, hadst thou rejected my sighs and tears! Let the Angels in paradise, the glorious choir of the Apostles, the noble army of the Martyrs, the holy bands of Virgins and Confessors give thee thanks in my behalf. Let the many souls of sinners, saved by thine intercession, who now enjoy in heaven the vision of thine unfading loveliness, give thanks to thee in my behalf. I would that all creatures might love thee in union with me, and that the whole world might repeat the refrain of my hymns of thanksgiving. What can I render to thee, O Queen, rich in mercy and magnificence? What remains of life I dedicate to thee and to the spreading of thy devotion, O Virgin of the Rosary of Pompeii, through whose invocation the grace of the Lord hath visited me. I will spread abroad devotion to thy Rosary, I will tell all men of the mercies thou hast obtained for me; I will evermore pro-

claim thy great goodness toward me, so that other sinners, as unworthy as I, may turn to thee in all confidence.

Glory be to the Father; Hail, holy Queen.

3. By what name shall I invoke thee, thou white dove of peace? Under what title shall I call upon thee whom the holy Doctors have named the Mistress of creation, the gate of life, the temple of God, the palace of light, the glory of the heavens, the Saint of saints, the wonder of wonders, the paradise of the Most High God? Thou art the treasurer of divine graces, the omnipotent answer to prayer, nay, the very mercy of God, which is shown toward the unfortunate. But I know, too, that it is pleasing to thy heart to be invoked as Queen of the Rosary in the Vale of Pompeii. And as I hail thee by this title, I perceive the sweetness of thy mystic name, O rose of paradise, transplanted into this valley of tears, to sweeten our miseries who are banished children of Eve; red rose of charity, more fragrant than all the spices of Libanus, who by the perfume of thy heavenly sweetness dost draw the hearts of sinners to the Heart of God in this thy valley of Pompeii. Thou art the rose of eternal freshness, watered by the streams of water from heaven; thou hast set thy roots in a land parched by a rain of fire; thou art a rose of spotless beauty, who in a place of desolation hast planted a garden of the delights of the Lord. May God be praised, who hath made thy name so wonderful! Bless, O ye peoples, bless the name of the Virgin of Pompeii, for all the earth is full of her loving-kindness.

Glory be to the Father; Hail, holy Queen.

4. In the midst of the tempests which have overwhelmed me, I have lifted up mine eyes to thee, thou new star of hope that hath risen in these latter days above the valley of ruin. From the depths of my bitterness I have lifted up my voice to thee, O Queen of the Rosary of Pompeii, and I have felt the power of that title so dear to thee. Hail, I shall ever cry, hail to thee, thou Mother of pity, fathomless ocean of grace, sea of goodness and compassion! Who shall be worthy to sing the new glories of thy Rosary, the fresh victories of thy chaplet? In this valley, where Satan devoured souls in olden times, thou hast prepared salvation for a world, that is tearing itself from the loving arms of Jesus in order to cast itself into the deadly embrace of Satan. Triumphantly dost thou trample underfoot the fragments of pagan temples, and upon the ruins of ancient idolatry thou hast established the throne of thine imperial sway. Thou hast changed the valley of death into a valley of resurrection and life; and in a land once dominated by thine enemy, thou hast built a city of refuge, where thou dost receive thy people in safety. Behold, thy children, scattered throughout the world, have erected thy throne there, as a witness to thy miracles, as a memorial of thy mer-

cies. From that throne thou hast called me to be among the sons of thy predilection; upon poor me thy merciful glance hath rested. May thy works be praised for ever, O Blessed Lady, and praised be the marvels wrought by thee in this valley of desolation and death.

Glory be to the Father; Hail, holy Queen.

5. Let every tongue speak of thy glory, dear Lady, and let the harmonious accord of our praises sound from evening even to the morning. May all generations call thee blessed and may all the coasts of earth and all the mansions of heaven re-echo the hymn of praise. Nay, I will call thee thrice blessed, in union with the Angels and Principalities; thrice blessed, with the angelical Powers, with the Virtues of heaven, with the supernal Dominations; most blessed will I proclaim thee with the Thrones, with the Cherubim and Seraphim. O Queen of salvation, cease not to turn thine eyes in pity upon this thy family, upon this nation, upon the Church universal. Above all, deny me not the greatest of graces; that is, let not my frailty ever separate me from thee. Grant that I may persevere even to the end in the love and faith wherewith my soul is on fire at this moment. Grant, also, that all of us, who come together in the beauty of thy sanctuary in Pompeii, may be of the number of the elect. O chaplet of the Rosary of my Mother, I press thee to my breast and I kiss thee in a spirit of profound reverence. Thou art the way that leads to the attainment of every virtue, the treasure of merits for paradise, the pledge of my predestination, the mighty chain that binds fast the enemy of our salvation, a source of peace to all who give thee due honor in this life, and a foretaste of victory to those who kiss thee at the hour of death. In that last hour, I shall look to thee, O Mother; thy coming will be the sign of my salvation, thy Rosary will open to me the gates of paradise. Amen.

Glory be to the Father; Hail, holy Queen.

℣. Pray for us, O Queen of the most holy Rosary;

℟. That we may be made worthy of the promises of Christ.

Let us pray.

O God and Father of our Lord Jesus Christ, who hast taught us to come to Thee with confidence and to call Thee: Our Father, who art in heaven, ah! good Lord, to whom it belongeth to have mercy and to pardon, graciously hear us through the intercession of the immaculate Virgin Mary, for we glory in the title of children of the Rosary; accept our humble thanks for the gifts we have received from Thee; and do Thou make the shrine which Thou hast set up in the sanctuary of Pompeii, every day more glorious and more lasting, through the merits of Jesus Christ our Lord. Amen.

An indulgence of 7 years on each day of the Novena or Triduum, if the prayers are said publicly in a church or public oratory.

An indulgence of 3 years on each day of a Novena or Triduum made privately.

A plenary indulgence, on the usual conditions, at the end of the exercise (Apostolic Brief, July 20, 1925; S. P. Ap., Nov. 15, 1927 and March 18, 1932) .

V

A PRAYER

404

O Virgin immaculate and Queen of the Rosary, in these days of dead faith and triumphant impiety, thou hast been pleased to establish thy throne as Queen and Mother in the ancient land of Pompeii, once the home of paganism. From that place, where men of old worshiped idols and evil spirits, do thou this day, as the Mother of divine graces scatter far and wide the treasures of heavens mercy. Ah, from that throne where thou reignest in mercy, turn, dear Mother, thine eyes of pity even upon me and be gracious unto me who have so great need of thine assistance. Show thyself to me, even as thou hast shown thyself to so many others, a true Mother of mercy: "Monstra te esse Matrem" (Show Thyself a Mother); while with all my heart I salute thee and invoke thee as my sovereign Lady and Queen of the most holy Rosary.

Hail, holy Queen.

An indulgence of 300 days (Apostolic Brief, July 20, 1925) .

NOTE: Another prayer for the conversion of non-Catholics is found under number 628.

Art. VI

OUR LADY OF MOUNT CARMEL

I

AN INVOCATION

405

O Queen, who art the beauty of Carmel, pray for us.

An indulgence of 300 days (S. P. Ap., Nov. 8, 1921).

Regína decor Carméli, ora pro nobis.

II

A PRAYER

406

O blessed Virgin, full of grace, Queen of all Saints, how sweet it is for me to venerate thee under the title of our Lady of Mount Carmel. It takes me back to the days of the prophet Elias, when thou wast prefigured on Mount Carmel under the form of the little cloud, from which, as it increased, there fell a kindly rain, symbolic of the sanctifying graces that come to us from thee. Even from the days of the Apostles, thou hast been honored under this mystic title; and today I am filled with joy at the thought that we are united with those first clients of thine, and in union with them we salute thee, saying: O beauty of Carmel, glory of Libanus, thou purest of lilies, mystic rose in the flowering garden of the Church. Meanwhile, O Virgin of virgins, be mindful of me in my misery, and show thyself my Mother. Shed upon me ever more and more the living light of that faith which made thee blessed; inflame me with that heavenly love wherewith thou didst love thy dear Son, Jesus Christ. I am filled with miseries both spiritual and temporal. I am straitened by many sorrows in body and soul, and I take refuge, like a child, in the shadow of thy motherly protection. Do thou, Mother of God, who hast such power and might, obtain for me from blessed Jesus, the heavenly gifts of humility, chastity, and meekness, which were the fairest ornaments of thine immaculate soul. Do thou grant me to be strong in the midst of the temptations and bitterness, which so often overwhelm my spirit. And when the days of my earthly pilgrimage are accomplished according to God's holy will, grant that my soul may obtain the glory of paradise, through the merits of Christ and thine intercession. Amen.

An indulgence of 500 days (Apostolic Brief, April 12, 1927; S. P. Ap., April 29, 1935).

Art. VII
THE BLESSED VIRGIN UNDER DIVERS TITLES

I
OUR LADY OF PITY

407
An Oration

Kneeling at thy most sacred feet, I venerate thee, great Queen of Heaven, with the deepest reverence, and I confess that thou art the Daughter of God, the Father, the Mother of the divine Word, and the Bride of the Holy Ghost. Thou art full of grace, virtue and the heavenly gifts; thou art the most pure temple of the Holy Trinity. Thou art the treasurer and dispenser of God's mercies. Thy pure heart is full to overflowing with charity, sweetness and tenderness for us, poor sinners; wherefore we name thee our Lady of divine Pity. Hence it is with sure confidence that I present myself before thee, our most loving Mother, afflicted and straitened on every side, and I beseech thee to make me feel the love thou hast for me, by granting me . . . . , if it is in conformity with the will of God and profitable to my salvation. Ah, I beseech thee, turn thy pure eyes upon me and upon all who are dear to me. Consider the cruel warfare waged by the world, the flesh and the devil against our souls, and see how many are perishing in the strife. Remember, most tender Mother, that we are thy children, purchased by the Precious Blood of thine only-begotten Son. Deign to pray for us without ceasing to the Blessed Trinity, that we may have the grace to be ever victorious over the devil, the world and all our perverse passions; that grace whereby the just may sanctify themselves ever more and more, sinners may be converted, heresies destroyed, unbelievers enlightened and the Jews brought to the light of faith. Ask this grace for us, dearest Mother, through the infinite goodness of God most high, the merits of thy most holy Son, the anxious care wherewith thou didst wait

upon Him, the love with which thou didst
cherish Him, the tears thou didst shed and
the sorrows thou didst undergo during His
Passion.   Amen.

An indulgence of 500 days (S. C. Ind., March 26, 1860; S. P. Ap.,
April 8, 1931 and June 14, 1949).

II
OUR LADY OF DIVINE PROVIDENCE

408
A Prayer

Mary, immaculate Virgin and Mother of
divine Providence, keep my soul with
the fulness of thy grace: do thou govern my
life and direct it in the way of virtue to the
fulfilment of the divine will.   Obtain for me
the pardon and remission of all my sins; be
thou my refuge, my protection, my defense
and my guide in my pilgrimage through the
world; comfort me in the midst of tribulation; bring me safe through every danger; in
the storms of adversity afford me thy sure
protection.   Obtain for me, O Mary, the
renewal of my heart within me, that it may
become a holy dwelling place for thy divine
Son Jesus; keep far from me, who am so weak
and miserable, every kind of sin, negligence,
lukewarmness, cowardice and human respect.   Dear Mother of divine Providence,
turn thy motherly gaze upon me, and, if
through weakness or malice, I have provoked
the threats of the eternal Judge and saddened
the Sacred Heart of my dear Jesus, do thou

cover me with the mantle of thy protection and I shall be safe. Thou art the Mother of Providence; thou art the Virgin of pardon; thou art my hope on earth. Grant that I may have thee as my Mother in the glory of heaven. Amen.

Hail Mary, *three times.*

An indulgence of 500 days (S. C. Ind., Feb. 27, 1886; S. P. Ap., Feb. 12, 1933 and June 10, 1949).

409
A Prayer

O Mother of mercy, help of Christians, most faithful minister of divine Providence, treasurer of all graces, remember that never in the world has it been heard that thou hast left him without comfort who has come to thee with true devotion. Wherefore I, trusting in thy tender pity and in thy most generous providence, bend low before thee, praying that thou wouldst hear my prayer.

Obtain for me a holy provision for the future, namely, graces for all my spiritual and temporal needs.

I fervently recommend to thy loving motherly heart our Holy Church, the Sovereign Pontiff, the conversion of sinners, the spread of the Catholic faith, and those souls chosen by our Lord, who are suffering the tormenting flames of purgatory, that they may soon be comforted with eternal refreshment. Amen.

An indulgence of 500 days (Pius X, Rescript in his own hand, exhib. Dec. 19, 1906; S. P. Ap., April 20, 1932 and June 12, 1949).

III

OUR LADY OF THE CENACLE

410

A Prayer

M ost holy Virgin of the Cenacle, our Mother, Mary immaculate, obtain for us, we humbly pray, the gifts of the Holy Spirit, that we may live in charity and persevere with one accord in prayer, under thy guidance and teaching, to the greater glory of God, and that we may labor both by word and work for the salvation of souls and may deserve to enter into everlasting life.

Graciously be near us, O our Lady of the Cenacle, in our present needs, and succor us by thy power, that Almighty God may be pleased to grant us, through thy pleading, the favor for which we earnestly pray. Amen.

An indulgence of 500 days (S. C. Ind., Dec. 14, 1889; S. P. Ap., March 15, 1934).

S anctíssima Virgo de Cœnáculo, Mater nostra, immaculáta María, ímpetra nobis, humíliter deprecámur, Spíritus Sancti dona, ut in caritáte vivéntes et in oratióne unanímiter perseverántes, duce te et magístra, ad maiórem Dei glóriam, exémplo et ópere animárum salúti adlaboráre et ad vitam íngredi mereámur ætérnam.

Adsis propítia, nostra Dómina de Cœnáculo, in præsénti necessitáte et tua nos virtúte succúrre, ut eam, quam eníxe rogámus, grátiam omnípotens et miséricors Deus tuis précibus indulgére dignétur. Amen.

IV

OUR LADY, HELP OF CHRISTIANS

411

A Prayer

I mmaculate Virgin, Mother of God and our Mother, Mary, thou seest the attacks that are everywhere made by the devil and the world upon the Catholic faith, in which, by God's grace, we intend to live and die, in order that we may attain to eternal glory. Do thou, the Help of Christians, renew thine ancient victories and save thy children. They entrust to thee their firm purpose never to enroll themselves in societies hostile to our holy religion; do thou, who art all holy, present to thy divine Son our good resolutions and obtain for us the grace we need to be unshaken in their observance even to the end of life. Console the visible Head of the Church, sustain the Catholic episcopate, protect the clergy and people who proclaim thee Queen; by the power of thine intercession hasten the day when all nations shall be gathered at the feet of the chief Shepherd. Amen.

Mary, Help of Christians, pray for us!

An indulgence of 500 days (S. C. Ind., Dec. 20, 1890; S. P. Ap., July 2, 1931).

412

A Prayer

V irgin most powerful, loving helper of the Christian people, how great thanks do we not owe thee for the assistance thou didst give our fathers, who, when they were threatened by the Turkish infidels, invoked thy maternal help by the devout recitation of thy Rosary! From heaven thou didst see their deadly peril; thou didst hear their voices imploring thy compassion; and their humble prayers, enjoined by the great Pope, Saint Pius the Fifth, were acceptable unto thee, and thou camest quickly to deliver them. Grant, dear Mother, that in like manner the prolonged sighs of the holy Bride of Christ in these our days may come to thy throne and engage thy pity; do thou, moved anew to compassion for her, rise once again to deliver her from the many foes who encompass her on every side.

Even now from the four quarters of the earth there arises to thy throne that lovéd prayer, to win thy mercy in these troublous times even as of old. Unhappily our sins hinder, or at least, retard its effect. Wherefore, dear Mother, obtain for us true sorrow for our sins and a firm resolution to face death itself rather than return to our former iniquities; we are sore distressed that, through our fault, thy help, of which we stand in such extreme need, should be denied or come too late.

Rise, then, O Mary, incline thyself to hear the prayers of the whole Catholic world, and beat flat to the ground the pride of those wretched men, who in their insolence blaspheme Almighty God and would destroy His Church, against which, according to the infallible words of Christ, the gates of hell shall never prevail. Let it be seen once more that when thou dost arise to protect the Church, her victory is sure. Amen.

An indulgence of 500 days (S. C. Ind., June 20, 1891; S. P. Ap., Nov. 16, 1935).

413
A Prayer

Most holy and immaculate Virgin Mary, our tender Mother and mighty Help of Christians, we dedicate ourselves wholly to thy dear love and holy service. We dedicate to thee our minds and all our thoughts, our hearts and all our affections, our bodies and all our senses and all our strength; we promise to be ever willing to labor for the greater glory of God and the salvation of souls.

Meanwhile, do thou, O incomparable Virgin, who hast ever been the helper of the Christian people, continue to show thyself to be so in these our days. Bring low the enemies of our holy religion and frustrate their wicked designs. Enlighten and strengthen our Bishops and our priests; keep them always in close union and obedience to the Pope, their infallible Teacher; preserve thoughtless youth from sin and irreligion; increase holy vocations and multiply the number of the sacred ministers, that by means of them the kingdom of Jesus Christ may be preserved amongst us and be extended even to the uttermost parts of the earth.

We pray thee, moreover, dear Mother, to keep thine eyes of mercy ever turned upon young men and maidens, who are exposed to so many dangers, as well as upon poor sinners and those who are dying; be thou, O Mary, to them all a source of sweet hope, thou who art the Mother of mercy and the Gate of heaven.

But also for ourselves do we pour forth our supplications, O mighty Mother of God. Teach us to show forth in our lives thy virtues, especially angelic purity, deep humility and burning love; so by our demeanor, our words and our example may we, according as it is given to us, be living images of thy blessed Son Jesus in the midst of the world, and make thee known and loved, in the sure hope that thus we may succeed in bringing many souls to salvation.

Grant unto us, O Mary, thou Help of Christians, to be gathered under thy maternal protection. May the thought of the love thou bearest toward thy devoted clients be unto us so great a source of strength as to make us victors over the enemies of our salvation, both in life and in death, that so we may come to stand about thee in the beauty of paradise. Amen.

An indulgence of 500 days (Apostolic Brief, March 10, 1900; S. P. Ap., Jan. 9, 1934).

414

A Prayer

O Mary, powerful Virgin, thou art the mighty and glorious protector of the Church; thou art the marvelous help of Christians; thou art terrible as an army in battle array; thou alone hast destroyed every heresy in the whole world. In the midst of our anguish, our struggles and our distress defend us from the power of the enemy and at the hour of our death receive our souls in paradise. Amen (St. John Bosco).

An indulgence of 3 years.

A plenary indulgence on the usual conditions, when this prayer has been devoutly recited every day for a month (S. P. Ap., Feb. 20, 1923 and July 29, 1933).

V

OUR LADY, QUEEN OF THE PROPHETS

415

A Prayer

To thee, O Queen of Prophets, O Vision of the Prophets, Mother of God and of His people, we have recourse in our necessities, confident that as thou art thyself the fulfilment of prophecy, thou wilt fulfil thine own, and amongst all generations wilt bring N. to call thee blessed. Say to the wanderers for whom we plead, and specially to N., "Thy light is come." One word from thee to thy Son, and the glory of the Lord will arise upon them and the eyes of the blind be opened, so that they, beholding the star, will follow it to the House of Bread; where finding thy Son with thee, they shall eat of the True Bread, and live forever, obtaining joy and gladness while sorrow and mourning shall flee away. O thou who art "prayerfully omnipotent," at whose petition thy Son worked His first miracle, beseech Him to say "I, the Lord, will suddenly do this thing in its time," and grant those for whom we pray, to draw water with joy out of the Saviour's fountains. May we all unite with thee, our Mother, in singing thy "Magnificat" to Him thy Son our Lord Jesus Christ, who with the Father and the Holy Ghost, liveth and reigneth one God, world without end. Amen.

An indulgence of 500 days (Apostolic Brief. Jan. 24, 1901; S. P. Ap., Oct. 13, 1933) .

VI
OUR LADY OF GOOD HOPE

416
A Prayer

O Mary immaculate, the precious name of Mother of Good Hope, with which we honor thee, fills our hearts to overflowing with the sweetest consolation and moves us to hope for every blessing from thee. If such a title has been given to thee, it is a sure sign that no one has recourse to thee in vain. Accept, therefore, with a mother's love our devout homage, as we earnestly beseech thee to be gracious unto us in our every need. Above all do we pray thee to make us live in constant union with thee and thy divine Son Jesus. With thee as our guide, we are certain that we shall ever walk in the right way; in such wise that it will be our happy lot to hear thee say on the last day of our life those words of comfort: "Come then, my good and faithful servant, enter thou into the joy of thy Lord." Amen.

An indulgence of 500 days (S. C. Ind., Jan. 26, 1901; S. P. Ap., Aug. 8, 1936) .

NOTE: The same indulgences are gained by those who, having been called to the religious life, insert the following words after: "thy divine Son Jesus":

"He has graciously chosen us to labor in His mystic vineyard. Ah, do thou who art ever watchful that its fruits may be plentiful, extend thy loving care to us, miserable sinners, that we may be enabled to succeed abundantly in our high undertaking. With thee as our guide," *as above.*

VII
OUR LADY OF REPARATION
417
A Prayer

Immaculate Virgin, refuge of sinners, thou who, in order to atone for the injuries done to Almighty God and the evils inflicted on men by sin, didst accept with resignation the death of thy divine Son, be ever propitious toward us, and in heaven, where thou dost reign gloriously, continue in our behalf thy work of zeal and love. We would be thy children: do thou still show thyself a Mother. Obtain from Jesus, our divine Redeemer, that He may be pleased to apply to our souls the fruits of His passion and death, and deliver us from the bonds of our iniquities. May He be our light in the midst of darkness, our strength in weakness, our refuge in the midst of peril; may He strengthen us by His grace and love in this world, and grant us to love Him, see Him and possess Him in the world to come. Amen.

An indulgence of 500 days (S. C. Ind., Aug. 24, 1904; S. P. Ap., April 28. 1934).

VIII

OUR LADY OF THE BLESSED SACRAMENT

418

A Prayer

O Virgin Mary, our Lady of the Blessed Sacrament, thou glory of the Christian people, joy of the universal Church, salvation of the whole world, pray for us, and awaken in all believers a lively devotion toward the Most Holy Eucharist, that so they may be made worthy to partake of the same daily.

An indulgence of 500 days (Pius X, Audience, Dec. 9, 1906; S. C. Ind., Jan. 23. 1907; S. P. Ap., Dec. 12, 1933).

IX

OUR LADY, COMFORTER OF THE AFFLICTED

419

A Prayer

I mmaculate Virgin Mary, Mother of God and our most compassionate Mother, we present ourselves in thy sight in all humility, and with full confidence we implore thee for thy maternal patronage.

Thou hast been proclaimed by Holy Church the Comforter of the afflicted; and to thee constant recourse is had by the sorrowful in their afflictions, the sick in their maladies, the dying in their agony, the poor in their straitened circumstances, those who stand in all manner of need in both public and private calamities; and from thee they all receive consolation and strength.

Our dearest Mother, turn upon us also, wretched sinners that we are, thy merciful eyes, and graciously accept our humble and confident prayers. Aid us in all our spiritual and temporal necessities, deliver us from all evil and especially from sin, which is the greatest evil, and from all danger of falling into it; obtain for us from thy Son Jesus every blessing of which thou seest we stand in need both in soul and body, and especially the greatest blessing of all, which is divine grace. Comfort our spirits, troubled and afflicted in the midst of the many dangers that threaten us, and the countless miseries and misfortunes that beset us on every side. This we ask through that immense joy which filled thy pure soul in the glorious Resurrection of thy divine Son.

Obtain tranquillity for Holy Church, help and comfort for her visible Head, the Roman Pontiff, peace for Christian princes, refreshment in their pains for the holy souls in purgatory, for sinners the forgiveness of their sins and for the just perseverance in well-doing. Receive us all, our most tender Mother, under thy loving and mighty protection, that we may be enabled to live virtuously, die holily and attain to everlasting happiness in heaven. Amen.

An indulgence of 500 days.

A plenary indulgence once a month for the daily recitation of this prayer, on condition of confession, Communion and a visit to a church or public oratory (S. C. Ind., Apr. 10, 1907; S. P. Ap., June 7, 1935) .

420

A Prayer

O Mary Immaculate, our Mother and Consolation, I take refuge in thy most loving heart with all the confidence of which I am capable; thou shalt be the dearest object of my love and veneration. To thee, who art the dispenser of the treasures of heaven, I shall always have recourse in my sorrows to have peace, in my doubts to have light, in my dangers to be defended, in all my needs to obtain thy assistance. Be therefore my refuge, my strength, my consolation, O Mary the Consoler! At the hour of my death, graciously receive the last sighs of my heart and obtain for me a place in thy heavenly home, where all hearts shall praise with one accord the adorable Heart of Jesus for evermore as well as thy most lovable heart, O Mary. Our tender Mother, Comforter of the afflicted, pray for us who have recourse to thee.

An indulgence of 500 days.

A plenary indulgence on the usual conditions if this prayer is devoutly repeated every day for a month (S. P. Ap., Jan. 15, 1921 and May 16, 1932).

X

IN HONOR OF OUR LADY OF RANSOM

421

A Devout Exercise

The faithful who devoutly take part in the public exercises of the seven Saturdays in honor of Our Lady of Ransom, and who, on one of the aforesaid Saturdays, visit a church of the Religious or of the Third Order of Our Lady of Ransom, or of a Confraternity of the same Order and title, or failing these, their own parish church, may gain:

An indulgence of 7 years on each of the Saturdays;

A plenary indulgence at the end of the exercises, on condition of confession, Communion and prayers for the intentions of His Holiness the Pope (Apostolic Brief, May 25, 1908; S. P. Ap., Apr. 29, 1931).

XI
OUR LADY OF GUADALUPE

422
A Visit to the Image

The faithful who devoutly visit an image of Our Lady of Guadalupe exposed in some church may gain:

An indulgence of 300 days once a day;

An indulgence of 7 years on the twelfth day of any month;

A plenary indulgence on the Feast of the Maternity of the B. V. M., on the last Sunday after Pentecost and on the 12th day of December, with the addition of confession, Communion and prayer for the intentions of the Sovereign Pontiff (S. C. Ind., July 8, 1908; S. P. Ap., May 12, 1931, Jan. 26, and March 18, 1932).

423
A Devout Exercise

The faithful who devoutly visit an image of the Virgin Mother of God of "Guadalupe," exposed in some church or public oratory, on any of the five Sundays immediately preceding the Feast of the Apparition of Our Lady of Guadalupe may gain:

A plenary indulgence, if they make their confession, receive Holy Communion and pray for the intentions of the Holy Father (S. P. Ap., May 12, 1931).

424
Prayer

O our Lady of Guadalupe, mystical rose, make intercession for Holy Church, protect the Sovereign Pontiff, help all those who invoke thee in their necessities, and since thou art the ever Virgin Mary and Mother of the true God, obtain for us from thy most holy Son the grace of keeping our faith, sweet hope in the midst of the bitterness of life, burning charity and the precious gift of final perseverance. Amen.

An indulgence of 500 days (Pius X, Audience, Aug. 18, 1908, exhib. Aug. 19, 1908; S. P. Ap., April 29, 1935).

XII
OUR LADY OF DELIVERANCE

425
An Invocation

Holy Mary, our Lady of Deliverance, pray for us and for the holy souls in purgatory.

An indulgence of 300 days (Holy Office, Jan. 22, 1914; S. P. Ap., April 23, 1936).

XIII
OUR LADY OF PERPETUAL HELP

426
An Invocation

Mother of Perpetual Help, pray for us.

An indulgence of 300 days (Holy Office Jan. 29, 1914; S. P. Ap., Oct. 4, 1933).

Mater de Perpétuo Succúrsu, ora pro nobis.

427
Prayers

I. Behold, O *Mother of Perpetual Help*, at thy feet a wretched sinner, who has recourse to thee and trusts in thee. O Mother of mercy, have pity on me; I hear all men call thee the refuge and hope of sinners: be therefore my refuge and my hope. Help me for the love of Jesus Christ: hold out thy hand to a fallen wretch, who commends himself to thee and dedicates himself to be thy servant for ever. I praise and thank God, who of His great mercy hath given me this confidence in thee, a sure pledge of my eternal salvation. Alas, it is only too true that in the past I have fallen miserably, because I did not come to thee. I know that with thy help I shall conquer; I know that thou wilt help me, if I commend myself to thee; but I am fearful lest in the occasions of sin I shall forget to call upon thee and so I shall be lost. This grace, then, do I ask of thee; for this I implore thee, as much as I can and know how to do; namely, that in the assaults of hell I may ever run to thy protection and may say to thee: Mary, help me; *Mother of Perpetual Help*, permit me not to lose my God.

Hail Mary, *three times.*

2. O *Mother of Perpetual Help*, grant me ever to be able to call upon thy powerful name, since thy name is the help of the living and the salvation of the dying. Ah, Mary most pure, Mary most sweet, grant that thy name from this day forth may be to me the very breath of life. Dear Lady, delay not to come to my assistance whenever I call upon thee; for in all the temptations that assail me, in all the necessities that befall me, I will never leave off calling upon thee, ever repeating: Mary, Mary. What comfort, what sweetness, what confidence, what tenderness fills my soul at the sound of thy name, at the very thought of thee! I give thanks to our Lord, who for my sake hath given thee a name so sweet, so lovable, so mighty. But I

am not content merely to speak thy name; I would utter it for very love of thee; it is my desire that love should ever remind me to name thee, *Mother of Perpetual Help*.

Hail Mary, *three times*.

3. O *Mother of Perpetual Help*, thou art the dispenser of every grace that God grants us in our misery; it is for this cause that He hath made thee so powerful, so rich, so kind, that thou mightest assist us in our miseries. Thou art the advocate of the most wretched and abandoned sinners, if they but come unto thee; come once more to my assistance, for I commend myself to thee. In thy hands I place my eternal salvation; to thee I entrust my soul. Enroll me among thy most faithful servants; take me under thy protection and it is enough for me: yes, for if thou protect me, I shall fear nothing; not my sins, for thou wilt obtain for me their pardon and remission; not the evil spirits, for thou art mightier than all the powers of hell; not even Jesus, my Judge, for He is appeased by a single prayer from thee. I fear only that through my own negligence I may forget to recommend myself to thee and so I shall be lost. My dear Lady, obtain for me the forgiveness of my sins, love for Jesus, final perseverance and the grace to have recourse to thee at all times, O *Mother of Perpetual Help*.

Hail Mary, *three times*.

An indulgence of 500 days (S. C. Rites, May 17, 1866; S. P. Ap., March 2, 1934).

XIV

OUR LADY OF GOOD COUNSEL

428

Devout Exercises

a) **T**he faithful who piously assist at devotions in honor of our Lady of Good Counsel, held publicly in a church or public oratory, on twelve successive Sundays, or if that be impossible on the respective Saturdays immediately preceding, may gain:

An indulgence of 7 years on anyone of the twelve successive Sundays;

A plenary indulgence upon the completion of the exercise, if they go to confession and Communion and pray for the intentions of His Holiness.

b) Those who piously assist at public devotions in honor of Our Lady of Good Counsel, held in a church or public oratory on the first Sunday of any month, or, if that should be impossible, on the Saturday immediately preceding, may gain:

An indulgence of 7 years;

A plenary indulgence on condition of confession, Communion and prayer for the intentions of the Holy Father (Apostolic Brief, Dec. 12, 1919; S. P. Ap., March 18, 1932).

429

A Prayer

Most glorious Virgin, chosen by the eternal Counsel to be the Mother of the eternal Word made flesh, thou who art the treasurer of divine graces and the advocate of sinners, I who am thy most unworthy servant have recourse to thee; be thou pleased to be my guide and counselor in this vale of tears. Obtain for me through the Most Precious Blood of thy divine Son, the forgiveness of my sins, the salvation of my soul and the means necessary to obtain it. In like manner obtain for Holy Church victory over her enemies and the spread of the kingdom of Jesus Christ upon the whole earth. Amen.

An indulgence of 500 days (S. C. for Extraord. Eccl. Affairs, Nov. 23, 1880; S. P. Ap., May 29, 1933 and June 8, 1949) .

XV
OUR LADY QUEEN OF PEACE

430
An Invocation

I mmaculate Queen of Peace, pray for us.

An indulgence of 300 days (Apostolic Brief, Feb. 9, 1924) .

I mmaculáta Regína Pacis, ora pro nobis.

431
A Prayer

M ost holy Virgin, Mother of God and our most loving Mother, by thy divine maternity thou didst merit to share in thy divine Son's prerogative of universal kingship; we, thy most humble servants and devoted children, feel ourselves comforted by the thought that, as it pleased the Redeemer of mankind to have Himself announced by the Prophets and by the Angels at Bethlehem under the glorious title of King of Peace, so too it must be pleasing to thee to hear thyself saluted and honored by us under the title of Queen of Peace, a title that is so dear to thy motherly heart; it is an invocation poured forth with great fervor from our hearts. May thy powerful intercession ward off from thy people all hatred and discord, and direct their hearts in the ways of peace and brotherhood, which Jesus Christ came to teach and enforce among men for the prosperity and safety of all, and in which paths Holy Church does not cease to guide our steps. Vouchsafe, O glorious Queen, to regard with kindly eyes and to crown with success the paternal solicitude, wherewith the Sovereign Pontiff, the Vicar on earth of thy divine Son, continually seeks to call together and unite the nations about the only center of saving Faith; grant that to us also in filial submission to our common Father, it may be given to correspond wholeheartedly with his salutary designs. Enlighten the rulers of our country as to those same designs; quicken and maintain peace and concord in our families, peace in our hearts and Christian charity throughout all the world. Amen.

An indulgence of 500 days.

A plenary indulgence once a month for the daily recitation of this prayer, on condition of confession, Communion and a visit to some church or public oratory (S. P. Ap., July 5, 1927 and July 12, 1932 and June 10, 1949).

XVI
OUR LADY MOTHER OF ORPHANS
432
An Invocation

Mother of orphans, pray for us.

An indulgence of 300 days (Apostolic Brief, Feb. 23, 1924).

Mater orphanórum, ora pro nobis.

XVII

OUR LADY MOTHER OF GRACE

433

A Prayer

M ost holy Mary, great Queen of heaven, the very treasure of life and ever-flowing channel of divine grace, by thine ineffable virtues thou wast so pleasing in the sight of God, that thou didst merit to conceive in thy virginal womb the very Author of life and of grace, Jesus Christ our Lord; and by becoming the Mother of the God-made man, thou didst become likewise the Mother of redeemed humanity. Mother, therefore, of grace and of life, of mercy and forgiveness, turn upon me thy motherly countenance; behold my many miseries both in body and soul; raise me up to a state of perfect friendship with Almighty God, obtain for me the grace of final perseverance. And since thy prayers, O Mary, are all-powerful with our Lord, permit me, miserable as I am, to choose thee as my special patroness. With the help of thy mighty intercession I am sure to obtain from thy divine Son all the graces necessary to serve God faithfully. In such wise thou wilt show thyself unto me the Mother of divine grace as indeed thou art, and I, thanks to the assistance obtained by thee, will be enabled to live in holiness on earth and hereafter will enjoy the happy lot of praising thee eternally in heaven. Amen.

An indulgence of 500 days (S. P. Ap., May 28, 1925, Oct. 9, 1933 and June 8, 1949).

XVIII
OUR LADY OF INTERCESSION
434
A Prayer

Most holy Mary, Our Lady of Intercession, whose maternal tenderness gathers in one embrace all the souls redeemed by the Precious Blood of thy Son Jesus, we come before thy royal throne with sadness in our hearts as we remember those who have gone before us, but also with unlimited confidence in thine intercession. Death, which burst asunder the bonds of earth, has not destroyed the affection which binds us to those who lived in the same faith as we do. O Mary, countless souls await with unutterable anxiety the assistance of our prayers, and the merits of our good works in that place of expiation. Urged by the charity of Jesus Christ, we raise our countenance and heart in supplication to thee, the compassionate Mother of all believers, in favor of those suffering souls. Make our prayers of good effect, O Mary; obtain for them the power to move the Heart of Jesus our Redeemer through thy motherly intercession. Let thine incomparable holiness supply the defects of our misery, thy love make good our languid affection, thy power strengthen our weakness. Grant, O Queen of heaven, that the ardent desire of the souls of the departed to be admitted to the Beatific Vision may soon be satisfied. We pray to thee, O Mother, especially for the souls of our relations, of priests, of those who were zealous in honoring thee, of those who did good to the souls of others, of those who wept with them and for them and, finally, for the souls of those who are forgotten.   Grant that one day, when we are all reunited in heaven, we may be able to rejoice in the possession of God, in the happiness of thy dear presence, in the fellowship of all the Saints, thanking thee forever for all the blessings thou hast obtained for us, O Mother, who art our unfailing comfort.   Amen.

Hail Mary *three times, and once* Eternal rest grant unto them, *etc.*

An indulgence of 500 days.

A plenary indulgence on the usual conditions once a month for the daily recitation of this prayer (S. P. Ap., Dec. 2, 1926 and Apr. 18, 1935).

XIX
OUR LADY OF LA SALETTE
435
An Invocation

Our Lady of la Salette, Reconciler of sinners, pray without ceasing for us who have recourse to thee.

An indulgence of 300 days (S. P. Ap., Nov. 7, 1927 and Dec. 12, 1933).

436
A Prayer

Remember, our Lady of la Salette, true Mother of sorrows, the tears which thou didst shed for me on Calvary; be mindful also of the unceasing care which thou dost exercise to screen me from the justice of God; and consider whether thou canst now abandon thy child, for whom thou hast done so much.   Inspired by this consoling thought,

I come to cast myself at thy feet, in spite of my infidelity and ingratitude. Reject not my prayer, O Virgin of reconciliation, convert me, obtain for me the grace to love Jesus Christ above all things and to console thee too by living a holy life, in order that one day I may be able to see thee in heaven. Amen.

An indulgence of 500 days (S. P. Ap., Nov. 7, 1927 and Dec. 12, 1933).

XX
OUR LADY QUEEN OF APOSTLES
437
An Invocation

Queen of the Apostles, pray for us.

An indulgence of 300 days (S. P. Ap., Nov. 20, 1930).

Regína Apostolórum, ora pro nobis.

XXI
OUR LADY REFUGE OF SINNERS
438
A Prayer

Almighty and merciful God, who in blessed Mary ever Virgin hast set up a refuge and a help for sinners, grant that we, under her protection, may be absolved from all our sins and may obtain the blessed effect of Thy great mercy. Through Christ our Lord. Amen (Roman Missal).

An indulgence of 3 years.

A plenary indulgence once a month on the usual conditions for the daily recitation of this prayer (S. P. Ap., July 20, 1934).

Omnípotens et miséricors Deus, qui in beáta semper Vírgine María peccatórum refúgium et auxílium collocásti, concéde, ut, ipsa protegénte, a culpis ómnibus absolúti, misericórdiæ tuæ efféctum felícem consequámur. Per Christum Dóminum nostrum. Amen (ex *Missali Romano*).

XXII
OUR LADY OF THE SACRED HEART
439
A Prayer

R emember, Our Lady of the Sacred Heart, what ineffable power thy divine Son hath given thee over His own adorable Heart. Filled with confidence in thy merits, we come before thee and implore thy protection. O heavenly Treasurer of the Heart of Jesus, that Heart which is the inexhaustible source of all graces, which thou mayest open to us at thy good pleasure, in order that from it may flow forth upon mankind the riches of love and mercy, light and salvation, that are contained therein; grant unto us, we beseech thee, the favors which we seek. . . . We can never, never be refused by thee, and since thou art our Mother, O our Lady of the Sacred Heart, graciously receive our prayers and grant our request. Amen.

An indulgence of 500 days.
A plenary indulgence on the usual conditions, if this prayer is devoutly recited every day for a month (S. P. Ap., April 5, 1949).

M emoráre, o Dómina Nostra a Sacro Corde, quam ineffábilem tibi poténtiam Fílius tuus divínus contúlerit in suum ipsíus Cor adorábile. Pleni nos fidúciæ in méritis tuis, accédimus implorántes tuum præsídium. O Cordis Iesu Thesaurária cæléstis, illíus Cordis, fontis inexháusti gratiárum ómnium, quod potes ipsa pro tua voluntáte reclúdere, ut défluant inde in hómines divítiæ amóris et misericórdiæ, lúminis et salútis, quæ in ipso continéntur; concéde nobis, obsecrámus, benefícia quæ pétimus. . . . Nulla nobis, nulla a te erit repúlsa, et, quóniam Mater Tu nostra es, o Dómina Nostra a Sacro Corde, preces nostras benígne habe et benígne exáudi. Amen.

BENEDI- CITE ++
OMNES + +ANGELI
DOMINI + DOMINUM

CHAPTER VI
THE HOLY ANGELS

Art. I
GENERAL INVOCATIONS OF THE HOLY ANGELS

440
An Invocation

Ye Angels and Archangels, ye Thrones and Dominations, ye Principalities and Powers, ye Virtues of the heavens, Cherubim and Seraphim, bless ye the Lord for ever (Roman Missal).

An indulgence of 300 days.

A plenary indulgence on the usual conditions, when this invocation has been recited with devotion every day for a month (S. P. Ap., Nov. 20, 1934).

Angeli, Archángeli, Throni et Dominatiónes, Principátus et Potestátes, Virtútes cælórum, Chérubim atque Séraphim, Dóminum benedícite in ætérnum (ex *Missali Romano*).

441
An Invocation

Bless the Lord, all ye His Angels: you that are mighty in strength, and execute His word.

Bless the Lord, all ye His hosts: ye ministers.

of His that do His will (Roman Missal).

An indulgence of 300 days.

A plenary indulgence on the usual conditions, for the daily recitation of these invocations throughout one month (S. P. Ap., July 8, 1935).

B enedícite Dóminum omnes Angeli eius; poténtes virtúte, qui fácitis verbum eius.

Benedícite Dómino omnes virtútes eius; minístri eius qui fácitis voluntátem eius (ex *Missali Romano*).

Art. II

SAINT MICHAEL THE ARCHANGEL

I

INVOCATIONS

442

S aint Michael the Archangel, defend us in the battle, that we perish not in the fearful judgment (Roman Missal).

An indulgence of 300 days.

A plenary indulgence on the usual conditions, for the devout recitation of this invocation every day for a month (S. C. Ind., Aug. 19, 1893; S. P. Ap., May 6, 1933).

S ancte Míchaël Archángele, defénde nos in prǽlio, ut non pereámus in treméndo iudício (ex *Missali Romano*).

443

S aint Michael, first champion of the Kingship of Christ, pray for us.

An indulgence of 300 days (Apostolic Brief, Jan. 11, 1927).

II

HYMN

Te splendor et virtus Patris

444

O Jesus! life-spring of the soul!
The Father's Power and Glory bright!

Thee with the Angels we extol;
From Thee they draw their life and light.
 Thy thousand, thousand hosts are spread,
Embattled o'er the azure sky;
But Michael bears Thy standard dread,
And lifts the mighty Cross on high.
 He in that sign the rebel powers
Did with their dragon prince expel:
And hurled them from the heaven's high
    towers,
Down like a thunderbolt to hell.
 Grant us with Michael still, O Lord,
Against the Prince of pride to fight;
So may a crown be our reward,
Before the Lamb's pure throne of light.
 To God the Father and the Son
And Holy Paraclete to Thee,
As evermore hath been before,
Be glory through eternity. Amen (tr. E. Caswall),.

Antiphon. Most glorious Prince, Michael
the Archangel, be ever mindful of us; here
and everywhere pray always for us to the
Son of God.
 ℣. Before the Angels will I sing praise unto
Thee, O my God:
 ℟. I will worship at Thy holy temple, and
praise Thy name.

Let us pray.

 O God, who in wondrous order dost ordain
and constitute the services of men and Angels; mercifully grant that our life may be
defended on earth by them that stand near
Thee, evermore ministering to Thee in heav-

en. Through Christ our Lord. Amen(Roman
Breviary) .
   An indulgence of 3 years.

   A plenary indulgence on the usual conditions, if the devout recitation of this hymn together with the versicles and prayer, performed daily, shall be continued for one month(S. C. Ind., May 6,
1817; S. P. Ap., May 18, 1935) .

      T e splendor et virtus Patris,
        Te vita, Iesu, córdium,
   Ab ore qui pendent tuo,
   Laudámus inter Angelos.

    Tibi mille densa míllium
   Ducum coróna mílitat;
   Sed éxplicat victor Crucem
   Míchaël salútis Sígnifer.

    Dracónis hic dirum caput
   In ima pellit tártara,
   Ducémque cum rebéllibus
   Cælésti ab arce fúlminat.

    Contra ducem supérbiæ
   Sequámur hunc nos Príncipem,
   Ut detur ex Agni throno
   Nobis coróna glóriæ.

    Patri, simúlque Fílio,
   Tibíque, Sancte Spíritus,
   Sicut fuit, sit iúgiter
   Sæculum per omne glória. Amen.

   Antiph.   Princeps gloriosíssime Míchaël Archángele, esto memor nostri; hic et ubíque semper precáre pro nobis Fílium Dei.

   ℣. In conspéctu Angelórum psallam tibi, Deus
meus:

   ℟. Adorábo ad templum sanctum tuum, et con-
fitébor nómini tuo.

Orémus.

   Deus, qui miro órdine Angelórum ministéria
hominúmque dispénsas, concéde propítius, ut a
quibus tibi ministrántibus in cælo semper assístitur,
ab his in terra vita nostra muniátur. Per Christum
Dóminum nostrum. Amen (ex *Breviario Romano*) .

III

A DEVOUT EXERCISE

445

The faithful who recite devoutly some prayers in honor of St. Michael the Archangel at any season of the year, with the intention of continuing the said prayers for nine successive days, may gain:

An indulgence of 5 years once each day;

A plenary indulgence, on the usual conditions, at the end of their novena (Pius IX, Audience, Jan. 3, 1849; S. C. Bishops and Religious, Jan. 28, 1850; S. C. Ind., Nov. 26, 1876; S. P. Ap., Feb. 9, 1933).

IV

PRAYERS

446

O glorious Prince of the heavenly host, Saint Michael the Archangel, defend us in the battle and in the fearful warfare that we are waging against the principalities and powers, against the rulers of this world of darkness, against the evil spirits. Come thou to the assistance of men, whom Almighty God created immortal, making them in His own image and likeness and redeeming them at a great price from the tyranny of Satan. Fight this day the battle of the Lord with thy legions of holy Angels, even as of old thou didst fight against Lucifer, the leader of the proud spirits and all his rebel angels, who were powerless to stand against thee, neither was their place found any more in heaven. And that apostate angel, transformed into an angel of darkness who still creeps about the earth to encompass our ruin, was cast headlong into the abyss together with his followers. But behold, that first enemy of mankind, and a murderer from the beginning, has regained his confidence. Changing himself into an angel of light, he goes about with the whole multitude of the wicked spirits to invade the earth and blot out the Name of God and of His Christ, to plunder, to slay and to consign to eternal damnation the souls that have been destined for a crown of everlasting life. This wicked serpent, like an unclean torrent, pours into men of depraved minds and corrupt hearts the poison of his malice, the spirit of lying, impiety and blasphemy, and the deadly breath of impurity and every form of vice and iniquity. These crafty enemies of mankind have filled to overflowing with gall and wormwood the Church, which is the Bride of the Lamb without spot; they have laid profane hands upon her most sacred treasures. Make haste, therefore, O invincible Prince, to help the people of God against the inroads of the lost spirits and grant us the victory. Amen.

An indulgence of 500 days (Leo XIII, Motu Proprio, Sept 25, 1888; S. P. Ap., May 4, 1934).

447

Saint Michael the Archangel, defend us in battle, be our protection against the wickedness and snares of the devil; may God rebuke him, we humbly pray; and do thou, O Prince of the heavenly host, by the power of God, thrust into hell Satan and all evil spirits who wander through the world for the ruin of souls. Amen.

An indulgence of 3 years.

A plenary indulgence once a month on the usual conditions, if this prayer is repeated daily (S. P. Ap., Nov. 12, 1932).

Sancte Míchaël Archángele, defénde nos in prælio, contra nequítias et insídias diáboli esto præsídium: Imperet illi Deus, súpplices deprecámur, tuque, Princeps milítiæ cæléstis, sátanam aliósque spíritus malígnos, qui ad perditiónem animárum pervagántur in mundo, divína virtúte in inférnum detrúde. Amen.

Art. III

SAINT GABRIEL THE ARCHANGEL

I

A DEVOUT EXERCISE

448

The faithful who devoutly recite some prayers in honor of St. Gabriel the Archangel at any season of the year, with the intention of continuing the same for nine successive days, may gain:

An indulgence of 5 years, once each day;

A plenary indulgence on the usual conditions, at the end of the novena (Pius IX, Audience, Jan. 3, 1849; S. C. of Bishops and Religious, Jan. 28, 1850; S. C. Ind., Nov. 26, 1876; S. P. Ap., June 2, 1933).

II

A PRAYER

449

O God, who amongst all the Angels didst choose the Archangel Gabriel to announce the mystery of Thine Incarnation; mercifully grant, that we who solemnly keep his feast on earth may feel the benefit of his patronage in heaven: who livest and reignest for ever and ever. Amen (Roman Missal).

An indulgence of 3 years.

A plenary indulgence on the usual conditions, if the daily devout recitation of this prayer is continued for a month (S. P. Ap., April 25, 1949).

Deus, qui inter céteros Angelos, ad annuntiándum incarnatiónis tuæ mystérium, Gabriélem Archángelum elegísti; concéde propítius, ut qui festum ejus celebrámus in terris, ipsíus patrocínium sentiámus in cælis: qui vivis et regnas in sǽcula sæculórum. Amen
ex *Missali Romano*).

Art. IV
SAINT RAPHAEL THE ARCHANGEL

I
A DEVOUT EXERCISE

450

The faithful who perform some devotions in honor of St. Raphael the Archangel at any season of the year, with the intention of so continuing for nine successive days, may gain:

An indulgence of 5 years, once each day;

A plenary indulgence on the usual conditions, at the end of their novena (Pius IX, Audience, Jan. 3, 1849; S. C. of Bishops and Religious, Jan. 28, 1850; S. C. Ind., Nov. 26, 1876; S. P. Ap., May 6, 1933).

II
A PRAYER

451

Vouchsafe, O Lord God, to send unto our assistance Saint Raphael the Archangel: and may he, who, we believe, evermore standeth before the throne of Thy Majesty, offer unto Thee our humble petitions to be blessed by Thee. Through Christ our Lord. Amen
(Roman Missal).

An indulgence of 3 years.

A plenary indulgence on the usual conditions, when this prayer has been said every day for one month (S. P. Ap., Nov. 22, 1934).

Dirígere dignáre, Dómine Deus, in adiutórium nostrum, sanctum Raphaélem Archángelum; et quem tuæ maiestáti semper assístere crédimus, tibi nostras exíguas preces benedicéndas assígnet. Per Christum Dóminum nostrum. Amen (ex *Missali Romano*).

NOTE: Prayers to St. Raphael the Archangel for emigrants are found under n. 664.

Art. V

THE GUARDIAN ANGEL

I

INVOCATION

452

A ngel of God, my guardian dear,
To whom His love commits me here;
Ever this day (*or* night) be at my side,
To light and guard, to rule and guide.
Amen.

An indulgence of 300 days.

A plenary indulgence once a month, on the usual conditions, for the daily recitation of this invocation.

A plenary indulgence on the usual conditions on the Feast of the holy Guardian Angels, if this invocation has been said frequently in the morning and evening throughout the preceding year.

A plenary indulgence at the hour of death, to be gained by the faithful who have been accustomed to say this invocation frequently during life, provided that they go to confession and Communion, or, at least, make an act of contrition, invoke the holy Name of Jesus, orally, if possible, or at least mentally, and accept death with resignation from the hand of God as the just punishment for their sins (Apostolic Brief, Oct. 2, 1795; S. C. Ind., June 11, 1796 and May 15, 1821; S. P. Ap., Oct. 27, 1935).

A ngele Dei, qui custos es mei, me tibi commíssum pietáte supérna hódie (*vel* hac nocte) illúmina, custódi, rege et gubérna. Amen.

II

A DEVOUT EXERCISE

453

T he faithful who devoutly recite some prayers in honor of their Guardian Angel at any season of the year, with the intention of persevering therein for nine successive days, may gain:

An indulgence of 5 years once, on any day;

A plenary indulgence on the usual conditions at the end of the novena (Pius IX, Audience Jan. 3, 1849; S. C. of Bishops and Religious, Jan. 28, 1850; S. C. Ind.. Nov. 26, 1876; S. P. Ap., Jan. 9, 1931) .

Art. VI
THE HOLY ANGEL WHO STRENGTHENED JESUS IN THE GARDEN OF OLIVES

I
INVOCATION

454

O holy Angel who didst strengthen Jesus Christ our Lord, come and strengthen us also; come and tarry not!

An indulgence of 300 days (Pius X, Rescript in his own hand, July 10, 1907, exhib. Dec. 15, 1910) .

II
PRAYER

455

I salute thee, holy Angel who didst comfort my Jesus in His agony, and with thee I praise the Most Holy Trinity for having chosen thee from among all the holy Angels to comfort and strengthen Him who is the comfort and strength of all that are in affliction. By the honor thou didst enjoy and by the obedience, humility and love wherewith thou didst assist the sacred Humanity of Jesus, my Saviour, when He was fainting for very sorrow at seeing the sins of the world and especially my sins, I beseech thee to obtain for me perfect sorrow for my sins; deign to strengthen me in the afflictions that now overwhelm me, and in all the other trials, to which I shall be exposed henceforth and, in particular, when I find myself in my final agony. Amen.

An indulgence of 500 days (S. P. Ap., Aug. 5, 1921 and Sept. 24, 1935).

CHAPTER VII
THE SAINTS
Art. II
IN HONOR OF SAINT JOHN THE BAPTIST

I
A DEVOUT EXERCISE

456

The faithful who devoutly offer some prayers in honor of St. John the Baptist, with the intention of so doing for nine continuous days, may gain:

An indulgence of 5 years once each day;

A plenary indulgence on the usual conditions, at the end of the novena (S. P. Ap., July 8, 1925; Nov. 15, 1927 and May 6, 1934).

II
PRAYERS

457

I. O glorious Saint John the Baptist, greatest prophet among those born of woman (Luke 7, 28), although thou wast sanctified in thy mother's womb and didst lead a most innocent life, nevertheless it was thy will to retire into the wilderness, there to devote thyself to the practice of austerity and penance; obtain for us of thy Lord the grace to be wholly detached, at least in our hearts, from earthly goods, and to practice Christian mortification with interior recollection and with the spirit of holy prayer.

Our Father, Hail Mary, Glory be, *etc.*

II. O most zealous Apostle, who, without working any miracle on others, but solely by the example of thy life of penance and the power of thy word, didst draw after thee the multitudes, in order to dispose them to receive the Messias worthily and to listen to His heavenly doctrine; grant that it may be given unto us, by means of the example of a holy life and the exercise of every good work, to bring many souls to God, but above all those souls that are enveloped in the darkness of error and ignorance and are led astray by vice.

Our Father, Hail Mary, Glory be.

III. O Martyr invincible, who, for the honor of God and the salvation of souls, didst with firmness and constancy withstand the impiety of Herod even at the cost of thine own life, and didst rebuke him openly for his wicked and dissolute life; by thy prayers obtain for us a heart, brave and generous, in order that we may overcome all human respect and openly profess our faith in loyal obedience to the teachings of Jesus Christ, our divine Master.

Our Father, Hail Mary, Glory be.

℣. Pray for us, Saint John the Baptist,

℟. That we may be made worthy of the promises of Christ.

Let us pray.

O God, who hast made this day to be honorable in our eyes by the Nativity (*or* commemoration) of blessed John, grant unto

Thy people the grace of spiritual joy, and direct the minds of all Thy faithful into the way of everlasting salvation. Through Christ our Lord. Amen.

An indulgence of 3 years.

An indulgence of 5 years once a day, if the prayers are said with the intention of completing a triduum.

A plenary indulgence on the usual conditions, at the close of the triduum (Pius X, Rescript in his own hand, Jan. 9, 1904, exhib. Jan. 11, 1904; S. P. Ap., Nov. 15, 1927 and Dec. 2, 1933).

Art. II

IN HONOR OF SAINT JOSEPH, SPOUSE OF THE B. V. M.

I

INVOCATIONS

458

Grant us, dear Joseph, to run life's pathway in innocent fashion:
May we for ever be safe under thy blest patronage (Roman Missal).

An indulgence of 300 days.

A plenary indulgence on the usual conditions, for the devout recitation of this invocation every day throughout a month (S. C. Ind., March 18, 1882; S. P. Ap., May 13, 1933).

Fac nos innócuam, Ioseph, decúrrere vitam,
Sitque tuo semper tuta patrocínio.

(ex *Missali Romano*).

459

O Saint Joseph, foster-father of our Lord Jesus Christ and true spouse of Mary the Virgin, pray for us.

An indulgence of 300 days once a day (Leo XIII, Motu Proprio, May 15, 1891).

460

The faithful, who in order to obtain the assistance of St. Joseph, the Spouse of the B. V. M., in the various needs of their spiritual and physical life devoutly invoke his holy name, are granted:

An indulgence of 300 days;

A plenary indulgence on the usual conditions, provided that they devoutly repeat this invocation every day for a month (**S. P. Ap., Oct. 22, 1940**).

II

THE LITTLE OFFICE

461

The faithful who devoutly recite the little Office of St. Joseph, Spouse of the B. V. Mary, may obtain:

An indulgence of 7 years;

A plenary indulgence once a month on the usual conditions, if the Office is recited daily (**S. P. Ap., May 10, 1921 and March 18, 1932**).

III

LITANY

462

Lord, have mercy on us.
Christ, have mercy on us.
Lord, have mercy on us.
Christ, hear us.
Christ, graciously hear us.
God, the Father of Heaven, have mercy on us.
God the Son, Redeemer of the world,
have mercy on us.
God, the Holy Ghost,   have mercy on us.
Holy Trinity one God,   have mercy on us.
Holy Mary,   pray for us.
Saint Joseph,   pray for us.
Renowned offspring of David,   pray for us.
Light of Patriarchs,   pray for us.
Spouse of the Mother of God,   pray for us.
Chaste guardian of the Virgin,   pray for us.

Foster-father of the Son of God, pray for us.
Diligent protector of Christ, pray for us.
Head of the Holy Family, pray for us.
Joseph most just, pray for us.
Joseph most chaste, pray for us.
Joseph most prudent, pray for us.
Joseph most strong, pray for us.
Joseph most obedient, pray for us.
Joseph most faithful, pray for us.
Mirror of patience, pray for us.
Lover of poverty, pray for us.
Model of artisans, pray for us.
Glory of home life, pray for us.
Guardian of virgins, pray for us.
Pillar of families, pray for us.
Solace of the wretched, pray for us.
Hope of the sick, pray for us.
Patron of the dying, pray for us.
Terror of demons, pray for us.
Protector of Holy Church, pray for us.
Lamb of God, Who takest away the sins of the world, spare us, O Lord.
Lamb of God, Who takest away the sins of the world, graciously hear us, O Lord.
Lamb of God, Who takest away the sins of the world, have mercy on us.

℣. He made him lord of His house:
℟. And ruler of all His substance.

Let us pray.

O God, who in Thine unspeakable Providence didst vouchsafe to choose blessed Joseph to be the spouse of Thy most holy Mother: grant, we beseech Thee, that we may deserve to have him as our intercessor in heaven, whom we venerate on earth as our protector: Who livest and reignest world without end. Amen.

An indulgence of 5 years.

A plenary indulgence on the usual conditions, if this litany together with its versicle and response, and the prayer are recited daily for a month (S. Cong. of Rites, March 18, 1909, exhib. March 19, 1909; S. P. Ap., March 21, 1935).

K yrie, eléison.
   Christe, eléison.
Kyrie, eléison.
Christe, audi nos.
Christe, exáudi nos.

Pater de cælis, Deus,	miserére nobis
Fili, Redémptor mundi, Deus,	miserére
Spíritus Sancte, Deus,	miserére
Sancta Trínitas, unus Deus,	miserére
Sancta María,	ora pro nobis
Sancte Ioseph,	ora
Proles David ínclyta,	ora
Lumen Patriarchárum,	ora
Dei Genitrícis Sponse,	ora
Custos pudíce Vírginis,	ora
Fílii Dei nutrície,	ora
Christi defénsor sédule,	ora
Almæ Famíliæ præses,	ora
Ioseph iustíssime,	ora
Ioseph castíssime,	ora
Ioseph prudentíssime,	ora
Ioseph fortíssime,	ora
Ioseph obedientíssime,	ora
Ioseph fidelíssime,	ora
Spéculum patiéntiæ,	ora
Amátor paupertátis,	ora
Exémplar opíficum,	ora
Domésticæ vitæ decus,	ora
Custos vírginum,	ora
Familiárum cólumen,	ora

Solátium miserórum,	ora
Spes ægrotántium,	ora
Patróne moriéntium,	ora
Terror dǽmonum,	ora
Protéctor sanctæ Ecclésiæ,	ora

Agnus Dei, qui tollis peccáta mundi, parce nobis, Dómine.

Agnus Dei, qui tollis peccáta mundi, exáudi nos, Dómine.

Agnus Dei, qui tollis peccáta mundi, miserére nobis.

℣. Constítuit eum dóminum domus suæ.

℟. Et príncipem omnis possessiónis suæ.

Orémus.

Deus, qui ineffábili providéntia beátum Ioseph sanctíssimæ Genitrícis tuæ Sponsum elígere dignátus es; præsta, quǽsumus; ut quem protectórem venerámur in terris, intercessórem habére mereámur in cælis: Qui vivis et regnas in sǽcula sæculórum. Amen.

IV

HYMNS

463

Te Ioseph celebrent agmina cælitum

Joseph! to thee by hosts on high
  And choirs of Christians, laud be paid!—
Saintly of life,—by purest tie
  Joined unto her, the glorious Maid.

When thou didst doubt thy wife's repute,
  And mark her great with motherhood,
The angel taught thee that her fruit
  Came from the Holy Ghost of God.

To clasp the Son, thy Lord, was thine,—
  To share His flight to Egypt's shore,—
With tears, to seek in Salem's shrine
  Him lost,—with joy, to find once more.

Death brings to other Saints their rest;
   Through toil they win the victor's place;—
Thou happier, like the Angels blest,
   Alive, hast seen God face to face.

Spare us, O Trinity most High!
   Grant that, with Joseph, we may gain
Thy starry realm, and ceaselessly
   There raise to Thee our thankful strain.
Amen (Roman Breviary, tr. R. F. Littledale).

An indulgence of 3 years.

A plenary indulgence on the usual conditions, for the daily recitation of this hymn for a month (S. P. Ap., Feb. 9, 1922 and July 13, 1932).

Te, Ioseph, célebrent ágmina Cǽlitum
   Te cuncti résonent Christíadum chori,
Qui, clarus méritis, iunctus es ínclytæ
Casto fœdere Vírgini.

Almo cum túmidam gérmine cóniugem
Admírans, dúbio tángeris ánxius,
Afflátu súperi Fláminis, Angelus
Concéptum púerum docet.

Tu natum Dóminum stringis, ad éxteras
Aegýpti prófugum tu séqueris plagas;
Amíssum Sólymis quæris et ínvenis,
Miscens gáudia flétibus.

Post mortem réliquos sors pia cónsecrat,
Palmámque eméritos glória súscipit:
Tu vivens, Súperis par, frúeris Deo,
Mira sorte beátior.

Nobis, summa Trias, parce precántibus,
Da Ioseph méritis sídera scándere:
Ut tandem líceat nos tibi pérpetim
Gratum prómere cánticum. Amen.
                    (ex *Breviario Romano*).

464

Salve, Ioseph, custos pie

H ail, dear Spouse of Mary mild,
   Tender Guardian of her Child,
Joseph, best of teachers, hail!

By thy prayers obtain salvation,
And of sin full condonation
   For the soul by guilt oppressed.

May we all through thee be freed
From the pain that is our meed
   For the evil we have done.

Thou impart to us all grace,
And in Heaven a blessed place;
   This we humbly ask of thee.

By thy prayer, when life is o'er,
May we reach the Heavenly shore,
   There to join angelic choirs.

May all those that are in woe,
Freed from sorrow, joyous go,
   When thou off'rest up thy prayer.

Make the nations leap for joy,
Save the sick from all annoy,
   Whilst thou prayest to thy Lord.

Joseph, hail, king David's son!
Help the flock by Jesus won,
   In the dreadful judgment day.

Do thou to our Saviour pray,
That He cast us not away,
   When death's angel doth appear.

While we live, defend us here:
After death, grant us good cheer
   In our fatherland above. **Amen.**

(tr. C.E.S.)

An indulgence of 3 years (S. P. Ap., April 28, 1934).

Salve, Ioseph, Custos pie
Sponse Vírginis Maríæ
Educátor óptime.

Tua prece salus data
Sit et culpa condonáta
Peccatrícis ánimæ.

Per te cuncti liberémur
Omni pœna quam merémur
Nostris pro crimínibus.

Per te nobis impertíta
Omnis grátia expetíta
Sit, et salus ánimæ.

Te precánte vita functi
Simus Angelis coniúncti
In cælésti pátria.

Sint et omnes tribuláti
Te precánte liberáti
Cunctis ab angústiis.

Omnes pópuli læténtur,
Aegrotántes et sanéntur,
Te rogánte Dóminum.

Ioseph, Fili David Regis,
Recordáre Christi gregis
In die iudícii.

Salvatórem deprecáre,
Ut nos velit liberáre
Nostræ mortis témpore.

Tu nos vivos hic tuére
Inde mórtuos gaudére
Fac cælésti glória. Amen.

V

DEVOUT EXERCISES

465

The faithful on any of seven continuous Sundays of the year that they may choose, if they devoutly recite the prayers set forth under n. 470 below, or, in case of some impediment thereto, say *Our Father*, *Hail Mary* and *Glory be* seven times, may gain:

An indulgence of 5 years;

A plenary indulgence, on the usual conditions (S. C. Ind., Feb. 1, and March 22, 1847; S. P. Ap., May 23, 1936).

466

The faithful who in the month of March or, if that is impossible, in any other month of the year, are present at public devotions in honor of St. Joseph, Spouse of the B. V. M., may gain:

An indulgence of 7 years, on any day of the month;

A plenary indulgence, if they take part in ten such exercises at least, and, moreover, go to confession, receive Holy Communion and pray for the intentions of His Holiness the Pope.

Those who perform their devotions to St. Joseph privately during the month of March, may gain:

An indulgence of 5 years once, on any day of the month;

A plenary indulgence on the usual conditions, if they perform such devotions daily through the entire month; but if public devotions are held, this indulgence is available only to those who are lawfully hindered from taking part therein (S. C. Ind., April 27, 1865; S. P. Ap., Nov. 21, 1933).

467

The faithful who devoutly take part in a public novena in honor of St. Joseph, Spouse of the B. V. M., in preparation for the Feast, may gain:

An indulgence of 7 years on any day;

A plenary indulgence, on condition of confession, Communion and prayer for the intentions of the Sovereign Pontiff, if they take part in the exercises of the novena for at least five days.

Those who perform their devotions privately at the aforesaid time, with the intention of so continuing for nine successive days, may gain:

An indulgence of 5 years once, on any day;

A plenary indulgence, on the usual conditions, at the end of the novena; but where such devout exercises are held publicly, this indulgence can be gained only by those who are lawfully hindered from being present at the public exercises (S. C. Ind., Nov. 26, 1876; S. P. Ap., March 4, 1935).

468

The faithful who on the first Wednesday of any month, perform some devout exercise in honor of St. Joseph, may gain:

An indulgence of 5 years;

A plenary indulgence on the usual conditions (S. P. Ap., April 1, 1921, Nov. 27, 1928 and May 13, 1933).

469

The faithful who before an image of St. Joseph, piously recite *Our Father*, *Hail Mary* and *Glory be*, with the invocation: *Saint Joseph, pray for me!* may gain:

An indulgence of 300 days;

A plenary indulgence on the usual conditions, if this pious practice is continued for an entire month (S. P. Ap., Oct. 12, 1936).

VI

PRAYERS

470

I. O chaste Spouse of Mary most holy, glorious Saint Joseph, great was the trouble and anguish of thy heart when thou wast minded to put away privately thine inviolate Spouse, yet thy joy was unspeakable, when the surpassing mystery of the Incarnation was made known to thee by the Angel!

By this thy sorrow and this thy joy we beseech thee to comfort our souls, both now and in the sorrows of our final hour, with the joy of a good life and a holy death after the pattern of thine own in the arms of Jesus and Mary.

Our Father, Hail Mary, Glory be.

II. O most blessed Patriarch, glorious Saint Joseph, who wast chosen to be the foster-father of the Word made flesh, thy sorrow at seeing the Child Jesus born in such poverty was suddenly changed into heavenly exultation when thou didst hear the angelic hymn, and didst behold the glories of that resplendent night.

By this thy sorrow and this thy joy, we implore thee to obtain for us the grace to pass over from life's pathway to hear the angelic songs of praise, and to rejoice in the shining splendor of celestial glory.

Our Father, Hail Mary, Glory be.

III. O glorious Saint Joseph, thou who didst faithfully obey the law of God, thy heart was pierced at the sight of the Most Precious Blood that was shed by the Infant Saviour during His Circumcision, but the Name of Jesus gave thee new life and filled thee with quiet joy.

By this thy sorrow and this thy joy, obtain for us the grace to be freed from all sin during life, and to die rejoicing, with the holy Name of Jesus in our hearts and on our lips.

Our Father, Hail Mary, Glory be.

IV. O most faithful Saint, who didst share the mysteries of our Redemption, glorious Saint Joseph, the prophecy of Simeon touching the sufferings of Jesus and Mary caused thee to shudder with mortal dread, but at the same time filled thee with a blessed joy for the salvation and glorious resurrection which, he foretold, would be attained by countless souls.

By this thy sorrow and this thy joy, obtain for us that we may be of the number of those who, through the merits of Jesus and the intercession of Mary the Virgin Mother, are predestined to a glorious resurrection.

Our Father, Hail Mary, Glory be.

V. O most watchful Guardian of the Incarnate Son of God, glorious Saint Joseph, what toil was thine in supporting and waiting upon the Son of the Most High God, especially in the flight into Egypt! Yet at the same time, how thou didst rejoice to have near thee always the very God Himself, and to see the idols of the Egyptians fall prostrate to the ground before Him.

By this thy sorrow and this thy joy, obtain for us the grace of keeping ourselves in safety from the infernal tyrant, especially by flight from dangerous occasions; may every idol of earthly affection fall from our hearts; may we be wholly employed in serving Jesus and Mary, and for them alone may we live and happily die.

Our Father, Hail Mary, Glory be.

VI. O glorious Saint Joseph, an angel on earth, thou didst marvel to see the King of Heaven obedient to thy commands, but thy consolation in bringing Jesus out of the land of Egypt was troubled by thy fear of Archelaus; nevertheless, being assured by the Angel, thou didst dwell in gladness at Nazareth with Jesus and Mary.

By this thy sorrow and this thy joy, obtain for us that our hearts may be delivered from harmful fears, that so we may rejoice in peace of conscience and may live in safety with Jesus and Mary, and, like unto thee, may die in their company.

Our Father, Hail Mary, Glory be.

VII. O glorious Saint Joseph, pattern of all holiness, when thou didst lose, through no fault of thine, the Child Jesus, thou didst seek Him sorrowing for the space of three days, until with great joy thou didst find Him again in the temple, sitting in the midst of the doctors.

By this thy sorrow and this thy joy, we supplicate thee, with our hearts upon our lips, to keep us from ever having the misfortune to lose Jesus through mortal sin; but if this supreme misfortune should befall us, grant that we may seek Him with unceasing sorrow until we find Him again, ready to show us His great mercy, especially at the hour of death; that so we may pass over to enjoy His presence in heaven, and there, in company with thee, may we sing the praises of His divine mercy forever.

Our Father, Hail Mary, Glory be.

Antiphon. And Jesus Himself was beginning about the age of thirty years, being (as it was supposed) the Son of Joseph.

℣. Pray for us, O holy Joseph,
℟. That we may be made worthy of the promises of Christ.

Let us pray.

O God, Who in Thine unspeakable Providence didst vouchsafe to choose blessed Joseph to be the Spouse of Thy most holy Mother: grant, we beseech Thee, that we may deserve to have him as our intercessor in heaven, whom we venerate on earth as our protector: Who livest and reignest world without end. Amen.

An indulgence of 5 years.

A plenary indulgence on the usual conditions, if these prayers are repeated with devotion daily for an entire month (Pius VII, Audience, Dec. 9, 1819; S. P. Ap., May 12, 1932).

471

I. In the miseries of this vale of tears, to whom shall we have recourse, if not to thee, to whom thy beloved Spouse Mary entrusted all her rich treasures, that thou mightest keep them to our advantage? "Go to my Spouse, Joseph," Mary seems to say to us, "and he will comfort you, he will deliver you from the misfortunes which now oppress you and will make you happy and contented." Do thou have pity on us, therefore, O Joseph, have pity on us through that love which thou didst cherish toward a Spouse so worthy and so amiable.

Our Father, Hail Mary, Glory be.

II. We are fully conscious that we have offended the justice of God by our sins and deserve His most severe chastisements. Now, what shall be our place of refuge? In what haven shall we find ourselves in safety? "Go to Joseph," Jesus seems to say to us, "Go to Joseph, in whom I was well pleased and

whom I had for my foster-father. To him,
as to a father, I have communicated all
power, that he may use it for your good according to his own desire." Pity us, therefore, O blessed Joseph, pity us, for the great
love thou didst bear toward a Son so admirable and so dear.

Our Father, Hail Mary, Glory be.

III. Unhappily, the sins we have committed call down upon us the heaviest scourges;
this we must confess. In what ark shall we
take refuge in order to be saved? Where shall
we find the blessed rainbow that shall give
us comfort and hope in the midst of our
affliction? "Go to Joseph," the eternal
Father seems to say to us, "go to him, who
took My place on earth with regard to My
Son made Man. I entrusted to his keeping
My Son who is the unfailing source of grace:
every grace, therefore, is in his hands." Pity
us, then, dear Joseph, pity us by thy great
love for Almighty God who hath been so
generous to thee.

Our Father, Hail Mary, Glory be.

An indulgence of 3 years.

A plenary indulgence on the usual conditions, when these
prayers are devoutly recited every day for a month (S. P. Ap.,
Sept. 30, 1936).

VII
PRAYERS

472

Remember, O most pure Spouse of the
Virgin Mary, Saint Joseph, my beloved
patron, that never hath it been heard that
any one invoked thy patronage and sought

thine aid without being comforted. Inspired
by this confidence, I come to thee and fervently commend myself to thee. Ah, despise
not my petition, dear foster-father of our
Redeemer, but accept it graciously. Amen.

An indulgence of 500 days (Apostolic Brief, June 26, 1863; S. P.
Ap., Jan. 20, 1933).

473

Saint Joseph, father and guardian of virgins, into whose faithful keeping were
entrusted Innocency itself, Christ Jesus, and
Mary, the Virgin of virgins, I pray and beseech thee through Jesus and Mary, those
pledges so dear to thee, to keep me from all
uncleanness, and to grant that my mind
may be untainted, my heart pure and my
body chaste; help me always to serve Jesus
and Mary in perfect chastity. Amen.

An indulgence of 3 years.
An indulgence of 7 years every day in March and on any Wednesday throughout the year.
A plenary indulgence, on the usual conditions, if this prayer is
devoutly repeated every day for an entire month (S. C. Ind., Feb. 4,
1877; S. P. Ap., May 18, 1936 and March 10, 1941).

Vírginum Custos et Pater, sancte Ioseph, cuius
fidéli custódiæ ipsa Innocéntia, Christus Iesus,
et Virgo vírginum María commíssa fuit, te per hoc
utrúmque caríssimum pignus Iesum et Maríam
óbsecro et obtéstor, ut me ab omni immundítia præ-
servátum, mente incontamináta, puro corde et casto
córpore Iesu et Maríæ semper fácias castíssime famulári. Amen.

474

O glorious Saint Joseph, chosen by God to
be the foster-father of Jesus, the chaste
spouse of Mary ever Virgin, and the head of
the Holy Family and then appointed by the

Vicar of Christ to be the heavenly patron and defender of the Church founded by Jesus, most confidently do I implore at this moment thy powerful aid for all the Church militant on earth. Do thou shield with thy truly paternal love especially the Supreme Pontiff and all the Bishops and priests who are in union with the Holy See of Peter. Be the defender of all who labor for souls amidst the trials and tribulations of this life, and cause all the peoples of the earth to submit themselves in a docile spirit to that Church which is the ark of salvation for all men.

Be pleased also, dear Saint Joseph, to accept this dedication of myself which I now make unto thee. I dedicate myself wholly to thee, that thou mayest ever be my father, my patron and my guide in the way of salvation. Obtain for me great purity of heart and a fervent devotion to the interior life. Grant that, following thine example, I may direct all my actions to the greater glory of God, in union with the Sacred Heart of Jesus and the immaculate heart of Mary and in union with thee. Finally pray for me that I may be a partaker in the peace and joy which were thine at the hour of thy holy death. Amen.

An indulgence of 500 days (S. C. Ind., July 18, 1885; S. P. Ap., Nov. 8, 1933).

475

Be mindful of us, O blessed Joseph, and intercede for us with thy foster-Son by the pleading of thy prayer: do thou, in like

manner, render the blessed Virgin Mary thy
Spouse, gracious unto us, for she is the
Mother of Him, who with the Father and the
Holy Ghost liveth and reigneth world with-
out end. Amen (St. Bernardine of Siena).

An indulgence of 3 years.
A plenary indulgence, on the usual conditions, if this prayer is
recited daily for a month in a spirit of devotion (S. C. Ind., Dec.
14, 1889; S. P. Ap., June 13, 1936).

Meménto nostri, beáte Ioseph, et tuæ oratiónis
suffrágio apud tuum putatívum Fílium intercéde; sed et beatíssimam Vírginem Sponsam tuam
nobis propítiam redde, quæ Mater est Eius, qui cum
Patre et Spíritu Sancto vivit et regnat per infiníta
sǽcula sæculórum. Amen (S. Bernardinus Senensis).

476

To thee, O blessed Joseph, do we have recourse in our tribulation, and, having
implored the help of thy thrice-holy Spouse,
we confidently invoke thy patronage also. By
that charity wherewith thou wast united to
the immaculate Virgin Mother of God, and
by that fatherly affection with which thou
didst embrace the Child Jesus, we beseech
thee and we humbly pray, that thou wouldst
look graciously upon the inheritance which
Jesus Christ hath purchased by His Blood,
and assist us in our needs by thy power and
strength. Most watchful guardian of the
Holy Family, protect the chosen people of
Jesus Christ; keep far from us, most loving
father, all blight of error and corruption:
mercifully assist us from heaven, most
mighty defender, in this our conflict with
the powers of darkness; and, even as of old

thou didst rescue the Child Jesus from the supreme peril of His life, so now defend God's Holy Church from the snares of the enemy and from all adversity; keep us one and all under thy continual protection, that we may be supported by thine example and thine assistance, may be enabled to lead a holy life, die a happy death and come at last to the possession of everlasting blessedness in heaven. Amen.

An indulgence of 3 years.

An indulgence of 7 years during the month of October, when said after the recitation of the Rosary and on any Wednesday throughout the year.

A plenary indulgence once a month, on the usual conditions, for the daily recitation of this prayer (Leo XIII, Encyclical Aug. 15, 1889; S. C. Ind., Sept. 21, 1889; S. P. Ap., May 17, 1927; Dec. 13, 1935 and March 10, 1941).

Ad te beáte Ioseph, in tribulatióne nostra confúgimus, atque, imploráto Sponsæ tuæ sanctíssimæ auxílio, patrocínium quoque tuum fidénter expóscimus. Per eam, quæsumus, quæ te cum immaculáta Vírgine Dei Genitríce coniúnxit, caritátem, perque patérnum, quo Púerum Iesum ampléxus es, amórem, súpplices deprecámur, ut ad hereditátem, quam Iesus Christus acquisívit Sánguine suo, benígnus respícias, ac necessitátibus nostris tua virtúte et ope succúrras. Tuére, o Custos providentíssime divínæ Famíliæ, Iesu Christi sóbolem eléctam; próhibe a nobis, amantíssime Pater, omnem errórum ac corruptelárum luem; propítius nobis, sospitátor noster fortíssime, in hoc cum potestáte tenebrárum certámine e cælo adésto; et sicut olim Púerum Iesum e summo eripuísti vitæ discrímine, ita nunc Ecclésiam sanctam Dei ab hostílibus insídiis atque ab omni adversitáte defénde: nosque síngulos perpétuo tege patrocínio, ut ad tui exémplar et ope tua suffúlti, sancte vívere, pie émori, sempiternámque in cælis beatitúdinem ássequi possímus. Amen.

477

O Joseph, virgin-father of Jesus, most pure Spouse of the Virgin Mary, pray every day for us to the same Jesus, the Son of God, that we, being defended by the power of His grace and striving dutifully in life, may be crowned by Him at the hour of death.

An indulgence of 500 days (Pius X, Rescript in his own hand, Oct. 11, 1906; exhib. Nov. 26, 1906; S. P. Ap., May 23, 1931).

O Ioseph, virgo Pater Iesu, puríssime Sponse Vírginis Maríæ, quotídie deprecáre pro nobis ipsum Iesum Fílium Dei, ut, armis suæ grátiæ muníti legítime certántes in vita, ab eódem coronémur in morte.

478

Glorious Saint Joseph, pattern of all who are devoted to toil, obtain for me the grace to toil in the spirit of penance, in order thereby to atone for my many sins; to toil conscientiously, putting devotion to duty before my own inclinations; to labor with thankfulness and joy, deeming it an honor to employ and to develop, by my labor, the gifts I have received from Almighty God; to work with order, peace, moderation, and patience, without ever shrinking from weariness and difficulties; to work above all with a pure intention and with detachment from self, having always before my eyes the hour of death and the accounting which I must then render of time ill-spent, of talents unemployed, of good undone, and of my empty pride in success, which is so fatal to the work of God. All for Jesus, all through Mary, all in imitation of thee, O Patriarch

Joseph! This shall be my motto in life and in death. Amen.

An indulgence of 500 days (Pius X, Rescript in his own hand, Nov. 23, 1906, exhib. March 15, 1907; S. P. Ap., March 28, 1933) .

479

S upported by the patronage of the Spouse of Thy most holy Mother, we pray Thee, O Lord, for Thy mercy; that Thou wouldst make our hearts despise all things earthly and love Thee, the true God, with perfect charity: Who livest and reignest world without end. Amen (Roman Missal) .

An indulgence of 3 years.

A plenary indulgence, once a month, on the usual conditions, if this prayer is devoutly repeated every day (S. P. Ap., Nov. 12, 1936) .

S anctíssimæ Genitrícis tuæ Sponsi patrocínio suf- fúlti, rogámus, Dómine, cleméntiam tuam: ut corda nostra fácias terréna cuncta despícere ac te verum Deum perfécta caritáte dilígere: Qui vivis et regnas in sǽcula sæculórum. Amen (ex *Missali Romano*) .

NOTE: A prayer to St. Joseph, for the hallowing of holydays, is found under n. 700.

Art. III

IN HONOR OF THE HOLY APOSTLES

I

THE HOLY APOSTLES, PETER AND PAUL

480

Invocation

D efend, O Lord, Thy people: and as they put their trust in the patronage of Thy holy Apostles, Peter and Paul, keep them ever by Thy protection. Through Christ our Lord. Amen (Roman Missal) .

An indulgence of 300 days.

A plenary indulgence on the usual conditions, for the daily recitation of this prayer when continued for a month (S. P. Ap., Nov. 22, 1934).

Prótege, Dómine, pópulum tuum; et Apostolórum tuórum, Petri et Pauli patrocínio confidéntem perpétua defensióne consérva. Per Christum Dóminum nostrum. Amen (ex *Missali Romano*).

481
A Pious Exercise

The faithful who devoutly assist at a public novena in honor of the holy Apostles, Peter and Paul, before their Feast, are granted:

An indulgence of 5 years, on any day of the novena;

A plenary indulgence, if they take part in the exercises of the novena on at least five days, and go to confession, receive Holy Communion and pray for the intentions of the Sovereign Pontiff.

Those, moreover, who at the aforesaid time offer their prayers privately in honor of the same holy Apostles, with the intention of so doing for nine consecutive days are granted:

An indulgence of 3 years once on any day;

A plenary indulgence, on the usual conditions, at the completion of the novena; but where such a novena is held publicly, only those who are lawfully prevented from attending the public service, may avail themselves of this latter indulgence (S. P. Ap., June 12, 1932).

482
Petitions

O holy Apostles, Peter and Paul, I choose you this day and for ever to be my special patrons and advocates; thee, Saint Peter, Prince of the Apostles, because thou art the Rock, upon which Almighty God hath built His Church; thee, Saint Paul, because thou wast fore-chosen by God as the Vessel of election and the Preacher of truth in the whole world. Obtain for me, I pray you, lively faith, firm hope and burning love; complete detachment from myself, contempt of the world, patience in adversity, humility in prosperity, attention in prayer, purity of heart, a right intention in all my works, diligence in fulfilling the duties of my state of life, constancy in my resolutions, resignation to the will of God and perseverance in the grace of God even unto death; that so, by means of your intercession and your glorious merits, I may be able to overcome the temptations of the world, the flesh and the devil, and may be made worthy to appear before the chief and eternal Shepherd of souls, Jesus Christ, who with the Father and the Holy Ghost liveth and reigneth for endless ages, to enjoy His presence and love Him forever.   Amen.

Our Father, Hail Mary, Glory be.

℣. Thou shalt make them princes over all the earth,

℟. They shall be mindful of Thy Name, O Lord.

Let us pray.

O God, whose right hand raised up blessed Peter, when he walked upon the water and began to sink, and thrice delivered his fellow-Apostle Paul from the depths of the sea, when he suffered shipwreck: graciously hear us and grant, by the merits of them both, that we also may attain unto everlasting glory: Who livest and reignest world without end.   Amen.

An indulgence of 500 days.

A plenary indulgence once a month, on the usual conditions, for the daily recitation of these petitions (S. C. Ind., June 18, 1876; S. P. Ap., July 21, 1931 and May 16, 1933).

II

SAINT PETER THE APOSTLE

483

Prayers

Thou art the Shepherd of the sheep, the Prince of the Apostles, unto thee were given the keys of the kingdom of heaven.

℣. Thou art Peter;

℟. And upon this rock I will build my Church.

Let us pray.

Raise us up, we beseech Thee, O Lord, by the apostolic assistance of blessed Peter, Thine Apostle: so that the weaker we are, the more mightily we may be helped by the power of his intercession: and that being perpetually defended by the same holy Apostle, we may neither yield to any iniquity, nor be overcome by any adversity. Through Christ our Lord. Amen.

An indulgence of 500 days.

A plenary indulgence, once a month, on the usual conditions, for the daily recitation of these prayers (S. C. Ind., June 22, 1782; S. P. Ap., May 18, 1935).

Tu es Pastor óvium, Princeps Apostolórum, tibi tráditæ sunt claves regni cælórum.

℣. Tu es Petrus,

℟. Et super hanc petram ædificábo Ecclésiam meam.

Oremus.

Apostólicis nos, Dómine, quæsumus, beáti Petri Apóstoli tui attólle præsídiis, ut quanto fragilióres sumus, tanto eius intercessióne validióribus auxíliis foveámur; et iúgiter apostólica defensióne muníti, nec succumbámus vítiis, nec opprimámur advérsis. Per Christum Dóminum nostrum. Amen.

484

Prayers

O glorious Saint Peter, who, in return for thy lively and generous faith, thy profound and sincere humility, and thy burning love, wast honored by Jesus Christ with singular privileges, and, in particular, with the leadership of the other Apostles and the primacy of the whole Church, of which thou wast made the foundation stone, do thou obtain for us the grace of a lively faith, that shall not fear to profess itself openly, in its entirety and in all of its manifestations, even to the shedding of blood, if occasion should demand it, and to the sacrifice of life itself in preference to surrender. Obtain for us likewise, a sincere loyalty to our holy mother, the Church; grant that we may ever remain most closely and sincerely united to the Roman Pontiff, who is the heir of thy faith and of thy authority, the one, true, visible Head of the Catholic Church, that mystic ark outside which there is no salvation. Grant, moreover, that we may follow, in all humility and meekness, her teaching and her counsels, and may be obedient to all her precepts, in order to be able here on earth to enjoy a peace that is sure and undisturbed, and to attain one day in heaven to everlasting happiness. Amen.

℣. Pray for us, Saint Peter the Apostle,

℟. That we may be made worthy of the promises of Christ.

Let us pray.

O God, who hast given unto Thy blessed Apostle Peter the keys of the kingdom of heaven, and the power to bind and loose: grant that we may be delivered, through the help of his intercession, from the bonds of all our sins: Who livest and reignest world without end. Amen.

An indulgence of 500 days.

A plenary indulgence once a month, on the usual conditions, if these prayers are repeated daily with devout sentiments (Apostolic Brief, April 27, 1916; S. P. Ap., Jan. 24, 1931).

NOTE: For the indulgences attached to visits to the tomb and image of St. Peter in the Vatican Basilica, see n. 774.

III

SAINT PAUL THE APOSTLE

485

Prayers

T hou art the Vessel of election, Saint Paul the Apostle, the Preacher of truth in the whole world.

℣. Pray for us, Saint Paul the Apostle,

℟. That we may be made worthy of the promises of Christ.

Let us pray.

Almighty and everlasting God, who, of Thy divine mercy, didst instruct Thy blessed

Apostle Paul what he should do that he might be filled with the Holy Ghost; by his admonitions directing us and his merits interceding for us, grant that we may serve Thee in fear and trembling and so be filled with the comfort of Thy heavenly gifts. Through Christ our Lord. Amen.

An indulgence of 500 days.

A plenary indulgence once a month, on the usual conditions, for the daily recitation of these prayers with devotion (Pius VII, Audience Jan. 23, 1806; S. P. Ap., Oct. 16, 1933).

Tu es vas electiónis, sancte Paule Apóstole, prædicátor veritátis in univérso mundo.

℣. Ora pro nobis, sancte Paule Apóstole,
℞. Ut digni efficiámur promissiónibus Christi.

Oremus.

Omnípotens sempitérne Deus, qui beáto Apóstolo tuo Paulo quid fáceret, ut implerétur Spíritu Sancto, divína miseratióne præcepísti; eius dirigéntibus mónitis et suffragántibus méritis concéde, ut serviéntes tibi in timóre et tremóre, cæléstium donórum consolatióne repleámur. Per Christum Dóminum nostrum. Amen.

486
Prayers

O glorious Saint Paul, who, from being a persecutor of the Christian name, didst become its most zealous Apostle, and who, to carry the knowledge of Jesus, our divine Saviour, to the uttermost parts of the earth, didst joyfully suffer prison, scourgings, stonings, shipwreck and all manner of persecutions, and who didst finish thy course by shedding the last drop of thy blood: obtain for us the grace to accept, as favors bestowed by the mercy of God, the infirmities, suffer-

ings and misfortunes of this life, that we
may not grow slack in our service of God by
reason of these vicissitudes of our exile, but
that we may the rather show ourselves ever
more devoted.   Amen.

℣. Pray for us, Saint Paul the Apostle,

℟. That we may be made worthy of the
promises of Christ.

Let us pray.

O God, who hast taught the multitude of
the Gentiles by the preaching of blessed Paul
the Apostle: grant unto us, we beseech Thee,
that we who keep his memory sacred, may
feel the might of his intercession before
Thee.   Through Christ our Lord.   Amen.

An indulgence of 500 days.

A plenary indulgence on the usual conditions if these prayers
are recited daily for a month (S. C. of the Prop. of the Faith, Jan.
13, 1905, document exhibited, Jan. 18, 1905; S. P. Ap., Aug. 8, 1936).

NOTE: Another prayer to St. Paul the Apostle for the publishing
of good books, is found under n. 709.

IV

SAINT JOHN, APOSTLE AND EVANGELIST

487

Prayer

O glorious Apostle, Saint John, who for
thy virginal purity wast so beloved by
Jesus as to merit to rest thy head upon His
divine bosom, and to be left, in His stead, as
a son to His most holy Mother, I implore thee
to set me on fire with a burning love for Jesus
and Mary. Obtain for me, I pray, this grace
from our Lord, that, even now, with my
heart set free from earthly affections, I may

be made worthy to be ever united to Jesus as His faithful disciple and to Mary as her devoted child both here on earth and then forever in heaven. Amen.

An indulgence of 300 days.

A plenary indulgence once a month, on the usual conditions, for the daily repetition of these prayers with devotion (S. C. Ind., Dec. 8, 1897; S. P. Ap., May 10, 1933 and June 10, 1949).

NOTE: A prayer to St. John the Apostle, to be said by priests, is found under n. 745.

V

SAINT JUDE THADDEUS, APOSTLE

488

Prayer

O glorious Saint Jude Thaddeus, by those sublime prerogatives, wherewith thou wast ennobled in thy lifetime, namely, thy kinship with our Lord Jesus Christ according to the flesh, and thy vocation to be an Apostle; by that glory which now is thine in heaven as the reward of thine apostolic labors and thy martyrdom: obtain for us from the Giver of every good and perfect gift all the graces whereof we stand in need in order to treasure up in our hearts the divinely inspired doctrines which thou hast transmitted to us in thy Epistle; that is to say, to build our edifice of perfection upon our most holy faith, praying by the grace of the Holy Spirit; to keep ourselves in the love of God, looking for the mercy of Jesus Christ unto eternal life; to strive by all means to help them that go astray; exalting thus the glory and majesty, the dominion and power of Him who is able to keep us without sin and to present us spotless with exceeding joy at the coming of our divine Saviour, the Lord Jesus Christ. Amen.

An indulgence of 300 days.

A plenary indulgence on the usual conditions, if this prayer is said with devotion every day for a month (S. C. Ind., Aug. 17, 1908, S. P. Ap., Feb. 21, 1933).

VI
SAINT JAMES THE APOSTLE

489
Prayer

O glorious Apostle, Saint James, who by reason of thy fervent and generous heart wast chosen by Jesus to be a witness of His glory on Mount Tabor, and of His agony in Gethsemane; thou, whose very name is a symbol of warfare and victory: obtain for us strength and consolation in the unending warfare of this life, that, having constantly and generously followed Jesus, we may be victors in the strife and deserve to receive the victor's crown in heaven. Amen.

An indulgence of 300 days.

A plenary indulgence once a month, on the usual conditions, for the daily recitation of this prayer with devotion (S. P. Ap., July 16, 1923 and June 12, 1949).

Art. IV
IN HONOR OF OTHER SAINTS

I
SAINT JOACHIM, FATHER OF THE B. V. MARY

490
Invocation

O Joachim, husband of holy Anne, father of the merciful Virgin, hither bring thy servants help for their salvation.

O Ióachim, sanctæ coniux Annæ, pater almæ
Vírginis, hic fámulis ferto salútis opem.

An indulgence of 300 days, once a day (Pius X, Rescript in his
own hand, May 28, 1906; exhib. June 16, 1906).

491
Prayer

O great and glorious Patriarch, Saint
Joachim, what joy is mine when I consider that thou wast chosen among all God's
holy ones to assist in the fulfilment of the
mysteries of God, and to enrich our earth
with the great Mother of God, Mary most
holy! By this singular privilege, thou hast
become most powerful with both the Mother
and her Son, so as to be able to obtain for us
the graces that are needful to us; with great
confidence I have recourse to thy mighty protection and I commend to thee all my needs
and those of my family, both spiritual and
temporal; and especially do I entrust to thy
keeping the particular favor that I desire and
look for from thy fatherly intercession. And
since thou wast a perfect pattern of the interior life, obtain for me the grace of interior
recollection and a spirit of detachment from
the transitory goods of this life, together
with a lively and enduring love for Jesus and
Mary. Obtain for me in like manner a sincere devotion and obedience to Holy Church
and the Sovereign Pontiff who rules over her:
to the end that I may live and die in faith
and hope and perfect charity, ever invoking
the holy Names of Jesus and Mary, and may
I thus be saved. Amen.

Our Father, Hail Mary, Glory be *three times*.

An indulgence of 300 days once a day.

A plenary indulgence on the usual conditions, if this prayer is recited daily for an entire month (S. C. Ind., March 20, 1886; S. P. Ap., Jan. 12, 1935).

492
Prayer

O great Patriarch, Saint Joachim, deserving by thy singular virtue to be chosen of old by divine Providence to give to the world that immaculate Queen, in whom all nations were to be blessed, and who, in her virginal bosom, was to bear the Saviour of the human race: we who are thy devout clients rejoice with thee in this thy great privilege, and implore thee to extend thy special protection to ourselves and our families. Do not, dear Saint, suffer the devil and sin to find a place in our hearts, nor the false maxims of the world to lead us astray; permit us not to live unmindful of eternity, for which we have been created. Obtain for us from God a firm and unshaken faith in opposition to the impieties and errors which are ever being spread abroad by the enemies of Holy Church and the Apostolic See; a sincere and constant devotion to the Vicar of Jesus Christ, the Roman Pontiff; and an unfailing courage in refuting calumnies against those things which are most sacred and venerable in our holy religion.

Do thou, who art powerful by reason of that love which thy holy daughter Mary bears toward thee, assist the cause of the Church, gain for her the victory for which she sighs, scatter the powers of darkness, destroy their pride and grant that the light of the true faith may shine resplendent in all minds. Grant us, above all, a tender and filial devotion to thy beloved daughter and our Mother, Mary most holy, so that we, honoring her daily with our devout homage, may be made worthy to be numbered by her amongst her children; and after the miseries of this exile may be brought to praise and bless the mercy of God forever in heaven.   Amen.

Our Father, Hail Mary, Glory be *three times*.

An indulgence of 300 days, once a day.

A plenary indulgence, once a month, on the usual conditions, for the daily recitation of this prayer with piety (Leo XIII, Motu propr., Aug. 16, 1890; S. P. Ap., July 8, 1936 and April 10, 1949).

II
SAINT ANNE, MOTHER OF THE B. V. MARY

493
Pious Practices

a) The faithful who devoutly say some prayers in honor of St. Anne, on Tuesday of any week, are granted:

An indulgence of 7 years;
A plenary indulgence, on the usual conditions.

Those who perform such a devotional exercise on nine successive Tuesdays are granted:

A plenary indulgence on the usual conditions (S. C. of the Holy Office Aug. 22, 1912; S. P. Ap., Nov. 15, 1927 and March 18, 1932).

b) The faithful who offer their devout supplications in honor of St. Anne with the intention of so continuing for nine successive days are granted:

An indulgence of 7 years, once on any day of the novena;

A plenary indulgence on the usual conditions, at the completion of the novena (Holy Office, Aug. 22, 1912; S. P. Ap., Nov. 15, 1927 and March 18, 1932).

494

Prayer

With my heart full of the most sincere veneration, I prostrate myself before thee, O glorious Saint Anne. Thou art that creature of privilege and predilection, who by thy extraordinary virtues and holiness didst merit from God the high favor of giving life to her who is the Treasury of all graces, blessed among women, the Mother of the Word Incarnate, the most holy Virgin Mary. By virtue of so lofty a privilege, do thou deign, O most compassionate Saint, to receive me into the number of thy true clients, for so I profess myself and so I desire to remain throughout my entire life.

Shield me with thine effectual patronage and obtain for me from God the power to imitate those virtues wherewith thou wast so plentifully adorned. Grant that I may know and weep over my sins in bitterness of heart. Obtain for me the grace of most active love for Jesus and Mary, and resolution to fulfil the duties of my state of life with faithfulness and constancy. Save me from every danger that confronts me in life, and help me at the hour of death, that so I may come in safety to paradise, there to sing with thee, O most happy mother, the praises of the

Word of God made Man in the womb of thy most pure daughter, the Virgin Mary. Amen.

Our Father, Hail Mary, Glory be, *three times*.

An indulgence of 300 days, once a day.

A plenary indulgence once a month, on the usual conditions, for the daily repetition of this prayer (S. C. Ind., March 20, 1886; S. P. Ap., Oct. 10, 1934).

III
IN HONOR OF SAINT ALOYSIUS GONZAGA, CONFESSOR

495
Devout Exercises

a) The faithful who devoutly visit a church or a public or (for those who legitimately use it) a semi-public oratory, where the Feast of St. Aloysius is being kept, may gain:

A plenary indulgence, if, in addition, they make their confession, receive Holy Communion and pray for the Holy Father's intentions (S. C. Ind., Nov. 22, 1729; Nov. 21, 1737 and April 12, 1742; S. P. Ap., April 15, 1937 and Dec. 10, 1949).

b) The faithful who, on any of the six Sundays immediately preceding the Feast of St. Aloysius Gonzaga, or on any of six consecutive Sundays that they may choose during the year, spend some time in devout meditations or prayers, or who perform some other exercises of devotion in honor of the same Saint, are granted:

A plenary indulgence on the usual conditions (S. C. Ind., Dec. 11, 1739 and Jan. 7, 1740).

c) The faithful who, on any one of the nine days immediately preceding the Feast of St. Aloysius Gonzaga, say some prayers with piety in honor of the Saint, are granted:

An indulgence of 500 days, once a day;

A plenary indulgence on the usual conditions, at the end of the novena (S. P. Ap., Sept. 25, 1936).

d) The faithful who before an image of St. Aloysius Gonzaga devoutly recite *Our Father, Hail Mary*, and *Glory be*, with the invocation:

Saint Aloysius, pray for me!
are granted:

An indulgence of 300 days;

A plenary indulgence once a month, on the usual conditions, if they repeat this devout homage daily (S. P. Ap., Sept. 25, 1936).

496
Prayers

Saint Aloysius, adorned with angelic virtues, I, thy most unworthy client, commend to thee most earnestly the chastity of my mind and body. I beseech thee, for the sake of thine angelic purity, to commend me to the immaculate Lamb, Christ Jesus, and to His most holy Mother, the Virgin of virgins; and to protect me from every grievous sin. Permit me not to defile myself by any spot of impurity; nay, when thou seest me in temptation or in the danger of sin, banish far from my heart every unclean thought and desire. Awaken in me the thought of eternity and of Jesus crucified; imprint deeply in my heart a lively sense of the holy fear of God; set me on fire with the love of God; grant me the grace to imitate thee on earth that I may worthily enjoy the possession of God in heaven with thee. Amen.

Our Father, Hail Mary, Glory be.

℣. Pray for us, Saint Aloysius,

℟. That we may be made worthy of the promises of Christ.

Let us pray.

O God, the Giver of all heavenly gifts, who in the angelic youth, Aloysius, didst join wondrous innocence with equal penance: be entreated by his merits and his prayers, and grant unto us who have not followed him in his innocence the grace to imitate him in his penance. Through Christ our Lord. Amen.

An indulgence of 300 days once a day.

A plenary indulgence once a month, on the usual conditions, for the daily and devout recitation of this prayer (S. C. Ind., March 6, 1802; S. P. Ap., June 19, 1933)

NOTE: Another prayer to St. Aloysius Gonzaga, to be said by young men, is found under n. 768; an invocation to be said by clerics, is found under n. 730.

IV
SAINT IGNATIUS LOYOLA, CONFESSOR

497
A Devout Exercise

The faithful who, on any of the ten Sundays preceding the Feast of St. Ignatius Loyola, or on any of ten consecutive Sundays that they may choose during the year, spend some time in devout meditations or prayers in honor of the Saint, or who perform some other acts of devotion, are granted:

A plenary indulgence on the usual conditions (S. C. Ind., Jan. 27, 1767 and Dec. 10, 1841).

498
A Prayer

O glorious Patriarch, Saint Ignatius, we humbly beseech thee to obtain for us from Almighty God, above all things else, deliverance from sin, which is the greatest of evils, and next, from those scourges wherewith the Lord chastises the sins of His people. May thine example enkindle in our hearts an effectual desire to employ ourselves continually in laboring for the greater glory of God and the good of our fellow-men; obtain for us, likewise, from the loving Heart of Jesus our Lord, that grace which is the crown of all graces, that is to say, the grace of final perseverance and everlasting happiness. Amen.

An indulgence of 300 days.

A plenary indulgence on the usual conditions, once a month, when this prayer has been recited daily (S. C. Ind., Feb. 5, 1885; S. P. Ap., May 20, 1933).

499
A PRAYER TO ST. IGNATIUS LOYOLA AND ST. FRANCIS XAVIER, CONFESSORS

Ye mighty heroes of the Christian faith, most worthy of our love, Saint Ignatius and Saint Francis, not only were you intimately associated here below in the same bonds of religion to procure the greater glory of God, but you also merited to be raised on the same day to the honors of our altars: obtain for me, your humble and devoted servant, the singular grace of knowing and loving the Lord Jesus in deed and in truth, that so, being faithful and constant in imitating your example, I may desire and seek, above every thing created, the eternal salvation of my soul and of all them that have been redeemed in the Most Precious Blood of Jesus. Amen.

An indulgence of 300 days.

A plenary indulgence once a month, on the usual conditions, for the daily repetition of this prayer with devotion (S. P. Ap., March 6, 1922).

V

SAINT FRANCIS XAVIER, CONFESSOR

500

(The Novena of Grace)

O Saint Francis Xavier, well beloved and full of charity, in union with thee, I reverently adore the Majesty of God; and since I rejoice with exceeding joy in the singular gifts of grace bestowed upon thee during thy life, and thy gifts of glory after death, I give Him hearty thanks for them; I beseech thee with all my heart's devotion to be pleased to obtain for me, by thy effectual intercession, above all things, the grace of a holy life and a happy death. Moreover, I beg of thee to obtain for me . . . *(here mention the spiritual or temporal favor to be prayed for)*. But if what I ask of thee so earnestly doth not tend to the glory of God and the greater good of my soul, do thou, I pray, obtain for me what is more profitable to both these ends. Amen.

Our Father, Hail Mary, Glory be.

On any of nine successive days that the faithful may select for obtaining some grace through the intercession of St. Francis Xavier, if they make use of the foregoing form of prayer, or on any day that they attend the exercises of the novena, of Grace, as above, held in some church or public oratory, they are granted:

An indulgence of 3 years;
A plenary indulgence on the usual conditions at the end of the exercises (S. C. Ind., March 23, 1904; S. P. Ap., May 20, 1933).

NOTE: If, for any reason, the above prayer cannot be said, it will suffice to say five times *Our Father*, *Hail Mary*, and *Glory be* (S. C. Ind., March 23, 1904).

(Novendialia a gratia)

O valde amábilis et caritáte plene, sancte Francísce Xavéri, tecum Maiestátem divínam reverénter adóro: et quóniam summópere gáudeo de singuláribus grátiæ donis, quæ ipsa tibi cóntulit in hac vita et glóriæ post mortem, ei máximas ago grátias, teque toto cordis afféctu déprecor, ut efficáci tua intercessióne præcípuam mihi grátiam velis obtinére sanctam vitam agéndi sanctéque moriéndi. Insuper te rogo, ut mihi ímpetres... *(hic exprimatur gratia sive spiritualis sive temporalis imploranda)*. Si vero id, quod a te supplíciter peto, ad Dei glóriam et ad maius bonum ánimæ meæ mínime confert, Tu, quæso, mihi ímpetres quod utríque est utílius. Amen.

Pater, Ave, Glória.

VI

SAINT STANISLAUS KOSTKA, CONFESSOR

501

Pious Practices

a) The faithful who visit for the purpose of prayer, a church or public oratory, or even a semi-public oratory (in the case of those who may lawfully use the latter), where the Feast of St. Stanislaus Kostka is being celebrated, may gain:

A plenary indulgence, if they make their confession, receive Holy Communion and pray for the intentions of His Holiness the Pope.

b) The faithful on any of the ten Sundays immediately preceding the Feast of St. Stanislaus Kostka, if they devote themselves to pious supplications in honor of the Saint, are granted:

A plenary indulgence on the usual conditions.

c) The faithful on any of the nine days that precede the Feast of St. Stanislaus Kostka, if they devoutly offer their prayers in honor of the Saint, may gain:

An indulgence of 500 days, once a day;

A plenary indulgence, on the usual conditions, at the end of the novena.

d) The faithful who devoutly recite before an image of this saint: *Our Father, Hail Mary*, and *Glory be*, adding the invocation:

Saint Stanislaus, pray for me!

may obtain:

An indulgence of 300 days;

A plenary indulgence on the usual conditions, if they perform this devotion daily for a month.

e) The faithful who take part in the retreat, known as the Retreat of Saint Stanislaus, may gain:

An indulgence of 100 days (S. C. Ind., March 3, 1827; S. P. Ap., Oct. 12, 1935).

502
Prayers

Saint Stanislaus, my patron most chaste, Angel of purity, I rejoice with thee in that singular gift of virginal purity which graced thy spotless heart; and I humbly beseech thee, obtain for me the strength to overcome temptations to impurity, and inspire me to continual vigilance in keeping intact the virtue of holy purity.

Our Father, Hail Mary, Glory be.

Saint Stanislaus, my patron most loving, Seraph of charity, I rejoice with thee in the glowing flame of love that kept thy pure and sinless heart always at peace and united to thy God: I humbly beseech thee to obtain for me such a flame of divine love as shall consume every affection for things of earth, and set me on fire with heavenly love alone.

Our Father, Hail Mary, Glory be.

Saint Stanislaus, my patron most tender and most powerful, Angel of purity and Seraph of love, I rejoice with thee in thy happy death, a death caused by thy longing to see Mary who was taken up bodily into heaven, and consummated by a mighty impulse of love toward her. I give thanks unto Mary who was pleased to hear and answer thy prayers, and I implore thee, by the glory of that thy happy death, to be the advocate and patron of my death. Intercede with Mary for me that my death, if not so happy as thine, may at least be peaceful under the protection of Mary, my Advocate, and of thee my special patron.

Our Father, Hail Mary, Glory be.

℣. Pray for us, O holy Stanislaus,
℞. That we may be made worthy of the promises of Christ.

Let us pray.

O God, who amongst the other wonderful works of Thy wisdom, hast bestowed the grace of ripe holiness on them of tender years: grant, we beseech Thee, that we, following in the footsteps of blessed Stanislaus and redeeming the time by unremitting labor, may hasten to enter into our eternal rest. Through Christ our Lord. Amen.

An indulgence of 300 days, once a day.

A plenary indulgence, on the usual conditions, if these prayers are said daily for a month with devotion (Pius IX, Rescript in nis own hand, March 21, 1847; S. C. Ind., July 10, 1854; S. P. Ap., Dec. 5, 1931).

VII
SAINT JOHN OF THE CROSS, CONFESSOR

503
A Prayer

O glorious Saint John of the Cross, great Doctor of the Church, who, from very longing to be configured to Jesus crucified, didst desire nothing more ardently, even to the last moment of thy holy life, than to suffer and to be despised and rejected of all men; and so great was thy thirst for suffering, that thy generous heart was filled with joy in the midst of most painful torments and afflictions; I beseech thee, dear Saint, by the glory thou didst merit by thy manifold sufferings, intercede for me with Almighty God and obtain for me love of suffering, together with grace and strength to endure all tribulations and adversities with dauntless courage; for these are the sure means of coming into the possession of that crown of glory which is prepared for me in heaven.   Ah yes, dear Saint, from that high and glorious throne where thou sittest triumphant, hear, I beseech thee, my earnest entreaties, that, following thee, I may become a lover of the Cross and of suffering and thus may merit to be thy companion in glory.   Amen.

An indulgence of 300 days.

A plenary indulgence, once a month, on the usual conditions, for the daily recitation of this prayer (S. C. Ind., Jan. 30, 1828; S. P. Ap., May 20 1934).

VIII

SAINT PIUS V, POPE AND CONFESSOR

504
Hymn

Belli tumultus ingruit

Wars and tumults fill the earth;
    Men the fear of God despise;
Retribution, vengeance, wrath,
Brood upon the angry skies.

Holy Pius, Pope sublime!
Whom, in this most evil time—
Whom, of Saints in bliss, can we
Better call to aid than thee?

None more mightily than thou
Hath, by holy deed or word,
Through the spacious earth below,
Spread the glory of the Lord.

    Holy Pius, etc.

Thine it was, O Pontiff brave!
Pontiff of eternal Rome!
From barbaric yoke to save
Terror-stricken Christendom.

    Holy Pius, etc.

When Lepanto's gulf beheld,
Strewn upon its waters fair,
Turkey's countless navy yield
To the power of thy prayer.

    Holy Pius, etc.

Who meanwhile with prophet's eye,
Didst the distant battle see,

And announce to standers-by
That same moment's victory.
  Holy Pius, etc.

Mightier now and glorified,
Hear the suppliant cry we pour;
Crush rebellion's haughty pride:
Quell the din of rising war.
  Holy Pius, etc.

At thy prayers may golden peace
Down to earth descend again;
License, discord, trouble cease;
Justice, truth and order reign.
  Holy Pius, etc.

To the Lord of endless days,
One Almighty Trinity,
Sempiternal glory, praise,
Honor, might and blessing be.   Amen.

(tr. E. Caswall).

An indulgence of 300 days (S. C. Ind., Oct. 2, 1830; S. P. Ap., Feb. 15, 1932)

Hymnus

Belli tumúltus íngruit;
  Cultus Dei contémnitur;
Ultríxque culpam pérsequens
Iam poena terris ímminet.

  Quem nos in hoc discrímine
  Cæléstium de sédibus
  Præsentiórem víndicem,
  Quam te, Pie, invocábimus?

Nemo, beáte Póntifex,
Intensióre róbore
Quam Tu, supérni Núminis
Promóvit in terris decus.
  Quem nos etc.

Ausísve fortióribus
Avértit a cervícibus,
Quod christiánis géntibus
Iugum parábant bárbari.
Quem nos etc.

Tu comparátis clássibus,
Votis magis sed férvidis
Ad ínsulas Echínadas
Fundis tyránnum Thráciæ.
Quem nos etc.

Absénsque eódem témpore,
Hostis fuit quo pérditus,
Vides, et adstántes doces
Pugnæ secúndos éxitus.
Quem nos etc.

Maióra qui cælo potes,
Tu súpplices nunc áspice;
Tu cívium discórdias
Compésce et iras hóstium.
Quem nos etc.

Precánte te, pax áurea
Terras revísat; ut Deo
Tuti queámus réddere
Mox lætióra cántica.
Quem nos etc.

Tibi, beáta Trínitas,
Uni Deo sit glória,
Laus et potéstas ómnia
Per sæculórum sæcula.   Amen.

505

Prayers

Ant. **P**ius, admirable Shepherd, ever
mindful of thy sheep, before the
highest Judge do thou intercede for all believers.

Let us pray.

O God, who in order to crush them that hate Thy Church and to restore Thy solemn worship, didst vouchsafe to choose Blessed Pius to be Thy great High Priest: grant us to be secure under his protection and so to continue in Thy service, that, having overcome all the wiles of our adversaries, we may enjoy a perpetual peace. Through Christ our Lord. Amen.

Our Father, Hail Mary, Glory be.

An indulgence of 300 days (Holy Office, Sept. 18, 1916).

Ant. Pie, pastor mirífice, tuárum memor óvium, sta coram summo iúdice pro pártibus fidélium.

Orémus.

Deus, qui, ad conteréndos Ecclésiæ tuæ hostes et ad divínum cultum reparándum, beátum Pium Pontíficem Máximum elígere dignátus es: fac nos ipsíus deféndi præsídiis et ita tuis inhærére obséquiis, ut, ómnium hóstium superátis insídiis, perpétua pace lætémur. Per Christum Dóminum nostrum. Amen.

Pater, Ave, Glória.

IX

SAINT CAMILLUS OF LELLIS, CONFESSOR

506

A Devout Exercise

The faithful who pray devoutly on any Sunday in honor of Saint Camillus of Lellis, with the intention of so continuing for seven successive Sundays, are granted:

A plenary indulgence on the usual conditions (S. C. Ind., Aug. 8, 1853; S. P. Ap., July 20, 1933).

NOTE: A prayer to St. Camillus for the sick is found under n. 668.

X

SAINT MICHAEL DE' SANTI, CONFESSOR

507

Prayer

O glorious Saint Michael, Seraph inflamed with the most ardent love of Jesus in the Blessed Sacrament, who didst spend thy nights and days in His real Presence and didst find there thy dearest joys, so that thou didst swoon away for very love: vouchsafe, I pray thee, to obtain for me a lively faith, a firm hope and an ardent love toward this inestimable Treasure, this precious Pledge of glory everlasting; in order that I may be able to be a fervent worshiper of Jesus in the Blessed Sacrament, and thereby rejoice with thee to behold Him face to face in an eternity of bliss. Amen.

Our Father, Hail Mary, Glory be.

An indulgence of 300 days (Pius IX, Rescript in his own hand, May 20, 1862; S. P. Ap., May 20, 1933 and June 10, 1949).

XI

SAINT PAUL OF THE CROSS, CONFESSOR

508

A Devout Exercise

The faithful who perform their devotions in honor of St. Paul of the Cross, with the intention of repeating the same for nine successive days, may gain:

An indulgence of 3 years, once each day;

A plenary indulgence on the usual conditions, at the end of the nine-days' exercise (Pius IX, Rescript in his own hand, Oct. 17, 1867; S. P. Ap., March 2, 1935).

509

A Prayer

O glorious Saint Paul of the Cross, on earth thou wast a mirror of innocence and a model of penance! O hero of saintliness, chosen by God to meditate day and night on the bitter Passion of His only-begotten Son, and to spread devotion thereto by word and deed as well as by means of thy religious family! O Apostle, mighty in word and work, thou didst spend thy life in bringing back to the foot of the Cross the erring souls of countless unfortunate sinners! Do thou mercifully look down once more from heaven upon my poor soul and hear my petitions. Obtain for me so great a love of Jesus suffering, that by constant meditation on His Passion I may make His sufferings mine. Let me realize in the deep Wounds of my Saviour the wickedness of my transgressions, and obtain from them, as from the fountain of salvation, the grace of bitter tears and an effectual resolution to imitate thee in thy penance, if I have not followed thine example of innocence. Obtain for me, also, Saint Paul, the favor that I now especially ask of thee, as I humbly kneel before thee. . . . Obtain, moreover, for our Holy Mother the Church, victory over Her foes; for sinners, the gift of conversion; for heretics, the grace of returning to the unity of the Catholic faith. Finally, intercede for me that I may, by the grace of God, die a holy death, and come at last to enjoy with thee His blessed

Presence in heaven for all eternity. Amen.
Our Father, Hail Mary, Glory be.

An indulgence of 300 days.

A plenary indulgence on the usual conditions, once a month, for the daily recitation of this prayer in a spirit of devotion (Pius IX, Rescript in his own hand, April 24, 1853 and April 20, 1868; S. P. Ap., Sept. 12, 1933).

510
A Prayer

O glorious Saint Paul of the Cross, who, by meditating on the Passion of Jesus Christ, didst attain to so high a degree of holiness on earth and of happiness in heaven, and, by preaching the same Passion, didst offer anew to the world the most certain cure for all its ills, obtain for us the grace to keep it ever deeply engraved in our hearts, that so we may be able to reap the same fruits both in time and in eternity. Amen.

Our Father, Hail Mary, Glory be.

An indulgence of 300 days.

A plenary indulgence on the usual conditions, for the daily devout repetition of this prayer for a month (Pius X, Rescript in his own hand, March 26, 1904; exhib. Sept. 17, 1904; S. P. Ap., Nov. 18, 1935).

XII
SAINT GREGORY VII, POPE AND CONFESSOR

511
A Prayer

O invincible defender of Holy Church's freedom, Saint Gregory of great renown, by that firmness thou didst show in maintaining the Church's rights against all her enemies, stretch forth from heaven thy mighty arm, we beseech thee, to comfort her and defend her in the fearful battle she must ever wage with the powers of darkness. Do thou, in an especial manner, give strength in this dread conflict to the venerable Pontiff who has fallen heir not only to thy throne, but likewise to the fearlessness of thy mighty heart; obtain for him the joy of beholding his holy endeavors crowned by the triumph of the Church and the return of the lost sheep into the right path. Grant, finally, that all may understand how vain it is to strive against that faith which has always conquered and is destined always to conquer: "this is the victory which overcometh the world, our faith." This is the prayer that we raise to thee with one accord; and we are confident, that, after thou hast heard our prayers on earth, thou wilt one day call us to stand with thee in heaven, before the eternal High Priest, who with the Father and the Holy Spirit liveth and reigneth world without end. Amen.

An indulgence of 300 days (S. C. Ind., Feb. 4, 1873; S. P. Ap., June 20, 1933 and April 12, 1949).

XIII
SAINT VINCENT DE PAUL, CONFESSOR

512
A Devout Exercise

The faithful who devoutly offer their prayers in honor of Saint Vincent de Paul, with the purpose of so doing for nine continuous days, may gain:

An indulgence of 3 years, once each day;

A plenary indulgence on the usual conditions, at the end of their novena (Pius IX, Audience Jan. 3, 1849; S. C. of Bishops and Religious, Jan. 28, 1850; S. C. Ind., Nov. 26, 1876; S. P. Ap., Oct. 15, 1936).

513
A Prayer

O glorious Saint Vincent, heavenly patron of all charitable associations and father of all who are in misery, whilst thou wast on earth thou didst never cast out any who came to thee; ah, consider by what evils we are oppressed and come to our assistance! Obtain from thy Lord help for the poor, relief for the infirm, consolation for the afflicted, protection for the abandoned, a spirit of generosity for the rich, the grace of conversion for sinners, zeal for priests, peace for the Church, tranquillity and order for all nations, and salvation for them all. Yea, let all men prove the effects of thy merciful intercession, so that, being helped by thee in the miseries of this life, we may be united to thee in the life to come, where there shall be no more grief, nor weeping, nor sorrow, but joy and gladness and everlasting happiness. Amen.

An indulgence of 300 days.

A plenary indulgence once a month, on the usual conditions, for the daily devout recitation of this prayer (S. C. Ind., June 23, 1885; S. P. Ap., May 20, 1933).

XIV

SAINT BENEDICT JOSEPH LABRE, CONFESSOR

514
Prayers

O wondrous pattern of Christian perfection, Saint Benedict Joseph, from thy earliest use of reason even to thy dying day,

thou didst keep unspotted the white robe of
innocence, and, forsaking all things and becoming a pilgrim on the earth, thou didst
gain naught therefrom save only suffering,
privations and reproaches. Miserable sinner
that I am, I kneel at thy feet, and return
thanks to the infinite goodness of the Most
High God who hath willed to imprint on thee
the living likeness of His crucified Son. At
the same time I am filled with confusion
when I consider how different is my life from
thine. Do thou, beloved Saint, have pity on
me! Offer thy merits before the throne of
the Eternal, and obtain for me the grace to
follow thine example and to direct my actions
according to the precepts and teachings of our
divine Master: thus let me learn to love His
sufferings and His humiliations, and to despise the pleasures and honors of earth: so
that neither the fear of the former, nor the
desire of the latter may ever induce me to
transgress His holy law. May I merit in this
manner to be acknowledged by Him and
numbered amongst the blessed of His Father.
Amen.

Our Father, Hail Mary, Glory be.

℣. Pray for us, O holy Benedict Joseph,
℟. That we may be made worthy of the
promises of Christ.

Let us pray.

O God, who didst cause Thy holy confessor,
Benedict Joseph, to cleave unto Thee alone

by his zeal for humility and his love for poverty: grant unto us, by the help of his merits, to despise all things earthly and to seek evermore the things that are heavenly. Through Christ our Lord. Amen.

An indulgence of 300 days (S. C. Ind., Jan. 21, 1882; S. P. Ap., July 9, 1934).

XV

SAINT FRANCIS OF ASSISI, CONFESSOR

515

Pious Practices

a) The faithful, on any one of the five Sundays immediately preceding the Feast of the sacred Stigmata of St. Francis of Assisi, or on any one of five successive Sundays that they shall choose once during the year, if they spend some time in meditations, prayers or other devotional exercises in honor of the same sacred Stigmata, may gain:

A plenary indulgence on the usual conditions (S. C. Ind., Nov. 21, 1885).

b) The faithful who visit a church or public oratory for the purpose of prayer on the Feast of St. Francis of Assisi, or on one of the seven days immediately following, may gain:

A plenary indulgence, if, in addition, they make their confession, receive Holy Communion and pray for the intentions of the Sovereign Pontiff.

c) The faithful who devote some time to prayer or other exercises of piety in honor of St. Francis, with the intention of so doing for nine successive days, or an entire month, may gain:

An indulgence of three years, once on any day;

A plenary indulgence on the usual conditions, at the end of the entire exercise (Apostolic Brief, Feb. 28, 1904; S. P. Ap., Oct. 20, 1933).

516

A HYMN

O divi amoris victima

O victim dear of heavenly love,
    Impurpled by thy fivefold sign,
Saint Francis, father of the poor,
Of Jesus' Cross a living shrine.

Thou, burning with the glowing flames
Of love of God and love of man,
Dost yearn for Christ to shed thy blood
And thrice dost try the seas to span.

Although denied thy heart's desire,
Thou lettest not thine ardour wane;
But kindled still with love divine
To stir new fires thou strivest amain.

Still living in thine Orders three,
Thou art found in many a savage clime;
And frozen hearts, warmed at thy flame,
Grow fervent with thy fire sublime.

So shalt thou crush the powers of hell,
Thy conquering arms our foes dismay;
When Holy Church doth seem to fail,
Still is thy mighty strength her stay.

Come, help us, father, while we pray,
Thy love within our hearts inspire,
Thy boundless love, that spreads abroad
The glowing brightness of its fire.

Praise we the Father and the Son,
Praise we the Holy Paraclete:
He grant us grace to emulate
Our father's spirit, as is meet.   Amen.

(tr. C. E. Spence) .

An indulgence of 300 days.

A plenary indulgence on the usual conditions, if this hymn is recited daily for a month (S. C. Ind., Sept. 13, 1893; S. P. Ap., Dec. 5, 1932).

Hymnus

O divi amóris víctima
   Quino cruénta vúlnere,
Francísce qui vivam Crucis
Christi refers imáginem.

Tu caritátis férvidis
Flammis adústus, sánguinem
Christo datúrus, bárbara
Ter cogitásti líttora.

Voti sed impos, non sinis
Languére flammas désides:
Et éxcitas cæléstia,
Flagrans amóre, incéndia.

In prole vivens éfferas
Pervádis oras; álgida
Gelu solúto, ut férveant
Ardóre sancto péctora.

Sic pertiméndis líividum
Armis Avérnum cónteris;
Virtútis et firmum latus
Templo labánti súbiicis.

Adsis, Pater, precántibus
Ignémque, late quo tua
Exársit ingens cáritas,
Accénde nostris méntibus.

Sit laus Patri et Fílio,
Sit ínclyto Paráclito,
Qui nos Paréntis óptimi
Det æmulári spíritum. Amen.

517
A PRAYER

O glorious Saint Francis, who, even in thy youth, with a generous heart didst renounce the comfort and ease of thy father's

house in order to follow Jesus more closely
in His humility and poverty, in His mortification and passionate love of the Cross, and
didst thereby merit to behold the miraculous
Stigmata impressed upon thy flesh and to
bear them about with thee, obtain for us
also, we pray, the grace of passing through
our life here below, as though insensible to
the ephemeral splendor of all earthly possessions, with our hearts constantly beating
with love of Jesus Crucified even in the dark-
est and saddest hours of life and with our
eyes ever serenely raised toward heaven, as
though already enjoying a foretaste of the
eternal possession of the infinite Good with
His divine and everlasting joys.

An indulgence of 300 days.
A plenary indulgence on the usual conditions, if this prayer is
devoutly recited every day for a month (S. P. Ap., Jan. 20, 1941).

518
A PRAYER

Lord Jesus Christ, who, when the world
was growing cold, didst renew in the
flesh of blessed Francis the sacred marks of
Thy Passion in order to inflame our hearts
with the fire of Thy love; mercifully grant
that, by his merits and prayers, we may always carry the cross and bring forth fruits
worthy of repentance: Who livest and reignest for ever and ever.   Amen.

An indulgence of 300 days.
A plenary indulgence on the usual conditions, if the daily recitation of this prayer is continued for a month (S. P. Ap., Jan. 20,
1941).

Dómine Iesu Christe, qui, frigescénte mundo, ad inflammándum corda nostra tui amóris igne, in carne beatíssimi Francísci Passiónis tuæ sacra Stígmata renovásti; concéde propítius, ut eius méritis et précibus crucem júgiter ferámus et dignos fructus pæniténtiæ faciámus: qui vivis et regnas in sǽcula sæculórum. Amen.

XVI
SAINT THOMAS AQUINAS, CONFESSOR

519
A Devout Exercise

The faithful who spend some time on Sunday in devout meditations and prayers, or other works of piety in honor of St. Thomas Aquinas, with the intention of continuing the same for six successive Sundays, may gain:

A plenary indulgence on the usual conditions (S. C. Ind., Aug. 21, 1886).

520
Prayer

Angelic Doctor, Saint Thomas, prince of theologians and model of philosophers, bright ornament of the Christian world, light of the Church and patron of all Catholic schools, who didst learn wisdom without guile and dost communicate it without envy, pray for us to the Son of God who is Wisdom itself, that, by the coming of the Spirit of Wisdom upon us, we may clearly understand that which thou didst teach, and, by imitating thee, may bring to completion that which thou didst do; that we may be made partakers both of thy doctrine and thy holiness, whereby thou didst shine on earth even as the sun; and finally that we may enjoy with thee in

heaven for evermore the most delectable
fruits of the same, praising together with
thee divine Wisdom through endless ages.
Amen.

An indulgence of 300 days, once a day.

A plenary indulgence once a month, on the usual conditions,
when this prayer is said daily with devotion (S. C. Ind., July 3,
1885; S. P. Ap., Nov. 8, 1933).

Doctor angélice sancte Thoma, theologórum princeps et philosophórum norma, præclárum christi-
áni orbis decus et Ecclésiæ lumen, scholárum ómnium
catholicárum cæléstis Patróne, qui sapiéntiam sine
fictióne didicísti et sine invídia commúnicas, ipsam
Sapiéntiam Fílium Dei deprecáre pro nobis, ut
veniénte in nos Spíritu sapiéntiæ, ea quæ docuísti in-
telléctu conspiciámus, et quæ egísti imitatióne com-
pleámus; doctrínæ et virtútis, quibus in terris solis
instar semper eluxísti, partícipes efficiámur; ac
tandem eárum suavíssimis frúctibus perénniter tecum delectémur in cælis, divínam Sapiéntiam col-
laudántes per infiníta sǽcula sæculórum. Amen.

XVII
SAINT ALPHONSUS M. DE' LIGUORI,
BISHOP AND CONFESSOR

521
A Prayer

O my glorious and well-beloved patron,
Saint Alphonsus, thou who didst toil
and suffer so abundantly to assure to men
the fruits of the Redemption, behold the
miseries of my poor soul and have pity on me.
By thy powerful intercession with Jesus and
Mary, obtain for me true repentance for my
sins together with their pardon and remission, a deep hatred of sin and strength ever-

more to resist all temptations. Share with me, I pray, at least a spark of that fire of love wherewith thy heart did ever burn; and grant that, following thy example, I may make the will of God the only rule of my life. Obtain for me likewise a fervent and lasting love of Jesus, and a tender and childlike devotion to Mary, together with the grace to pray without ceasing and to persevere in the service of God even to the end of my life, that so I may finally be united with thee in praising God and most holy Mary through all eternity. Amen.

An indulgence of 300 days.

A plenary indulgence on the usual conditions, if this prayer is said devoutly every day for a month (S. C. Ind., June 18, 1887; S. P. Ap., Feb. 12, 1933).

XVIII
SAINT VINCENT FERRER, CONFESSOR

522
A Prayer

O glorious Apostle and wonder-worker, Saint Vincent Ferrer, new Angel of the Apocalypse and our loving patron, receive our humble prayer, and send down upon us a plentiful shower of divine favors. By the fire of love in thy heart, obtain for us from the Father of mercies the pardon and remission of all our sins, steadfastness in faith, and perseverance in good works, that so we may live as good and fervent Christians and become worthy of thy powerful patronage. Extend thy protection to our bodies also, and deliver

us from sickness. Keep our fields from hurtful tempests and storms of hail, and banish
all misfortunes far from us. Blessed by thy
favors both in body and soul, we shall ever be
thy devoted clients, and one day we shall
come to heaven to join with thee in praising
God through all eternity. Amen.

An indulgence of 300 days S. C. Ind., Sept. 17, 1887; S. P. Ap.,
Jan. 20, 1931).

523
A Prayer

O Saint Vincent, glorious worker of miracles, who in thy lifetime didst convert
so many sinners by preaching the last judgment, grant that we too, by meditating on
the four last things, may be enabled to obtain from Almighty God through thine intercession the healing of all our spiritual
maladies. Let thy heart be tender toward
us, O mighty Saint: stretch forth thy hand
over us, and obtain for us those graces for the
welfare of both soul and body, which we so
earnestly ask of thee. Amen.

An indulgence of 300 days S. P. Ap., June 22, 1935).

XIX
THE SEVEN HOLY FOUNDERS OF THE
ORDER OF THE SERVANTS OF MARY, CONFESSORS

524
A Prayer

O glorious Patriarchs, the seven holy
Founders of the Order of the Servants
of Mary, you who by reason of your sublime

holiness were worthy to be called by the
Blessed Virgin to found in the Church a new
religious Order dedicated to fostering and
spreading devotion towards her and the
honoring of her sorrows; you who were separated from the world in the solitude of
Monte Senario and were given to the most
severe penances, nourishing your hearts with
meditation on the eternal truths and the
infinite love of God towards us; you who
were constrained by the bonds of charity,
and with your mission of peace gave to the
world a noble example of brotherly love; obtain for us a tender devotion to Jesus Crucified and to the Queen of Martyrs, an ardent
longing for an interior life, for mortification
and penance, and for a burning charity towards our neighbor, which may increase our
zeal in every good work. Amen.

An indulgence of 300 days.

A plenary indulgence on the usual conditions, provided that this
prayer is devoutly recited every day for a month (S. C. Ind., Feb.
22, 1888; S. P. Ap., Jan. 12, 1932 and June 14, 1949) .

525
PRAYERS

I. **O** glorious Patriarchs, who during your
life in the world, amid the lewd man-
ners of your time, ever kept alive in your
hearts the fire of divine love and in your
conduct the holiness of the Christian way of
life, obtain for us such grace that being inflamed with heavenly love and drawn by the
fragrance of your virtues we may live always

in conformity with the maxims of the Gospel and the rules of Christian living.

II. O glorious Patriarchs, who in docile obedience to Mary's invitation overcame the most formidable difficulties of family ties and turned your backs to the world and all its promises of happiness and fortune; obtain for us such grace that we may renounce the deceitful and contemptible pleasures of earth and may ever turn our thoughts and affections to the inestimable riches of heaven.

III. O glorious Patriarchs, humble dwellers in the wilderness of Monte Senario, you who in constant and fervent prayer, in continual study of the Sacred Books, in harsh and unremitting penance, led there a life more like that of angels than that of men; obtain for us, likewise, the grace to fulfil daily all the duties of the Christian life, so as to sanctify every moment of our lives on earth and to grow in merit for the life that is eternal.

IV. O tender lovers of Jesus Crucified and devoted servants of the Queen of Martyrs, who by contemplating the sufferings of our Redeemer and the sorrows of her who shared His redeeming work fed the flames of divine love within yourselves, obtain for us the grace to grow in the love and knowledge of Jesus Crucified and of Mary the Queen of Martyrs.

V. O glorious Holy Founders of the Order of the Servants of Mary, summoned by the same Queen of Heaven to establish a new religious family in the Church, obtain for us the grace to be ever docile to the divine inspirations by a prompt and willing obedience thereto, and to serve Jesus and Mary faithfully in that state of life to which it has pleased Divine Providence to call us.

VI. O zealous Apostles of the Crucified and of Our Lady of Sorrows, who at the sight of a world estranged from God and torn asunder by discord left the solitude of Monte Senario and burning with love preached the Crucified and the Queen of Martyrs, and everywhere brought the blessings of peace and tranquillity; obtain for us the grace to live always with all men in the bonds of Christian charity and to practise always and everywhere the apostolate of the love of brotherhood.

VII. Angels of purity, seraphs of love, and martyrs of penance, you glorious seven Holy Founders, who after a life spent in the exercise of the most sublime virtue were rewarded by a happy passage from this place of exile to your heavenly home and were raised by Holy Church to the highest honors of the altar, from your place in glory where you reign with Christ turn your eyes towards us; obtain for us the grace to be able after a holy life to join your blest society in the glories of paradise, there to sing with you forever hymns of love and gratitude.

An indulgence of 300 days.

A plenary indulgence on the usual conditions, when these prayers have been devoutly repeated every day for an entire month (S. C. Ind., Apr. 21, 1888; S. P. Ap., Jan. 12, 1932 and June 14, 1949).

XX

SAINT JOHN BERCHMANS, CONFESSOR

526

Devout Practices

a) The faithful on any one of the five Sundays immediately preceding the Feast of St. John Berchmans, if they say prayers in honor of this Saint, may gain:

An indulgence of 7 years;

A plenary indulgence on the usual conditions (S. C. Ind., May 17, 1890; S. P. Ap., Feb. 22, 1921 and March 18, 1932).

b) The faithful who visit with devotion a church or a public oratory, or (for those who are lawfully entitled thereto) a semi-public oratory, where the Feast of St. John Berchmans is being kept, may gain:

A plenary indulgence, if they make their confession, receive Holy Communion and pray for the intentions of the Sovereign Pontiff.

c) The faithful on any of the nine days immediately preceding the Feast of St. John Berchmans, if they say some devout prayers in honor of the Saint, may gain:

An indulgence of 500 days once a day;

A plenary indulgence on the completion of the novena, on the usual conditions.

d) The faithful who devoutly say *Our Father*, *Hail Mary* and *Glory be*, together with the invocation, *"Saint John, pray for me,"* before a likeness of the Saint, may gain:

An indulgence of 300 days;

A plenary indulgence on the usual conditions, provided that they perform this act of devotion daily for one month (S. P. Ap., Sept. 25, 1936 and Dec. 10, 1949).

527

Prayers

Saint John, angelic youth, sweet-scented flower of innocence, stalwart soldier of the Company of Jesus, ardent defender of

the Immaculate Conception of the Blessed
Virgin, whom the all-wise Providence of God
hath set forth as a light and pattern, in order
that He might reveal in thee the treasures of
that holiness which consisteth in the devoted
and holy fulfilment of the common duties of
life, I earnestly beseech thee to make me
ever constant and faithful in observing the
duties of my state of life, pure in heart, fearless and strong against the enemies of my
eternal salvation, and cheerfully obedient to
the promptings of God's holy will. By thy
singular devotion to the loving Mother of
Jesus Christ, who looked upon thee also as
her dear son, obtain for me the grace of a
fervent love for Jesus and Mary, together
with the power of drawing many others to
love them in like manner. Wherefore, dear
Saint John, I choose thee as my special
patron, humbly beseeching thee to make me
zealous in the things that pertain to the
praise of God, and to assist me by thy mighty
help, to lead a life filled with good works.
Finally, when the hour of death cometh, do
thou, of thy loving-kindness, cherish in me
those motions of humble confidence, which,
at the moment of thy departure from this
world to thy mansion in the skies, as thou
didst lovingly clasp to thy breast the image of
Jesus Crucified, together with Mary's rosary
and thy book of rules, impelled thee to utter
these sweet words: "These three things are
my dearest possessions; with these I am
content to die."

℣. Pray for us, Saint John,
℟. That we may be made worthy of the promises of Christ.

Let us pray.

Grant, we beseech Thee, O Lord God, unto Thy faithful servants, to copy the pattern of innocence and faithfulness in Thy service, wherewith the angelic youth, John, did consecrate to Thee the very flower of his years. Through Christ our Lord. Amen.

An indulgence of 300 days, once a day.

A plenary indulgence on the usual conditions, if this prayer is said with devotion every day for an entire month (S. P. Ap., Feb. 22, 1921 and May 20, 1935)

O angélice iúvenis Ioánnes, innocéntiæ flos suáviter fragrans, in Societáte Iesu miles strénue, immaculátæ Conceptiónis beatíssimæ Vírginis propugnátor ardentíssime, quem próvidens Dei sapiéntia lumen et exémplar propósuit ut thesáuros eius sanctitátis reveláret quæ in commúnis vitæ rebus pie sanctéque præstándis est constitúta, te veheménter déprecor, ut me reddas in offíciis vitæ meæ servándis constánter fidélem, corde purum, contra salútis ætérnæ hostes impávidum et fortem, divínæ voluntátis mónita prompto ánimo exsequéntem. Per singulárem tuam devotiónem erga amantíssimam Iesu Christi Matrem, quæ te étiam ut fílium hábuit sibi caríssimum, id mihi ímpetra, ut et Iesum et Maríam fervénter amem, simúlque ut in eórum amórem possim étiam quamplúres álios allícere. Ideo te, o sancte Ioánnes, éligo singulárem mihi patrónum, supplíciter exórans, ut in iis, quæ ad Dei laudem sunt, me álacrem effícias, auxilióque iuves, quo vitam bonis opéribus refértam tránsigam. Tua me dénique benevoléntia, cum mortis hora advéniat, iis fove húmilis fidúciæ afféctibus qui tibi iam in cæléstem sedem evolatúro, manibúsque ad pectus peramánter

admovénti Iesu Crucifíxi imáginem et Deiparéntis
Rosárium et regulárum libéllum, ea dulcíssima verba
inspirárunt: "Hæc tria sunt mihi caríssima; cum his
libénter mórior."

℣. Ora pro nobis, sancte Ioánnes,
℟. Ut digni efficiámur promissiónibus Christi.

Orémus.

Concéde, quǽsumus, fámulis tuis, Dómine Deus,
ea innocéntiæ ac fidelitátis exémpla in tuo servítio
sectári, quibus angélicus iúvenis Ioánnes ætátis suæ
florem consecrávit. Per Christum Dóminum nostrum. Amen.

XXI
SAINT LOUIS, BISHOP AND CONFESSOR

528
A Prayer

To thee do we have recourse in prayer,
Saint Louis, lily of virginity, bright and
shining star, and vessel of holiness. Through
thine intercession pour forth the blessings of
heaven upon the Catholic nations to which
thou art allied, and over which thou hast
been set by God as their protector. Do thou
entreat Almighty God and the immaculate
Virgin, that the Christian peoples may once
again be quickened by the faith of their
fathers, that charity may burn fervently
amongst them, and that their way of life
may be made conformable to the law of God.
Obtain true peace and concord for both rulers
and people, the victory of our Holy Mother
the Church over her enemies, perfect freedom for the Vicar of Christ in his sacred
government of souls, and eternal happiness

in heaven for all of us who implore thy mighty assistance. Amen.

An indulgence of 300 days (S. C. Ind., June 12, 1894; S. P. Ap., Dec. 12, 1933).

Ad te súpplices confúgimus, sancte Ludovíce, lílium virginitátis, stella fulgens et vas sanctitátis. Supra cathólicas natiónes quibus affinitáte coniúngeris, et quarum a Deo protéctor es constitútus, cæléstes grátias intercessióne diffúnde. Deum ac immaculátam Vírginem deprecáre, ut in christiáno pópulo avórum fides rursum excitétur, férveat cáritas morésque componántur. Intercéde veram princípibus ac cívibus concórdiam, sanctæ Matri Ecclésiæ contra hostes triúmphum, Christi in terris Vicário plenam in sacro animárum regímine libertátem nobísque ómnibus tuum implorántibus auxílium ætérnam in cælo felicitátem. Amen.

XXII

SAINT ANTHONY, ABBOT AND CONFESSOR

529

A Prayer

O glorious Saint Anthony, who upon hearing only one word of the Gospel didst forsake the riches and the ease of thy family, thy native land and the world, in order to retire into the wilderness; who, in spite of the heavy burden of advanced age and the ravages of severe penance, didst not hesitate to leave thy solitude to rebuke openly the impiety of heretics and to restore wavering Christians to a firmer hold upon their faith with all the zeal of a confessor desirous of martyrdom; who through thy conquest of self and the excellence of thy virtues wast endowed by Our Lord with miraculous power

over animate and inanimate nature; do thou
obtain for us the grace to be ever zealous in
the cause of Christ and His Church and to
persevere even unto death in our imitation
of thee, in our belief in revealed truth, and
in our keeping of the commandments and
the counsels of the Gospel; to the end that,
having faithfully followed in thy footsteps
here on earth, we may be enabled to become
sharers in thy heavenly glory through all the
ages of eternity.   Amen.

Our Father, Hail Mary, Glory be *three
times.*

An indulgence of 300 days (S. C. Ind., June 3, 1896; S. P. Ap.,
May 9, 1934 and May 15, 1949) ·

XXIII

SAINT ANTHONY OF PADUA, CONFESSOR

530

Devout Practices

a) The faithful who devoutly recite *Our Father,*
Hail Mary and *Glory be*, thirteen times in
honor of St. Anthony of Padua, may gain:

An indulgence of 300 days once a day (S. C. Ind., June 9, 1896;
S. P. Ap., Nov. 18, 1935) ·

b) The faithful who spend some time in devout
meditations or prayers, or who perform some other
acts of piety in honor of St. Anthony of Padua, on
Tuesday or Sunday of any week, with the intention
of so doing for thirteen Tuesdays or Sundays without interruption, may gain:

A plenary indulgence on the usual conditions (Apostolic Brief,
March 1, 1898) ·

531

A Responsory

Si quæris miracula

I f, then, thou seekest miracles,
Death, error, all calamities,
The leprosy and demons flee,
The sick, by him made whole, arise.

The sea withdraws and fetters break,
And withered limbs he doth restore,
While treasures lost are found again,
When young or old his help implore.

All dangers vanish from our path,
Our direst needs do quickly flee;
Let those who know repeat the theme:
Let Paduans praise Saint Anthony.

The sea withdraws, *etc.*

To Father, Son let glory be,
And Holy Ghost eternally.

The sea withdraws, *etc.* (tr. cento) .

℣. Pray for us, O blessed Anthony,
℟. That we may be made worthy of the promises of Christ.

Let us pray.

Let Thy Church, O God, be gladdened by the solemn commemoration of blessed Anthony Thy Confessor: that she may evermore be defended by Thy spiritual assistance, and merit to possess everlasting joy. Through Christ our Lord. Amen.

An indulgence of 300 days, once a day.

A plenary indulgence once a month, on the usual conditions, if this responsory, together with its versicles and prayer, be said daily(S. C. Ind., Jan. 25, 1866; S. P. Ap., Jan. 30, 1936) .

Responsorium

Si quæris mirácula,
  Mors, error, calámitas,
Dæmon, lepra fúgiunt,
Ægri surgunt sani.

Cedunt mare, víncula:
Membra, resque pérditas
Petunt et accípiunt
Iúvenes et cani.

Péreunt perícula,
Cessat et necéssitas;
Narrent hi, qui séntiunt,
Dicant Paduáni.

Cedunt mare, víncula, etc.
Glória Patri et Fílio et Spirítui
Sancto.
  Cedunt mare, víncula, etc.
℣. Ora pro nobis, beáte Antóni,
℟. Ut digni efficiámur promissiónibus Christi.

Orémus.

Ecclésiam tuam, Deus, beáti Antónii Confessóris tui commemorátio votíva lætíficet, ut spirituálibus semper muniátur auxíliis et gáudiis pérfrui mereátur ætérnis. Per Christum Dóminum nostrum. Amen.

532

A Prayer of Petition

O wondrous Saint Anthony, glorious by reason of the fame of thy miracles, who hadst the happiness of receiving within thine arms our blessed Lord under the guise of a little child, obtain for me of His bounty this favor that I desire from the bottom of my heart. Thou who wast so gracious unto poor sinners, regard not the lack of merit on the part of him who calls upon thee, but consider the glory of God, which will be exalted once more through thee, to the salvation of my soul and the granting of the petition that I now make with such ardent yearning.

As a pledge of my gratitude, I beg thee to accept my promise to live henceforth more agreeably to the teachings of the Gospel, and to be devoted to the service of the poor whom thou didst ever love and still dost love so greatly; bless this my resolution and obtain for me the grace to be faithful thereto even until death. Amen.

An indulgence of 300 days, once a day.

A plenary indulgence once a month, on the usual conditions, for the daily recitation of this prayer (Leo XIII, Audience, May 6, 1899; S. C. Ind., May 15, 1899; S. P. Ap., Dec. 7, 1936).

533
A Prayer of Thanksgiving

O glorious wonder-worker, Saint Anthony, father of the poor and comforter of the afflicted, thou who hast come with such loving solicitude to my assistance, and hast comforted me so abundantly: behold me at thy feet to offer thee my heartfelt thanks. Accept, therefore, this offering and with it my earnest promise which I now renew, to live always in the love of Jesus and my neighbor. Continue to shield me graciously with thy protection, and obtain for me the final grace of being able one day to enter the kingdom of heaven, there to sing with thee the everlasting mercies of God. Amen.

An indulgence of 300 days, once a day.

A plenary indulgence, on the usual conditions, if the prayer has been devoutly recited every day for an entire month (S. C. Ind., July 13, 1896; S. P. Ap., March 4, 1933)

XXIV
SAINT JOHN OF MATHA, CONFESSOR

534
A Prayer

Glorious Saint John of Matha, thou wast inflamed with an ardent love of God and a tender compassion toward thy neighbor, and therefore wast chosen by God Himself to found the famous Order of the Most Holy Trinity, wherein thou didst spend thy days in glorifying this venerable mystery and in rescuing unhappy Christians from bondage; do thou obtain for us the grace to pass our days in like manner, glorifying the Most Holy Trinity and doing good to our neighbor with the deeds of Christian charity, that so we may hereafter obtain the happy lot of rejoicing in heaven in the Beatific Vision of the Father, and of the Son, and of the Holy Ghost. Amen.

An indulgence of 300 days once a day.

A plenary indulgence on the usual conditions, when this prayer has been devoutly recited every day for a month (S. C. Ind., March 16, 1897; S. P. Ap., Sept. 20, 1931)

XXV
SAINT PETER FOURIER, CONFESSOR

535
A Prayer

Most glorious Saint Peter Fourier, lily of purity, pattern of Christian perfection, perfect model of priestly zeal, by that glory which has been granted thee in heaven, turn one kind glance upon us and come to our assistance before the throne of the Most High. During thy earthly life, guided by thy favorite maxim: "to harm no one, to give help to all," thou didst spend thine entire life in giving aid to the wretched, counsel to the doubtful, and consolation to the afflicted; thou didst draw back to the paths of virtue those who had gone astray. Now that thou art so powerful in heaven, continue thy task of giving help to all and be our watchful defender, so that, through thine intercession, we, being delivered from all temporal misfortunes and confirmed in our faith and in our love, may be victors over the wiles of the enemies of our salvation, and may be enabled one day with thee to praise and bless our Lord through all eternity. Amen.

An indulgence of 300 days.

A plenary indulgence once a month, on the usual conditions, if this prayer is said daily with devotion (S. C. Ind., May 27, 1897; S. P. Ap., June 26, 1934 and May 22, 1949).

XXVI
SAINT JOSEPH CALASANCTIUS, CONFESSOR

536

A Prayer

Saint Joseph Calasanctius, protector of youth, great servant of our Lord, who didst work such marvels in their behalf; thou who, having made thyself a mirror for them of burning charity, of unwearied patience, of deep humility, of angelic purity and of every other heroic virtue, by a holy example, by words full of the Spirit of God, didst inspire them to flee dangerous occasions, to hate sin, to detest vicious courses, and to love piety and devotion, and thus didst guide countless souls to heaven; thou who didst obtain for them the visible benediction of the Child Jesus and His holy Mother, obtain the like for us, thy humble and devoted servants; obtain for us a lasting hatred for sin, victory in the midst of temptation, and help in time of danger, so that, by living in the perfect observance of the law of God, we may attain to eternal salvation.   Amen.

An indulgence of 300 days.

A plenary indulgence on the usual conditions, if this prayer is said with devotion every day for a month (Leo XIII, Audience, Oct. 19, 1897; S. P. Ap., April 12, 1932 and June 12, 1949).

XXVII
SAINT BLASE, BISHOP AND MARTYR

537
A Prayer

O glorious Saint Blase, who by thy martyrdom didst leave to the Church a precious witness to the faith, obtain for us the grace to preserve within ourselves this divine gift, and to defend, without human respect, both by word and example, the truth of that same faith, which is so wickedly attacked and slandered in these our times. Thou who didst miraculously restore a little child when it was at the point of death by

reason of an affliction of the throat, grant us
thy mighty protection in like misfortunes;
and, above all, obtain for us the grace of
Christian mortification together with a faithful observance of the precepts of the Church,
which may keep us from offending Almighty
God. Amen.

An indulgence of 300 days (S. C. of the Propagation of the Faith,
exhib. Aug. 16, 1902; S. P. Ap., March 20, 1936).

XXVIII
SAINT STEPHEN, PROTOMARTYR

538
Prayers

Ant. The Apostles chose Stephen the
deacon, a man full of faith and
of the Holy Ghost, whom the Jews stoned
whilst he prayed, saying: "Lord Jesus, receive my spirit, and lay not this sin to their
charge."

℣. By the merits and prayers of blessed
Stephen,
℟. Be merciful, O God, to Thy people.

Let us pray.

Almighty and everlasting God, who didst
consecrate the first-fruits of Thy martyrs in
the blood of blessed Stephen the deacon;
grant, we beseech Thee, that he may pray for
us, even as he also prayed for his persecutors,
to our Lord Jesus Christ thy Son, who liveth
and reigneth world without end. Amen.

An indulgence of 300 days once a day.

A plenary indulgence on the usual conditions on the two Feast-days of St. Stephen (Aug. 3 and Dec. 26), if this antiphon together with its versicle and prayer is also said devoutly on each of the nine days immediately preceding either of the above-mentioned days (S. C. Ind., Jan. 23, 1904 and June 8, 1904) .

Ant. Elegérunt Apóstoli Stéphanum levítam, plenum fide et Spíritu Sancto, quem lapidavérunt Iudǽi orántem et dicéntem: "Dómine Iesu, áccipe spíritum meum, et ne státuas illis hoc peccátum."

℣. Méritis et précibus beáti Stéphani,

℟. Propítius esto, Dómine, pópulo tuo.

Orémus.

Omnípotens sempitérne Deus, qui primítias Mártyrum in beáti Levítæ Stéphani sánguine dedicásti; tríbue, quǽsumus, ut pro nobis intercéssor exsístat, qui pro suis étiam persecutóribus exorávit Dóminum nostrum Iesum Christum Fílium tuum, qui vivit et regnat in sǽcula sæculórum. Amen.

XXIX
SAINT HOMOBONUS, CONFESSOR

539

A Prayer

Our defender, father of the poor, pattern of meekness, prayer and devotion, by the charity wherewith thou didst love God above all things, and that generous love which led thee to assist the poor, make intercession for us to our Saviour, in order that we, by imitating here on earth thy virtues and, above all, thy spirit of charity, may be enabled to attain one day to thy company and that of all the Saints in blessing and praising the Lord of glory in our heavenly homeland. Amen.

An indulgence of 300 days (Apostolic Brief, Feb. 8, 1904; S. P. Ap., May 12, 1934) .

XXX
SAINT JOHN BAPTIST DE LA SALLE, CONFESSOR

540

A Prayer

O glorious John Baptist de la Salle, Apostle of children and young folk, be thou, from the heights of heaven, our guide and our patron. Offer thy prayers for us and help us, that we may be kept free from every stain of error and corruption, and remain ever faithful to Jesus Christ and to the infallible Head of His Church. Grant that we, practising the virtues of which thou hast been so wondrous an example, may be made partakers of thy glory in heaven, our true country. Amen.

An indulgence of 300 days.

A plenary indulgence on the usual conditions, if this prayer is said daily for a month (S. C. Ind., Nov. 28, 1906; S. P. Ap., Sept. 25, 1935) .

XXXI
SAINT DOMINIC, CONFESSOR

541

A Devout Exercise

The faithful who on Tuesday of each week spend some time in devout meditations or prayers in honor of St. Dominic or perform some other act of piety, with the intention of repeating this act of homage for fifteen continuous Tuesdays, may obtain:

A plenary indulgence on the usual conditions (S. C. Holy Office, May 6, 1915 and Nov. 25, 1915; S. P. Ap., May 20, 1935) .

542

Prayers

I. O glorious Saint Dominic, thou who wast a model of mortification and purity, by punishing thy innocent body with scourges, with fastings and with watchings, and by keeping inviolate the lily of thy virginity, obtain for us the grace to practise penance with a generous heart and to keep unspotted the purity of our bodies and our hearts.

Our Father, Hail Mary, Glory be.

II. O great Saint, who, inflamed with divine love, didst find thy delight in prayer and intimate union with God; obtain for us to be faithful in our daily prayers, to love Our Lord ardently, and to observe His commandments with ever increasing fidelity.

Our Father, Hail Mary, Glory be.

III. O glorious Saint Dominic, who, being filled with zeal for the salvation of souls, didst preach the Gospel in season and out of season and didst establish the Order of Friars Preachers to labor for the conversion of heretics and poor sinners, pray thou to God for us, that He may grant us to love all our brethren sincerely and to cooperate always, by our prayers and good works, in their sanctification and eternal salvation.

Our Father, Hail Mary, Glory be.

℣. Pray for us, Saint Dominic,
℟. That we may be made worthy of the promises of Christ.

Let us pray.

Grant, we beseech Thee, Almighty God, that we who are weighed down by the burden

of our sins may be raised up by the patronage
of blessed Dominic Thy Confessor. Through
Christ our Lord. Amen.

An indulgence of 300 days.

A plenary indulgence on the usual conditions, when these prayers together with versicle and prayer have been recited daily for
a month (S. C. Ind., July 21, 1883; S. P. Ap., Mar. 16, 1934 and June
2, 1949).

XXXII
SAINT PASCHAL BAYLON, CONFESSOR

543

Responsory
Paschalis admirabilis

Paschal, illustrious is thy name,
But brighter glows thy virtue's fame;
With many a sign thy works are crowned;
Through thee God's gifts to men abound.
From Heaven look down, we humbly pray,
On us who seek thine aid this day;
Remove the evil that we dread,
And grant us what we ask instead.
And when to Heaven's high feast we go,
The nuptial robe on us bestow,
That Christ our strength and food may be,
In death and for eternity.
From Heaven look down, *etc.*
Glory be to the Father, and to the Son, and
to the Holy Ghost.
From Heaven look down, *etc.* (Tr. anon.).

℣. Pray for us, O blessed Paschal,
℟. That we may be made worthy of the
promises of Christ.

Let us pray.

O God, who hast glorified blessed Paschal
Thy Confessor by a wonderful love for the

sacred mysteries of Thy Body and Blood:
mercifully grant that we also, like him, may
deserve to taste the spiritual sweetness of
this divine Supper: Who livest and reignest
world without end. Amen.

An indulgence of 300 days once a day.

A plenary indulgence on the usual conditions, for the daily and
devout recitation of this responsory together with its versicle and
prayer through an entire month (S. P. Ap., Aug. 3, 1917).

Responsorium

Paschális admirábilis,
  Qui, clárior virtútibus,
Signísque fulgens plúrimis,
Supréma confers múnera.

Adésto nobis, quǽsumus,
Opem tuam rogántibus,
Et, quæ timémus, ámove,
Quæ postulámus, ádiice.

Mensæ parátæ cǽlitus
Fac nos rite assídere,
Ut robur et viáticum
Possímus inde súmere.

Adésto nobis, etc.
Glória Patri, et Fílio,
Et, Spirítui Sancto.
Adésto nobis, etc.

℣. Ora pro nobis, beáte Paschális,
℟. Ut digni efficiámur promissiónibus Christi.

Orémus.

Deus, qui beátum Paschálem, Confessórem tuum,
mirífica erga Córporis et Sánguinis tui sacra mystéria
dilectióne decorásti: concéde propítius; ut, quam ille
ex hoc divíno convívio spíritus percépit pinguédinem,
eámdem et nos percípere mereámur: Qui vivis et
regnas in sǽcula sæculórum. Amen.

XXXIII
SAINT GABRIEL OF THE SORROWFUL MOTHER, CONFESSOR

544
Devout Practices

a) The faithful who visit in the spirit of devotion a church or public oratory, or even a semi-public oratory (in the case of those who may lawfully use the latter), where the Feast of St. Gabriel of the Sorrowful Mother is being kept, may gain:

A plenary indulgence, on condition of confession, Holy Communion and prayer for the intentions of the Sovereign Pontiff.

b) The faithful, who devoutly recite *Our Father*, *Hail Mary* and *Glory be*, adding the invocation, *"Saint Gabriel, pray for me,"* before a representation of St. Gabriel of the Sorrowful Mother, may gain:

An indulgence of 300 days;

A plenary indulgence on the usual conditions, if they perform this devout exercise daily for a month (S. P. Ap., Sept. 25, 1936 and Dec. 10, 1949).

545
A Prayer of Petition

Let us adore and give thanks to God the Father everlasting, who, of the great love He bore us, was pleased to send His only-begotten Son into the world to suffer and die on the gibbet of the Cross; and let us beseech Him, for the sake of His Passion and death and by the intercession of Saint Gabriel, that most loving follower of our crucified Lord, to grant us the favor for which we pray. . . .

Our Father, Hail Mary, Glory be.

Let us adore and give thanks to God the eternal Son, who, becoming man and dying for us upon the Cross, left us Mary most holy to be our Mother; and let us beseech Him, by the merits of this sorrowful Virgin Mother and by the intercession of Saint Gabriel, who was her most devoted servant, to grant us the favor for which we pray. . . .

Our Father, Hail Mary, Glory be.

Let us adore and give thanks to God the eternal Spirit, who of His infinite goodness communicates Himself to our souls to make them holy; and let us beseech Him, by the merit of the same divine goodness and by the intercession of Saint Gabriel, who in a special manner shared therein and corresponded thereto, to grant us the favor for which we pray. . . .

Our Father, Hail Mary, Glory be.

℣. Pray for us, Saint Gabriel,

℟. That we may be made worthy of the promises of Christ.

Let us pray.

O God, who didst teach blessed Gabriel to have the sorrows of Thy most dear Mother in perpetual remembrance, and through her didst glorify him with the fame of holiness and miracles; grant unto us, by his intercession and example, so to share the sorrows of Thy Mother that we may be saved by her maternal protection: Who livest and reignest world without end. Amen.

An indulgence of 300 days once a day.

A plenary indulgence once a month, on the usual conditions, if these prayers have been recited daily with devotion (S. P. Ap., Oct. 25, 1920 and July 20, 1934).

XXXIV
SAINT PHILIP NERI, CONFESSOR

546
Invocation

Lowly Saint Philip, make intercession to the immaculate Virgin Mother of God for me.

An indulgence of 100 days.
A plenary indulgence on the usual conditions, if this invocation is repeated every day for a month (S. P. Ap., April 7, 1921).

Húmilis sancte Philíppe, deprecáre immaculátam Vírginem ac Dei Genitrícem pro me.

547
Prayers for Every Day of the Week
SUNDAY
A prayer to obtain the virtue of humility

O my glorious patron, Saint Philip, thou who wast so humble as to consider thyself a useless servant and unworthy of human praise but deserving the contempt of all, to such a degree as to renounce by every means the honors offered thee on numerous occasions by the Supreme Pontiffs themselves, thou seest what an exaggerated esteem I have for myself, how readily I judge and think ill of others, how ambitious I am even in well-doing, and how much I allow myself to be disturbed and influenced by the good or bad opinion which others entertain of me. Dear Saint, obtain for me a truly humble heart, so that I may rejoice at being despised, may feel no resentment at being overlooked, nor be unduly elated by praise, but rather let me seek to be great in the eyes of God alone.

Our Father, Hail Mary, Glory be.

MONDAY
A prayer to obtain the virtue of patience

My holy Advocate, Saint Philip, thou whose heart was so serene in the midst of adversity, whose spirit was so devoted to suffering, thou who when thou wast persecuted by the envious, or calumniated by the wicked who sought to discredit thee, or sorely tried by Our Lord with many persistent and painful maladies, didst endure it all with an admirable tranquillity of heart and mind; obtain for me also the spirit of fortitude in all the tribulations of this life. Thou seest how perturbed and indignant I become at every light affliction, how angry and resentful at every insignificant contradiction, and how unable I am to remember that the cross is the only way to paradise. Obtain for me perfect patience and readiness like thine in carrying the crosses which Our Lord daily gives me to carry, so that I may be made worthy to rejoice with thee in our eternal reward in heaven.

Our Father, Hail Mary, Glory be.

TUESDAY
A prayer to obtain the virtue of purity

O glorious Saint Philip, thou who didst ever preserve intact the lily of chastity to such a degree that the splendor of this fair virtue shone forth in thy eyes, and so transformed thy whole body that it gave forth a delightful fragrance that consoled and inspired to devotion everyone who came

into thy presence, obtain for me from the
Holy Spirit that grace which thou didst obtain for so many of thy spiritual children,
the grace of defending, preserving and increasing within me that virtue which is so
great, so fair, so necessary.

Our Father, Hail Mary, Glory be.

WEDNESDAY
A prayer to obtain the love of God

Saint Philip, I am filled with admiration
at the great miracle wrought in thee by
the Holy Spirit, when He poured forth His
charity so abundantly into thy heart that it
was dilated, even physically, to such an extent that two of thy ribs were broken. I
marvel, too, at the pure and glowing love of
God, which fired thy soul to such warmth
that thy countenance was illumined with
heavenly light and thou wast caught up into
an ecstasy so as to be desirous of shedding
thy blood to make Him known and loved by
the heathen nations. What shame I feel
when I observe the coldness of my heart towards God, whom nevertheless I know to be
the supreme and infinite Good. I love the
world, which attracts me but cannot make
me happy; I love the flesh, which tempts me
but cannot satisfy my heart; I love riches,
which I cannot enjoy, save for a few, fleeting
moments. When shall I learn from thee to
love nothing else except God, the only and
incomprehensible Good? Make me, O holy
Patron, through thy intercession, begin to

love God from this day forth at least, with all my mind, with all my strength, even until that happy hour when I shall love Him in a blessed eternity.

Our Father, Hail Mary, Glory be.

THURSDAY
A prayer to obtain the love of one's neighbor

O glorious Saint, who didst employ thyself wholly in favor of thy neighbor, esteeming, sympathizing with, and assisting everyone; who in the whole of thy life-time didst make everyone's salvation thy special care, never refusing the labor involved nor reserving for thyself either time or convenience, in order to win all to God, obtain for me, I pray thee, a like charity towards my neighbor, even such as thou didst entertain for thy many devoted clients, in order that I too may love everyone with a charity that is pure and disinterested, giving a helping hand to everyone, sympathizing with everyone, and treating everyone, even my enemies, with that sweetness of manner, and that eager desire for their good, with which thou wast able to overcome and convert thy very persecutors.

Our Father, Hail Mary, Glory be.

FRIDAY
A prayer to obtain detachment from worldly goods

Great Saint, thou who didst prefer a life of poverty and obscurity to one of ease and comfort which was thine by inheritance,

obtain for me the grace of never attaching
my heart to the fleeting goods of this life.
Do thou, who didst desire to become so poor
as to be reduced to beggary and not to find
anyone willing to give thee even the barest
means of livelihood, obtain for me also a love
of poverty, so that I may turn all my thoughts
to the things that are eternal.   Thou who
didst wish to live in a lowly station rather
than to be advanced to the highest dignities
of the Church, intercede for me that I may
never seek after honors, but may be content
with that station in life in which it has
pleased Our Lord to place me.   My heart is
too much preoccupied with the vain and
passing things of earth; but do thou, who
didst ever inculcate this great maxim: "And
then?", which brought about so many wonderful conversions, obtain for me that this
saying may ever remain so firmly fixed in my
mind that I may despise the nothingness of
this world, and may make God the only object of my affections and my thoughts.

Our Father, Hail Mary, Glory be.

SATURDAY

A prayer to obtain the grace of perseverance

O my holy patron, Philip, thou who didst
always persevere in well-doing, who
didst preach the need of perseverance, and
didst admonish us to pray for perseverance
continually from Almighty God through the
intercession of the Blessed Virgin; thou who
didst desire that thy spiritual children should

not overload themselves with devotional practices, but rather that they should persevere in those which they had already undertaken, thou seest how easily I grow weary of the good works I have begun and forget my good resolutions so often repeated. I have recourse to thee, in order that thou mayest obtain for me the great grace of never forsaking my God again, of never again losing His grace, of being faithful to my religious exercises, and of dying in the embrace of my Lord, fortified with the holy Sacraments and rich in merits for eternal life.

Our Father, Hail Mary, Glory be.

An indulgence of 300 days for each of these prayers.

A plenary indulgence on the usual conditions, if they have been devoutly recited for four continuous weeks (S. C. Ind., May 17, 1852; S. P. Ap., Jan. 12, 1932 and June 8, 1949).

XXXV

SAINT FIDELIS OF SIGMARINGEN
PROTOMARTYR OF THE PROPAGATION OF THE FAITH

548

Responsory

Fidelis Vir tu nomine

Thy name, Fidelis, doth proclaim
   Thy living faith and doctrine's fame;
False teachers bow before thy word,
Thy blood bears witness to thy Lord.

   Let Heaven's light, to thee we pray,
Within our hearts and minds hold sway;
Let faith and hope and holy love
Shine in us brightly from above.

Through thee the halt, the lame, the blind,
New health and strength and light do find;
To speechless tongues, speech thou dost give;
Thou makest dying infants live.

Let Heaven's light, to thee we pray,
Within our hearts and minds hold sway:
Let faith and hope and holy love
Shine in us brightly from above.

Glory be to the Father, and to the Son,
And to the Holy Ghost.

Let Heaven's light, to thee we pray,
Within our hearts and minds hold sway.

As it was in the beginning,
is now, and ever shall be,
world without end.   Amen.

Let faith and hope and holy love
Shine in us brightly from above.

(tr. C. E. Spence).

Antiphon.   Be thou faithful unto death,
and I will give thee a crown of life.

℣. Pray for us, O blessed Fidelis,

℟. That we may be made worthy of the
promises of Christ.

Let us pray.

O God, who hast vouchsafed to glorify
blessed Fidelis, inflamed with seraphic ardor
of spirit, with the palm of martyrdom and
the fame of miracles in the propagation of
the true faith: by his merits and intercession, we beseech Thee so to strengthen us by
Thy grace in faith and charity, that we may

deserve to be found faithful in Thy service unto death. Through Christ our Lord. Amen.

An indulgence of 300 days, once a day.

A plenary indulgence on the usual conditions, if this responsory, together with the versicles and prayer, is said with devotion every day for a month(S. P. Ap., May 1, 1923 and July 21, 1935) .

Responsorium

Fidélis Vir tu nómine,
  Doctrína, fide, clárior,
Tu verbo vincens hæresim,
Firmásti fidem sánguine.

Nostris precámur méntibus
Cæléste lumen ímpetra;
Ut fides, spes et cáritas
In nobis semper fúlgeant.

Qui cæcos, claudos, débiles,
Illústras, sanas, róboras,
Mutis loquélam tríbuis,
A morte infántes éripis,

Nostris precámur méntibus
Cæléste lumen ímpetra:
Ut fides, spes et cáritas
In nobis semper fúlgeant.

Glória Patri, et Fílio,
Et Spirítui Sancto.

Nostris precámur méntibus
Cæléste lumen ímpetra.

Sicut erat in princípio,
Et nunc, et semper,
Et in sæcula sæculórum. Amen.

Ut fides, spes et cáritas
In nobis semper fúlgeant.

Ant. Esto fidélis usque ad mortem, et dabo tibi corónam vitæ.

℣. Ora pro nobis, beáte Fidélis,
℟. Ut digni efficiámur promissiónibus Christi.

Orémus.

Deus, qui beátum Fidélem, seráphico spíritus ardóre succénsum, in veræ fídei propagatióne martýrii palma et gloriósis miráculis decoráre dignátus es, eius, quǽsumus, méritis et intercessióne, ita nos per grátiam tuam in fide et caritáte confírma, ut in servítio tuo fidéles usque ad mortem inveníri mereámur. Per Christum Dóminum nostrum. Amen.

XXXVI
SAINT COLUMBANUS, CONFESSOR

549

A prayer to St. Columbanus for missionaries is found under n. 618.

XXXVII
SAINT NICHOLAS, BISHOP AND CONFESSOR

550
Invocation

Saint Nicholas, glorious Confessor of Christ, assist us in thy loving kindness.

An indulgence of 100 days (S. P. Ap., Jan. 28, 1924).

Sancte Nicoláë, Conféssor Christi glorióse, adésto nobis pius ac propítius.

551
A Prayer of Impetration

Glorious Saint Nicholas, my special patron, from thy throne in glory where thou dost enjoy the presence of God, turn thine eyes in pity upon me and obtain for me from our Lord the graces and helps that I need in my spiritual and temporal necessities (and especially this favor ......, provided that it be profitable to my salvation). Be mindful, likewise, O glorious and saintly

Bishop, of our Sovereign Pontiff, of Holy Church, and of all Christian people. Bring back to the right way of salvation all those who are living steeped in sin and blinded by the darkness of ignorance, error and heresy. Comfort the afflicted, provide for the needy, strengthen the fearful, defend the oppressed, give health to the infirm; cause all men to experience the effects of thy powerful intercession with the supreme Giver of every good and perfect gift. Amen.

Our Father, Hail Mary, Glory be.

℣. Pray for us, O blessed Nicholas,

℟. That we may be made worthy of the promises of Christ.

Let us pray.

O God, who hast glorified blessed Nicholas, Thine illustrious Confessor and Bishop, by means of countless signs and wonders, and who dost not cease daily so to glorify him; grant, we beseech Thee, that we, being assisted by his merits and prayers, may be delivered from the fires of hell and from all dangers. Through Christ our Lord. Amen.

An indulgence of 300 days (S. P. Ap., Jan. 28, 1924 and May 17, 1932).

XXXVIII
SAINT FRANCIS OF PAOLA, CONFESSOR
552
A Devout Exercise

The faithful on any of thirteen consecutive Fridays which they purpose to devote to the pious exercise known as "The Thirteen Fridays in honor of St. Francis of Paola," which consists of the recitation of the *Our Father* and the *Hail Mary* thirteen times on each Friday, if they complete the aforesaid recitation, may gain:

A plenary indulgence on the usual conditions **(Apostolic Brief, Dec. 8, 1928)**.

XXXIX
SAINT PEREGRINE LAZIOSI, CONFESSOR

553
A Prayer

O glorious wonder-worker, Saint Peregrine, thou who didst answer the divine call with a ready spirit, forsaking all the comforts of a life of ease and all the empty honors of the world, to dedicate thyself to God in the Order of His most holy Mother; thou who didst labor manfully for the salvation of souls, meriting the title of "Apostle of Emilia"; thou who, in union with Jesus crucified, didst endure the most painful sufferings with such patience as to deserve to be healed miraculously by Him with a touch of His divine hand from an incurable wound in thy leg: obtain for us, we pray, the grace to answer every call from God; enkindle in our hearts a consuming zeal for the salvation of souls; deliver us from the infirmities that so often afflict our wretched bodies; and obtain for us the grace of perfect resignation to the sufferings which it shall please Him to send us; so may we, imitating thy virtues and tenderly loving our crucified Lord and His sorrowful Mother, be enabled to merit glory everlasting in paradise. Amen.

Our Father, Hail Mary, Glory be.

An indulgence of 300 days (S. P. Ap., April 26, 1932 and Sept. 9, 1936).

XL
SAINT LAWRENCE, MARTYR

554
Prayers

O glorious Saint Lawrence, Martyr and Deacon, who, being subjected to the most bitter torments, didst not lose thy faith nor thy constancy in confessing Jesus Christ, obtain in like manner for us such an active and solid faith, that we shall never be ashamed to be true followers of Jesus Christ, and fervent Christians in word and in deed.

Our Father, Hail Mary, Glory be.

℣. Pray for us, O holy Lawrence,

℟. That we may be made worthy of the promises of Christ.

Let us pray.

Grant, we beseech Thee, Almighty God, the grace to quench the flames of our vices, Thou who didst enable blessed Lawrence to overcome his fiery torments. Through Christ our Lord. Amen.

An indulgence of 300 days, once a day.
A plenary indulgence on the usual conditions, if these prayers are said devoutly every day for a month (S. P. Ap., Nov. 22, 1934).

XLI
SAINT PANCRATIUS, MARTYR

555
A Prayer

O glorious Saint Pancratius, who, in the flower of youth, which for thee was especially rich in the promises of the world,

didst renounce all, with true greatness of
mind, to embrace the faith and to serve our
Lord Jesus Christ in a spirit of burning love
and profound humility; and who didst joyfully offer thy life for Him in a sublime martyrdom: now that thou art all-powerful with
Him, hear our prayers. Obtain for us a lively
faith that shall be a shining light upon our
earthly path; an ardent love of God above all
things and of our neighbor as ourselves; a
spirit of detachment from the good things of
earth and a contempt for the vanities of this
world; the grace of true humility in the
exemplary profession of the Christian life.
We pray thee in especial manner for all
young men. Remember that thou art the patron of youth; do thou, therefore, by thine
intercession, make all young men clean of
heart and fervent in piety, and bring them
safe to our Lord. Do thou obtain for all of
us the happiness of heaven. Amen.

An indulgence of 300 days(S. P. Ap., March 1, 1935; Dec. 12, 1936)

XLII
SAINT JOHN BOSCO, CONFESSOR
556
A Prayer

O glorious Saint John Bosco, who in order
to lead young people to the feet of the
divine Master and to form them in the light
of faith and Christian morality didst heroi-
cally sacrifice thyself to the very end of thy
life and didst found a proper religious Institute destined to endure and to bring to the
farthest boundaries of the earth thy glorious

work, obtain also for us from Our Lord a holy love for young people who are exposed to so many seductions in order that we may generously spend ourselves in supporting them against the snares of the devil, in keeping them safe from the dangers of the world, and in guiding them, pure and holy, in the path that leads to God.

An indulgence of 300 days.
A plenary indulgence on the usual conditions, if this prayer is devoutly recited every day for a month (S. P. Ap., Feb. 25, 1941).

XLIII
SAINT TARCISIUS, MARTYR
557
Prayers

O unvanquished martyr of the faith, Saint Tarcisius, who wast inflamed with the most intense affection for the Holy Eucharist and didst enjoy the happiness of dying united to Jesus in the Eucharistic species, we beseech thee to obtain for us from Our Lord that our hearts also may be filled with a like love in receiving Him frequently into our breast and above all in the final moments of our lives, and so united with Him we may enter into a blessed eternity. Amen.

℣. Pray for us, O blessed Tarcisius.
℟. That we may be made worthy of the promises of Christ.

Let us pray.

Grant, we beseech Thee, Almighty God, that even as we praise Thy mighty works in

the passion of Saint Tarcisius, so we may
obtain Thy forgiveness through his loving
entreaties. Through Christ our Lord. Amen.

An indulgence of 300 days (S. P. Ap., May 26, 1941).

XLIV
IN HONOR OF SAINT EUGENE I, POPE AND CONFESSOR
558
A Prayer

O Jesus, great High Priest of the new and
eternal Testament, who sittest at the
right hand of the Father as our perpetual
Advocate and who art pleased to abide here
below all days from age to age with Thy beloved Spouse the Church, and with Thy
Vicar who governs it, Thou, O divine Prince
of the pastors of Thy flock, hast deigned to
glorify upon the seat of Peter Thy servant
and Pontiff Eugene, and in the midst of the
wickedness of his times to make him a model
for us, meek under the assaults of his enemies, invincible in his defence of the faith, a
kindly father and a vigilant teacher in his
pastoral office; oh! through his merits, which
are Thy grace and glory, lend a gracious ear
to his intercession with Thee and hear our
prayer. May Thy kingdom come, O immortal King of Ages; may Thy truth reach the
ends of the earth, that truth which Thou
didst bring down to us from Heaven, and
may it enkindle in all hearts that fire which
Thou desirest should be enkindled upon the
earth. This is the earnest desire which con-
strains the paternal heart of Thy Vicar; a

desire for reconciliation between Thee and men; a desire for truth and goodness in the souls of men; a desire to comfort the tears of so many mothers and so many children; a desire for concord and forgiveness among the nations of the earth, a desire for justice and peace. Enlighten Thy Vicar, dear Jesus, console him in his sorrows and in his universal solicitude; renew in him the spirit of the holy Pontiff, who intercedes for him before Thee. Speak, O Lord, that powerful word that will transform the spirits of men; change hatred into love; restrain the fury of human passions; assuage the sufferings and dry the tears of the unfortunate; give an increase of virtue and mutual resignation in families; give peace to the nations and the peoples; so that the Church, founded by Thee upon the rock that is Peter in order to unite all mankind around Thy altar of life and salvation, may invoke Thee in tranquillity, may worship Thee and exalt Thee for ever and ever. Amen.

An indulgence of 500 days.

A plenary indulgence on the usual conditions, once a month, when this prayer has been devoutly recited every day for a month (S. P. Ap., May 31, 1941).

XLV
SAINT ELIZABETH, WIDOW

559
A Prayer

D ear Saint Elizabeth, chosen vessel of the highest virtues, thou didst show to the world, by thy shining example, what things can be wrought in a Christian soul by charity, faith and humility.

Thou didst make use of all the powers of thy soul in loving thy God alone; thou didst love Him with a love so pure and fervent that thou wast made worthy to enjoy upon earth a foretaste of those heavenly favors and blessings that are bestowed upon the souls invited to the marriage of the adorable Lamb of God.

Illuminated by supernatural light and resolute faith, thou didst show thyself to be a true child of the Gospel, giving refreshment to Jesus Christ in the person of thy neighbor and making Him the only object of thy love. Hence, thou didst find all thy joy in conversing with the poor and needy, serving them, wiping away all tears from their eyes, consoling them and assisting them with all manner of kindly offices in sickness and in the other miseries to which our human nature is subject.

Thou thyself becamest poor in order to relieve poverty in thy neighbor: poor, that is to say, in the goods of this world, in order to be made rich in the goods of heaven.

So great was thy humility that thou didst exchange thy royal throne for a miserable hovel, and thy queenly attire for the lowly habit of the seraphic St. Francis; thou didst, moreover, subject thyself, though sinless, to a life of privation and penance, and didst embrace with holy joy the Cross of our divine Saviour, accepting gladly, after His divine

example, the insults and unjust persecutions
of thy fellow-men. In such wise didst thou
forget the world and thyself in order to
remember God alone.

O most amiable Saint, the object of God's
predilection, vouchsafe to protect our souls
and help us to become ever more acceptable
to Jesus. From the heights of heaven, turn
thy pitying eyes upon us, thine eyes one look
of which sufficed on earth to heal the most
distressing maladies of thy people.

In this our age, which is so wicked and corrupt, so indifferent to the things of God, we
run to thy protection with the utmost confidence that thou wilt obtain for us from
our Lord light for our minds and strength
for our wills, thereby enabling us to attain
to true peace of soul.

Defend and guard us in our perilous journey through life; intercede for the pardon
and remission of all our sins; and reveal to
us the way whereby we may enter with thee
into the possession of the kingdom of God.
Amen.

An indulgence of 300 days(Apostolic Brief, Aug. 9, 1861; S. P.
Ap., Oct. 3, 1935 and April 24, 1949) .

XLVI

SAINT AGNES, VIRGIN AND MARTYR

560

Prayers

I. O singular example of virtue, glorious
Saint Agnes, by the living faith which
animated thee from thy tenderest years, and

rendered thee so pleasing to God that thou didst merit the martyr's crown: obtain for us the grace to keep our holy faith inviolate within us, and to profess ourselves Christians sincerely in word and work; may our open confession of Jesus before men cause Him to bear a favorable witness to us before His eternal Father.

Our Father, Hail Mary, Glory be.

II. O invincible Martyr, Saint Agnes most renowned, by thy confidence in God's help, when, being condemned by the impious Roman prefect to see the lily of thy purity stained and trampled in the mire, thou didst not despair, still trusting firmly in the God who giveth His angels charge over them that trust in Him: we beseech thee by thine intercession to obtain for us from Almighty God the forgiveness of all our sins and the sure confidence that He will bestow upon us life everlasting and the means necessary to merit it.

Our Father, Hail Mary, Glory be.

III. O courageous maiden, Saint Agnes most pure, by the burning love with which thy heart was on fire, and which preserved thee from harm in the midst of the flames of passion and of the stake, where the enemies of Jesus Christ sought to destroy thee: obtain for us from Almighty God that every unclean flame may be extinguished in us and only that fire, which Jesus Christ came to enkindle upon the earth, may burn within us; so that, after spending a blameless life in the practice of this fair virtue, we shall be worthy to have a share in the glory thou didst merit by the purity of thy heart and by thy martyrdom.

Our Father, Hail Mary, Glory be.

An indulgence of 300 days, once a day.

A plenary indulgence on the usual conditions, once a month for the daily and devout recitation of these prayers (S. C. Ind., Jan. 16, 1886; S. P. Ap., May 20, 1933 and May 20, 1949).

XLVII
SAINT LUCY, VIRGIN AND MARTYR

561

Prayers

I. **B**y that admirable faith, which thou hadst, O glorious Saint Lucy, when thou didst declare to the tyrant that no one would have been able to take from thee the Holy Spirit, Who dwelt in thy heart as in His temple, obtain for me from Our Lord that I may be so blessed as to live always in a holy and salutary fear of losing His grace, and to flee from everything that might be the occasion of my suffering so grievous a loss.

Our Father, Hail Mary, Glory be.

II. By that singular predilection, O glorious Saint Lucy, which thy immaculate Spouse, Jesus Christ, had for thee, when by an unheard of miracle He rendered thee immovable in spite of all the attempts of thy enemies to drag thee into a place of sin and infamy, obtain for me the grace never to yield to the temptations of the world, the flesh, and the devil, and to fight constantly against their assaults by the continual mortification of all my senses.

Our Father, Hail Mary, Glory be.

III. By that glowing love which thou hadst for Jesus, O glorious Saint Lucy, when, after being consecrated to Him by an irrevocable vow, thou didst refuse the most eligible suitors and, after distributing all thy goods to feed the poor, thou didst also sacrifice thy life by the sword that passed through thy neck, obtain for me the grace to burn constantly with a holy love, by means of which I may be ready to renounce all earthly goods and to endure all evils rather than to become, even in the slightest degree, unfaithful to Jesus.

Our Father, Hail Mary, Glory be.

℣. Pray for us, O blessed Lucy,
℟. That we may be made worthy of the promises of Christ.

Let us pray.

Mercifully hear us, O God of our salvation, that even as we rejoice in the constant faith of blessed Lucy, thy Virgin and Martyr, so we may be instructed in sentiments of loving devotion. Through Christ our Lord. Amen.

An indulgence of 300 days once a day.

A plenary indulgence on the usual conditions, if these prayers together with the versicle and prayer are repeated daily for a whole month (S. C. Ind., Feb. 27, 1886; S. P. Ap., Dec. 10, 1935 and May 20, 1949).

562
Prayer

Dear Saint Lucy, whose name doth signify the light, we come to thee filled with confidence: do thou obtain for us a holy light that shall make us careful not to walk in the ways of sin, nor to remain enshrouded in the darkness of error. We ask also, through thy intercession, for the preservation of the light of our bodily eyes and for abundant grace to use the same, according to the good pleasure of God without any hurt to our souls. Grant, O Lucy, that, after venerating thee and giving thee thanks for thy powerful protection here on earth, we may come at length to share thy joy in paradise in the everlasting light of the Lamb of God, thy beloved Bridegroom, even Jesus. Amen.

An indulgence of 300 days, once a day.

A plenary indulgence on the usual conditions, if the daily recitation of this prayer is continued for a month (S. C. Ind., Dec. 29, 1907; S. P. Ap., June 7, 1936).

XLVIII
SAINT JULIANA FALCONIERI, VIRGIN

563
Prayer

O faithful bride of Jesus and humble servant of Mary, Saint Juliana, thou who by practicing the most heroic virtues, especially the virtue of penance and the love of Jesus in His Sacrament didst arrive at the highest peak of Christian perfection and didst merit to be fed miraculously with the

Bread of Angels in thy last agony; obtain for me the grace to live a holy life in the exercise of every Christian duty and to be able to receive at the moment of death the comfort of the holy Sacraments in order to come with thee to the blessed happiness of heaven. Amen.

An indulgence of 300 days (S. C. Ind., July 20, 1889; S. P. Ap., May 28, 1932 and June 10, 1949).

XLIX

SAINT MARGARET OF CORTONA, PENITENT

564

A Prayer

O most glorious Saint Margaret, true pearl whom Almighty God with so great love plucked from the hand of the infernal enemy who possessed thee, in order that, by means of thy wonderful conversion, holy life and most precious death, He might move all poor sinners to forsake sin, by doing good and avoiding evil as well as all sinful occasions: obtain for us, thy faithful clients, from thy exalted place in heaven, a place to which thy tears and thy penance elevated thee, the grace of a sincere repentance, a lively sorrow for our sins and, after a holy life spent, like thine, in the love of Jesus Crucified, the grace of a happy death and a crown of glory in paradise. Amen.

Our Father, Hail Mary, Glory be.

An indulgence of 300 days (S. C. Ind., Jan. 12, 1897; S. P. Ap., Jan. 26, 1932).

L

SAINT TERESA, VIRGIN

565

A Prayer

O Saint Teresa, seraphic Virgin, beloved spouse of thy crucified Lord, thou who on earth didst burn with a love so intense toward thy God and my God, and now dost glow with a brighter and purer flame in paradise: obtain for me also, I beseech thee, a spark of that same holy fire which shall cause me to forget the world, all things created, and even myself; for thou didst ever greatly desire to see Him loved by all men. Grant that my every thought and desire and affection may be continually employed in doing the will of God, the supreme Good, whether I am in joy or in pain, for He is worthy to be loved and obeyed everlastingly. Obtain for me this grace, thou who art so powerful with God; may I be all on fire, like thee, with the holy love of God. Amen (St. Alphonsus M. de' Liguori) .

An indulgence of 300 days.

A plenary indulgence on the usual conditions, if this prayer is said devoutly every day for a month(S. C. Ind., April 22, 1898 and S. P. Ap., Feb. 12, 1934) .

LI

SAINT BRIDGET, QUEEN OF SWEDEN, WIDOW

566

A prayer for the conversion of non-Catholics is found under n. 629.

LII
SAINT RITA, WIDOW
567
A Prayer

O God, who didst vouchsafe to communicate so great grace to Saint Rita that she imitated Thine example in the love of enemies and bore in her heart and on her countenance the sacred marks of Thy love and passion: grant, we beseech Thee, by her merits and intercession, that we may love our enemies and ever contemplate with deep contrition the sorrows of Thy Passion: Who livest and reignest world without end. Amen.

An indulgence of 300 days, once a day.

A plenary indulgence on the usual conditions, if the daily recitation of this prayer is continued for a month (Pius X, Rescript in his own hand, March 8, 1905, exhib., March 28, 1905; S. P. Ap., Feb. 15, 1935).

568
A Prayer

O glorious Saint Rita, thou who didst share in a marvelous manner the sorrowful Passion of our Lord Jesus Christ, obtain for me the grace to suffer in patience the miseries of this life, and be my refuge in all my necessities.

An indulgence of 300 days, once a day.

A plenary indulgence, on the usual conditions, once a month, for the devout recitation of this prayer every day (Pius X, Audience, July 30, 1906, exhib., Aug. 11, 1906; S. P. Ap., March 2, 1936).

LIII
SAINT CATHERINE, VIRGIN AND MARTYR
569

Prayers to be said by those engaged in teaching are found under nn. 761 and 762.

LIV

SAINT FRANCES OF ROME, WIDOW

570

A Prayer

B right jewel of the Order of Saint Benedict, illustrious Saint Frances of Rome, thou who wast led by divine Providence through various stations in life, that thou mightest be a pattern of every virtue, to maidens, to matrons and to widows, pray for us to our divine Saviour that we may be detached from the vanities of the world and may be able, under the guiding hand of our Guardian Angel, to grow daily in the love of God, of His Church and of our neighbor, and finally to be made partakers in heaven of thy felicity. Amen.

An indulgence of 300 days.

A plenary indulgence on the usual conditions, if the devout repetition of this prayer is performed daily throughout an entire month (S. P. Ap., April 7, 1919 and Sept. 21, 1934).

LV

SAINT MARGARET MARY ALACOQUE, VIRGIN

571

A Devout Exercise

T he faithful who recite with devotion *Glory be to the Father*, etc., three times, together with the invocation: *Saint Margaret, pray for me*, before a representation of St. Margaret Mary Alacoque, are granted:

An indulgence of 300 days;

A plenary indulgence on the usual conditions, if they perform this act of devotion daily for a month (S. P. Ap., Nov. 26, 1936).

572

Prayers

Saint Margaret Mary, thou who wast made a partaker of the divine treasures of the Sacred Heart of Jesus, obtain for us, we beseech thee, from this adorable Heart, the graces we need so sorely. We ask these favors of thee with unbounded confidence. May the divine Heart of Jesus be pleased to bestow them upon us through thy intercession, so that once again He may be loved and glorified through thee. Amen.

℣. Pray for us, O blessed Margaret;

℟. That we may be made worthy of the promises of Christ.

Let us pray.

O Lord Jesus Christ, who didst wondrously open the unsearchable riches of Thy Heart to blessed Margaret Mary, the Virgin: grant unto us, by her merits and our imitation of her, that we may love Thee in all things and above all things, and may be worthy to have our everlasting dwelling in the same Thy Sacred Heart: Who livest and reignest world without end. Amen.

An indulgence of 300 days, once a day.

A plenary indulgence on the usual conditions, if these prayers are said every day for a month (S. P. Ap., June 22, 1922 and Nov. 6. 1935).

LVI
SAINT JOAN OF ARC, VIRGIN

573
An Invocation

Saint Joan of Arc, Apostle of the kingship of Christ, pray for us.

An indulgence of 300 days (Apostolic Brief, Jan. 11, 1927).

LVII
SAINT THERESA OF THE CHILD JESUS, VIRGIN

574
An Invocation

O Saint Theresa of the Child Jesus, Patroness of the Missions, pray for us.

An indulgence of 100 days (Apostolic Brief, July 9, 1928).

575
A Devout Exercise

a) The faithful who devoutly recite thrice the doxology: *Glory be to the Father*, etc., together with the invocation: *Saint Theresa of the Child Jesus, pray for me*, before an image of Saint Theresa, may gain:

An indulgence of 300 days;

A plenary indulgence on the usual conditions, if this act of devotion is repeated daily for a month.

b) The faithful who devoutly visit a church or public oratory, or even a semi-public oratory (in the case of those who may lawfully use the latter), where the Feast of St. Theresa of the Child Jesus is being kept, may gain:

A plenary indulgence, if, in addition, they make their confession, receive Holy Communion and pray for the intentions of the Sovereign Pontiff (S. P. Ap., Sept. 30, 1935 and Dec. 19, 1949).

576
Prayers

O marvelous Saint Theresa of the Child Jesus, who, in thy brief mortal career, didst become a mirror of angelic purity, of daring love and of whole-hearted surrender to Almighty God, now that thou art enjoying the recompense of thy virtues, turn thine eyes of mercy upon us who trust in thee. Obtain for us the grace to keep our hearts and minds pure and clean like unto thine, and to abhor in all sincerity whatever might tarnish ever so slightly the luster of a virtue so sublime, a virtue that endears us to thy heavenly Bridegroom. Ah, dear Saint, grant us to feel in every need the power of thy intercession; give us comfort in all the bitterness of this life and especially at its latter end, that we may be worthy to share eternal happiness with thee in paradise. Amen.

℣. Pray for us, O blessed Theresa,
℟. That we may be made worthy of the promises of Christ.

Let us pray.

O Lord, who hast said: "Unless you become as little children, you shall not enter into the kingdom of heaven"; grant us, we beseech Thee, so to walk in the footsteps of thy blessed Virgin Theresa with a humble and single heart, that we may attain to everlasting rewards: Who livest and reignest world without end. Amen.

An indulgence of 300 days, once a day.

A plenary indulgence on the usual conditions, if these prayers are said daily with devotion for an entire month (S. P. Ap., July 2, 1925 and Sept. 30, 1935).

577
A Prayer

O God, who didst inflame with Thy spirit of love the soul of Saint Theresa of the Child Jesus, grant that we too may love Thee and make Thee loved exceedingly. Amen.

An indulgence of 300 days, once a day.

A plenary indulgence on the usual conditions, provided that the daily recitation of this prayer be continued for a month (S. P. Ap., April 20, 1932 and Oct. 25, 1936).

NOTE: Prayers to St. Theresa of the Child Jesus in behalf of Missions among the heathen are found under nn. 619 and 620; for the conversion of Russia, under n. 632.

LVIII
SAINT LUCY FILIPPINI, VIRGIN

578
A Prayer

O Saint Lucy, who, not content with sanctifying thyself by the fervent and constant practise of the choicest virtues, didst devote thyself zealously to the particular mission of instructing young girls and women in the mysteries of the faith and the precepts of Christian morality, and didst found also a special Institute for Teachers, which was to perpetuate thy work with piety and learning, obtain also for us from thy heavenly Bridegroom the grace not only to live holily, but also to pour forth upon other souls His sweet radiance of light and love, in order that in the eventide of our lives we may close our eyes to the fugitive light of earth and open them in the blessed light of eternity. Amen.

An indulgence of 300 days.

A plenary indulgence on the usual conditions, if this oration is devoutly recited every day for a month (S. P. Ap., May 16, 1939).

LIX

SAINT CATHARINE OF SIENA
PRIMARY PATRON OF ITALY

579
A Prayer

O Saint Catharine, thou lily of virginity and rose of charity who didst adorn the garden of Saint Dominic, heroine of Christian zeal who wast chosen like Saint Francis to be the special Patron of Italy, to thee we have recourse with confidence, invoking thy mighty protection upon ourselves and upon the whole Church of Christ, thy Beloved, in whose Heart thou didst drink of the inexhaustible fountain of all grace and all peace for thee and for the world. From that divine Heart thou didst draw the living water of virtue and concord in families, of upright conduct in young people, of union among the discordant nations, of renewal of public morality and of brotherly love, which is compassionate and benevolent towards the unfortunate and suffering, and didst teach us by thy example how to unite the love of Christ with the love of country.

If thou lovest the land of Italy and its people entrusted to thee, if pity for us moves thee, if that tomb is dear to thee in which Rome venerates and honors thy virginal remains, oh! graciously turn thine eyes and thy favor upon our pain and upon our prayer, and fulfil our desires.

Defend, assist, and comfort thy fatherland and the world. Under thy protection and thy guidance be the sons and daughters of Italy, our hearts and our minds, our labors and our hopes, our faith and our love; that faith and that love which formed thy very life and made thee the living image of Christ crucified in thy intrepid zeal for His Spouse, Holy Church.

O heroic and holy messenger of union and peace for the Church of Christ, thou who didst restore the successor of Peter to the Apostolic Roman See in the splendor of its authority and teaching office, protect and console him in his paternal and universal solicitude, in his anxious cares and in his counsels for the salvation and the tranquillity of the peoples of the earth; revive, preserve, and increase in us and in all faithful Christians, O heavenly Patroness, the affection and the filial submission which thou didst cherish for him and for the fold of Christ in a world at peace. Amen (Pope Pius XII)

An indulgence of 500 days.

A plenary indulgence on the usual conditions, if this prayer is devoutly recited every day for a month (Pius XII, Rescript in his own hand, March 7, 1942, document exhibited, March 24, 1942; S. P. Ap., June 18, 1949).

580

A Prayer

O admirable Saint Catharine, thou who
didst merit to make of thy whole life
the noblest holocaust, constantly inspiring
thyself to a most ardent love for Jesus, the
Lamb without blemish, and for His beloved
Spouse the Church, whose rights thou didst
strenuously affirm and support in troubled
times, obtain, likewise, for us the grace not
only to pass unscathed through the corruption of this world, but also to remain un-
shakably faithful to the Church, in word, in
deed, in example, to see always, and to make
others see, in the Vicar of Christ our anchor,
as it were, in the storms of life, the beacon
light that points the way to the harbor of
safety in the dark night of our times and of
men's souls.

An indulgence of 300 days.
A plenary indulgence on the usual conditions, when this prayer
has been recited daily for a month (S. P. Ap., Dec. 12, 1940).

LX

ONE'S OWN PATRON SAINT

581

A Prayer

O heavenly Patron, in whose name I glory,
pray ever to God for me: strengthen me
in my faith; establish me in virtue; guard me
in the conflict; that I may vanquish the foe
malign and attain to glory everlasting. Amen.

An indulgence of 300 days.

A plenary indulgence on the usual conditions, if this prayer is said devoutly every day for a month (S. C. of the Holy Office, July 24, 1912; S. P. Ap., June 10, 1927) ·

Cæléstis Patróne, cuius nómine glórior, semper precáre pro me apud Deum: in fide confírma; in virtúte róbora; in pugna tuére, ut victor de hoste malígno glóriam ætérnam cónsequi mérear. Amen.

CHAPTER VIII
FOR THE FAITHFUL DEPARTED

REQUIEM ETERNAM DONA EIS OMINE ET LUX PERPETUA UCEAT EIS

I

INVOCATIONS

582

E ternal rest grant unto them, O Lord; and let perpetual light shine upon them. May they rest in peace. Amen.

An indulgence of 300 days, applicable only to the holy souls (S. C. Ind., Feb. 13, 1908; S. P. Ap., May 17, 1927).

R équiem ætérnam dona eis Dómine; et lux perpétua lúceat eis. Requiéscant in pace. Amen.

583

M erciful Lord Jesus, grant them everlasting rest.

An indulgence of 300 days, applicable only to the holy souls (S. C. of the Holy Office, March 18, 1909).

P ie Iesu Dómine, dona eis réquiem sempitérnam.

II

THE OFFICE OF THE DEAD

584

T he faithful who recite with devotion:
  a) Matins and Lauds may gain:

An indulgence of 7 years;

  b) Only one Nocturn, with Lauds:

An indulgence of 5 years;

c) Vespers:

An indulgence of 5 years;

d) Matins, or at least one Nocturn, with Lauds daily for a month:

A plenary indulgence on the usual conditions.

The same indulgences may be gained by those who devoutly assist at the Office of the Dead and follow the singing of the psalms and lessons, either by reading them devoutly, or with pious meditations and prayers (**Apostolic Brief, April 2, 1921; S. P. Ap., June 15, 1936**).

III

PSALMS AND SEQUENCE

585

The faithful who devoutly recite the 129th Psalm, *De profundis* or who say the *Our Father*, *Hail Mary* and the versicle *Eternal rest*, in supplication for the faithful departed, may gain:

An indulgence of 3 years;

An indulgence of 5 years every day in November;

A plenary indulgence on the usual conditions, if this pious practice is repeated daily for a month (**Apostolic Brief, Aug. 11, 1736; S. P. Ap., May 29, 1933 and Nov. 20, 1940**).

586

The faithful who devoutly recite the 50th Psalm, *Miserere* for the souls detained in purgatory, may gain:

An indulgence of 3 years;

A plenary indulgence once a month, on the usual conditions, for the daily recitation of the same (**S. P. Ap., March 9, 1934**).

587

SEQUENCE

Dies iræ, dies illa

Day of wrath and doom impending,
David's word with Sibyl's blending,
Heaven and earth in ashes ending!

O what fear man's bosom rendeth,
When from heaven the Judge descendeth,
On whose sentence all dependeth!

Wondrous sound the trumpet flingeth,
Through earth's sepulchres it ringeth,
  All before the throne it bringeth.

Death is struck, and nature quaking,
All creation is awaking,
  To its Judge an answer making.

Lo! the book exactly worded,
Wherein all hath been recorded;
  Thence shall judgment be awarded.

When the Judge His seat attaineth,
And each hidden deed arraigneth,
  Nothing unavenged remaineth.

What shall I, frail man, be pleading?
Who for me be interceding,
  When the just are mercy needing?

King of majesty tremendous,
Who dost free salvation send us,
  Fount of pity, then befriend us!

Think, kind Jesu!—my salvation
Caused Thy wondrous Incarnation;
  Leave me not to reprobation.

Faint and weary Thou hast sought me,
On the Cross of suffering bought me;
  Shall such grace be vainly brought me?

Righteous Judge! for sin's pollution
Grant Thy gift of absolution,
  Ere that day of retribution.

Guilty, now I pour my moaning,
All my shame with anguish owning;
  Spare, O God, thy suppliant groaning!

Through the sinful woman shriven,
Through the dying thief forgiven,
  Thou to me a hope hast given.

Worthless are my prayers and sighing,
Yet, good Lord, in grace complying,
  Rescue me from fires undying.

With Thy sheep a place provide me,
From the goats afar divide me,
  To Thy right hand do thou guide me.

When the wicked are confounded,
Doomed to shame and woe unbounded,
  Call me, with thy Saints surrounded.

Low I kneel, with heart's submission,
See, like ashes my contrition!
  Help me in my last condition!

Ah! that day of tears and mourning!
From the dust of earth returning,
  Man for judgment must prepare him:

Spare, O God, in mercy spare him!
Lord, all-pitying, Jesu blest,
  Grant them thine eternal rest.   Amen.

(Roman Missal).   (tr. W. J. Irons).

An indulgence of 3 years.

A plenary indulgence once a month, on the usual conditions, if this sequence is recited daily in a spirit of devotion (S. P. Ap., March 9, 1934).

Sequentia

Dies iræ, dies illa,
  Solvet sæclum in favílla:
Teste David cum Sibýlla.

  Quantus tremor est futúrus,
Quando Iudex est ventúrus,
Cuncta stricte discussúrus!

Tuba mirum spargens sonum
Per sepúlcra regiónum
Coget omnes ante thronum.

Mors stupébit et natúra,
Cum resúrget creatúra
Iudicánti responsúra.

Liber scriptus proferétur,
In quo totum continétur,
Unde mundus iudicétur.

Iudex ergo cum sedébit,
Quidquid latet, apparébit:
Nil inúltum remanébit.

Quid sum miser tunc dictúrus?
Quem patrónum rogatúrus?
Cum vix iustus sit secúrus?

Rex treméndæ maiestátis,
Qui salvándos salvas gratis,
Salva me, fons pietátis.

Recordáre, Iesu pie,
Quod sum causa tuæ viæ,
Ne me perdas illa die.

Quærens me, sedísti lassus:
Redemísti, crucem passus;
Tantus labor non sit cassus.

Iuste Iudex ultiónis,
Donum fac remissiónis
Ante diem ratiónis.

Ingemísco tamquam reus;
Culpa rubet vultus meus:
Supplicánti parce, Deus.

Qui Maríam absolvísti,
Et latrónem exaudísti,
Mihi quoque spem dedísti.

Preces meæ non sunt dignæ;
Sed tu bonus fac benígne
Ne perénni cremer igne.

Inter oves locum præsta,
Et ab hædis me sequéstra,
Státuens in parte dextra.

Confutátis maledíctis,
Flammis ácribus addíctis,
Voca me cum benedíctis.

Oro supplex et acclínis,
Cor contrítum quasi cinis:
Gere curam mei finis.

Lacrymósa dies illa,
Qua resúrget ex favílla
Iudicándus homo reus.

Huic ergo parce, Deus;
Pie Iesu Dómine,
Dona eis réquiem. Amen.

(ex *Missali Romano*).

IV
DEVOUT EXERCISES

588

The faithful who devoutly offer prayers at any season of the year in intercession for the souls of the faithful departed, with the intention of so continuing for seven or nine successive days, may obtain:

An indulgence of 3 years once each day;

A plenary indulgence on the usual conditions at the end of their seven or nine days of prayer (Pius IX, Audience Jan. 5, 1849; S. C. of Bishops and Religious, Jan. 28, 1850; S. C. Ind., Nov. 26, 1876; S. P. Ap., May 28, 1933).

589

The faithful who recite prayers or perform other devout exercises in supplication for the faithful departed during the month of November, may gain:

An indulgence of 3 years once on each day of the month;

A plenary indulgence on the usual conditions, if they perform these devotions daily for the entire month.

Those who, during the aforesaid month, take part in public services held in a church or public oratory in intercession for the faithful departed may gain:

An indulgence of 7 years on each day of the month;

A plenary indulgence, if they attend these exercises on at least fifteen days and, in addition, go to confession, receive Holy Communion and pray for the intentions of the Sovereign Pontiff (S. C. Ind., Jan. 17, 1888; S. P. Ap., Oct. 30, 1932).

590

The faithful, as often as they visit a church or public oratory, or even a semi-public oratory (if they may lawfully use the same), in order to pray for the dead on the day on which the Commemoration of All the Faithful Departed is celebrated or on the Sunday immediately following, may gain:

A plenary indulgence applicable only to the souls detained in purgatory, on condition of confession and Communion, and the recitation six times during each visit of *Our Father*, *Hail Mary* and *Glory be* for the intentions of the Sovereign Pontiff (S. C. of the Holy Office, June 25, 1914 and Dec. 14, 1916; S. P. Ap., July 5, 1930 and Jan. 2, 1939).

591

All Masses that are celebrated at any altar by any priest within the period of eight days from the Commemoration of All Souls inclusive, enjoy the same privilege as if they were offered on a privileged altar, but only in favor of the soul for whom they are applied (S. C. Ind., May 19, 1761; Benedict XV, Ap. Const., "Incruentum Altaris," Aug. 10, 1915; Can. 917, No. 1, Code of Canon Law; S. P. Ap., Oct. 31, 1934 and June 12, 1949).

592

The faithful who during the period of eight days from the Commemoration of All Souls inclusive, visit a cemetery in a spirit of piety and devotion, and pray, even mentally, for the dead, may gain:

A plenary indulgence on the usual conditions, on each day of the Octave, applicable only to the dead.

Those who make such a visit, and pray for the Holy Souls, on any day in the year, may gain:

An indulgence of 7 years, applicable only to the departed (S. P. Ap., Oct. 31, 1934).

V

THE HEROIC ACT OF CHARITY

593

a) The faithful who make the heroic act in favor of the souls detained in purgatory, may gain:

A plenary indulgence, applicable only to the dead:

1° on any day that they receive Holy Communion, if they have made their confession and visited some church or public oratory and prayed for the intentions of the Sovereign Pontiff;

2° on any Monday of the year, or if some impediment arises, on the following Sunday, if they attend Mass in supplication for the faithful departed and moreover fulfill the usual conditions.

b) Priests, who make the aforesaid heroic act, may enjoy the indult of a personal privileged altar every day of the year (S. C. Ind., Sept. 30, 1852 and Nov. 20, 1854; S. P. Ap., Jan. 26, 1932).

VI

PRAYERS

594

Prayers for every day of the week

SUNDAY

O Lord God omnipotent, I beseech Thee by the Precious Blood, which Thy divine Son Jesus shed in the Garden, deliver the souls in purgatory, and especially that one which is the most forsaken of all, and bring it into Thy glory, where it may praise and bless Thee for ever. Amen.

Our Father, Hail Mary, Eternal rest, *etc.*

MONDAY

O Lord God omnipotent, I beseech Thee by the Precious Blood which Thy divine Son Jesus shed in His cruel scourging, deliver the souls in purgatory, and among them all, especially that soul which is nearest to its entrance into Thy glory, that it may soon begin to praise Thee and bless Thee for ever. Amen.

Our Father, Hail Mary, Eternal rest, *etc.*

TUESDAY

O Lord God omnipotent, I beseech Thee by the Precious Blood of Thy divine Son Jesus that was shed in His bitter crowning with thorns, deliver the souls in purgatory, and among them all, particularly that soul which is in the greatest need of our prayers, in order that it may not long be delayed in praising Thee in Thy glory and blessing Thee for ever. Amen.

Our Father, Hail Mary, Eternal rest, *etc.*

WEDNESDAY

O Lord God omnipotent, I beseech Thee by the Precious Blood of Thy divine Son Jesus that was shed in the streets of Jerusalem whilst He carried on His sacred shoulders the heavy burden of the Cross, deliver the souls in purgatory and especially that one which is richest in merits in Thy sight, so that, having soon attained the high place in glory to which it is destined, it may praise Thee triumphantly and bless Thee for ever. Amen.

Our Father, Hail Mary, Eternal rest, *etc.*

THURSDAY

O Lord God omnipotent, I beseech Thee by the Precious Body and Blood of Thy divine Son Jesus, which He Himself on the night before His Passion gave as meat and drink to His beloved Apostles and bequeathed to His Holy Church to be the perpetual Sacrifice and life-giving nourishment of His faithful people, deliver the souls in purgatory, but most of all, that soul which was most devoted to this Mystery of infinite love, in order that it may praise Thee therefor, together with Thy divine Son and the Holy Spirit in Thy glory for ever. Amen.

Our Father, Hail Mary, Eternal rest, *etc.*

FRIDAY

O Lord God omnipotent, I beseech Thee by the Precious Blood which Jesus Thy divine Son did shed this day upon the tree of the Cross, especially from His sacred Hands and Feet, deliver the souls in purgatory, and particularly that soul for whom I am most bound to pray, in order that I may not be the cause which hinders Thee from admitting it quickly to the possession of Thy glory where it may praise Thee and bless Thee for evermore. Amen.

Our Father, Hail Mary, Eternal rest, *etc.*

SATURDAY

O Lord God omnipotent, I beseech Thee by the Precious Blood which gushed forth from the sacred Side of Thy divine Son Jesus in the

presence and to the great sorrow of His most
holy Mother, deliver the souls in purgatory
and among them all especially that soul which
has been most devout to this noble Lady, that
it may come quickly into Thy glory, there to
praise Thee in her, and her in Thee through
all the ages.   Amen.

Our Father, Hail Mary, Eternal rest, *etc.*

An indulgence of 500 days for each of these prayers (S. C. Ind.,
Nov. 18, 1826; S. P. Ap., Jan. 26, 1932).

595

Most loving Jesu, I humbly beseech Thee,
that Thou Thyself wouldst offer to
Thine eternal Father in behalf of the Holy
Souls in purgatory, the Most Precious Blood
which poured forth from the sacred wounds
of Thine adorable Body, together with Thine
agony and death.   And do thou likewise, O
sorrowful Virgin Mary, present unto Him,
together with the dolorous Passion of thy
dear Son, thine own sighs and tears, and all
the sorrows thou didst suffer in His suffering,
in order that, through the merits of the same,
refreshment may be granted to the souls
now suffering in the fiery torments of purgatory, so that, being delivered from that
painful prison, they may be clothed with
glory in heaven, there to sing the mercies of
God for ever and ever.   Amen.

Absolve, O Lord, the souls of all the faithful departed from every bond of sin, that
with Thy gracious assistance they may deserve to escape the judgment of vengeance
and enjoy the blessedness of everlasting light.

℣. Eternal rest give unto them. O Lord,
℟. And let perpetual light shine upon them.
℣. From the gates of hell,
℟. Deliver their souls, O Lord.
℣. May they rest in peace.
℟. Amen.
℣. O Lord, hear my prayer.
℟. And let my cry come unto Thee.

Let us pray.

O God, the Creator and Redeemer of all the faithful; grant unto the souls of Thy servants and handmaids the remission of all their sins: that through our devout supplications they may obtain the pardon they have always desired. Who livest and reignest world without end. Amen.
Eternal rest, etc.

An indulgence of 3 years.

A plenary indulgence on the usual conditions, if these prayers are said daily for a month (S. C. Ind., Sept. 15, 1888; S. P. Ap., April 25, 1934).

596

My Jesus, by the sorrows Thou didst suffer in Thine agony in the Garden, in Thy scourging and crowning with thorns, in the way to Calvary, in Thy crucifixion and death, have mercy on the souls in purgatory, and especially on those that are most forsaken; do Thou deliver them from the dire torments they endure; call them and admit them to Thy most sweet embrace in paradise.
Our Father, Hail Mary, Eternal rest, *etc.*

An indulgence of 500 days (S. C. Ind., Dec. 14, 1889 and Nov. 28 1903; S. P. Ap., Oct. 29, 1931).

597

O Lord Jesus Christ, King of glory, deliver the souls of all the faithful departed from the pains of hell and from the
bottomless pit; deliver them out of the lion's
mouth, lest hell should swallow them up,
lest they fall into the outer darkness; but let
Thy standard-bearer, Saint Michael, bring
them back into Thy holy light, which Thou
didst promise of old to Abraham and to his
seed (Roman Missal).

An indulgence of 3 years.

A plenary indulgence once a month on the usual conditions, if
this prayer is devoutly said daily (S. P. Ap., Sept. 12, 1935).

Dómine Iesu Christe, Rex glóriæ, líbera ánimas
ómnium fidélium defunctórum de pœnis inférni
et de profúndo lacu; líbera eas de ore leónis, ne
absórbeat eas tártarus, ne cadant in obscúrum; sed
sígnifer sanctus Míchaël repræséntet eas in lucem
sanctam, quam olim Abrahæ promisísti et sémini
eius.   (ex *Missali Romano*).

598

O God, who hast commanded us to honor
our father and our mother; in Thy
mercy have pity on the souls of my father
and mother, (*or*, the soul of my father, *or*
the soul of my mother,) and forgive them
their trespasses (*or*, forgive him his trespasses, *or*, forgive her her trespasses); and
make me to see them (*or*, him, *or*, her)
again in the joy of everlasting brightness.
Through Christ our Lord.   Amen (Roman Missal).

An indulgence of 3 years.

A plenary indulgence on the usual conditions, if the devout
recitation of this prayer be continued every day for a month (S. P.
Ap., Sept. 12, 1935).

Deus, qui nos patrem et matrem honoráre præcepísti; miseróre cleménter animábus patris et matris meæ[1] eorúmque peccáta dimítte: meque eos in ætérnæ claritátis gáudio fac vidére. Per Christum Dóminum nostrum. Amen (ex *Missali Romano*)

599

O God, who in the ranks of the Apostolic Priesthood hast caused Thy servants to be invested with the pontifical or priestly dignity; grant, we beseech Thee, that they also may be joined unto the everlasting fellowship of the same Thy priests. Through Christ our Lord. Amen (Roman Missal)

An indulgence of 3 years.

A plenary indulgence once a month, on the usual conditions, if this prayer is said daily (S. P. Ap., Oct. 25, 1936)

Deus, qui inter apostólicos sacerdótes fámulos tuos pontificáli seu sacerdotáli fecísti dignitáte vigére, præsta, quǽsumus, ut eórum quoque perpétuo aggregéntur consórtio. Per Christum Dóminum nostrum. Amen (ex *Missali Romano*)

600

(For a man deceased)

Incline Thine ear, O Lord, unto our prayers, wherein we humbly pray Thee to show Thy mercy upon the soul of Thy servant N., whom Thou hast commanded to pass out of this world, that Thou wouldst place him in the region of peace and light, and bid him be a partaker with Thy Saints. Through Christ our Lord. Amen.

[1] Si pro patre tantum recitetur oratio, dicatur: *ánimæ patris mei eiusque peccáta dimítte; meque eum* . . . — Si pro matre tantum, dicatur: *ánimæ matris meæ eiusque peccáta dimítte; meque eam* . . .

(For a woman deceased)

We beseech Thee, O Lord, according to Thy loving-kindness, have mercy upon the soul of Thy handmaidenN., and, now that she is set free from the defilements of this mortal flesh, restore her to her heritage of everlasting salvation. Through Christ our Lord. Amen (Roman Missal).

An indulgence of 500 days for each prayer.

A plenary indulgence on the usual conditions, if either of these prayers is said devoutly every day for a month (S. P. Ap., March 14, 1923 and June 24, 1936).

NOTE: A prayer to Our Blessed Lady of Intercession for the faithful departed is found under n. 434.

Pro defuncto nominatim

Inclína, Dómine, aurem tuam ad preces nostras, quibus misericórdiam tuam súpplices deprecámur, ut ánimam fámuli tui N., quam de hoc sǽculo migráre iussísti, in pacis ac lucis regióne constítuas et Sanctórum tuórum iúbeas esse consórtem. Per Christum Dóminum nostrum. Amen.

Pro defuncta nominatim

Quǽsumus Dómine, pro tua pietáte miserére ánimæ fámulæ tuæ N., et a contágiis mortalitátis exútam, in ætérnæ salvatiónis partem restítue. Per Christum Dóminum nostrum. Amen (ex *Missali Romano*).

CHAPTER IX
FOR SPECIAL OCCASIONS

DIRIGATUR ORATIO EA SUM IN CON DOMINE ✝ SICUT INCEN- SPECTU TUO

EUCHARISTIC CONGRESSES

I

PRAYER FOR THE SUCCESS OF EUCHARISTIC CONGRESSES

601

O Jesus, who art really, truly and substantially present in the Blessed Sacrament to be the food of our souls, deign to bless and bring to a successful issue all Eucharistic congresses and gatherings, and especially the coming congress. . . . Be Thou the inspiration of their labors, resolutions and vows; accept graciously the solemn homage there rendered to Thee; enkindle the hearts of priests and faithful, of parents and children, so that frequent and daily Communion as well as the early Communion of little children may be held in honor in all the countries of the world; and grant that the Kingship of the Sacred Heart over human society may everywhere be acknowledged. Sacred Heart of Jesus, bless the Congress. Saint Paschal Baylon, pray for us.

An indulgence of 300 days.

A plenary indulgence on the usual conditions, when this prayer has been devoutly recited every day for a month (S. P. Ap., March 11, 1924 and June 21, 1927).

NOTE: The same indulgences are attached to any other prayer for Eucharistic Congresses that is approved by the local Ordinary (S. P. Ap., June 21, 1927).

II

INDULGENCES AT THE TIME OF THE CONGRESS INTERNATIONAL, NATIONAL, REGIONAL OR DIOCESAN

602

a) In the place where the Congress is being held, as long as it continues, the faithful are granted:

A plenary indulgence on the usual conditions, once only.

A plenary indulgence, if the faithful devoutly take part in the solemn Eucharistic procession, with which the Congress is usually closed, and in addition, go to confession and receive Holy Communion.

A plenary indulgence on the usual conditions, for those who are present for the Papal Blessing and receive it in a spirit of true devotion.

An indulgence of 15 years, if they visit the Blessed Sacrament exposed for public adoration, according to the prescriptions of n. 148 above.

An indulgence of 7 years, if they are present at any sacred function appointed by the moderators of the Congress; likewise if they participate in any gathering or session of the Congress.

An indulgence of 100 days, if they perform any work of religion in a spirit of penance for the success of the Congress.

b) Elsewhere, the faithful are granted:

A plenary indulgence to be gained only once, from the day of the public opening of the Congress until the last full day of the same, anywhere in the world, if the Congress is international in scope; otherwise, in the whole country, region or diocese respectively, on the usual conditions, provided that a prayer is said in some church or public oratory for the happy outcome of the Congress.

An indulgence of 300 days, as often as the faithful pray for the well-being of the Congress, or perform some good work or make an offering, even after the Congress is closed (**Apostolic Brief, March 7, 1924; S. P. Ap., June 12, 1933**).

III

INDULGENCES AT THE TIME OF A CONGRESS IN A RURAL VICARIATE, DEANERY, MOTHER-CHURCH WITH SUCCURSAL CHAPELS OR PARISH

603

The same indulgences are granted as above for major Congresses, (except the indulgences of the Papal Blessing which does not take place); in such a way, however, that the indulgences cannot be gained outside the place of the Congress, but only within the limits of the rural vicariate, deanery, plebanian district, or parish respectively (Apostolic Brief, March 7, 1924).

Art. II

FOR VOCATIONS TO THE PRIESTHOOD AND THE RELIGIOUS LIFE

I

Invocations

604

O Mary, Queen of the clergy, pray for us; obtain for us many and holy priests.

An indulgence of 300 days (S. P. Ap., Jan. 16, 1923).

605

O Lord, grant unto Thy Church saintly priests and fervent religious.

An indulgence of 300 days (S. P. Ap., July 27, 1923).

606

Send forth, O Lord, laborers into Thy harvest (Roman Missal).

An indulgence of 500 days.

A plenary indulgence once a month on the usual conditions, if this prayer is said every day (S. P. Ap., Nov. 22, 1934).

Mitte, Dómine, operários in messem tuam.

(ex *Missali Romano*).

II

A Devout Exercise

607

The faithful who spend at least half an hour in prayer before the Blessed Sacrament in any church or public oratory to obtain vocations to the priesthood, and who, in addition, go to confession and receive Holy Communion, may gain:

A plenary indulgence (S. P. Ap., May 24, 1921 and June 24, 1936).

III

Prayers

608

The faithful who recite with devotion any prayer approved by ecclesiastical authority, in order to obtain from Almighty God priestly and religious vocations, may gain:

An indulgence of 7 years;

A plenary indulgence on the usual conditions, if the daily recitation of such a prayer be continued for an entire month (S. P. Ap., May 17, 1927 and March 18, 1932).

Art. III

FOR MISSIONS IN PAGAN COUNTRIES

I

Devout Exercises

609

The faithful who give assistance to the sacred Missions either by means of alms or their own personal work, or who encourage others to do the same, whenever they devoutly recite the invocation *Jesus, our way, our truth, and our life, have mercy on us*, may gain:

An indulgence of 300 days (S. C. Prop. of the Faith, April 26, 1857, exhib. May 9, 1857; S. P. Ap., June 2, 1933 and June 14, 1949).

610

The faithful who receive Holy Communion once a month and devoutly recite some prayers for the Missions, may gain:

A plenary indulgence, if, besides, they go to confession and visit some church or public oratory (S. P. Ap., **June 6, 1923**) .

611

A Missionary Day

a) The faithful who on the last Sunday but one of October, or some other appointed by the local Ordinary, according to the regulations of the Rescript of the Sacred Congregation of Rites, April 14, 1926, take part in one of the sacred functions usually celebrated for the Missions, and offer their devout prayers for the conversion of pagans, may gain:

An indulgence of 7 years.

Those moreover, who make their confession, receive Holy Communion, and pray as above, may gain:

A plenary indulgence.

b) The faithful in places where a Missionary Day is not observed, who on the last Sunday but one in October, visit some church or public oratory and pray for the conversion of pagans, may gain:

An indulgence of 7 years.

A plenary indulgence, if moreover they make their confession and receive Holy Communion (S. C. **Rites, April 14, 1926; exhib.** Nov. 16, 1927; S. P. Ap., Aug. 30, 1934 and March 25, 1936) .

II

Prayers

612

O God, the everlasting Creator of all things, remember that the souls of unbelievers were made by Thee and formed in Thine own image and likeness. Remember that Jesus, Thy Son, endured a most bitter

death for their salvation. Permit not, I beseech Thee, O Lord, that Thy Son should be
any longer despised by unbelievers, but do
Thou graciously accept the prayers of holy
men and of the Church, the Spouse of Thy
most holy Son, and be mindful of Thy mercy.
Forget their idolatry and unbelief, and grant
that they too may some day know Him
whom Thou hast sent, even the Lord Jesus
Christ, who is our Salvation, our Life and
Resurrection, by whom we have been saved
and delivered, to whom be glory for endless
ages.   Amen (St. Francis Xavier).

An indulgence of 500 days.

A plenary indulgence on the usual conditions, if the prayer is
devoutly recited daily for a month (Pius IX, Rescript in his own
hand, May 24, 1847, exhib. Sept. 30, 1862; S. P. Ap., Dec. 6, 1918 and
Oct. 23, 1935).

A etérne rerum ómnium efféctor Deus, meménto
abs te ánimas infidélium procreátas, eásque ad
imáginem et similitúdinem tuam cónditas.   Meménto
Iesum, Fílium tuum, pro illórum salúte atrocíssimam
subiísse necem.   Noli, quæso, Dómine, ultra permíttere, ut Fílius tuus ab infidélibus contemnátur, sed
précibus sanctórum virórum et Ecclésiæ, sanctíssimi
Fílii tui Sponsæ, placátus, recordáre misericórdiæ
tuæ et, oblítus idololatríæ et infidelitátis eórum, éffice
ut ipsi quoque agnóscant aliquándo quem misísti
Dóminum Iesum Christum, qui est salus, vita et
resurréctio nostra, per quem salváti et liberáti sumus, cui sit glória per infiníta sæcula sæculórum.
Amen (S. Franciscus Xaverius).

613

O praise the Lord, all ye nations: praise
Him, all ye peoples; for His mercy is
confirmed upon us: and the truth of the
Lord remaineth for ever (Ps. 116).

℣. Let the people praise Thee, O God.
℞. Let all the people praise Thee.

Let us pray.

O God, our Protector, behold and look upon the face of Thy Christ, who gave Himself a redemption for all, and grant that from the rising of the sun even to the going down, Thy Name may be great among the Gentiles, and in every place sacrifice and a clean oblation may be offered unto Thy Name. Through the same Christ our Lord.   Amen.

An indulgence of 3 years.

A plenary indulgence on the usual conditions, when these prayers have been recited daily for a month (S. P. Ap., Nov. 9, 1920 and June 5, 1936).

Laudáte Dóminum, omnes gentes: laudáte eum, omnes pópuli; quóniam confirmáta est super nos misericórdia eius et véritas Dómini manet in ætérnum (Ps. CXVI).

℣. Confiteántur tibi pópuli, Deus.
℞. Confiteántur tibi pópuli omnes.

Orémus.

Protéctor noster, áspice, Deus, et réspice in fáciem Christi tui: qui dedit redemptiónem semetípsum pro ómnibus, et fac ut ab ortu solis usque ad occásum magnificétur nomen tuum in géntibus, ac in omni loco sacrificétur et offerátur nómini tuo oblátio munda. Per eúmdem Christum Dóminum nostrum.   Amen.

614

Have mercy on us, O God of all, and behold us; and send Thy fear upon all the nations that seek not after Thee, that they may know Thee, that there is no God but only Thou, and may tell forth Thy wondrous works. Make the time short, and remember the end, that they may declare Thy wonderful works, and let all the ends of the earth fear Thee.

℣. Make a joyful noise unto God, all the earth;

℟. Serve the Lord with gladness.

Let us pray.

Almighty and everlasting God, who seekest not the death of sinners, but always that they may live; graciously receive our prayer, and deliver the heathen from the worship of idols and gather them into Thy Holy Church unto the praise and glory of Thy name. Through Christ our Lord. Amen.

An indulgence of 3 years.

A plenary indulgence on the usual conditions, when these prayers are recited daily for a month (S. P. Ap., Nov. 9, 1920 and July 12, 1933).

Miserére nostri, Deus ómnium, et réspice nos et immítte timórem tuum super gentes, quæ non exquisiérunt te, ut cognóscant, quia non est Deus nisi Tu, et enárrent magnália tua. Festína tempus, et meménto finis, ut enárrent mirabília tua et métuant te omnes fines terræ.

℣. Iubiláte, omnis terra.

℟. Servíte Dómino in lætítia.

Orémus.

Omnípotens sempitérne Deus, qui non mortem peccatórum, sed vitam semper inquíris: súscipe propítius oratiónem nostram, et líbera pagános ab idolórum cultúra et ággrega Ecclésiæ tuæ sanctæ, ad laudem et glóriam nóminis tui. Per Christum Dóminum nostrum. Amen.

615

O Mary most merciful, the refuge of sinners, hear our supplications and pray to Thy Son, that Almighty God may take away all iniquity from the hearts of the heathen; that, having forsaken their idols, they may turn to the living and true God, and His only Son, Christ our Lord and God.

℣. Confounded be all they that worship graven images;

℟. And that glory in their idols.

Let us pray.

O God, who wilt have all men to be saved and to come to the knowledge of the truth: send forth, we beseech Thee, laborers into Thy harvest and grant them to speak Thy word with all confidence; that Thy word may run and be glorified, and that all peoples may know Thee, the only true God, and Him whom Thou hast sent, Jesus Christ Thy Son, our Lord: Who liveth and reigneth with Thee world without end. Amen.

An indulgence of 3 years.

A plenary indulgence once a month on the usual conditions, if these prayers are devoutly said daily (S. P. Ap., Nov. 9, 1920 and June 5, 1932).

O clementíssima María, refúgium peccatórum, adésto supplicatiónibus nostris et ora Fílium tuum, ut Deus omnípotens áuferat iniquitátem a córdibus paganórum; ut, relíctis idólis suis, convertántur ad Deum vivum et verum, et únicum Fílium eius Christum Deum et Dóminum nostrum.

℣. Confundántur omnes, qui adórant sculptília.

℟. Et qui gloriántur in simulácris suis.

Orémus.

Deus, qui omnes hómines vis salvos fíeri et ad agnitiónem veritátis veníre: mitte, quæsumus, operários in messem tuam et da eis cum omni fidúcia loqui verbum tuum; ut sermo tuus currat et clarificétur, et omnes gentes cognóscant te, solum Deum verum, et quem misísti Iesum Christum Fílium tuum, Dóminum nostrum: Qui tecum vivit et regnat in sæcula sæculórum. Amen.

616

O God of love! In all humility and confidence I offer Thee the immaculate Heart of Mary together with the loving Heart of Jesus our Lord, who gave Himself upon the Cross of Calvary and still offers Himself upon the altar to sanctify and save the souls of men. In loving union with this sacrifice of infinite value, I offer Thee my whole being, O my God, and all my prayers and sufferings, all my sorrows and labors, my life and my death, in order to fulfil Thy divine will in my own soul, to sanctify all missionaries and their native clergy, to obtain the grace of perseverance for their converts as well as the conversion of all sinners and unbelievers in their missions.

An indulgence of 500 days.

A plenary indulgence on the usual conditions, if this act of oblation is devoutly said daily for a month (S. P. Ap., Nov. 25, 1920 and June 5, 1933).

617

Most loving Lord Jesus Christ, who hast redeemed the world by the shedding of Thy Most Precious Blood, turn Thine eyes in mercy upon our poor humanity, which still lies, for the most part, sunk in the darkness of error and in the shadow of death, and grant that the light of Thy truth may shine gloriously upon all mankind. Multiply, O Lord, the apostles of Thy gospel, give them new fervor, and bless with Thy grace their zeal and their labors and make them fruitful; that by means of them all unbelievers may know Thee and be converted to Thee, their Creator and their Redeemer. Call back to Thy fold all who have gone astray, and restore to the bosom of Thy one, true Church all who are in rebellion against her. Hasten, dear Saviour, the happy day when Thy kingdom shall truly come upon earth; draw all men to Thy loving Heart, so that all may be partakers of the unspeakable blessings of Thy redemption in the everlasting bliss of heaven. Amen.

An indulgence of 500 days.

A plenary indulgence on the usual conditions, for the daily recitation of this prayer throughout a month (S. P. Ap., May 18, 1926 and July 9, 1931).

618

O blessed Columbanus, who, in thy zeal for the extension of Christ's kingdom, and the salvation of souls, didst spend thy life in suffering and exile, assist and protect, we humbly implore thee, the missionaries of our day, who have devoted their lives to preaching the Gospel throughout the world. Obtain for them, we beseech thee, that prudence and fortitude, by which thou didst overcome the dangers which beset thy path, and that firm faith and ardent charity which enabled thee to endure gladly the privations of this life, for the love of Christ. Assist and protect us also, dear Saint Columbanus, so to live for God's glory, that when our pilgrimage through life is over, we may enjoy with thee the eternal rest of heaven. Through Christ our Lord. Amen.

An indulgence of 300 days (S. P. Ap., Jan. 5, 1924 and June 5, 1935).

619

Saint Theresa of the Child Jesus, thou who hast been rightly proclaimed the Patroness of Catholic missions throughout the world, remember the burning desire which thou didst manifest here on earth to plant the Cross of Christ on every shore and to preach the Gospel even to the consummation of the world; we implore thee, according to thy promise, to assist all priests and missionaries and the whole Church of God.

An indulgence of 300 days once a day.

A plenary indulgence on the usual conditions, if this prayer is devoutly said every day for a month (Apostolic Brief, July 9, 1928; S. P. Ap., May 20, 1935).

NOTE: An invocation to St. Theresa of the Child Jesus, Patroness of the Missions, is found under n. 574.

620

O glorious virgin St. Theresa, whom the Vicar of Jesus Christ on earth hath chosen to be the heavenly Patroness of the Missions, for which cause all missionaries confess thee to be their Patroness and call upon thy name; we fly to thee with heartfelt affection, beseeching thee that thou wouldst take under thy special protection these generous souls who are filled with the Spirit of God and whose hearts are on fire with the love of Jesus Christ and of their neighbor; they have freely forsaken their families and native land; with great courage they make light of every manner of sacrifice, painful toil, countless dangers, and even death itself which may perchance overtake them, and their only joy is the thought that they are able to suffer and die for the sake of Jesus Christ. Hence they go forth gladly into distant and barbarous places in order to declare to the peoples that dwell therein the work of redemption which was accomplished for their souls also by the Lord Jesus Christ.

In this valley of tears thou didst follow these athletes of the faith, these heroic souls, with special affection, thus opening to them thy virgin heart; thou didst offer for their salvation thy fervent prayers to God; thou didst endure bitter sorrow and cruel penance that God, the Saviour of the world, might be pleased to sustain them in their sacred and difficult ministry. Now that thou art in heaven, adorned with greater glory, and seeing Jesus, face to face, whom thou didst love so much and from whom thou didst receive assurance of mutual love, do thou pray and make intercession for them. May they be enabled, through thy singular assistance, to bring many souls to Jesus, souls who were redeemed by His Precious Blood but who still sit in the darkness and shadow of death un-

der the domination of the evil spirit. This
in truth is likewise their own earnest desire;
in order that they may see it fulfilled, do
thou obtain for them that increase of grace
and holiness which is so necessary for the
fruitful exercise of this apostolic ministry.
Sustain them in their many labors, comfort
them in their sorrows, help them in their
grievous privations and ask of God a special
blessing in their behalf, which shall raise
them up and reward with abundant fruit
the task which they are to accomplish in
spreading the Kingdom of Christ on earth
with such heartfelt love and self-sacrificing
devotion.

O glorious virgin Saint Theresa, heavenly
Patroness of the Missions, hear and answer
us.

An indulgence of 300 days, once a day.

A plenary indulgence once a month, on the usual conditions,
provided that this prayer be said daily with devotion (S. P. Ap.,
Nov. 25, 1936).

O gloriósa virgo Terésia, quam Iesu Christi
Vicárius in terris cæléstem Missiónum Patrónam elégit, ideóque Missionáles te ipsórum Patrónam faténtur et ínvocant, nos máximo cordis
afféctu ad te confúgimus, ut sub tua peculiári tutéla
generósas istas ánimas recípias, quæ spíritu Dei
replétæ et veheménti caritáte erga Iesum Christum
ac próximum deflagrántes, pátria familiáque sponte
relíctis, cuiúslibet géneris sacrifícia, aspérrimos labóres, perícula innúmera, persecutiónes ac ipsam
mortem, ex his ómnibus forte sequutúram, viríli
ánimo posthabéntes et solum gaudéntes pro Iesu
Christi causa se posse pati ac étiam mori, in longín-
quas et bárbaras regiónes se cónferunt, ut pópulis
eásdem incoléntibus opus redemptiónis, peráctæ a

Iesu Christo étiam pro ipsórum animábus, libentíssime annuntiáre nitántur.

Tu quæ in hac lacrimárum valle, virgíneum cor
patefáciens, hos fídei athlétas et heróës peculiári
amóre prosecúta es, atque pro ipsórum salúte férvi-
das Deo preces obtulísti, acérbos dolóres durásque
pœnas tolerásti, ut Deus mundi Salvátor in sancto ac
difficili ministério eos sustinére dignarétur: nunc in
cælo glória maióre redimíta, própius contémplans
Iesum, quem valde amásti et a quo mútui amóris
sensus excepísti, pro iísdem exoráre atque intercédere velis. Ipsi, ope tua singulári, innúmeras
ánimas ad Iesum addúcere queant, quæ tamen redémptæ eius pretióso Sánguine adhuc in ténebris et
in umbra mortis sedent sub dæmonis império. Hoc
revéra válidum est etiam ipsórum desidérium, pro
quo expléndo eísdem ímpetra augméntum grátiæ et
sanctitátis, ádeo necessárium ut reápse éfficax sit
huiúsmodi apostólicum ministérium. Eósdem in tot
labóribus sústine, in dolóribus consoláre, in tot grá-
vibus privatiónibus ádiuva atque a Deo in ipsórum
favórem speciálem benedictiónem expósce, quæ súb-
levet eorúmque valde fecúndet opus, quod tanto
cordis afféctu ac sacrifício pro dilatándo Christi
regno in terris sunt expletúri.

O gloriósa virgo Terésia, cæléstis Missiónum
Patróna, exáudi nos.

Art. IV
FOR THE CONVERSION OF NON-CATHOLICS

I
INVOCATION

621

That Thou wouldst vouchsafe to bring
back into the unity of the Church all
that stray, and to lead all unbelievers to the
light of the Gospel, we beseech Thee to hear
us, O Lord.

An indulgence of 300 days.

A plenary indulgence on the usual conditions, for the daily recitation of this invocation for a whole month (S. P. Ap., May 18, 1926, Nov. 15, 1927 and May 20, 1949).

NOTE: Another invocation is found under n. 233.

Ut omnes errántes ad unitátem Ecclésiæ revocáre et infidéles univérsos ad Evangélii lumen perdúcere dignéris: te rogámus, Dómine, audi nos.

II

A DEVOUT EXERCISE FOR THE UNITY OF THE CHURCH

622

Ant. That they all may be one, as Thou, Father, in me and I in Thee, that they also may be one in us; that the world may believe that Thou hast sent me.

℣. I say to thee, that thou art Peter,

℟. And upon this rock I will build my Church.

Let us pray.

Lord Jesus Christ, Who didst say to Thine Apostles: peace I leave with you, my peace I give unto you, look not upon my sins, but upon the faith of Thy Church; and vouchsafe unto her that peace and unity which is agreeable to Thy will: Who livest and reignest God forever and ever. Amen.

An indulgence of 300 days during the octave of prayers for the unity of the Church from the Feast of the Chair of St. Peter in Rome (Jan. 18) to the Feast of the Conversion of St. Paul (Jan. 25).

A plenary indulgence on the usual conditions at the end of the devout exercise (Apostolic Brief, Feb. 25, 1916; S. P. Ap., Nov. 15, 1927 and Dec. 10, 1946).

Ant. Ut omnes unum sint, sicut Tu, Pater, in me et ego in te, ut et ipsi in nobis unum sint; ut credat mundus quia Tu me misísti.

℣. Ego dico tibi, quia Tu es Petrus, ℟. Et super hanc petram ædificábo Ecclésiam meam.

Orémus.

Domine Iesu Christe, qui dixísti Apóstolis tuis: Pacem relínquo vobis, pacem meam do vobis; ne respícias peccáta mea, sed fidem Ecclésiæ tuæ; eámque secúndum voluntátem tuam pacificáre et coadunáre dignéris: qui vivis et regnas Deus per ómnia sǽcula sæculórum. Amen.

III

PRAYERS

623

O God, who guidest that which is gone astray, and gatherest that which is scattered, and keepest that which is gathered together; we beseech Thee, mercifully pour forth upon the Christian people the grace of Thy unity; that they may reject the spirit of dissension and unite themselves to the true Shepherd of Thy Church, and may thus be enabled to serve Thee worthily. Through Christ our Lord. Amen (Roman Missal).

An indulgence of 3 years.

A plenary indulgence on the usual conditions, if this prayer is said with devotion every day for a month (S. P. Ap., Nov. 22, 1934.

Deus, qui erráta córrigis, et dispérsa cóngregas, et congregáta consérvas: quǽsumus, super pópulum christiánum tuæ uniónis grátiam cleménter infúnde; ut divisióne reiécta, vero pastóri Ecclésiæ tuæ se úniens, tibi digne váleat famulári. Per Christum Dóminum nostrum. Amen (ex Missali Romano).

624

Almighty and everlasting God, whose will it is that all men should be saved and that none should perish, look upon the souls that are deceived by the guile of Satan, in order that the hearts of them that have gone astray may put aside all the perverseness of heresy, and, being truly repentant, may return to the unity of Thy truth. Through Christ our Lord. Amen (Roman Missal).

An indulgence of 3 years.

A plenary indulgence on the usual conditions, when this prayer has been devoutly recited every day for a month (S. P. Ap., May 15, 1937).

O mnípotens sempitérne Deus, qui salvas omnes et néminem vis períre, réspice ad ánimas diabólica fraude decéptas, ut omni hærética pravitáte depósita, errántium corda resipíscant et ad veritátis tuæ rédeant unitátem. Per Christum Dóminum nostrum. Amen (ex *Missali Romano*).

625

L ord Jesu, merciful Saviour of the world, we humbly beseech Thee by Thy Most Sacred Heart, that all the straying sheep may turn unto Thee, the Shepherd and Bishop of their souls: Who livest and reignest world without end. Amen.

An indulgence of 500 days (Pius X, Rescript in his own hand, Oct. 26, 1905, exhib. Nov. 3, 1905; S. P. Ap., June 5, 1933).

D ómine Iesu, clementíssime Salvátor mundi, te per sacratíssimum Cor tuum súpplices exorámus, ut omnes oves errántes ad te Pastórem et Epíscopum animárum suárum convertántur: Qui vivis et regnas in sǽcula sæculórum. Amen.

626

O Mary, Mother of mercy and Refuge of sinners, we beseech thee, be pleased to look with pitiful eyes upon poor heretics and schismatics. Thou who art the Seat of Wisdom, enlighten the minds that are miserably enfolded in the darkness of ignorance and sin, that they may clearly know that the Holy Catholic Church is the one true Church of Jesus Christ, outside of which neither holiness nor salvation can be found. Call them to the unity of the one fold, granting them the grace to accept all the truths of our holy Faith, and to submit themselves to the Supreme Roman Pontiff, the Vicar of Jesus Christ on earth; that so, being united with us in the sweet chains of divine charity, there may soon be one only fold under the same one Shepherd; and may we all, O glorious Virgin, sing forever with exultation: Rejoice, O Virgin Mary, thou only hast destroyed all heresies in the whole world. Amen.

Hail Mary, *three times.*

An indulgence of 500 days (S. C. Prop. of the Faith, Dec. 30, 1868; S. P. Ap., March 18, 1936 and June 10, 1949).

627

O Virgin immaculate, thou who by a singular privilege of grace wast preserved from original sin, look in pity upon our separated brethren, who are nevertheless thy children, and call them back to the center of unity. Not a few of them, although separated from the Church, have kept a certain veneration for thee; and do thou, generous as thou art, reward them for it, by obtaining for them the grace of conversion.

Thou wast conqueror of the infernal serpent from the first instant of thy existence; renew even now, for it is now more necessary than ever before, thine ancient triumphs; glorify thy divine Son, bring back to Him the sheep that have strayed from the one fold and place them once more under the guidance of the universal Shepherd who holds the place of thy Son on earth; let it be thy glory, O Virgin who destroyest all heresies, to restore unity and peace once more to all the Christian people.

An indulgence of 500 days.

A plenary indulgence on the usual conditions, on the Feasts of the Immaculate Conception, the Nativity, the Annunciation, the Purification, and the Assumption of the B. V. M., if this prayer is recited with devotion.

A plenary indulgence on the usual conditions, for the daily, devout recitation of this prayer throughout an entire month (S. C. Ind., Feb. 1, 1896; S. P. Ap., Feb. 15, 1935 and June 11, 1938).

628
To Our Lady of the Rosary of Pompeii

O merciful Queen of the Rosary of Pompeii, thou, the Seat of Wisdom, hast established a throne of fresh mercy in the land that once was pagan, in order to draw all nations to salvation by means of the chaplet of thy mystic roses: remember that thy divine Son hath left us this saying: "Other sheep I have that are not of this fold; them also must I bring, and they shall hear my voice; and there shall be one fold, and one Shepherd." Remember likewise that on Calvary thou didst become our Co-Redemptrix, by virtue of the crucifixion of Thy heart cooperating with Thy Crucified Son in the salvation of the world; and from that day thou didst become the Restorer of the human race, the Refuge of sinners and the Mother of all mankind. Behold, dear Mother, how many souls are lost every hour! Behold, how countless millions of those who dwell in India, in China, and in barbarous regions do not yet know our Lord Jesus Christ! See, too, how many others are indeed Christians and are nevertheless far from the bosom of Mother Church which is Catholic, Apostolic and Roman! O Mary, powerful mediator, advocate of the human race, full of love for us who are mortal, the life of our hearts, blessed Virgin of the Rosary of Pompeii, graciously hear our prayers; let not the Precious Blood and the fruits of Redemption be lost for so many souls. From thy chosen shrine in Pompeii where thou dost nothing else save dispense heaven's favors upon the afflicted, grant that a ray of thy heavenly light may shine forth to enlighten those many blinded understandings and to enkindle so many cold hearts. Intercede with thy divine Son and obtain grace for all the pagans, Jews, heretics and schismatics in the whole world to receive supernatural light and to enter with joy into the bosom of the true Church. Hear the confident prayer of the Supreme Pontiff, that all nations may be joined in the one faith, may know and love Jesus Christ, the blessed fruit of thy womb, who liveth and reigneth with the Father and the Holy Spirit world without end. And then all men shall love thee also, thou who art the salvation of the world, arbiter and dispenser of the treasures of God, and Queen of mercy in the valley of Pompeii. And glorifying thee, the Queen of Victories, who by means of thy Rosary, dost trample upon all heresies, they shall acknowledge that thou givest life to all the nations, since there must be a fulfilment of the prophecy in the Gospel: "All generations shall call me blessed."

An indulgence of 500 days (Apostolic Brief, July 20, 1925; S. P. Ap., Aug. 24, 1934).

629

To Saint Bridget, Queen of Sweden, Widow

With trusting hearts we turn to thee, blessed Bridget, in these hostile and unbelieving days, to implore thine intercession in behalf of those who are separated from the Church of Jesus Christ. By that clear knowledge thou didst have of the bitter sufferings of our crucified Redeemer, the price of our salvation, we offer thee our supplications to obtain the grace of faith for those who are outside the one true fold, that so the sheep who are scattered may return to the one true Shepherd, our Lord Jesus Christ. Amen.

Saint Bridget, fearless in thy service of God, pray for us. Saint Bridget, patient in the midst of suffering and humiliation, pray for us. Saint Bridget, wonderful in thy love for Jesus and Mary, pray for us.

Our Father, Hail Mary, Glory be.

An indulgence of 300 days once a day (S. C. Ind., July 5, 1905; S. P. Ap., Oct. 23. 1928).

630
To obtain the reunion of the Christians of the East

O Lord, who hast united the various nations in the confession of Thy name, we pray Thee for the Christian peoples of the East. Mindful of the high place they held of old in Thy Church, we beg of Thee to inspire them with an ardent desire to regain that place, in order to form, with us, one only fold under the guidance of one and the same Shepherd. Grant that their hearts may be docile to hear the voice of their holy Doctors, who are likewise our Fathers in the faith. Let a spirit of concord and charity, which is a sign of Thy presence among the faithful, hasten the day when our prayers shall be united to theirs, so that every nation and every tongue may acknowledge and glorify our Lord Jesus Christ. Amen.

An indulgence of 500 days.

A plenary indulgence once a month, on the usual conditions, for the daily recitation of this prayer (Apostolic Brief, April 15, 1916; S. P. Ap., May 22, 1937) .

631
Invocation for the Conversion of Russia

Saviour of the world, save Russia.

An indulgence of 300 days (S. P. Ap., Nov. 24, 1924) .
Salvátor mundi, salva Rússiam.

632
Prayer to Saint Theresa of the Child Jesus
for the Conversion of Russia

O loving and compassionate Saint, deign to comfort our Russian brethren, the victims of a long and cruel persecution of the

Christian name; obtain for them perseverance in the faith, progress in the love of God
and of their neighbor, and in confidence
toward the most holy Mother of God; prepare for them holy priests who shall make
reparation for the blasphemies and sacrileges
committed against the holy Eucharist; grant
that angelic purity, especially in the young,
and every Christian virtue may once more
flourish amongst them, to the end that this
noble people, being delivered from all slavery
and returning freely to the one fold entrusted by the loving Heart of the Risen
Christ to Saint Peter and his successors,
may at length taste the joy of glorifying the
Father and the Son and the Holy Spirit in
the fellowship of the holy Catholic Church.
Amen.

An indulgence of 300 days.

A plenary indulgence on the usual conditions, if this prayer is
said devoutly every day for a month (S. P. Ap., Aug. 19, 1929).

Art. V

MISSIONS FOR THE PEOPLE

I

A PRAYER FOR THE SUCCESS OF A MISSION

633

O Jesus, most holy Redeemer, our Master
and our King, it is to Thy Sacred Heart,
that ocean of love and goodness, that we owe
the inestimable blessing of a mission. Touched
with compassion at the sight of our miseries
and the eternal unhappiness that threatens
us, Thou hast resolved to save us. The missionaries who are coming to us are Thy

representatives; in Thy person they will break for us the bread of God's Word and will bring to us the joy of forgiveness. Grant, O Lord, that we may be faithful to Thy grace and correspond zealously with the advances of Thy mercy. Let the preaching of Thy eternal truths enlighten and quicken our minds, and deeply move our hearts, so that we may realize our shortcomings and sincerely repent of them. To the poor souls plunged in the darkness of ignorance and error do Thou grant the light of faith. To those who have saddened Thee by a wicked life, do Thou give the grace of a sincere conversion. Bestow fresh fervor upon the lukewarm, and upon the just true progress in the way of virtue. Send forth Thy Holy Spirit upon all of us, and the face of this parish (*or* this place) shall be renewed. And thou, O Mary, immaculate Virgin and Mother of Perpetual Help, thou art the refuge and advocate of poor sinners; the more guilty they are, the more claim they have upon thy tenderness. It is for this reason that we make bold to implore thy powerful and motherly protection with all confidence. Our salvation is in Thy hands, plead our cause and intercede for us with thy divine Son. Saint N . . . , Patron of the parish of N . . . , pray for us during the blessed days of this Mission. Amen.

An indulgence of 500 days in places, where missions have been publicly announced beforehand to the people, up to the beginning of the same (S. C. of the Holy Office, Feb. 27, 1913, S. P. Ap., May 17, 1935)

II

A PRAYER AFTER A MISSION

634

J esus Christ, who for my sake didst will to be nailed to the Cross, I give Thee thanks for all the benefits of Thy love which Thou hast bestowed upon me during this sacred mission. Behold, once again I am persuaded that only one thing is needful, that is to say, the salvation of my one and only immortal soul. Wherefore I firmly resolve to avoid mortal sin above all things, as well as every voluntary and proximate occasion thereof, especially the sin of. . . , which has been the chief cause of my spiritual ruin. Further, I earnestly desire to avoid venial sin and all perverse attachment thereto; and I engage myself to fulfil faithfully and conscientiously all the duties of my state of life, and to direct my entire life according to Thy most holy will. Moreover, I promise Thee, good Jesus, to be instant in prayer every day of my life, and to have recourse to prayer, especially when temptation presses upon me. I resolve to keep holy the Lord's day, and to approach Thy holy Table frequently and devoutly. Finally I offer unto Thee my whole life and, in particular, my labors and my sufferings. Bless me and all who have taken part with me in this sacred mission. Give me, Lord Jesus, Thy Mother to be my special Patroness, and be Thou my consolation and my joy even to the blessed end of my life. Amen.

An indulgence of 500 days, within the year that follows a mission (S. C. of the Holy Office, Jan. 29, 1914; S. P. Ap., May 17, 1935).

NOTE: For indulgences granted to those who attend the sacred sermons during the missions see n. 692c.

I esu Christe, qui pro me cruci affígi voluísti, grátias tibi ago pro cunctis amóris tui benefíciis, quæ hisce sacrárum Missiónum diébus mihi contulísti. En íterum mihi persuásum est ante ómnia oportére, ut salvem ánimam meam, únicam et immortálem. Ideóque fírmiter propóno in primis omne peccátum lethále vitáre omnémque voluntáriam atque próximam peccáti occasiónem, máxime vero ... quæ præ céteris mihi nocuménto fuit. Sed étiam peccáto veniáli omníque ad ipsum pravo afféctui pro víribus obsístere volo. Promítto tibi, me ómnia status vel offícii mei múnera fidéliter atque religióse adimpletúrum, totámque vitam meam iuxta sanctíssimam voluntátem tuam institutúrum. Insuper promítto tibi, o bone Iesu, me quotidiánis oratiónibus instáre velle, præsértim vero, tentatióne urgénte, ad oratiónem confúgere. Diem domínicam sanctificáre volo et ad Mensam sanctam tuam frequénter et devóte accédere. Dénique totam vitam meam tibi óffero, máxime labóres meos atque dolóres. Bénedic mihi et ómnibus qui mecum huic sacræ Missióni interfuérunt. Da mihi, Dómine Iesu, Matrem tuam in patrónam singulárem et esto solátium et gáudium meum usque ad vitæ meæ beátum finem. Amen.

III

MISSION CROSSES

635

T he faithful who devoutly make a visit to a cross erected in memory of a Mission may gain:

A plenary indulgence on the usual conditions, on the day of the erection or blessing of the mission cross, on the anniversary of the same, on the Feasts of the Finding (May 3) and of the Exaltation (September 14) of the Holy Cross, or on any of the seven days following any of the above.

The faithful who salute the aforesaid cross with some external mark of reverence and say one *Our Father, Hail Mary,* and *Glory be,* in honor of our Lord's Passion, may gain:

An indulgence of 5 years (S. C. of the Holy Office, Aug. 13, 1913; S. P. Ap., March 18, 1932).

NOTE: The cross to be erected must be of durable and handsome material; it must be fastened in a definite place or sustained by a firm base; it must be blessed by the priest who preached the sacred mission; further, the consent of the local Ordinary must be obtained.

Art. VI
FOR A HAPPY DEATH

I
INVOCATIONS

636

Jesus, Mary and Joseph, I give you my heart and soul.

Jesus, Mary and Joseph, assist me in my last agony.

Jesus, Mary and Joseph, let me breathe forth my spirit in peace with you.

An indulgence of 7 years for each invocation.

A plenary indulgence on the usual conditions, for the recitation of each of the foregoing invocations every day for a month (S. C. Ind., April 28, 1807; S. P. Ap., Oct. 12, 1936).

637

From a sudden and unprovided death, deliver us, O Lord.

An indulgence of 300 days (S. P. Ap., Nov. 12, 1935).

A subitánea et improvísa morte líbera nos, Dómine.

NOTE: An invocation for a happy death, addressed to God, is found under n. 19; to the B. V. M., under n. 307; to the Holy Family of J. M. J., under n. 273.

II

AN ACT OF ACCEPTING ONE'S OWN DEATH FROM THE HAND OF GOD

638

The faithful who at any time in their lives, from a sincere spirit of love of God and with at least a contrite heart, express their intention of accepting calmly and gladly from the hand of God whatsoever manner of death it may please Him to send them, together with all its pain, anguish and suffering, may gain:

An indulgence of 7 years;

A plenary indulgence at the hour of death, if they have devoutly made such an act at least once in their lifetime, after having fulfilled the usual conditions (S. C. Ind., March 9, 1904; Holy Office, Nov. 16, 1916; S. P. Ap., March 18, 1932).

III

PIOUS EXERCISES

639

Prayers

Remember, O Virgin Mother of God, when thou shalt stand in the sight of the Lord, to speak good things for us and to turn away His indignation from us.

Holy Mother, pierce me through,
In my heart each wound renew,
   Of my Saviour crucified.

Let me to my latest breath,
In my body bear the death
   Of that dying Son of thine.

Be to me, O Virgin, nigh
Lest in flames I burn and die
   In that awful judgment day.

Christ, when Thou shalt call me hence,
Be Thy Mother my defense,
  Be Thy Cross my victory.

While my body here decays,
May my soul Thy goodness praise
  Safe in paradise with Thee.   Amen.

℣. Pray for us, O most sorrowful Virgin,
℞. That we may be made worthy of the promises of Christ.

Let us pray.

Let intercession be made for us, we beseech Thee, O Lord Jesus Christ, now and at the hour of our death, before the throne of Thy mercy, by the blessed Virgin Mary, Thy Mother, whose most holy soul was pierced by a sword of sorrow in the hour of Thy bitter Passion. Through Thee, Jesus Christ, Saviour of the world, who with the Father and the Holy Ghost livest and reignest world without end.   Amen.

Hail Mary, *three times.*
℣. Our Lady of a happy death,
℞. Pray for us.
℣. Saint Joseph,
℞. Pray for us.

An indulgence of 3 years.

The faithful who complete a novena, reciting daily and devoutly the prayers set forth above, may gain:

A plenary indulgence on the usual conditions (Apostolic Brief, March 22, 1918; S. P. Ap., June 15, 1935).

Recordáre, Virgo Mater Dei, dum stéteris in conspéctu Dómini, ut loquáris pro nobis bona et ut avértat indignatiónem suam a nobis.

Sancta Mater, istud agas,
Crucifíxi fige plagas
Cordi meo válide.

Fac ut portem Christi mortem,
Passiónis fac consórtem
Et plagas recólere.

Flammis ne urar succénsus,
Per te, Virgo, sim defénsus
In die iudícii.

Christe, cum sit hinc exíre,
Da per Matrem me veníre
Ad palmam victóriæ.

Quando corpus moriétur,
Fac ut ánimæ donétur
Paradísi glória. Amen.

℣. Ora pro nobis, Virgo dolorosíssima.
℟. Quæ iuxta crucem Iesu constitísti.

Orémus.

Intervéniat pro nobis, quǽsumus, Dómine Iesu Christe, nunc et in hora mortis nostræ, apud tuam cleméntiam beáta Virgo María, Mater tua, cuius sacratíssimam ánimam in hora tuæ passiónis dolóris gládius pertransívit. Per te, Iesu Christe, Salvátor mundi, qui cum Patre et Spíritu Sancto vivis et regnas in sæcula sæculórum. Amen.

Ter Ave, María.
℣. Nostra Dómina a bona morte,
℟. Ora pro nobis.
℣. Sancte Ioseph,
℟. Ora pro nobis.

640
Rhyme
Ave, Mater dolorosa

Mother, hail, immersed in woes,
Thou the Martyrs' earliest rose,
Hear my cry, to thee I pray:

Grant that in death's agony,
Putting all my trust in thee,
  I may win the just soul's peace.

By that sorrow, like a sword,
At the holy Simeon's word,
  Piercing through thy heart and soul:
Grant that in death's agony, *etc.*

By that sorrow, whelming thee,
When to Egypt thou dost flee,
  So to save thy holy Child:
Grant that in death's agony, *etc.*

By that sorrow, when in tears,
Seeking Jesus midst His peers,
  Thou dost find Him once again:
Grant that in death's agony, *etc.*

By that sorrow, racking thee,
When thy Son's Cross thou dost see
  Bowing Him beneath its weight:
Grant that in death's agony, *etc.*

By that sorrow, fixed in thee,
Whilst He hangs upon the tree,
  Thou thyself a victim too:
Grant that in death's agony, *etc.*

By that sorrow, when thy breast
Now enfolds that body blest
  Taken down from off the Cross:
Grant that in death's agony, *etc.*

By that sorrow, when the tomb
Takes Him from thee to its gloom,
  Loving Mother, Virgin blest:
Grant that in death's agony, *etc.*

Christ, when Thou shalt call me hence,
Be Thy Mother my defense,
Be Thy Cross my victory.   Amen.

(tr. C. E. Spence).

An indulgence of 500 days.

A plenary indulgence once a month, on the usual conditions, if
this rhyme is devoutly recited every day (Apostolic Brief, March
22, 1918; S. P. Ap., July 24, 1931).

NOTE: Other prayers are found under n. 204.

Rhythmus

Ave, Mater dolorósa,
Martyrúmque prima rosa,
Audi vocem súpplicis:

Fac, ut mortis in agóne,
Tua fidens protectióne,
Iusti pacem gáudeam.

Per dolórem, o María,
Tibi Senis prophetía
Velut ense, cónditum:

Fac, ut mortis in agóne, etc.

Per dolórem, quem tulísti,
In Ægyptum quum fugísti,
Ut salváres Púerum:

Fac, ut mortis in agóne, etc.

Per dolórem, quando mœrens,
Inter notos Iesum quærens,
Revocábas pérditum:

Fac, ut mortis in agóne, etc.

Per dolórem, qui te pressit,
Dulcis Natus quum procéssit
Fractus ligni póndere:

Fac, ut mortis in agóne, etc.

Per dolórem cordi infíxum,
Dum spectábas Crucifíxum,
Sacra simul víctima:

Fac, ut mortis in agóne, etc.

Per dolórem, quando Christi
Corpus ulnis excepísti,
E cruce depósitum:

Fac, ut mortis in agóne, *etc.*

Per dolórem, dum condébas,
Pia Mater, et linquébas,
In sepúlcro Fílium:

Fac, ut mortis in agóne, *etc.*

Christe, cum sit hinc exíre,
Da per Matrem me veníre
Ad palmam victóriæ.
Amen.

IV

PRAYERS

641

O most merciful Lord Jesus, by Thine agony and sweat of Blood, by Thy precious death, deliver us, we beseech Thee, from a sudden and unprovided death. O most kind Lord Jesus, by Thy most sharp and ignominious scourging and crowning with thorns, by Thy holy Cross and bitter Passion, by Thy loving-kindness, we humbly pray that Thou wouldst not suffer us to die unprovided with Thy holy Sacraments. O dearly beloved Lord Jesus, by all Thy labors and sorrows, by Thy Precious Blood and sacred Wounds, by those Thy last words on the Cross: "My God, my God, why hast Thou forsaken me?" and those others: "Father, into Thy hands I commend my spirit," we most earnestly beseech Thee to deliver us from a sudden death. Grant us, we pray, room for repentance; grant us a happy passing in Thy grace, that so we may be able to

love Thee, praise Thee and bless Thee forever. Amen.

Our Father, Hail Mary, Glory be to the
Father.

An indulgence of 500 days.
A plenary indulgence on the usual conditions, when this prayer
has been devoutly said every day for a month (S. C. Ind., March 2,
1816; S. P. Ap., May 12, 1933).

642

O Mary, conceived without sin, pray for
us who have recourse to thee; O refuge
of sinners, Mother of the dying, forsake us
not at the hour of our death; obtain for us
the grace of perfect sorrow, sincere contrition, the pardon and remission of our sins, a
worthy receiving of the holy Viaticum, and
the comfort of the Sacrament of Extreme
Unction, in order that we may appear with
greater security before the throne of the just
but merciful Judge, our God and our Redeemer. Amen.

An indulgence of 500 days (Secretariat of Briefs, March 11, 1856;
S. P. Ap., March 7, 1932).

O María sine labe concépta, ora pro nobis, qui confúgimus ad te; o Refúgium peccatórum, Mater
agonizántium, noli nos derelínquere in hora éxitus
nostri, sed ímpetra nobis dolórem perféctum,
sincéram contritiónem, remissiónem peccatórum
nostrórum, sanctíssimi Viátici dignam receptiónem,
Extrémæ Unctiónis Sacraménti corroboratiónem, ut
magis secúri præsentári valeámus ante thronum iusti
sed et misericórdis Iúdicis, Dei et Redemptóris
nostri. Amen.

643

G rant unto us, Lord Jesus, ever to follow
the example of Thy holy Family, that
in the hour of our death Thy glorious Virgin

Mother together with blessed Joseph may come to meet us and we may be worthily received by Thee into everlasting dwellings: Who livest and reignest world without end. Amen (Roman Missal).

An indulgence of 3 years.
A plenary indulgence on the usual conditions, for the devout repetition of this prayer every day for a month (S. C. Ind., March 25, 1897; S. P. Ap., Nov. 22, 1934).

Fac nos, Dómine Iesu, sanctæ Famíliæ tuæ exémpla iúgiter imitári, ut in hora mortis nostræ, occurrénte gloriósa Vírgine Matre tua cum beáto Joseph, per te in ætérna tabernácula récipi mereámur: Qui vivis et regnas in sǽcula sæculórum. Amen (ex *Missali Romano*).

644

Lord Jesus Christ, who willest that no man should perish, and to whom supplication is never made without the hope of mercy, for Thou saidst with Thine own holy and blessed lips: "All things whatsoever ye shall ask in My name, shall be done unto you"; I ask of Thee, O Lord, for Thy holy Name's sake, to grant me at the hour of my death full consciousness and the power of speech, sincere contrition for my sins, true faith, firm hope and perfect charity, that I may be able to say unto Thee with a clean heart: Into Thy hands, O Lord, I commend my spirit: Thou hast redeemed me, O God of truth, who art blessed for ever and ever. Amen (St. Vincent Ferrer).

An indulgence of 3 years once a day (S. C. of the Holy Office, June 5, 1913; S. P. Ap., Dec. 12, 1933 and June 14, 1949).

Dómine Iesu Christe, qui néminem vis períre, et cui numquam sine spe misericórdiæ supplicátur, nam Tu dixísti ore sancto tuo et benedícto: Omnia quæcúmque petiéritis in nómine meo, fient vobis; peto a te, Dómine, propter nomen sanctum tuum, ut in artí-culo mortis meæ des mihi integritátem sensus cum loquéla, veheméntem contritiónem de peccátis meis, veram fidem, spem ordinátam, caritátem perféctam ut tibi puro corde dícere váleam: In manus tuas, Dómine, comméndo spíritum meum: redemísti me, Deus veritátis, qui es benedíctus in sǽcula sæculó-rum.   Amen (S. Vincentius Ferrerius).

645

O my adorable Creator, I ask of Thee the greatest of all Thy graces, that is to say, a holy death. No matter how greatly I have hitherto abused the life Thou gavest me, grant me the grace to end it in Thy holy love.

Let me die, like the holy Patriarchs, for-saking this valley of tears without sadness, to enter into the joy of eternal rest in my own true country.

Let me die, like the glorious Saint Joseph, in the arms of Jesus and Mary, repeating in turn each of these sweet Names which I hope to bless throughout eternity.

Let me die, like the immaculate and blessed Virgin, in the purest love and desire to be reunited to the only object of my love.

Let me die, like Jesus on the Cross, with the most lively sentiments of hatred for sin, of charity toward Thee, O heavenly Father, and of perfect resignation in my agony. Holy Father, into Thy hands I commend my spirit. Be merciful unto me.

Jesus, who didst die for me, grant me the grace of dying in an act of perfect love for Thee.

Holy Mary, Mother of God, pray for me now and at the hour of my death.

My Guardian Angel, my holy Patron Saints, forsake me not at the hour of my death.

Saint Joseph, obtain for me the grace of dying the death of the just. Amen.

O my God, sovereign Lord of life and of death, who, by an immutable decree for the punishment of sin, hast determined that all men must die, behold me humbly kneeling before Thy dread Majesty, resigned and submissive to this law of Thy justice. With all my heart I detest my past sins, by which I have deserved death a thousand times; and for this cause I accept death in reparation for my sins and in obedience to Thy holy will. Yes, great God, send death upon me where Thou wilt, when Thou wilt, and in what manner Thou wilt. Meantime I shall avail myself of the days which it shall please Thee to bestow upon me, to detach myself from this world and to break every tie that holds me in bondage to this place of exile, and to prepare myself to appear with sure confidence before Thy judgment seat. Wherefore I surrender myself without reserve into the hands of Thy fatherly Providence. May Thy divine will be done now and for evermore! Amen.

An indulgence of 500 days once a day (S. P. Ap., Jan. 15, 1920 and Aug. 18, 1936).

646

My journey toward eternity, dear Lord, is encompassed round about by powerful enemies of my soul. I live in fear and trembling, especially at the thought of the hour of death, on which my eternity will depend, and of the fearful struggle that the devil will then have to wage against me, knowing that little time is left for him to accomplish my eternal ruin. I desire, therefore, O Lord, to prepare myself for it from this hour, by offering Thee this day, in view of my last hour, those protestations of faith and love for Thee, which are so effectual in repressing and bringing to naught all the crafty and wicked arts of the enemy and which I resolve to oppose to him at that moment of such grave consequence, even though he should dare alone to attack with his deceits the peace and tranquillity of my spirit.

I N.N., in the presence of the Most Holy Trinity, the blessed Virgin Mary, my holy Guardian Angel and the entire heavenly host, protest that I wish to live and die under the standard of the Holy Cross. I firmly believe all that our Holy Mother, the Catholic and Apostolic Roman Church, believes and teaches. It is my steadfast intention to die in this holy faith, in which all the holy Martyrs, Confessors and Virgins of Christ have died, as well as all those who have saved their souls.

If the devil should tempt me to despair because of the multitude and grievousness of my sins, I protest that from this day forth I firmly hope in the infinite mercy of God, which will not suffer itself to be overcome by my sins, and in the Precious Blood of Jesus which has washed them all away.

If the devil should assail me with temptations to presumption by reason of the small amount of good which by the help of God I may have been able to accomplish, I confess from this day forth that I deserve hell a thousand times by my sins and I entrust myself wholly to the infinite goodness of God, through Whose grace alone I am what I am.

Finally, if the evil spirit should suggest to me that the pains inflicted upon me by our Lord in that last hour of my life are too heavy to bear, I protest now that all will be as nothing in comparison with the punishments I have deserved throughout life. I thank God that He should deign to give me by these sufferings an opportunity in this life to discharge my debt to Him, which I should have to pay hereafter in the pains of purgatory.

In the bitterness of my soul I call to remembrance all my years; I see my iniquities, I confess them and detest them. Ashamed and sorrowful I turn to Thee, my God, my Creator and my Redeemer. Forgive me, O Lord, by the multitude of Thy mercies; forgive Thy servant whom Thou hast redeemed by Thy Precious Blood.

My God, I turn to Thee, I call upon Thee, I trust in Thee; to Thine infinite goodness I commit the entire reckoning of my life. I have sinned exceedingly; enter not into judgment with Thy servant, who surrenders to Thee and confesses his guilt. Of myself I cannot make satisfaction unto Thee for my countless sins: I have not wherewith to pay

Thee, and my debt is infinite. But Thy Son hath shed His Blood for me, and greater than all mine iniquity is Thy mercy.

O Jesus, be my Saviour! At the hour of my fearful crossing to eternity put to flight the enemy of my soul; grant me grace to overcome every difficulty, Thou who alone doest mighty wonders.

Lord, according to the multitude of Thy tender mercies I shall enter into Thy dwelling place. Trusting in Thy pity, I commend my spirit into Thy hands!

May the Blessed Virgin Mary and my Guardian Angel accompany my soul into the heavenly country. Amen. (From the works of St. Pompilio M. Pirrotti).

An indulgence of 3 years.

A plenary indulgence on the usual conditions, for the daily recitation of this prayer for a month (S. P. Ap., Feb. 6, 1934 and May 15, 1937).

647

Almighty and merciful God, who hast bestowed upon mankind the medicine of salvation and the gift of everlasting life: mercifully look upon us Thy servants and restore the souls which Thou hast made, that in the hour of their passing they may deserve to be cleansed from all sin and set before Thee, their Creator, by the hands of Thy holy Angels. Through Christ our Lord. Amen (Roman Missal).

An indulgence of 3 years.

A plenary indulgence once a month on the usual conditions, if this prayer is said devoutly every day (S. P. Ap., Sept. 9, 1935).

Omnípotens et miséricors Deus, qui humáno géneri et salútis remédia et vitæ ætérnæ múnera contulísti: réspice propítius nos fámulos tuos et ánimas réfove, quas creásti, ut in hora éxitus eárum absque peccáti mácula tibi Creatóri suo per manus sanctórum Angelórum repræsentári mereámur. Per Christum Dóminum nostrum. Amen (ex *Missali Romano*).

648

Lord Jesu, pour into us the spirit of Thy love, that in the hour of our death we may be worthy to vanquish the enemy and attain unto the heavenly crown: Who livest and reignest world without end. Amen (Roman Missal).

An indulgence of 3 years.

A plenary indulgence on the usual conditions, provided that this prayer is devoutly said every day for a month (S. P. Ap., Apr.21, 1936).

Dómine Iesu, spíritum nobis tuæ dilectiónis infúnde, ut in hora éxitus nostri hostem víncere et ad cæléstem mereámur corónam perveníre: Qui vivis et regnas in sǽcula sæculórum. Amen (ex *Missali Romano*).

649

Grant, we beseech Thee, O Lord, that in the hour of our death we may be refreshed by Thy holy Sacraments and delivered from all guilt, and so deserve to be received with joy into the arms of Thy mercy. Through Christ our Lord. Amen (Roman Missal).

An indulgence of 3 years.

A plenary indulgence on the usual conditions, if the daily recitation of this prayer is continued for one month (S. P. Ap., Nov. 11, 1936).

Da, quǽsumus Dómine, ut in hora mortis nostræ Sacraméntis refécti et culpis ómnibus expiáti, in sinum misericórdiæ tuæ læti súscipi mereámur.   Per

Christum Dóminum nostrum. Amen (ex *Missali Romano*).

Art. VII

MISCELLANEOUS DEVOTIONS

I

PRAYERS FOR THE SOVEREIGN PONTIFF

650

Invocation

L ord Jesus, shelter our Holy Father the Pope under the protection of Thy Sacred Heart. Be Thou his light, his strength and his consolation.

An indulgence of 300 days (S. P. Ap., Jan. 18, 1924 and June 19, 1933).

651

A Day Dedicated to the Soverign Pontiff

T he faithful who devoutly assist at any of the religious services held every year, on a day dedicated to the Sovereign Pontiff, either to celebrate solemnly the praises of the Roman Pontiff and to call to mind the countless benefits which he has hitherto bestowed upon the whole world, or to give thanks to God for the preservation of the life of the supreme Ruler of the Church and at the same time to obtain from Almighty God the help he needs in ruling the Church, exposed as she is to so many dangers, may gain:

An indulgence of 10 years, if a prayer for the intentions of his Holiness is added;

A plenary indulgence, if in addition they go to confession, receive Holy Communion and pray for the intentions of the Pope (S. C. Ap., Dec. 29, 1933).

652

Versicle and Response

℣. Let us pray for our Pontiff N.

℟. The Lord preserve him, and give him life, and make him to be blessed upon the earth, and deliver him not up to the will of his enemies (Roman Breviary).

Our Father, Hail Mary.

An indulgence of 3 years.

A plenary indulgence on the usual conditions, when this prayer has been devoutly said every day for a month (S. C. Ind., Nov. 26, 1876; S. P. Ap., Oct. 12, 1931).

℣. Orémus pro Pontífice nostro N.

℟. Dóminus consérvet eum, et vivíficet eum, et beátum fáciat eum in terra, et non tradat eum in ánimam inimicórum eius (ex *Breviario Romano*).

Pater, Ave.

653
Prayer

O Lord, we are the millions of believers, humbly kneeling at Thy feet and begging Thee to preserve, defend and save the Sovereign Pontiff for many years. He is the Father of the great fellowship of souls and our Father as well. On this day, as on every other day, he is praying for us also, and is offering unto Thee with holy fervor the sacred Victim of love and peace.

Wherefore, O Lord, turn Thyself toward us with eyes of pity; for we are now, as it were, forgetful of ourselves, and are praying above all for him. Do Thou unite our prayers with his and receive them into the bosom of Thine infinite mercy, as a sweet savor of active and fruitful charity, whereby the children are united in the Church to their Father. All that he asks of Thee this day, we too ask it of Thee in union with him.

Whether he weeps or rejoices, whether he hopes or offers himself as a victim of charity for his people, we desire to be united with him; nay more, we desire that the cry of our hearts should be made one with his. Of Thy great mercy grant, O Lord, that not one of us may be far from his mind and his heart in the hour that he prays and offers unto Thee the Sacrifice of Thy blessed Son. At the moment when our venerable High Priest, holding in His hands the very Body of Jesus Christ, shall say to the people over the Chalice of benediction these words: "The peace of the Lord be with you always," grant, O Lord, that Thy sweet peace may come down upon our hearts and upon all the nations with new and manifest power. Amen.

An indulgence of 500 days once a day (Leo XIII, Audience May 8, 1896; S. P. Ap., Jan. 18, 1934).

654
A Prayer

O God, the Shepherd and Ruler of all Thy faithful people, mercifully look upon Thy servant N., whom Thou hast chosen as the chief Shepherd to preside over Thy Church; grant him, we beseech Thee, so to edify, both by word and example, those over whom he hath charge, that he may attain unto everlasting life, together with the flock committed unto him. Through Christ our Lord. Amen (Roman Missal).

An indulgence of 3 years.

A plenary indulgence on the usual conditions, if this prayer is devoutly said every day for a month (S. P. Ap., Nov. 22, 1934).

Deus ómnium fidélium pastor et rector, fámulum tuum N., quem pastórem Ecclésiæ tuæ præésse voluísti, propítius réspice: da ei, quǽsumus, verbo et exémplo, quibus præest, profícere; ut ad vitam, una cum grege sibi crédito, pervéniat sempitérnam. Per Christum Dóminum nostrum. Amen (ex *Missali Romano*).

655
A Prayer

Almighty and everlasting God, have mercy upon Thy servant N., our Supreme Pontiff, and direct him, according to Thy loving-kindness, in the way of eternal salvation; that, of Thy gift, he may ever desire that which is pleasing unto Thee and may accomplish it with all his might. Through Christ our Lord. Amen (Roman Ritual).

An indulgence of 3 years.

A plenary indulgence once a month on the usual conditions, for the daily devout recitation of this prayer (S. P. Ap., March 10. 1935).

Omnípotens sempitérne Deus, miserére fámulo tuo Pontífici nostro N., et dírige eum secúndum tuam cleméntiam in viam salútis ætérnæ: ut, te donánte, tibi plácita cúpiat et tota virtúte perfíciat. Per Christum Dóminum nostrum. Amen (ex *Rituali Romano*).

II
PRAYERS TO OBTAIN FROM GOD
THE SANCTIFICATION OF THE CLERGY

656
An Invocation

Jesus, Saviour of the world, sanctify Thy priests and sacred ministers.

An indulgence of 300 days (S. P. Ap., Dec. 15, 1936; Apr. 12, 1937).

Iesu, Salvátor mundi, sanctífica sacerdótes et levítas tuos.

657
A Day dedicated to the Sanctification of the Clergy

The faithful who on the first Thursday or Saturday of any month, on Holy Thursday, on the Feast of Our Lady, Queen of Apostles, or on the Birthdays of the Holy Apostles, in some church or public oratory, or even a semi-public oratory (in the case of those who may lawfully use the latter), perform the devout exercise of offering to God the holy Sacrifice of the Mass and Holy Communion, as well as all their prayers and good works done that day, in behalf of the priests and sacred ministers of the Church, that our Lord Jesus Christ, the eternal High Priest, may sanctify them and make them to be priests after His own Heart, may gain:

A plenary indulgence, if in addition, they make their confession and pray for the intentions of His Holiness, the Pope.

If, however, they devoutly perform this same pious exercise on other days of the year, they may gain:

An indulgence of 7 years (S. P. Ap., Dec. 15, 1936 and April 12, 1937).

658
An Act of Oblation

O Jesus, humbled in the Eucharist to be the source and center of charity of the Catholic Church and the strength of souls, we offer Thee our prayers, our actions, our sufferings in behalf of Thy priests, to the end that each day may behold the wider extension of the Kingdom of Thy Sacred Heart.

An indulgence of 300 days once a day (S. P. Ap., April 8, 1919).

659
A Prayer

O Jesus, eternal High Priest, divine Sacrificer, Thou who in an unspeakable burst of love for men, Thy brethren, didst cause the Christian priesthood to spring forth from Thy Sacred Heart, vouchsafe to pour forth upon Thy priests continual living streams of infinite love.

Live in them, transform them into Thee; make them, by Thy grace, fit instruments of Thy mercy; do Thou act in them and through them, and grant, that they may become wholly one with Thee by their faithful imitation of Thy virtues; and, in Thy Name and by the strength of Thy spirit, may they do the works which Thou didst accomplish for the salvation of the world.

Divine Redeemer of souls, behold how great is the multitude of those who still sleep in the darkness of error; reckon up the number of those unfaithful sheep who stray to the edge of the precipice; consider the throngs of the poor, the hungry, the ignorant and the feeble who groan in their abandoned condition.

Return to us in the person of Thy priests; truly live again in them; act through them and pass once more through the world, teaching, forgiving, comforting, sacrificing and renewing the sacred bonds of love between the Heart of God and the heart of man. Amen.

An indulgence of 300 days once a day.

A plenary indulgence on the usual conditions, if the daily recitation of this prayer is continued for a month (Pius X, Rescript in his own hand, March 3, 1905, exhib. Feb. 13, 1911; S. P. Ap., May 17, 1927).

660
A Prayer

O God, who hast appointed Thine only-begotten Son to be the eternal High Priest for the glory of Thy Majesty and the salvation of mankind; grant that they whom He hath chosen to be His ministers and the stewards of His mysteries, may be found faithful in the fulfilment of the ministry which they have received. Through the same Christ our Lord. Amen (Roman Missal).

An indulgence of 3 years.
A plenary indulgence on the usual conditions, for the daily and devout recitation of this prayer throughout an entire month (S. P. Ap., Dec. 15, 1936).

Deus, qui ad maiestátis tuæ glóriam et géneris humáni salútem, Unigénitum tuum summum atque ætérnum constituísti Sacerdótem; præsta, ut quos minístros et mysteriórum suórum dispensatóres elégit, in accépto ministério adimpléndo fidéles inveniántur. Per eúmdem Christum Dóminum nostrum. Amen (ex *Missali Romano*).

III
PRAYERS FOR MILITARY CHAPLAINS
661

The faithful who devoutly recite *Our Father*, *Hail Mary* and *Glory be*, five times, in honor of the Sacred Heart of Jesus, in order to obtain the preservation of military chaplains in purity and holiness of life, may gain:

An indulgence of 300 days (S. P. Ap., Nov. 12, 1934).

IV
A PRAYER FOR CHILDREN
662

O Jesus, friend of little children, Thou who, from Thy tenderest years, didst manifestly grow in wisdom and grace, before

God and men; Thou who, at the age of twelve years, sitting in the temple in the midst of the Doctors, didst listen to them with attention, didst ask questions of them in all humility, and didst win their admiration by the prudence and wisdom of Thy words; Thou who didst receive the little children so gladly, blessing them and saying to Thine Apostles: "Suffer the little children to come unto Me, for of such is the kingdom of heaven," inspire me, even as Thou didst inspire Saint Peter Canisius, the model and guide of the perfect catechist, with a deep respect and holy affection for little children, sincere zeal and devotion in teaching them the elements of Christian doctrine, and a special aptitude for making them understand its mysteries and love its beauty. I ask it of Thee, my Jesus, through the intercession of the Blessed Virgin Mary. Amen.

An indulgence of 300 days once a day (Pius X, Rescript in his own hand, Nov. 23, 1906, exhib. March 15, 1907).

V

PRAYERS FOR EMIGRANTS

663

A Prayer to Jesus Christ

O Jesus, who in the very first days of Thine earthly life wast compelled, together with Mary, Thy loving Mother, and Saint Joseph, to leave Thy native land and to endure in Egypt the misery and discomforts of poor emigrants, turn Thine eyes upon our brethren, who, far away from their dear country and from all that is dear to them, are not infrequently constrained to struggle with the difficulties of a new life, and who are likewise often exposed to grave dangers and snares for their immortal souls.

Be Thou their guide in their uncertain journey, their help in trouble, their comfort in sorrow; keep them safe in their faith, holy in their lives, and faithful to their children, their wives, and their parents; grant, O Lord, that we may be able to embrace them affectionately once more in their native land, and hereafter to live inseparably united to them at the foot of Thy throne in our heavenly country.   Amen.

An indulgence of 350 days (Pius XI, Audience Oct. 26, 1928; exhib. Nov. 19, 1928; S. P. Ap., Aug. 22, 1936).

664
Prayers to St. Raphæl the Archangel

I. Saint Raphael the Archangel, thou wast a faithful companion to the young man, Tobias, on his long journey from Syria to Media, rescuing him from many dangers and, in particular, from the danger of death in the river Tigris; we beseech thee with all our hearts to be a safe guide and an Angel of consolation to our dear ones on the long journey which they must undertake in order to remove to foreign lands; do thou keep them far from all dangers of body and soul, and grant that they may come in safety to the haven of their desire.

Glory be to the Father, *etc.*

II. Saint Raphael the Archangel, arriving

in Media thou didst bestow upon the young man, Tobias, extraordinary favors, going thyself to the city of Rages to receive the money from Gabelus, and causing him to find a worthy spouse in Sara, when she was delivered from the slavery of the demon, and enriching him with the goods of fortune; look, we humbly beseech thee, upon our dear ones who find themselves in foreign lands; do thou in like manner extend unto them thy heavenly protection, prospering their labors to the benefit of our beloved families and saving them from the many snares which will be laid for their souls, so that they may be enabled to preserve the precious gift of faith and to conform their lives to its teaching.

Glory be to the Father, *etc.*

III. Saint Raphael the Archangel, who faithful to thy mission didst bring back safe and sound to Syria the young man, Tobias, enriching his house with blessings and graces, and even restoring the gift of sight to his blind father; ah, fulfil thy task in behalf of our dear emigrants. Bring them back in thine own good time, safe and sound, to our dear families, and grant that their return may be a source of consolation, prosperity and every choice blessing; and we too, like the family of Tobias, will thank thee for all thy tender care and will unite ourselves to thee in praising, blessing and thanking the Giver of every good and perfect gift. Amen.

Glory be to the Father, *etc.*

℣. Pray for us, Saint Raphael the Archangel,

℟. That we may be made worthy of the promises of Christ.

Let us pray.

O God, who didst give Thy blessed Archangel Raphael unto Thy servant Tobias to be his fellow-traveler; grant unto us, Thy servants, that the same may ever keep us and shield us, help us and defend us. Through Christ our Lord. Amen.

An indulgence of 300 days once a day (S. C. of the Holy Office, Feb. 17, 1910; S. P. Ap., Aug. 22, 1936).

VI
PRAYERS FOR THOSE WHO ARE UNDERTAKING A JOURNEY OR A WALK
665

In the way of peace direct us, O Lord.
We praise and venerate
All the heavenly princes,
But especially Raphael,
Faithful physician
And companion true,
Who with Heaven's power
Bindeth fast the demon.

℣. God hath given His Angels charge over thee.

℟. To keep thee in all thy ways.

Let us pray.

O God, who didst give the blessed Archangel Raphael unto Thy servant Tobias to be his fellow-traveler; grant unto us, Thy servants, that the same may ever keep us and shield us, help us and defend us. Through Christ our Lord. Amen.

Let us go forward in peace,
In the name of the Lord. Amen.

The faithful who, being about to make a journey or take a walk, recite these prayers in honor of St. Raphael the Archangel in a spirit of devotion, are granted:

An indulgence of 500 days;

A plenary indulgence on the usual conditions, if they recite them daily for an entire month (S. P. Ap., Jan. 25, 1946).

In viam pacis dírige nos, Dómine.

Collaudámus venerántes
Omnes cæli príncipes,
Sed præcípue fidélem
Médicum et cómitem
Raphaélem in virtúte
Alligántem dǽmonem.

℣. Angelis suis Deus mandávit de te. ℟. Ut custódiant te in ómnibus viis tuis.

Orémus.

Deus, qui beátum Raphaélem Archángelum Tobíæ fámulo tuo cómitem dedísti in via: concéde nobis fámulis tuis ut eiúsdem semper protegámur custódia et muniámur auxílio. Per Christum Dóminum nostrum. Amen.

Procedámus in pace.
In nómine Dómini. Amen.

VII
A PRAYER FOR BENEFACTORS

666

May it please Thee, O Lord, to reward with eternal life all those who do good to us for Thy Name's sake. Amen (Roman Breviary).

An indulgence of 300 days (S. C. Ind., Dec. 17, 1892; S. P. Ap., June 17, 1933).

R etribúere dignáre, Dómine, ómnibus nobis bona faciéntibus propter nomen tuum vitam ætérnam. Amen (ex *Breviario Romano*).

VIII
PRAYERS FOR THE SICK

667
A Devout Practice

T he faithful who visit the sick in hospitals in order to perform the works of charity, may gain:

An indulgence of 7 years (Pius VI, Audience, Feb. 28, 1778; S. P. Ap., Feb. 16, 1932).

668
A Prayer

O glorious Saint Camillus, special patron of the sick poor, thou who for forty years, with truly heroic charity, didst devote thyself to the relief of their temporal and spiritual necessities, be pleased to assist them now even more generously, since thou art blessed in heaven and they have been committed by Holy Church to thy powerful protection. Obtain for them from Almighty God the healing of ali their maladies, or, at least, the spirit of Christian patience and resignation that may sanctify them and comfort them in the hour of their passing to eternity; at the same time obtain for us the precious grace of living and dying after thine example in the practice of divine love. Amen.

Our Father, Hail Mary, Glory be to the Father.

An indulgence of 300 days.

A plenary indulgence on the usual conditions, if this prayer is said devoutly every day for a month (S. C. Ind., Feb. 27, 1894; S. P. Ap., April 24, 1931).

IX

PRAYERS FOR THE DYING

669

A Devout Practice

The faithful who lovingly commend to Almighty God those who are in their last agony throughout the whole world, in order to obtain for them the grace of a happy death, may gain:

An indulgence of 300 days (Pius X, Rescript in his own hand, Oct. 26, 1907; S. C. Ind., Dec. 18, 1907; S. P. Ap., April 10, 1932).

670

Prayers

Eternal Father, by the love Thou bearest toward Saint Joseph, who was chosen by Thee from among all men to exercise Thy divine fatherhood over Thy Son made Man, have mercy on us and upon all poor souls who are in their agony.

Our Father, Hail Mary, Glory be to the Father.

Eternal Son of God, by the love Thou bearest toward Saint Joseph who was Thy most faithful Guardian upon earth, have mercy on us and upon all poor souls who are in their agony.

Our Father, Hail Mary, Glory be to the Father.

Eternal Spirit of God, by the love Thou bearest toward Saint Joseph, who guarded with such tender care most holy Mary, Thy beloved Spouse, have mercy on us and upon all poor souls who are in their agony.

Our Father, Hail Mary, Glory be to the Father.

An indulgence of 500 days once a day (S. C. Ind., May 17, 1884; S. P. Ap., Feb. 29, 1931).
NOTE: Other prayers are found under n. 204.

671
A Prayer

O most merciful Jesus, lover of souls, I beseech Thee, by the agony of Thy Most Sacred Heart and by the sorrows of Thine immaculate Mother, wash clean in Thy Blood the sinners of the whole world who are now in their agony and who are to die this day. Amen.

℣. Heart of Jesus, who didst suffer death's agony.
℟. Have mercy on the dying.

An indulgence of 300 days.
A plenary indulgence once a month on the usual conditions, if this prayer is said with devotion thrice daily at three distinct times (S. C. Ind., Feb. 2, 1850; S. P. Ap., May 15, 1933).

O clementíssime Iesu, amátor animárum, óbsecro te, per agoníam Cordis tui sanctíssimi et per dolóres Matris tuæ immaculátæ, lava in Sánguine tuo peccatóres totíus mundi nunc pósitos in agonía et hódie moritúros. Amen.
℣. Cor Iesu in agonía factum,
℟. Miserére moriéntium.

A PRAYER FOR PARISH PRIESTS
672

Almighty and merciful God, who didst bestow upon the blessed Curé of Ars wonderful pastoral zeal and great fervor for prayer and penance, grant, we beseech Thee, that by his example and intercession, our parish priests may be able to gain the souls of their brethren for Christ, and with them attain to everlasting glory. Through the same Christ our Lord. Amen.

An indulgence of 300 days (S. P. Ap., Jan. 26, 1949).

XI
THE INDULGENCES OF "THE HOLY LAND"

673

The faithful who carry upon their persons or who reverently keep at home crosses, crucifixes, chaplets, small statues, medals and other objects of piety that have been touched to places in the Holy Land or to the sacred Relics preserved there, are granted the so-called Indulgences of "the Holy Land," which are the same as the Apostolic Indulgences (Innocent XI, Const. "Unigeniti," Jan. 28, 1688; S. C. Ind., June 4, 1721, and Aug. 18, 1895; S. P. Ap., June 12, 1923 and Jan. 26, 1932).

NOTE: The Apostolic Indulgences are those which the Sovereign Pontiff imparts to the faithful who possess a chaplet, rosary, cross, crucifix, small statue or medal blessed by the Sovereign Pontiff or by a priest having faculties to give such blessing. Each Pope sets forth his own list of these indulgences.

XII
FOR THOSE WHO SERVE HOLY MASS

674

The faithful who devoutly serve a priest who is offering the sacrifice of the Mass, may gain:

An indulgence of 3 years (S. P. Ap., May 13, 1937).

XIII
PRAYERS TO BE SAID AFTER THE CELEBRATION
OF LOW MASS

675

Hail Mary, *thrice.*

Hail, holy Queen, *etc.*

℣. Pray for us, O holy Mother of God,

℞. That we may be made worthy of the promises of Christ.

Let us pray.

O God, our refuge and our strength, look down in mercy upon Thy people who cry unto Thee, and by the intercession of the glorious and immaculate Virgin Mary, Mother of God, with blessed Joseph, her Spouse, and Thy blessed Apostles, Peter and Paul, and all Thy Saints, mercifully and graciously hear the prayers which we pour forth for the conversion of sinners and for the freedom and exaltation of our holy Mother the Church. Through the same Christ our Lord. Amen.

Holy Michael the Archangel, defend us in battle; be our protection against the wickedness and snares of the devil: may God rebuke him, we humbly pray, and do thou, O Prince of the heavenly host, by the power of God, thrust into hell Satan and all wicked spirits who wander through the world for the ruin of souls. Amen.

The faithful who devoutly recite these prayers kneeling, with the priest who has just celebrated a private Mass at which they have assisted, are granted:

An indulgence of 10 years (S. Cong. of Rites, Jan. 6, 1884 and Nov. 24, 1915; S. P. Ap., May 30, 1934).

Moreover, if the invocation: *Most Sacred Heart of Jesus, have mercy on us*, (Cor Iesu sacratíssimum, miserére nobis) be added three times:

An indulgence of 7 years (S. C. Ind., June 17, 1904; S. P. Ap., March 18, 1932).

Ter Ave, María.
Salve, Regína.
℣. Ora pro nobis, sancta Dei Génitrix,
℟ Ut digni efficiámur promissiónibus Christi.

Orémus.

Deus, refúgium nostrum et virtus, pópulum ad te clamántem propítius réspice, et intercedénte gloriósa et immaculáta Vírgine Dei Genitríce María cum beáto Ioseph eius Sponso, ac beátis Apóstolis tuis, Petro et Paulo, et ómnibus Sanctis, quas pro conversióne peccatórum, pro libertáte et exaltatióne sanctæ Matris Ecclésiæ preces effúndimus, miséricors et benígnus exáudi. Per eúmdem Christum Dóminum nostrum. Amen.

Sancte Míchaël Archángele, defénde nos in prǽlio, contra nequítias et insídias diáboli esto præsídium: Imperet illi Deus, súpplices deprecámur, tuque, Princeps milítiæ cæléstis, Sátanam aliósque spíritus malígnos, qui ad perditiónem animárum pervagántur in mundo, divína virtúte in inférnum detrúde. Amen.

XIV

ASSISTING AT THE FIRST MASS OF NEWLY-ORDAINED PRIESTS AND KISSING THE PALMS OF THEIR HANDS

676

a) The faithful who devoutly assist at the first Mass of any priest, may gain:

An indulgence of 7 years;

A plenary indulgence, if they are kinsmen of the newly ordained priest within the third degree (inclusive) of consanguinity, and further have obtained the remission of their sins, received the Bread of Heaven and prayed for the intentions of His Holiness the Pope (S. C. Ind., Jan. 16, 1886; S. P. Ap., March 18, 1932).

b) Those who devoutly kiss the palms of the hands of a newly ordained priest, both on the day of ordination and on the day of the first Mass are granted:

An indulgence of 100 days (S. P. Ap., Dec. 29, 1934).

NOTE: The indulgences granted to a priest celebrating his first Mass are found under n. 742.

XV

KISSING THE RING OF THE SOVEREIGN PONTIFF, OF A CARDINAL, OF A BISHOP, AND OF A PREFECT APOSTOLIC

677

The faithful who devoutly kiss the ring:
a) Of the Sovereign Pontiff, are granted:

An indulgence of 300 days;

b) Of a Cardinal:

An indulgence of 100 days;

c) Of a Patriarch, Archbishop, Bishop, or Prefect Apostolic:

An indulgence of 50 days (S. C. of the Holy Office, March 18, 1909; S. P. Ap., Dec. 29, 1934 and Nov. 21, 1945).

XVI

THE SIGN OF THE CROSS

678

The faithful, as often as they devoutly sign themselves with the sign of the Cross, with the invocation of the Most Holy Trinity: *"In the Name of the Father,"* etc., are granted:

An indulgence of 3 years.

Whenever they make the same holy sign with blessed water, they may gain:

An indulgence of 7 years (Apostolic Brief, July 28, 1863 and March 23, 1866; S. P. Ap., Feb. 10, 1935 and June 14, 1949).

XVII

THE RENEWAL OF ONE'S BAPTISMAL VOWS

679

The faithful who, at the end of a mission or retreat, or at any season of the year, devoutly assist at the pious ceremony held in parochial and other churches with the permission of the Ordinary in accordance with the rules and formulas laid down by him, in which the promises made in the reception of Baptism are solemnly renewed, may gain:

A plenary indulgence, if, in addition, they make their confession, receive Holy Communion and pray for the intentions of the Sovereign Pontiff (S. C. Ind., Feb. 27, 1907; S. P. Ap., June 21, 1927).

NOTE: The following formula is proposed as an example:

I renounce Satan and all his pomps and all his works, and I promise to cling to Christ with all faithfulness.

NOTA: Ad exemplum, sequens proponitur formula:

Abrenúntio Sátanæ et ómnibus pompis eius et ómnibus opéribus eius, et promítto me Christo fidéliter adhæsúrum.

XVIII
PRAYERS TO IMPLORE GOD'S HELP
BEFORE ANY ACTION

680
A Prayer

Go before us, O Lord, we beseech Thee, in all our doings with Thy gracious inspiration, and further us with Thy continual help, that every prayer and work of ours may begin from Thee, and by Thee be duly ended. Through Christ our Lord. Amen.

An indulgence of 300 days (S. P. Ap., Dec. 14, 1934).

Actiónes nostras, quæsumus Dómine, aspirándo præveni et adiuvándo proséquere: ut cuncta nostra orátio et operátio a te semper incípiat et per te cœpta finiátur. Per Christum Dóminum nostrum. Amen.

681
A Devout Practice

The faithful who on the first day of the year join in the devout chanting of the hymn "Veni Creator" in a church, public or semi-public oratory (in the case of those who may lawfully use the latter),

in order to pray for God's help throughout the course
of the year, are granted:

An indulgence of 10 years;

A plenary indulgence, if they go to confession, receive Holy
Communion and pray for the intentions of His Holiness the Pope
(S. P. Ap., Aug. 10, 1936) .

682

A Prayer

before assembly to transact some public business

We are come, O God the Holy Ghost, we
are come before Thee, hindered indeed by our many and grievous sins, but
especially gathered together in Thy Name.
Come unto us and be with us; vouchsafe to
enter our hearts; teach us what we are to do
and whither we ought to tend; show us what
we must accomplish, in order that, with Thy
help, we may be able to please Thee in all
things. Be Thou alone the author and the
finisher of our judgments, who alone with
God the Father and His Son dost possess a
glorious Name.

Suffer us not to disturb the order of justice, Thou who lovest equity above all things;
let not ignorance draw us into devious paths,
nor partiality sway our minds, neither let
respect of riches or persons pervert our judgment; but unite us to Thee effectually by the
gift of Thine only grace, that we may be one
in Thee and may never forsake the truth;
inasmuch as we are gathered together in Thy
Name, so may we in all things hold fast to
justice tempered by pity, that so in this life

our judgment may in no wise be at variance with Thee and in the life to come we may attain to everlasting rewards for deeds well done. Amen.

An indulgence of 5 years (S. P. Ap., March 8, 1934 and May 20, 1949).

Adsumus, Dómine Sancte Spíritus, ádsumus peccáti quidem immanitáte deténti, sed in nómine tuo speciáliter congregáti. Veni ad nos et esto nobíscum et dignáre illábi córdibus nostris; doce nos quid agámus, quo gradiámur et osténde quid effícere debeámus, ut, te auxiliánte, tibi in ómnibus placére valeámus. Esto solus suggéstor et efféctor iudiciórum nostrórum, qui solus cum Deo Patre et eius Fílio nomen póssides gloriósum.

Non nos patiáris perturbatóres esse iustítiæ qui summam díligis æquitátem; non in sinístrum nos ignorántia trahat, non favor infléctat, non accéptio múneris vel persónæ corrúmpat; sed iunge nos tibi efficáciter solíus tuæ grátiæ dono, ut simus in te unum et in nullo deviémus a vero; quátenus in nómine tuo collécti, sic in cunctis teneámus cum moderámine pietátis iustítiam, ut et hic a te in nullo disséntiat senténtia nostra et in futúrum pro bene gestis consequámur præmia sempitérna. Amen.

XIX
PRAYERS OF THANKSGIVING

683
A Prayer

We give Thee thanks, Almighty God, for all Thy blessings: Who livest and reignest for ever and ever. Amen.

An indulgence of 300 days (S. P. Ap., Dec. 14, 1934).

Agimus tibi grátias, omnípotens Deus, pro univérsis benefíciis tuis: Qui vivis et regnas in sæcula sæculórum. Amen.

684
The Ambrosian Hymn

a) The faithful who, to give thanks to God for blessings received, devoutly recite the Ambrosian hymn *Te Deum laudamus* are granted:

An indulgence of 5 years.

b) Those who on the last day of the year assist at the singing of this hymn in a church, public or semi-public oratory (in the case of those who lawfully use the same), in order to give thanks to God for the blessings received from Him during the whole year, are granted:

An indulgence of 10 years;

A plenary indulgence with the addition of confession and Holy Communion, and prayer for the intentions of the Holy Father (S. P. Ap., Aug. 10, 1936).

685
Devout Practices

a) The faithful who devoutly assist at the religious service, to return thanks to the Most Holy Trinity for blessings received and to implore God's help, held publicly during the last half-hour of the old year and the first half-hour of the new year, and pray for the intentions of the Sovereign Pontiff, are granted:

An indulgence of 10 years;

A plenary indulgence with the addition of confession and Communion.

If they perform this pious exercise privately, for some time at least, immediately before and after midnight, they may gain:

An indulgence of 7 years;

A plenary indulgence on the usual conditions; but where such a public service is held, this indulgence can be gained only by those who are lawfully prevented from assisting at the public service (Apostolic Brief, Dec. 5, 1876; S. P. Ap., Dec. 9, 1932).

b) The faithful who resolve to perform a pious exercise of thanksgiving for the blessings conferred by Almighty God on the human race, arranged for the various days of the week (from Sunday to Saturday) according to a form approved by ecclesiastical authority, may gain:

An indulgence of 300 days, once on each day of the week;

A plenary indulgence on the usual conditions, if this devout exercise is continued for four successive weeks (S. C. of the Holy Office, May 6, 1909).

XX
THE GRADUAL AND PENITENTIAL PSALMS

686

The faithful who devoutly recite the Gradual Psalms or the seven Penitential Psalms, are granted:

An indulgence of 7 years (S. Pius V, Bull '*Quod a nobis*,' July 9, 1568 and '*Superni Omnipotentis Dei*', April 15, 1571; S. P. Ap., March 18, 1932).

XXI
THE LITANY OF THE SAINTS

687

a) The faithful who on the feast of St. Mark the Evangelist or on the Rogation days devoutly assist at the sacred ceremony proper to these days in churches or in public oratories are granted:

An indulgence of 10 years;

A plenary indulgence if they have obtained the forgiveness of their sins, received Holy Communion and prayed for the intentions of the Holy Father.

b) Those, however, who on the aforementioned days when the sacred function mentioned above does not take place, recite the Litany of the Saints, are granted:

An indulgence of 7 years.

c) Those who on the other days of the year piously recite the same Litany are granted:

An indulgence of 5 years;

A plenary indulgence on the usual conditions, if they recite the same Litany daily for an entire month (S. P. Ap., July 10, 1935, and March 21, 1941).

XXII

MENTAL PRAYER

688

The faithful who devote at least a quarter of an hour to mental prayer, are granted:

An indulgence of 5 years;

A plenary indulgence on the usual conditions, if they do this every day for a month (Benedict XIV, Apostolic Brief, Dec. 16, 1746; S. P. Ap., June 19, 1933).

XXIII

SPIRITUAL EXERCISES AND THE MONTHLY RECOLLECTION

689

a) The faithful who take part in a retreat in common with others, and devoutly assist at the sacred conferences, are granted:

An indulgence of 7 years for each of the aforementioned conferences;

A plenary indulgence on the usual conditions, if they devoutly assist at one third at least of the same conferences.

b) Those, however, who participate in a monthly recollection held in common, are granted:

An indulgence of 10 years (S. P. Ap., June 26, 1937, and July 8, 1939).

XXIV

EXAMINATION OF CONSCIENCE

690

The faithful who examine their consciences and sincerely detest their sins together with a firm purpose of amendment are granted:

An indulgence of 500 days;

A plenary indulgence on the usual conditions, if they perform this exercise daily for a month (S. P. Ap., Nov. 16, 1938).

XXV
PRAYERS
TO ASK PARDON FOR SIN

691

I confess to Almighty God, to blessed Mary ever Virgin, to blessed Michael the Archangel, to blessed John the Baptist, to the holy Apostles Peter and Paul and to all the Saints, that I have sinned exceedingly in thought, word, and deed: through my fault, through my fault, through my most grievous fault. Therefore I beseech blessed Mary ever Virgin, blessed Michael the Archangel, blessed John the Baptist, the holy Apostles Peter and Paul, and all the Saints, to pray to the Lord our God for me.

The faithful who, conscious of their sins, with a truly contrite heart sincerely acknowledge themselves to be sinners before God, and confessing their guilt by this humble confession, recommend themselves to the prayers of the blessed Virgin Mary and the whole heavenly court with all earnestness are granted:

An indulgence of 300 days.

Those, moreover, who following the spirit of holy Mother Church make this confession to God before receiving Holy Communion, are granted:

An indulgence of 500 days (S. P. Ap., Dec. 30, 1940).

Confíteor Deo omnipoténti, beátæ Maríæ semper Vírgini, beáto Michaéli Archángelo, beáto Joánni Baptístæ, sanctis Apóstolis Petro et Paulo et ómnibus Sanctis, quia peccávi nimis cogitatióne, verbo et ópere: mea culpa, mea culpa, mea máxima culpa. Ideo precor beátam Maríam semper Vírginem, beátum Michaélem Archángelum, beátum Joánnem Baptístam, sanctos Apóstolos Petrum et Paulum, et omnes Sanctos, oráre pro me ad Dóminum Deum nostrum.

XXVI
ASSISTANCE AT THE EXPLANATION OF THE GOSPEL AND OTHER SACRED DISCOURSES
692

a) **T**he faithful who devoutly and attentively assist at the explanation of the Gospel on Sundays and the more solemn Feasts, as given during Mass, are granted:

An indulgence of 7 years;

A plenary indulgence twice a month, if they are present at such an instruction at least twice a month, as above, and moreover go to confession, receive Holy Communion and pray for the intentions of the Sovereign Pontiff.

b) As often as they hear a sermon attentively and devoutly, they are granted:

An indulgence of 5 years.

c) Those, however, who devoutly attend the sermons delivered in Lent, in Advent, and during a Mission, are granted:

An indulgence of 7 years for any one of the aforementioned sermons;

A plenary indulgence, on the usual conditions, if they hear at least a third of these same sermons in a spirit of devotion (S. C. Ind., July 31, 1756 and Dec. 12, 1784; S. P. Ap., Nov. 8, 1931 and July 8, 1939).

XXVII
CHRISTIAN DOCTRINE
693

The faithful who devote a half hour but not less than twenty minutes to teaching or studying Christian doctrine, may gain:

An indulgence of 3 years;

A plenary indulgence on the usual conditions twice a month, if the above practice is done at least twice a month (Apostolic Brief, March 12, 1930; S. P. Ap., May 26, 1949).

XXVIII
THE READING OF HOLY SCRIPTURE
694

a) **T**he faithful who spend at least a quarter of an hour in reading Holy Scripture with the reverence due to the Word of God and after the manner of spiritual reading, may gain:

An indulgence of 3 years.

b) Those, however, who read at least a few verses of the Gospel and further kiss the book of the Gospels, devoutly reciting one of the following invocations: Through the Gospel's words may our sins be blotted out (*Per evangélica dicta deleántur nostra delícta*)—May the reading of the Gospel be our health and protection (*Evangélica léctio sit nobis salus et protéctio*)—May Christ, the Son of God, teach us the words of the Holy Gospel (*Verba sancti Evangélii dóceat nos Christus, Fílius Dei*), are granted:

An indulgence of 500 days;

A plenary indulgence on the usual conditions, if they perform this act daily for an entire month, as given above;

A plenary indulgence at the hour of death, if they have frequently performed this devout exercise during their lives, provided that they have made their confession and received holy Communion or are at least contrite, and invoke devoutly the most holy Name of Jesus with their lips, if possible, otherwise in their hearts and accept death patiently from the hand of God as the just penalty for sin (S. C. Ind., Dec. 13, 1898; S. P. Ap., Mar. 22, 1932 and Apr. 24, 1945).

XXIX
THE PAPAL BLESSING
695

The faithful who with sentiments of piety and devotion receive the Blessing given by the Supreme Pontiff Urbi et Orbi, even by means of radio, may gain:

A plenary indulgence on the usual conditions (S. P. Ap., June 15, 1939).

XXX
THE DIVINE PRAISES
IN REPARATION FOR BLASPHEMIES
696

Blessed be God.
Blessed be His holy Name.
Blessed be Jesus Christ, true God and true Man.

Blessed be the Name of Jesus.

Blessed be His Most Sacred Heart.

Blessed be Jesus in the Most Holy Sacrament of the Altar.

Blessed be the great Mother of God, Mary most holy.

Blessed be her holy and Immaculate Conception.

Blessed be the name of Mary, Virgin and Mother.

Blessed be Saint Joseph, her most chaste Spouse.

Blessed be God in His Angels and in His Saints.

An indulgence of 3 years.

An indulgence of 5 years, if these prayers are said publicly.

A plenary indulgence on the usual conditions, if these Praises are said daily for a month (Pius VII, Audience July 23, 1801; S. C. Ind., Aug. 8, 1847 and Feb. 2, 1897; S. Cong. of Rites, Feb. 23, 1921; S. P. Ap., Dec. 12, 1935).

XXXI

A CHRISTIAN GREETING

697

a) ℣. Praised be Jesus Christ. ℞. Amen, *or* For ever.

b) ℣. Praised be Jesus and Mary. ℞. Today and for ever.

c) ℣. Glory be to the Sacred Heart of Jesus. ℞. Glory be to the immaculate Heart of Mary.

The faithful whenever they greet one another with one of the above salutations, or with one similar to these, may gain:

An indulgence of 300 days;

A plenary indulgence on the usual conditions once a month, if they habitually observe this devout practice (Pius X, Rescript in his own hand, May 30, 1908, exhib. May 2, 1912; Holy Office, March 27, 1913 and June 26, 1913; S. P. Ap., Aug. 5, 1936).

a) ℣. Laudétur Iesus Christus. ℟. Amen, *vel* In sǽcula.

b) ℣. Laudétur Iesus et María. ℟. Hódie et semper.

c) ℣. Vive le sacré Cœur de Jésus. ℟. Vive le Cœur immaculé de Marie.

XXXII
THE INDULGENCES OF THE PORTIUNCULA
698

If for some special reason it seems advisable to allow this indulgence to be gained in a semi-public oratory, only those belonging to the community or group of the faithful for whose convenience the oratory was erected may avail themselves of the said indulgence.

The faculty is hereby granted to local Ordinaries, to parish priests and even to rectors of churches which enjoy the privilege of the indulgence, of transferring the day for gaining the indulgence from the second day of August, if this should fall on a day not a Sunday, to the Sunday immediately following, when a reasonable cause seems to make this advisable.

Those who wish to gain this indulgence must confess their sins, and if necessary, obtain absolution, receive Holy Communion, and visit a church or oratory possessing the privilege, and there pray for the intentions of the Supreme Pontiff in the usual manner: *i. e.*, they must say at least six times *Our Father*, *Hail Mary* and *Glory be*, at each visit, which they may repeat at will in order to gain the indulgence as often as they desire. (See the decree of the S. P. Ap., July 10, 1924, concerning the regulations for granting and gaining the Indulgence of the Portiuncula.—Cf. the Acta Apostolicæ Sedis, vol. xvi, page 345.)

All cathedral and parochial churches, and moreover other churches and oratories—for which, especially in the larger parishes, the convenience of the faithful, according to the prudent judgment of the Ordinaries of places, seems to demand it—can obtain the privilege of the Portiuncula from the Sacred Penitentiary upon a petition for it with a recommendation from the Ordinary (S. P. Ap., May 1, 1939; Cf. the Acta Apostolicæ Sedis, vol. xxxi, page 226).

XXXIII
A PRAYER FOR THE PRESERVATION OF THE FAITH
699

O my Redeemer, will that terrible moment ever come, when but few Christians shall be left who are inspired by the spirit of faith, that moment when Thine indignation shall be provoked and Thy protection shall be taken from us? Have our vices and our evil lives irrevocably moved Thy justice to take vengeance, perhaps this very day, upon Thy children? O Thou, the author and finisher of our faith, we conjure Thee, in the bitterness of our contrite and humbled hearts, not to suffer the fair light of faith to be extinguished in us. Remember Thy mercies of old, turn Thine eyes in compassion upon the vineyard planted by Thine own right hand, and watered by the sweat of the Apostles, by the precious blood of countless Martyrs and by the tears of so many sincere penitents, and made fruitful by the prayers of so many Confessors and innocent Virgins. O divine Mediator, look upon those zealous souls who raise their hearts to Thee and pray without ceasing for the maintenance of that most precious gift of Thine, the true faith. We beseech Thee, O God of justice, to hold back the decree of our rejection, and to turn away Thine eyes from our vices and regard instead the adorable Blood shed upon the Cross, which purchased our salvation and daily intercedes for us upon our altars. Ah, keep us safe in the true Catholic and Roman faith. Let sickness afflict us, vexations waste us, misfortunes overwhelm us! But preserve in us Thy holy faith; for if we are rich with this precious gift, we shall gladly endure every sorrow, and nothing shall ever be able to change our happiness. On the other hand, without this great treasure of faith, our unhappiness would be unspeakable and without limit! O good Jesus, author of our faith, preserve it pure within us; keep us safe in the bark of Peter, faithful and obedient to his successor and Thy Vicar here on earth, that so the unity of Holy Church may be maintained, holiness fostered, the Holy See protected in freedom, and the Church universal extended to the benefit of souls. O Jesus, author of our faith, humble and convert the enemies of Thy Church; grant true peace and concord to all Christian kings and princes and to all believers; strengthen and preserve us in Thy holy service, to the end that we may live in Thee and die in Thee. O Jesus, author of our faith, let me live for Thee and die for Thee. Amen (St. Clement Hofbauer).

An indulgence of 500 days once a day (S. C. Ind., April 11, 1888; S. P. Ap., July 10, 1933).

XXXIV
A PRAYER FOR THE SANCTIFICATION OF FESTIVAL DAYS

700

M ost glorious Patriarch Saint Joseph, obtain, we beseech Thee, from our Lord Jesus Christ His most plentiful blessings upon all those who keep festival days holy; and grant that those who profane them may realize, while there is yet time, how great is the evil they commit and the punishments they draw upon themselves both in this present life and in the life to come; and grant that they may be speedily converted.

O most faithful Saint Joseph, thou who in thine earthly life wast ever faithful in keeping the law of God, grant that the day may soon come, when all Christian people shall refrain from those works that are forbidden on festival days, devote themselves earnestly to the salvation of their souls and give glory to God: Who liveth and reigneth for ever and ever.   Amen.

An indulgence of 300 days (Pius X, Audience May 30, 1905, exhib. Dec. 1, 1905; S. P. Ap., May 17, 1935).

XXXV
PRAYERS FOR PEACE

701
Prayers

G ive peace in our times, O Lord, because there is none other that fighteth for us, but only Thou, O our God.

℣. Peace be within thy walls,

℟. And abundance within thy towers.

Let us pray.

O God, from whom all holy desires, all right counsels and all just works do proceed; give unto Thy servants that peace which the world cannot give, that both our hearts may be set to obey Thy commandments, and also that we, being delivered from the fear of our enemies, may pass our time, under Thy protection, in rest and quietness. Through Christ our Lord. Amen (Roman Missal).

An indulgence of 3 years.

A plenary indulgence on the usual conditions, if these prayers are said with devotion daily for a month (S. C. Ind., May 18, 1848; S. P. Ap., April 15, 1934).

Da pacem, Dómine, in diébus nostris, quia non est álius, qui pugnet pro nobis, nisi tu, Deus noster.

℣. Fiat pax in virtúte tua,

℟. Et abundántia in túrribus tuis.

Orémus.

Deus, a quo sancta desidéria, recta consília et iusta sunt ópera: da servis tuis illam, quam mundus dare non potest, pacem; ut et corda nostra mandátis tuis dédita, et hóstium subláta formídine, témpora sint tua protectióne tranquílla. Per Christum Dóminum nostrum. Amen (ex *Missali Romano*).

702

A Prayer

Graciously give peace, O Lord, in our days, that, being assisted by help of Thy mercy, we may ever be free from sin and safe from all disturbance. Through Christ our Lord. Amen (Roman Missal).

An indulgence of 3 years.

A plenary indulgence on the usual conditions, when the prayer has been said with devotion daily for a month (Holy Office, Aug. 5, 1915; S. P. Ap., June 10, 1927 and March 3, 1932).

Da, Dómine, propítius pacem in diébus nostris, ut, ope misericórdiæ tuæ adiúti, et a peccáto simus semper líberi et ab omni perturbatióne secúri. Per Christum Dóminum nostrum. Amen (*ex Missali Romano*).

703

A Prayer

Lord Jesus Christ, who didst say unto Thine Apostles: "Peace I leave with you, my peace I give unto you, not as the world giveth, do I give unto you," regard not our sins but Thy merits, and grant unto all Thy servants, that they whom the Almighty Father hath created and governeth, and whom Thou hast redeemed with Thy Precious Blood and hast ordained unto everlasting life, may love one another with all their hearts for Thy sake, and may be made one in spirit and rejoice in Thy perpetual peace. Lord Jesus Christ, concerning whom the Prophet hath said: "And all kings of the earth shall adore Him, all nations shall serve Him," extend Thy reign over the whole human race. Send upon all men the light of Thy faith, deliver them from all the snares and bonds of passion, and direct them to heavenly things; and graciously grant, that the states and nations may be united by means of Thine immaculate Bride, Holy Church, and, through the intercession of the blessed Virgin Mary, Queen of Peace, may serve Thee in all humility; and that all tongues and peoples may form one great choir, to praise Thee both day and night, to bless Thee, to exalt Thee, O King of the nations and the Ruler thereof, O Prince of Peace, immortal King of ages. Amen.

An indulgence of 500 days (Apostolic Brief, Aug. 25, 1923; S. P. Ap., Feb. 16, 1932).

Dómine Iesu Christe, qui dixísti Apóstolis tuis: "Pacem relínquo vobis, pacem meam do vobis, non quómodo mundus dat ego do vobis", ne respícias peccáta nostra sed mérita tua, et concéde ómnibus fámulis tuis, ut quos creávit Pater omnípotens atque gubérnat, quosque Tu pretióso Sánguine redemísti et ad vitam ætérnam destinásti, omnes altérutrum toto corde propter te diligéntes, cor unum fiant et perénni tua pace læténtur. Dómine Iesu Christe, de quo cécinit Prophéta: "Et adorábunt eum omnes reges terræ, omnes gentes sérvient ei", regnum tuum ad genus humánum univérsum exténde. Super omnes hómines fídei tuæ lumen immítte, a passiónum illécebris vinculísque eos líbera, atque ad cæléstia dírige: et concéde propítius, ut civitátes nationésque per immaculátam Sponsam tuam Ecclésiam sanctam coniúnctæ, beatíssima Vírgine María Regína Pacis intercedénte, tibi humíllime famuléntur; et ex ómnibus linguis et pópulis unus exístat chorus, qui, die ac nocte, te laudet, te benedícat, te exáltet, o Rex géntium et dominátor eárum, o Princeps pacis, o sæculórum Rex immortális. Amen.

704
A Prayer

O God, who art the author and lover of peace, in knowledge of whom is eternal life, whose service is a kingly state; defend us Thy humble servants from all assaults of our enemies; that we, surely trusting in Thy defense, may not fear the power of any adversa-

ries. Through Christ our Lord. Amen

(Roman Missal) .

An indulgence of 3 years.

A plenary indulgence on the usual conditions, provided that this prayer is said with devotion daily for an entire month (S. P. Ap., Nov. 28, 1934) .

D eus, auctor pacis et amátor, quem nosse, vívere, cui servíre, regnáre est: prótege ab ómnibus impugnatiónibus súpplices tuos; ut qui in defensióne tua confídimus, nullíus hostilitátis arma timeámus. Per Christum Dóminum nostrum. Amen (ex *Missali Romano*) .

NOTE: An invocation to Jesus for peace is found under n. 82; to Jesus Christ the King, under n. 268.

XXXVI
PRAYERS FOR THE CONSECRATION OF FAMILIES

705
Consecration to the Sacred Heart of Jesus

O Most Sacred Heart of Jesus, Thou didst reveal to the blessed Margaret Mary Thy desire to rule over Christian families; behold, in order to please Thee, we stand before Thee this day, to proclaim Thy full sovereignty over our family. We desire henceforth to live Thy life, we desire that the virtues, to which Thou hast promised peace on earth, may flower in the bosom of our family; we desire to keep far from us the spirit of the world, which Thou hast condemned. Thou art King of our minds by the simplicity of our faith; Thou art King of our hearts by our love of Thee alone, with which our hearts are on fire and whose flame we shall keep alive by frequently receiving the

Holy Eucharist. Be pleased, O Sacred Heart, to preside over our gathering together, to bless our spiritual and temporal affairs, to ward off all annoyance from us, to hallow our joys and comfort our sorrows. If any of us has ever been so unhappy as to fall into the misery of displeasing Thee, grant that he may remember, O Heart of Jesus, that Thou art full of goodness and mercy toward the repentant sinner. And when the hour of separation strikes and death enters our family circle, whether we go or whether we stay, we shall all bow humbly before Thine eternal decrees. This shall be our consolation, to remember that the day will come, when our entire family, once more united in heaven, shall be able to sing of Thy glory and Thy goodness forever. May the immaculate Heart of Mary and the glorious Patriarch Saint Joseph vouchsafe to offer Thee this our act of consecration, and to keep the memory thereof alive in us all the days of our lives.

Glory to the Heart of Jesus, our King and our Father!

a) The members of a family, on the day when for the first time the family is consecrated to the Sacred Heart of Jesus, if they recite the above prayer before a likeness of the Sacred Heart, are granted:

An indulgence of 7 years;

A plenary indulgence, if they fulfil the usual conditions.

b) The members of a family, on the day when this consecration is renewed each year, if they make use of the same prayer before a likeness of the Sacred Heart of Jesus, are granted:

An indulgence of 3 years;

A plenary indulgence, if they fulfil the usual conditions (Pius X, Rescript in his own hand, May 19, 1908, exhib. June 15, 1908; Benedict XV, Letter, April 27, 1915; S. P. Ap., Dec. 10, 1923 and March 18, 1932).

O sacratíssimum Cor Iesu, Tu beátæ Margarítæ Maríæ desidérium regnándi super christiánas famílias pandidísti: ecce ut tibi placeámus ádsumus hódie, ut plenum tuum super nostram famíliam impérium proclamémus. Vólumus deínceps tuam vitam vívere, vólumus in sinu famíliæ nostræ florére virtútes, quibus Tu in terris pacem promisísti, vólumus longe arcére a nobis spíritum mundi, quem Tu damnásti. Tu regnábis in mente nostra fídei nostræ simplicitáte, in corde nostro tui solíus amóre, quo flagrábit erga te et cuius vivam servábimus flammam frequénti divínæ Eucharístiæ receptióne. Dignáre, Cor divínum, nobis præésse in unum conveniéntibus, benedícere negótiis spirituálibus et temporálibus, arcére moléstias, sanctificáre gáudia, pœnas leváre. Si quando mísere quis nostrum in tantam ærúmnam incíderit ut te afflígat, fac in memóriam illi rédigas, Cor Iesu, te cum peccatóre, quem pænitet, plenum esse bonitátis et misericórdiæ. Et quum hora separatiónis insonúerit et mors in famíliæ nostræ sinum luctum intúlerit, nos omnes, sive abeúntes sive manéntes, tuis ætérnis decrétis nos subiiciémus. Hoc solátio erit nobis, ánimo recogitáre ventúrum esse diem, in quo tota família nostra, in cælo coniúncta, tuam glóriam, tua benefícia in ætérnum cantáre póterit. Dignétur Cor immaculátum Maríæ, dignétur gloriósus Patriárcha sanctus Ioseph tibi hanc consecratiónem offérre, eiúsque vivam in nobis síngulis diébus vitæ nostræ conserváre memóriam.

Vivat Cor Iesu, Regis et Patris nostri!

NOTE: The same indulgences may be gained under the usual conditions by the members of other institutes (a religious community, a parish, a college or school, etc.), both on the day when the consecration is made for the first time and each year on the day when it is renewed, provided that they make use of a form approved by the Ordinary (S. P. Ap., Dec. 30, 1923).

706

A Consecration to the Holy Family of J. M. J.

O Jesus, our most loving Redeemer, who having come to enlighten the world with Thy teaching and example, didst will to pass the greater part of Thy life in humility and subjection to Mary and Joseph in the poor home of Nazareth, thus sanctifying the Family that was to be an example for all Christian families, graciously receive our family as it dedicates and consecrates itself to Thee this day. Do Thou defend us, guard us and establish amongst us Thy holy fear, true peace and concord in Christian love: in order that by conforming ourselves to the divine pattern of Thy family we may be able, all of us without exception, to attain to eternal happiness.

Mary, dear Mother of Jesus and Mother of us, by thy kindly intercession make this our humble offering acceptable in the sight of Jesus, and obtain for us His graces and blessings.

O Saint Joseph, most holy Guardian of Jesus and Mary, assist us by thy prayers in all our spiritual and temporal necessities; that so we may be enabled to praise our divine Saviour Jesus, together with Mary and thee, for all eternity.

Our Father, Hail Mary *and* Glory be *three times.*

An indulgence of 500 days.

A plenary indulgence on the usual conditions, if this prayer is repeated with devotion every day for a month (S. P. Ap., June 1, 1923 and Oct. 20, 1935).

707
A Prayer

O God of goodness and mercy, to Thy fatherly protection we commend our family, our household and all that belongs to us. We commit all to Thy love and keeping; do Thou fill this house with Thy blessings even as Thou didst fill the holy House of Nazareth with Thy presence.

Keep far from us, above all things else, the taint of sin, and do Thou alone reign in our midst by Thy law, by Thy most holy love and by the exercise of every Christian virtue. Let each one of us obey Thee, love Thee and set himself to imitate in his own life Thine example, that of Mary, Thy Mother and our Mother most loving, and that of Thy blameless guardian, Saint Joseph.

Preserve us and our house from all evils and misfortunes, but grant that we may be ever resigned to Thy divine will even in the sorrows which it shall please Thee to send us. Finally give unto all of us the grace to live in perfect harmony and in the fulness of love toward our neighbor. Grant that every one of us may deserve by a holy life the comfort of Thy holy Sacraments at the hour of death. O Jesus, bless us and protect us.

O Mary, Mother of grace and of mercy, defend us against the wicked spirit, reconcile us with Thy Son, commit us to His keeping, that so we may be made worthy of His promises.

MISCELLANEOUS   565   SPECIAL OCCASIONS

Saint Joseph, foster-father of our Saviour, guardian of His holy Mother, head of the Holy Family, intercede for us, bless us and defend our home at all times.

Saint Michael, defend us against all the wicked cunning of hell.

Saint Gabriel, make us to understand the holy will of God.

Saint Raphael, keep us free from all sickness and from every danger to our lives.

Our holy Guardian Angels, keep our feet safely on the path of salvation both day and night.

Our holy Patrons, pray for us before the throne of God.

Yea, bless this house, O God the Father, who hast created us; O God the Son, who hast suffered for us upon the holy Cross, and Thou, O Holy Spirit, who hast sanctified us in holy Baptism. May the one God in three divine Persons preserve our bodies, purify our minds, direct our hearts and bring us all to everlasting life.

Glory be to the Father, glory be to the Son, glory be to the Holy Ghost! Amen.

An indulgence of 500 days once a day (S. C. Ind., Jan. 19, 1889; S. P. Ap., March 2, 1933).

708
A Prayer

Guard, we beseech Thee, O Lord, through the intercession of Blessed Mary ever Virgin, this family from all adversity; and as we humbly bow before Thee with all our hearts, graciously protect us, in Thy mercy, from all the snares of the enemy. Through Christ our Lord. Amen (Roman Missal).

An indulgence of 3 years.

A plenary indulgence on the usual conditions, when this prayer has been recited daily for a month (S. P. Ap., Nov. 27, 1934).

D efénde, quæsumus Dómine, beáta María semper Vírgine intercedénte, istam ab omni adversitáte famíliam; et toto corde tibi prostrátam, ab hóstium propítius tuére cleménter insídiis. Per Christum Dóminum nostrum. Amen (ex *Missali Romano*).

XXXVII

A PRAYER FOR THE PRINTING OF GOOD BOOKS

709

O glorious Apostle of the Gentiles, Saint Paul, who with such zeal didst busy thyself in destroying at Ephesus those books which thou knewest well would have perverted the minds of the faithful: turn upon us thy gracious eyes also at this present day. Thou seest how an unbelieving and licentious press is attempting to rob our hearts of the precious treasure of faith and spotless morals. Enlighten, we beseech Thee, O holy Apostle, the minds of so many perverted writers, that they may cease once for all to do harm to souls with their evil doctrines and lying insinuations; move their hearts to hate the evil that they have done and are doing to the chosen flock of Jesus Christ. For us, too, obtain the grace of being ever docile to the voice of the Supreme Pontiff, that so we may never allow ourselves to indulge in the reading of bad books, but may seek instead to read and, so far as it is given to us, to diffuse those books which by their salutary doctrine shall assist all of us to promote the greater glory of God, the exaltation of His Church and the salvation of souls.   Amen.

An indulgence of 300 days once a day (S. C. of the Holy Office, Dec. 10, 1908 and Jan. 23, 1909; S. P. Ap., March 4, 1931).

XXXVIII

AN INVOCATION TO BE SAID WHEN PEOPLE ARE ENGAGED IN MAKING AND REPAIRING THE ORNAMENTS OF CHURCHES AND LITURGICAL VESTMENTS

710

Jesus, the way, the truth, and the life, have mercy on us.

The faithful who devote themselves without compensation to the making and repairing of church ornaments and liturgical vestments, either privately or in institutes founded for this purpose, as often as they devoutly recite the above invocation, while engaged in this work, that they may thus sanctify their labor still more, may gain:

An indulgence of 300 days   S. P. Ap., June 2, 1933 and June 14, 1949.

Jesu, via, véritas et vita, miserére nobis.

XXXIX

A PRAYER FOR CHOOSING A STATE OF LIFE

711

O my God, Thou who art the God of wisdom and good counsel, Thou who readest in my heart a sincere desire to please Thee alone and to direct myself in regard to my choice of a state of life, in conformity with Thy holy will in all things; by the intercession of the most holy Virgin, my Mother, and of my Patron Saints, grant me the grace to know that state of life which I ought to choose, and to embrace it when known, in order that thus I may seek Thy glory and increase it, work out my own salvation and deserve the heavenly reward which Thou hast promised to those who do Thy holy will. Amen.

An indulgence of 300 days once a day (Pius X, Rescript in his own hand, May 2, 1905, exhib. May 6, 1905; S. P. Ap., May 18, 1937).

XL
PRAYERS TO OBTAIN THE GIFT OF CONTINENCE

712
An Invocation

Let my heart, O Lord, be made immaculate, that I may not be ashamed.

An indulgence of 300 days (S. P. Ap., Oct. 10, 1934).

Fiat, Dómine, cor meum immaculátum, ut non confúndar.

713
An Invocation

Make my heart and my body clean, holy Mary.

An indulgence of 300 days (S. P. Ap., Dec. 15, 1935).

Munda cor et corpus meum, sancta María.

714
A Prayer

Lord, burn our reins and our hearts with the fire of Thy Holy Spirit, that we may serve Thee with chaste bodies and pure minds. Through Christ our Lord. Amen
(Roman Missal).

An indulgence of 3 years.

A plenary indulgence on the usual conditions, if this prayer is devoutly recited every day for a month (S. P. Ap., Jan. 6, 1935).

U re igne Sancti Spíritus renes nostros et cor nostrum, Dómine; ut tibi casto córpore serviámus et mundo corde placeámus. Per Christum Dóminum nostrum. Amen (ex *Missali Romano*).

715
A Prayer

G rant, we beseech Thee, Almighty and everlasting God, that we may attain to purity of mind and body through the inviolate virginity of the most pure Virgin Mary. Amen.

An indulgence of 500 days (S. P. Ap., March 27, 1936).

NOTE: Other invocations for begging the grace of continence are found under nn. 354, 358, 387.

D a, quæsumus, omnípotens ætérne Deus, ut per integérrimam virginitátem puríssimæ Vírginis Maríæ, puritátem mentis et córporis consequámur. Amen.

XLI
A PRAYER TO OBTAIN THE GRACE OF A DEVOUT LIFE

716

G rant me, O merciful God, to desire eagerly, to investigate prudently, to acknowledge sincerely, and to fulfil perfectly those things that are pleasing to Thee, to the praise and glory of Thy holy Name.

Do Thou, my God, order my life; and grant that I may know what Thou wilt have me to do; and give me to fulfil it as is fitting and profitable to my soul.

Grant me, O Lord my God, the grace not to faint either in prosperity or adversity, that I be not unduly lifted up by the one, nor unduly cast down by the other. Let me neither rejoice nor grieve at anything, save what either leads to Thee or leads away from Thee. Let me not desire to please anyone, nor fear to displease anyone save only Thee.

Let all things that pass away seem vile in my eyes, and let all things that are eternal be dear to me. Let me tire of that joy which is without Thee, neither permit me to desire anything that is outside Thee. Let me find joy in the labor that is for Thee; and let all repose that is without Thee be tiresome to me.

Give me, my God, the grace to direct my heart towards Thee, and to grieve continually at my failures, together with a firm purpose of amendment.

O Lord my God, make me obedient without gainsaying, poor without despondency, chaste without stain, patient without murmuring, humble without pretense, cheerful without dissipation, serious without undue heaviness, active without instability, fearful of Thee without abjectness, truthful without double-dealing, devoted to good works without presumption, ready to correct my neighbor without arrogance, and to edify him by word and example, without hypocrisy.

Give me, Lord God, a watchful heart which shall be distracted from Thee by no vain thoughts; give me a generous heart which shall not be drawn downward by any un-

worthy affection; give me an upright heart
which shall not be led astray by any perverse
intention; give me a stout heart which shall
not be crushed by any hardship; give me a
free heart which shall not be claimed as its
own by any unregulated affection.

Bestow upon me, O Lord my God, an understanding that knows Thee, diligence in
seeking Thee, wisdom in finding Thee, a way
of life that is pleasing to Thee, perseverance
that faithfully waits for Thee, and confidence that I shall embrace Thee at the last.
Grant that I may be chastised here by penance, that I may make good use of Thy gifts
in this life by Thy grace, and that I may
partake of Thy joys in the glory of heaven:
Who livest and reignest God, world without
end.   Amen (St. Thomas Aquinas).

An indulgence of 3 years once a day.

A plenary indulgence on the usual conditions, provided that the
daily recitation of this prayer be continued for a month (S. C. Ind.,
Jan. 17, 1888; S. P. Ap., July 31, 1936).

Concéde mihi, miséricors Deus, quæ tibi sunt
plácita, ardénter concupíscere, prudénter investi-
gáre, veráciter agnóscere, et perfécte adimplére ad
laudem et glóriam Nóminis tui.

Ordina, Deus meus, statum meum; et quod a me
requíris, ut fáciam, tríbue ut sciam; et da éxsequi
sicut opórtet et éxpedit ánimæ meæ.

Da mihi, Dómine Deus meus, inter próspera et
advérsa non defícere, ut in illis non extóllar, et in
istis non déprimar. De nullo gáudeam vel dóleam,
nisi quod ducat ad te, vel abdúcat a te. Nulli placére
áppetam, vel displicére tímeam nisi tibi.

Viléscant mihi, Dómine, ómnia transitória, et cara
mihi sint ómnia ætérna. Tædeat me gáudii quod est
sine te. nec áliud cúpiam quod est extra te. Deléctet

me, Dómine, labor, qui est pro te; et tædiósa sit mihi omnis quies, quæ est sine te.

Da mihi, Deus meus, cor meum ad te dirígere, et in defectióne mea cum emendatiónis propósito constánter dolére.

Fac me, Dómine Deus meus, obediéntem sine contradictióne, páuperem sine deiectióne, castum sine corruptióne, patiéntem sine murmuratióne, húmilem sine fictióne, hílarem sine dissolutióne, matúrum sine gravédine, ágilem sine levitáte, timéntem te sine desperatióne, verácem sine duplicitáte, operántem bona sine præsumptióne, próximum corrípere sine elatióne, ipsum ædificáre verbo et exémplo sine simulatióne.

Da mihi, Dómine Deus, cor pérvigil, quod nulla abdúcat a te curiósa cogitátio: da nóbile, quod nulla deórsum trahat indígna afféctio: da rectum, quod nulla seórsum oblíquet sinístra inténtio: da firmum, quod nulla frangat tribulátio: da líberum, quod nulla sibi víndicet violénta afféctio.

Largíre mihi, Dómine Deus meus, intelléctum te cognoscéntem, diligéntiam te quæréntem, sapiéntiam te inveniéntem, conversatiónem tibi placéntem, perseverántiam fidénter te exspectántem, et fidúciam te panéliter amplecténtem. Da tuis pœnis hic afflígi per pæniténtiam, tuis benefíciis in via uti per grátiam, tuis gáudiis in pátria pérfrui per glóriam: Qui vivis et regnas Deus per ómnia sæcula sæculórum. Amen (S. Thomas Aquinas).

XLII
PRAYERS AGAINST THE PERSECUTORS OF THE CHURCH

717
An Invocation

That Thou wouldst vouchsafe to bring low the enemies of holy Church, we beseech Thee to hear us (Roman Ritual).

An indulgence of 300 days (S. P. Ap., Sept. 1, 1936).

Ut inimícos sanctæ Ecclésiæ humiliáre dignéris, te rogámus, audi nos (ex *Rituali Romano*).

718
A Prayer

Graciously hear the prayers of Thy Church, we beseech Thee, O Lord; that her enemies and all heresies may be brought to naught, and that she may serve Thee in perfect security and freedom. Through Christ our Lord. Amen (Roman Missal).

An indulgence of 3 years.

A plenary indulgence on the usual conditions, when this prayer has been said with devotion every day for a month (S. P. Ap., March 9, 1934).

Ecclésiæ tuæ, quǽsumus Dómine, preces placátus admítte: ut, destrúctis adversitátibus et erróribus univérsis, secúra tibi sérviat libertáte. Per Christum Dóminum nostrum. Amen (ex *Missali Romano*).

NOTE: A prayer to the B. V. Mary in behalf of the Church is found under n. 412.

XLIII
A PRAYER IN TIME OF EARTHQUAKE

719

O God, who hast established the earth upon firm foundations, graciously receive the prayers of Thy people: and, having utterly removed the dangers of the shaken earth, turn the terrors of Thy divine wrath into the means of the salvation of mankind; that they who are of the earth, and unto earth shall return, may rejoice to find themselves citizens of heaven by means of a holy life. Through Christ our Lord. Amen (Roman Missal).

An indulgence of 500 days (S. P. Ap., Dec. 20, 1932).

D eus, qui fundásti terram super stabilitátem suam, súscipe preces pópuli tui: ac treméntis terræ perículis pénitus amótis, divínæ tuæ iracúndiæ terróres in humánæ salútis remédia convérte; ut qui de terra sunt, et in terram reverténtur, gáudeant se fíeri sancta conversatióne cæléstes. Per Christum Dóminum nostrum. Amen. (ex *Missali Romano*).

XLIV
IN THE TIME OF TRIAL
720
An Invocation

R egard, O Lord, our humility and forsake us not in the time of tribulation.

An indulgence of 300 days(S. P. Ap., Jan. 20, 1941).

R éspice, Dómine, ad humilitátem nostram et non déseras nos in témpore tribulatiónis.

721
An Invocation

I deserve to suffer these things, O Lord, for I have sinned!

The faithful who devoutly make this act of humility in their trials and tribulations, whether spiritual or temporal, are granted:

An indulgence of 300 days(S. P. Ap., Mar. 28, 1941).

M érito hæc pátior, Dómine, quia peccávi!

722
A Prayer

D espise not, Almighty God, Thy people who cry out to Thee in their affliction, but for the glory of Thy Name, being appeased assist those who are in tribulation. Through Christ our Lord. Amen.

An indulgence of 3 years(S. P. Ap., Jan. 20, 1941).

Ne despícias, omnípotens Deus, pópulum tuum in afflictióne clamántem, sed propter glóriam nóminis tui, tribulátis succúrre placátus. Per Christum Dóminum nostrum. Amen.

723
A Prayer

O God, our refuge and our strength, mercifully regard Thy people who cry to Thee, and turn away the scourges of Thy anger, which we justly deserve for our sins. Through Christ our Lord. Amen.

An indulgence of 3 years (S. P. Ap., April 7, 1941)·

Deus, refúgium nostrum et virtus, pópulum ad te clamántem propítius réspice atque flagélla tuæ iracúndiæ, quæ pro peccátis nostris merémur, avérte. Per Christum Dóminum nostrum. Amen.

XLV
AT THE TIME OF ANY CALAMITY

724
An Invocation

From all dangers, deliver us, O Lord.

An indulgence of 300 days (S. P. Ap., June 18, 1949)·

A perículis cunctis, líbera nos, Dómine.

725
A Prayer

O God, Who knowest us to be set in the midst of so great dangers, that, by reason of the frailty of our nature, we cannot stand upright, grant us such health of mind and body, that those evils which we suffer for our sins we may overcome through Thine assistance. Through Christ our Lord. Amen

(Roman Missal)·

An indulgence of 500 days (S. P. Ap., March 10, 1939)·

Deus, qui nos in tantis perículis constitútos, pro humána scis fragilitáte non posse subsístere, da nobis salútem mentis et córporis, ut ea, quæ pro peccátis nostris pátimur, te adiuvánte vincámus. Per Christum Dóminum nostrum. Amen (ex *Missali Romano*).

726
Prayers

Help us, O God, our Saviour; and for the glory of Thy Name deliver us: and forgive us our sins for Thy Name's sake.

℣. For the glory of Thy holy Name deliver us,

℟. And forgive us our sins for Thy Name's sake.

Let us pray.

Mercifully hear the prayers of Thy people, we beseech Thee, O Lord, that we who are justly afflicted for our sins, may be mercifully delivered from the same for the glory of Thy holy Name. Through Christ our Lord. Amen.

An indulgence of 3 years (S. C. Ind., Nov. 8, 1849; S. P. Ap. June 14, 1935 and May 12, 1949).

Adiuva nos, Deus salutáris noster, et propter glóriam Nóminis tui líbera nos, et propítius esto peccátis nostris propter Nomen tuum.

℣. Propter glóriam Nóminis tui líbera nos,

℟. Et propítius esto peccátis nostris propter Nomen tuum.

Orémus.

Preces pópuli tui quæsumus, Dómine, cleménter exáudi, et qui iuste pro peccátis nostris afflígimur, pro glória Nóminis tui misericórditer liberémur. Per Christum Dóminum nostrum. Amen.

PART II

IN FAVOR OF CERTAIN GROUPS
OF PERSONS

BEATI qui HABIT ant in DOMO tua DOMINE +

I
AN INVOCATION
TO BE SAID BY CANDIDATES FOR THE PRIESTHOOD

727

O good Jesus, grant that I may become a priest after Thine own Heart.

An indulgence of 300 days (Apostolic Brief, Feb. 11, 1924; S. P. Ap., June 18, 1949)·

O bone Iesu, fac ut sacérdos fiam secúndum Cor tuum.

II
PRAYERS TO BE SAID BY ALL CLERICS
AND BY OTHERS WHO ASPIRE TO THE SACRED MINISTRY

728
An Invocation

Put upon me, O Lord, the new man who is created according to God in justice and the holiness of truth.   Amen.

All those who are being trained in Seminaries, Colleges, and Monasteries for the priesthood, as well as clerics of every rank and order, as often as they make the sign of the cross and recite the above invocation while vesting themselves with a surplice, may gain:

An indulgence of 300 days (S. C. Ind., Dec. 1, 1907)·

Indue me, Dómine, novum hóminem, qui secúndum Deum creátus est in iustítia et sanctitáte veritátis. Amen.

729
An Invocation

H eart of Jesus, Victim of love, make me a living victim for Thee, holy and pleasing unto God.

An indulgence of 300 days (S. P. Ap., May 13, 1937).

C or Iesu, caritátis víctima, fac me tibi hóstiam vivéntem, sanctam, Deo placéntem.

730
An Invocation

S aint Aloysius, exemplar of clerics and their protector, pray for me.

An indulgence of 300 days (S. P. Ap., April 15, 1941).

S ancte Aloísi clericórum exémplar et præsídium, ora pro me.

731
Recitation of the Divine Office
in the presence of the Blessed Sacrament

A ll ecclesiastics, including those who have received the first tonsure, as well as the novices and students of Religious Communities, whether they are bound by rule to the recitation of the Divine Office or not, if they devoutly recite the entire Office, even though interrupted, in the presence of the Blessed Sacrament, when it is exposed for public adoration or reserved in the Tabernacle, may gain the same indulgences as ecclesiastics in Holy Orders, as stated below in n. 736 a) and b) (S. P. Ap., March 31, 1937).

732

Clerics to be ordained are granted on the day when they receive a major Order:

A plenary indulgence on the usual conditions (S. P. Ap., Dec. 18, 1939).

III

PRAYERS TO BE SAID
BY CLERICS IN HOLY ORDERS AND BY PRIESTS

A) FOR A HOLY LIFE

733

A Prayer

Dearest Jesus, who of Thy great goodness hast called me to be Thy follower in preference to countless others and hast raised me to the high dignity of Thy priesthood, bestow upon me abundantly, I pray, Thy divine help in fulfilling my duties in a right spirit. I beseech Thee, Lord Jesus, to stir up in me Thy grace both today and always, that grace which is in me by reason of the laying on of hands of the bishop. O mighty Physician of souls, heal me in such wise that I may never be entangled in sinful habits, but that I may renounce them all and be enabled to please Thee even to the day of my death. Amen.

An indulgence of 500 days once a day (S. C. Ind., Aug. 14, 1884; S. P. Ap., June 19, 1933).

Iesu dilectíssime, qui ex singulári benevoléntia me præ millénis homínibus ad tui sequélam et ad exímiam Sacerdótii dignitátem vocásti, largíre mihi, precor, opem tuam divínam ad offícia mea rite obeúnda. Oro te, Dómine Iesu, ut resúscites hódie et semper in me grátiam tuam, quæ fuit in me per impositiónem mánuum episcopálium. O potentíssime animárum médice, sana me táliter, ne revólvar in vítia; et cuncta peccáta fúgiam tibíque usque ad mortem placére possim. Amen.

734

A Prayer to obtain the grace of preserving chastity

Lord Jesus Christ, bridegroom of my soul, the beloved of my heart, nay, my very heart and soul, I throw myself upon my knees in Thy sight, and most earnestly implore Thee to give me grace to keep the faith I solemnly gave unto Thee in the reception of Subdeaconship. Wherefore, O sweetest Jesus, let me deny all ungodliness; let me ever be a stranger to carnal desires and earthly lusts which war against the soul, and, with Thy help, let me preserve my chastity unspotted.

O Mary most holy and immaculate, the Virgin of virgins, and our loving Mother, make clean my heart and my soul ever more and more; obtain for me the fear of the Lord and a great distrust of myself.

Saint Joseph, guardian of Mary's virginity, keep my soul free from every sin.

All ye holy Virgins who follow the Lamb whithersoever He goeth, be ever watchful over me, a sinner, lest at any time I go astray from the most pure Heart of Jesus and transgress by thought, word or deed.   Amen.

An indulgence of 500 days (S. C. Ind., March 16, 1889; S. P. Ap., May 4. 1932).

Dómine Iesu Christe, sponse ánimæ meæ, delíciæ cordis mei, imo cor meum et ánima mea, ante conspéctum tuum génibus me provólvo, ac máximo ánimi ardóre te oro atque obtéstor, ut mihi des serváre fidem a me tibi solémniter datam in receptióne Subdiaconátus. Ideo, o dulcíssime Iesu, ábnegem omnem impietátem, sim semper aliénus a

carnálibus desidériis et terrénis concupiscéntiis, quæ
mílitant advérsus ánimam, et castitátem te adiuvánte
intemeráte servem.

O sanctíssima et immaculáta María, Virgo vírginum et Mater nostra amantíssima, munda in dies cor
meum et ánimam meam, ímpetra mihi timórem
Dómini et singulárem mei diffidéntiam.

Sancte Ioseph, custos virginitátis Maríæ, custódi
ánimam meam ab omni peccáto.

Omnes sanctæ Vírgines divínum Agnum quocúmque sequéntes, estóte mei peccatóris semper
sollícitæ, ne cogitatióne, verbo aut ópere delínquam
et a castíssimo Corde Iesu unquam discédam. Amen.

B) FOR THE DUE FULFILMENT OF THEIR SACRED DUTIES

735
A Prayer before reciting the Divine Office

O Lord, open Thou my mouth to bless
Thy holy Name; cleanse my heart also
from all vain, evil and wandering thoughts;
enlighten my understanding, kindle my affections, that I may be able to recite this
Office worthily, attentively and devoutly,
and may deserve to be heard in the presence
of Thy divine Majesty. Through Christ our
Lord. Amen.

Lord, in union with that divine intention,
wherewith Thou Thyself didst praise God
whilst Thou wast on earth, I offer these Hours
(*or* this Hour) unto Thee (Roman Breviary).

An indulgence of 3 years (S. P. Ap., Nov. 17, 1933).

The same indulgence may be gained by the faithful, who recite
this prayer devoutly before saying the divine Office, when it is
recited for any reason (S. P. Ap., Dec. 3, 1949).

Aperi, Dómine, os meum ad benedicéndum Nomen
sanctum tuum; munda quoque cor meum ab
ómnibus vanis, pervérsis et aliénis cogitatiónibus;

intelléctum illúmina, afféctum inflámma, ut digne, atténte ac devóte hoc Offícium recitáre váleam, et exaudíri mérear ante conspéctum divínæ Maiestátis tuæ.   Per Christum Dóminum nostrum.   Amen.

Dómine, in unióne illíus divínæ intentiónis, qua ipse in terris laudes Deo persolvísti, has tibi Horas (*vel* hanc tibi Horam) persólvo (ex *Breviario Romano*).

736
The Recitation of the Divine Office
in the presence of the Blessed Sacrament

a) Clerics in Holy Orders, who devoutly recite the entire Divine Office, even when separated into parts, before the Blessed Sacrament whether exposed for public adoration or reserved in the Tabernacle, are granted:

A plenary indulgence, if they make their confession, receive Holy Communion and pray for the intentions of the Holy Father (S. P. Ap., Oct. 23, 1930).

b) Those, however, who recite only a part of the Divine Office before the Blessed Sacrament, as above, are granted:

An indulgence of 500 days for each canonical Hour (S. P. Ap., May 18, 1933).

c) Moreover, those clerics who have duly obtained the commutation of the Divine Office into other prayers, if they recite these prayers devoutly before the Blessed Sacrament, as above, may gain:

A plenary indulgence, on condition of confession, Holy Communion and prayer for the intentions of the Holy Father (S. P. Ap., Nov. 7, 1932).

737
A Prayer
to be said after reciting the Divine Office

To the most Holy and undivided Trinity, to the Manhood of our Lord Jesus Christ crucified, to the fruitful Virginity of the most blessed and most glorious Mary ever Virgin,

and to the congregation of all the Saints be
ascribed everlasting praise, and to us be
granted the foregiveness of all our sins, world
without end. Amen.

℣. Blessed be the womb of the Virgin Mary,
which bore the Son of the Eternal Father.

℟. And blessed be the breasts which gave
suck to Christ our Lord (Roman Breviary).

Our Father *and* Hail Mary.

An indulgence of 3 years (S. P. Ap., Dec. 1, 1933).

The same indulgence is granted to the faithful, who devoutly
recite this prayer after saying the divine Office, for whatever reason
it has been recited (S. P. Ap., Dec. 3, 1949).

Sacrosánctæ et indivíduæ Trinitáti, Crucifíxi Dómini nostri Iesu Christi humanitáti, beatíssimæ
et gloriosíssimæ sempérque Vírginis Maríæ fecúndæ
integritáti, et ómnium Sanctórum universitáti sit
sempitérna laus, honor, virtus et glória ab omni
creatúra, nobísque remíssio ómnium peccatórum, per
infiníta sǽcula sæculórum. Amen.

℣. Beáta víscera Maríæ Vírginis quæ portavérunt
ætérni Patris Fílium,

℟. Et beáta úbera quæ lactavérunt Christum
Dóminum (ex *Breviario Romano*).

Pater *et* Ave.

NOTE: Clerics in Holy Orders and priests who, having completed
the Divine Office, shall recite the above prayer on bended knees,
unless they are hindered therefrom, have been granted by Pope
Leo X the condonation of the shortcomings and faults committed
by them from human frailty in saying the Office (S. C. Ind., July
26, 1855).

738
*A Prayer for the grace of preaching holily
and fruitfully*

Give me, O Lord, a mild and judicious
eloquence which shall keep me from
being puffed up and exalted above my brethren by reason of Thy gifts. Put into my

mouth, I beseech Thee, words of consolation and edification and exhortation through Thy Holy Spirit, that I may be enabled to exhort the good to better things, and, by word and example, to recall to the straight way of Thy righteousness those who walk perversely. Let the words which Thou shalt give Thy servant, be like to sharp javelins and burning arrows that shall pierce and enkindle unto Thy fear and holy love the minds of all them that hear me. Amen (St. Anselm, Bishop, Confessor and Doctor).

An indulgence of 500 days, if this prayer is said before preaching the Word of God (S. C. Ind., July 12, 1907; S. P. Ap., July 13, 1934).

Da mihi, Dómine, et mitíssimam et sapiéntem eloquéntiam, qua nésciam inflári et de tuis bonis super fratres extólli. Pone, quæso, in ore meo verbum consolatiónis et ædificatiónis et exhortatiónis per Spíritum Sanctum tuum, ut et bonos váleam ad melióra exhortári, et eos, qui advérse gradiúntur, ad tuæ rectitúdinis líneam revocáre verbo et exémplo. Sint verba, quæ déderis servo tuo, tamquam acutíssima iácula et ardéntes sagíttæ, quæ pénetrent et incéndant mentes audiéntium ad timórem et amórem tuum. Amen (S. Anselmus, Ep. Conf. Doct.).

IV
PRAYERS TO BE SAID BY PRIESTS
A) TO OBTAIN HOLINESS OF LIFE

739
An Invocation

O good Jesu, grant that I may be a priest after Thine own Heart.

An indulgence of 300 days (Apostolic Brief, Feb. 11, 1924).

O bone Iesu, fac ut sim sacérdos secúndum Cor tuum.

740

A Prayer

Almighty and merciful God, graciously attend to my humble prayers; and make me, Thy servant, whom Thou hast appointed to dispense Thy heavenly mysteries, through no merits of mine own, but only of the infinite bounty of Thy mercy, a worthy minister at Thy sacred altar, that what is set forth by my voice may be confirmed by Thy hallowing grace. Through Christ our Lord. Amen Roman Missal).

An indulgence of 3 years.
A plenary indulgence on the usual conditions, when this prayer has been repeated daily for a month (S. P. Ap., Nov. 15, 1936).

Omnípotens et miséricors Deus, humilitátis meæ preces benígnus inténde, et me fámulum tuum, quem nullis suffragántibus méritis, sed imménsa cleméntiæ tuæ largitáte cæléstibus mystériis servíre tribuísti, dignum sacris altáribus fac minístrum, ut quod mea voce deprómitur, tua sanctificatióne firmétur. Per Christum Dóminum nostrum. Amen (ex *Missali Romano*).

741

A Prayer

O Almighty God, let Thy grace assist us, that we who have undertaken the office of Priesthood, may be able to wait upon Thee worthily and devoutly, in all purity, and with a good conscience. And if we cannot live in so great innocency of life as we ought to do, grant to us at the least worthily to lament the sins that we have committed; and in the spirit of humility, and with the full purpose of a good will, to serve Thee more earnestly for the time to come. Through Christ our lord. Amen(The Imitation of Christ, book IV, chap. xi, n. 7).

An indulgence of 500 days(S. P. Ap., Nov. 15, 1936).

Adiuvet nos grátia tua, omnípotens Deus, ut qui offícium sacerdótale suscépimus, digne ac devóte tibi in omni puritáte et consciéntia bona famulári valeámus. Et si non póssumus in tanta innocéntia vitæ conversári, ut debémus, concéde nobis tamen digne flere mala, quæ géssimus, et in spíritu humili- tátis ac bonæ voluntátis propósito tibi fervéntius de cétero deservíre. Per Christum Dóminum nostrum. Amen. (De Imit. Chr., lib. IV, c. XI, n. 7).

742
The Celebration of a First Mass

Priests offering Holy Mass for the first time are granted:

A plenary indulgence, if, in addition, they atone for their sins in sacramental confession and pray according to the mind of the Sovereign Pontiff(S. C. Ind., Jan. 16, 1886).

NOTE: Indulgences for the faithful who assist at the first Mass of a priest, and who kiss the palms of his hands reverently, are to be found under n. 676.

743
Prayers to be said by Priests before and after making
their own sacramental confession

a) *Before confession*

Accept my confession, O most tender and merciful Lord Jesus Christ, my soul's only hope of salvation; and give me, Thy priest, I pray, true contrition and tears to mine eyes, that I may weep night and day for all my shortcomings in humility and clean- ness of heart. My Lord and God, accept my prayers. Saviour of the world, good Jesu, who gavest Thyself to the death of the Cross to save sinners, look upon me, a miserable sinner, calling upon Thy holy Name, and regard not my wickedness in such wise as to forget Thy goodness; and if I have done that which deserves Thy condemnation, Thou hast not lost that whereby Thou art wont to save. Spare me, therefore, Thou who art my Saviour, and have pity on my sinful soul. Loose its bonds, heal its wounds. O most gracious Lord, by the merits of Thy pure and inviolate Mother Mary ever Virgin, whom Thou hast bequeathed especially unto Thy priests to be their Mother, and by the merits of all Thy Saints, send out Thy light and Thy truth into my soul, and show me all my shortcomings in truth which I am bound to confess, and assist and teach me to unfold them fully and with a contrite heart: Who livest and reignest God, for ever and ever. Amen.

b) *After confession*

Let this my confession, I beseech Thee, O Lord, be pleasing and acceptable in Thy sight, by the merits of Thy blessed and ever Virgin Mother Mary and of all Thy Saints; and whatsoever is wanting, now or at any other time, in sufficient contrition, or in sincerity and integrity of confession, do Thou, of Thy loving kindness and mercy, supply and deign thereby to hold me more fully and perfectly absolved in heaven: Who livest and reignest God world without end. Amen.

An indulgence of 500 days (S. C. Ind., Aug. 19, 1882; S. P. Ap.,
Sept. 18, 1936).

a) *Ante confessionem*

Súscipe confessiónem meam, piíssime ac clementíssime Dómine Iesu Christe, única spes salútis
ánimæ meæ; et da mihi, sacerdóti tuo, óbsecro, contritiónem cordis et lácrimas óculis meis, ut défleam
diébus ac nóctibus omnes negligéntias meas cum
humilitáte et puritáte cordis. Dómine Deus meus,
súscipe preces meas. Salvátor mundi, Iesu bone, qui
te crucis morti dedísti, ut peccatóres salvos fáceres,
réspice me míserum peccatórem invocántem Nomen
tuum, et noli sic atténdere malum meum, ut oblivi-
scáris bonum tuum; et si commísi unde me damnáre
potes, tu non amisísti unde salváre soles. Parce ergo
mihi, qui es salvátor meus et miserére peccatríci
ánimæ meæ. Solve víncula eius, sana vúlnera.
Emítte ígitur, piíssime Dómine, méritis puríssimæ
et immaculátæ semper Vírginis Genitrícis tuæ
Maríæ, quam tuis præsértim sacerdótibus in Matrem
reliquísti, et Sanctórum tuórum, lucem tuam, veri-
tátem tuam in ánimam meam, quæ omnes deféctus
meos in veritáte mihi osténdat, de quibus confitéri me
opórtet, atque iuvet et dóceat ipsos plene et contríto
corde explicáre: Qui vivis et regnas Deus per ómnia
sǽcula sæculórum. Amen.

b) *Post confessionem*

Sit tibi, Dómine, óbsecro, méritis beátæ semper
Vírginis Genitrícis tuæ Maríæ et ómnium Sanctórum grata et accépta ista conféssio mea; et
quidquid mihi défuit nunc et álias de sufficiéntia
contritiónis, de puritáte et integritáte confessiónis,
súppleat píetas et misericórdia tua et secúndum
illam dignéris me habére plénius et perféctius abso-
lútum in cælo: Qui vivis et regnas Deus per ómnia
sǽcula sæculórum. Amen.

744

A Form of Consecrating Priests to the
Most Sacred Heart of Jesus

Lord Jesus, who art our most loving Redeemer and a Priest for ever, look mercifully on us, Thy humble suppliants, whom Thou hast been pleased to call Thy friends and partakers of Thy priesthood. We are Thine; we wish to be Thine forever: therefore to Thy Most Sacred Heart which Thou hast shown to oppressed humanity as their only safe refuge, we dedicate and devote ourselves wholly this day. Thou who hast promised plenteous fruit in the divine ministry to those priests who are devoted to Thy Sacred Heart, make us, we beseech Thee, fit workmen in Thy vineyard, truly meek and humble, filled with the spirit of devotion and patience, so fired with love of Thee that we shall never cease to enkindle and quicken the same fire of love in the hearts of the faithful. Renew our hearts, therefore, in the fire of Thy Heart, so that henceforth we shall desire nothing save to promote Thy glory and win for Thee the souls whom Thou didst redeem by Thy Precious Blood. Show Thy mercy, good Shepherd, chiefly to those priests, our brethren, if there be any such, who, walking in the vanity of sense, have saddened Thee and Thy beloved Spouse, Holy Church, by their lamentable falling away from Thee. Grant us grace to bring them back to Thine embrace, or, at least, to atone for their crimes, to repair the harm they

have done, and to lessen the sorrow they
have caused Thee, by the consolation of our
love.   Allow each one of us, finally, to pray
to Thee in the words of Saint Augustine: "O
sweet Jesus, live Thou in me, and let the living coal of Thy love burn brightly in my
spirit, and grow into a perfect conflagration;
let it burn perpetually on the altar of my
heart, let it glow in my marrow, let it blaze
up in the most secret places of my soul; in
the day of my consummation let me be
found totally consumed thereby in Thy
presence, who with the Father and the Holy
Ghost livest and reignest one God for ever
and ever.   Amen.

An indulgence of 3 years.

An indulgence of 7 years on the day of the monthly retreat.

A plenary indulgence on the usual conditions at the end of a
course of "Spiritual Exercises" (Pius X, Rescript in his own hand,
Aug. 17, 1908, exhib. Nov. 14, 1908; S. P. Ap., Oct. 24, 1935).

Dómine Iesu, Redémptor noster amantíssime et
Sacérdos in ætérnum, nos súpplices tuos, quos
appelláre amícos et sacerdótii tui partícipes fácere
dignátus es, propítius réspice. Tui sumus; tui perpétuo esse vólumus: ideo sacratíssimo Cordi tuo,
quod tamquam únicum salútis perfúgium laboránti
humáno géneri ostendísti, dedicámus nos hódie totos
et addícimus. Tu, qui sacerdótibus, Cordis tui cultó-
ribus, úberes divíni ministérii fructus promisísti, fac
nos, quǽsumus, idóneos in vínea tua operários, vere
húmiles et mites, spíritu devotiónis et patiéntiæ
plenos, ita flagrántes amóre tui, ut eúmdem caritátis
ignem in ánimis fidél um excitáre et fovére non
cessémus. Nostra ígitur corda incéndio tui Cordis
ínnova, ut iam nihil áliud studeámus, quam tuam
promovére glóriam et ánimas tibi lucrári, quas
pretióso Sánguine redemísti. Miserére, Pastor bone,

præsértim sacerdótum, fratrum nostrórum, si qui, ambulántes in vanitáte sensus sui, te et diléctam Sponsam tuam, Ecclésiam, lacrimábili defectióne contristárunt. Concéde nobis ad tuum compléxum eos redúcere, aut certe ipsórum expiáre delícta, resarcíre damna, et dolórem, quo te affíciunt, amóris nostri consolatióne minúere. Sine, dénique, te quisque nostrum exóret his Augustíni verbis: O dulcis Iesu, vivas Tu in me, et concaléscat spíritu meo vivus carbo amóris tui, et excréscat in ignem perféctum; árdeat iúgiter in ara cordis mei, férveat in medúllis meis, flagret in abscónditis ánimæ meæ; in die consummatiónis meæ consummátus invéniar apud te, qui cum Patre et Spíritu Sancto vivis et regnas Deus in sǽcula sæculórum. Amen.

745
A Prayer to Saint John, Apostle and Evangelist

Let us rejoice with thee, blessed John, who, by a privilege of special love, wast honored by Christ Jesus above all the other disciples: being held worthy to recline upon His bosom at the Last Supper, and to be entrusted with His holy Mother at the hour of His death. We know that thou didst deserve this on account of thy special gift of chastity; because, being chosen as a virgin by our Lord, thou didst remain a virgin for ever. Accordingly, since thou didst imbibe the living streams of the Gospel from its very source, the bosom of our Lord, thou didst speak more fully and more sublimely of the divinity of Christ; and since thou didst catch thy flame of love from the fire burning in His Sacred Heart, we do not wonder that thou wast the only disciple to accompany Jesus in His Passion, and thereafter didst write such burning words that thou art rightly called "the Apostle of love." Moreover, it behooves us, who are the ministers of Christ and stewards of the mysteries of God, by the gift of His goodness, to lift our eyes to thee, who hast been set before us as an example for our imitation: it is likewise meet, and we ask it of thee in great humility, that thou wouldst assist us as our own special Patron before Jesus and Mary. Grant us, therefore, to walk worthy of the vocation wherewith we are called; in particular that we may perform our priestly tasks with due purity of mind and body; fired with zeal for the glory of God, may we attain to intimate fellowship with the Heart of Jesus, and console the most holy Virgin, who was given from the Cross to be a Mother to all of us after thee, by the kindly offices of our ardent affection, even as thou didst do. Finally grant, that after this mortal life we may be numbered with the elders, whom thou didst see clothed in white raiment and sitting round the throne of the spotless Lamb, Who is worthy to receive honor, blessing and glory for endless ages. Amen.

An indulgence of 300 days.

A plenary indulgence on the usual conditions on the Feast of St. John, Ap. and Ev. (Pius X, Rescript in his own hand, July 9, 1908; exhib. Oct. 22, 1908).

Congaudémus tibi, beáte Ioánnes, qui, privilégio amóris præcípui, céteris discípulis áltius honorátus es a Christo Iesu: dignus hábitus, qui supra pectus eius in cœna recúmberes, et cui Matrem ipse suam moritúrus commendáret. Scimus, id te meruís-

se propter speciálem prærogatívam castitátis; quia
virgo eléctus a Dómino, virgo in ævum permansísti.
Ita, quum fluénta Evangélii de ipso domínici péctoris
fonte potásses, ubérius et sublímius áliis de Christi
divinitáte locútus es; quumque de ipso divíni Cordis
incéndio amóris flammam concepísses, non mirámur
te unum discípulum Iesu patiénti adhæsísse indiví-
duum cómitem, ac deínceps tália scripsísse, ut
mérito appellátus sis caritátis Apóstolus. Decet
enímvero nos, qui, divínæ bonitátis múnere, minístri
Christi sumus et dispensatóres mysteriórum Dei,
intuéri te, tamquam propósitum nobis ad imitándum
exémplar: decet autem te, quod súpplices quæsumus,
nobis apud Iesum et Maríam adésse patrónum pró-
prium et peculiárem. Fac ígitur, ut digne ambulé-
mus vocatióne, qua vocáti sumus; præsértim, ut ea,
qua par est, mentis et córporis puritáte, sacerdotália
obeámus múnia; incénsi stúdio divínæ glóriæ, ín-
timam familiaritátem sacratíssimi Cordis Iesu consequámur, et Vírginem sanctíssimam, datam de
Cruce nobis ómnibus post te Matrem, perstudiósæ
pietátis offíciis, quemádmodum Tu fecísti, recreé-
mus. Dénique præsta, ut post mortálem vitam inter
senióres numerémur, quos vidísti amíctos vesti-
méntis albis sedére circa thronum Agni immaculáti,
qui dignus est accípere honórem, benedictiónem et
glóriam in sǽcula sæculórum. Amen.

746

A Prayer
to be said by priests
on the Anniversary of their Ordination

Most lovable Jesus, today, the anniversary
of the day on which, in spite of my
misery, Thou didst deign to raise me to the
dignity of the Priesthood by an impulse of
Thy goodness, and to make me Thy minister
and messenger as well as the dispenser of
Thy sublime mysteries of wisdom and grace,

my heart is filled with joy and grateful memories towards Thee because of this singular favor conferred upon me, but it is afflicted with sadness and grief, inasmuch as I have not corresponded with this great gift in the manner or to the extent I should have done. To my mind, as it reviews the past, there comes a brilliant light, even though it is somewhat obscured by the darkness: Thou, indeed, O Jesus, both in Thy light and in my darkness, dost shine by reason of Thy mercy, and from my heart bursts forth an exultant hymn of glory.

O Lord, while I acknowledge and deplore in all humility my unworthiness I earnestly beseech the continual help of Thy infinite goodness, assisted by which I may be able to conform my life to the high office committed to me, enlightened thereby may I be enabled to impart daily to my fellow-men richer fruits of Thy Redemption, finally strengthened thereby may I be strong enough to continue on this mortal journey in a worthy manner, until my last day shall dawn, when, having finished my earthly pilgrimage, I may lay my weary head upon Thy bosom, and enjoy for ever Thy light and peace.

Most holy Virgin, thou who didst receive on Calvary at the foot of the Cross in the person of the beloved disciple all priests under thy maternal protection, pray for me.

An indulgence of 500 days.

A plenary indulgence on the usual conditions (S. P. Ap., Jan. 8, 1939) .

Amabilíssime Iesu, hódie, anniversário die, ex quo, miséria mea non obstánte, ex impúlsu bonitátis tuæ me ad sacerdotálem dignitátem evéhere dignátus es, meque minístrum tuum réddere ac núntium dispensatorémque sublímium sapiéntiæ et grátiæ mysteriórum tuórum, meus ánimus tum iucunditáte, amóre gratáque memória erga te afficitur ob accéptum singuláre benefícium, tum étiam mæstítia ac dolóre afflígitur, quandóquidem non débita ratióne, non débito modo huic múneri respóndi. Menti meæ, prætérita respiciénti témpora, lux refúlgens, sed obumbráta ténebris, occúrrit; Tu vero, o Iesu, tam in luce tua, quam in ténebris meis ob misericórdiam tuam enítes, meóque ex péctore glóriæ hymnus exsúltans deprómitur.

O Dómine, dum indignitátem meam humíliter agnósco ac deplóro, perénne infinítæ bonitátis tuæ auxílium eníxe déprecor, qua adiútus vitam meam ad sublíme munus mihi commíssum conformáre queam, qua illuminátus uberióres cotídie fructus Redemptiónis tuæ homínibus impertíre possim, qua dénique roborátus hoc mortále iter digne pérsequi váleam, usque dum postrémus dies elucéscat, quo, terréna peregrinatióne perácta, fatigátum caput in sinum tuum reclínem, tuáque luce ac pace iúgiter pérfruar.

Sanctíssima Virgo, quæ in Calvária iuxta Crucem per diléctum discípulum Ioánnem sacerdótes omnes in matérnam tutélam tuam excepísti, deprecáre pro me.

TO FULFIL WORTHILY THE SACRED OFFICES COMMITTED TO THEM

747

The Prayers set forth in the Roman Missal for the devotion of Priests, to be said, according to their opportunity before celebrating Mass:

a)

Antiphon: Ne reminiscáris, Dómine, *etc.*
Ps. 83: Quam dilécta tabernácula tua, *etc.*
Ps. 84: Benedixísti, Dómine, terram tuam, *etc.*
Ps. 85: Inclína, Dómine, aurem tuam, *etc.*
Ps. 115: Crédidi, *etc.*
Ps. 129: De profúndis clamávi ad te, Dómine, *etc.*
Ant.: Ne reminiscáris, Dómine, *etc.*
Kýrie eléison, *etc.* Pater noster, *etc.*
Versicles: Ego dixi, Dómine, *etc.*
Prayers: Aures tuæ pietátis, *etc.*

An indulgence of 5 years.

A plenary indulgence, if the aforesaid prayers are recited daily for a month, in addition to confession and prayer for the intentions of the Holy Father.

b)

Prayers of Saint Ambrose for every day of the week: Summe Sacerdos, *etc.*

Prayer of Saint Ambrose: Ad mensam dulcíssimi convívii, *etc.*

Prayer to the B. V. M.: O Mater pietátis, *etc.*

Prayers to Saint Joseph: O felícem virum, *etc.*

Prayer to all Angels and Saints: Angeli, Archángeli, *etc.*

Prayer to the Saint, in whose honor Mass is being celebrated: O Sancte N. , ecce ego, *etc.*

An indulgence of 3 years for each of the above prayers (S. C. Ind., Dec. 20, 1884, Feb. 17, 1883 and Feb. 4, 1877; S. P. Ap., Oct. 3, 1936) .

NOTE: For the prayer of St. Thomas Aquinas, *Omnípotens semipiterne Deus*, see n. 158.

748

a) Priests, who recite devoutly the prayers contained in the Roman Missal to be said while they are putting on the priestly vestments, are granted:

An indulgence of 100 days for each prayer.

b) The same indulgence is granted to Bishops, who devoutly recite the prayers to be said by them when they assume the pontifical vestments (S. P. Ap., Jan. 14, 1940) .

749

A Form of directing one's intention before Mass

I wish to celebrate Mass and consecrate the Body and Blood of our Lord Jesus Christ after the use of the Holy Roman Church to the praise of Almighty God and of all the Court of heaven, to my own benefit and that of all the Church militant: for all who have commended themselves to my prayers, in general and in particular, and for the happy estate of the holy Roman Church. Amen.

Joy and peace, amendment of life, room for sincere repentance, the grace and comfort of the Holy Spirit, perseverance in good works be given to us by the almighty and merciful Lord. Amen.

An indulgence of 500 days (Gregory XIII; S. P. Ap., July 12, 1935).

Ego volo celebráre Missam et confícere Corpus et Sánguinem Dómini nostri Iesu Christi iuxta ritum sanctæ Románæ Ecclésiæ ad laudem omnipoténtis Dei totiúsque Cúriæ triumphántis, ad utilitátem meam totiúsque Cúriæ militántis: pro ómnibus, qui se commendavérunt oratiónibus meis in génere et in spécie, ac pro felíci statu sanctæ Románæ Ecclésiæ. Amen.

Gáudium cum pace, emendatiónem vitæ, spátium veræ pæniténtiæ, grátiam et consolatiónem Sancti Spíritus, perseverántiam in bonis opéribus tríbuat nobis omnípotens et miséricors Dóminus. Amen.

750

The Prayers set forth in the Roman Missal for the devotion of Priests to be said, according to their opportunity, after celebrating Mass:

a)

Antiphon: Tríum puerórum, *etc.*
Canticle: Benedícite, *etc.*
Ps. 150: Laudáte Dóminum, *etc.*
Ant.: Trium puerórum, *etc.*
Kýrie eléison, *etc.* Pater noster, *etc.*
Versicles: Confiteántur tibi, Dómine, *etc.*
Prayers: Deus, qui tribus púeris, *etc.*

An indulgence of 5 years.

A plenary indulgence, if the aforesaid prayers are said daily for
an entire month, sacramental confession and prayer for the intentions of His Holiness being added thereto.

b)

Prayer of St. Bonaventure: Transfíge, dulcíssime
Dómine, *etc.*

Prayer to the B. V. M.: O María, Virgo et Mater,
etc.

Prayer to the Saint in whose honor Mass has been
celebrated: Sancte N., in cuius honórem, *etc.*

Prayers of St. Alphonsus M. de' Liguori for each
day of the week: Amantíssime Iesu, *etc.*

An indulgence of 3 years for each of the aforesaid prayers (S. C.
Ind., Dec. 20, 1884; S. P. Ap., Nov. 16, 1917 and Oct. 3, 1936).

NOTE: For the prayer of St. Thomas Aquinas: *Grátias tibi ago,*
etc., see n. 160: for the hymn: *Adóro te devôte*, etc., n. 166: for
the invocations *Anima Christi*, etc., n. 131: for the prayer of St.
Ignatius Loyola: *Suscipe, Dómine*, etc., n. 52; for the prayer:
Vírginum custos, etc., n. 473.

751

A Prayer to be said after celebrating Mass

I beseech Thee, sweetest Lord Jesus Christ,
let Thy Passion be my strength, whereby
I may be fortified, protected and defended:
let Thy wounds be my meat and drink,
wherewith I may be fed and filled to overflowing with spiritual joy: let the sprinkling
of Thy Blood be to me a cleansing from all

my sins: let Thy death be to me life unfailing, and Thy Cross my everlasting glory. In these let me find refreshment, exultation, healing and sweetness in my heart: Who livest and reignest world without end. Amen.

An indulgence of 3 years (S. C. Ind., Dec. 11, 1846).

Priests who say the above prayer after Mass, with the right dispositions and devoutly kneeling (if possible), will receive the remission of all shortcomings and faults committed by them through human frailty in offering the Holy Sacrifice (S. C. of the Holy Office, Aug. 29, 1912).

O bsecro te, dulcíssime Dómine Iesu Christe, ut pássio tua sit mihi virtus, qua múniar, prótegar atque deféndar: vúlnera tua sint mihi cibus potúsque, quibus pascar, inébrier atque delécter: aspérsio Sánguinis tui sit mihi ablútio ómnium delictórum meórum: mors tua sit mihi vita indefíciens, crux tua sit mihi glória sempitérna. In his sit mihi reféctio, exsultátio, sánitas et dulcédo cordis mei: Qui vivis et regnas in sæcula sæculórum. Amen.

752
Another Prayer after the celebration of Mass

O most illustrious Virgin and Mother of our Lord Jesus Christ, who didst worthily bear in thy sacred womb the very Creator of all things, whose most holy Body and Blood I have just received, vouchsafe to make intercession to Him in my behalf, that whatsoever I have omitted or committed in this unutterable Sacrament whether through ignorance, negligence or irreverence, may be graciously pardoned by the same, Thy dear Son, in answer to thy most holy prayers. Amen.

An indulgence of 3 years (Pius XI, Rescript in his own hand, Oct. 18, 1926, exhib. Nov. 6, 1926; S. P. Ap., June 15, 1937).

O sereníssima Virgo et Mater Dómini nostri Iesu Christi, quæ in tuo sacratíssimo útero portáre meruísti ipsum rerum ómnium Creatórem, cuius sacratíssimum Corpus et Sánguinem recépi, apud ipsum pro me intercédere dignéris, ut quidquid per ignorántiam, negligéntiam, irreverentiámque in hoc ineffábili Sacraménto omísi vel commísi, idem diléctus Fílius tuus, sanctíssimis tuis précibus exorátus, condonáre dignétur. Amen.

753
A Prayer to be said by Confessors
before they hear the confessions of the faithful

Give me, O Lord, the wisdom that sitteth by Thy throne, that I may be enabled to judge Thy people with justice, and Thy poor and humble ones with true judgment. Grant me so to handle the keys of the Kingdom of heaven, that I may open it to none who ought to be shut out, nor shut out any to whom I ought to open. Let my intention be pure, my zeal sincere, my charity long-suffering, and my labor fruitful. Let me be kind without laxity, severe without harshness; let me not look down upon the poor man, nor flatter the rich man. Give me sweetness that I may draw sinners unto Thee; give me prudence in asking questions; give me skill in instruction. Bestow upon me, I beseech Thee, zeal in withdrawing sinners from evil courses, diligence in establishing them in goodness, and earnestness in moving them to a better life: maturity in my answers, rightness in my counsels, light in obscure matters, insight in intricate cases, and victory over all difficulties; let me not be involved in useless talk, nor corrupted by shameful avowals; may I save others, without myself becoming a castaway.   Amen.

An indulgence of 500 days (S. C. Ind., March 27, 1854; S. P. Ap., May 12, 1933).

Da mihi, Dómine, sédium tuárum assistrícem sapiéntiam, ut sciam iudicáre pópulum tum in iustítia, et páuperes tuos in iudício. Fac me ita tractáre claves regni cælórum, ut nulli apériam cui claudéndum sit, nulli claudam cui aperiéndum sit. Sit inténtio mea pura, zelus meus sincérus, cáritas mea pátiens, labor meus fructuósus. Sit in me lénitas non remíssa, aspéritas non sevéra; páuperem ne despíciam, díviti ne áduler. Fac me ad alliciéndos peccatóres suávem, ad interrogándos prudéntem, ad instruéndos perítum. Tríbue, quæso, ad retrahéndos a malo solértiam, ad confirmándos in bono sedulitátem, ad promovéndos ad melióra indústriam: in respónsis maturitátem, in consíliis rectitúdinem, in obscúris lumen, in impléxis sagacitátem, in árduis victóriam: inutílibus collóquiis ne detínear, pravis ne contáminer: álios salvem, meípsum non perdam.   Amen.

754

Priests, who with attentive care and abounding charity assist the sick, or help them to die a Christian death, if they are near death, are granted:

An indulgence of 10 years (S. P. Ap., Dec. 20, 1940).

V

PRAYERS TO BE SAID BY RELIGIOUS

755
An Invocation

Heart of Jesus, Victim of charity, make me a living sacrifice to Thee, holy, and pleasing unto God.

Religious who say the above invocation with the intention of promoting the more exact observance of their religious vows are granted:

An indulgence of 300 days (S. C. Ind., Feb. 27, 1907; S. P. Ap., Feb. 3, 1931).

Cor Iesu, caritátis víctima, fac me tibi hóstiam vivéntem, sanctam, Deo placéntem.

756
The Renewal of Religious Vows

The Religious of any Order or Congregation, who privately renew their religious vows with at least a contrite heart, after celebrating Holy Mass or receiving Holy Communion, may gain:

An indulgence of 3 years (S. P. Ap., April 10, 1937).

757
A Prayer

Lord Jesus, by the merits and prayers of the Virgin Mary, of Saint N. (*here insert the name of the Saint according to the Order*) and of all the holy Founders, pour out upon me and my brethren, and upon the religious of the entire world, the spirit of faith, sacrifice, prayer, humility, docility and charity. Grant, O my Jesus, that this spirit of charity may be truly supernatural, universal, understanding, long-suffering, joyous and fruitful. Amen.

An indulgence of 500 days (S. C. of the Holy Office, Feb. 1, 1912; S. P. Ap., April 10, 1934).

758
Recitation of the Divine Office
in the presence of the Blessed Sacrament

a) Nuns and other religious women living in communities, who are bound to the daily recitation of the Divine Office by the constitutions of their Institute, if they recite the entire Office, even when this is done at intervals, before the Blessed Sacrament, whether exposed for public adoration or reserved in the Tabernacle, are granted:

A plenary indulgence, if, in addition, they go to confession, receive Holy Communion and pray for the intentions of the Sovereign Pontiff (S. P. Ap., Dec. 5, 1930).

b) Any of the aforesaid women who recite a part only of the Divine Office before the Blessed Sacrament, are granted:

An indulgence of 500 days for each canonical Hour (S. P. Ap., May 18, 1933).

VI
PRAYERS TO BE SAID BY TEACHERS
759
An Invocation

Teach me goodness and discipline and knowledge, O Lord: for I have believed Thy commandments (Ps. 118, 66).

An indulgence of 300 days (Pius X, Rescript in his own hand, May 14, 1908; S. C. Ind., Sept. 12, 1908).

Bonitátem et disciplínam et sciéntiam doce me, Dómine; quia mandátis tuis crédidi (Ps. CXVIII, 66).

760
AN INVOCATION

Seat of wisdom, pray for us.

Teachers, who at the beginning of class devoutly recite once the Angelical salutation with this invocation, are granted:

An indulgence of 300 days (S. P. Ap., Nov. 10, 1940).
Sedes sapiéntiæ, ora pro nobis.

761
A Prayer

O glorious Virgin and Martyr, Saint Catherine, who, by thy wonderful knowledge, thy zeal for the faith and thy glorious martyrdom, hast gained for Jesus Christ so great a harvest of souls, we choose thee, whose patronage hath been so often implored by the most learned men, as the protector and patroness of our studies and our teaching. Obtain for us, who are thy clients, a wholehearted love for Jesus Christ our Saviour, a burning zeal to make Him known and loved, an unwavering attachment to the Catholic faith and to the teachings of Holy Church. May our Lord, through thine intercession, be pleased to bestow upon all who teach others the fulness of the gifts of the Holy Spirit; may they join to true knowledge sure and effectual methods, purity of faith, integrity of life and a humble distrust of themselves. Ask Jesus, thy Spouse, to have pity on all those who are being taught; may He preserve them from irreligious or indifferent masters, from perverse or erroneous doctrines; may He give them a right spirit, a docile heart and the grace to make progress in their studies according to the designs of His supreme wisdom. Finally, glorious Saint, implore from the Father of lights such an outpouring of grace upon the instruction of youth, that after they have studied, loved and practiced Thy divine law, they may all of them, both masters and pupils, come at last to the holy mount, which is Jesus Christ. Amen.

An indulgence of 300 days (S. C. Ind., April 29, 1907; S. P. Ap., Aug. 10, 1933).

762

A Prayer

O glorious Saint Catherine, wise and prudent virgin, thou who didst set the knowledge of Jesus Christ above all other knowledge, obtain for us the grace to remain inviolably attached to the Catholic faith, and to seek in our studies and in our teaching only the extension of the Kingdom of Jesus Christ our Lord and of His Holy Church both in ourselves and in the souls of others. Amen.

An indulgence of 300 days (S. C. Ind., April 29, 1907; S. P. Ap., Oct. 20, 1935).

VII

PRAYERS TO BE SAID BY STUDENTS

763

An Act of Consecration

Under thy patronage, dear Mother, and invoking the mystery of thine Immaculate Conception, I desire to pursue my studies and my literary labors: I hereby solemnly declare that I am devoting myself to these studies chiefly to the following end: that I may the better contribute to the glory of God and to the spread of thy veneration among men. I pray thee, therefore, most loving Mother, who art the Seat of Wisdom, to bless my labors in thy loving-kindness. Moreover I promise with true affection and a willing spirit, as it is right that I should do, to ascribe all the good that shall accrue to me therefrom, wholly to thine intercession for me in God's holy presence. Amen.

An indulgence of 300 days once a day (S. C. Ind., Nov. 18, 1882; S. P. Ap., Aug. 5, 1932).

Sub patrocínio tuo, Mater dulcíssima, et invocáto immaculátæ Conceptiónis tuæ mystério, stúdia mea laborésque litterários prósequi volo: quibus me protéstor hunc máxime ob finem incúmbere, ut mélius divíno honóri tuóque cúltui propagándo insérviam. Oro te ígitur, Mater amantíssima, sedes sapiéntiæ, ut labóribus meis benígne fáveas. Ego vero, quod iustum est, pie libentérque promítto, quidquid boni mihi inde succésserit, id me tuæ apud Deum intercessióni totum accéptum relatúrum. Amen.

764

A Prayer

O Creator ineffable, who of the riches of Thy wisdom didst appoint three hierarchies of Angels and didst set them in wondrous order over the highest heavens, and who didst apportion the elements of the world most wisely: do Thou, who art in truth the fountain of light and wisdom, deign to shed upon the darkness of my understanding the rays of Thine infinite brightness, and remove far from me the twofold darkness in which I was born, namely, sin and ignorance. Do Thou, who givest speech to the tongues of little children, instruct my tongue and pour into my lips the grace of Thy benediction. Give me keenness of apprehension, capacity for remembering, method and ease in learning, insight in interpretation, and copious eloquence in speech. Instruct my beginning, direct my progress, and set Thy seal upon the finished work, Thou, who art true God and true Man, who livest and reignest world without end. Amen (St. Thomas Aquinas).

An indulgence of 7 years (Pius XI, Encyclical "Studiorum Ducem," June 29, 1923; S. P. Ap., March 18, 1932).

Creator ineffábilis, qui de thesáuris sapiéntiæ tuæ tres Angelórum hierarchías designásti et eas super cælum empýreum miro órdine collocásti, atque univérsi partes elegantíssime distribuísti: Tu, inquam, qui verus fons lúminis et sapiéntiæ díceris ac superéminens princípium, infúndere dignéris super intelléctus mei ténebras tuæ rádium claritátis, dúplices, in quibus natus sum, a me rémovens ténebras, peccátum scílicet et ignorántiam. Tu, qui linguas infántium facis disértas, linguam meam erúdias atque in lábiis meis grátiam tuæ benedictiónis infúndas. Da mihi intelligéndi acúmen, retinéndi capacitátem, addiscéndi modum et facilitátem, interpretándi subtilitátem, loquéndi grátiam copiósam. Ingréssum ínstruas, progréssum dírigas, egréssum cómpleas. Tu, qui es verus Deus et Homo, qui vivis et regnas in sæcula sæculórum. Amen (S. Thomas Aquinas).

765
A Prayer

O most holy Virgin Mary, who didst bear Jesus our Saviour and didst shed the everlasting Light upon the world, O Mother of divine knowledge, whose merciful intercession hath procured the grace of increasing in knowledge and piety for countless minds that were rude and ignorant, I choose thee as the guide and patroness of my studies.

By thine intercession, O Mother of fruitful studies, may the Holy Spirit fill my spirit with light and fortitude, prudence and humility; may He give me a good will, intelligence, memory and ability in sufficient measure, and above all, a spirit of docility both in mind and heart, that I may proceed in all things according to the counsels of divine Wisdom.

Defend me, good Mother, against the spirit of pride and presumption, of vain curiosity and instability; keep me from every occasion of stumbling, from all erroneous opinion, and from all things that might corrupt my faith and disturb the clearness of my understanding, the purity of my heart, and the peace of my soul.

Grant, O Mary, that, under thy protection, I may ever be submissive to the directions and teachings of Holy Church, my mother, and may advance in the way of truth and virtue surely, courageously and without wavering; at length may I attain to the knowledge, the love and the everlasting possession of Jesus Christ, thy Son, our Lord. Amen.

An indulgence of 500 days (Pius X, Rescript in his own hand, April 26, 1907, exhib. April 27, 1907; S. P. Ap., Sept. 18, 1933).

O sanctíssima Virgo María, quæ Salvatórem Iesum genuísti, Lumen ætérnum mundo effudísti, o Mater divínæ sciéntiæ, cuius pia intercéssio innúmeris méntibus incúltis et ignorántibus mirabíliter prógredi in sciéntia et pietáte obtínuit, te studiórum meórum præsidem ac patrónam éligo.

Per tuam intercessiónem, o Mater bonórum studiórum, Spíritus Sanctus ánimam meam ímpleat lúmine et fortitúdine, prudéntia et humilitáte; det mihi voluntátem rectam, intelligéntiam, memóriam, facilitátem sufficiéntem, docilitátem præsértim mentis et cordis, ut in ómnibus, secúndum divínæ Sapiéntiæ consília, prógredi possim.

Defénde me, o bone Mater, advérsus spíritum supérbiæ, præsumptiónis, vanæ curiositátis et incon-

stántiæ; præsérva me ab omni scándalo, ab omni
erróre, ab iis ómnibus qui possent fidem meam corrúmpere, luciditátem intelléctus, puritátem cordis,
pacem ánimæ meæ turbáre.

Fac, o María, ut, sub tuo patrocínio, semper sub-
míssus directiónibus et doctrínis sanctæ Ecclésiæ,
Matris meæ, cum securitáte, fortitúdine et constántia
incédere possim in viam veritátis et virtútis, et tandem pervenire ad cognitiónem, amórem et ætérnam
possessiónem Iesu Christi, Dómini nostri, Fílii tui.
Amen.

VIII
AN INVOCATION TO BE RECITED
BY THOSE WHO DO MENTAL OR PHYSICAL LABOR

766

The faithful, as often as they raise their mind to
God by reciting some invocation in the midst of their
duties or work, are granted:

An indulgence of 300 days(S. P. Ap., Mar. 22, 1941).

IX
A PRAYER TO BE SAID BY CHILDREN

767

Sweetest Jesus, who, being subject as a
child to Mary and Joseph at Nazareth,
didst leave to children an excellent pattern
of affection and obedience to parents, and of
wondrous reverence for all men, grant, I
most earnestly beseech Thee, that I may
strive to see Thee always and in all things, so
that as my years increase, I too may increase
in Thy grace and love: Who livest and reignest world without end. Amen.

An indulgence of 300 days(Apostolic Brief, June 25, 1924; S. P.
Ap., May 20, 1937).

Dulcíssime Iesu, qui puer, Názaræ, Maríæ et Ioseph súbditus, exémplar præclárum púeris reliquísti pietátis et obediéntiæ in paréntes atque exímiæ in omnes reveréntiæ, fac, piíssime rogo, ut semper et in ómnibus intuéri te stúdeam, ut crescéntibus annis, grátia et amóre tui crescam: Qui vivis et regnas in sǽcula sæculórum. Amen.

X

A PRAYER TO BE SAID BY YOUNG MEN

768

O most glorious Saint Aloysius, who hast been honored by the Church with the fair title of "angelic youth," because of the life of utmost purity thou didst lead here on earth, I come before thy presence this day with all the devotion of my mind and heart. O perfect exemplar, kind and powerful patron of young men, how great is my need of thee! The world and the devil are trying to ensnare me; I am conscious of the ardor of my passions; I know full well the weakness and inconstancy of my age. Who shall be able to keep me safe, if not thou, O Saint of angelic purity, the glory and honor, the loving protector of youth? To thee, therefore, I have recourse with all my soul, to thee I commit myself with all my heart. I hereby resolve, promise and desire to be especially devout toward thee, to glorify thee by imitating thy extraordinary virtues and in particular thy angelic purity, to copy thy example, and to promote devotion to thee among my companions. O dear Saint Aloysius, do thou guard and defend me always, in order that, under thy protection and following thy example, I may one day be able to join with thee in seeing and praising my God for ever in heaven. Amen.

An indulgence of 300 days once a day.

A plenary indulgence on the usual conditions, if this prayer is devoutly said daily for a month (S. C. Ind., June 12, 1894; S. P. Ap., June 29, 1933).

XI
A PRAYER TO THE MOST SACRED HEART OF JESUS
TO BE SAID BY MARRIED FOLK IN THEIR OWN BEHALF

769

O Most Sacred Heart of Jesus, King and center of all hearts, dwell in our hearts and be our King: grant us by Thy grace to love each other truly and chastely, even as Thou hast loved Thine immaculate Bride, the Church, and didst deliver Thyself up for her.

Bestow upon us the mutual love and Christian forbearance that are so acceptable in Thy sight, and a mutual patience in bearing each other's defects; for we are certain that no living creature is free from them. Permit not the slightest misunderstanding to mar that harmony of spirit which is the foundation of that mutual assistance in the many and varied hardships of life, to provide which woman was created and united inseparably to her husband.

Grant, O Lord God, that between us there may be a constant and holy rivalry in striving to lead a perfect Christian life, by virtue of which the divine image of Thy mystic union with Holy Church, imprinted upon us

on the happy day of our marriage, may shine
forth more and more clearly. Grant, we
beseech Thee, that our good example of
Christian living may be a source of inspiration to our children to spur them on to conform their lives also to Thy holy Law; and
finally, after this exile, may we be found
worthy, by the help of Thy grace, for which
we earnestly pray, to ascend into heaven,
there to be joined with our children for ever,
and to praise and bless Thee through everlasting ages.   Amen.

NOTE:—If they have no children, instead of the words: "Grant,
O Lord God, etc. . . . Amen", let them pray as follows:

Grant, O Lord God, that between us there
may be a constant and holy rivalry in our
efforts to lead a truly Christian life, by virtue
of which the divine image of Thy mystic
union with Thy Holy Church, which Thou
didst deign to impress upon us on the happy
day of our marriage, may shine forth more
and more clearly; and so living may we, both
of us, ascend into heaven and be found
worthy to praise Thee and bless Thee for ever.
Amen.

An indulgence of 300 days (S. P. Ap., Dec. 11, 1923 and Nov. 25,
1936).

Sacratíssimum Cor Iesu, Rex et centrum ómnium
córdium, hábita et regna in córdibus nostris et
fac per grátiam tuam, ut nosmetípsos ínvicem caste
et vere diligámus sicut Tu immaculátam tuam Sponsam, Ecclésiam, dilexísti ac temetípsum pro ea tradi-
dísti.

Concéde nobis mútuam illam caritátem et christiánam indulgéntiam tibi summópere acceptíssimam,
mutuámque in tolerándis deféctibus nostris patién-

tiam; persuásum enim habémus nullam creatúram iísdem carére. Noli permíttere ut vel mínimum detriméntum cápiat plena ac suávis illa animórum concórdia, fundaméntum altérni illíus adiutórii in váriis plurimísque vitæ necessitátibus, quod finem constítuit propter quem creáta fuit múlier et viro suo inseparabíliter iuncta.

Inter nos, Dómine Deus, fac regnet perénne ac sanctum vitæ summópere christiánæ certámen, vi cuius magis magísque divína illa tui mýstici coniúgii cum sancta Ecclésia imágo illucéscat, quam fausto die uniónis nostræ in nobis imprímere dignátus fuísti. Præsta, quǽsumus, ut bonum vitæ nostræ exémplum fíliis nostris inservíre queat, tamquam potens stímulus ad suam vitam tuæ sanctæ legi conformándam; ac tandem post hoc exsílium in cælum ascendámus, ubi, favénte tua grátia quam eníxe exoptámus, simul cum ipsis perpétuo consístere, teque in ætérnum laudáre ac benedícere mereámur. Amen.

NOTA.—Si coniuges filiis destituuntur, *loco verborum:*

Inter nos, Dómine Deus . . . mereámur. Amen, *haec dicantur:*

Inter nos, Dómine Deus, fac regnet perénne ac sanctum vitæ summópere christiánæ certámen, vi cuius magis magísque illucéscat divína illa imágo, quam fausto die uniónis nostræ imprímere dignátus es, scílicet mýstici tui coniúgii cum sancta Ecclésia, atque ita utríque ad cælum ascendámus teque in ætérnum laudáre ac benedícere mereámur. Amen.

XII
A PRAYER TO BE SAID BY PARENTS IN BEHALF OF THEIR CHILDREN

770

O Lord God, who hast called us to holy matrimony and hast been pleased to render our union fruitful, thus making glad the sublime state of life wherein Thou hast placed us, by a certain likeness to Thine own infinite fruitfulness; we heartily recommend to Thee our dear children; we entrust them to Thy fatherly care and all-powerful protection, that they may grow daily in Thy holy fear, may lead a perfect Christian life and may be a source of consolation, not only to us who have given them life, but also and chiefly to Thee, who art their Creator.

Behold, O Lord, in what a world they must pass their lives; consider the cunning flatteries whereby the sons of men everywhere endeavor to deprave their minds and hearts with false doctrine and wicked example. Be watchful, O Lord, to help and defend them; grant us the grace to be able to guide them aright in the paths of virtue and in the way of Thy commandments, by the righteous pattern of our own life and practice, and our perfect observance of Thy holy law and that of our Holy Mother the Church; and in order that we may do so faithfully, make us certain of the grave danger that awaits us at the hands of Thy divine justice. Nevertheless all our efforts will be unavailing, unless Thou, O almighty and merciful God, shalt make them fruitful by Thy heavenly blessing.

This Thy blessing, therefore, we humbly ask of Thee, from the bottom of our hearts, trusting in Thy great goodness and mercy hitherto shown unto us; we ask it for ourselves and for the children whom Thou hast been graciously pleased to give unto us. We dedicate them to Thee, O Lord, do Thou keep them as the apple of Thine eye, and protect them under the shadow of Thy wings; do Thou make us worthy to come at last to heaven, together with them, giving thanks unto Thee, our Father, for the loving care Thou hast had of our entire family and praising Thee through endless ages. Amen.

An indulgence of 300 days (S. P. Ap., Nov. 25, 1936).

Dómine Deus, qui nos ad matrimónium ádvocans, illud effícere fecúndum dignátus es, sublimémque hunc statum, in quo a te pósiti sumus, quadam fecunditátis tuæ infinítæ imágine lætíficas; tibi dilectíssimos líberos nostros ardénter commendámus. Ipsos in tua patérna tutéla atque omnipoténti patrocínio collocámus, ut semper in sancto tui timóre succréscant, vitam pénitus christiánam tradúcant, et non solum nobis, qui eis vitam dédimus, sed præsértim tibi, eorúmdem Creatóri, solátium áfferant.

Vide, Dómine, úbinam géntium ipsi versántur; vide cállida blandiménta quibus úndique hómines eórum mentes animúmque fallácibus doctrínis pravísque exémplis corrúmpere conántur. Ad ipsórum auxílium ac defensiónem, Dómine, vígila; nobísque concéde, ut, de permágno perículo quod ante tuam divínam iustítiam prorsus exstat certióres facti, recto nostræ vitæ nostrorúmque morum exémplo, perfectíssima tuæ sanctæ legis ac Matris Ecclésiæ observántia, eos per virtútis ac mandatórum tuórum sémitas perdúcere valeámus; cuncta vero ópera nostra inánis evádet nisi Tu, omnípotens et miséricors Deus, tua cælésti benedictióne eam fecúndam reddíderis.

Hanc ígitur benedictiónem, ex imo corde ac fidéntes bonitáte magna et favóre nobis concéssis, a te pétimus pro nobis atque fíliis quos nobismetípsis donáre voluísti. Tibi, Dómine, eos consecrámus; Tu eos custódi tamquam tuórum oculórum pupíllam et sub alárum tuárum eósdem prótege, et éffice ut una

simul cum ipsis ad cælum perveníre valeámus, grátias agéntes pro custódia quam, amábilis Pater, totíus
famíliæ nostræ habuísti, et te in ætérna sǽcula laudántes. Amen.

XIII

A PRAYER TO BE SAID BY CHILDREN
IN BEHALF OF THEIR PARENTS

771

Almighty and everlasting God, who, in the
secret counsels of Thine ineffable Providence, hast been pleased to call us into life
by means of our parents, who thus partake
of Thy divine power in our regard, mercifully
hear the prayer of filial affection which we
offer to Thee in behalf of those to whom
Thou hast given a share of Thy fatherly
mercy, in order that they might lavish upon
us in our journey through life the consoling
gift of Thy holy and generous love.

Dear Lord, fill our parents with Thy choicest blessings; enrich their souls with Thy
holy grace; grant that they may faithfully
and constantly guard that likeness to Thy
mystic marriage with Thy Church, which
Thou didst imprint upon them on the day of
their nuptials. Fill them with the spirit of
holy fear, which is the beginning of wisdom,
and continually move them to impart the
same to their children; in such wise may
they ever walk in the way of Thy commandments, and may their children be their joy
in this earthly exile and their crown of glory
in their home in heaven.

Finally, Lord God, grant that both our

father and our mother may attain to extreme old age and enjoy perpetual health in mind and body; may they deserve to sing Thy praises forever in our heavenly country in union with us, their children, giving Thee most hearty thanks that Thou hast bestowed upon them in this valley of tears the great gift of a share in the light of Thy infinite fruitfulness and of Thy divine fatherhood. Amen.

An indulgence of 300 days (S. P. Ap., Nov. 25, 1936).

Omnípotens sempitérne Deus, qui per arcána tuæ ineffábilis providéntiæ consília, ad vitam nos vocáre dignátus es ópera paréntum nostrórum pro nobis tuam potestátem reveréntium, exáudi filiális pietátis oratiónem quam tibi offérimus pro iis, quibus paternórum tuórum víscerum misericórdiam communicásti, ut super nostrum vitæ currículum tuæ sanctæ ac generósæ dilectiónis levámen effúnderent.

Imple, Dómine, singuláribus tuis benedictiónibus paréntes nostros; ipsórum ánimum tua sancta grátia adáuge; præsta ut ipsi fidéliter ac semper mýstici tui cum Ecclésia connúbii imáginem custódiant, quam die suárum nuptiárum in eis sculpsísti. Tui sancti timóris spíritu, qui est sapiéntiæ princípium, eósdem reple, et quovis moménto ipsis suáde ut eúmdem in fíliis suis infúndant atque ita semper in via mandatórum tuórum incédant, utque et in hoc terréno exsílio gáudium ipsórum, et in cælésti pátria corónam efformáre váleant. Tandem, Dómine Deus, éffice ut utríque ad extrémam senectútem, perpétua mentis et córporis sanitáte gaudéntes, perveníre queant, ut simul nobíscum, suis fíliis, tuas laudes in cælésti pátria cantáre perénniter mereántur et úberes grátias agant ob magnum donum eísdem oblátum, ipsis concedéndo, in hac lacrimárum valle, lumen tuæ infínitæ fecunditátis tuæque divínæ paternitátis. Amen.

NOTE.—A prayer for deceased parents is found under n. 599.

XIV

A VISIT TO A CHURCH
TO BE MADE BY DEAF-MUTES AND THEIR INSTRUCTORS

772

Catholic deaf-mutes and their teachers and instructors, who devoutly visit any church or public oratory on the XI Sunday after Pentecost, are granted:

A plenary indulgence, if in addition they have obtained the pardon of their sins, have received holy Communion, and have devoutly prayed for the intention of the Sovereign Pontiff (S. P. Ap., Nov. 15, 1943).

APPENDIX

INDULGENCES
ATTACHED TO VISITING
CERTAIN HOLY PLACES IN ROME

INTROIBO DALTARE DEIADDEUM QUILAETIFI-CATJUVENTU TEM MEAM

I

A ROMAN PILGRIMAGE

773

The faithful who visit the more important sanctuaries of the Holy City, may gain:

A plenary indulgence, to be gained on the day of their departure, if they confess their sins, approach the holy Table and pray for the intentions of his Holiness, the Pope (S. P. Ap., April 4, 1932).

II

A VISIT TO THE VATICAN BASILICA ALSO TO THE TOMB AND STATUE OF SAINT PETER, APOSTLE, IN THE SAME BASILICA

774

a) The faithful, who, having confessed their sins and received Holy Communion, visit the Vatican Patriarchal Basilica with pious sentiments, and there devoutly recite six times the *Our Father*, *Hail Mary*, and *Glory be* for the intention of the Sovereign Pontiff on each visit, are granted:

A plenary indulgence as often as they do this.

b) The faithful who recite the *Our Father*, *Hail Mary*, and *Glory be*, three times before the tomb of St. Peter, the Apostle, in the Vatican Basilica, in gratitude to Almighty God for the privileges granted by Him to the same holy Apostle, may gain:

An indulgence of 7 years.

c) Those who devoutly kiss the foot of the bronze statue of St. Peter, which stands in the aforesaid Basilica and pray for the intentions of the Holy Father, may gain:

An indulgence of 50 days (Apostolic Brief, May 15, 1857; S. P. Ap., March 18, 1932 and Jan. 12, 1935).

III

THE VISIT TO THE SO-CALLED "SEVEN ALTARS" IN THE VATICAN BASILICA

775

The faithful who visit the following Seven Altars in the Vatican Basilica: 1° the Gregorian altar of the Blessed Virgin; 2° that of Sts. Processus and Martinian; 3° that of St. Michael the Archangel; 4° that of St. Petronilla, Virgin; 5° that of Our Lady of the Pillar; 6° that of the holy Apostles Simon and Jude; 7° that of St. Gregory the Great, may gain:

An indulgence of 7 years for the visit to each of the seven altars, if they recite any prayer they may choose in honor of the Titular Saint of the altar;

A plenary indulgence on the Feast Day of the Titular Saint of a given altar, if they visit that altar as above, and confess their sins, receive Holy Communion and pray for the intentions of the Sovereign Pontiff;

A plenary indulgence, if they visit the seven altars in the aforesaid manner on the same day, according to the rule laid down in canon 923 of the Code of Canon Law, with the addition of confession, Communion and prayers for the intentions of the Pope (S. P. Ap., Oct. 2, 1935).

IV

A VISIT TO THE LATERAN ARCHBASILICA

776

The faithful, who after confession and Holy Communion, devoutly visit the Lateran Archbasilica and there piously recite six times the *Our Father*, *Hail Mary*, and *Glory be* for the intention of His Holiness on each visit, are granted:

A plenary indulgence as often as they do this (Apostolic Brief, Nov. 9, 1939).

V

A VISIT TO THE SACRED CRIB OF OUR LORD JESUS CHRIST
IN THE BASILICA OF SAINT MARY MAJOR

777
Prayer

I adore Thee, O incarnate Word, the true Son of God from all eternity, and the true Son of Mary in the fulness of time. As I adore Thy divine Person and the sacred Humanity thereto united, I feel myself drawn to venerate likewise the poor Crib that welcomed Thee, when Thou wast a little Child, and which was, in very truth, the first throne of Thy love. Would that I could fall prostrate before it with the simplicity of the shepherds, with the faith of Joseph, and the love of Mary! Would that I too could bend low to venerate this precious memorial of our salvation with the spirit of mortification, poverty and humility, with which Thou, the Lord of heaven and earth, didst choose a manger to be the resting place of Thy dear limbs! And do Thou, O Lord, who didst deign in Thine infancy to be laid in this manger, pour into my heart a drop of that joy which must have been experienced at the sight of Thy lovely infancy and of the wonders that accompanied Thy birth; by virtue of this Thy holy birth, I implore Thee to give peace and good-will to all the world, and, in the name of all mankind, to render perfect thanksgiving and infinite glory to Thine eternal Father, with whom, in the unity of the Holy Spirit, Thou livest and reignest one God, world without end. Amen.

An indulgence of 500 days (Apostolic Brief, Oct. 1, 1861; S. P. Ap., Feb. 21, 1933).

VI

A VISIT TO THE SCALA SANTA

778

The faithful who devoutly ascend on their knees the Scala Santa (or Holy Stairs) in the city of Rome, whilst meditating on the Passion of our Lord Jesus Christ, are granted:

An indulgence of 9 years for each step, even if the ascent be interrupted;

A plenary indulgence, whenever they make the entire ascent, and confess their sins, partake of the Eucharistic Table and offer their prayers for the intentions of the Holy Father.

The same indulgence of 9 years is granted to the faithful, who on their knees make the ascent of one or the other of the two stairs to the right and left of the Scala Santa, from All Saints' Day to the end of the Octave of All Souls' Day, from Christmas Day to the Epiphany inclusive, as well as during the whole of Lent (S. C. Ind., Sept. 2, 1817 and July 23, 1898; Pius X, Rescript in his own hand, Feb. 26, 1908; S. P. Ap., Feb. 6, 1925).

VII

THE VISIT TO THE SO-CALLED "SEVEN CHURCHES"

779

The faithful who in one day, according to the rule of canon 923 of the Code of Canon Law, complete the devout visitation of the Seven Basilicas of the city of Rome, to wit, St. Peter's in the Vatican, St. Paul's outside the Walls, St. John Lateran, St. Mary Major, St. Sebastian's, St. Lawrence outside the Walls, and Holy Cross in Jerusalem, reciting in each Basilica *Our Father*, *Hail Mary*, and *Glory be*, five times before the altar of the Blessed Sacrament and the same prayers once more for the intentions of His Holiness the Pope, adding also some prayer, according to their liking, to the Blessed Virgin Mary and to the Titular Saint of the respective Basilicas, and substituting, in memory of the Passion of our Lord in the Basilica of the Holy Cross in Jerusalem, the Apostles' Creed and the versicle "*We Adore Thee, O Christ*," etc., for the prayer to the titular Saint, may gain:

A plenary indulgence for the visit to each of the Basilicas, on condition of confession and Holy Communion; in such a way, however, that if they are accidentally hindered from completing the entire pilgrimage through no fault of their own, they are not deprived by this interruption of the indulgences which they have gained by the visits already completed (S. P. Ap., Jan. 15, 1935).

VIII
VISITS TO THE CHURCHES OF THE STATIONS

780

The faithful who on the days appointed in the Roman Missal, a) devoutly visit the churches of the Stations in Rome and attend the sacred functions which are held there, either in the morning or afternoon, according to custom or the express command of the Ordinary, may gain:

A plenary indulgence, on condition of confession, Communion and prayer for the intentions of the Sovereign Pontiff;

b) in a Stational church, where no public service is held, if they recite the *Our Father*, *Hail Mary*, and *Glory be*, five times in the presence of the Blessed Sacrament, three times before the Holy Relics exposed for veneration and at least once for the intentions of the Sovereign Pontiff, they may gain:

A plenary indulgence, if they confess their sins and receive the Bread of Heaven;

c) If they merely visit the church of the Station and recite the prayers mentioned in b) above, they may gain:

An indulgence of 10 years (S. P. Ap., April 12, 1932).

IX
THE PENITENTIAL WAND

781

The faithful, who on any day of the year, approach the minor Penitentiaries in the Lateran, Vatican,

Ostian, and Liberian Basilicas and allow themselves to be touched by the penitential wand, if animated by sentiments of Christian humility and sincere contrition, are granted:

An indulgence of 300 days, once a day.

T hose, however, who present themselves to the most Eminent Cardinal, the major Penitentiary, when he is fulfilling his office on the appointed greater days of the week in the four Basilicas just mentioned, and allow themselves to be touched by the penitential wand in a similar manner, if animated by the same sentiments as above, are granted:

An indulgence of 7 years(S. P. Ap., July 20, 1942) .

ADDENDA to THE RACCOLTA

INDULGENCED PRAYERS AND DEVOTIONS APPROVED
BY THE SACRED PENITENTIARY APOSTOLIC SINCE
1950

I

INDULGENCE FOR CARRYING THE ROSARY

The faithful who devoutly carry about their person a Rosary of the Blessed Virgin Mary that has been properly blessed may gain an Indulgence of 500 days once a day, if they kiss the Rosary and at the same time devoutly recite these words of the Angelic Salutation:

Hail, Mary, full of grace; the Lord is with thee: blessed art thou among women, and blessed is the fruit of thy womb, Jesus.
(Pius XII. Audience March 12, 1953.)

Ave, María, grátia plena; Dóminus tecum: benedícta tu in muliéribus, et benedíctus fructus ventris tui Jesus.

II

PRAYER TO THE MOTHER MOST ADMIRABLE

Hail, Mary, full of grace, glorious light reflecting the splendor of the three divine Persons. Thy name, O Mary, is like a balm poured out on our wounds providing us sinners with the help that we ask for in continual sighing. The Lord is with thee, O Mary, as thou art with us, O kind and gracious star, to enlighten thy children, who ever look up to thee from their exile for guidance and consolation amid the sorrows of this vale of tears. Blessed art thou among women, for the Lord has chosen thee to be the Mother of the Word Incarnate and never permitted thy surpassing beauty to be tarnished by the stain of sin. Blessed is the fruit of thy womb, Jesus, since it was through thee that there was given to us the one and only Savior, who has redeemed us from

627

death and opened again the gates of heaven. Holy
Mary, Mother of God, pray for us, who must still
struggle here on earth. Be thou ever our refuge so
that in the blessed hour of death we may be worthy
to behold thy fair countenance in the brightness of
eternal glory. Amen.

The faithful provided they are at least duly contrite, can gain an indulgence of 300 days as often
they devoutly recite the above prayer; a plenary
indulgence on the usual conditions, if they persevere
daily in this devout practice throughout the entire
month (Pius XII, Audience May 12, 1953).

Oratio ad Matrem Admirabilem

Ave, María, grátia plena, lux fúlgida, in qua tres
divínæ Persónæ relúcent. Nomen tuum, o María,
vulnéribus nostris est bálsamum effúsum, nobísque
peccatóribus auxílium quod semper suspirámus.
Dóminus tecum, sicut tu, o María, nobíscum es, ut
fílios illúmines, dírigas eósque consoléris qui mísere
peregrinántur in hac lacrymárum valle, in te óculos
intendéntes, o nostra propítia stella. Benedícta tu
in muliéribus, quia Dóminus te elégit, ut sis Mater
incarnáti Verbi, nunquam permíttens ut labe peccáti
pulchritúdo tua suavíssima maculétur. Benedíctus
fructus ventris tui, Jesus, quia per te nobis datus est
únicus Salvátor, qui a morte nos redémit nobísque
cælórum portam íterum áperit. Sancta María, Mater
Dei, ora pro nobis, qui in terris nunc pugnam susti-
némus. Esto nobis semper refúgium, ut in mortis
benedícta hora suávem tuam fáciem in splendóre
æternitátis spectáre valeámus. Amen.

ROSARY OF THE SEVEN DOLORS

The faithful who piously recite the Rosary of the
Seven Dolors of the Blessed Virgin Mary in the
presence of the Blessed Sacrament publicly exposed
or even reserved in the tabernacle may gain:

Plenary indulgence once a day on condition of Confession and
Communion (S.P. Ap., Jan. 15, 1954).

PRAYER TO THE BLESSED VIRGIN MARY
Composed by Pope Pius XII

O Virgin, fair as the moon, in whom the heavens rejoice, upon whose face the blessed gaze, and whom the Angels acknowledge as their model; make us, thy children, like unto thee by shedding upon our souls a ray of thy beauty such as will not grow dim with passing time, but will shine for all eternity.

O Mary, thou mystic sun, reawaken life wherever there is death, and cast thy light on souls where shadows fall. Let thy image be mirrored in the faces of thy children, and grant us to reflect thy light and thy ardor.

O Mary, powerful as an army, grant victory to our ranks. We are so weak, and our proud enemy unceasingly rages against us. But under thy standard we have the sure hope of conquering him, for he knows the power of thy heel and trembles at the majesty of thy countenance.

Save us, O Mary, fair as the moon, bright as the sun, powerful as an army set in array, whose strength lies not in hate but in the most glowing love. Amen.

The faithful, provided that they are at least duly contrite, can gain an indulgence of 500 days as often as they devoutly recite the above prayer.(Pius XII, January 17, 1956.)

PRAYER TO MARY, MOST HOLY, MOTHER OF ORPHANS
Composed by Pope Pius XII

Hail, O Virgin most pure and Queen most powerful, whom the human family addresses with the sweetest name of Mother, we cannot call upon an earthly mother either because we have never known one or because we have been deprived very early of the support of a mother's sweet care. Therefore we have recourse to thee, confident that thou wilt show thyself a Mother to us in particular. If our sad plight moves men's hearts with sentiments of pity, compassion and love towards us, will not thy most tender heart be moved still more seeing as thou art the most loving, the most affectionate and the most merciful of all pure creatures.

O true Mother of all orphans, we take refuge in thy Immaculate Heart, certain to find therein all comfort and consolation for our lonely hearts. We place full confidence in thee trusting that thy maternal hand will guide and sustain us in the difficult journey through this life.

Bless all who assist us and protect us in Thy name; reward our benefactors and those noble souls who sacrifice their lives for us. But above all, be thou ever a Mother unto us, by moulding our hearts, by enlightening our minds, by regulating our will, by adorning our souls with all virtue and by driving away those hostile to our welfare who would prefer to destroy us forever.

Finally, most loving Mother, our joy and our hope, lead us to Jesus, the blessed fruit of thy womb, so that if we lack the sweet tenderness of an earthly mother, we may become so much more worthy of thee in this life and in the eternal hereafter may rejoice in thy maternal affection and in thy company together with that of thy divine Son who with the Father and the Holy Spirit lives and reigns forever and ever. Amen.

An indulgence of 1000 days (S. P. Ap. August 28, 1956).

PRAYERS TO OBTAIN THE SANCTIFICATION OF THE CLERGY
Composed by Pope Pius XII

I

PRAYER TO BE SAID BY PRIESTS

O Lord Jesus Christ, eternal High Priest, Good Shepherd and Fountain of Life, who hast numbered us among thy priests not through any merits of ours but by the special bounty of Thy most Sacred Heart, mercifully grant unto us an abundance of Thy gifts that we may be able to fulfill those priestly promises which we have made by the inspiration of Thy grace. Since Thou didst sanctify Thyself for us that we also may be truly sanctified (John 17, 19), and since Thou art our Way, grant that we may never depart from Thee so that becoming well versed in Thy teaching and faithful in the keeping of Thy commandments we may reflect in our conduct the image and kind dispositions of Thy Sacred Heart. Thus in Thee and through Thee we shall in all things be found pleasing to the heavenly Father.

May perfect justice together with prudence shine forth in our lives and let robust fortitude be tempered by the restraints of chaste temperance. With pure faith abiding in our hearts, may they be consoled by the hope of immortal blessings, and become inflamed with the fires of heavenly love from Thy Sacred Heart, the burning furnace of charity. Grant that we may be ever diligent in meditating on thy words, radiant with the brightness of Thy eternal wisdom for the enlightenment of our minds. Thus from that very pasture in which we are fed, we can feed the sheep of Thy flock committed to our care. May the enemies of Thy Gospel stand in awe as they witness the strong bonds of unity that knit us so closely together. May they never have occasion to observe in our conduct anything with which to find fault with Thy Church, our spotless and immaculate Mother. Finally, may we ever prefer Thy glory to our own personal gain, and grant us to persevere to our last breath in the fruitful performance of duty with an upright will and a pure conscience. Then after death be Thou, who art now our Teacher and Companion, our eternal reward in the glory of the Saints, who livest and reignest with God the Father in the unity of the Holy Ghost for ever and ever. Amen.

An indulgence of 1000 days (S. P. Ap. May 4, 1956).

Dómine Iesu, Póntifex ætérne, Pastor bone, fons vitæ, qui nos, nullis nostris suffragántibus méritis, ex peculiári Sacratíssimi Cordis tui múnere in sacerdótum tuórum órdinem aggregásti, ad illa implénda vota, quæ grátia tua méntibus nostris aspírat, auxiliántis misericórdiæ tuæ nobis larga dona concéde. Tu qui pro nobis sanctificásti teípsum, ut simus et ipsi sancti in veritáte (cfr. Ioan. XVII, 19), fac, ut a via, quæ tu es, numquam digrediéntes, in doctrína tua sollértes, in exsequéndis legis tuæ præcéptis fidéles, suavíssimi Cordis tui imáginem in nostros mores referámus, et in te et per te in ómnibus rebus Patri placeámus cælésti.

Respléndeat in nobis cum prudéntia omnis forma iustítiæ, et castæ temperántiæ moderatióni fortitúdinis robur adiungátur. Péctori nostro sincéra fides insídeat, immortálium bonórum spes solácii rorem infúndat; ibíque cæléstis ignis flamméscat, quem Cor tuum fornax ardens caritátis accéndat. Fac ut in verbis tuis, in quibus ætérna sapiéntia refúlget, iugis meditátio nostra versétur, et unde ipsi páscimur, oves gregis tui, curam nostram, pascámus. Qui Evangélio tuo adversántur, unitátis nostræ vereántur compáginem, neque ullo modo in nobis quidquam deprehéndant, quod Ecclésiæ tuæ, Matri nostræ, expérti rugæ et máculæ, ímputent. Fac dénique ut non nostras utilitátes, sed tuam glóriam sectántes, usque ad extrémum hálitum in offício nostro, rectæ voluntátis consciéntia pura, perstémus; et cum corpus nostrum moriétur, te, quem in terris habémus ductórem et cómitem, in Sanctórum splendóribus ætérnum præmium sortiámur. Qui vivis et regnas cum Deo Patre in unitáte Spíritus Sancti per ómnia sæcula. Amen.

II

PRAYER TO BE SAID BY THE LAITY

O Jesus, eternal High Priest, Good Shepherd, Font of Life, who by a special favor of Thy most tender Heart hast given to us our priests in order to accomplish in us those holy ideals with which thy grace inspires our hearts, let thy mercy, we beseech Thee, come to the aid of our priests.

Grant them, O Jesus, lively faith in their works, unshakeable hope in their trials and fervent charity in their intentions. May Thy word, radiant with eternal Wisdom, become through continual meditation, the never-failing nourishment of their interior life; may the examples of Thy Life and Passion be renewed in their conduct and sufferings for our instruction and as a light and consolation in our sorrows.

Grant, O Lord, that our priests, free from all earthly attachments and solicitous for Thy glory alone, may persevere to their last breath in the fulfillment of duty and in purity of conscience. And when in death they deliver into your hands a task well done may they have in Thee, Lord Jesus, their Master on earth, the eternal reward of the crown of justice in the glory of the Saints. Amen.

An indulgence of 1000 days   (S. P. Ap. July 17, 1956).

INDEX

ANALYTICAL AND ALPHABETICAL

(The references are to the numbers prefixed to the prayers, etc.)

Act of Charity, Heroic, 593.

Adoration, Acts of:
To the Holy Trinity, 12a, 45.
To God, 46, 61, 63.
To Jesus Christ, 95, 99.
To the Holy Eucharist, 137, 146–147, 177–178.
To Jesus Crucified, 191.

Agnes (St.), Virgin and Martyr: Prayers, 560.

Agony, For those in their last: Invocation, 229, 239; prayers, 204, 670; devout exercise, 669; prayer, 671.

Alms for missions, 609.

Aloysius (St.), Gonzaga:
Devotions in honor of, 495; prayers, 496; prayer to be said by young men, 768; invocation to be said by clerics, 730; prayer by him, 343.

Alphonsus (St.), M. de' Liguori:
Prayer, 521; prayers and invocations composed by, 15, 99, 182, 334, 335, 342, 358, 565.

Altar, privileged:
During the period of eight days from the Commemoration of All Souls inclusive, 591; during the Forty Hours' Adoration, 169; Visit to the seven altars in the Vatican Basilica, 775.

Altars, The Seven, in the Vatican Basilica: a visit, 775.

Ambrosian Hymn, 684.

Angels, The Holy:
Invocations, 440, 441, 452, 454; prayer, 455.

Guardian (See *Guardian Angel*).

Angelus, The, 331

Anne (St.), mother of the B. V. M.:
Devotions, 493; prayer, 494.

Annunciation of the B. V. M.:
A novena, 326; prayer on the feast of, 627.

Anthony (St.), Abbot:
Prayer, 529.

Anthony (St.) of Padua:
Devotions, 530; responsory (Si quaeris miracula), 531; prayer of impetration, 532; prayer of thanksgiving, 533.

Apostles, The Holy:
St. Peter, 480–484.
St. Paul, 480–482, 485–486, 709.
St. John, 487, 745.
St. Jude Thaddæus, 488.
St. James, 489.

Apostles, Queen of (B. V. M.):
Invocation, 437.

Archangels, The:
St. Michael, 442–447.
St. Gabriel, 448–449.
St. Raphael, 450–451, 664–665.

Archbasilica, Lateran (See *Visits*).

Assembly about to transact public business (See *Divine Help*).

Assistance of the sick, by priests, 754.

Assumption of the B. V. M.:
A novena, 326; prayer on the feast of, 627.

August, Month of:
Dedicated to the Most Pure Heart of Mary, 389.
Augustine, (St.): A prayer by him, 341.

Badge of the Sacred Heart, 251.
Baptismal Vows, Renewal of, 679.
Basilica, Vatican (See *Visits*).
Benedict (St.), Joseph Labre: Prayers, 514.
Benefactors: prayers for, 666.
Bernardine (St.), of Siena: A prayer by, 475.
Bible: Reading of, 694.
Bishops:
Kissing the ring, 677c.
Prayers to be said by them when they assume the Pontifical vestments, 748b.
Blase (St.), Bishop and Martyr: Prayer, 537.
Blasphemers: invocation for the conversion of, 241.
Blasphemy: acts of reparation for, 8, 696.
Against the B. V. M., 328–329.
Against the Immaculate Conception, 367.
Blessed Sacrament:
Accompanying the Bl. Sacr. when It is carried as Viaticum or in solemn procession to the sick, 143–144.
Visit to Repository on Holy Thursday or Good Friday, 145.
In public processions, 150. (See *Eucharist.*)
Blessed Sacrament, Our Lady of the:
Prayer for daily Communion, 418.
Blessing, Papal, given by Pope, 695.
Bonaventure (St.):
Prayer by him, 66.

Books:
Prayer to St. Paul the Apostle for the printing of good books, 709.
Bridget (St.):
Prayer for the conversion of non-Catholics, 566, 629.

Calamity, Invocation, 724; prayer, 725; prayers in time of, 726.
Camillus (St.) de Lellis:
Devotions, 506; prayer for the sick, 668.
Candidates for the priesthood:
Invocation to be said by them, 727.
Cardinals of the holy Roman Church:
Kissing the ring, 677b.
Carmel, Our Lady of Mount:
Invocation, 405; prayer, 406.
Catechism, See *Christian Doctrine.*
Catechists, 693.
Catherine (St.), Virgin and Martyr:
Prayers, 569, 761–762.
Catherine (St.) of Siena:
Prayers, 402, 579–580.
Cemetery:
Visit to, 592.
Cenacle, Our Lady of the:
Prayer, 410.
Chaplains, military (See *Clerics*).
Chaplet:
In honor of the Sacred Heart of Jesus, 255.
of the Holy Ghost, 286.
of the twelve stars, 330.
of B. V. M. of the Rosary, 395.
Charity:
Invocation to obtain, 74; prayer for an increase of, 42; heroic act, 593. (See *Theological virtues*).
Chastity:
Prayer to be said by clerics in Holy Orders and by priests

to implore the grace of preserving chastity, 734. (See *Continence*).

Child Jesus:
Devotions, 123–125; prayers, 126–130.

Children:
Invocation to Jesus for, 78.
First Communion, 151–152.
Prayer to Jesus the Friend of children, 662.
Prayer to be said by children, 767.
Prayer to be said by them for their living parents, 771.
for deceased parents, 598.

Christian Doctrine, 693.

Christmas: (See *Nativity*).

Church:
Prayers for the, 107, 219, 288, 385, 412, 476, 511; prayers against the persecutors of the, 717–718. Visit to a church (See *Visits*).

Circumcision of Our Lord:
Prayer on the feast of, 129.

Clement Hofbauer, (St.):
A prayer by him, 699.

Clergy:
To implore holiness for the: invocation, 656.
Act of oblation, 658; prayers, 659–660.
A day dedicated to the sanctification of, 657. (See *Priests, Clerics*).

Clerics:
Prayers for military chaplains for their preservation in holiness of life, 661.
Prayers to be said by clerics: Invocations, 729–730.
When putting on the surplice, 728.
Reciting the Divine Office before the Blessed Sacrament, 731.
On the day when they receive a major Order, 732.

Clerics in Holy Orders, prayers to be said by them:

To lead a holy life, 733, 416.
To preserve their chastity, 734.
Before and after the Divine Office, 735, 737.
Recitation of the Divine Office before the Blessed Sacrament, 736.
For grace to preach holily and fruitfully, 738.
(See *Priests, Clergy*).

Colleges, Consecration of: to the Sacred Heart of Jesus, 705 note.

Columbanus (St.):
A prayer for missions to the heathen, 549, 618.

Comforter of the Afflicted (B. V. M.):
Prayers, 419–420.

Communion, Holy:
Prayer for daily Communion, 101, 163, 418.
First Communion, 151–152.
Prayers before, 153–158, 351, 691.
Prayers after, 131, 159–162.
Spiritual communion, 164.
For the missions, 610.
For gaining indulgences, XIII (Can. 931).

Commutation of pious exercises, XV (Can. 935).

Conception, Immaculate (B. V. M.):
Invocations, 353–359.
Little Office, 360.
Devotions, 361–367.
Prayers, 368–372.
Prayers to be said on the feast of, 96, 373–374, 627.
Prayer for the conversion of non-Catholics, 627.
For a happy death, 642.

Confession, Sacramental: prayers to be said by Priests:
Before and after their own confession, 743.
Before they hear confessions, 753.

For gaining indulgences, XIII
(Can. 931).
Confidence, Our Lady of:
Invocation, 302; prayer, 416.
Confiteor, 691.
Congress, Eucharistic:
Prayer in preparation for, 601
Indulgences, 602–603.
Conscience, Examination of:
Indulgence, 690.
Consecration:
To God, 56.
To Jesus the Eternal Wisdom
through Mary, 96.
To the Sacred Heart of Jesus,
257–260.
To the Holy Ghost, 289.
To the B. V. M., 336, 340.
To the Pure Heart of Mary,
390–391.
Consecration of Families:
To the Holy Family, 706.
To the Sacred Heart of Jesus,
705.
**Consecration of groups of the
faithful.** (e.g.,religious com-
munities, parishes, colleges,
schools, etc.) to the Sacred
Heart of Jesus, 705 note.
Of priests to the Sacred Heart
of Jesus, 744.
Of students to the B.V. M.,763.
Continence, to obtain:
Invocations, 354, 358, 387,
712–713.
Prayers, 496, 547, 560, 714–
715. (See *Chastity*).
Contrition, Act of: 36, 286.
Conversion:
Of non-Catholics, 621–632.
Of sinners, 229.
Of lapsed Catholics, 233.
Of blasphemers, 241.
Of Russia, 631–632.
Corpus Christi, Feast of:
Sequence, 167.
Prayers for a novena, 170.
The Feast and its Octave, 171.
A triduum during the Octave,
172.
Prayer on the feast of, 185.

Crib of Our Lord Jesus Christ:
A visit to the Basilica of St.
Mary Major in Rome, 777.
Cross, The Holy:
Invocations, 186–188.
Stations of the Cross, 194.
Prayers, 210, 212.
Mission Cross, 635.
Sign of the Cross, 678. (See
Jesus Crucified).

Day, New Year's:
Devotions, 681.
Day, the last day of the year:
An act of thanksgiving on,
684b, 685a.
Devotion for the last half-
hour of, 685a.
Day:
Meaning of, XII (Can. 923).
Eucharistic, 176
For the Missions, 611.
Dedicated to the Pope, 651.
Dedicated to the Sanctifica-
tion of the Clergy, 657.
On New Year's Day, prayers
for God's help, 681.
On the last day of the year,
prayers of Thanksgiving,
684b, 685a.
For the Sanctification of feast
days, 700.
Plenary Indulgence on the day
of reception of major Or-
ders, 732.
Prayer to be said by priests on
the anniversary of their
ordination, 746.
Deaf-Mutes: Indulgence for
Visit to a church, 772
Death, A happy (bona mors):
Invocations, 19, 40, 239, 273,
307, 636–637.
To escape eternal death, 107.
Act of accepting one's own
death at the hands of God,
638.
Devotions, 204, 639–640;
prayers, 641–649. (See
Hour of death, Agony).

December, Month of:
Devoted to the Immaculate Conception of the B. V. M., 364.

Dedication of mankind to Jesus Christ the King, 271.

Deliverance, Our Lady of: Invocation, 425.

Devotions in honor of:
The Holy Trinity, 47–48; the Name of Jesus, 118–120; the Infant Jesus, 123–125; the Blessed Sacrament, 168–176; Jesus Crucified, 195–198; the Precious Blood, 217; the Sacred Heart, 248–254; Jesus Christ the King, 270; the Holy Ghost, 284–285.

The B. V. M., 325–327; the Immaculate Conception, 361–367; Our Lady of Sorrows, 379–382; the Pure Heart of Mary, 388–389; Our Lady of the Rosary, 396–398; Our Lady of Ransom, 421; Our Lady of Guadalupe, 422–423; Our Lady of Good Counsel, 428. St. Michael the Archangel, 445; St. Gabriel the Archangel, 448; St. Raphael the Archangel, 450; the Guardian Angel, 453; St. Joseph, 465–469. (See also *Novena* and *Triduum*).

Divine Help:
Invocation for, 20.
To implore before any action, 680.
On the first day of the year, 681.
Before assembly to transact some public business, 682.

Divine Praises, The: 696.

Dominic (St.):
Devout exercise, 541; prayers, 402, 542.

Doxology, 47.
With ejaculation, 119.

Earthquake:
Prayer in time of, 719.

Eastern Churches:
Prayer for their return to unity, 630.

Edmund (St.):
Prayer of, 55.

Ejaculations: (See *Invocations*).

Elizabeth (St.):
Prayer, 559.

Emigrants:
Prayer to Jesus for, 663; to St. Raphael the Archangel, 664.

Ephrem (St.), the Syrian:
Prayer of, 371.

Epiphany of our Lord:
Prayer on the feast of, 130.

Erring brethren:
Invocation for their conversion, 233 (See *Non-Catholics*).

Eucharist, The Blessed:
Acts of faith before, 79, 133; invocations, 131–141; devotions, 142–150.
First Communion, 151–152.
Prayers before Communion, 153–158, 351, 691.
Thanksgiving after Communion, 131, 159–162.
Prayer for the spread of daily Communion, 163, 418.
Spiritual Communion, 164.
Hymn, rhythm, and sequence, 165–167; devout practices, 168–176.
Acts of adoration, reparation, and thanksgiving, 177–179; prayers, 180–185.

Eucharistic Congress, (See *Congress*).

Eucharistic Day, 176.

Eucharistic Month, 175.

Eugene I (St.), Pope:
Prayer, 558.

Evening Prayers: (See *Night prayers*).

Examination of Conscience:
Indulgence, 690.
Exercises:
For vocations to the priest-hood and the religious life, 607.
For foreign missions, 609–611.
For a happy death, 639–640.
For the sick, 667.
For those in their last agony, 669.
Exercises, Spiritual: 689a.
(See *Retreats* and *Missions*).
Expectation of the B. V. M.:
Novena, 326.
Exposition, Forty Hours', 169.

Faith:
Prayer for the increase of, 38.
Prayer, 42.
Acts of faith before the Blessed Sacrament, 79, 133.
Prayer for the preservation of, 699.
Invocation to obtain unity in faith, 30 (See *Theological Virtues*).
Faithful Departed, The:
Invocations, 13, 229, 582–583; prayers, 107, 219, 594–600.
Office, 584; psalms and sequence, 585–587.
Devout practices, 588–592; heroic act of charity, 593.
Prayer for deceased parents, 598;
For deceased priests, 599.
For deceased person by name, 600.
To Our Lady of Intercession, 434.
Family, Consecration of the Christian:
To the Sacred Heart, 705.
To the Holy Family of J.M.J., 706.
Invocation, 236; prayers, 707–708.
Recitation of rosary in a family group, 395b.

Family, The Holy:
Invocations, 273–274, 636; prayers, 275, 276, 643;
Consecration of families to, 706.
Father, God the:
Prayers, 65–69, 125, 219, 220.
Feast Days:
Prayer for the sanctification of, 700.
Fidelis (St.) of Sigmaringen:
Responsory, 548.
First Friday:
In honor of the Sacred Heart, 252.
Five Wounds, The:
(See *Wounds*).
Forty Hours' Adoration:
Exposition of the Blessed Sacrament, 169.
Founders, The Seven Holy, of the Order of the Servants of Mary.
Prayers, 524–525.
Frances (St.) of Rome:
Prayer, 570.
Francis (St.) of Assisi:
Devout practice, 515; hymn, 516.
Prayers, 517–518.
Prayer of, 95.
Francis (St.) of Paula:
A devout exercise, 552.
Francis (St.) Xavier:
Prayer, 499; the novena of grace, 500.
Friday, First:
In honor of the Sacred Heart, 252.
Friday, Good: (See *Good Friday*).
Fridays:
5 Fridays before the Feast of the Sacred Heart, 254.
7 Fridays before the Feast of the Seven Sorrows of Mary, 382.
13 Fridays in honor of St. Francis of Paula, 552.

Gabriel (St.) the Archangel:
Devout practice, 448; prayer, 449.

Gabriel (St.) of the Sorrowful Virgin:
Devotions, 544; prayers to, 545.

Gemma (St.) Galgani:
Prayers by, 209.

Genuflection, before the Blessed Sacrament, 146a and b.

Good Counsel, Our Lady of:
Devout practices, 428; prayer, 429.

Good Friday:
A visit to the Blessed Sacrament in the repository, 145.
Tenebrae, 189.
Meditation on the Passion for 3 hours, 195.
Prayer, 214.
Meditation in honor of Our Lady Sorrowing, 379.

Good Hope, Our Lady of:
Prayer, 416.
Recitation of the doxology before a Crucifix on any Friday, 196.
Recitation of prayers at the sound of the bell in memory of our dying Saviour, 197.

Gospel:
Assistance at the explanation of, 692a.

Grace, Our Lady of:
Prayer, 433.

Gradual Psalms: 686.

Greeting, A Christian, 697.

Gregory (St.) Vii:
Prayer, 511.

Grignion de Montfort (St.), L. M.:
Prayer by, 96.

Guadalupe, Our Lady of:
Visit to her image, 422; devout exercise, 423; prayer, 424.

Guardian Angel:
Invocation, 452; devout practice, 453.

Heart of Jesus:
(See *Sacred Heart*).

Heart of Mary:
Invocations, 386–387.
Devout practices, 388–389.
Act of Consecration, 390–391.
Prayers, 392–393.

Help (See *Divine Help*).

Help of Christians, Our Lady:
Prayers, 411–414.

Heroic Act of Charity, 593.

Holy Ghost:
Invocations, 277–281; sequence, 282; hymn, 283; devotions, 284–285; chaplet, 286; prayers, 287–291.
Prayer before assembly to transact some public business, 682.

Holy Hour, the: 168.

Holy Land:
Indulgences of the, 673.

Holy Thursday:
Visit to the Blessed Sacrament, 145; Tenebrae, 189.

Holy Week:
Visit to the Blessed Sacrament in the repository on Holy Thursday or Good Friday, 145.
Meditation on Our Lord's Passion on Good Friday, 195.
Office of Tenebrae, 189.

Homobonus, (St.):
Prayer, 539.

Hope:
Prayer for an increase of, 42 (See *Theological virtues*).

Hope, Our Lady of Good:
Prayer, 416.

Hour of Death:
Plenary indulgences to be gained at, 4, 36, 113, 292, 332–333, 367b, 452, 638, 694.

Humility:
Invocation to obtain, 387; prayer, 547.

Hymns in honor of:
The Name of Jesus, 115–117.
The Blessed Sacrament, 165.
Jesus Crucified, 193.

Precious Blood, 216.
Sacred Heart, 246–247.
Holy Ghost, 283.
B. V. M., 321–324.
St. Michael the Archangel, 444.
St. Joseph, 463–464.
St. Pius V, 504.
St. Francis of Assisi, 516.

Ignatius (St.) of Loyola:
Devout exercises, 497; prayers, 498–499.
Prayer of St. Ignatius, 52.
Images:
Prayers before an image:
Of Christ Crucified, 196, 201.
Of the Sacred Heart, 248, 260.
Of the B. V. M., 327, 342.
Of Our Lady of the Rosary of Pompeii, 400.
Of Our Lady of Guadalupe, 422.
Of St. Joseph, 469.
Of St. Aloysius, 495d.
Of St. Stanislaus Kostka, 501d.
Of St. John Berchmans, 526d.
Of St. Gabriel of the Sorrowful Mother, 544b.
Of St. Margaret Mary Alacoque, 571.
Of St. Theresa of the Infant Jesus, 575a.
Imitation of Christ:
Prayers from, 98, 741.
Immaculate Conception of the B. V. M.:
Invocations, 353–359.
Little Office, 360.
Devotions, 361–367; prayers, 368–372.
Prayers to be said on the feast of, 96, 373–374, 627.
Prayer for the conversion of non-Catholics, 627.
Indulgences:
Application of XIII (Can. 930).
Attached to one and same thing, XIV, (Can. 933).

Attached to Rosaries, cessation of, XII, (Can. 924); inability to hold Rosaries, XVI, footnote 6b.
Cessation of, XIV (Can. 934, No. 2). See also footnote 5, XVI.
Communion for gaining of, XIII, (Can. 931).
Conditions, usual, for gaining, explained, IX, No. 4.
Confession for gaining, XIII (Can. 931).
Daily plenary, XII (Can. 921).
"Day," meaning of, XII (Can. 923).
Deaf-Mutes, XV (Can. 936); 772.
Intention required for, XII (Can. 925, No. 2).
For work to which already bound, XIV (Can. 932).
Partial, frequency of, XIII, (Can. 928, No. 2).
Plenary: usual conditions for, IX, No. 4; for feasts of Our Lord and Blessed Virgin, XI, (Can. 921); daily, XI, (Can. 921); attached to feasts, XII, (Can. 922); state of grace required for, XII, (Can. 925); "day," meaning of, XII, (Can. 923); confession for, XIII, (Can. 931, Nos. 1, 2, 3).
Prayers, how they may be said for gaining, XIV, (Can. 934, No. 3).
Prayer for intentions of Sovereign Pontiff, for gaining, XIV (Can. 934). See also XV, footnote, 4, a.
State of grace required for gaining, XII, (Can. 925).
Infant Jesus: (See *Child Jesus*).
Instructors of deaf-mutes:
Indulgence for visit to a church, 772.
Intercession, Our Lady of:
Prayer, 434.

James (St.) The Apostle:
Prayer, 489.
January, Month of:
Dedicated to the Holy Name
of Jesus, 118.
Jerome (St.) Emilian:
Prayer of, 71.
Jesus Christ:
Invocations, 70–94.
Acts of adoration and thanks-
giving, 95.
Act of Consecration, 96;
prayers, 97–112.
Name of Jesus, 113–122, 274.
Child Jesus, 123–130.
In the Blessed Sacrament,
131–185.
Jesus Crucified, 186–214.
Precious Blood, 215–222.
Sacred Heart, 223–267.
Jesus Christ the King, 268–
272.
Jesus Crucified:
Ejaculation during the eleva-
tion at Mass, 132a.
Invocations, 186–188.
Office of Tenebrae, 189.
Office of the Passion, 190.
Adoration and thanksgiving,
191–192; hymn, 193.
Stations of the Cross, 194.
Devotions, 195–198.
The Five Wounds, 199–203.
Seven Last Words on the
Cross, 204.
Prayers, 205–214. (See *Cross,
The Holy*).
Joachim (St.):
Invocation, 490; prayers, 491–
492.
Joan (St.) of Arc:
Invocation, 573.
John (St.), the Apostle and
Evangelist:
Prayer, 487.
Prayer to be said by priests,
745.
John (St.), the Baptist:
Devotion, 456; prayers, 457.
John (St.) Berchmans:
Devotions, 526; prayers, 527.

John (St.) Bosco:
Prayer of, 556.
John (St.) of the Cross:
Prayer, 503.
John (St.) Baptist de la Salle:
Prayer, 540.
John (St.) of Matha:
Prayer, 534.
Joseph (St.) Calasanctius:
Prayer to, 536.
Prayer composed by, 330.
Joseph (St.), Spouse of the
B. V. M.:
Invocations, 273–274, 458–
460, 636.
Little Office, 461.
Litany, 462; hymns, 463–464;
devotions, 465–469; pray-
ers, 470–479.
For the sanctification of holy-
days, 700.
Prayer before celebrating
Mass, 747b.
Journey:
Prayers for those undertaking
a, 665.
Jude (St.) the Apostle:
Prayer, 488.
Juliana (St.) Falconieri:
Prayer, 563.
July, Month of:
Dedicated to the Precious
Blood, 217; prayer, 219.
June, Month of:
Dedicated to the Sacred
Heart, 253.

King, Jesus Christ the:
Invocations, 82, 268–269.
Novena or triduum, 270.
Act of dedication, 271.
Prayer, 272
Kingdom of Christ:
Invocations, 82, 228, 268, 573.
Kissing the palms of the
hands:
Of newly-ordained priests,
676b.
Kissing the ring:
Of a Pope, a Cardinal, a

Bishop, or a Prefect Apostolic, 677.
Knowledge:
Prayers to obtain, 520, 763–765. (See *Students, Wisdom*).

Labor, mental or physical:
Invocation in the midst of, 766.
Labre (St.) Benedict Joseph:
Prayers, 514.
Last day of the Year:
Prayers of thanksgiving, 684b, 685a.
Lawrence (St.) Martyr:
Prayer, 554.
Leonard (St.) of Port Maurice:
Invocation by, 70.
Litanies:
Holy Name of Jesus, 114.
Sacred Heart, 245.
B. V. M., 319.
St. Joseph, 462.
All Saints, 687; on the feast of St. Mark, Evangelist, 687a.
Louis (St.), Bishop and Confessor:
Prayer, 528.
Lucy (St.), Virgin and Martyr:
Prayers, 561–562.
Lucy (St.) Filippini:
Prayer, 578.

Magnificat: canticle of the B. V. M., 320.
March, Month of:
In honor of St. Joseph, 466.
Margaret (St.) of Cortona:
Prayer, 564
Margaret (St.) Mary Alacoque:
Devotion, 571; prayers to, 572.
Prayers by, 69, 232.
Mark (St.) the Evangelist:
Litany of the Saints on the feast of, 687a.

Married People: prayers to be said by, 769–770.
Mary, The Blessed Virgin:
Invocations, 80, 292–317, 713.
Thanksgiving for the gifts bestowed upon, 47.
Invocation of the name of, 292.
Little Office, 318.
Litany, 319.
Magnificat, 320.
Hymns, 321–324; devotions, 325–327.
Act of reparation, 328–329.
The crown of twelve stars, 330.
Prayers to, 331–352.
Immaculate Conception, 353–374.
Mary Sorrowing, 375–385.
Heart of Mary, 386–393.
The Holy Rosary, 394–404.
Our Lady of Mount Carmel, 405–406.
Mary, The Blessed Virgin under divers titles:
Our Lady of Pity, 407.
Of Divine Providence, 408–409.
Of the Cenacle, 410.
Help of Christians, 411–414.
Queen of Prophets, 415.
Mother of Confidence, 302, 416.
Our Lady of Reparation, 417.
Our Lady of the Blessed Sacrament, 418.
Comforter of the Afflicted, 419–420.
Our Lady of Ransom, 421.
Our Lady of Guadalupe, 422–424.
Our Lady of Deliverance, 425.
Our Lady of Perpetual Help, 426–427.
Our Lady of Good Counsel, 428–429.
Queen of Peace, 430–431.
Mother of Orphans, 432.
Mother of Grace, 433.
Our Lady of Intercession, 434.

Our Lady of La Salette, 435–436.
Queen of the Apostles, 437.
Refuge of Sinners, 438.
Our Lady of the Sacred Heart, 439.
Mass:
On Christmas Eve, 123a.
In reparation for injuries to the Blessed Sacrament, 174b.
Invocations during the elevation, 132–133.
Invocations after the Consecration, 139.
Act of Offering, 68.
Adoration at the sound of the Consecration bell, 142.
Application in reparation, 173.
Serving at Mass, 674.
After a low Mass, 675.
First Mass, assisting at it, 676; indulgence for priest saying Mass the first time, 742.
Prayer before and after celebrating, 747–752.
May, Month of:
In honor of the B. V. M., 325.
Mental Prayer, 688.
Michael (St.) Archangel:
Invocations, 442–443; hymn, 444; devotion, 445; prayers, 446–447.
Michael (St.) de'Santi:
Prayer, 507.
Mission Day: 611.
Missions for the Faithful:
Prayer for success of, 633; prayer after, 634.
Mission Crosses, 635.
Missions to the Heathen:
Invocation to St. Theresa of the Child Jesus, 574.
Assisting, 609.
Devotions, 609–611.
Mission day, 611.
Prayers, 612–620.
Missions, Parochial:
Prayers, 633–634.

Month of:
January, 118; March, 466; May, 325; June, 253; July, 217, 219; August, 389; September, 381; October, 398; November, 589; December, 364; Eucharistic, 175.
Devotions, Beginning and conclusion of, X, No. 8.
Monthly recollection, 689b.
Morning Prayers:
Invocation, 21; doxology, 47; prayers, 60–61, 108, 331.
Mount Carmel, Our Lady of:
Invocation, 405; prayer, 406.

Name of God:
Ejaculations, 8.
Name of Jesus:
Invocations, 113, 119, 274.
Litany, 114; hymns, 115–117.
Devotions, 118–120; prayers, 121–122.
Name of Joseph:
Invocation, 274, 460.
Name of Mary:
Invocation, 274, 292.
Nativity of Our Lord:
Midnight Mass and Office, 123a and b.
Nativity of the B. V. M.:
Novena, 326.
Prayer on the feast of, 627.
New Year's Day:
Prayers for divine assistance, 681.
Nicholas (St.), Bishop and Confessor:
Invocation, 550; prayer, 551.
Night Prayers:
Invocation, 21; doxology, 47 prayers, 62–63, 99, 331.
Non-Catholics, prayers for the conversion of:
Invocations, 233, 621; devout exercise for the unity of the Church, 622; prayers, 623–632.
Noon, Prayers at:
Doxology, 47; prayers, 331.

November, Month of: 589; recitation of Psalm De profundis, 585.

Novena:
Before the Nativity of Our Lord, 124.
From the 16th to the 24th day of any month, 125.
Before the Feast of Corpus Christi, 170.
Of reparation to the Blessed Sacrament, 174.
In honor of the Holy Trinity, 48.
Of the Sacred Heart, 250.
Of Christ the King, 270.
Of the Holy Ghost, 284.
Of the Nativity, Presentation, Annunciation, Visitation, Expectation, Purification and Assumption of the B. V. M., 326; of the Immaculate Conception, 361; of Mary Sorrowing, 380; of the Pure Heart of Mary, 388; of Our Lady of the Rosary, 396; of Our Lady of the Rosary of Pompeii, 402–403.
Of St. Michael the Archangel, 445; of St. Gabriel the Archangel, 448; of St. Raphael the Archangel, 450; of the Guardian Angel, 453.
Of St. John the Baptist, 456; of St. Joseph, 467; of Ss. Peter and Paul, 481; of St. Anne, 493b; of St. Aloysius Gonzaga, 495c; of St. Francis Xavier, 500; of St. Stanislaus Kostka, 501c; of St. Paul of the Cross, 508; of St. Vincent de Paul, 512; of St. Francis of Assisi, 415c; of St. John Berchmans, 526c.
For the faithful departed, 588.

Nuns:
Recitation of the Divine Office before the Blessed Sacrament by, 758. (See *Religious*.)

Octave, Unity, 622.

October Month of:
In honor of the Holy Rosary, 398.

Offerings for the Missions, 609.

Office, Divine:
Assistance at the Divine Office on Christmas Eve, 123b.
Recitation of, before the Blessed Sacrament:
For all clerics, 731.
For those in Holy Orders, 736.
For nuns, 758.
Prayers before and after, 735, 737.

Offices:
Tenebrae, 189.
Passion of Our Lord, 190.
Sacred Heart, 244.
B. V. M., 318; Immaculate Conception, 360.
St. Joseph, 461.
The faithful departed, 584.

Ordination, Prayer on anniversary of, 746.

Ornaments of Churches:
Prayer to be said when engaged in making or repairing, 710.

Orphans, Our Lady of:
Ejaculation, 432.

Pancratius (St.), Martyr:
Prayer, 555.

Pardon for sins: 27, 691.

Parents:
Prayer to be said by them, for their children, 770; by children for their parents, 771.

Parishes, their consecration to the Sacred Heart, 705, note.

Paschal (St.) Baylon:
Responsory, 543.

Passion of Our Lord:
Office, 190.

Meditation on Good Friday, 195.
Devout practice at the sound of the bell on Friday, 197.
Pastors:
Prayer for them, 672.
Patron Saint:
Prayer, 581.
Paul (St.) the Apostle:
Invocation, 480; devout practice, 481; prayers, 482, 485–486; for the publishing of good books, 709.
Paul (St.) of the Cross:
Devout exercise, 508; prayers, 509–510.
Peace:
Invocations for, 82, 243, 268; prayers, 107, 701–704 (See *Queen of Peace*).
Peace, Our Lady Queen of:
Invocation, 430; prayer, 431. (See *Peace*)
Penitential Psalms, 686.
Penitential Wand:
Indulgences, 781.
Pentecost:
Prayer on feast of, 291.
Peregrine (St.) Laziosi (Pellegrino):
Prayer, 553.
Perpetual Help, Our Lady of:
Invocation, 426; prayers, 427.
Peter (St.) the Apostle:
Invocation, 480; devout exercise, 481; prayers, 482–484.
Visit to the tomb and statue in the Vatican Basilica, 774.
Peter (St.) Fourier:
Prayer, 535.
Philip (St.) Neri:
Invocation, 246; prayers, 547.
Pilgrimage, Roman, 773.
Pity, Our Lady of:
Prayers, 407.
Pius V (St.) Pope:
Hymn, 504; prayers, 505.
Pompeii, Our Lady of: (See *Rosary*).

Pope, The:
Invocation for, 650.
Day dedicated to, 651.
Prayers, 385, 511, 558, 652–655.
Prayers for the intentions of, XIV (Can. 934). See also XV, footnote 4, a.
Kissing the ring of, 677a.
Blessing of, also by radio, 695.
Portiuncula: a plenary indulgence *toties quoties*, on the 2nd of August, 698.
Praises, Divine, 696.
Prayer, mental, 688.
Prayers or devotions in honor of:
The Child Jesus, 125–126.
The Five Wounds, 200.
The Precious Blood, 220.
The Holy Eucharist, 177–178.
The Seven Last Words on the Cross, 204.
The B. V. M.: Our Lady of Sorrows, 383; the Pure Heart of Mary, 392; Our Lady of the Rosary of Pompeii, 402–403.
St. John the Baptist, 457; St. Joseph, 470–471.
Prayers to be said by certain classes of persons:
Clerics in Holy Orders and priests, 733–735; 737–738.
Priests, 740–741; 743–753.
Religious, 757.
Teachers, 761–762.
Students, 763–765.
Children, 767, 771.
Young men, 768.
Married persons, 769.
Parents, 770.
Preachers:
Prayer to be said by, 738.
Precious Blood, The:
Ejaculation at the elevation in Mass, 132b and c.
Invocation, 215.
Hymn, 216.
Devotions in July, 217.
Prayers, 218–222.

Prefect Apostolic:
Kissing the ring of, 677c.
Presentation of the B. V. M.:
A novena in honor of, 326.
Priesthood:
Invocation to be said by aspirants to, 727.
Priests:
Newly-ordained, 676a, 742; kissing the palms of their hands, 676b.
Prayer for a deceased priest, 599.
Prayers to be said by priests: invocation, 739; for sanctity of life, 416, 733, 740–741; for the preservation of chastity, 734; before and after the Office, 735, 737; recitation of the Office before the Blessed Sacrament, 736; for the grace of preaching holily and fruitfully, 738; indulgence at First Mass, 742; before and after confession, 743; form of consecration to the Sacred Heart, 744; to St. John the Apostle, 745; prayer on the anniversary of ordination, 746; before celebrating Mass, 747–749; after celebrating Mass, 750–752; before hearing confessions, 753; assisting the sick, 754. (See *Clergy* and *Clerics*).
Privileged Altars:
During the period of eight days from the Commemoration of All Souls inclusive, 591.
During the Forty Hours Adoration, 169.
Indult of a personal privileged altar on the final day of June when this month is solemnly celebrated in honor of the Sacred Heart, 253.
For priests who make the heroic act of charity, 593b.

Processions, Eucharistic, 144, 150.
Prophets, Queen of:
Prayer, 415.
Providence, Mother of Divine:
Prayers, 408–409.
Psalms:
De Profundis, 585.
Miserere, 586.
Gradual and penitential, 686.
Public religious exercises, explained, X, No. 7.
Purification of the B. V. M.:
A novena in honor of, 326; prayer on the feast of, 627.
Purity: (See *Continence*).

Ransom, Our Lady of:
A devout exercise, 421.
Raphael (St.) Archangel:
A devout practice, 450; prayer, 451.
Prayers for emigrants, 664; for those taking a journey or a walk, 665.
Reading Sacred Scripture:
Indulgence for, 694.
Recollection, monthly:
Held in common, 689b.
Refuge of Sinners, Our Lady:
Prayer, 438.
Religious:
Prayers to be said by religious: invocation, 755; renewal of religious vows, 756; prayer, 757; recitation by nuns of Divine Office before the Blessed Sacrament, 758.
Religious Communities:
Consecration to the Sacred Heart, 705 note.
Reparation:
Of injuries offered to the Blessed Sacrament, 173–174; to the B. V. M., 328–329.
Of blasphemies against God, 8, 696; against the B. V. M., 328–329, 367.

Reparation, Acts of:
To the Blessed Sacrament, 178–179.
To the Sacred Heart of Jesus, 256–257.
To the B. V. M., 328–329.
Reparation, Our Lady of:
Prayer, 417.
Repository:
Visit on Holy Thursday or Good Friday, 145.
Responsory, in honor of:
St. Anthony of Padua, 531.
St. Paschal Baylon, 543.
St. Fidelis of Sigmaringen, 548.
Retreat:
In common with others, 689a.
Of St. Stanislaus Kostka, 501e.
Reverences:
At the sound of the Consecration bell, 142.
When passing a church or oratory, where the Blessed Sacrament is reserved, 146c.
To the Blessed Sacrament upon entering a church, 147.
Genuflection before the Blessed Sacrament, 146a and b.
Rhythms:
Adoro te devote, 166.
Ave Mater dolorosa, 640.
Ring of Pope, Cardinal, Bishop or Prefect Apostolic:
Indulgence for kissing, 677.
Rita (St.) Widow:
Prayers, 567–568.
Rogation days:
Litany of the Saints, 687a.
Roman Pilgrimage, 773.
Rosary of the B. V. M.: (Our Lady of the Rosary):
Invocation, 394; recitation of the Rosary, 395; devotions, 396–398; prayer, 399.
Rosary of Pompeii, Our Lady of the:
Visit to the image, 400.
Supplication, 401.
Prayers of impetation for a novena or triduum, 402.

Prayers for a novena or triduum of thanksgiving, 403.
Prayer, 404.
For the conversion of non-Catholics, 628.
Rosary of the Seven Dolors of the B. V. M.:
Recitation of, 628.
Russia, for the conversion of:
Invocation, 631; prayer, 632.
Sacred Heart of Jesus, The:
Invocations, 77, 223–243.
Little Office, 244.
Litanies, 245; hymns, 246–247; devotions, 248–254.
Chaplet, 255.
Acts of reparation and consecration, 256–260.
Prayers, 181, 261–267.
Consecration of families, 705.
Consecration of priests, 744.
Sacred Heart, Our Lady of:
Prayer, 439.
Salette, Our Lady of La:
Invocation, 435; prayer, 436.
Salutation, A Christian, 697.
Sanctity: Invocations for obtaining, 15, 303.
Saturdays:
The 12 first Saturdays in honor of the Immaculate Conception, 365.
The 12 Saturdays before the Feast of the Immaculate Conception, 366.
The 1st Saturday of each month in reparation for blasphemies against Mary Immaculate, 367.
The 15 Saturdays in honor of Our Lady of the Rosary, 397.
The 7 Saturdays in honor of Our Lady of Ransom, 421.
Scala Santa:
Visit to the, 778.
Schools:
Dedication of, to the Sacred Heart, 705 note.
Scripture:
Indulgence for reading, 694.

September, Month of:
Dedicated to the Sorrows of Mary, 381.

Sepulchre, or Repository:
Visit to the Blessed Sacrament reserved in, 145.

Sequences:
Lauda Sion (Bl. Sacr.), 167.
Veni Sancte (Holy Ghost), 282.
Stabat Mater, 378.
Sancta Mater (B. V. M. Sorrowing), 639.
Dies irae, (the Holy Souls), 587.

Sermons:
Indulgence for those who hear them, 692, b, c.

Seven Altars in the Vatican Basilica: a visit to, 775.

Seven Holy Founders of the Servites: (See *Founders*).

Sick, The:
Indulgence for accompanying the Blessed Sacrament when It is carried to the sick, 143–144.
Devotions for the sick, 667.
Prayer, 668.
For priests assisting the sick, 754.

Sins:
To obtain pardon for: 27, 691.

Sinners:
An invocation for the conversion of, 229.
Prayers to obtain pardon for sins, 27, 691.
Prayer to our Lady, Refuge of, 438.

Sorrows (Dolors) of the B. V. M.:
Invocations, 375–377; sequence, 378; devotions, 379–382; prayers, 383–385; rhyme, 640.

Spirit, Holy: (See *Holy Ghost*).

Spiritual Communion, 164.
Spiritual visit to the Blessed Sacrament, 149.

Spiritual Exercises: 689a. (See *Missions* and *Retreats*).

State of life:
Prayer for choosing, 711.

Stational churches in Rome:
Visit to, 780.

Statue of (St.) Peter:
Visit to, in Vatican Basilica, 774c.

Stanislaus (St.) Kostka:
Devotions, 501; prayers, 502.

Stephen (St.) Protomartyr:
Prayers, 538.

Students: Prayers to be said by, 520, 763–765. (See *Knowledge, Wisdom*).

Suffrage, Our Lady of: (See *Intercession*).

Sundays:
The 7 Sundays in honor of the Immaculate Conception, 363.
The 12 first Sundays in honor of the Immaculate Conception, 365.
The 15 Sundays in honor of our Lady of the Rosary, 397.
The 5 Sundays in honor of Our Lady of Guadalupe, 423.
The 12 Sundays (and the first of each month) in honor of Our Lady of Good Counsel, 428.
The 7 Sundays in honor of St. Joseph, 465.
The 6 Sundays in honor of St. Aloysius Gonzaga, 495b.
The 10 Sundays in honor of St. Ignatius of Loyola, 497.
The 10 Sundays in honor of St. Stanislaus, 501b.
The 7 Sundays in honor of St. Camillus of Lellis, 506.
The 5 Sundays in honor of St. Francis of Assisi, 515a.
The 6 Sundays in honor of St. Thomas Aquinas, 519.
The 5 Sundays in honor of St. John Berchmans, 526a.
The 13 Sundays in honor of St. Anthony of Padua, 530b.
Indulgence for deaf-mutes on

the XI Sunday after Pente-
cost, 772.
Supplication:
To the B. V. M. of Pompeii,
401.
Surplice:
Invocation to be said by
clerics when putting on, 728.

Tarcisius (St.), Martyr:
Prayers, 557.
Teachers:
Of Christian Doctrine, 693.
Prayers to be said by: invo-
cations, 759–760; prayers to
St. Catherine, 761–762.
Te Deum, 684.
Tenebrae:
Office of, 189.
Teresa (St.) of Avila, Virgin:
Prayer, 565.
Thanksgiving, Prayers of:
To the Blessed Trinity, 16b,
45, 47.
To God, 9.
To God the Father, 123.
After Communion, 159–162.
To the Holy Eucharist, 177.
To Jesus Crucified, 192.
To Our Lady of Pompeii, 403.
To St. Anthony of Padua, 533.
After any action, 683–684a.
On the last day of the year,
684b, 685a.
Through the week, 685b.
Theological Virtues, The:
Acts of, 36–44, 79, 133.
Prayers to obtain, 65.
**Theresa (St.) of the Child
Jesus:**
Invocation, 574; devotions,
575; prayers, 576–577.
For missions to the heathen,
619–620.
For the conversion of Russia,
632.
Thomas (St.) Aquinas.
Devotion, 519; prayer to, 520.
Prayers by, 158, 160, 716, 764.
Thursday:
Holy: (See *Holy Thursday*).

First Thursday of any month:
act of adoration and thanks-
giving, 177.
Tomb of St. Peter, Visit to, in
Vatican Basilica, 774b.
Toties Quoties Indulgence:
On the day on which the
month dedicated to the Sa-
cred Heart is closed, 253.
The Way of the Cross, 194.
For recitation of the Rosary
before the Blessed Sacra-
ment, 395c.
On All Souls' Day, 590.
On the 2nd of August (*the
Portiuncula*), 698.
Visit to Vatican Basilica, 774a;
visit to Lateran Basilica, 776.
Trials, in time of:
Invocations, 720–721; prayers,
722–723.
Tribulations (See *Trials*).
Triduum:
Within the Octave of Corpus
Christi, 172.
In honor of Christ the King,
270.
In honor of Our Lady of Pom-
peii, 402–403.
In honor of St. John the Bap-
tist, 457.
Trinity, The Holy (*Triune
God*):
Invocations, 1–35.
Acts of the theological virtues,
36–44.
Acts of adoration and thanks-
giving, 45–46, 61, 63.
Devotions, 47–48; prayers,
49–64.
Prayer on the feast of, 64.
Tuesdays:
In honor of St. Anne, 493a.
The 13 Tuesdays in honor of
St. Anthony of Padua, 530b.
The 15 Tuesdays in honor of
St. Dominic, 541.

Unity:
Invocation, to obtain unity of
minds and hearts, 10.

Invocation to obtain unity in faith, 30.

Octave, 622.

Prayer for the reunion of Eastern Christians with the Apostolic See, 630.

Devout exercise for the unity of the church, 622

Usual conditions for plenary indulgence, IX, No. 4.

Vestments, Liturgical:

Invocation to be said by those making or repairing, 710.

Prayers to be said by priests and Bishops when putting on liturgical vestments, 748.

Viaticum:

Indulgence for accompanying the, 143.

Vincent (St.) Ferrer:

Prayers to, 522–523.

Vincent (St.) de Paul:

Devotions, 512; prayer, 513.

Vincent (Bl.) Pallotti:

Prayer by, 370.

Virtues, Theological: (See *Theological Virtues*).

Visitation of the B. V. M.:

Indulgences for a novena in honor of, 326.

Visits:

To a cemetery, 592.

To a church on the following feasts: Holy Name of Jesus, 120; Sacred Heart, 249; St. Aloysius Gonzaga, 495a; St. Stanislaus Kostka, 501a; St. Francis of Assisi, 515b; St. John Berchmans, 526b; St. Gabriel of the Sorrowful Mother, 544a; St. Theresa of the Child Jesus, 575b; visit of a church by deaf-mutes, 772.

To an image, (See *Image*).

To the Crib in the Basilica of St. Mary Major in Rome, 777.

To the Blessed Sacrament, 145, 148–149, 171; upon entering a church, 147.

To the Scala Santa in Rome, 778.

To the Vatican Basilica, 774a.

To the Lateran Archbasilica, 776.

To the Seven Altars in the Vatican Basilica, 775.

To the Seven Churches in Rome, 779.

To the tomb and statue of St. Peter in the Vatican Basilica, 774 b and c.

To the Churches of the Stations in Rome, 780.

Vocations to the priesthood and the religious life:

Invocations, 604–606; devotion, 607; prayers, 608.

Vows:

Renewal of Baptismal vows, 679.

Renewal of religious vows, 756.

Walking:

Prayers for those taking a walk, 665

Wand, penitential:

Indulgences, 781.

Way of the Cross, 194.

Wednesday, the 1st W. of the month in honor of St. Joseph, 468.

Wednesday in Holy Week:

Tenebrae, 189.

Wisdom, The Eternal:

Consecration to Jesus through Mary, 96 (See *Knowledge, Students*).

Words, The Seven Last:

Meditation, 195; prayers in memory of, 204.

Wounds, The Five:

Invocation, 199; devotion, 198; prayers, 200–203; hymn, 216.

Young Men:

Prayer to be said by, 768.

INDEX OF MORE FREQUENTLY USED
PRAYERS

Angelus, The, 331
Anima Christi, 131
Ave Maris, 321
Behold O my most loving Jesus, 181
Blessed be holy and immaculate, 356
Divine Praises, 696
En ego, 201
Eternal Father, I unite, 68
Eternal Father, I offer, 219
Genuflection, 146
Give peace, 701
Gloria Patri 3 times, 47
Glorious St. Joseph, 478
Grant me Thy grace, 98
Grant us, dear Joseph, 458
Grant us, Lord Jesus, 643
Guardian of Virgins, 473
Hail, Holy Queen, 332
Hail, Saving Victim, 132
Heart of Jesus burning, 225
Heart of Jesus, I put my trust in Thee, 226
Holy, Holy, Holy, 2
Holy Mother, pierce, 198
Holy Spirit, Spirit of Truth, 277
I adore Thee, eternal Father, 177
Immaculate Queen of peace, 430
In thy conception, 353
Jesus, Mary, Joseph, 255
Jesus, Mary, Joseph, I give, 636
Jesus meek, 227
Jesus my God, 72
Jesus Son of David, 73
Litany of Bl. Virgin, 319
Litany of Holy Name, 114
Litany of Sacred Heart, 245
Lord Jesus Christ, Thou only, 86

Lord Jesus Christ, in union, 97
Lord Jesu, most merciful, 625
Magnificat, 320
Mary, 292
Mary most sorrowful, 376
Mary Mother of God, 294
Mary our hope, 299
May, month, 325
May the most just, 4
Memorare, 339
My God and my all, 5
My God, grant, 6
My Jesus mercy, 70
My Lord Jesus Christ, 182
My Lord and my God, 133
My loving Jesus out of, 260
My Queen, 340
Most dear Lord Jesus Christ, 127
Most holy Virgin immaculate, 342
Most holy and immaculate Virgin Mary, 413
Most Sacred Heart of Jesus, 242; Mass, 675
Most sweet Jesus, Redeemer, 271
New Year, 685
Novena Pentecost, 284
O Holy Spirit, Creator, 288
O Holy Mary, my Mistress, 343
O Joseph, virgin, 477
O Mary conceived, 357
O Mary, conceived (prayer), 642
O Mary, thou didst, 355
O Lord Omnipotent, 51
O Most Holy Heart of Jesus, shower, 262
O Heart most pure of . . . . Mary, 387
O Sacrament most holy, 136

xxxv

O most merciful Jesus, 671
O Sacrum Convivium, 180
O Virgin Mary, Our Lady of Blessed Sacrament, 418
O sweetest Jesus, 256
O sweetest Jesu, 163
Omnipotence of the Father, 53
Prayers after Low Mass, 675
Precious Blood, Offering of, 219
Rosary, 395
Saint Michael the Archangel, 442

Saviour of World, save Russia, 631
Saint Joseph, foster-father, 459
Sign of Cross, 678
Sequence for Pentecost, 282
Suscipe, 52
Sweet Heart of Jesus, 224, 237.
Sweetest Jesus, 71
Sweet Heart of Mary, 386
Veni Creator, 283
Virgin Mother of God, 305
Virgin most holy, 337
We fly, 333

CONTENTS

DECREE.................................... VII
PREFACE................................... IX
CANONS................................... XI

PART I
In Favor Of All The Faithful

CHAPTER I
THE TRIUNE GOD

I. Ejaculations and Invocations

1. To the King of ages..................... 3
2. Holy, Holy, Holy...................... 3
3. With all our heart...................... 4
4. May the most just will of God........... 4
5. My God and my all..................... 4
6. My God, grant (*from the Italian*).......... 5
7. My God, my only Good (*from the French*).. 5
8. Blessed be the Name.................... 5
9. My God, I give Thee thanks............. 5
10. My God, make us to be of one mind (*from the French*)....................... 5
11. Teach me, O Lord...................... 6
12. (*a*) O Most Holy Trinity, I adore Thee... 6
   (*b*) O Most Holy Trinity, make me love Thee............................ 6
   (*c*) O Most Holy Trinity, sanctify me..... 6
   (*d*) Abide with me, O Lord............. 6
13. My God, pour forth Thy blessings (*from the French*).......................... 6
14. O God, be merciful.................... 7
15. O God, Thou art all-powerful (*from the Italian*)........................... 7
16. (*a*) Holy God, Holy Strong One.......... 7
   (*b*) To Thee be praise.................. 7
17. Blessing and glory..................... 7
18. Keep me, O Lord...................... 8
19. Into Thy hands, O Lord................ 8
20. O God, come unto my assistance.......... 8
21. Vouchsafe, O Lord..................... 9

22. Deliver me, O Lord.................... 9
23. O Lord, reward us...................... 9
24. O Lord, remember not.................. 9
25. O praise the Lord..................... 10
26. Holy Trinity, One God................ 10
27. From all sin deliver.................. 10
28. Lord, I fear thy justice.............. 10
29. All through thee...................... 11
30. Most Holy Trinity, we adore.......... 11
31. Lord, save us........................ 11
32. Thy will be done..................... 11
33. O merciful Lord...................... 12
34. Lord, I am nothing................... 12
35. Lord, I am my own enemy.............. 12

II. *Acts of the Theological Virtues and of Contrition*
36. Acts of faith, hope, charity and contrition.. 12
37. My God, I believe in Thee............ 13
38. Lord, increase our faith............. 13
39. My God, I love Thee (*from the French*).... 13
40. I believe in Thee.................... 13
41. O my soul, love the love............ 14
42. Almighty and everlasting God......... 14
43. I believe in God the Father......... 14
44. I believe in one God, the Father.... 15

III. *Acts of Adoration and Thanksgiving*
45. Most Holy Trinity (*from the Italian*)...... 17
46. I adore Thee, O God (*from the French*).... 18

IV. *Pious Practices*
47. Recitation of the doxology............ 19
48. Making a novena to the Trinity....... 19

V. *Prayers*
49. Almighty and everlasting God......... 20
50. Of Thy tender mercy.................. 20
51. O Lord Omnipotent (*from the Italian*)...... 21
52. Receive, O Lord...................... 22
53. Omnipotence of the Father........... 22
54. O Lord, our God (*from the Spanish*)....... 23
55. Into Thy hands (*from the French*)......... 23
56. I vow and consecrate (*from the French*).... 24
57. In order that I may (*from the French*)...... 24

58. Most Holy Trinity (*from the Italian*)...... 25
59. Grant, we beseech Thee................. 25
60. Lord God Almighty.................... 26
61. I adore thee . . . this night............. 26
62. Visit, we beseech Thee................. 27
63. I adore thee . . . this day.............. 27
64. O God, thou who art one in nature........ 28

CHAPTER II
God the Father

Prayers............................... 29
65. O Father of mercies........... 29
66. O holy Lord, Father Almighty........... 30
67. O God, who in the Transfiguration........ 31
68. Eternal Father, I offer Thee (*from the Italian*)............................ 31
69. Eternal Father, I offer unto Thee (*from the French*)........................ 32

CHAPTER III
God the Son

Art. I—The Lord Jesus Christ................. 33
I. *Ejaculations and Invocations*................... 33
70. My Jesus, mercy (*from the Italian*)........ 33
71. Sweetest Jesus........................ 33
72. Jesus, my God........................ 33
73. Jesus, Son of David.................... 34
74. O my Jesus (*from the Italian*)............. 34
75. Jesus Christ, Son of the living God........ 34
76. Jesus, I live for Thee.....................34
77. O Jesus, life eternal (*from the French*).... 35
78. O Jesus, the friend of little children (*from the Italian*)........................ 35
79. Thou art the Christ.................... 35
80. Blessed be Jesus Christ (*from the Italian*).. 35
81. Jesus, for love of Thee................. 35
82. O Jesus, Son of the living God........... 36
83. O Jesus, with all my heart.............. 36
84. O Jesus, be to me Jesus................ 36
85. Christ Jesus, my helper................. 36

86. Lord Jesus Christ........................ 37
87. O Jesus, grant (*from the Italian*).......... 37
88. Lord Jesus, let me know myself........... 37
89. Lamb of God, who takest away.......... 38
90. All honor, laud and glory be.............. 39
91. Grant unto us, Thy servants............. 39
92. O sweetest Jesus, hide me in Thy Sacred
        Heart............................... 39
93. Lord Jesus, through thine infant cries...... 40
94. My dearest Jesus...................... 40
II. An Act of Adoration and Thanksgiving......... 40
95. We adore Thee........................ 40
III. An Act of Consecration...................... 41
96. O Eternal and Incarnate Wisdom (*from
        the French*)......................... 41
IV. Prayers.................................. 44
97. Lord, Jesus Christ...................... 44
98. Grant me Thy grace.................... 45
99. Jesus Christ my God (*from the Italian*).... 45
100. O Jesus, my Saviour (*from the German*)... 46
101. Our sins, O Lord (*from the Italian*)........ 47
102. O Jesus, Son of the glorious Virgin Mary
        (*from the French*)..................... 47
103. Our Lord Jesus Christ (*from the Italian*).. 48
104. Lord Jesus, I unite myself (*from the French*) 48
105. O Jesus! I come to Thee (*from the French*) 49
106. My Lord Jesus Christ (*from the Italian*)... 50
107. O Jesus our Saviour (*from the Italian*)...... 50
108. O Lord God............................ 50
109. Deliver me, Lord Jesus Christ............ 51
110. We offer Thee, Lord Jesus.............. 51
111. O dearly beloved Word of God........... 52
112. Change my heart, O Jesus............... 52
Art. II—IN HONOR OF THE MOST HOLY NAME OF JESUS 52
I. Invocation................................. 52
113. Jesus............................... 52
II. Litany.................................. 53
114. Litany of the Holy Name.................53
III. Hymns................................. 59
115. Jesus the very thought of Thee.......... 59

CONTENTS

116. O Jesus, Thou the beauty art............ 60
117. O Jesus, King most wonderful............ 61

IV. *Devout Practices*........................... 63
118. For the month of January............... 63
119. Recitation of the doxology with an ejacu-
      lation........................... 63
120. Visit to a church on the Feast........... 63

V. *Prayers*................................. 64
121. O good Jesu.......................... 64
122. O God, who didst appoint............... 64

Art. III—THE INFANT JESUS.................... 65

I. *Pious Exercises*........................... 65
123. (a) Presence at midnight Mass of Christmas 65
      (b) Presence at Matins and Lauds........ 65
124. Novena before Christmas............... 65
125. Novena from the 16th to the 24th of any
      month (*from the Italian*)............. 66

II. *Prayers*................................... 67
126. Jesu, Sweetest Child................... 68

III. *Prayers*................................. 75
127. Most dear Lord Jesus Christ (*from the
      Italian*)........................... 75
128. O divine Infant (*from the Italian*)......... 75
129. Eight days being passed................. 76
130. At thy birth, O Jesus.................. 77

Art. IV—JESUS IN THE BLESSED SACRAMENT...... 79

I. *Ejaculations and Invocations*.................. 79
131. Soul of Christ, be my sanctification....... 79
132. (a) Hail, saving Victim................. 80
      (b) Hail, Precious Blood................. 80
      (c) Be mindful, O Lord................. 80
133. My Lord and my God................... 80
134. O Jesus in the Blessed Sacrament........ 81
135. Praise and adoration................... 81
136. O Sacrament most holy (*from the Italian*).. 81
137. I adore Thee every moment (*from the
      Italian*)........................... 82
138. O Saving Victim...................... 82

139. Blessed is He that cometh................. 82
140. Very Bread, good Shepherd............... 83
141. Hail true Body......................... 84

II. Acts of Adoration............................ 84
142. Adoration of the Host during the elevation
     at Mass............................ 84
143. Accompanying the Bl. Sacr. when carried
     as Viaticum........................ 84
144. Accompanying the Bl. Sacr. when carried
     to the sick......................... 84
145. Visit to the Bl. Sacr. on Holy Thursday or
     Good Friday........................ 84
146. Genuflection before the Bl. Sacr........... 85
147. Adoration of the Bl. Sacr. on entering a
     church............................. 85
148. Visiting the Bl. Sacr..................... 86
149. Visiting the Bl. Sacr. in spirit............. 86
150. Walking in a procession of the Bl. Sacr..... 86

III. First Communion........................... 86
151. Receiving, or being present at............ 86
152. A Prayer by those who instruct for First
     Communion (*from the French*)........ 87

IV. Prayers before Communion................... 87
153. As the hart panteth..................... 87
154. Come, O Lord.......................... 88
155. Let the receiving....................... 88
156. Lord, I am not worthy................... 89
157. The Body of Our Lord................... 89
158. Almighty and everlasting God............ 89

V. Thanksgiving after Communion................ 91
159. How delectable is the Sweetness (*from the
     Italian*)........................... 91
160. I give Thee thanks..................... 92
161. My Lord Jesus Christ (*from the Italian*).. 93
162. O Lord Jesus Christ, Son of the living God.. 94

*VI. Prayer for fostering the Practice of Daily Com-
     munion*.............................. 94
163. O Sweetest Jesu (*from the Italian*)........ 94

VII. An Act of Spiritual Communion............. 95

CONTENTS

164. Formulas.............................. 95
    (a) My Jesus, I believe.................. 96
    (b) At thy feet, O my Jesus............. 96
VIII. Hymn, Rhythm and Sequence............... 96
165. Sing, my tongue....................... 96
166. O Godhead, hid........................ 99
167. Laud, O Sion, thy Salvation.............. 102
IX. Pious Practices............................ 107
168. The Holy Hour........................ 107
169. Solemn Exposition of the Bl. Sacr......... 107
170. Novena before Feast of Corpus Christi..... 109
171. Feast and Octave of Corpus Christi........ 109
172. Triduum during the Octave of Corpus Christi........................... 109
173. Having a Mass said in reparation......... 110
174. A Pious Exercise of Reparation........... 110
175. The Eucharistic Month.................. 111
176. The Eucharistic Day.................... 111
X. Acts of Adoration, Reparation and Thanksgiving.. 111
177. I adore Thee, Eternal Father (*from the Italian*)............................ 111
178. I adore Thee profoundly (*from the Italian*). 113
179. With that profound humility (*from the Italian*)............................ 116
XI. Prayers.................................. 117
180. O sacred banquet....................... 117
XII. Prayers................................. 119
181. Behold, O my most loving Jesus (*from the Italian*)............................ 119
182. O my Lord Jesus Christ (*from the Italian*).. 119
183. I adore Thee, O Jesus.................. 121
184. O my God, I firmly believe (*from the French*). 122
185. Throughout the year, O Jesus........... 122
Art. V—JESUS CRUCIFIED...................... 123
I. Ejaculations and Invocations................... 123
186. The Cross is my sure salvation........... 123
187. Hail, O Cross......................... 124
188. By the sign of the holy Cross........... 124
II. Offices of the Passion....................... 124
189. Office of Tenebræ...................... 124

190. The Little Office................................. 125
III. Acts of Adoration and Thanksgiving............ 125
191. We adore Thee, O Christ................... 125
192. Lord, I give Thee thanks (*from the Italian*) 125
IV. Hymn.. 126
193. The royal banners forward go.............. 126
V. The Way of the Cross............................ 128
194. Indulgences for making the Way of the Cross 128
VI. Pious Exercises................................. 129
195. The Three Hours' Agony on Good Friday.. 129
196. Saying certain prayers on any Friday...... 129
197. Praying at the sound of the bell on any
     Friday.. 129
198. Praying in memory of the Five Wounds.... 130
VII. Prayers in honor of the Five Wounds.......... 130
199. O good Jesus within Thy wounds......... 130
200. My dearest Lord (*from the Italian*)........ 131
201. Behold, O good and sweetest Jesus........ 132
202. O God, who by the Passion............... 133
203. Grant, Lord Jesus Christ................. 134
*VIII. Prayers in memory of the Seven Words on the
     Cross*... 134
204. Dear Jesu, who for love of me (*from the
     Italian*)....................................... 135
IX. Prayers... 140
205. O God, who for the redemption........... 140
206. My divine Saviour (*from the Italian*)....... 141
207. Behold me at Thy feet (*from the Italian*)... 142
208. O Jesus, who in Thy bitter Passion (*from
     the Italian*)................................. 143
209. O my crucified God (*from the Italian*)...... 143
210. Assist us, O Lord.......................... 144
211. O God, who for our sake.................. 145
212. O God, who didst will..................... 145
213. Lord Jesus Christ.......................... 146
214. O Jesus, Who by reason of Thy burning love. 146
Art. VI—IN HONOR OF THE MOST PRECIOUS BLOOD.. 147
I. Invocation....................................... 147
215. We therefore pray Thee................... 147

II. Hymn...................................... 147
   216. Hail, Holy Wounds.................... 147

III. Devout Exercise........................... 150
   217. For the month of July................. 150

IV. Prayers.................................. 150
   218. O Precious Blood *(from the Italian)*........ 150
   219. Eternal Father, I offer Thee *(from the Italian)*............................. 151
   220. Eternal Father, I offer Thee the merits *(from the Italian)*.................... 151
   221. Lord Jesus Christ....................... 153
   222. Almighty and everlasting God............ 154

Art. VII—THE MOST SACRED HEART OF JESUS..... 155

I. Ejaculations and Invocations................... 155
   223. May the Sacred Heart of Jesus *(from the French)*........................... 155
   224. Sweet Heart of my Jesus *(from the Italian)*. 155
   225. Heart of Jesus, burning with love......... 155
   226. Heart of Jesus, I put my trust *(from the French)*............................. 155
   227. Jesus, meek and humble of heart.......... 156
   228. Sacred Heart of Jesus *(from the French)*.. 156
   229. Divine Heart of Jesus *(from the Italian)*... 156
   230. Sacred Heart of Jesus, I believe *(from the French)*............................. 156
   231. Glory, love and thanksgiving *(from the French)*............................. 156
   232. O Heart of love *(from the French)*......... 156
   233. Sweet Heart of Jesus, have mercy......... 157
   234. All for Thee *(from the Italian)*............. 157
   235. Sacred Heart of Jesus, mayest Thou *(from the French)*........................ 157
   236. Sacred Heart of Jesus, protect *(from the French)*............................. 157
   237. Sweet Heart of Jesus, be my love......... 157
   238. Sacred Heart of Jesus, I give myself *(from the French)*........................ 157
   239. Sacred Heart of Jesus, strengthened *(from the Italian)*........................ 158

240. Sacred Heart of Jesus, let me love Thee (*from the Italian*)........................ 158
241. Sacred Heart of Jesus, convert (*from the Italian*)............................ 158
242. Most Sacred Heart of Jesus, have mercy... 158
243. Most sweet Heart of Jesus............... 158
II. *The Little Office*........................... 159
244. Indulgences........................... 159
III. *The Litany*............................... 159
245. Litany, with versicles and prayer......... 159
IV. *Hymns*.................................... 164
246. O Heart, thou ark where lies the law...... 164
247. Jesu! Creator of the world................ 166
V. *Pious Practices*............................ 167
248. Visiting an image of the Sacred Heart..... 167
249. Visiting a church on the Feast...... 167
250. Making a novena before the Feast........ 168
251. Wearing the badge of the Sacred Heart..... 168
252. Indulgences for the First Friday devotions. 168
253. For the month dedicated to the Sacred Heart 169
254. Making the five Fridays before the Feast... 170
VI. *Chaplet*.................................... 170
255. My most loving Jesus (*from the Italian*)... 170
VII. *Acts of Reparation and Consecration*.......... 173
256. O sweetest Jesus, Thou dost pour forth.... 173
257. O most merciful Heart of Jesus (*from the Spanish*)............................ 177
258. I give myself and consecrate (*from the French*)............................ 179
259. My most loving Jesus (*from the Italian*)... 180
260. My loving Jesus (*from the Italian*)......... 181
VIII. *Prayers*.................................... 182
261. O divine Heart of Jesus................. 182
262. O Most Holy Heart of Jesus, shower Thy blessings (*from the Italian*)........... 183
263. O most Holy Heart of Jesus, fountain of every blessing (*from the Italian*)...... 183
264. I hail Thee, O Sacred Heart (*from the Italian*)............................ 183

265. O God, who dost deign................. 184
266. Grant, we beseech Thee................. 184
267. Reveal Thy Sacred Heart to me.......... 185

Art. VIII—JESUS CHRIST THE KING............. 185

I. *Invocations*................................ 185
268. Jesus, King and center.................. 185
269. Christ conquers......................... 186
II. *A Devout Exercise*......................... 186
270. Making novena or triduum before the Feast 186
III. *Act of Dedication of the Human Race*.......... 186
271. Most Sweet Jesus, Redeemer............. 186
IV. *Prayer*................................... 189
272. O Christ Jesus, I acknowledge Thee (*from
the French*)......................... 189

Art. IX—THE HOLY FAMILY.................... 189

I. *Invocations*................................ 189
273. Jesus, Mary and Joseph most kind........ 189
274. Jesus, Mary and Joseph................. 190
II. *Responsory Prayers*......................... 190
275. Jesus, Mary and Joseph, bless us (*from the
Italian*)............................ 190
III. *Prayer*................................... 191
276. Lord, Jesus Christ, who, being made....... 191

CHAPTER IV
GOD THE HOLY GHOST

I. *Invocations*................................ 193
277. O Holy Spirit, Spirit of Truth... 193
278. O Holy Spirit, Sweet Guest.............. 193
279. God the Holy Ghost.................... 193
280. May the grace of the Holy Spirit......... 194
281. May our hearts be cleansed............. 194
II. *Sequence for Pentecost*...................... 194
282. Come, Thou holy Paraclete.............. 194
III. *Hymn for Pentecost*......................... 196
283. Come, Holy Ghost, Creator blest......... 196

IV. Devout Exercises............................ 198
    284. Making a novena before the Feast of
        Pentecost........................... 198
    285. The doxology recited seven times......... 199
V. Chaplet.................................... 199
    286. A Chaplet of the Holy Spirit............. 199
VI. Prayers.................................. 203
    287. Come, Holy Ghost, fill the hearts......... 203
VII. Prayers................................. 204
    288. O Holy Spirit, Creator.................... 204
    289. O Holy Spirit, divine Spirit (*from the
        French*)........................... 204
    290. Come, Holy Ghost...................... 205
    291. O Holy Spirit, who.................... 205

CHAPTER V
The Most Blessed Virgin Mary

Art. I—GENERAL DEVOTIONS TO THE BLESSED VIRGIN MARY

I. Ejaculations and Invocations.................. 209
    292. Mary.................................. 209
    293. Vouchsafe that I may praise thee......... 209
    294. O Mary, Mother of God (*from the Italian*). 210
    295. Thou who wast a Virgin................. 210
    296. Our Lady of Lourdes.................... 210
    297. My Mother, deliver me.................. 211
    298. O Mary, bless this house (*from the Italian*). 211
    299. O Mary, our hope (*from the Italian*)...... 211
    300. Mother of love......................... 211
    301. Holy Mary, deliver us.................. 211
    302. My Mother, my hope................... 212
    303. O Virgin Mary, Mother of Jesus (*from the
        Italian*)........................... 212
    304. Mother of mercy (*from the Italian*)....... 212
    305. O Mary, Virgin Mother of God........... 212
    306. O Mary, make me to live in God......... 212
    307. O Mary, Mother of grace................ 212
    308. Remember, O Virgin Mother of God....... 213
    309. Bless us, Mary, Maiden mild............. 213
    310. Thou art my Mother.................... 213

CONTENTS

311. Blessed art thou 213
312. Most high Queen 214
313. Draw us after thee 214
314. Pray for us, O holy Mother of God 214
315. Holy Mary, Virgin Mother of God 215
316. Rejoice, O Virgin Mary 215
317. O Mary, may thy children 215

II. *The Little Office* 215
318. Indulgences 215

III. *Litany* 216
319. The Litany of Loreto 216

IV. *Canticle, Hymns and Antiphons* 220
320. My soul doth magnify the Lord 220
321. Hail, thou star of ocean 221
322. O glorious Virgin, ever blest 223
323. Alma Redemptoris Mater 224
324. Ave Regina cælorum 225

V. *Devout Exercises* 226
325. The month of May 226
326. Making a novena for Feasts of the B.V.M. .. 226
    (a) the Nativity 226
    (b) the Presentation 226
    (c) the Annunciation 226
    (d) the Visitation 226
    (e) the Expectation 226
    (f) the Purification 226
    (g) the Assumption 226
327. Praying before an image of the B.V.M. 227

VI. *Act of Reparation* 227
328. Most glorious Virgin Mary (*from the Italian*) . 227
329. Prayer in reparation for insults offered to
    B.V.M. (*from the Italian*) 228

VII. *The Crown of Twelve Stars* 229
330. Let us offer praise (*from the Italian*) 229

VIII. *Prayers* 231
331. (a) The Angelus 231
    (b) Regina Cœli 232

CONTENTS

IX. *Prayers*................................. 233
  332. Hail, holy Queen........................ 233
  333. We fly to thy patronage................. 234
  334. Prayers for every day of the week (*from che Italian*)........................ 235
      Sunday   — Behold, O Mother of God................ 235
      Monday   — O Queen of Heaven, most holy Mary...... 236
      Tuesday   —· Most holy Mary....... 237
      Wednesday — O Mother of God...... 238
      Thursday   — O Queen of Heaven, thou who sittest enthroned............ 239
      Friday   — O Mary, thou art the noblest.............. 240
      Saturday   — O my most holy Mother. 241
  335. O Mother of God, Mary most holy (*from the Italian*).......................... 242
  336. I venerate thee (*from the Italian*).......... 244
  337. Virgin most holy, Mother of the Word Incarnate (*from the Italian*)........... 244
  338. O most excellent........................ 245
  339. The Memorare.......................... 247
  340. My Queen, my Mother.................. 247
  341. O Blessed Virgin Mary.................. 248
  342. Most holy Virgin (*from the Italian*)........ 250
  343. O holy Mary, my Mistress................ 251
  344. O Mary, crowned with stars (*from the Italian*)............................. 251
  345. Majestic Queen of Heaven (*from the French*)............................. 253
  346. O Mary, my dear Mother and mighty Queen (*from the Italian*).................... 253
  347. May we be assisted...................... 254
  348. Grant, we beseech Thee, O Lord.......... 255
  349. Holy Mary, be thou a help............... 255
  350. Hail, most gracious..................... 256
  351. O Mother of tender mercy............... 256
  352. O Mary, my dear Mother................ 257

CONTENTS

Art. II—The Immaculate Conception of the B.V.M.   258

I. Ejaculations and Invocations..................   258
   353. In thy Conception......................   258
   354. To thee, O Virgin Mother (*from the Italian*).   258
   355. O Mary, thou didst enter the world (*from the Italian*)............................   258
   356. Blessed be the holy (*from the Italian*)......   258
   357. O Mary, conceived without sin (*from the Italian*)............................   259
   358. By thine Immaculate Conception.........   259
   359. Thou art all fair, O Mary...............   259
II. The Little Office............................   260
   360. Indulgences.........................   260
III. Devout Practices...........................   260
   361. Novena for the Feast...................   260
   362. The Seven Days' Devotion of St. Bonaventure...........................   261
   363. The seven successive Sundays............   261
   364. The month of December.................   261
   365. The first Saturday or first Sunday of each month...........................   261
   366. The twelve Saturdays immediately preceding the Feast.......................   262
   367. The first Saturday of each month........   262
IV. Prayers....................................   262
   368. O Virgin Immaculate, who wast pleasing (*from the Italian*)....................   262
   369. O Virgin Immaculate, Mother of God (*from the Italian*)....................   263
   370. Immaculate Mother of God..............   263
   371. O pure and immaculate..................   265
   372. O God, who by the Immaculate Conception.   266
   373. Most holy Virgin, who, being predestined..   266
   374. O Mary, Mother of God and Mother of us.   268
Art. III—The Blessed Virgin Sorrowing........   269

I. Invocations..................................   269
   375. Holy Mother, pierce me through.........   269
   376. Mary most sorrowful (*from the Italian*)....   270
   377. Virgin most sorrowful..................   270

II. Sequence............................... 270
   378. Stabat Mater.......................... 270
III. Devout Exercises........................... 274
   379. Prayers on Good Friday................ 274
   380. Novena at any time.................... 275
   381. The month of September....... 275
   382. The seven Fridays preceding each Feast of
        B.V.M. Sorrowing................... 275
IV. Prayers....................................... 275
   383. I grieve for thee (*from the Italian*)......... 275
V. Prayers.. 278
   384. Mary, most holy Virgin (*from the Italian*).. 278
   385. Most holy Virgin and Mother............ 278

Art. IV—THE MOST PURE HEART OF MARY....... 279

I. Invocations.................................... 279
   386. Sweet Heart of Mary (*from the Italian*)..... 279
   387. O Heart most pure (*from the Italian*)...... 279
II. Devout Exercises............................. 279
   388. Indulgences for novena.................. 279
   389. The month of August.................... 280
III. An Act of Consecration...................... 280
   390. O Mary, Virgin most powerful (*from the
        French*)............................. 280
   391. Queen of the most holy Rosary........... 281
IV. Prayers...................................... 283
   392. Immaculate Virgin, who (*from the Italian*). 284
V. A Prayer..................................... 286
   393. O Heart of Mary....................... 286

Art. V—THE HOLY ROSARY..................... 287

(A) AS PRACTISED IN THE UNIVERSAL CHURCH

I. An Invocation................................. 287
   394. Queen of the most holy Rosary........... 287
II. The Recitation of the Rosary................... 287
   395. Indulgences for reciting the Rosary........ 287
III. Devout Exercises............................. 288
   396. Indulgences for novena to Our Lady of the
        Rosary............................. 288

CONTENTS

397. The devotion of the fifteen Saturdays...... 288
398. The month of October.................. 289

IV. A Prayer................................ 289
  399. Queen of the most Holy Rosary (*from the Italian*).......................... 289

(B) As Practised in the Valley of Pompeii..... 290

I. A Visit.................................. 290
  400. Visiting an image of Our Lady of Pompeii. 290

II. A prayer to be said at midday on the 8th day of May and the first Sunday of October.... 290
  401. O august Queen of victories (*from the Italian*).......................... 290

III. Prayers for a novena or a triduum............ 294
  402. O Saint Catherine of Siena.............. 294

IV. Prayers for a novena or triduum of thanksgiving. 300
  403. Behold me at thy knees (*from the Italian*).. 300

V. A Prayer................................ 306
  404. O Virgin immaculate (*from the Italian*).... 306

Art. VI—Our Lady of Mount Carmel.......... 307

I. Invocation.............................. 307
  405. O Queen who art the beauty of Carmel.... 307

II. A Prayer................................ 307
  406. O blessed Virgin, full of grace (*from the Italian*).......................... 307

Art. VII—The Blessed Virgin under divers titles 308

I. Our Lady of Pity............................ 308
  407. *An Oration*—Kneeling at thy (*from the Italian*).......................... 308

II. Our Lady of Divine Providence.............. 310
  408. *Prayer*—Mary, immaculate Virgin (*from the Italian*)........................ 310
  409. *Prayer*—O Mother of mercy (*from the Italian*).......................... 311

III. Our Lady of the Cenacle.................. 312
  410. *Prayer*—Most holy Virgin of the Cenacle (*from the Italian*)................... 312

liv CONTENTS

IV. Our Lady, Help of Christians.................. 313
    411. *A Prayer*—Immaculate Virgin (*from the Italian*)............................. 313
    412. *A Prayer*—Virgin most powerful (*from the Italian*)............................. 313
    413. *A Prayer*—Most holy and immaculate Virgin (*from the Italian*)................ 315
    414. *A Prayer*—O Mary, powerful Virgin (*from the Italian*)........................ 316
V. Our Lady, Queen of Prophets.................. 317
    415. *A Prayer*—To thee, O Queen of Prophets (*original English prayer*)............. 317
VI. Our Lady of Good Hope...................... 318
    416. *A Prayer*—O Mary immaculate (*from the Italian*)............................. 318
VII. Our Lady of Reparation..................... 319
    417. *A Prayer*—Immaculate Virgin, refuge of sinners (*from the Italian*)............. 319
VIII. Our Lady of the Blessed Sacrament.......... 320
    418. *A Prayer*—O Virgin Mary (*from the Italian*). 320
IX. Our Lady, Comforter of the Afflicted........... 320
    419. *A Prayer*—Immaculate Virgin Mary (*from the Italian*)........................ 320
    420. *A Prayer*—O Mary Immaculate (*from the French*)............................. 322
X. Our Lady of Ransom......................... 322
    421. Devout exercise of the Seven Saturdays... 322
XI. Our Lady of Guadalupe...................... 323
    422. Visiting the image....................... 323
    423. The devotion of the Five Sundays......... 323
    424. *Prayer*—Our Lady of Guadalupe (*from the Spanish*)............................. 323
XII. Our Lady of Deliverance.................... 324
    425. *An Invocation*—Holy Mary, our Lady of Deliverance (*from the Italian*)......... 324
XIII. Our Lady of Perpetual Help................ 324
    426. *An Invocation*—Mother of Perpetual Help. 324
    427. *Prayers*—Behold, O Mother of Perpetual Help (*from the Italian*)............... 324

CONTENTS lv

XIV. Our Lady of Good Counsel.................. 327
  428. *A Devout Exercise*...................... 327
      (*a*) on 12 successive Sundays or Saturdays 327
      (*b*) on the first Sunday, or the preceding
            Saturday of any month.............. 327
  429. *A Prayer*—Most glorious Virgin (*from the
            Italian*)........................... 327
XV. Our Lady, Queen of Peace.................. 328
  430. *An Invocation*—Immaculate Queen of Peace. 328
  431. *A Prayer*—Most holy Virgin (*from the
            Italian*)........................... 328
XVI. Our Lady, Mother of Orphans.............. 329
  432. *An Invocation*—Mother of Orphans, pray
            for us............................. 329
XVII. Our Lady, Mother of Grace............... 330
  433. *A Prayer*—Most holy Mary, great Queen
            of Heaven (*from the Italian*)......... 330
XVIII. Our Lady of Intercession............... 331
  434. *A Prayer*—Most holy Mary, our Lady of
            Intercession (*from the Italian*)........ 331
XIX. Our Lady of La Salette.................... 332
  435. *An Invocation*—Our Lady of La Salette
            (*from the French*).................. 332
  436. *A Prayer*—Remember, our Lady of La
            Salette (*from the French*)............. 332
XX. Our Lady, Queen of Apostles............... 333
  437. *An Invocation*—Queen of the Apostles, pray
            for us............................. 333
XXI. Our Lady, Refuge of Sinners.............. 333
  438. *A Prayer*—Almighty and merciful God.... 333
XXII. Our Lady of the Sacred Heart............ 334
  439. *A Prayer*—Remember, our Lady.......... 334

CHAPTER VI
THE HOLY ANGELS

Art. I—GENERAL INVOCATIONS OF THE HOLY ANGELS. 335
  440. *An Invocation*—Ye Angels and Archangels. 335
  441. *An Invocation*—Bless the Lord, all ye His
            Angels............................. 335

Art. II—SAINT MICHAEL THE ARCHANGEL.......... 336

I. Invocations................................. 336
   442. Saint Michael the Archangel, defend us... 336
   443. Saint Michael, first champion of the King-
       ship of Christ (*from the French*)....... 336
II. Hymn..................................... 336
   444. O Jesus, life-spring of the soul............ 336
III. Devout Exercise........................... 339
   445. Novena in honor of St. Michael........... 339
IV. Prayers.................................. 339
   446. O glorious Prince (*from the Italian*)....... 339
   447. Saint Michael the Archangel.............. 340

Art. III—SAINT GABRIEL THE ARCHANGEL......... 341

   448. I. *A Devout Exercise*—Novena in honor of
       St. Gabriel......................... 341
   449. II. *A Prayer*—O God, who amongst all.... 341

Art. IV—SAINT RAPHAEL THE ARCHANGEL......... 342

   450. I. *A Devout Exercise*—Novena in honor of
       St. Raphael........................ 342
   451. II. *A Prayer*—Vouchsafe, O Lord God.... 342

Art. V—THE GUARDIAN ANGEL.................. 343

   452. I. *Invocation*—Angel of God. my guardian
       dear.............................. 343
   453. II. *A Devout Exercise*—Novena in honor of
       one's Guardian Angel................ 343

Art. VI—THE HOLY ANGEL WHO STRENGTHENED
     JESUS IN THE GARDEN OF OLIVES..... 344

   454. I. *Invocation*—O holy Angel who didst
       strengthen......................... 344
   455. II. *Prayer*—I salute thee, holy Angel (*from
       the Italian*)........................ 344

CHAPTER VII
THE SAINTS

Art. I—IN HONOR OF SAINT JOHN THE BAPTIST..... 345

I. A Devout Exercise............................ 345
   456. Novena in honor of St. John the Baptist... 345

CONTENTS lvii

II. Prayers...................................... 345
    457. O glorious Saint John (*from the Italian*).... 345

Art. II—IN HONOR OF SAINT JOSEPH, SPOUSE OF THE
    B.V.M.. 347

I. Invocations.................................... 347
    458. Grant us, dear Joseph.................... 347
    459. O Saint Joseph, foster-father of our Lord
        (*from the Italian*).................... 347
    460. Joseph................................... 347

II. The Little Office............................. 348
    461. Indulgences............................. 348

III. The Litany.................................. 348
    462. Litany with Versicles and Prayer.......... 348

IV. Hymns....................................... 351
    463. Joseph, to thee by hosts on high.......... 351
    464. Hail, dear Spouse of Mary mild........... 353

V. Devout Exercises.............................. 354
    465. The seven Sundays...................... 354
    466. The month of March.................... 355
    467. Novena before the Feast................. 355
    468. The first Wednesday of any month........ 355
    469. Visiting an image of the Saint............ 356

VI. Prayers...................................... 356
    470. O chaste Spouse of Mary (*from the Italian*). 356
    471. In the miseries of this vale of tears (*from the
        Italian*)............................... 360

VII. Prayers..................................... 361
    472. Remember, O most pure Spouse (*from the
        Italian*)............................... 361
    473. Saint Joseph, father and guardian......... 362
    474. O glorious Saint Joseph (*from the Italian*). 362
    475. Be mindful of us, O blessed Joseph........ 363
    476. To thee, O blessed Joseph............... 364
    477. O Joseph, virgin-father of Jesus........... 366
    478. Glorious Saint Joseph, pattern (*from the
        French*)............................... 366
    479. Supported by the patronage.............. 367

CONTENTS

Art. III—In honor of the Holy Apostles........ 367

I. The Holy Apostles, Peter and Paul.............. 367
    480. Invocation—Defend, O Lord, Thy People.. 367
    481. A Pious Exercise—Novena prayers........ 368
    482. Petitions—O holy Apostles, Peter and Paul
         (from the Italian).................... 368

II. Saint Peter the Apostle...................... 370
    483. Prayers—Thou art the Shepherd.......... 370
    484. Prayers—O glorious Saint Peter (from the
         Italian)............................. 371

III. Saint Paul the Apostle..................... 372
    485. Prayers—Thou art the Vessel of election... 372
    486. Prayers—O glorious Saint Paul (from the
         French)............................. 373

IV. Saint John, Apostle and Evangelist............ 374
    487. Prayer—O glorious Apostle (from the
         Italian)............................. 374

V. Saint Jude Thaddeus, Apostle.................. 375
    488. Prayer—O glorious Saint Jude Thaddeus
         (from the Italian).................... 375

VI. Saint James the Apostle...................... 376
    489. Prayer—O glorious Apostle, Saint James
         (from the Italian).................... 376

Art. IV—In honor of other Saints.............. 376

I. Saint Joachim, Father of the B.V.M..............376
    490. Invocation—O Joachim, husband of holy
         Anne................................. 376
    491. Prayer—O great and glorious Patriarch
         (from the Italian).................... 377
    492. Prayer—O great Patriarch (from the Italian). 378

II. Saint Anne, Mother of the B.V.M.............. 379
    493. Pious Practices
         (a) for every Tuesday.................. 379
         (b) for a novena...................... 379
    494. Prayer—With my heart full (from the
         Italian)............................. 380

III. Saint Aloysius Gonzaga, Confessor . . . . , 381
    495. *Devout Exercises*
        (*a*) Visiting a church on the Feast 381
        (*b*) The devotion of the six Sundays 381
        (*c*) Novena before the Feast 381
        (*d*) Visit an image of the Saint 381
    496. *Prayers*—Saint Aloysius, adorned (*from the Italian*) 382

IV. Saint Ignatius Loyola, Confessor 383
    497. *A Devout Exercise*—The devotion of the ten Sundays 383
    498. *A Prayer*—O glorious Patriarch, Saint Ignatius (*from the Italian*) 383
    499. *A Prayer* to St. Ignatius Loyola and St. Francis Xavier 384

V. Saint Francis Xavier, Confessor 385
    500. The Novena of Grace 385

VI. Saint Stanislaus Kostka, Confessor 386
    501. *Pious Practices*
        (*a*) Visiting a church on the Feast 386
        (*b*) The devotion of the ten Sundays 386
        (*c*) Novena before the Feast 386
        (*d*) Visiting an image of the Saint 387
        (*e*) Making the Retreat of Saint Stanislaus 387
    502. *Prayers*—Saint Stanislaus, my patron (*from the Italian*) 387

VII. Saint John of the Cross, Confessor 389
    503. *Prayer*—O glorious Saint John of the Cross (*from the Italian*) 389

VIII. Saint Pius V, Pope and Confessor 390
    504. *Hymn*—Wars and tumults fill the earth . . . 390
    505. *Prayers*—Pius, admirable Shepherd 392

IX. Saint Camillus of Lellis, Confessor 393
    506. *A Devout Exercise*—The devotion of the seven Sundays 393

X. Saint Michael de' Santi, Confessor 394
    507. *Prayer*—O glorious Saint Michael (*from the Italian*) 394

XI. Saint Paul of the Cross, Confessor 394

508. *A Devout Exercise*—Novena in honor of the
Saint 394

509. *A Prayer*—O glorious Saint Paul of the
Cross (*from the Italian*) 395

510. *A Prayer*—O glorious Saint Paul of the
Cross (*from the Spanish*) 396

XII. Saint Gregory VII, Pope and Confessor 396

511. *A Prayer*—O invincible defender (*from the
Italian*) 396

XIII. Saint Vincent de Paul, Confessor 397

512. *A Devout Exercise*—Novena in honor of the
Saint 397

513. *A Prayer*—O glorious Saint Vincent (*from
the Italian*) 398

XIV. Saint Benedict Joseph Labre, Confessor 398

514. *Prayers*—O wondrous pattern (*from the
Italian*) 398

XV. Saint Francis of Assisi, Confessor 400

515. *Pious Practices*—
(*a*) The devotion of the five Sundays 400
(*b*) Visiting a church on the Feast 400
(*c*) Novena in honor of the Saint 400

516. *Hymn*—O victim dear of heavenly love 401

517. *A Prayer*—O glorious St. Francis, (from the
Italian) 402

518. *A Prayer*—Lord Jesus Christ, who 403

XVI. Saint Thomas Aquinas, Confessor 404

519. *A Devout Exercise*—The devotion of the six
Sundays 404

520. *Prayer*—Angelic Doctor, Saint Thomas ... 404

*XVII. Saint Alphonsus M. de'Liguori, Bishop and
Confessor* 405

521. *A Prayer*—O my glorious and well-beloved
patron (*from the Italian*) 405

XVIII. Saint Vincent Ferrer, Confessor 406

522. *A Prayer*—O glorious Apostle and wonder-
worker (*from the Italian*) 406

523. *A Prayer*—O Saint Vincent, glorious worker
of miracles (*from the Italian*) 407

*XIX. The Seven Holy Founders of the Order of the
      Servants of Mary, Confessors* 407
524. *A Prayer*—O glorious Patriarchs (*from the
      Italian*) 407
525. *Prayers*—O glorious Patriarchs (*from the
      Italian*) 408

XX. Saint John Berchmans, Confessor 411
526. *Devout Practices*—
     (*a*) The devotion of the five Sundays 411
     (*b*) Visiting a church on the Feast 411
     (*c*) Novena before the Feast 411
     (*d*) Visiting an image of the Saint 411
527. *Prayers*—Saint John, angelic youth 411

XXI. Saint Louis, Bishop and Confessor 414
528. *A Prayer*—To thee do we have recourse... 414

XXII. Saint Anthony, Abbot and Confessor 415
529. *A Prayer*—O glorious Saint Anthony 415

XXIII. Saint Anthony of Padua, Confessor 416
530. *Devout Practices*—
     (*a*) Reciting thirteen times the Our Father,
        Hail Mary and Glory be 416
     (*b*) The devotion of the thirteen Tuesdays
        or Sundays 416
531. *A Responsory*—If, then, thou seekest mir-
     acles 417
532. *Prayer of Petition*—O wondrous Saint
     Anthony (*from the Italian*) 418
533. *Prayer of Thanksgiving*—O glorious won-
     der-worker (*from the Italian*) 419

XXIV. Saint John of Matha, Confessor 420
534. *A Prayer*—Glorious Saint John of Matha
     (*from the Italian*) 420

XXV. Saint Peter Fourier, Confessor 420
535. *A Prayer*—Most glorious Saint Peter
     Fourier (*from the Italian*) 420

XXVI. Saint Joseph Calasanctius, Confessor 421
536. *A Prayer*—Saint Joseph Calasanctius, pro-
     tector (*from the Italian*) 421

XXVII. Saint Blase, Bishop and Martyr 422
  537. *A Prayer*—O glorious Saint Blase (*from the Italian*) 422

XXVIII. Saint Stephen, Protomartyr 423
  538. *Prayers*—The Apostles chose Stephen 423

XXIX. Saint Homobonus, Confessor 424
  539. *A Prayer*—Our defender, father of the poor (*from the Italian*) 424

XXX. Saint John Baptist de la Salle, Confessor 425
  540. *A Prayer*—O glorious John Baptist de la Salle (*from the French*) 425

XXXI. Saint Dominic, Confessor 425
  541. *A Devout Exercise*—Devotion of the fifteen Tuesdays 425
  542. *Prayers*—O glorious St. Dominic (*from the Italian*) 425

XXXII. Saint Paschal Baylon, Confessor 427
  543. *Responsory*—Paschal, illustrious is thy name 427

XXXIII. Saint Gabriel of the Sorrowful Mother, Confessor 429
  544. *Devout Practices*—
    (*a*) Visiting a church on the Feast 429
    (*b*) Visiting a representation of the Saint. 429
  545. *Prayer of Petition*—Let us adore and give thanks (*from the Italian*) 429

XXXIV. Saint Philip Neri, Confessor 431
  546. *Invocation*—Lowly Saint Philip 431
  547. *Prayers* for every day of the week (*from the Italian*) 431
    Sunday   — O my glorious Patron. 431
    Monday   — My holy advocate, Saint Philip 432
    Tuesday   — O glorious Saint Philip. 432
    Wednesday — Saint Philip, I am filled. 433
    Thursday   — O glorious Saint 434
    Friday   — Great Saint 434
    Saturday   — O my holy patron 435

CONTENTS

lxiii

*XXXV. Saint Fidelis of Sigmaringen, Protomartyr
of the Propagation of the Faith* 436
548. *Responsory*—Thy name, Fidelis, doth proclaim 436

XXXVI. Saint Columbanus, Confessor 439
549. Prayer for Missionaries—see n. 618 439

XXXVII. Saint Nicholas, Bishop and Confessor ... 439
550. *Invocation*—Saint Nicholas, glorious Confessor 439
551. *Prayer of Impetration*—Glorious Saint
Nicholas (*from the Italian*) 439

XXXVIII. Saint Francis of Paola, Confessor 440
552. *A Devout Exercise*—The devotion of the
thirteen Fridays 440

XXXIX. Saint Peregrine Laziosi, Confessor 441
553. *A Prayer*—O glorious wonder-worker
(*from the Italian*) 441

XL. Saint Lawrence, Martyr 442
554. *Prayers*—O glorious Saint Lawrence (*from
the Italian*) 442

XLI. Saint Pancratius, Martyr 442
555 *A Prayer*—O glorious Saint Pancratius
(*from the Italian*) 442

XLII. Saint John Bosco, Confessor 443
556. *A Prayer*—O glorious Saint John Bosco
(*from the Italian*) 443

XLIII. Saint Tarcisius, Martyr 444
557. *Prayers*—O unvanquished martyr (*from
the Italian*) 444

XLIV. In honor of Saint Eugene I, Pope and Confessor 445
558. *A Prayer*—O Jesus, great High-Priest 445

XLV. Saint Elizabeth, Widow 446
559. *A Prayer*—Dear Saint Elizabeth (*from the
Italian*) 446

XLVI. Saint Agnes, Virgin and Martyr 448
560. *Prayers*—O singular example (*from the
Italian*) 448

lxiv CONTENTS

XLVII. Saint Lucy, Virgin and Martyr 450
561. *Prayers*—By that admirable faith (*from the Italian*) 450
562. *Prayer*—Dear Saint Lucy (*from the Italian*). 452

XLVIII. Saint Juliana Falconieri, Virgin 452
563. *A Prayer*—O faithful bride of Jesus (*from the Italian*) 452

XLIX. Saint Margaret of Cortona, Penitent 453
564. *A Prayer*—O most glorious Saint Margaret (*from the Italian*) 453

L. Saint Teresa, Virgin 454
565. *A Prayer*—O Saint Teresa, seraphic Virgin. 454

LI. Saint Bridget, Queen of Sweden, Widow 454
566. A Prayer for the conversion of non-Catholics, see n. 629 454

LII. Saint Rita, Widow 455
567. *A Prayer*—O God, who didst vouchsafe (*from the Spanish*) 455
568. *A Prayer*—O glorious Saint Rita (*from the Italian*) 455

LIII. Saint Catherine, Virgin and Martyr 455
569. A Prayer for those engaged in teaching, see n. 761 and 762 455

LIV. Saint Frances of Rome, Widow 456
570. *A Prayer*—Bright jewel of the Order (*from the Italian*) 456

LV. Saint Margaret Mary Alacoque, Virgin 456
571. *A Devout Exercise*—Praying before a representation of the Saint 456
572. *Prayers*—Saint Margaret Mary (*from the Italian*) 457

LVI. Saint Joan of Arc, Virgin 458
573. *An Invocation*—Saint Joan of Arc (*from the French*) 458

LVII. Saint Theresa of the Child Jesus, Virgin 458
574. *An Invocation*—O Saint Theresa of the Child Jesus (*from the Italian*) 458

CONTENTS

575. *A Devout Exercise—*
    (a) Praying before a representation of the Saint............................ 458
    (b) Visiting a church on the Feast........ 458
576. *Prayers—O marvelous Saint Theresa (from the Italian)*......................... 459
577. *A Prayer—O God, who didst inflame (from the French)*......................... 460
LVIII. *Saint Lucy Filippini, Virgin*............... 460
    578. *A Prayer—O Saint Lucy (from the Italian)*. 460
LIX. *Saint Catherine of Siena, Primary Patron of Italy*................................. 461
    579. *A Prayer—O Saint Catherine (from the Italian)*........................... 461
    580. *A Prayer—O admirable Saint Catherine (from the Italian)*.................... 463
LX. *One's own Patron Saint*..................... 463
    581. *A Prayer—O heavenly Patron*............ 463

CHAPTER VIII
For the Faithful Departed

I. *Invocation*.................................... 466
    582. Eternal rest grant unto them............. 466
    583. Merciful Lord Jesus, grant............... 466
II. *The Office of the Dead*........................ 466
    584. Indulgences............................. 466
III. *Psalms and Sequence*........................ 467
    585. De Profundis........................... 467
    586. Miserere mei, Deus...................... 467
    587. Dies iræ, dies illa...................... 467
IV. *Devout Exercises*............................ 471
    588. Novena for the souls of the faithful departed.................................. 471
    589. The month of November................. 471
    590. The plenary indulgence "toties quoties" for All Souls' Day........................ 472
    591. Altars privileged on All Souls' Day and during the Octave.................... 472

592. Visiting a cemetery..................... 472
V. *The Heroic Act of Charity*..................... 473
   593. Indulgences for the Heroic Act............ 473
VI. *Prayers*...................................... 473
   594. Prayers for every day of the week (*from
       the Italian*)......................... 473
   595. Most loving Jesu (*from the Italian*)......... 476
   596. My Jesus, by the sorrows (*from the Italian*). 477
   597. O Lord Jesus Christ..................... 478
   598. O God, who hast commanded............. 478
   599. O God, who in the ranks of the Apostolic.. 479
   600. (*a*) For a man deceased................. 479
       (*b*) For a woman deceased.............. 480

CHAPTER IX
For Special Occasions
Art. I—Eucharistic Congresses

I. *Prayer for the success of Eucharistic Congresses*.. 482
   601. O Jesus, who art really (*from the French*).. 482
II. *During any such Congress, international, national,
    regional or diocesan*.................. 483
   602. Indulgences........................... 483
III. *During any such Congress in a rural Vicariate,
    Deanery, Mother-Church with suc-
    cursal chapels or Parish*.............. 484
   603. Indulgences........................... 484

Art. II—For Vocations to the Priesthood
and the Religious Life

I. *Invocations*................................. 484
   604. O Mary, Queen of the clergy (*from the
    French*)............................. 484
   605. O Lord, grant unto Thy Church (*from the
    French*)............................. 484
   606. Send forth, O Lord, laborers............. 484
II. *Devout Exercise*............................ 485
   607. Prayer before the Blessed Sacrament...... 485

CONTENTS

III. Prayers.................................. 485
  608. Indulgences for any prayer approved by
       ecclesiastical authority............... 485

Art. III—For Missions in Pagan Countries

I. Devout Exercises........................... 485
  609. Donating alms or personal work to the
       Missions........................... 485
  610. Receiving Holy Communion for the Mis-
       sions............................. 486
  611. Observing the Missionary Day........... 486

II. Prayers................................... 486
  612. O God, the everlasting Creator.......... 486
  613. O praise the Lord...................... 487
  614. Have mercy on us, O God............... 488
  615. O Mary, most merciful................. 490
  616. O God of love (*from the French*)........... 491
  617. Most loving Lord Jesus (*from the Italian*). 491
  618. O blessed Columbanus (*original English
       prayer*)........................... 492
  619. Saint Theresa of the Child Jesus (*from the
       Italian*)........................... 493
  620. O glorious virgin Saint Theresa.......... 493

Art. IV—For the Conversion of Non-Catholics

I. Invocation................................. 496
  621. That Thou wouldst vouchsafe........... 496

II. A Devout Exercise for the Unity of the Church... 497
  622. Octave of Prayers..................... 497

III. Prayers................................. 498
  623. O God, who guidest.................... 498
  624. Almighty and everlasting God........... 498
  625. Lord Jesu, merciful Saviour............. 499
  626. O Mary, Mother of mercy (*from the Italian*). 499
  627. O Virgin, immaculate (*from the Italian*)... 500
  628. O merciful Queen of the Rosary of Pompeii
       (*from the Italian*).................... 501
  629. With trusting hearts (*from the Italian*).... 503

630. O Lord, who hast united the various nations (*from the Italian*).................... 504

631. For the conversion of Russia—*Invocation* Saviour of the world................. 504

632. For the conversion of Russia—Prayer to Saint Theresa of the Child Jesus: O loving and compassionate Saint (*from the French*)........................ 504

Art. V—Missions for the People

I. A Prayer for the success of a Mission............ 505

633. O Jesus, most holy Redeemer (*from the French*)............................ 505

II. A Prayer after a Mission...................... 507

634. Jesus Christ, who for my sake............ 507

III. Mission Crosses............................ 508

635. Indulgences............................ 508

Art. VI—For a Happy Death

I. Invocations.................................. 509

636. Jesus, Mary and Joseph, I give you my heart (*from the Italian*).............. 509

637. From a sudden and unprovided death..... 509

II. An Act of accepting one's own death from the hand of God........................... 510

638. Conditions and indulgences.............. 510

III. Pious Exercises............................ 510

639. *Prayers*—The "Recordare": Remember, O Virgin Mother..................... 510

640. *Rhyme*—Mother, hail, immersed in woes.. 512

IV. Prayers.................................. 515

641. O most merciful Lord Jesus (*from the Italian*)............................ 515

642. O Mary, conceived without sin.......... 516

643. Grant unto us, Lord Jesus.............. 516

644. Lord Jesus Christ...................... 517

645. O my adorable Creator (*from the Italian*). 518

646. My journey toward eternity, dear Lord (*from the Italian*).................... 519

CONTENTS

647. Almighty and merciful God............. 522
648. Lord Jesu, pour into us the spirit of Thy
     love.............................. 523
649. Grant, we beseech Thee................ 523

Art. VII—Miscellaneous Devotions

I. *For the Sovereign Pontiff*..................... 524
   650. *Invocation*—Lord Jesus, shelter our Holy
        Father *(from the French)*............ 524
   651. A Day dedicated to the Sovereign Pontiff. 524
   652. Versicle and Response.................. 524
   653. *Prayer*—O Lord, we are the millions of
        believers *(from the Italian)*............ 525
   654. *Prayer*—O God, the Shepherd and Ruler. 526
   655. *Prayer*—Almighty and everlasting God... 527
II. *For the Sanctification of the Clergy*............. 527
   656. *Invocation*—Jesus, Saviour of the world... 527
   657. A Day dedicated to the Sanctification of
        the clergy........................... 528
   658. *An Act of Oblation*—O Jesus, humbled
        (from the French).................... 528
   659. *A Prayer*—O Jesus, eternal High Priest
        (from the French).................... 528
   660. *A Prayer*—O God, who hast appointed... 530
III. *For Military Chaplains*...................... 530
   661. Devoutly reciting certain prayers for them. 530
IV. *For Children*............................. 530
   662. *A Prayer*—O Jesus, friend of little children
        (from the French).................... 530
V. *For Emigrants*............................. 531
   663. *A Prayer*—O Jesus, who in the very first
        days *(from the Italian)*............... 531
   664. *Prayers*—Saint Raphael the Archangel
        (from the Italian).................... 532
VI. *Prayers for those undertaking a journey or a walk*. 534
   665. In the way of peace direct us............. 534
VII. *For Benefactors*........................... 535
   666. *A Prayer*—May it please Thee, O Lord.... 535
VIII. *For the Sick*............................. 536

667. *A Devout Practice*—Visiting the Sick....... 536
668. *A Prayer*—O glorious Saint Camillus (*from the Italian*)......................... 536
IX. *For the Dying*............................... 537
669. *A Devout Practice*—Commending the dying to God............................ 537
670. *Prayers*—Eternal Father, by the love (*from the Italian*).................... 537
671. *A Prayer*—O most merciful Jesus......... 538
X. *A Prayer for Parish Priests*.................. 538
672. Almighty and merciful................... 538
XI. *The Indulgences of "the Holy Land"*........... 539
673. Conditions for gaining the indulgences..... 539
XII. *For those who serve Holy Mass*.............. 539
674. Indulgences........................... 539
XIII. *Prayers after the celebration of Low Mass*.... 539
675. Prayers............................... 539
XIV. *Assisting at the First Mass of Newly-ordained Priests and Kissing the palms of their hands*............................. 541
676. Indulgences........................... 541
XV. *Kissing the ring of the Sovereign Pontiff, of a Cardinal, a Bishop or a Prefect Apostolic* 542
677. Indulgences........................... 542
XVI. *The Sign of the Cross*...................... 542
678. Indulgences........................... 542
XVII. *The Renewal of One's Baptismal Vows*....... 542
679. Indulgences........................... 542
XVIII. *To obtain God's help before any action*...... 543
680. *Prayer*—Go before us, O Lord............ 543
681. *A Devout Practice*—Being present at the chanting of the *Veni Creator* on New Year's Day......................... 543
682. *A Prayer before assembling to transact some public business*—We are come, O God. 544
XIX. *Prayers of Thanksgiving*.................... 545
683. *Prayer*—We give Thee thanks, Almighty God................................ 545

684. The *Te Deum laudamus*................ 546
685. *Devout Practices—*
    (*a*) Presence at a thanksgiving service during the last half-hour of the old year and the first half-hour of the new year 546
    (*b*) Thanking God for the blessings conferred on the human race........... 546
XX. The Gradual and Penitential Psalms......... 547
686. Indulgences........................... 547
XXI. The Litany of the Saints.................... 547
687. Indulgences........................... 547
XXII. Mental Prayer.......................... 548
688. Indulgences........................... 548
XXIII. Spiritual Exercises and the Monthly Recollection........................... 548
689. Indulgences........................... 548
XXIV. Examination of Conscience............... 548
690. Indulgences........................... 548
XXV. Prayers to ask Pardon for Sin............. 549
691. I confess to Almighty God (*the confiteor*)... 549
XXVI. Assistance at the Explanation of the Gospel and other Sacred Discourses........ 550
692. Indulgences........................... 550
XXVII. Christian Doctrine..................... 550
693. Indulgences........................... 550
XXVIII. The Reading of Holy Scripture.......... 550
694. Indulgences........................... 550
XXIX. The Papal Blessing..................... 551
695. Plenary Indulgence..................... 551
XXX. The Divine Praises in reparation for blasphemies........................... 551
696. Blessed be God (*from the Italian*)......... 551
XXXI. A Christian Greeting.................... 552
697. (*a*) Praised be Jesus Christ............. 552
    (*b*) Praised be Jesus and Mary.......... 552
    (*c*) Glory be to the Sacred Heart (*from the French*)........................... 552

XXXII. The Indulgences of the Portiuncula........ 553
  698. Conditions for gaining them.............. 553
XXXIII. For the Preservation of the Faith........ 554
  699. *A Prayer*—O my Redeemer (*from the Italian*)............................ 554
XXXIV. For the Sanctification of Festival Days..... 556
  700. *A Prayer*—Most glorious Patriarch, Saint Joseph (*from the Italian*)............. 556
XXXV. For Peace............................ 556
  701. *Prayers*—Give peace in our times, O Lord. 556
  702. *A Prayer*—Graciously give peace, O Lord. 557
  703. *A Prayer*—Lord Jesus Christ who didst say. 558
  704. *A Prayer*—O God, who art the Author..... 559
XXXVI. For the Consecration of Families.......... 560
  705. *Consecration to the Sacred Heart*—O Most Sacred Heart....................... 560
  706. *A Consecration to the Holy Family*—O Jesus, our most loving Redeemer (*from the Italian*)............................ 563
  707. *A Prayer*—O God of goodness and mercy (*from the Italian*)..................... 564
  708. *A Prayer*—Guard, we beseech Thee, O Lord............................. 565
XXXVII. For the Printing of Good Books.......... 566
  709. *A Prayer*—O glorious Apostle of the Gentiles (*from the Italian*)............... 566
XXXVIII. While Making or Repairing Liturgical Ornaments or Vestments.............. 567
  710. *An Invocation*—Jesus, the way, the truth, and the life, have mercy on us....... 567
XXXIX. For Choosing a State of Life............. 567
  711. *A Prayer*—O my God, Thou who art (*from the Italian*)......................... 567
XL. To obtain the gift of continence................ 568
  712. *An Invocation*—Let my heart, O Lord..... 568
  713. *An Invocation*—Make my heart and my body clean........................ 568
  714. *A Prayer*—Lord, burn our reins and our hearts........................... 568
  715. *A Prayer*— Grant we beseech Thee........ 569

XLI. *To obtain the grace of a devout life*............ 569
    716. *A Prayer*—Grant me, O merciful God..... 569
XLII. *Against the Persecutors of the Church*....... 572
    717. *An Invocation*—That Thou wouldst vouch-
        safe................................. 572
    718. *A Prayer*—Graciously hear the prayers.... 573
XLIII. *In time of earthquake*..................... 573
    719. *A Prayer*—O God, who hast established.... 573
XLIV. *In the Time of Trial*..................... 574
    720. *An Invocation*—Regard, O Lord........... 574
    721. *An Invocation*—I deserve to suffer these
        things............................... 574
    722. *A Prayer*—Despise not, Almighty God.... 574
    723. *A Prayer*—O God, our refuge............ 575
XLV. *At the time of any calamity*................. 575
    724. *An Invocation*—From all dangers........ 575
    725. *A Prayer*—O God, Who knowest.......... 575
    726. *Prayers*—Help us, O God, our Saviour..... 576

PART II

In Favor of Certain Groups of Persons

I. *An Invocation to be said by candidates for the
    priesthood*.......................... 578
    727. O good Jesus, grant that I may become.... 578
II. *Prayers to be used by all clerics and others who
    aspire to the sacred ministry*........... 578
    728. *An Invocation*—Put upon me, O Lord, the
        new man........................... 578
    729. *An Invocation*—Heart of Jesus, Victim of
        love............................... 579
    730. *An Invocation*—Saint Aloysius, exemplar of
        clerics............................. 579
    731. *Recitation of the Divine Office in the Presence
        of the Blessed Sacrament*.............. 579
    732. *On the day of Reception of a Major Order*.... 579
III. *Prayers to be said by all clerics in Holy Orders
    and priests*.......................... 580

(A) FOR A HOLY LIFE............................ 580
   733. *A Prayer*—Dearest Jesus................. 580
   734. *A Prayer to obtain the grace of preserving*
      chastity—Lord Jesus Christ........... 581

(B) FOR THE DUE FULFILLMENT OF THEIR SACRED
     DUTIES............................ 582
   735. *A Prayer before reciting the Divine Office*—
      "Aperi, Domine".................... 582
   736. *The Recitation of the Divine Office in the*
      Presence of the Blessed Sacrament.... 583
   737. *A Prayer after the recitation of the Divine*
      Office—"Sacrosanctæ"................ 583
   738. *A Prayer for the grace of preaching holily and*
      fruitfully............................ 584

IV. *Prayers to be said by Priests*................. 585

(A) TO OBTAIN HOLINESS OF LIFE................. 585
   739. *An Invocation*—O good Jesu, grant........ 585
   740. *A Prayer*—Almighty and merciful God..... 586
   741. *A Prayer*—O Almighty God, let Thy grace. 586
   742. *Indulgences for the celebration of a First*
      Mass............................. 587
   743. *Prayers to be said by Priests before and after*
      their own sacramental Confession..... 587
      (a) *before Confession*—Accept my confes-
        sion............................. 587
      (b) *after Confession*—Let this my confession 588
   744. *A form of consecrating Priests to the Most*
      Sacred Heart of Jesus—Lord Jesus,
      who art........................... 590
   745. *A Prayer to St. John, Apostle and Evan-*
      gelist—Let us rejoice................. 592
   746. *A Prayer to be said on the Anniversary of*
      Ordination........................ 594

(B) TO FULFIL WORTHILY THE SACRED OFFICES COM-
     MITTED TO THEM................... 596
   747. *Preparation for Mass*................... 596
   748. *Prayers to be said while putting on the*
      sacred vestments.................... 597

CONTENTS

749. *A Form of directing one's intention before Mass* 598
750. *Thanksgiving after Mass* 598
751. *A Prayer to be said after celebrating Mass* .. 599
752. *Another Prayer after the celebration of Mass*. 600
753. *A Prayer to be said by Confessors before they hear the confessions of the faithful— Give me, O Lord* 601
754. *Assistance to the sick* 602

V. *Prayers to be recited by Religious* 602
755. *An Invocation—Heart of Jesus, Victim of charity* 602
756. *The Renewal of Religious Vows* 603
757. *A Prayer—Lord Jesus, by the merits (from the French)* 603
758. *Recitation of the Divine Office in the presence of the Blessed Sacrament* 603

VI. *Prayers to be said by teachers* 604
759. *An Invocation—Teach me goodness and discipline* 604
760. *An Invocation—Seat of Wisdom* 604
761. *A Prayer—O glorious Virgin and Martyr (from the French)* 604
762. *A Prayer—O glorious Saint Catherine (from the French)* 606

VII. *Prayers to be said by students* 606
763. *An Act of Consecration—Under thy patronage, dear Mother* 606
764. *A Prayer—O Creator ineffable* 607
765. *A Prayer—O most holy Virgin Mary* 608

VIII. *An Invocation to be recited by those who do mental or physical labor* 610
766. Indulgences 610

IX. *A Prayer to be said by children* 610
767. Sweetest Jesus, who, being subject 610

X. *A Prayer to be said by young men* 611
768. O most glorious Saint Aloysius (from the Italian) 611

SET UP, PRINTED, AND BOUND BY BENZIGER BROTHERS, INC., N. Y.

CONTENTS

XI. *A Prayer to be said by married folk in their own
behalf*.............................. 612
769. O Most Sacred Heart of Jesus........... 612
XII. *A Prayer to be said by parents in behalf of their
children*.......................... 614
770. O Lord God, who hast called us.......... 614
XIII. *A Prayer to be said by children in behalf of
their parents*..................... 617
771. Almighty and everlasting God........... 617
XIV. *A visit to a church to be made by Deaf-mutes and
their Instructors*.................... 619
772. Plenary indulgence.................... 619

APPENDIX
Indulgences attached to visiting certain
holy places in Rome

I. *A Roman Pilgrimage*........................ 621
773. Indulgences............................ 621
II. *Visiting the Vatican Basilica, the tomb and statue
of St. Peter in the same Basilica*....... 621
774. Indulgences............................ 621
III. *Visiting the "Seven Altars" in the Vatican
Basilica*........................... 622
775. Indulgences............................ 622
IV. *A Visit to the Lateran Archbasilica*.......... 622
776. Plenary indulgence "toties quoties"........ 622
V. *Visiting the Sacred Crib of our Lord in the Basilica
of Saint Mary Major*................ 623
777. *Prayer*—I adore Thee, O incarnate Word
(*from the Italian*).................... 623
VI. *Visiting the Scala Santa*................... 624
778. Indulgences............................ 624
VII. *Visiting the "Seven Churches"*.............. 624
779. Indulgences............................ 624
VIII. *Visiting the Churches of the Stations*......... 625
780. Indulgences............................ 625
IX. *The Penitential Wand*.................... 625
781. Indulgences............................ 626

SUPPLEMENT TO THE RACCOLTA

PRAYER FOR CHRISTIAN FAMILIES
Composed by Pope Pius XII

O Lord, God of goodness and mercy, who in the midst of an evil and sinful world hast presented to the society of the redeemed the Holy Family of Nazareth as a spotless mirror of piety, justice and love, behold how the family is being undermined on all sides, every effort being made to desecrate it by stripping it of faith, religion and morals.

Regard the work of Thy own hands. Safeguard in our homes the domestic virtues, for these alone will ensure us harmony and peace.

Come and stir up the champions of the family. Bestir the modern apostles so that in Thy Name, bearing the message of Jesus Christ and exhibiting holiness of life, they may revive the doctrines of conjugal fidelity for married couples, the exercise of authority by parents, obedience on the part of children and modesty on the part of girls. Grant also through the efforts of these apostles, that the home favored by Thee with many blessings may again become an object of esteem and love in the minds and hearts of all.

It is through the examples of the divine model of Nazareth that the Christian family is to be restored in Jesus Christ and to recover its former respect and dignity. Then every home will again become a sanctuary and in every household will be rekindled the flame of faith to teach patience in adversity and moderation in prosperity and to promote order, peace and harmony in all things.

Under Thy paternal gaze, O Lord, and with confidence in Thy Providence and in the loving patronage of Jesus, Mary and Joseph, the family will become a sanctuary of virtue and a school of wisdom. It shall prove, as Christ has promised, a haven of rest against life's burdens. In the sight of the world it shall render glory to Thee, O Father, and to Thy Son, Jesus, until

1

the day when, through Him, we shall, together with
all His members, sing the divine praises in the eternal
ages to come. Amen.

The faithful provided they are at least duly contrite, can gain an
indulgence of 1000 days as often as they devoutly recite the above
prayer (S.P. Ap., Jan. 13, 1957).

PRAYER FOR RELIGIOUS VOCATIONS
Composed by Pope Pius XII

O Lord Jesus Christ, sublime model of all perfection, Thou art ever urging onward all privileged
souls in their high aspiration towards the goal of religious life; and, moreover, Thou dost also strengthen
them through the powerful force of Thy example and
the efficacious influence of Thy grace so that they
may be able to follow Thee in such a noble way of
life; grant then that many, recognizing Thy sweet
inspirations, may have the will to correspond with
them by embracing the religious state and so enjoy in
it Thy special care and tender predilection.

Grant in like manner that there may never be
wanting those angels of Thy charity, who will repre-
sent Thee day and night at the cradle of the orphan,
at the bedside of the suffering, by the side of the aged
and the sick, who perhaps have no one on earth to
whom they may look for sympathy and a helping
hand. Grant that humble schools, like lofty pulpits,
may ever re-echo Thy voice, teaching the way to
heaven and the duties proper to each one's state in
life. May no land, ever so wild and remote, be deprived of the preaching of the Gospel, whereby the
invitation is extended to all peoples to enter into Thy
Kingdom. Increase and multiply the flames which are
to spread throughout the world that fire in which the
immaculate holiness of Thy Church is to shine forth in
all its splendor. May there flourish in every place gardens of chosen souls who by contemplation and penance make reparation for the sins of men and invoke
Thy mercy upon them. Grant that the continuous self-
sacrifice of these hearts, the snow-white purity of

these souls and their eminent virtues may keep ever alive the perfect example of the children of God which Thou didst will to make manifest to men by Thy coming into this world.

To these armies of Thy dearly beloved souls send a large number of good vocations, souls steadfast and firm in their resolve to make themselves worthy of their high calling and to become a credit to the holy institute to which they aspire, by exact religious observance, by diligence in prayer, by constant mortification and by the perfect conformity of their will with Thine in all things.

Enlighten, O Lord Jesus, many generous souls with the fiery glow of the Holy Spirit, who is substantial and eternal love, and by the powerful intercession of Thy most dear Mother Mary, stir up and preserve in them the fire of Thy love, unto the glory of the Father and the same Holy Spirit, who together with Thee live and reign for ever and ever. Amen.

An indulgence of 10 years.

A plenary indulgence on the usual conditions if this prayer is repeated every day for a month (**S.P. Ap., Feb. 9, 1957**).

PRAYER TO OUR LADY OF LOURDES
Composed by Pope Pius XII

Immaculate Virgin of Lourdes, in compliance with your loving invitation, we kneel before you in the lowly grotto where you appeared in order to point out the way of prayer and penance to those who had strayed and to distribute to those sorely beset by bitter anguish the graces and marvels of your queenly bounty.

Accept, compassionate Queen, the praise and prayers which all peoples and nations address to you with confidence.

O shining vision of Paradise, dispel the shadows of error from our minds with the light of Faith. O mystical Rose, comfort dejected souls with the heavenly fragrance of Hope. O inexhaustible source of life-giving waters, refresh our barren hearts with the waves of Divine Love.

Grant that we, your children, strengthened in affliction, protected in danger, supported in our struggles, may so love and serve your Divine Son as to merit eternal joys at the foot of your heavenly throne. Amen.

The faithful, provided they are at least duly contrite, can gain an indulgence of three years as often as they devoutly recite the above prayer at the Lourdes Grotto (S.P. Ap., May 10, 1957).

PRAYER TO MARY, MOST HOLY QUEEN
TO BE RECITED BY CHRISTIAN WOMEN
Composed by Pope Pius XII

"Hail, full of grace, blessed art thou among women" (Luke 1, 28, 42). We implore thee, O Mary, to extend to us thy daughters, the hand of thy maternal protection. We who draw near to thy queenly throne as thy handmaidens are ready to do thy bidding and are resolved, with thy help, to realize in ourselves and in our sisters the ideals of truth and Christian perfection.

As we gaze upon thee, O spotless maiden and favorite of the heavenly Father, our minds are lost in admiration! O Virgin, Spouse of the Holy Spirit! O tender Mother of Jesus! Obtain for us from thy Divine Son the grace so to imitate thy noble virtues that they may be reflected in every age and circumstance of our life.

May we be pure and upright in our thought and conduct; pleasant, loving and understanding companions to our husbands; careful, watchful and prudent mothers to our children; wise administrators of household affairs; exemplary citizens of our beloved fatherland; faithful children of the Church, ever docile to her guidance in our thoughts and actions.

Help us, O dearly beloved Mother, to have a sincere regard for the duties of our state in life that our homes may become centers of spiritual life and active charity, schools in which consciences are rightly formed, and gardens wherein virtues may thrive. Come to our aid in our social and public life, also, that we may be examples of profound faith and ever-edifying Christian conduct, of incorrupt integrity and sound equilibrium based on the most solid religious principles.

Bless us in our intentions and in our works, that, as we undertake them through thy inspiration, so by thy help it may be granted to us to see their abundant fruits in time and eternity. Amen.

An indulgence of 3 years (S.P. Ap., May 22, 1957).

PRAYER TO BE SAID BY PHYSICIANS
Composed by Pope Pius XII

O Divine Physician concerned for the welfare of both body and soul, Jesus, our Redeemer, who during Thy life on earth didst manifest a special love for the sick and by Thy almighty power didst restore them to health by the mere touch of Thy hand, we who are called to the arduous tasks of the medical profession adore Thee and acknowledge Thee as our model and firm support.

May our minds, hearts and hands always be guided by Thee so that we may merit the honor and praise which the Holy Spirit pronounces in commendation of our profession (Ecclus. 38).

Grant us to realize more fully that we are instruments of Thy mercy, called to cooperate with Thee in the work of safeguarding the welfare of human beings and promoting their development.

Enlighten our understanding, so hard pressed by the innumerable ailments of the human body, in order that, by the right use of modern scientific knowledge in the diagnosis of diseases, we may not be misled by mere symptoms but discover their true causes. We shall then feel safe in prescribing the remedies which Thy Providence has supplied.

Increase Thy love in our hearts so that, seeing Thee in the sick, especially in such as are most forsaken, we may reward their complete confidence in us by exhibiting a continuous and unwearied solicitude for their welfare.

Grant that, following Thy example, we may always show fatherly kindness in our sympathy, sincerity in giving advice, diligence in our attendance, freedom from all practices of deception, and gentleness in breaking the sad news when confronted with the mystery of death. Above all, help us to be firm in upholding Thy law concerning the sacredness of human life against the false dictates of egoism and unregulated lower instincts.

As physicians who take glory in Thy Name, we promise that in all our activity we shall take into account the observance of the moral order and be regulated by its laws.

Grant, finally, that we ourselves, by a truly Christian life and by the conscientious fulfillment of the duties of our profession, may merit some day to hear from Thy lips the sentence of beatification promised to all those who visit Thee in the person of Thy sick brethren: "Come, blessed of My Father, take possession of the Kingdom prepared for you" (Matth. 25, 34). Amen.

Physicians, provided they are at least duly contrite, can gain an indulgence of three years as often as they devoutly recite the above prayer (S.P. Ap., May 10, 1957).

PIOUS EXERCISE IN HONOR OF THE MYSTERIES OF THE INFANCY OF OUR LORD JESUS CHRIST

The faithful who, on any of the twelve successive Sundays that they choose, spend some time in prayers and devout meditations in honor of the mysteries of the Infancy of our Lord Jesus Christ may gain:

A plenary indulgence on the usual conditions (S.P. Ap., June 4, 1957).

PRAYER FOR THE CHURCH OF SILENCE
Composed by Pope Pius XII

O Lord Jesus, King of martyrs, Thou art the comfort of the afflicted and firm support of all who suffer for love of Thee and by reason of their loyalty to Thy Spouse Holy Mother the Church. In Thy mercy give ear to our fervent prayers in behalf of our brethren of the "Church of Silence" that they may never be disheartened in the struggle nor waver in the faith; rather may they taste the sweetness of the consolations reserved by Thee for those souls whom Thou dost vouchsafe to number among Thy companions on the hill of the cross.

To those who must suffer torment and violence, hunger and fatigue, be Thou the invincible strength sustaining them in their trials and assuring them of the rewards pledged by Thee to those who persevere unto the end.

Many, on the other hand, are exposed to moral constraints, which oftentimes prove much more dangerous inasmuch as they are more deceitful; to such then be Thou the light to enlighten their mind, so that they may clearly see the straight path of truth; be Thou also to them a source of strength for the support of their will so that they may triumph in every crisis and never yield to any vacillation or weakness.

Finally, there are those who find it impossible to profess their faith openly, to lead a normal Christian life, to receive the holy sacraments frequently, and to converse familiarly with their spiritual guides. To such be Thou Thyself a hidden altar, an invisible temple, a plenitude of grace and a fatherly voice, helping and encouraging them, providing a remedy for their aching hearts and filling them with joy and peace.

May they be helped by our fervent prayer; let our fraternal solidarity assure them that they are not alone. May their example redound to the edification of the whole Church; especially may it be profitable to us who regard them with so much affection.

Grant, O Lord, that their period of trial be shortened and that very soon all, including also their converted oppressors, may enjoy the freedom of serving and worshipping Thee, who with the Father and the Holy Spirit livest and reignest for ever and ever. Amen

An indulgence of 3 years (S.P. Ap., July 16, 1957).

PRAYER FOR VOCATIONS TO THE PRIESTHOOD
Composed by Pope Pius XII

Lord Jesus, High Priest and universal Shepherd, Thou hast taught us to pray, saying: "Pray the Lord of the harvest to send forth laborers into His harvest" (Matt. 9, 38). Therefore we beseech Thee graciously to hear our supplications and raise up many generous souls who, inspired by Thy example and supported by Thy grace, may conceive the ardent desire to enter the ranks of Thy sacred ministers in order to continue the office of Thy one true priesthood.

Although Thy priests live in the world as dispensers of the mysteries of God, yet their mission demands that they be not men of this world. Grant, then, that the insidious lies and vicious slanders directed against the priesthood by the malignant enemy and abetted by the world through its spirit of indifference and materialism may not dim the brilliance of the light with which they shine before men, nor lessen the profound and reverent esteem due to them. Grant that the continual promotion of religious instruction, true piety, purity of life and devotion to the highest ideals may prepare the groundwork for good vocations among youth. May the Christian family, as a nursery of pure and pious souls, become the unfailing source of good vocations, ever firmly convinced of the great honor that can redound to our Lord through some of its numerous offspring. Come to the aid of Thy Church, that always and in every place she may have at her disposal the means necessary for the reception, promotion, formation and mature development of all the good vocations that may arise. For the full realization of all these things, O Jesus, who art most zealous for the welfare and salvation of all, may Thy graces continually descend from heaven to move many hearts by their irresistible force: first, the silent invitation; then generous co-operation; and finally perseverance in Thy holy service.

Art Thou not moved to compassion, O Lord, seeing the crowds like sheep without a shepherd, without anyone to break for them the bread of Thy word, or to lead them to drink at the fountains of Thy grace, so that they are continually in danger of becoming a prey to ravening wolves? Does it not grieve Thee to behold so many unploughed fields where thorns and thistles are allowed to grow in undisputed possession? Art Thou not saddened that many of Thy gardens, once so green and productive, are now on the verge of becoming fallow and barren through neglect?

O Mary, Mother most pure, through whose compassion we have received the holiest of priests; O glorious Patriarch St. Joseph, perfect model of co-operation with the divine call; O holy priests, who in heaven compose a choice choir about the Lamb of God: obtain for us many good vocations in order that the Lord's flock, through the support and government of vigilant shepherds, may attain to the enjoyment of the most delightful pastures of eternal happiness.

An indulgence of 10 years.

A plenary indulgence once a month, on the usual conditions, for the daily recitation of this prayer (S.P. Ap., Nov. 6, 1957).

PRAYER TO BE RECITED BY CATHOLIC TEACHERS
Composed by Pope Pius XII

O Word Incarnate, Teacher of teachers, our most loving Jesus, who didst deign to come into the world and, out of Thy infinite wisdom and inexhaustible goodness, point out to men the way to heaven, mercifully hear the humble prayers of those who follow Thy footsteps, thereby giving expression to their desire to be Catholic teachers worthy of the name and making known to souls the faith that will surely lead to Thee and through Thee to eternal happiness.

Grant us the light, not only to avoid falling into the pitfalls of error, but also to penetrate the truth so as to acquire that luminous clarity whereby that which is the most essential turns out to be the most simple and therefore best adapted to the intelligence even of children, in whom especially Thy divine simplicity is reflected. Visit us, then, with the help of Thy Spirit, the Creator, so that in accordance with Thy mandate we may be able to give appropriate and adequate instructions in the doctrines of faith.

Give us the ability to adapt ourselves to the still immature minds of our pupils, to foster their fine, youthful energy, to have a sympathetic understanding for their deficiencies, to support their spirit of restlessness. Give us the power to become little without neglecting our line of duty even as Thou, O Lord, didst become as one of us without leaving the exalted throne of Thy divinity.

Above all, however, fill us with Thy Spirit of love: love for Thee, Teacher unique and excelling, so that we may gladly sacrifice ourselves in Thy holy service; love for our holy profession, regarding it as a most noble calling rather than mere employment; loving concern for our personal sanctification, as the primal source of energy in all our work and apostolate; love of truth, not allowing ourselves to be turned aside from it; love for souls which we must pattern and form according to the standards of truth and goodness; love for our students, helping them to become exemplary citizens and loyal sons of the Church; love for our dearly beloved youth and for our children, like the love of a father, but more elevated, more conscious and more pure than mere natural paternal love.

And thou, most holy Mother Mary, under whose loving care the youthful Jesus grew in wisdom and in grace, be our intercessor at the side of Thy divine Son and obtain for us an abundance of heavenly graces in order that our work may redound to the honor and glory of Him who with the Father and the

Holy Ghost liveth and reigneth for ever and ever. Amen.

An indulgence of 1000 days (**S.P. Ap., December 28, 1957**).

PRAYER TO BE RECITED BY THE MEMBERS OF A CHRISTIAN FAMILY
Composed by Pope Pius XII

O Holy Family, Trinity of the earth, O Jesus, Mary and Joseph, sublime models and protectors of Christian families, to you do we have recourse, not only to find comfort in the sweet contemplation of your loving examples, but also to implore your protection and to promise constant fidelity in the paths you have pointed out to us.

Your peace, your unalterable serenity refreshes our troubled souls in the midst of the continuous stress and strain of life's burdens. We are thus given eloquent proof that only in a home adorned and embellished with the virtues you have exemplified can our hearts find the peace and happiness they so earnestly desire.

But how could such a tender plant as the family be defended against the burning heat of unbridled passions, against the insidious spirit of rebellion that asserts itself almost everywhere, against the raging storm of present-day life which seems bent on overthrowing everything? How else except by causing its roots to penetrate deeply into the noble soil of Christian piety; by imploring for it continuous streams of divine grace, especially through the reception of the Holy Sacraments in common; by animating it with a true spirit of faith which will enable us to surmount the materialistic concept of life; by joining all its branches closely together through the strong bonds of a love which, were it not also supernatural, would pass away like all things here below; by strengthening it from within through the firm resolution, made by each one, to fulfill our duties in everything that the right order of the family requires; by supporting it in the severe trials of this earthly exile where sometimes people are without even a decent home or suffer from a lack of the bare necessities of life.

In the midst of the present confusion of ideas with which minds are often disturbed, we loudly proclaim the sanctity, the unity and divine mission of the Christian family as the cell of society and of the Church, and each at our post — parents and children — humbly but firmly pledge ourselves to do all in our power in order that such holy ideals may become a reality in the world.

Help us, O Joseph, mirror of the most admirable paternity in the diligent concern that thou didst manifest for the Saviour and for the Virgin, ever faithful to the divine inspirations; come to our aid, O Mary, the most loving, the most faithful and the most pure of all spouses and mothers; assist us, O Jesus, who, as our light and model in all things, didst will to become the most submissive of children. Be always near to us, all ye three, in times of joy and in times of sadness, in our work and in our rest, in our anxieties and in our hopes, be near to those who are born and to those who die.

Finally, obtain for us that all homes, made holy through the imitation of yours, may become for all their members schools of virtue, sanctuaries of holiness, a sure way to that eternal happiness which we confidently hope for through your intercession. Amen.

An indulgence of 1000 days (S.P. Ap., December 30, 1957).

PRAYER TO BE RECITED BY
CATHOLIC MEMBERS OF LEGISLATIVE BODIES
AND BY CATHOLIC POLITICIANS
Composed by Pope Pius XII

Great and eternal God, Creator and Lord of all things, foremost Legislator and supreme Ruler, all power emanates from Thee and depends on Thee; and those whose duty is to legislate, determine in Thy name what is just or unjust, as a reflection of Thy divine wisdom. Therefore we, the Catholic members of parliament (Congress) and Catholic politicians, upon whom rests the burden of a grave responsibility that places us at the center of the whole nation, implore Thy aid for the fulfillment of our office that we intend to accept and exercise for the greater spiritual and material welfare of our people.

Grant us such a sense of duty as will cause us to omit no preparation or effort for the realization of this noble end. Grant us also that objectivity and sound realism which will guide us on every occasion to a clear perception of that which seems the best. Grant that we may never deviate from that sound impartiality which dictates that we labor without unjust preferences for the good of all. Grant also that we may never fail in loyalty to our people, nor in firm adherence to the principles which we openly profess, nor in the noble resolve to preserve ourselves above all possible corruption and base selfish ambitions.

Help us to be calm in our deliberations and to be immune from all passion except such as is inspired by the honest quest after truth. May our resolutions be in conformity with Thy precepts even if the service of Thy will should demand sufferings and sacrifices. May we, even in our own little way, endeavor to imitate that rectitude and holiness according to which Thou in Thy providence dost direct and govern everything for Thy greater glory and for the true well-being of human society and of all Thy creatures.

Hear us, O Lord, in order that our minds may never be without Thy light, nor our wills without Thy strength, nor our hearts without the warmth of Thy love, for we ought to have a tender love for our people. Keep far from us every form of human ambition and every kind of lust for illicit gain. Inspire us with a real, lively and profound sentiment of what constitutes a sound social order wherein full regard is had for law and justice. Finally as a supreme reward grant us some day to enjoy Thy blessed presence for all eternity, in union with all those who have been entrusted to our care. Amen.

An indulgence of 3 years (S.P. Ap., January 27, 1958).

PRAYER FOR MISSION EXERCISES
Composed by Pope Pius XII

O Jesus, Divine Missioner, during Thy life on earth Thou wast consumed with an ardent zeal for the glory of Thy Father and for the redemption of souls. Therefore Thou didst deign to become the messenger and propagator of that Kingdom of holiness and grace which was to be for mankind the ark of mercy and salvation. Hear then, we beseech Thee, the earnest supplications of us, Thy unworthy ministers, who are called to continue Thy mission, as also of us, the faithful, who desire to enjoy the salutary effects of these sacred days of reconciliation and sanctification.

Grant to us missioners a ray of Thy spirit, whereby we may be taught to sacrifice ourselves without reserve, to exhibit understanding and fatherly kindness without weakness; to be firm and resolute without harshness; to be discreet and prudent, having no vain fear of the world and its judgments. Impart to us Thy light for discerning the needs of men and peoples; Thy zeal and Thy strength so as to be unyielding when faced with lukewarmness and obstacles; the charm and power of Thy grace whereby we may move hearts and bring them gently to Thy divine feet.

To this end, however, grant us the precious gift of Thy love, which is a love for Thee, for Thy Church and for souls and which ought at all times to be the inspiration of our undertakings and the prime source of the energy needed to bring them to a successful conclusion.

Since we, the faithful, expect to obtain from this holy mission a profound spiritual renewal in individuals, in families and in society, grant that we may never fail in the true humility necessary for the devout and attentive acceptation of the instructions imparted to us, in the sincerity needed for their effective application to ourselves and in the honesty of intention that must underlie any serious resolution to reform if our life in the future is to be better and more holy than in the past and in the present.

We beg of Thee, O Lord, the forgiveness for our sins; we ask also for a blessing upon our resolutions that they may be strengthened and become fruitful, and for the right ordering of our lives such as will not allow us to ever be separated from Thee.

All ye Saints, who became holy yourselves by exercises like these, come to our aid! And thou, Mother of God and our Mother, deign to be present at all the exercises of this mission, ennobling them with the fragrance of thy all-powerful intercession, so that those who now implore thee with a childlike confidence may one day be led by thee before the throne of thy Divine Son, who with the Father and the Holy Spirit, liveth and reigneth for ever and ever. Amen.

An indulgence of 3 years. It can be gained both by priests who preach the mission and the faithful who attend, on the condition that the usual prayers are recited with devotion and contrition. (S.P. Ap., May 21, 1958)

PRAYER TO BE RECITED BY YOUNG WOMEN
Composed by Pope Pius XII

With hearts bubbling over with the fondest aspirations, we, "the flower of youth" prostrate ourselves at Thy feet, O Lord Jesus, "who givest joy to our youth." By this act of homage we desire to offer to Thee the beatings of our hearts as one who with a trembling hand places a flower upon Thy altar, in order to know Thee better — the Infinite Truth, who alone can quench our thirst for the ideal; to love Thee ever more and more — the Ineffable Good, who art the ultimate object of our highest aspirations; and to follow Thee closely — the Supreme Norm of all perfection.

May Thy presence, like a soft gentle breeze accompany us on our journey through this violent and restless world. May Thy spotless purity, like the heav-

enly dawn, never disappear from our view when
confronted by an arrogant materialism whose vileness
is so harmful and seeks to engulf us in darkness. May
Thy strength, all-powerful and meek, be a sure support sustaining us in our frailty and helping us in
our weakness when face to face with those wiles and
allurements whose glamour is designed to ensnare us.

Like a ray of light we would like to clearly illustrate
and set forth an example of a life of living faith animated with love. In the intimacy of our homes we will
strive to keep our union and affection always on a
supernatural plane through grace. In our social relations we will endeavor to adhere always to the high
standard of justice and love, as a visible sign of a
Christian program of life. In our studies and work we
will seek to breathe forth and inspire peace and joy
like one sowing a garden with the most precious seeds.
In the choice of our state in life we will entrust ourselves with the most loving confidence to Thy divine
will. We will make every effort to live always a life
of prayer and sacramental grace, in union with Thee
and in submission to Thy will, exhibiting that filial
sentiment which should adorn all our actions with a
beautiful aroma, thus sealing them as holy and meri-
torious.

And do thou, O Mary, our most loving Mother, Immaculate Lily, give heed to the earnest prayers of
these your daughters, who like lowly flowers of the
field, are all but lost in the meadows of this world, yet
raise aloft their stems in sacrifice before the altar of
the Lord. Present then our offering, O mighty advocate, and help us to spend all the days of our life in
the most faithful imitation of Thy virtues, for the
greater glory of Thy most beloved Son, who together
with the Father and the Holy Spirit lives and reigns
for ever and ever. Amen.

An indulgence of 3 years (S.P. Ap., March 7, 1958).

PRAYER TO SAINT JOSEPH, WORKMAN
TO BE RECITED BY WORKMEN
Composed by Pope Pius XII

O glorious Patriarch, Saint Joseph, humble and just artisan of Nazareth, thou hast given to all Christians and particularly to us an example of a perfect life through diligent labor and admirable union with Jesus and Mary.

Assist us in our daily work in order that we, Catholic artisans, may also see in it an effective means of glorifying God, of sanctifying ourselves, and of being a useful member in the society in which we live. These should be the highest ideals for all our actions.

O dearest Protector, obtain for us from the Lord humility and simplicity of heart, love for our work and kindness towards our fellow-laborers; conformity to God's will in the unavoidable trials of this life together with joy in bearing them; recognition of our specific social mission and a sense of responsibility; the spirit and discipline and prayer; docility and respectfulness towards superiors; the spirit of brotherhood towards our equals; charity and indulgence with our dependents. Accompany us in times of prosperity when the opportunity is given for an honest enjoyment of the fruits of our labors; sustain us in our hours of sadness, when heaven seems to be shut in our regard, and even the very tools with which our hands toil appear to rebel against us.

Grant that, in imitation of thee, we may keep our eyes fixed on our Mother, Mary, thy dearest Spouse, who as she spun silently in a corner of thy shop would let the sweetest smile course over her lips. Besides, may we never take our eyes off Jesus, who was busily occupied with thee at the carpenters bench, in order that we in like manner may lead on earth a peaceful and a holy life, a prelude to the life of eternal happiness that awaits us in heaven for ever and ever. Amen.

An indulgence of 3 years (S.P. Ap., March 11, 1958).

PRAYER TO BE SAID BY CHRISTIANS
CONFINED IN PRISON
Composed by Pope Pius XII

O Divine Prisoner of the sanctuary, who for love of us and for our salvation hast willed not only to enclose Thyself within the narrow limits of human nature and thereafter to conceal Thyself under the veils of the sacramental species, but also to live continually in the tabernacle-cell, give heed to our prayers which ascend to Thee from within these barred and walled enclosures, and by which we desire to make known to Thee our love as well as our grief and the urgent need we feel for Thee in our distress, especially in the privation of our freedom, which causes us so much pain.

To some of us perhaps a voice out of the depth of conscience says that we are not guilty, and that it is only through a deplorable miscarriage of justice that we are now in this prison. We shall then find comfort in the remembrance that Thou, the most exalted and most innocent of victims, wast also condemned to death.

Or perhaps on the contrary we are moved to look downwards, to feel ashamed and to strike our breast. In that case also we are not without a remedy, for we can have recourse to Thy protection, with the assurance that Thou canst restrain all error, pardon all sin and restore Thy grace generously to all who return to Thee in a spirit of penance.

Finally, because of so many relapses into sin sometimes even the best of men have given up all hope in us, and we ourselves hardly know whence to begin the new road to rehabilitation. All this however notwithstanding, we can hear in the inner recesses of our soul the whisper of a word of confidence and consolation; it is Thy word promising to help us with thy light and grace if we will to return to a good life.

Grant, O Lord, that we may never forget that this is a period of trial and a most favorable opportunity for purifying the soul, for practicing the highest virtues and acquiring greater merits. Grant that our saddened hearts may not be penetrated with hatred, which is a blight to the human heart, or with distrust, which leaves no room for the feeling of brotherhood, or with rancor, which is the forerunner of evil designs. May we always bear in mind that in taking away the freedom of the body, no one can deprive us of that of the spirit, which in the long hours of our solitude can raise its thoughts and fix them on Thee in order to know Thee better and to love Thee daily more and more.

Grant, O Divine Redeemer, help and resignation to our dear ones who bewail our absence. Give peace and tranquillity to this world which has rejected us, which however we love and to which we have promised in the future our cooperation as good citizens. Finally, obtain for us that our sufferings may serve as a salutary example for many souls, preserving them from the danger of following in our footsteps. But above all grant us the grace to believe firmly in Thee, to have a childlike trust in Thee and never to fail in the love of Thee, who with the Father and the Holy Spirit liveth and reigneth for ever and ever. Amen.

An indulgence of 3 years (**S.P. Ap.,** April 10, 1958).

IMPRIMATUR
☒ Francis Cardinal Spellman
Archbishop of New York

November 26, 1958

PRAYER TO BE SAID BY MOTORISTS
Composed by Pope John XXIII

O God, the Father Almighty, Thou hast created man in Thine own image, infusing into his body an immortal soul which sighs for Thee, and in its journeys over the highways of faith seeks its rest in union with Thee. Grant to us motorists, who have to travel over the roads of this world in the service of our brethren, a sense of our grave responsibility and point out to us the way of charity and prudence.

O Jesus, Word Incarnate, who here below didst cross over land and sea, to escape from enemies, to heal the sick, to preach the kingdom of heaven, make us energetic and persevering in good works and keep us ever in Thy grace.

O Virgin Immaculate, thou wast a support to the Child Jesus on the way during the time of exile, a guide in his journeys as a young man to the Holy City, and a companion at His side in the ascent to Calvary. Now that thou hast been taken up into heaven, and art the Queen of the world, the Mother of goodness and of mercy, the way to heaven and the gateway thereof, be propitious toward us during our earthly journey, defend us against the dangers of body and soul to which we are continually exposed, and make us kind and patient towards our neighbor in return for the confidence he places in us.

O heavenly spirits who travel through space as messengers of the Most High, O Saints of heaven, above all, you who were Apostles and Missionaries, bearers of Christ, obtain for us a living faith which directs our life to God and keeps us always in readiness for the final journey towards the eternal Father and where together with you we may praise God forever and ever. Amen.

An indulgence of 3 years (S.P. Ap., June 5, 1959).

**PRAYER TO BE SAID BY SEMINARIANS
IN BEHALF OF THEIR PARENTS**
Composed by the S. C. of Seminaries and Universities

Our Father, Hail Mary and Glory be to the Father.

I. To God the Father

℣. I bend my knees before the Father of our Lord Jesus Christ;

℟. From whom all fatherhood in heaven and on earth receives its name (Eph. 3, 14-15).

Prayer

O God, who hast commanded us to honor our father and mother, grant, we beseech Thee, that our parents, while humbly engaged in Thy service, may be free from all adversities, and by Thy help may be deemed worthy to gain everlasting rewards: Who livest and reignest world without end. Amen.

II. To Christ the Son of God

℣. Let Thy Father and Thy Mother be joyful,
℟. And let her rejoice that bore Thee (Prov. 23, 25).

Prayer

O Lord Jesus Christ, who, in the days of Thy subjection to Mary and Joseph, didst advance in age, wisdom and grace; mercifully grant that, through their intercession, to the joy and gladness of our parents, while devoutly guarding the divine call in accordance with Thy will, we may learn goodness, discipline and knowledge: Who with the Father and the Holy Spirit livest and reignest world without end. Amen.

III. To the Holy Spirit

℣. His parents took Jesus up to Jerusalem,
℟. To present Him to the Lord (Luke 2, 22).

Prayer

O Holy Spirit, fill the hearts of our parents; and grant that as many as possible in the Christian family may be influenced by their example to gladly offer their sons to the Lord unto the glory of Thy Name, for the welfare of the Church and the salvation of souls: Who livest and reignest world without end. Amen.

The following indulgences are granted to Seminarians:

(1) An indulgence of 500 days;

(2) A plenary indulgence on the usual conditions, if this prayer is devoutly said daily for a month (S.P. Ap., August 13, 1959).

Pater, Ave et Gloria.

I. Ad Deum Patrem

℣. Flecto génua mea ante Patrem Dómini Nostri Iesu Christi;
℟. Exo quo omnis patérnitas in cælis et in terra nominátur (Eph. 3, 14-15).

Oratio

Deus qui nos patrem et matrem honoráre præcepísti: præsta, quæsumus, ut paréntes nostri, tibi humíliter serviéntes, ab ómnibus sint adversitátibus líberi, et ad præmia sempitérna, te auxiliánte, perveníre mereántur. Qui vivis et regnas in sæcula sæculórum. Amen.

II. Ad Christum Dei Filium

℣. Gáudeat Pater tuus et Mater tua,
℟. Et exúltet quæ génuit te (Prov. 23, 25).

Oratio

Dómine Iesu Christe, qui Maríæ et Ioseph súbditus, ætáte, sapiéntia et grátia profecísti: concéde propítius, ut, eórum suffragántibus méritis, nos, cum paréntum nostrórum gáudio et exultatióne, divínam vocatiónem secúndum propósitum tuum pie custodiéntes, bonitátem et disciplínam et sciéntiam addíscere valeámus. Qui cum Patre et Spiritu Sancto vivis et regnas in sæcula sæculórum. Amen.

III. Ad Spíritum Sanctum

℣. Tulérunt Íesum paréntes eius in Ierúsalem,
℟. Ut sísterent eum Dómino (Luc. 2, 22).

Oratio

R eple, Sancte Spíritus, nostrórum corda paréntum; et fac, ut, eórum exémplo, quamplúrimi de pópulo christiáno, ad glóriam Nóminis tui, in Ecclésiæ bonum et animárum salútem, fílios suos Dómino commodáre lænténtur. Qui cum Patre et Fílio vivis et regnas in sæcula sæculórum. Amen.

DEVOUT EXERCISE KNOWN AS THE "HOLY HOUR"

The faithful who privately perform for an entire hour the devout exercise known as the "Holy Hour," in any church, public or semi-public oratory (if they may lawfully make use of the latter), in order to venerate the Passion and Death of our Lord Jesus Christ, and to worship and meditate upon the burning love whereby He was led to institute the Holy Eucharist, may gain:

An indulgence of 10 years (see above n. 168).

A plenary indulgence, provided that they make their confession, receive Holy Communion and pray for the intentions of the Sovereign Pontiff (S.P. Ap., August 13, 1959).

PRAYER FOR THE CHURCH OF SILENCE
Composed by Pope John XXIII

O Jesus, Son of God, who out of love for Thy Church didst deliver Thyself up for her in order to sanctify her and cause her to appear in Thy presence glorious and without spot (Eph. 5, 23-27), behold with eyes of pity the afflictions which Thy mystical Spouse is suffering in certain parts of the Catholic world, particularly now in the vast country of China.

Thou art fully aware, O Lord, of the traps that endanger the souls of Thy faithful; Thou knowest the calumnies uttered by innuendo against Thy Shepherds, Thy ministers and Thy faithful followers, who are eager for the spread of the Gospel and Thy kingdom, which is not of this world! How persistent and pernicious are the efforts to tear asunder the seamless garment of Thy Spouse, the one, holy, catholic, Roman Church, by separating the local hierarchy and community from the one center of truth, authority and salvation, the See of Peter!

Confronted with such an evil spectacle, we first of all ask Thee to pardon the offenses inflicted on Thee. Indeed, the words addressed by Thee to Saul of Tarsus on the way to Damascus: "Saul, Saul, why dost thou persecute Me" (Acts 9, 4), so true in olden and recent history, can be applied also to our own day.

We, however, will always trust in the power of the sublime words which Thou didst address to Thy Father when lifted up on the Cross: "Father, forgive them, for they do not know what they are doing" (Luke 23, 34). As Thy sacrifice was the source of universal salvation, so by Thy grace, may the martyrdom which the Church, Thy Spouse and our Mother, suffers in various places, redound to the salvation of all men!

O Prince of peace, grant that the bishops and priests, the religious and laity may everywhere and always be "careful to preserve the unity of the Spirit in the bond of peace" (Eph. 4, 3). May Thy almighty power overcome every human contingency so that the Shepherds and the flocks may remain obedient to the voice of the one universal Shepherd, the Bishop of Rome, who feels in his heart a sense of responsibility from that supreme aspiration of love: "Holy Father, keep in Thy name those whom thou hast given Me, that they may be one even as We are" (John 17, 11).

Finally, O Redeemer, look graciously upon the merits and prayers of Thy Mother and our Mother, the majestic Queen of the Missions and of the universal Church; regard also the labors, the sacrifices and the blood of the countless martyrs for the Faith who everywhere have borne and still bear witness to Thee. Above all, however, be mindful of Thy precious Blood, shed for many unto the remission of sins, and grant Thy peace to China and to the whole world inasmuch as hope, victory and peace are had only through Thee, our Lord and immortal King of ages and nations.

An indulgence of 3 years (S.P. Ap., January 23, 1959).

INVOCATION TO JESUS CHRIST, KING

O Jesus, King of love, I have confidence in Your merciful goodness.

An indulgence of 300 days.

A plenary indulgence on the usual conditions, if this prayer is devoutly recited every day for a month (S.P. Ap., December 12, 1958).

KISSING THE WEDDING RING

Married partners who kiss the wife's wedding ring, whether individually or together, and at the same time devoutly recite the following prayer at least with a contrite heart:

Grant unto us, O Lord, that loving Thee we may love one another and live in accordance with Thy holy law.

or another prayer similar to this, may gain:

An indulgence of 300 days, once on the day of their wedding (S.P. Ap., November 23, 1959).

IMPRIMATUR
✠ Francis Cardinal Spellman
Archbishop of New York

March 7, 1960

PRAYER TO OUR LADY OF GOOD HOPE
TO BE SAID BY SEMINARIANS
Composed by Pope John XXIII

O Holy Virgin, our Lady of Good Hope, O kind and gracious Mother of Seminarians throughout the world, thy presence in the Cenacle was a source of great joy to the first Apostles of the Gospel as with moving hearts they awaited the coming of the Holy Ghost.

Look favorably upon us whose hearts are vibrating with the same expectations of grace and of a holy priestly zeal that helps others also to be holy.

As thou hast been our morning star so be thou ever the serene joy of our vocation, the guardian of our purity, the inspiration for good works in the service of Jesus and of the souls redeemed by His Blood, as also of His Church which though afflicted at times, remains ever invincible and glorious.

What joy it is for us Seminarians throughout the world to be able to say individually and collectively: We are thy work, O Mary. What exultation to be able to say always and without fail in every event of our lives: We have no fear whatsoever because thou, O Mary, art and ever shall be our hope, our Mother for ever and ever.

An indulgence of 7 years if devoutly recited by seminarians with at least a contrite heart.

A plenary indulgence once a month, on the usual conditions if this prayer has been devoutly recited every day for a month (S.P. Ap., April 7, 1961).

KISSING THE FOOT OF THE STATUE OF ST. PETER
IN THE VATICAN BASILICA IN ROME

The faithful who devoutly kiss the foot of the bronze statue of St. Peter, the Apostle, which stands in the vatican Patriarchal Basilica and say the invocation:

St. Peter, pray for us.

having at least a contrite heart, may gain:

An indulgence of 3 years (S.P. Ap., June 5, 1961).

THE DEVOUT OFFERING OF DAILY WORK

1. The faithful who offer to God in the morning the work of the whole day, whether manual or mental, using any formula they may choose, may gain a plenary indulgence on the usual conditions.

2. The faithful as often as they devoutly offer to God the work they are engaged in, whether mental or manual, using any invocation they may choose and having at least a contrite heart may gain an indulgence of 500 days. (S.P. Ap., Nov. 25, 1961).

FIVE PRAYERS TO BE RECITED BEFORE OR AFTER COMMUNION

I. I hate and detest each and every one of my sins and all the sins committed by others from the beginning of the world until this very hour as well as those that will be committed from now until the end of the world: indeed, if I were able, I would prevent them by the grace of God. This grace I humbly implore.

II. I praise and commend all good works, performed from the beginning of the world until this very hour, as well as those that will be performed from now until the end of the world: indeed, if I were able, I would multiply them by the grace of God. This grace I humbly implore.

III. Whatever I do, say, and think, I intend all for the greater glory of God, with all those good intentions that the Saints had in the past or will have in the future or can even now have.

IV. I pardon and forgive with my whole heart all my enemies, all who calumniate me, all who detract me, all who in any way injure me or desire evil against me.

V. Would that I could save all men by dying for each and every one! I would gladly do it by the grace of God. This grace, without which I can do nothing, I humbly implore.

The faithful, provided they are at least duly contrite, can gain an indulgence of 3 years for devoutly reciting the above prayers before or after Communion; a plenary indulgence, once a month, on the usual conditions, for the daily recitation of this prayer throughout an entire month (S.P. Ap., May 5, 1962).

PRAYER FOR THE NEEDS OF OTHERS

O Lord God almighty, Father of Christ Thy Blessed Son, Thou hearest the prayers of those who devoutly call on Thee and knowest also the prayers of those who are silent. We give Thee thanks because Thou hast deemed us worthy to partake of Thy holy mysteries which Thou hast given to us for the firm conviction in the wholesome truths of faith, for the preservation of piety and for the remission of sins, inasmuch as the name of Thy Christ is called upon by us who are united to Thee. Thou hast set us apart from the company of the wicked, join us then with those who are consecrated to Thee; strengthen us in truth through the coming of the Holy Spirit; reveal to us the things of which we are ignorant; supply the things that are wanting; confirm us in the knowledge we possess. Preserve priests in Thy service without reproach; keep rulers in peace; magistrates in justice; the weather mild; fruits in abundance; the world in almighty providence. Calm warlike nations; convert the erring; sanctify Thy people; preserve virgins; keep married folk faithful; strengthen the chaste; bring infants to maturity; make firm the newly baptized; instruct the catechumens and make them worthy to be admitted to baptism; gather us all together into the kingdom of heaven, in Christ Jesus our Lord, together with whom may there be glory, honor, and veneration to Thee and the Holy Spirit forever. Amen.

(From the Apostolic Constitutions, VIII, c. 15.)

The faithful, provided they are at least duly contrite, can gain an indulgence of 3 years for devoutly reciting the above prayer; a plenary indulgence, once a month, on the usual conditions, for the daily, devout recitation of this prayer throughout an entire month (S.P. Ap., May 5, 1962).

THE SCOUT'S PRAYER TO MARY
Composed by Pope John XXIII

O Mary! Your name has been on my lips and in my heart from the very outset of my life.

From my infancy I have learned to love you as a mother, to call upon you in time of danger, to confide in your intercession.

Behold my soul's ardent desire to seek after truth, to practice virtue, to be prudent and just, courageous and patient, to be a brother to all.

O Mary! Support my resolve to live as a faithful disciple of Jesus for the edification of the Christian society and the joy of the Holy Catholic Church.

I greet you, Mother, in the morning and in the evening; I call upon you from the highway; from you I hope for inspiration and encouragement to fulfill the sacred obligations of my vocation on earth, to give glory to God and to attain to eternal salvation.

O Mary! Like you at Bethlehem and on Golgotha, I too wish to remain always by the side of Jesus. He is the immortal king of ages and of nations. Amen.

Scouts may gain:

(1) An indulgence of 500 days, as often as, with at least a contrite heart, they devoutly recite the above prayer;

(2) A plenary indulgence on the usual conditions, once a month, for the daily, devout recitation of this prayer throughout an entire month. (S.P. Ap., Aug. 19, 1962).

THE DEVOUT OFFERING OF DAILY SUFFERING

1. The faithful who offer to God in the morning the sufferings of the whole day, whether of body or of soul, using any formula they may choose, may gain a plenary indulgence on the usual conditions. (When, however, the faithful are legitimately impeded, confessors, according to Canon 935 of the Code of Canon Law are empowered to impose some other good works.)

2. The faithful as often as they devoutly offer to God some present suffering, whether of body or of soul. using any invocation they may choose, and having at least a contrite heart may gain an indulgence of 500 days (S.P.Ap., June 4, 1962).

IMPRIMATUR
✠ Francis Cardinal Spellman
Archbishop of New York

Dec. 12, 1962